International Cultural Differences

The International Library of Management

Series Editor: Keith Bradley

Titles in the Series:

International Cultural Differences

Edited by

Gordon Redding
University of Hong Kong

Dartmouth
Aldershot · Brookfield USA · Singapore · Sydney

Published by
Dartmouth Publishing Company Limited
Gower House
Croft Road
Aldershot
Hants GU11 3HR
England

Dartmouth Publishing Company
Old Post Road
Brookfield
Vermont 05036
USA

British Library Cataloguing in Publication Data
International Cultural Differences. –
(International Library of Management)
I. Redding, S.G. II. Series
658.001

Library of Congress Cataloging-in-Publication Data
Redding, S.G.
        International cultural differences / edited by S.G. Redding.
        p. cm. — (The International library of management)
        Includes bibliographical references and index.
        ISBN 1-85521-422-9 (HB)
        1. Management—Social aspects. 2. International business
enterprises—Management—Cross-cultural studies. 3. Corporate
culture—Cross-cultural studies. 4. Intercultural communication.
I. Title II. Series.
HD38.R358 1995
658.3′041—dc20
                                                                                    95–22890
                                                                                    CIP

ISBN 1 85521 422 9

Printed in Great Britain by Galliard (Printers) Ltd, Great Yarmouth

Contents

PART III   SPECIAL ASPECTS OF MANAGING ACROSS CULTURES: BUSINESS ENVIRONMENTS, MANAGING EXPATRIATES AND MANAGING ALLIANCES

PART IV   SUCCESSFUL CROSS-CULTURAL MANAGEMENT

PART V   THE PROGRESS OF UNDERSTANDING

Acknowledgements

The editor and publishers wish to thank the following for permission to use copyright material.

Academy of Management Review for the essays: Geert Hofstede (1984), 'The Cultural Relativity of the Quality of Life Concept', *Academy of Management Review*, **9**, pp. 389–98; J. Stewart Black, Mark Mendenhall and Gary Oddou (1991), 'Toward a Comprehensive Model of International Adjustment: An Integration of Multiple Theoretical Perspectives', *Academy of Management Review*, **16**, pp. 291–317; Nakiye Avdan Boyacigiller and Nancy J. Adler (1991), 'The Parochial Dinosaur: Organizational Science in a Global Context', *Academy of Management Review*, **16**, pp. 262–90.

Administrative Science Quarterly for the essay: Max Boisot and John Child (1988), 'The Iron Law of Fiefs: Bureaucratic Failure and the Problem of Governance in the Chinese Economic Reforms', *Administrative Science Quarterly*, **33**, pp. 507–27.

Andes Press Agency for photograph included in the essay: Peter L. Berger (1994), 'The Gross National Product and the Gods', *The McKinsey Quarterly*, **1**, pp. 97–110.

Annual Reviews Inc. for the essay: Roger M. Keesing (1974), 'Theories of Culture', *Annual Review of Anthropology*, **3**, pp. 73–97. © 1974 by Annual Reviews Inc.

California Management Review for the essay: Sangjin Yoo and Sang M. Lee (1987), 'Management Style and Practice of Korean Chaebols', *California Management Review*, **XXIX**, pp. 95–110. Copyright © 1987 by The Regents of the University of California. By permission of The Regents.

The Centre for East Asian Cultural Studies for Unesco for the essay: Yang Tien-yi (Kan Toshio) (1989), 'Japanese-Style Management: Socio-Economic and Cultural Factors', *East Asian Cultural Studies* (now *The Centre for East Asian Cultural Studies for Unesco*), **XXVIII**, pp. 13–44.

Elsevier Science Ltd for the essay: Philippe Lasserre and Jocelyn Probert (1994), 'Competing on the Pacific Rim: High Risks and High Returns', *Long Range Planning*, **27**, pp. 12–35.

Lawrence Erlbaum Associates Ltd for the essay: S.G. Redding and Michael Hsiao (1990), 'An Empirical Study of Overseas Chinese Managerial Ideology', *International Journal of Psychology*, **25**, pp. 629–41.

Sally and Richard Greenhill for photographs included in the essay: Peter L. Berger (1994), 'The Gross National Product and the Gods', *The McKinsey Quarterly*, **1**, pp. 97–110.

Series Preface

The International Library of Management brings together in one series the most significant and influential articles from across the whole range of management studies. In compiling the series, the editors have followed a selection policy that is both international and interdisciplinary. The articles that are included are not only of seminal importance today, but are expected to remain of key relevance and influence as management deals with the issues of the next millennium.

The Library was specifically designed to meet a great and growing need in the field of management studies. Few areas have grown as rapidly in recent years, in size, complexity, and importance. There has been an enormous increase in the number of important academic journals publishing in the field, in the amount published, in the diversity and complexity of theory and in the extent of cross-pollination from other disciplines. At the same time, managers themselves must deal with increasingly complex issues in a world growing ever more competitive and interdependent. These remarkable developments have presented all those working in the field, whether they be theorists or practitioners, with a serious challenge. In the absence of a core series bringing together this wide array of new knowledge and thought, it is becoming increasingly difficult to keep abreast of all new important developments and discoveries, while it is becoming ever-more vital to do so.

The International Library of Management aims to meet that need, by bringing the most important articles in management theory and practice together in one core, definitive series. The Library provides management researchers, professors, students, and managers themselves, with an extensive range of key articles which, together, provide a comprehensive basis for understanding the nature and importance of the major theoretical and substantive developments in management science. The Library is the definitive series in management studies.

In making their choice, the editors have drawn especially from the Anglo-American tradition, and have tended to exclude articles which have been widely reprinted and are generally available. Selection is particularly focused on issues most likely to be important to management thought and practice as we move into the next millennium. Editors have also prefaced each volume with a thought-provoking introduction, which provides a stimulating setting for the chosen articles.

The International Library of Management is an essential resource for all those engaged in management development in the future.

KEITH BRADLEY
Series Editor
The International Library of Management

Introduction

Comparative management theory, in an organized form, dates from the early 1960s. Not surprisingly, its emergence coincided with the early stages of internationalization by US corporations and the issues to which that process gave rise. Concern about understanding differences was given a major boost in the 1980s by the onslaught of East Asian competition in world markets and the dynamism of Pacific Asia as a region for investment and economic growth. There were of course companies operating across international boundaries before that – European history is replete with success stories going back hundreds of years – but there was then no body of thought called management theory within which the issues could be analysed. Companies worked out their own solutions, many with high intelligence and sensitivity to what was possible and appropriate. We include some historical perspective here in a study of the British adaptation to the role of managing the Indian Raj (Chapter 18).

The formalization of the attempt to understand organization and management, still largely an American-dominated process, has, over the last 30 years, grappled with the problem of providing advice to managers working abroad. In applying the methods of social science across a spectrum of approaches, it has achieved moderate success. This volume charts that progress by presenting examples of the craft of achieving understanding. They are supplemented by essays which stand back and review progress.

There are two particularly challenging difficulties which stand in the way of offering international managers clear and simple guidelines. Firstly the issues are extremely complex, while the tracing of cause and effect is a frustrating exercise. Secondly the response by researchers has tended to segment the problem into tiny pieces; by understanding more and more about less and less, it has been difficult to create general theories to connect things up. These results are understandable given the nature of the problem being examined and the way academic research is normally subdivided, but the consequence is that many practitioners in the field, typically running a department in a multinational abroad, are still working things out as they go along, basing their assessment of the local situation on anecdote and informal wisdom accumulated in the firm and in the local network of foreign businessmen.

And yet progress has been made. A number of major breakthroughs in understanding have been achieved and the discipline is much more sophisticated overall than in the 1960s. It has continued to draw in ideas from related fields such as anthropology, sociology, development economics and management theory, and it continues to attract scholars. The problems of complexity and causation remain, but in a sense always will with the study of human society.

How, then, may we understand the progress of the discipline so far? How also may readers at the same time achieve an understanding of what is currently known and usable for transmission to practitioners? And how may people personally interested in undertaking research be pointed towards new and fruitful enquiry? To achieve all of these aims the book is designed in five parts which respectively

I   explain how culture is seen and how its effects are traced, along with all the other influences which affect different kinds of organization;

II   describe the main differences for as many countries as possible;

III   examine particular aspects of organizing and managing to learn how cultural differences work to influence them;

IV   present successful examples from the world of organization to show how cultural influences can be managed;

V   review progress to date in understanding, knowledge gaps and future research needs.

While following this sequence, the core of the volume is the second section describing main differences. There will inevitably be some overspill between parts, as many essays address more than one theme, but that will serve to remind the reader of the interconnectedness of the problems addressed and the value of taking an over-arching perspective.

How Culture is Seen

The specification of what culture is has occupied many scholars in and around its core discipline of anthropology, but also in sociology and social psychology. At one point, almost as a gesture of despair, one famous study recorded 260 different definitions of culture (Kroeber and Kluckholn 1952). A major intellectual breakthrough in grappling with the concept and presenting an explanation of its workings was the 1966 book by Berger and Luckmann, *The Social Construction of Reality*. In this they argued cogently that societies collectively define their own frameworks for creating meaning out of the multiple impressions in which life is embedded. These frameworks are shared and also evolve as societies change. In some societies they are clearer and sharper than in others. There are certain human universals, such as the tendency to live in families, pair bonding, care of children. But there are also areas of life which display great variety from society to society, for instance in interpersonal behaviour, eating traditions, the understanding of authority, etc.

In a review of the topic in Chapter 1, Keesing presents an argument for understanding culture as the 'rules of the game', but with the important qualification that culture is the aggregate of many individual perceptions of what others see as the rules. In other words, if a society is to be coherent, there must be organizing principles shared by people. This echoes the social construction of reality argument and illustrates the gradual consensus emerging over the meaning of culture.

Such an approach was given powerful support in the now-dominant work of Hofstede whose 1980 book, *Culture's Consequences*, marked a major breakthrough in providing a working definition of culture based on strong empirical evidence. His work is represented here by Chapter 2, which challenges the underlying assumptions of much textbook management theory. The four dimensions which he derived to define culture are now widely used by scholars in comparative analysis, although the precise mechanics of their working remain to be studied in greater detail in most countries.

The role of religion in shaping cultural norms has been discussed extensively in the huge volume of scholarship initiated by Weber's classic treatise *The Protestant Ethic and the Spirit of Capitalism*. Work in the same tradition has discussed religious influence on modern

Japanese economic systems (Jacobs 1958), on modern Chinese business (Redding 1990) and on modern third world entrepreneurship (Martin 1990). As a little understood but intriguing special case, the role of Buddhism is discussed in Chapter 3 by Pryor, included here in preference to the repetition of more accessible arguments on other religions.

As scholars have accumulated more refined means of studying organizations, the question of the 'embeddedness' of organizations in particular societies has come to be better understood although by no means universally accepted. The discipline of economics, for instance, has tended to persist with its underlying assumption that the influences on human behaviour are universal and directly comparable. This assumption is challenged in a widely-cited paper by Granovetter (Chapter 4).

Another important perspective, that of the 'institutionalists', argues that the cultural and social history of a society will create certain institutional frameworks, such as systems of government, of education and of accessing capital, which are the main determinants of current systems of management. This rich and complex sociological approach, seeing culture as prior to but not necessarily the centrepiece of explanation, is represented in Chapter 5 by Whitley on the emergence of alternative 'business systems'.

It can thus be seen that agreement is common on culture being, in Hofstede's phrase, the 'collective programming of the mind' – the software which guides the workings of the hardware of surface behaviour and social structures. But there is less agreement on how culture can help to explain variations in systems of managing and organizations. Hofstede would argue that the psychological contribution is prime. Whitley that institutions are prime. Granovetter that institutions are embedded in a collective programming and that both are necessary. Clearly there are explanatory preferences which people follow according to their own intellectual training; clearly, too, the various components or stages of a complex process need to be acknowledged. Suffice it to say that mental programming will interact with the accidents and movements of social history to produce a specific institutional context. Modern organizations will then reflect that context, but they will also reflect deeper and earlier tendencies relating to trust, authority and cooperation.

Differences between Countries

Comparing cultures almost always begins with the assumption that the best way of identifying a culture is by the use of national boundaries. This is clearly justifiable in the case of, say, Japan or Portugal, but is more problematic in countries of mixed culture such as Malaysia or the United States. The reader is thus warned that cultural boundaries may not be comparable in their degree of clarity, but the convention or convenience of using countries as cultural entities is so little questioned that it pervades virtually all research in comparative management.

The work of Hofstede already presented in Part I establishes the most commonly used framework for country comparisons and explains its major components in a general theory of cultural difference. However two alternative approaches running in parallel with that of Hofstede are also widely used. They are those of Laurent and of Trompenaars, represented here in Chapters 6 and 7. These explanations tend to focus more on behaviour in organizations than does Hofstede's rather encyclopaedic framework, thus providing useful insights for the manager operating across national boundaries. Laurent's work is particularly well grounded in European data.

Different traditions of organizing and managing have contributed in recent years to the highly competitive development of Pacific Asia. Insights into these alternative structures, contrasting in so many ways with the standard Western textbook model, are provided in three papers from that region – one on Japanese management by Yang, one on Korean Chaebols by Yoo and Lee and one on the Chinese family business by Redding and Hsiao (Chapters 8 to 10).

The variety within Africa and South America can be acknowledged and represented here only briefly in two papers by Ahiauzu and by Amado and Brasil respectively (Chapters 11 and 12). The larger issues of societal movement from pre-modern to modern, relevant to the developing world generally, are illustrated in an important paper by Boisot and Child examining the context of change in China and its implications for organization (Chapter 13). They discuss the transition processes of steadily increasing institutionalization by taking the case of codifying and diffusing information, arguing that modern economic systems require support structures in the body of society (often called civil society) before they can reach their full potential. Underlying these considerations is the dilemma of trust and how societies manage it. This important distinguishing feature, so crucial to explaining variations in the way organizations operate, is discussed in Chapter 14 by Inzerilli on the networking structures of small business in Italy.

Special Aspects of Managing across Cultures

The impact of culture on organizations is most evident in the 'people dimensions' of managing. Where an organization's systems (derived as they may be from the assumptions of one culture) directly confront the assumptions of another carried in the head of an employee, the point of contact is clear and sharp. Thus an insensitive Western appraisal system might totally override Chinese norms about 'face'.

However, the influence of culture is not strictly limited to the domain of human resources. Its influence is visible in organization structures, in systems of communication, in decision processes and locations for decision, in the setting of strategy, in the typical array of stakeholders, in the varying penetration of professionalism, in performance norms and in much else. Patterns of causation which illuminate these phenomena are scattered throughout this book. In Part III we concentrate on three examples of cultural influences reaching beyond HRM.

The first, by Lasserre and Probert, is concerned with environmental variation, not all of which is necessarily cultural, but which, in sum, is often perceived by the expatriate manager in summary gross terms as 'working in a different culture'. The perceived threat of working in circumstances where the rules are different – and where simply finding out what they are is difficult – may be imagined. The research effectively illustrates the great variation among Pacific Asian countries in the forms and degrees of societal order faced by practising managers in tackling their external organizational work.

The paper by Black, Mendenhall and Oddou serves to illustrate the value of integrating multiple perspectives in the interests of progress in understanding. The literature on the management of expatriate assignments is now at a point where new directions are needed and the repetition of existing research shunned. Much has been learned about the actual experiences of executives as they adjust to foreign assignments. What is now required is more research on the control processes used by firms, on preparation and on the way local environments affect expatriate behaviour.

Parkhe's paper on the management of joint ventures deals with the increasingly common problems of managing strategic alliances as they become both more frequent and more complex. It illustrates that breakdown occurs most frequently because of misunderstanding in the more nebulous areas of meaning and in those fields of agreement which are implicit rather than easily measurable. This is obviously a rich field for those interested in the subtleties and pitfalls of cross-cultural communication. The practical implications are clearly substantial.

Successful Cross-Cultural Management

We begin here with a history lesson. British interests in India from around 1600 to 1858 were the responsibility of one company – the East India Company – precursor to the Indian Civil Service of the Raj. From the perspective of the late 20th century there may be much to regret about colonialism as a political structure, and there is no intention here to imply otherwise. From the standpoint of cross-cultural management, however, this provides one of the most intriguing success stories in terms of adaptation and efficient administration. It is told well in Stening's historical review, with potent implications for today's globalizing companies.

Globalizing is of course the ultimate challenge for the human resources function of a large company, and its achievement is fraught with difficulty. A recent study by Sparrow, Schuler and Jackson maps out the terrain and deals clearly with the question of convergence. The original convergence theory (Kerr *et al* 1960) was later revised by Kerr (1983) who concluded that, although managerial systems may appear to be converging, large and significant differences remain in the realm of the mind which affect the detail of behaviour. In other words, culture is not being homogenized. We remain persistently different despite appearances to the contrary.

In recent years successful management has tended to recognize a different level of culture from that of society at large – namely corporate culture. The two interconnect but, because of their separate workings and origins, a manager needs to understand each in its own right. Schneider's paper is a useful guide to disentangling the complexity.

The Progress of Understanding

The progress of social science works at two levels: the generation of ideas about causation and the testing of those ideas in the real world. The two are inevitably connected as they feed off each other. The essential difficulty is how to draw boundaries around the issue of interest in such a way that key parts of the explanation are not cut off from the account. Adding to this difficulty is the fact that organizations and societies are constantly changing and evolving.

An inevitable feature of the literature is that different disciplines work at different levels. The analysis of individual characteristics and behaviour in cross-cultural psychology is a rich and rewarding field of study with a large literature. Changing the focus to social psychology introduces different frameworks and leads to topic areas such as leadership behaviour, group dynamics and the study of interaction in communications, in conflict management, in negotiation and decision processes. In comparative organization theory, the focus shifts again as the object of study is the coordination system itself, introducing another different literature.

Two further levels exist. The newly emerging field of business systems theory explains the larger business system which connects organizations together in a particular economy, and in this theory culture retains a part in the explanation. Finally there is the macro level analysis of national economic success and failure, typified by the concerns of bodies such as the World Bank. In this field, where economics paradigms predominate, the impact of culture tends to be acknowledged only grudgingly, although this volume indicates that culture is inevitably there.

The important lesson both for those seeking to understand what is already known and for those seeking greater knowledge through research, is to avoid confusing the various levels of analysis. As the levels shift, so too do the analytical tools. The theoretical frameworks at each level reflect the issues of interest at that level which in turn define (a) the main factors that have to be included and (b) the degree of specificity with which they should be analysed.

The problems affecting research progress in this complex field mainly derive from the pigeon-holing resorted to in the face of the complexities involved. In other words the different levels are not talking to each other. Insights from any level can enrich the others and tend to do so when transferred. Occasionally a larger framework, crossing and integrating disciplines, is proposed in order to alleviate this problem; Part V provides examples of recent attempts to do so.

Chapter 21 by Boyacigiller and Adler reviews the performance of cross-cultural research in the 1980s, reaching sobering conclusions about its weakness in North America at a time when companies might be considered most in need of its results. Berger's essay on economic culture opens up a brave new set of vistas and presents a rich new conceptual framework for understanding the interaction of culture and economic life. Finally, in Chapter 23, Redding summarizes and criticizes the work in comparative management of the last 30 years; he points to the need for more conceptual sophistication and greater research adventurousness as conditions for progress.

One final observation is perhaps pertinent. It is that some of the richest insights into the understanding of culture's workings have come from ethnographic studies. In his classic 1973 call for better methods, Geertz introduced the term 'thick description' – the close, detailed study of activities on the ground as they occur. The difficulty here is that such work does not lend itself to the journal article format. A second difficulty is that the numbers-obsessed economics paradigm, with its naive epistemology for handling causation in social science, has become imperialist, resulting in a rash of quantitative reporting of investigations. These are in fact crucial to scientific progress, but they do need to be rooted in theory development and connected to larger frameworks. Regrettably many of them have not been.

The forces of globalization are now so powerful that cross-cultural managerial competence is becoming a strategic question for many large companies. This may precipitate greater research efforts in future years, hopefully yielding new insights to aid understanding. In the long run, given the danger of simplistic packaged solutions to complex problems, it is the increase in the level of understanding of why other people behave as they do that will lead to the most effective managerial responses.

References

Berger, P.L. and T. Luckmann (1966), *The Social Construction of Reality*, London: Pelican.

Geertz, C. (1973), *The Interpretation of Cultures*, New York: Basic Books.

Hofstede, G. (1980), *Culture's Consequences*, London: Sage Publications.

Jacobs, N. (1958), *The Origin of Modern Capitalism and Eastern Asia*, Hong Kong: University of Hong Kong Press.

Kerr, C. (1983), *The Future of Industrial Societies*, Cambridge MA: Harvard University Press.

Kerr, C., J.T. Dunlop, F.H. Harbison and C.A. Myers (1960), *Industrialism and Industrial Man*, Cambridge MA: Harvard University Press.

Kroeber, A. and C. Kluckholn (1952), 'Culture: a critical review of concepts and definitions', Cambridge MA: Papers of the Peabody Museum of American Archeology and Ethnology, Harvard University.

Martin, D. (1990), *Tongues of Fire: the Explosion of Protestantism in Latin America*, Oxford: Blackwell.

Redding, S.G. (1990), *The Spirit of Chinese Capitalism*, New York: de Gruyter.

Weber, M. (1958), *The Protestant Ethic and the Spirit of Capitalism*, New York: Scribners.

References

Part I
How Culture is Seen

[1]

THEORIES OF CULTURE

Roger M. Keesing[1]
Institute of Advanced Studies. Australian National University
Canberra A.C.T., Australia

INTRODUCTION

"Yanomamö culture," "Japanese culture," "the evolution of culture," "nature vs culture": we anthropologists are still using that word, and we still think it means something. But looking across at our primate relatives learning local traditions, using tools, and manipulating symbols, we can no longer say comfortably that "culture" is the heritage of learned symbolic behavior that makes humans human. And standing amid the swirling tides of change and individual diversity, we can no longer say comfortably that "a culture" is the heritage people in a particular society share. Moreover, we increasingly realize that the holistic, humanistic view of culture synthesized by Kroeber and Kluckhohn includes too much and is too diffuse either to separate analytically the twisted threads of human experience or to interpret the designs into which they are woven.

The challenge in recent years has been to narrow the concept of "culture" so that it includes less and reveals more. As Geertz argues, "cutting the culture concept down to size . . . [into] a narrowed, specialized, and . . . theoretically more powerful concept" (30, p. 4) has been a major theme in modern anthropological theorizing.[2] And predictably, modern anthropologists have not agreed on the best way to narrow and sharpen the central conceptual tool they have inherited from their elders.

In the pages that follow, I will summarize recent rethinkings of "culture" as

---

[1] I am indebted to the Center for Advanced Study in the Behavioral Sciences, Stanford, California, for providing an idyllic setting where this review could be written, and to Bridget O'Laughlin. Mervyn Meggitt, Triloki Nath Pandey, and Gregory Bateson for their helpful suggestions.

[2] Implicit in this view is an assumption shared by most of us, I think: that "culture" does not have some true and sacred and eternal meaning we are trying to discover; but that like other symbols, it means whatever we use it to mean; and that as with other analytical concepts, human users must carve out—and try to partly agree on—a class of natural phenomena it can most strategically label.

73

falling into four focal areas. Having highlighted work being done in each area,[3] I will seek to clarify the terminological, philosophical, and substantive issues that divide major theorists. In the process, I will consider the implications of these rethinkings for a number of classic anthropological questions: How have cultures developed and what forces shape them? How are cultures learned? How do shared symbolic systems transcend individual thought worlds? How different and unique are cultures? Do universal patterns underlie diversity? How is cultural description to be possible?

CULTURES AS ADAPTIVE SYSTEMS

An important expansion of cultural theory has come from viewing cultures in evolutionary perspective. A widened bridge between studies of hominid evolution and studies of human social life has led us to see more clearly that the human biological design is open-ended, and to perceive the way its completion and modification through cultural learning make human life viable in particular ecological settings. Applying an evolutionary model of natural selection to cultural constructions on biological foundations has led anthropologists to ask with increasing sophistication how human communities develop particular cultural patterns.

A vast literature, popular and technical, has dealt with the interweaving and relative importance of biological and cultural components of human behavior. Aggression, territoriality, sex roles, facial expression, sexuality, and other domains where cultural and biological are interwoven have been endlessly and often mindlessly discussed. From all this, we shall draw two brief conclusions, then pass on. First, any notion that if we peel off the layers of cultural convention we will ultimately find Primal Man and naked human nature underneath is both sterile and dangerous: we need a complex interactional model, not a simplistically stratigraphic one (19, 25). Second, either extreme ethological or extreme cultural determinism can now be sustained by ideology and faith but not by sober science. Just how biological templates are transformed and elaborated into cultural patterns will have to be worked out for each realm; and that will take careful and imaginative research designs and patient exploration, not polemics and sensationalism.

How human cultures are distinctive, despite the continuities in hominid evolution, has been extensively reviewed by Holloway (45), Alland (2, 3), Montagu (59), and others. A crucial issue here is how and at what stage vocal language evolved and what its immediate precursors were (44). If the evidence that an elaborated vocal language is less than 100,000 years old holds up, a vast period looms when

---

[3] I will *not* list exhaustively the publications where "culture" is used or cultural theory is applied or developed. Since that would include a substantial proportion of the writings in anthropology, this would not only be impossible, but trivial and unrevealing: a focus on high points and highlights is clearly demanded in a review article concerned with refinement of theory, not accumulation of substance.

early humans lived in bands, made tools, hunted in well-planned forays, probably lived in pair-bond family relationships—a period of two million years or more of proto-human social life without a fully elaborated code for symbolic communication. Our understanding of what makes humans human and how cultures evolved will doubtless unfold and change excitingly in the next few years.

From the standpoint of cultural theory, however, the major developments have come from evolutionary / ecological approaches to cultures as adaptive systems. The major spawning grounds of evolutionary / ecological rethinkings have been Michigan and Columbia. The foundations laid by Leslie White have been creatively recast by such scholars as Sahlins, Rappaport, Vayda, Harris, Carneiro; and by such theory-minded archeologists as the Binfords, Flannery, Longacre, Sanders, Price. and Meggers. The rapprochement of a theoretical archeology with ecological anthropology emerges as one of the major developments of the past decade.

That is not to imply that consensus prevails about how cultures are best conceptualized or how and why they develop and change. The recent exchanges between Service (75) and Harris (42), Marxist critiques of Harris' cultural materialism, the gulfs between cultural ecology and the human ecology conceived by Vayda & Rappaport (81), the sectarian wars within "the new archeology," all attest to diversity and disagreement. Given this sectarian diversity, most scholars working in this tradition (I will for shorthand call them "cultural adaptationists")[4] agree on some broad assumptions.

(*a*) Cultures are systems (of socially transmitted behavior patterns) that serve to relate human communities to their ecological settings. These ways-of-life-of-communities include technologies and modes of economic organization, settlement patterns, modes of social grouping and political organization, religious beliefs and practices, and so on. When cultures are viewed broadly as behavior systems characteristic of populations, extending and permuting somatic givens, whether we consider them to be patterns *of* or patterns *for* behavior is a secondary question.

> Culture is all those means whose forms are not under direct genetic control ... which serve to adjust individuals and groups within their ecological communities (Binford 11, p. 323)

> The culture concept comes down to behavior patterns associated with particular groups of peoples, that is to "customs" or to a people's "way of life" (Harris 41, p. 16).

(*b*) Cultural change is primarily a process of adaptation and what amounts to natural selection.

> Man is an animal and. like all other animals, must maintain an adaptive relationship with his surroundings in order to survive. Although he achieves this

---

[4] A term which, however disagreeable, lacks the aura of ancient battles, rusting weapons, and buried protagonists that "cultural evolutionists" conjures to mind.

adaptation principally through the medium of culture, the process is guided by the same rules of natural selection that govern biological adaptation (Meggers 56, p. 4).

Seen as adaptive systems, cultures change in the direction of equilibrium within ecosystems; but when balances are upset by environmental, demographic, technological, or other systemic changes, further adjustive changes ramify through the cultural system. Feedback mechanisms in cultural systems may thus operate both negatively (toward self-correction and equilibrium) and positively (toward disequilibrium and directional change).

(c) Technology, subsistence economy, and elements of social organization directly tied to production are the most adaptively central realms of culture. It is in these realms that adaptive changes usually begin and from which they usually ramify. However, different conceptions of how this process operates separate the "cultural materialism" of Harris from the social dialectics of more authentic Marxists or the "cultural evolutionism" of Service and distinguish the cultural ecologists of the Steward tradition from human ecologists such as Rappaport and Vayda. However, all (except perhaps the Rappaport of most recent vintage) would view economies and their social correlates as in some sense primary, and ideational systems—religion, ritual, world view—as in some sense secondary, derived, or epiphenomenal.

Service's charges of monistic reductionism are misplaced here (see 42, 75). Harris' analytical strategy expresses an expectation, not an assumption:

> Similar technologies applied to similar environments tend to produce similar arrangements of labor in production and distribution, and . . . these in turn call forth similar kinds of social groupings, which justify and coordinate their activities by means of similar systems of values and beliefs (41, p. 4).

In assigning "priority to the study of the material conditions of sociocultural life," Harris—like other articulate proponents of related views—does not invoke a simple "prime-mover," but a complex of them (he himself speaks of "demo-techno-econo-environmental conditions"); and he and other cultural adaptationists leave room for cases where an ideology, home grown or imported, transforms the social and economic order. Marxist critics of Harris also stress—rightly, I think—the importance of conflicts and contradictions in the social order, not simply adaptation, in generating and guiding processes of social and cultural change.

(d) The ideational components of cultural systems may have adaptive consequences—in controlling population, contributing to subsistence, maintaining the ecosystem, etc; and these, though often subtle, must be carefully traced out wherever they lead:

> . . . It is necessary to consider the total culture when analyzing adaptation. Superficially, it might be assumed that attention could be confined to aspects directly related to the environment . . . [But] whether analysis begins with religious

practices, social organization, or some other sector of a cultural complex, . . . [it] will . . . reveal functional relationships with other categories of behavior that are adaptive (Meggers 56, p. 43).

The most striking recent elaboration of this view has been Rappaport's impressive analysis of Tsembaga Maring ritual cycles as components in an adaptive system (65); and more recently, his suggestion that ritual systems and the cultural frame of sanctity play a central part in mediating cultural adaptation (66–68).

IDEATIONAL THEORIES OF CULTURE

In contrast to the diverse adaptationist theorists of culture stand a number of theorists who see cultures as ideational systems. Here I will distinguish three rather different ways of approaching cultures as systems of ideas.

Cultures as Cognitive Systems

Another major theme of the last 15 years has been the emergence of an explicit cognitive anthropology. In practice, "the new ethnography" has been mainly an exploration of systems of folk classification ("ethnoscience," "ethnographic semantics"). But beyond the anthropological study of other peoples' butterfly collecting has emerged a new and important view of culture as cognition.

Cultures are seen as systems of knowledge. To quote Ward Goodenough:

A society's culture consists of whatever it is one has to know or believe in order to operate in a manner acceptable to its members. Culture is not a material phenomenon; it does not consist of things, people, behavior, or emotions. It is rather an organization of these things. It is the form of things that people have in mind, their models for perceiving, relating, and otherwise interpreting them (32, p. 167).

Culture . . . consists of standards for deciding what is, . . . for deciding what can be, . . . for deciding what one feels about it, . . . for deciding what to do about it, and . . . for deciding how to go about doing it (33, p. 522).

Goodenough contrasts this ideational sense of culture with the sense used by the adaptationists we have discussed, who conceive culture to be the "pattern of life within a community—the regularly recurring activities and material and social arrangements" (33, p. 521; 34–37).

So reconceived, cultures are epistemologically in the same realm as language (Sassure's *langue* or Chomsky's competence), as inferred ideational codes lying behind the realm of observable events.

In this conceptualization, language is a subsystem of culture; and explorers in cognitive anthropology have hoped or assumed that linguistic methods and models will be appropriate to other cultural realms: hence componential analysis, emic vs etic, eliciting frames, etc. [See Keesing's argument (48) that cognitive anthropologists have made this jump too lightly, and have borrowed from a now outmoded taxonomic linguistics.] But in the last several years, attention has begun to turn from the uniqueness of cultural systems to a search for universal patterns (48).

Analyses of cultures as cognitive systems have not progressed very far beyond a mapping of limited and neatly bounded semantic domains. Significant attempts to formalize the cultural knowledge needed to stage performances or operate in limited social situations have been made by Frake (18), Metzger & Williams (57), Wallace (83), Spradley (77), Agar (1), and others; but it is striking in retrospect that the messianic optimism of early cognitive anthropology has yielded so few fragments of cultural description.

Moreover, it has yielded few even tentative sketch maps of the overall structure and organization of cultures as cognitive systems (see e.g. 50, p. 123; 34, pp. 258–59; 37; 78). Not only has the notion of a "cultural grammar" proved unproductive and inadequate in the face of the staggering richness and complexity of human knowledge and experience; "new ethnographers" have not set out even an empty blueprint of how an overall cognitive system might be organized, and hence how the bits and pieces offered in demonstration might fit into a wider design. Such a lack of broad vision, I believe, has obscured the magnitude of the realms of culture not amenable to the surface probings of formal ethnography. I have argued (48, 49) that the new transformational linguistics gives some valuable insights about how cultural knowledge underlying the surface structures so far mapped might be organized; below I will argue that burgeoning research in artificial intelligence can yield further insights.

Cultures as Structural Systems

On the continent, Lévi-Strauss has continued to elaborate his view of men's symbolic worlds and the processes of mind that generate them; and in the last decade, structuralist approaches have had profound impact on many scholars trained in the Anglo-American tradition.

Lévi-Strauss' writings on culture and mind have not only been sweepingly influential; as sacred texts, they have elicited an ever-widening stream of exegetical literature.[5] I will not add substantially to that stream. Here only a few points will serve to place the Lévi-Straussian position in relation to those that precede and follow. Lévi-Strauss views cultures as shared symbolic systems that are cumulative *creations of mind*; he seeks to discover in the structuring of cultural domains—myth, art, kinship, language—the principles of mind that generate these cultural elaborations. Material conditions of subsistence and economy constrain (but do not *explain*) lived-in worlds; but especially in myth, they leave thought-of worlds free reign. The physical world humans live in provides the raw materials universal processes of mind elaborate into substantively diverse but formally similar patterns. The mind imposes culturally patterned order, a logic of binary contrast, of relations and transformations, on a continuously changing and often

---

[5] Literary critics have a tendency to be ponderous, obscure, and intellectually pretentious, in counterpoint to the textured beauty of the texts they seek to illuminate; and Lévi-Strauss' exegetes and apologists have with rare exceptions (notably Boon 12) carried on this tradition.

random world. The gulf between the cultural realm, where man imposes his arbitrary order, and the realm of nature becomes a major axis of symbolic polarity: "nature vs culture" is a fundamental conceptual opposition in many—perhaps all—times and places. Lévi-Strauss, especially in *Mythologiques*, is more concerned with "Culture" than with "a culture": he sees American Indian mythic structures as overlapping, interconnected patterns that transcend not only the cognitive organization of individual Bororo or Winnebago or Mandan actors, but in a sense transcend as well the boundaries of language and custom that divide different peoples.

Cultures as Symbolic Systems

Another avenue of approach to culture, related to but distinct from both the American cognitivist and continental structuralist approaches, has been to treat cultures as systems of shared symbols and meanings (13). On the continent, this avenue has been most extensively explored by Louis Dumont.[6] In the United States, the most notable pioneers have been two anthropological heirs to the Parsonian tradition: Clifford Geertz and David Schneider.

Geertz' powerful view of culture, illumined by a broad humanistic scholarship, has become increasingly systematic. Like Lévi-Strauss, Geertz is at his best when he draws on general theory to interpret ethnographic particulars; unlike Lévi-Strauss, he finds these particularities in the richness of real people in real life: a cockfight, a funeral, a sheep theft. His texts are not disembodied and decontextualized myths or customs, but humans engaging in symbolic action.

Geertz sees the cognitive view of Goodenough and the "new ethnographers" as reductionistic and spuriously formalistic. Meanings are not "in people's heads"; symbols and meanings are shared by social actors—between, not in them; they are public, not private.[7] Cultural systems are ideational, but in the sense that a Beethoven quartet is ideational—beyond or between its manifestations in individual minds or concrete performances. Cultural patterns, he says, are not reified or metaphysical: like rocks and dreams "they are things of this world."

Geertz sees his view of culture as *semiotic*. To study culture is to study shared codes of meaning. Borrowing from Ricoeur a broader sense of "text," Geertz recently has treated a culture as "an assemblage of texts" (29, p. 26; cf. 13). Anthropology thus becomes a matter of *interpretation*, not decipherment (in this, Geertz contrasts his own approach with Lévi-Strauss' (see Geertz 28 and 29, p. 36, f.n. 38);[8] and interpretation becomes "thick description" that must be deeply embedded in the contextual richness of social life.

Geertz has no ethnoscience optimism that the cultural code can be formalized as

---

[6] Dumont's important ideas will not, due to limitations of space, be reviewed here.

[7] In this Geertz draws on Husserl, Wittgenstein, and Ryle.

[8] Note a further central contrast between Lévi-Strauss and Geertz, especially as drawn by the former: Lévi-Strauss' rejection [as argued in *L'Homme Nu* (54)] of the subjectivist orientation of phenomenology, which Geertz follows in drawing on Schutz and on the Parsonian actor frame of reference.

a grammar, no Lévi-Straussian glibness at decoding: interpreting cultural texts is a slow and difficult task. How a culture as an assemblage of texts fits together is nowhere made clear (presumably, Geertz would agree that we are still in the early stages of finding that out). When he has stepped back to generalize about religion, ideology, and common sense as cultural systems and about Balinese concepts of time and person (24, 26, 27, 30, 31), some picture of the relation between cultural domains begins to emerge. His view of the wider patterning of culture emerges most vividly in an extension of Wittgenstein's analogy between our language and an old city, "a maze of little streets and squares" that are the precipitate of time, surrounded by a neat reticulate design of planned modern sections—the formal languages of mathematics and science. Cultures are, Geertz argues, like old cities. The ones anthropologists usually study, unlike our own, have few if any planned suburbs (and that, he argues, makes somewhat spurious the anthropological effort to find in the wandering streets of those ideational cities the sectors that correspond to our neatly planned suburbs of philosophy, law, or science). The analogy is vivid; and Geertz has made a notable effort to explore some sectors of several old and tangled cities, to convey the subtle spirit of the streets as well as their rough map, and to generalize about the corresponding sectors of different cities. The overall plan of these cultural cities cannot yet be seen. Elsewhere, Geertz warns against the danger of the analyst mapping a culture in such a way as to maximize and neaten its integration and internal consistency—where in fact only partial integration and often disconnectedness and internal contradiction exist. He creates another vivid metaphor:

> ... The problem of cultural analysis is as much a matter of determining independencies as interconnection, gulfs as well as bridges. The appropriate image, if one must have images, of cultural organization, is neither the spider web nor the pile of sand. It is rather more the octopus, whose tentacles are in large part separately integrated, neurally quite poorly connected with one another and with what in the octopus passes for a brain, and yet who nonetheless manages to get around and to preserve himself, for a while anyway, as a viable, if somewhat ungainly entity (27, pp. 66–67).

A related but somewhat different tack has been taken by David Schneider. Like Geertz, Schneider began from a Parsonian framework, but he, too, has developed it in a distinctive way (drawing heavily on the insights of Dumont).

Schneider's view of culture is clearly expressed in his introduction to *American Kinship: A Cultural Account.* Culture, he tells us, is a system of symbols and meanings. It comprises categories or "units," and "rules" about relationships and modes of behavior. The epistemological status of cultural units or "things" does not depend on their observability; both ghosts and dead people are cultural categories. Nor are rules and categories to be inferred directly from behavior; they exist, as it were, on a separate plane. "The definition of the units and the rules is *not* based on, defined by, drawn from, constructed in accord with, or developed in terms of the observations of behavior in any direct, simple sense" (71, p. 6). And, as Schneider's analysis of kinship makes clear, he believes that analysis of cultures as systems of symbols can profitably be carried out independently of the "actual states of affairs" one can observe as events and behaviors. There are, he admits, important questions to be asked about the connections between the plane of cultural symbols and the plane of observable events so that one can "discover how the cultural constructs are generated, the laws governing their change, and in just what ways they are systematically, related to the actual states of affairs of life" (71, p. 7); but in his recent work, he has chosen to leave those tasks to others.

More recently, Schneider (72), has expanded and clarified his conception of culture. He distinguishes a level of "how-to-do-it" rules or *norms* that tell an actor how to navigate in his social world. But he wants in cultural analysis to take one further step back, to distinguish "the system of symbols and meanings embedded in the normative system, but . . . a distinct aspect of it [which] . . . can easily be abstracted from it":

> By symbols and meanings I mean the basic premises which a culture posits for life: what its units consist in; how those units are defined and differentiated; how they form an integrated order or classification; how the world is structured; in what parts it consists and on what premises it is conceived to exist, the categories and classifications of the various domains of the world of man and how they relate one with another, and the world that man sees himself living in (72, p. 38).

Since Schneider's contrast between "normative" and "cultural" levels is conceptually important, it is worth quoting him at greater length as he clarifies it:

> Where the normative system . . . is Ego centered and particularly appropriate to decision-making or interaction models of analysis, culture is system-centered . . . Culture takes man's position vis-à-vis the world rather than *a* man's position on how to get along in this world as it is given. . . . Culture concerns the stage, the stage setting, and the cast of characters; the normative system consists in the stage directions for the actors and how the actors should play their parts on the stage that is so set (72, p. 38; see also 73).

Schneider goes on to contrast his approach to cultural analysis with Geertz'. He sees the latter as bound—as Parsons himself has been—by Weberian assumptions: a domain of the *social system* (kinship or religion or economics or politics) is carved out, and the corresponding cultural realm is analyzed. A purely cultural analysis can fruitfully trace interconnections of symbols, premises, and principles of order wherever they lead; and a map of the cultural system *as a separate level* will, he argues, look very different than an interpretation of the cultural correlates of social institutions. In the end, he calls for a pure cultural analysis "uncontaminated by the study of its social system"; and only after this logically prior task, for the tracing of interconnectedness between cultural, social, and psychological planes, so as to understand the social life of a people or the actions of individuals.

CULTURES AND SOCIOCULTURAL SYSTEMS

In seeking to clarify the issues that divide major theorists of culture, we begin with no expectation that an eclectic composite can be reached with which they would agree: any statement about culture on which Marvin Harris and David Schneider could agree would probably be vacuous. And being eclectic would lead back toward the broad and clumsy culture concepts of the past.

Nonetheless, a conceptual sorting out will be useful, not to reconcile the disagreements, but to identify their nature and source. Some of them are philosophical and some substantive; some could be resolved by empirical evidence, some could not. Each of the theoretical positions or approaches I have sketched has strengths and vulnerabilities. By underlining strengths and exposing vulnerabilities hidden beneath eloquent rhetoric, some ways of joining strength to strength and guarding exposed flanks, and some paths for future research, may usefully emerge.

A first contrast in sorting out these conceptualizations of culture parallels is drawn by Goodenough. I will call (with considerable precedent) the patterns-of-life-of-communities *sociocultural systems.* Sociocultural systems represent the social realizations or enactments of ideational designs-for-living in particular environments. A settlement pattern is an element of a sociocultural system, not an element of a cultural system in this sense. (The same conceptual principles might yield densely clustered villages or scattered homesteads, depending on water sources, terrain, arable land, demography, and the peaceful or headhunting predilections of the neighboring tribe.) A mode of subsistence technology similarly is part of a sociocultural system, but not strictly speaking part of a cultural system (people with the same knowledge and set of strategies for subsisting might be primarily horticulturalists in one setting and primarily fishermen in another, might make adzes of flint in one setting or shells in another, might plant taro on one side of a mountain range or yams on the other side).

What cultural adaptationists are talking about are, in this sense, sociocultural systems-in-environments. It is these systems that are adaptive or maladaptive, that are subject in some way to natural selection. Ideational designs for living, patterns of shared meanings and systems of knowledge and belief, are crucially important subsystems of ways-of-life-in-environments. The latter are complex systems in the cybernetic sense, in which complex circuits connect ecological, demographic, ideational, and other subsystems.[9] How these circuits are interconnected, how information ramifies through them, and how homeostatic processes and directional change operate are (or can be) empirical questions for investigation, not articles of faith and ideological polemic.

[Note that this conceptualization of culture as an ideational system does not then correspond to the distinction drawn by Harris and some other cultural adaptationists between the economic domain (subsistence, technology, social organization of productive units) and the ideational realm (religion, ideology, law, art, etc). Knowledge and strategy about environments and ways of extracting subsistence from them, about making tools, about forming work groups, are as

---

[9] That these subsystems, or elements of them, may be from different ontological realms is, in the perspective of cybernetics, irrelevant (66).

much a part of the ideational realm I am calling "culture" as patterns of cosmological belief or religious ritual.][10]

That throws Goodenough, Lévi-Strauss, Geertz, and Schneider in one camp (from which the clashing of symbols can be heard in the distance). It does so in a way that most new archeologists and ecological / evolutionary cultural anthropologists can probably accept as a possible—if not necessarily productive—conceptual strategy. At least they would mainly agree that what they are interested in are sociocultural systems[11] and how they develop and change. One can then investigate how ideational systems operate in this process of adaptation and change, both in terms of internal structure (how are changes in ideas about subsistence strategy related to changes in ideas about kinship or changes in ideas about religious ritual?) and in relation to other subsystems (how are ideas about choosing postmarital residence related to increased population or increased agricultural production?).

CULTURES AS IDEATIONAL SYSTEMS: PARADOXES AND PROBLEMS

The theorists of cultures as ideational systems, whom we have thrown into one noisy camp, remain to be sorted out. These modern theorists share an important premise that partly distinguishes them from their intellectual predecessors. As Singer (76) has noted, the two parallel traditions of American cultural anthropology and British social anthropology each entailed a kind of intellectual imperialism: for the former, social patterns were one realm of the culture; for the latter, especially Radcliffe Brown, cultural patterns are crystallized in social structure "as institutionalized and standarized modes of behavior and thought whose normal forms are socially recognized in the explicit or implicit rules to which the members of a society tend to conform" (76, p. 532). The dangers of swallowing the social into the cultural or the cultural into the social have been vividly portrayed by Geertz:

> Either culture is regarded as wholly derivative from the forms of social organization . . . or the forms of social organization are regarded as behavioral embodiments of cultural patterns. In either case . . . the dynamic elements in social change which arise from the failure of cultural patterns to be perfectly congruent with the forms of social organization are largely incapable of formulation (22, p. 992).

He, Goodenough, Lévi-Strauss, Schneider, and other major modern theorists share the premise that cultural and social realms are distinct though interrelated: neither is a mere reflection of the other—each must be considered in its own right.

[10] Note, however, that the distinction I have drawn is characteristically observed in Marxist analysis.

[11] Many, such as the Binfords, have used that designation as more or less interchangeable with "cultural systems."

Such a conceptual untangling is basic to the refinements of theory and narrowings of the "culture" concept of the last 20 years.

The heart of the conceptual disagreements between these scholars is the problem of what to do about a basic paradox of human social life: When individuals engaging in social relations—even if there are only two of them—share common meanings, common understandings of one another's acts, then these shared meanings are greater than the sum of their "parts," their realizations in individual minds. Social meanings transcend, by some mysterious alchemy of minds meeting, the individuation of private experience. Social thinkers have struggled with this paradox for decades, even for centuries; yet *consciences collectives* still confound analytical dissection.

Goodenough's solution is to describe "culture" as an idealized systematization of an individual cognitive world, one that could enable an outsider to produce culturally appropriate responses in the range of social situations a native actor would encounter—to decide in culturally "grammatical" ways "what is, . . . what can be. . . . how one feels about it, . . . what to do about it, . . . and how to go about doing it." Thus what is shared is reduced to an idealized individual actor's point of view (one who, like Chomsky's hypothetical speaker-hearer, knows his culture perfectly). Goodenough's cognitive model would thus be a composite of the cultural knowledge of individuals in different social niches. Yet he, like the linguists, leaves room to deal with subcultural variations and individual differences (33, 34 37). Goodenough is by no means as simplistic a cognitive reductionist as Geertz portrays him to be:

> People learn as individuals. Therefore, if culture is learned, its ultimate locus must be in individuals rather than in groups. . . . Cultural theory must [then] explain in what sense we can speak of culture as being shared or as the property of groups . . . and what the processes are by which such sharing arises. . . . We must . . . try to explain how this analytically useful construct relates to . . . the social and psychological processes that characterize men in groups (37, p. 20).

Goodenough carefully distinguishes seven related ideational senses of "culture" that systematically relate the cognitive worlds of individuals to the collective ideas and behavior of populations (37, pp. 41–42).

Lévi-Strauss sees cultures as transcending individual actors, even as transcending in a sense ethnic boundaries; yet collective representations reflect and reveal the structures and processes of the individual minds of which they are cumulative creations.

Geertz takes the alchemy of shared meanings as basic, but—following Wittgenstein, Husserl, and Ryle—not as mysterious. Public traffic in symbols is very much of this world, not (he would argue) of a Platonic reified imaginary one. Geertz presumably would agree that cultures are "located in time and space by the temporal and spatial distribution of the individuals bearing them" (6, p. 86): but cultures are, as it were, *between* the minds of these individuals, not *in* them. Schneider wants to go a step further, it seems, toward a "methodological essentialist" position (63, pp. 28–29) that a culture in some sense exists "in its own right independently of its imperfect manifestations in the thoughts and actions of its bearers" (6, p. 86). In distinguishing the normative system from the system of cultural symbols and meanings, Schneider explicitly abstracts above and away from the perspective of an individual actor. This level of disembodied symbols, freed from their moorings in the world of social action and situational context, exists in the cognitive world of the cultural theorist; but only ego-centered *perspectives on it* exist in the cognitive worlds of his subjects.

This raises another facet of the basic paradox of the transcendence of shared symbols. Each actor perceives the way of life of his people as in some sense *external*. We do have a perspective on what we construe to be the game our fellows are playing (we also unconsciously assume—through cultural learning—many elements of the world in which we see it being played and view it with emotions subtly shaped by cultural experience). Perceiving "the system," one has some free rein to try to beat it, join it, change it, etc (53).

Moreover, the immediate life space each of us mainly moves in is a world not of roles and institutions and abstract rules, but of individual people and places that are intimately known. We live our lives mainly in familiar phenomenological space whose particularities guide our response. We call cultural roles and rules—based on the general and abstract, not the concrete and individual—into play mainly on the periphery of our immediately familiar space, when dealing with strangers or bureaucracies, or engaging in passing encounters with salesclerk or policeman (encounters much less frequent in the small-scale societies of most of the human past). In this sense, the knowledge that enables individuals to act in "culturally appropriate" ways is only a part of what they know that enables them to live in groups.

There are, moreover, fuzzy but important differences between a collective ideational system and the psychodynamics of the individual—differences theorists of "culture and personality" have sought for years to untangle.

All this means that any effort to reduce cultural systems to the cognitive system of an idealized individual actor is fraught with danger.

> In such a way, extreme subjectivism is married to extreme formalism, with the expected result, an explosion of debate as to whether particular analyses ... reflect what the natives "really" think or are merely clever simulations ... The cognitive fallacy—that culture consists of "mental phenomena which can ... be analyzed by formal methods similar to those of mathematics and logic" (80) is as destructive of an effective use of the concept as the behaviorist and idealist fallacies to which it is a misdrawn correction ... Culture ... is no more ... a psychological phenomenon, a characteristic of someone's mind, ... than ... Tantrism, genetics [or] the progesssive form of the verb (Geertz 30, pp. 11–13).[12]

[12] As noted, Geertz errs in attributing a naively reductionist cognitive view to Goodenough himself; for though Goodenough "places culture in the minds and hearts of men," he is in fact highly sophisticated in his discussion of culture as a composite of what is shared and public; and his most recent synthesis develops a view fairly close to the one I will attempt (37).

But the other horn of the conceptual dilemma—to cut "culture" free of the individual minds through which it is realized—poses dangers as well.

First, the structure of cultural systems is created, shaped, and constrained by individual minds and brains. What forms cultures take depend on what individual humans can think, imagine, and learn, as well as on what collective behaviors shape and sustain viable patterns of life in ecosystems. Cultures must be thinkable and learnable as well as livable.

Without informing our models of cultures with deepening knowledge of the structures and processes of mind, our cultural analyses may turn out to be mere literary exercises. Schneider complains that Geertz—in shaping his cultural analyses around religious institutions (or agricultural or economic ones)—distorts the patterning of cultures as ideational systems. But does Schneider, having moved to an ethereal level of symbols and meanings transcending individual minds, have a spurious freedom to draw his own designs when he thinks he is tracing other peoples'? Schneider has trained a number of students to expect great diversity in the cultural realm of kinship symbols; and not surprisingly, they have found it. Exploring a transcendent level of cultural symbols wherever they seem to lead, we may similarly discover radical diversity in other realms. But many of us are convinced that the diversity is to substantial degree a spurious artifact of the pursuit of cultural symbols unconstrained by the way humans think and learn and communicate, and the social settings in which they act. Time will resolve the question of whether kinship systems are in fact radically diverse symbolic realms, or permutations of the same basic system—so that an Australian Aborigine could drop in on New Guinea tribesmen or desert Bedouin and understand immediately, even through linguistic filters, what kinship discourse was about.

This raises, though obliquely, the question of universals. Are there in nonlinguistic culture universal patterns paralleling the ones emerging in language? In linguistics, the emergence of a universal grammar underlying surface syntactic diversity (and obviating any strong form of Whorfian relativism) has been a major theme of the last decade. Especially in recent generative semantics, the deepest structures of sentences are seen as propositions in a universal "natural logic" that encodes meanings—a logic very similar to that formalized by Boole in his much-maligned *Laws of Thought* (1854) where he sought "to investigate the fundamental laws of those operations of the mind by which reasoning is performed . . . and . . . to collect . . . some probable intimations concerning the nature and constitution of the human mind." Lévi-Strauss has of course sought to find universal processes of thought in the stuff of cultures: he could well have used the same words as Boole to describe his own enterprise, though the linguistic models he borrows are mainly the relatively static formalisms of structuralist phonology.

What is important is that this seems an auspicious time to seek cultural universals, though not to assume them, for language may turn out to be a quite specialized subsystem of logic and transduction (48, 49). And what universals there turn out to be will—most interestingly, at least—be universals of process, of logic, of structure, of organizational principles, rather than of substance (48, 69).

The sterility of seeking common denominators in the substantive stuff of culture has been eloquently argued by Geertz (25).

To what degree universals of language would reflect innately specified rules, logics, or structures is open to serious debate. Chomsky has argued for detailed innate specification; Piaget and others have countered that general cognitive principles and strategies may underlie both linguistic competence and acquisition of other cognitive abilities; and Piaget contends that highly complex hierarchical cognitive systems are built on minimally programmed foundations through the progressive unfolding or more and more complex "theories" about the world, each built on and reorganized from the previous one (62). If there turn out to be important universals of cultural structure (in this formal, not substantive, sense), it is not yet clear how much genetic programming and how much progressive cognitive refinement would underlie them.

Such frontier questions underline the urgency of not divorcing a conception of culture from our burgeoning knowledge of the mind. Geertz, concerned to bring the enlightenment of phenomenology, linguistic philosophy, and hermeneutics to anthropology, would do well to remember that it has been revolutions in science (evolution, relativity, quantum theory, cybernetics, molecular biology, linguistics) that have progressively transformed modern philosophy, not the reverse. A revolutionary advance in our understanding of the organization of intelligence—in a broad cybernetic sense that includes coding at a genetic, cellular, organismic, and ecosystemic level as well as in mind and brain—is now in its early stages.[13] In the international quest—not interdisciplinary but *superdisciplinary*—to unite a formal theory of intelligence and communication with an emerging theoretical biology and the empirical sciences of cognition (4, 60, 64), the human brain and its opposite face, the mind, represent the ultimate challenge, the most complex known natural systems:

> The human brain integrates the facts that it acquires through experience and other forms of learning into a model of the world. New facts are interpreted in the light of the model ... Understanding ... such world models, their neutral organization, their dependence upon environment and culture, are fundamental and difficult questions that cut across many scientific disciplines (14, p. 437).

More than a decade ago, Geertz noted early advances on these fronts and their potential importance (23); and in 1965, he wrote that "culture is best seen not as complexes of concrete behavior patterns—customs, usages, traditions, habit clusters— ... but as a set of control mechanisms—plans, recipes, rules, instructions (what computer engineers call 'programs')—for the governing of behavior" (25, p. 57). But he has not, I think, fully explored the implications of these insights. We

---

[13] Intelligence in this sense refers not simply to brains, real or artificial, but to formal representations of systems that display "biological" or "mental" properties of self-organization, goal-direction, and information processing characteristic of living systems. "Formal biology in this sense ... would ... be ... a theory of *all* organisms, both natural and artificial" (51, p. 49).

88   KEESING

will be poorly served if we weather the next revolutionary storms in philosophy poring over Husserl, Ryle, and Wittgenstein.[14]

Finally, treating the realm of cultural symbols as shared and public, as transcending the minds of individuals, raises the danger not only of the cultural interpreter creating a spuriously integrated and internally consistent symbolic design (recall Geertz' octopus analogy), but also of his hiding diversity and obscuring change. It seems likely that a range of diversity in individual versions of the "common" culture is not simply a social imperfection, but an adaptive necessity: a crucial resource that can be drawn on and selected from in cultural change. The most abstract cultural premises about what things there are and how they are related to one another and to human life may be relatively uniform and slow to change. But specific plans and patterns for human action and understanding are diverse (37, 78, 84), and unlike Beethoven quartets, they change.

But we are still left between the horns of a conceptual dilemma: on the one hand, of cognitive reductionism that misses the magic of shared symbols and the only partial overlap between the psychological world of the individual and the code of cultural meanings and conventions; and on the other, of a spuriously autonomous and spuriously uniform world of cultural symbols freed from the constraints of the mind and brain by which cultures are created and learned and through which they are realized.

TOWARD A CONCEPTUAL UNTANGLING

Perhaps the conceptual distinction between "competence" and "performance" that linguists are struggling to maintain can provide an avenue of escape from this dilemma. Linguistic competence is a model of the knowledge of his language a native speaker *draws on* in speaking and hearing (the processes of linguistic performance). In the Chomskyan linguistics of the mid-1960s, primary concern was with the competence of an idealized speaker-hearer who knows his language perfectly. But increased sophistication in the transformational camp, and pressures from Labov and his fellow "variationists," increasingly lead theorists to deal with diversity. How and at what level the linguistic competence of individuals varies has become a hotly debated issue that will be carefully studied in the next few years. Whether we analytically create a uniform idealized competence or plot differences in the competence of subgroups (dialects) or individuals (idiolects) becomes a question of heuristic strategy geared to the problem of the moment. Competence remains distinguishable from performance.[15]

It seems potentially possible to distinguish analytically a *cultural competence* that does not incorporate the whole psychological world of each individual, and that allows us to avoid both horns of the conceptual dilemma.

[14] As Bateson points out (10), there are serious problems of logical typing involved in the conceptualization of culture that have yet to be sorted out. Cybernetic modeling, drawing on increasing understanding of the formal structure of heterarchical systems, may be crucially important in this regard.

Culture, conceived as a system of competence shared in its broad design and deeper principles, and varying between individuals in its specificities, is then not all of what an individual knows and thinks and feels about his world. It is his *theory of what his fellows know, believe, and mean,* his theory of the code being followed, the game being played, in the society into which he was born (see also 37). It is this theory to which a native actor *refers* in interpreting the unfamiliar or the ambiguous, in interacting with strangers (or supernaturals), and in other settings peripheral to the familiarity of mundane everyday life space; and with which he creates the stage on which the games of life are played. We can account for the individual actor's perception of his culture as external (and as potentially constraining and frustrating); and we can account for the way individuals then can consciously use, manipulate, violate, and try to change what they conceive to be the rules of the game. But note that the actor's "theory" of his culture, like his theory of his language, may be in large measure unconscious. Actors follow rules of which they are not consciously aware, and assume a world to be "out there" that they have in fact created with culturally shaped and shaded patterns of mind.

We can recognize that not every individual shares precisely the same theory of the cultural code, that not every individual knows about all sectors of the culture. Thus a cultural description is always an abstracted composite. Depending on the heuristic purposes at hand, we, like the linguists, can plot the distribution of variant versions of competence among subgroups, roles, and individuals. And, like the linguists, we can study the processes of change in conceptual codes as well as in patterns of social behavior (37).

Such a conception of culture as an idealized body of competence differentially distributed in a population, yet partially realized in the minds of individuals, allows us to bring to bear a growing body of knowledge about the structure of mind and brain and the formal organization of intelligence. Even though no one native actor knows all of the culture, and each has a variant version of the code, culture in this view is ordered not simply as a collection of symbols fitted together by the analyst but as a *system of knowledge,* shaped and constrained by the way the human brain acquires, organizes, and processes information and creates "internal models of reality" (16, 38, 39). Such a conception of culture frees us potentially from the dangers of both cognitive reductionism and ethereal idealism.

To this point I have suggested that we look to linguistics for conceptual guidance. However, the linguists—having distinguished competence from performance—have chosen mainly to study only the former. This has not only given modern linguistics an aura of ivory tower scholasticism in a world where language has been an instrument of oppression and a force of division. It has unnecessarily separated advances in linguistics from advances in psychology, anthropology, and biology. And as Labov and others have pointed out, it has progressively narrowed

---

[15] The main difficulties have come in maintaining the boundary between linguistic competence and cultural knowledge in the face of the need to study presuppositions. The permeability of that boundary need not concern the anthropologist, who begins on the messy side linguistis want to avoid if they can (48, 52).

the data base of linguistic inquiry so that a large edifice teeters precariously on a thin edge of intuition.[16]

I am convinced that if anthropologists conceptualize culture as epistemologically and logically parallel to linguistic competence, they should do so only within a wider concern with sociocultural "performance." An ideational conception of culture "will serve us badly if we take the abstract system we have created out of the flux of the phenomenal world and examine 'it' to see how 'it' is put together. But 'culture' could serve us well if we use it to help untangle the vastly complex skeins of interconnectedness in that world" (48, p. 326).

I am thus agreeing with Schneider that cultures as ideational systems should be explored and mapped in their own terms, not in terms of the domains of social life; but I am disagreeing with his conclusion that the study of culture can profitably be pursued "uncontaminated" by the study of the social and ecological settings in which humans act.

Let me make my reasons explicit.

1. The questions that mainly concern anthropologists are only partly questions about cultures as ideational systems. We want to understand how human groups organize and sustain their social life; how biology and experience interact as individuals become functioning members of a society, and how the nature of that experience shapes personalities; how different—and how similar—are human modes of thought and perception in different times and places; how ways of life change, and what shapes the form they take in particular settings.

We cannot understand other people's lives simply by mapping their culture—though (contra Harris 40) we cannot understand or even adequately record events in their world without understanding their "internal models of reality" (see 15, 37). I have elsewhere illustrated this with Trobriand examples (47, p. 404; 50, p. 441). A competence model of Trobriand culture would tell us what classes of things, people, and events there are and what kind of a world they are situated in, and it would give rules for how to garden, trace descent, exchange, and reside. But it would tell us nothing about residence patterns, descent groups, agricultural production, or the flow of exchange—or even how many Trobrianders there are and where they live.

2. The magic of shared symbols, of minds meeting, is not a magic that occurs on some ethereal cultural plane; as Geertz, phenomenologists, and ethnomethodologists are vividly aware, it is a magic enacted in social settings. It is embedded in public encounters. "The mind is not even a metaphorical 'place' . . . The chessboard, the platform, the scholar's desk, the judge's bench, the lorry-driver's seat, the studio, and the football field are among its places" (70, quoted in 23). Meanings are shared by people whose conceptions of their culture are not identical; and that is more than a matter of common denominators or even of "equivalences" (84). But it is a magic achieved not in a hypothetical vacuum, a

---

[16] Or more precisely, on native speakers' competence in communicating their intuitions about sentences proferred by a linguist.

symbolic realm, but in the collective application of the general to the particular, the private to the social.

3. To understand change and diversity, we must see cultures as elements in complex cybernetic systems of humans-in-environments. An ideational model of culture, in isolation, prevents our understanding change and adaptation. As part of a more complex conceptual scheme, however, such a model of culture enriches our understanding of change and helps us to correct overly simplistic ecological / adaptationist models.

Cultures must generate viable patterns-of-life in ecosystems (or more precisely, they must not generate nonviable ones). But that does not mean that natural selection prunes and shapes ideational systems in any simple and direct way. Patterns of social life in a community are not a simple enactment of shared cultural programs. As Homans has observed, "the central problem of the social sciences remains that posed, in his own language and in his own age, by Hobbes: How does the behavior of individuals create the characterisitics of groups?" (46, p. 106). The behavior of individuals is guided, channeled, and constrained by cultural principles and rules about the game of life and how it is to be played. But it is individuals, making choices, pursuing strategies, maximizing values, forming coalitions, that generate the patterns of social life[17] (5, 7–9, 46). The rules of the game are themselves generated and changed by the patterns of play they guide, in a continuing dialectic.

It is how humans live, not how they conceptualize the game of life, that is directly shaped by selective pressures. Moreover, the superbrain that enables humans to solve survival problems in a wide range of environments imposes costs of its own: ritual, myth, cosmology, and magic may be adaptations to the pressures of the human psyche—to anxieties, frustrations, fears, and questionings—as much as they are adaptations to the pressures of the external environment.

4. To study cultures as ideational systems without mapping the complex cybernetic circuits[18] that link them to social systems, to ecosystems, and to the psychology and biology of individuals would turn cultural analysis into an arcane pursuit isolated from surrounding disciplines at a stage when a fantastic burst of scientific knowledge—with human survival as the stakes—is being launched: a burst that should relegate to the realm of Ptolemaic astronomy (or at least pre-Watson-Crick genetics) previous theories in ecology, the neurosciences, psychology, and related fields.

5. In the course of this advance, an irony may loom increasingly large: cultures as systems of knowledge may turn out to be only partly describable in the formal languages we command. Despite impressive progress in cybernetic modeling of the way the central nervous system processes and organizes information, there is a vast gulf between the models and what the brain achieves efficiently and almost

---

[17] Cf Freilich's distinction between "proper" and "smart" in his rather different conceptualization of the cultural and social realms (21).

[18] In the sense explored by Rappaport (66–68).

instantly. Some progress is being made to close this gap, and to unravel the mysteries of the living brain[19] (see, e.g. 4, 64).

But even as scientists begin to write ethnographies for robots and to explore mathematically and biologically the structure of "memory" (61, 64, 79)—of internal models of reality—many facets of mind resist formal representation. Interestingly, it is not the highly intellective logical functions of mind, but the evolutionarily old, unconscious, "automatic" functions that resist analysis.[20]

That suggests that there may be some fundamental obstacles, perhaps more evolutionary than Gödelian, to our laying bare in any formal way what humans "know" that enables them to do what they do. George Miller's warnings vividly suggest the dilemma:

> Given that we can know rules that have not yet been formulated [as in our implicit knowledge of grammatical rules], could we know rules that govern the operations of the human mind that the human mind, given its present level of intelligence and symbolic machinery, cannot make explicit? (58, p. 192).[21]

The point is not to digress about artificial intelligence research, but to warn that despite a vast concentration of brainpower, the possibility of analyzing a cultural system in any complete sense and of discovering and describing its structure remains far on the horizon—and may forever remain so. To abstract out a level of "cultural symbols" in the way Schneider proposes seems to me to offer a spurious sense of escape from this dilemma. That the anthropologist's mind can invent such a "level" attests to the remarkable powers that make humans human; but it does little to clarify how they perceive, think, and act.

It is partly Geertz' realization that the cultural grammars of the "new ethnographers" are so impossible to achieve in the face of the vast intricacy of what humans know about their world—the subtle shadings of understanding and mood and meaning that defy representation in formal algorithms—that leads him to aspire at most to thick description, to interpretation rather than "decoding" or explanation. I disagree with him if that means abandoning to cyberneticians the task of progressively filling in those segments and sectors that yield to under-

---

[19] Cybernetic modeling helps to clarify the relationship of "mind language" to "brain language"; but as Mackay (55, p. 465) argues, even if all operations of mind could ultimately be linked to processes of brain, there would still be an important need for "mind language." Neurophysiological reductionism is as defeating as any other form of reductionism.

[20] "Good progress has been made in the art of programming. For instance, it took an automaton only a few minutes to prove over 200 theorems from Whitehead & Russell's *Principia Mathematica*, some of these proofs being even more elegant than the known ones. But the robot's ability has peculiar limits. For example, no automaton has so far been built which in the matter of reading handwritten addresses can match even a mediocre post office sorter. . . Some functions . . . having a primitive and far from intellectual nature, are much more difficult to automate than certain other functions which we regard as typically intellectual. . . . *It is for those functions which take place unconsciously that no satisfactory automata have been built*" (74, p. 46; cf 17, 85).

[21] Von Foerster's cryptic remark expresses the same insight: "The Laws of Nature are written by man. The laws of biology must write themselves" (82, p. 5).

standing: they will do so less well without our collaboration than they would if we shared with them our insights into the varying patterns and richness of cultural experience. But I agree with him that as those enterprises advance we must remain rooted in the immediacies of interpreting real humans in real settings.

6. A final urgent argument for embedding an ideational conception of culture in the real social and ecological world is that "culture," like other heuristic concepts of social science,[22] should be potentially self-extinguishing. Like the linguists' notion of competence, it may in the longer run turn out to be a scaffolding that needs to be dismantled when more solid and enduring structures can be built.

It remains an open question to what degree human action actually is guided by a general conceptual code, a theory of the world and the game of social life that can be disentangled from the particularities and immediacies of each individual's unique experience and life space. John Haviland's recent study of gossip in Zinacantan from a cognitive perspective poses important doubts:

> We ordinarily have thought of one's cultural competence as composed of codes. . . . The conceptual schemata have, we assume, an independent existence prior to any particular configuration of animals, any set of actual kin, any actual political operation. . . . But in gossip the . . . contingencies determine the general principles—for they are all there is. In gossip, the world becomes more than ideal schemes and codes. . . . Much of an actor's cultural competence rests on a vast knowledge of contingent fact, raw unconnected trivia. . . .
>
> Watching people operate on their cultural rules through gossip also shows us the folly of our belief that culture *provides* sets of ideal rules which apply to particular con-figurations of people, places, things, and events. The contingencies of life themselves restructure the rules, even change them in time. . . In gossip . . . one's whole under-standing of the cultural code depends on the particular setting, on the configuration of past experience and knowledge, which is suddenly relevant to the application of rules and standards to the fact in question (43, pp. 279–80).[23]

Do human actors conceptualize "the system" in some systematic way and use this generalized model to guide action and understanding in concrete social situations? If not, a generalized composite model of cultural competence will in the long run serve us badly in understanding performance in the concrete settings of real life. We do not yet know.

Haviland reaches a conclusion similar to Geertz': that at least for the present, we can best aspire to understanding and interpretation, not to prediction and explanation. (Gossip, at once text and native commentary on texts, offers par-ticularly rich insights.) Moreover, it may be precisely in exploring the phe-nomenological world of the familiar and immediate, the everyday and mun-dane, that we stand to gain the most crucial knowledge of how humans perceive, understand, and act.

[22] See Bateson (10) on "dormitive principles" in social science.

[23] Quoted with permission from Dr. Haviland's PhD dissertation (43), which is being extensively revised for publication as a book.

94 KEESING

CONCLUSION

We need to work, I think, on many fronts. Interpreting cockfights in Bali and gossip in Zinacantan illuminates the human condition from one important perspective, even though—or perhaps *because*—what makes it possible for anthropologists and participants cannot be neatly codified. Studies of ritual and ecological adaptation in New Guinea illuminate another side, an interconnectedness we would, with less broad view of the systemic complexity of nature, have missed. At the same time, attempts to map cultures as ideational systems in the light of an emerging understanding of mind and brain should enable clearer insights into the organization of experience and the nature and depth of variation in the thought worlds of men.

Conceiving culture as an ideational subsystem within a vastly complex system, biological, social and symbolic, and grounding our abstract models in the concrete particularities of human social life, should make possible a continuing dialectic that yields deepening understanding. Whether in this quest the concept of culture is progressively refined, radically reinterpreted, or progressively extinguished will in the long run scarcely matter if along the way it has led us to ask strategic questions and to see connections that would otherwise have been hidden.

Literature Cited

1. Agar, M. 1973. *Ripping and Running: A Formal Ethnography of Urban Heroin Addicts.* New York: Seminar Press
2. Alland, A. 1972. *The Human Imperative.* New York: Columbia Univ. Press
3. Alland, A. 1973. *Evolution and Human Behavior.* New York: Doubleday. 2nd ed.
4. Arbib, M. 1973. *The Metaphorical Brain.* New York: Wiley
5. Bailey, F. 1969. *Stratagems and Spoils: A Social Anthropology of Politics.* New York: Schocken
6. Barnes, J. A. 1971. *Three Styles in the Study of Kinship.* London: Tavistock
7. Barth, F. 1966. Models of social organization. *Roy. Anthropol. Inst. Occas. Pap. 23*
8. Barth, F. 1966. Anthropological models and social reality. *Proc. Roy. Soc. B* 165:20–35
9. Barth, F. 1967. On the study of social change. *Am. Anthropol.* 69: 661–69
10. Bateson, G. 1972. *Steps to an Ecology of Mind.* Philadelphia: Intext
11. Binford, L. R. 1968. Post-Pleistocene adaptations. In *New Perspectives in Archaeology*, ed. L. R. Binford, S. R. Binford, 313–42. Chicago: Aldine. 373 pp.
12. Boon, J. A. 1972. *From Symbolism to Structuralism: Lévi-Strauss in Literary Tradition.* Oxford: Blackwell; New York: Harper and Row
13. Boon, J. A. 1972. Further operations of 'Culture' in anthropology: A synthesis of and for debate. *Soc. Sci. Quart.*
14. Bremermann, H. J. 1970. Principles of natural and artificial intelligence. In *Principles and Practice of Bionics*, ed. H. E. Von Gierke. W. D. Keidel, H. L. Oestreicher, 425–46. Slough, England: Technivision
15. Chomsky, N. 1959. Review of verbal behavior by B. F. Skinner. *Language* 35:26–59
16. Craik, K. J. W. 1943. *The Nature of Explanation.* Cambridge: Cambridge Univ. Press
17. Dreyfus, H. L. 1972. *What Computers Can't Do: A Critique of Artificial Reason.* New York: Harper and Row
18. Frake, C. O. 1964. A structural description of Subanun 'religious behavior.' In *Explorations in Cultural Anthropology*, ed. W. H. Goodenough, 111–29

New York: McGraw-Hill
19. Freeman, J. D. 1970. Human nature and culture. In *Man and the New Biology*. ed. R. G. Slatyer et al. 50–75. Canberra: Aust. Nat. Univ. Press
20. Freilich, M. 1972. Manufacturing culture: Man the scientist. See Ref. 21. 267–323
21. Freilich, M., Ed. 1972. *The Meaning of Culture: A Reader in Cultural Anthropology*. Lexington, Mass: Xerox Corp.
22. Geertz, C. 1957. Ritual and social change: A Javanese example. *Am. Anthropol.* 59: 991–1012
23. Geertz, C. 1962. The growth of culture and the evolution of mind. In *Theories of the Mind*, ed. J. Scher, 713–40. Glencoe, Ill.: Free Press
24. Geertz, C. 1964. Ideology as a cultural system. In *Ideology and Discontent*, ed. D. Apter, 47–56. Glencoe, Ill.: Free Press
25. Geertz, C. 1965. The impact of the concept of culture on the concept of man. In *New Views on the Nature of Man*, ed. J. R. Platt, 93–118. Univ. Chicago Press
26. Geertz, C. 1966. Religion as a cultural system. In *Anthropological Approaches to the Study of Religion*, ed. M. Banton, 1–46. London: Tavistock
27. Geertz, C. 1966. *Person, Time and Conduct in Bali: An Essay in Cultural Analysis.* Yale Southeast Asia Program. Cult. Rep. Ser. No. 14
28. Geertz, C. 1967. The cerebral savage: on the work of Claude Lévi-Strauss. *Encounter* 28: 25–32
29. Geertz, C. 1972. Deep play: notes on the Balinese cockfight. *Daedalus* 101: 1–37
30. Geertz, C. 1973. *The Interpretation of Culture.* New York: Basic Books
31. Geertz, C. n.d. Common sense as a cultural system. Forthcoming in *Antioch Review*
32. Goodenough, W. H. 1957. Cultural anthropology and linguistics. In *Report of the Seventh Annual Round Table Meeting on Linguistics and Language Study*, ed. P. Garvin. Washington, D. C.: Georgetown Univ. Monogr. Ser. Lang. and Ling. 9
33. Goodenough, W. H. 1961. Comment on cultural evolution. *Daedalus* 90: 521–28
34. Goodenough. W. H. 1963. *Cooperation in Change.* New York: Russell Sage Found.
35. Goodenough, W. H., Ed. 1964. Introduction to *Explorations in Cultural Anthropology*, 1–24. New York: McGraw-Hill
36. Goodenough, W. H. 1970. *Description and Comparison in Cultural Anthropology.* Chicago: Aldine
37. Goodenough, W. H. 1971. *Culture, Language, and Society.* McCaleb Module in Anthropology. Reading, Mass: Addison-Wesley
38. Gregory, R. L. 1969. On how little information controls so much behavior. In *Towards a Theoretical Biology*, Vol. I. ed. C. H. Waddington. Chicago: Aldine
39. Gregory, R. L. 1970. Information processing in biological and artificial brains. In *Principles and Practice of Bionics*, ed. H. E. Von Gierke, W. D. Keidel, H. L. Oestreicher, 73–80. Slough, England: Technivision
40. Harris, M. 1964. *The Nature of Cultural Things.* New York: Random House
41. Harris, M. 1968. *The Rise of Cultural Theory.* New York: Crowell
42. Harris, M. 1969. Monistic determinism: Anti-service. *Southwest J. Anthropol.* 25.2: 198–206
43. Haviland, J. B. 1972. *Gossip, Gossips and Gossiping in Zinacantan.* PhD thesis. Harvard Univ., Cambridge. 281 pp.
44. Hewes, G. W. 1973. Primate communication and the gestural origin of language. *Curr. Anthropol.* 14: 5–24
45. Holloway, R. J. Jr. 1969. Culture: a human domain. *Curr. Anthropol.* 10: 395–407
46. Homans, G. C. 1967. *The Nature of Social Science.* New York: Harcourt, Brace & Jovanovitch
47. Keesing, R. M. 1970. Toward a model of role analysis. In *A Handbook of Method in Cultural Anthropology*, ed. R. Naroll, R. Cohen, 423–53. Garden City, NY: Natural History Press
48. Keesing, R. M. 1972. Paradigms lost: the new ethnography and the new lin-

96   KEESING

guistics. *Southwest. J. Anthropol.* 28: 299–332

49. Keesing, R. M. 1974. Transformational linguistics and structural anthropology. *Cultural Hermeneutics.* In press

50. Keesing, R. M., Keesing, F. M. 1971. *New Perspectives in Cultural Anthropology.* New York: Holt, Rinehart & Winston

51. Laing, R. 1972. Artificial organisms and autonomous cell rules. *J. Cynbern.* 2, 1: 38–49

52. Lakoff, G. 1971. Presupposition and relative well-formedness. In *Semantics: An Interdisciplinary Reader,* ed. L. Jakobovits, D. Steinberg, 329–40. Cambridge Univ. Press

53. LeVine, R. A. 1973. *Culture, Behavior, and Personality.* Chicago: Aldine

54. Lévi-Strauss, C. 1971. *Mythologiques, IV: L'Homme Nu.* Paris: Plon

55. MacKay, D. M. 1970. Digits and analogues. See Ref. 39, 459–66

56. Meggers, B. J. 1971. *Amazonia: Man and Nature in a Counterfeit Paradise.* Chicago: Aldine

57. Metzger, D., Williams, G. 1963. A formal ethnographic analysis of Tenejapa Ladino weddings. *Am. Anthropol.* 65: 1072–1101

58. Miller, G. A. 1970. Four philosophical problems of psycholinguistics. *Phil. Sci.* June: 183–99

59. Montagu, M. F. A., Ed. *Culture: Man's Adaptive Dimension.* London: Oxford Univ. Press

60. Newell, A. 1970. Remarks on the relationship between artificial intelligence and cognitive psychology. In *Theoretical Approaches to Non-Numerical Problem Solving,* ed. R. Banerji, D. Mesarovic. Berlin: Springer-Verlag

61. Norman, D. A., Ed. 1970. *Models of Human Memory.* New York: Academic

62. Piaget, J. 1970. Piaget's Theory. In *Carmichael's Manual of Child Psychology,* ed. P. H. Mussen, 1: 803–32. New York: Wiley. 3rd ed.

63. Popper, K. A. 1961. *The Poverty of Historicism.* London: Routledge and Kegan Paul

64. Pribram, K. H., Broadbent, D. E., Eds.

1970. *Biology of Memory.* New York: Academic

65. Rappaport, R. 1967. *Pigs for the Ancestors: Ritual in the Ecology of a New Guinea People.* New Haven: Yale Univ. Press

66. Rappaport, R. 1971. Ritual, sanctity, and cybernetics. *Am. Anthropol.* 73: 59–76

67. Rappaport, R. 1971. The sacred in human evolution. *Ann. Rev. Ecol. System.* 2:22–44

68. Rappaport, R. 1971. Nature, culture, and ecological anthropology. In *Man, Culture and Society,* ed. H. Shapiro, 237–67. Oxford Univ. Press

69. Rosch, E. 1974. Universals and cultural specifics in human categorization. In *Cross-Cultural Perspectives on Learning,* ed. R. Breslin, W. Lonner, S. Bochner. New York: Sage

70. Ryle, G. 1949. *The Concept of Mind.* New York: Barnes and Noble

71. Schneider, D. 1968. *American Kinship: A Cultural Account.* Englewood Cliffs, N. J.: Prentice-Hall

72. Schneider, D. 1972. What is kinship all about? In *Kinship Studies in the Morgan Memorial Year,* ed. P. Reinig, 32–63. Washington, D. C.: Anthropol. Soc. Washington

73. Schneider, D., Smith, R. 1973. *Class Differences and Sex Roles in American Kinship.* Englewood Cliffs, N. J.: Prentice-Hall

74. Schuh, J. F. 1969. What a robot can and cannot do. In *Survey of Cybernetics: A Tribute to Norbert Weiner,* ed. J. Rose, 29–46. New York: Gordon and Breach

75. Service, E. R. 1968. The prime-mover of cultural evolution. *Southwest. J. Anthropol.* 24.4: 396–409

76. Singer, M. 1968. Culture. *Int. Encycl. Soc. Sci.* 3: 527–43

77. Spradley, J. P. 1970. *You Owe Yourself a Drunk: An Ethnography of Urban Nomads.* Boston: Little, Brown

78. Spradley, J. P. 1972. Foundations of cultural knowledge. In *Culture and Cognition: Rules, Maps, and Plans,* ed. J. P. Spradley, 3–40. San Francisco: Chandler. 400 pp.

79. Tulving, E., Donaldson, W., Eds. 1972.

Organization of Memory. New York: Academic

80. Tyler, S. A. 1969. Introduction. In *Cognitive Anthropology*, ed. S. A. Tyler, 1–23. New York: Holt, Rinehart & Winston

81. Vayda, A. P., Rappaport, R. A. 1968. Ecology, cultural and noncultural. In *Introduction to Cultural Anthropology*, ed. J. A. Clifton, 477–97. Boston: Houghton Mifflin

82. Von Foerster, H. 1972. Responsibilities of competence. *J. Cybern.* 2, 2: 1–6

83. Wallace, A. F. C. 1965. Driving to work. In *Context and Meaning in Cultural Anthropology*, ed. M. E. Spiro. Glencoe, Ill.: Free Press

84. Wallace, A. F. C. 1970. *Culture and Personality*. New York: Random House. 2nd ed.

85. Walter, W. G. 1969. Neurocybernetics: communication and control in the living brain. In *Survey of Cybernetics*, ed. J. Rose. London: Gordon and Breach

[2]

Academy of Management Review, 1984, Vol. 9, No. 3, 389-398.

The Cultural Relativity of the Quality of Life Concept[1]

GEERT HOFSTEDE
Institute for Research on
Intercultural Cooperation
The Netherlands

Research data on dominant work-related values patterns in 53 countries and regions are used to suggest how definitions of the quality of life are affected by national culture patterns.

What people see as the meaning of their lives and the kind of living they consider desirable or undesirable are matters of personal choice par excellence. However, personal choices are affected by the cultural environment in which people are brought up. Thus one can expect definitions of the quality of life concept to be culturally dependent as well. For example, in some cultures the quality of life is strongly associated with the degree of satisfaction of material needs. In others, it is associated with the degree to which people succeed in subduing and reducing their material needs.

One facet of a people's quality of life is their quality of work life. The relative contribution of the quality of work life to the quality of life is, in itself, a matter of personal and cultural choice. Charles F. Kettering is quoted as saying:

> I often tell my people that I don't want any fellow who has a job working for me. What I want is a fellow whom a job has. I want the job to get the fellow and not the fellow to get the job. And I want that job to get hold of this young man so hard that no matter where he is the job has got him for keeps. I want that job to have him in its clutches when he goes to bed at night, and in the morning I want that same job to be sitting on the foot of his bed telling him it's time to get up and go to work. And when a job gets a fellow that way, he's sure to amount to something. (Whyte, 1969, p. 31).

This statement is attributed to a classical U.S. businessman. It is an extreme of a manifestation of a culture in which the quality of work life is associated with a very central place of work in a people's life

concepts. It is a product of a society stressing job challenge, achievement, and the satisfaction of intrinsic needs. However, there are other societies in which the primary loyalties of individuals are their parents, relatives, or clan. Life fulfillment consists of living up to those loyalties. In such a society, a high quality job is one allowing individuals to fulfill obligations to their families (Kiggundu, 1982).

This paper deals primarily with cultural aspects of the quality of *work* life. However, *work* first must be placed in the wider context of total life patterns; that is, the quality of (total) life must be kept in mind. At the level of culture, work and life cannot and should not be separated. "Quality," by definition, is a matter of values. It relates to standards for "good" and "bad." Values depend partly on personal choices, but to a large extent what one considers good or bad is dictated by one's cultural context. In this paper, conclusions about the cultural relativity of the Quality of Life concepts are based on data about the cultural relativity of values.

Value Patterns

A shorthand definition of a value is a broad preference for one state of affairs over others. Culture can be defined as the collective programming of the mind which distinguishes the members of one category of people from those of another. Elsewhere (Hofstede, 1979b, 1980) the present author has reported on research into national differences in work-related value patterns in 40 countries. Later on (Hofstede, 1983), this research was extended to another 10 countries and 3 multicountry regions, so that it now encompasses 50 countries and 3 regions.

---

[1]An earlier version of this paper was presented at the 20th International Congress of Applied Psychology, Edinburgh, Scotland, 1982.

Paper-and-pencil answers on 32 value questions by matched samples of employees of subsidiaries of the same multinational business corporation in all these countries were used to study the relationship between nationality and mean value scores. In a factor analysis of 32 mean scores for each of the 40 countries (an ecological factor analysis), three factors together explained 49 percent of the variance in means (Hofstede, 1980). Afterwards, several reasons led to the splitting of one of these factors into two parts. Thus four dimensions were created. Together they explained about half of the differences in mean value scores among the 40 nations. Each country could be given an index score on each of these four dimensions.

The subsequent phase of the research was devoted to the validation on other populations of the four dimensions. This showed their meaningfulness outside the subsidiaries of this one multinational corporation. About 40 other studies were found that compared conceptually related data for between 5 and 40 of the countries involved. These studies produced qualitative outcomes that correlated significantly with one or more of the four dimensions scores (Hofstede, 1980).

The labels chosen for the four dimensions, and their interpretations, are as follows:

1. *Power distance,* as a characteristic of a culture, defines the extent to which the less powerful person in a society accepts inequality in power and considers it as normal. Inequality exists within any culture, but the degree of it that is tolerated varies between one culture and another. "All societies are unequal, but some are more unequal that others" (Hofstede, 1980, p. 136).

2. *Individualism,* as a characteristic of a culture, opposes collectivism (the word is used here in an anthropological, not a political, sense). Individualist cultures assume individuals look primarily after their own interests and the interests of their immediate family (husband, wife, and children). Collectivist cultures assume that individuals—through birth and possibly later events—belong to one or more close "in-groups," from which they cannot detach themselves. The in-group (whether extended family, clan, or organization) protects the interest of its members, but in turn expects their permanent loyalty. A collectivist society is tightly integrated; an individualist society is loosely integrated.

3. *Masculinity,* as a characteristic of a culture, op-poses femininity. Masculine cultures use the biological existence of two sexes to define very different social roles for men and women. They expect men to be assertive, ambitious, and competitive, to strive for material success, and to respect whatever is big, strong, and fast. They expect women to serve and to care for the nonmaterial quality of life, for children, and for the weak. Feminine cultures, on the other hand, define relatively overlapping social roles for the sexes, in which neither men nor women need to be ambitious or competitive. Both sexes may go for a different quality of life than material success and may respect whatever is small, weak, and slow. In both masculine and feminine cultures, the dominant values within political and work organizations are those of men. In masculine cultures these political/organizational values stress material success and assertiveness. In feminine cultures they stress other types of quality of life, interpersonal relationships, and concern for the weak.

4. *Uncertainty avoidance,* as a characteristic of a culture, defines the extent to which people within a culture are made nervous by situations that they consider to be unstructured, unclear, or unpredictable, and the extent to which they try to avoid such situations by adopting strict codes of behavior and a belief in absolute truths. Cultures with a strong uncertainty avoidance are active, aggressive, emotional, security-seeking, and intolerant. Cultures with a weak uncertainty avoidance are contemplative, less aggressive, unemotional, accepting of personal risk, and relatively tolerant.

Country scores on the four dimensions have been plotted in Figures 1 and 2. Exhibit 1 lists the countries and regions and the abbreviations used. Figure 1 plots power distance against individualism/collectivism. There is a statistical association between power distance and the collectivist end of the individualism/collectivism (I/C) dimension ($r = -.67$ across the original 40 countries). This association, however, is caused by the correlation of both power distance and individualism with national wealth. (The countries' per capita GNP correlates $-.65$ with the power distance index and .82 with the individualism index.) If one controls for national wealth, the correlation between power distance and collectivism disappears. In the ecological factor analysis of 32 values questions mean scores for 40 countries, power distance plus collectivism showed up on one factor. Their joint relationship with wealth and the disap-

Figure 1
A Power Distance × Individualism/Collectivism Plot for
Fifty Countries and Three Regions[a]

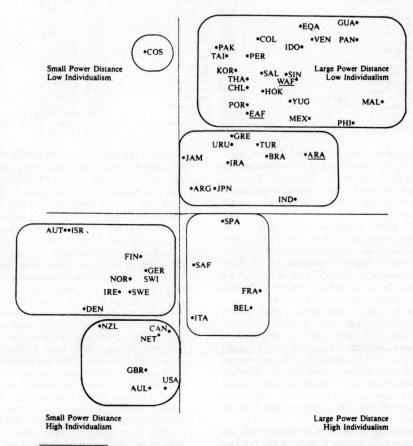

POWER DISTANCE INDEX (PDI)

Small Power Distance
Low Individualism

•COS

•EQA GUA•
•COL •VEN PAN•
•PAK
TAI• •PER IDO•

Large Power Distance
Low Individualism

KOR•
THA• •SAL •SIN
CHL• WAF•
•HOK
POR• •YUG MAL•
•EAF MEX• PHI•

•GRE
URU• •TUR
•JAM •BRA •ARA
•IRA
•ARG •JPN IND•

INDIVIDUALISM INDEX (IDV)

AUT••ISR

•SPA

FIN•
•GER •SAF
NOR• SWI
IRE• •SWE FRA•
•DEN BEL•
•ITA

•NZL CAN•
NET•

GBR•
AUL• USA•

Small Power Distance
High Individualism

Large Power Distance
High Individualism

[a]For country abbreviations see Exhibit 1.

Exhibit 1
Country Abbreviations
(For Figures 1 and 2)

ARA	Arab countries (Egypt, Lebanon, Lybia, Kuwait, Iraq, Saudi-Arabia, U.A.E.)	GER	Germany	PAN	Panama
		GRE	Greece	PER	Peru
ARG	Argentina	GUA	Guatemala	PHI	Philippines
AUL	Australia	HOK	Hong Kong	POR	Portugal
AUT	Austria	IDO	Indonesia	SAF	South Africa
BEL	Belgium	IND	India	SAL	Salvador
BRA	Brazil	IRA	Iran	SIN	Singapore
CAN	Canada	IRE	Ireland	SPA	Spain
CHL	Chile	ISR	Israel	SWE	Sweden
COL	Colombia	ITA	Italy	SWI	Switzerland
COS	Costa Rica	JAM	Jamaica	TAI	Taiwan
DEN	Denmark	JPN	Japan	THA	Thailand
EAF	East Africa (Kenya, Ethiopia, Zambia)	KOR	South Korea	TUR	Turkey
		MAL	Malaysia	URU	Uruguay
EQA	Equador	MEX	Mexico	USA	United States
FIN	Finland	NET	Netherlands	VEN	Venezuela
FRA	France	NOR	Norway	WAF	West Africa (Nigeria, Ghana, Sierra Leone)
GBR	Great Britain	NZL	New Zealand		
		PAK	Pakistan	YUG	Yugoslavia

pearance of their intercorrelation when the author controlled for wealth is one of the two reasons why he split this factor into two dimensions. The other reason is that power distance (inequality) and collectivism (social integration) are conceptually two different issues.

Figure 2 plots masculinity/femininity against uncertainty avoidance. In this case there is no statistical association between the two dimensions (correlation across the original 40 countries, $r = .12$). These two dimensions are directly based on two separate factors in the ecological factor analysis of 32 values questions mean scores for 40 countries.

Because of the joint association of power distance and collectivism with national wealth, the Third World countries in Figure 1 tend to be separated from the wealthy countries. The former are in the upper right hand corner and the latter are in the lower part of the diagram. However, masculinity and uncertainty avoidance are both unrelated to national wealth. Thus, in Figure 2 wealthy countries and Third World countries are found in all four quadrants of the diagram.

Work-related values differ by occupation as well as by nationality (Hofstede, 1972, 1979a). There are striking differences in the saliency of work goals if one goes from unskilled workers via clerical workers and technicians to professionals and managers. Professionals, technicians, and managers stress the content of their jobs. Clerks, managers, and technicians stress the social context (interpersonal relationships). Skilled workers and technicians stress security and

earnings; and unskilled stress only benefits and physical conditions (Hofstede, 1972). These occupational differences affect attempts at "humanization of work" (Hofstede, 1979a). They dynamics of the humanization of work movements are such that the "humanizers" tend to be managers and professionals. But the people whose work is to be humanized tend to be clerks and unskilled workers. Thus, there is a real danger of the humanizers trying to increase the quality of work life of these other employees (clerks and unskilled) based on their own (the humanizers') work values of what represents a high quality job; in particular, by trying to make the jobs more interesting. This helps to explain the lack of support for many attempts at improving the quality of work life from the workers and the unions that represent them (for an example from India, see Singh, 1982). In spite of the low priority that workers tend to give to job content factors, however, making the job more interesting *does* increase the workers' satisfaction with it (Hofstede, 1979a). If an increase in job satisfaction is wanted, the humanizers' attempts at making jobs more interesting are justified. Their problem becomes one of what is the best strategy to adopt in order to gain the support of employees and unions, without which support the humanization revolution is unlikely to succeed.

Occupational differences in work values can be seen as superimposed on the national patterns (Hofstede, 1980). In the cross-national research referred to earlier, the occupation effect was eliminated because the comparison was based on matched sam-

Figure 2
A Masculinity/Femininity × Uncertainty Avoidance Plot
for Fifty Countries and Three Regions[a]

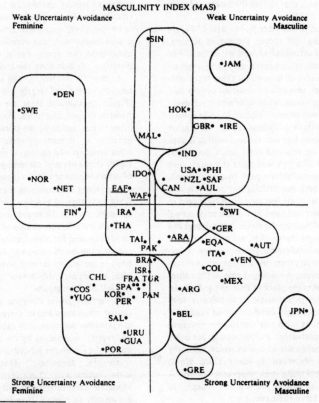

MASCULINITY INDEX (MAS)

Weak Uncertainty Avoidance
Feminine

Weak Uncertainty Avoidance
Masculine

UNCERTAINTY AVOIDANCE INDEX (UAI)

•SIN

•JAM

•DEN
•SWE   HOK•
              GBR• •IRE
MAL•
      •IND
        USA• •PHI
IDO•   •NZL •SAF
•NOR   EAF   CAN   •AUL
  •NET WAF•
FIN•   IRA•   •SWI
        •THA   •GER
        TAI• •ARA •EQA   •AUT
        PAK•   ITA• •VEN
        BRA•   •COL
        ISR•
    CHL FRA TUR   •MEX
  •COS SPA••   •ARG
  •YUG KOR• PAN
        PER
        SAL•   •BEL   JPN•
        •URU
        •GUA
        •POR
                    •GRE

Strong Uncertainty Avoidance
Feminine

Strong Uncertainty Avoidance
Masculine

[a]For country abbreviations see Exhibit 1.

ples of people in the same occupation from country to country. In any practical quality of work life problem, an account should be taken of both the nationality and the occupational level of the people involved. A useful way of measuring the occupational level is by the number of years of formal education necessary for their occupation (Hofstede, 1980).

In addition to the differences due to nationality and occupation, one is likely to find differences between one organization and another. Organizations have their own subcultures (Hofstede, 1982a, 1982b),

which reflect the values of their founders and the ways in which they were set up. Particular organizations may have particular objectives related to the quality of life that are reflected in the needs of the people who work for them (for an example, see De Bettignies and Hofstede, 1977).

Power Distance, Individualism. and the Quality of Life

Although occupational and organizational differences have to be considered, the focus of this paper is national differences considers differences on the dimension of power distance and I/C (Figure 1). A society's position on the I/C continuum will have a strong impact on the self-concept of its members and on the way in which they define the quality of their lives (Kanungo, 1982).

In an individualistic society (lower part of Figure 1) a high quality life means individual success, achievement, self-actualization, and self-respect. The capitalist economic system prevalent in and originating from these countries is based on enlightened self-interest. However, in a collective society (upper half of Figure 1), a high quality life is defined much more in family and group terms. Children in collectivistic societies learn to think of themselves as "we" rather than "I." Whoever has success and wealth is supposed to let his/her relatives and friends share in it. The satisfaction of a job well done (by one's own standard) is an individualistic goal. In a collectivistic society, people seek the satisfaction of a job well recognized. Students are less motivated by a need to master their subject and more by a desire to pass their examinations and acquire the status that a degree can provide. Preserving face—that is, preserving the respect from one's reference groups—is the collectivistic alternative to preserving self-respect in the individualistic cultures. Avoiding shame in the collectivistic society takes the place of avoiding guilt in the individualistic one. In Southeast Asian cultures, such as Indonesia (upper right-hand corner of Figure 1), preserving harmony with one's social environment is a powerful motivator. People would probably define a high quality life as one in which harmony is achieved and preserved. In many Third World countries, national unity is an important symbol. A criterion for a high quality job will be the degree to which they can serve their country.

In the individualistic society, job life and private life are sharply set apart, in both time and mind. Not so in the collectivistic society. People accept the job invading their private life. But they also expect the employer to take account of family problems and allow time to fulfill family duties, which may be many. Most importantly, in individualistic work organizations, the task comes before the relationship. In collectivistic work organizations the relationship has precedence over the task. This is because a society in which people think of themselves as "we," not "I," also will teach people to distinguish between

"us" and "them." Others are classified as belonging to "our" in-group, or not belonging, and the way others are treated depends on their group membership. In order to perform a task together, or to do business together, there must be time to develop a relationship with the other person, allowing him/her to be "adopted" into the in-group. Developing such a relationship will take time—anything from two minutes to two years—but it is an essential precondition for achieving the task.

A society's position on the power distance continuum is correlated largely with its position on I/C (Figure 1), although there are exceptions, such as Austria, France, and India. Power distance, among other things, indicates the strength of the need for dependence on more powerful people among the adult members of a society. If this is low (left side of Figure 1), the norm of subjecting oneself to the power of others is undesirable. Everyone should have a say in everything that concerns them. This may be difficult to realize in practice. Small power distance societies, such as Denmark and Sweden, often go through considerable rituals of democratization to satisfy the need for consultation without necessarily contributing much to actual decisions. Status differences are suspect in small power distance societies. Ideal leaders are "democrats" who loyally execute the will of their groups.

In medium power distance societies such as the United States and Canada, consultation is usually appreciated but not necessarily expected. "Participative leadership" is initiated by the participative leader, not by the rebellious subordinate. Ideal leaders are resourceful "democrats"—that is, individuals with some outstanding characteristics people enjoy. Moderate status differences and privileges for leaders are socially acceptable. However, laws and rules are expected to apply to superiors and subordinates alike.

In large power distance societies (right of the vertical line in Figure 1), subordinates have strong dependence needs. They usually aspire to democracy as an impersonal ideal. Subordinates expect superiors to behave autocratically and not to consult them. They may even be uncomfortable if superiors consult them. Ideal superiors in such a culture are benevolent autocrats or paternalists, "good fathers" on whom they like to depend. Everybody expects superiors to enjoy privileges. Moreover, laws and rules differ for superiors and subordinates. In

In addition, status symbols are widely used and contribute to the superiors' authority in the eyes of subordinates.

This set of connotations should make it clear that equality, participation, industrial democracy, and leadership mean different things for the quality of work life in societies at different positions on the power distance scale. North Americans are often appalled and uncomfortble at the legally required co-determination procedures in countries such as Sweden or Germany. They suppose a degree of subordinate initiative and basic equality not in the American book.

On the other hand, North and West Europeans have trouble with the vertical society of nearly all Third World countries. They believe the first thing these Third World countries need is the elimination of their power inequalities. However, after a certain time in those countries they usually adopt "neocolonial" attitudes. This means the North and West Europeans start behaving towards the native lower classes just as does the native ruling class. Third World citizens in Western countries often initially feel lost. This is because of the lack of dependable superiors to take a personal attitude towards them and give clear orders.

Differences in I/C and power distance affect the feasibility of socio-technical interventions. This is because different societies define the "socio" element in the system quite differently, as should be clear from the previous paragraphs. Should the "system" include family relationships? What degree of consultation and visible leadership makes people feel comfortable? These are missing considerations in the classical Anglo-American imported socio-technical approach. Changes in the system are brought about in various ways in different cultures. In small power distance societies people can accept new and less powerful roles and still continue functioning. The larger a society's power distance the more the system is identified with one or more powerful individuals. Thus, change comes about by decree from the center of power or by revolution, changing the center of power.

Kanungo (1982) suggests that differences in the cultural environment also affect the appropriateness of research instruments. Instruments developed by and for the North American mind are too often exported indiscriminately to other cultures. These instruments overemphasize items related to North American (individualist, medium power distance) values and lack

items related to other cultures' values. As an example, Kanungo uses the emphasis on intrinsic need satisfaction of most instruments for measuring the quality of work life. Even the classification of needs as "intrinsic" and "extrinsic" ceases to make sense in cross-national research (Hofstede, 1980). These instruments need to be redesigned and the entire research paradigm merits redefinition (Morrow, 1983).

So far, this paper has presented a static view of the cultural choices of nations. Obviously, cultures do change over time. For the indices plotted in Figures 1 and 2, shifts have been measured over a 4-year period, 1968-1972 (Hofstede, 1980). These show a consistent increase in individualism, which can be proven to follow, rather that precede, the increase in wealth in the countries concerned. These countries show a mixed picture for power distance. On the one hand, greater equality is expected. On the other hand, these are signs that the powerful are not prepared to reduce their power, at least in the large power distance societies. The stress in the large power distance systems increases. There is no sign whatsoever of a convergence among countries. Although cultures change, their differences remain remarkably stable.

Masculinity, Uncertainty Avoidance, and the Quality of Life

Figure 2 shows the masculinity/femininity × uncertainty avoidance plots. These plots denote the prevalent standards in a country for the quality of work life in different ways than Figure 1. The differences among countries in Figure 2 are unrelated to whether the country is wealthy or poor. Both dimensions relate to human motivation. Masculinity in society relates to the desirability of achievement; femininity relates to interpersonal relationships (not, as in the case of collectivism, with relatives and in-group members, but with people in general). Uncertainty avoidance relates to the acceptability in a society of personal risk-taking (weak uncertainty avoidance) versus an emphasis on personal security (strong uncertainty avoidance).

The consequence of country differences along these two dimensions is that management conceptions about the motivation of employees, common in North America, do not necessarily apply abroad. To illustrate consider the cultural limitations of two North American motivation theories highly popular among managers: McClelland's achievement motivation theory and Maslow's hierarchy of human needs. Both are either implicitly or explicitly considered by many managers as applying universally to the human race.

McClelland (1961) has published scores for the need for achievement (n_{Ach}) in a large number of countries, based on a content analysis of children's readers from around 1925 and around 1950. Across 22 contries, McClelland's n_{Ach} scores (1925 data) show a multiple correlation of $r = .74$ with a low uncertainty avoidance index and a high masculinity index. That is, what McClelland indentified as n_{Ach} follows a diagonal in Figure 2 from lower left (low n_{Ach}) to upper right (high n_{Ach}) (Hofstede, 1980). It is remarkable that McClelland's 1925 data, not his 1950 data, show significant correlations. It is likely that the traditional children's readers from 1925 reflected basic national values more purely than do the modernized readers from 1950 (Hofstede, 1980). The countries in which McClelland's n_{Ach} is strong are characterized by weak uncertainty avoidance (personal risk-taking) and strong masculinity. McClelland's n_{Ach} may represent one particular combination of cultural choices. Defining n_{Ach} as a desirable end-state for the world as a whole is McClelland's personal values choice. It is also a highly ethnocentric one. McClelland predicted the fastest economic growth for countries with high n_{Ach} scores. This prediction did not come true in the 1960-1980 period.

With the help of Figure 2, another theory that can be unmasked as ethnocentric is Maslow's (1954) hierarchy of human needs. Empirical evidence of its cultural limitations is found in the classical 14-country study by Haire, Ghiselli, and Porter, 1966. In Haire et al.'s study, managers were asked to rate the importance to them of, and their satisfaction with, the fulfillment of a number of needs. These needs were chosen to represent the five levels of Maslow's hierarchy (from low to high: security—social—esteem—autonomy—self-actualization). Although Haire et al. never drew this conclusion from their data, the only nationality group that ordered their need importance almost, and their need satisfaction exactly, in the Maslow order was the U.S. managers. The other nationalities showed more or less deviant patterns. The present author concluded (Hofstede, 1980) the ordering of needs in Maslow's hierarchy represents a value choice—Maslow's value choice. This choice was based on his mid-twentieth

century U.S. middle class values. First, Maslow's hierarchy reflects individualistic values, putting self-actualization and autonomy on top. Values prevalent in collectivist cultures, such as "harmony" or "family support," do not even appear in the hierarchy. Second, the cultural map of Figure 2 suggests even if just the needs Maslow used in his hierarchy are considered—the needs will have to be ordered differently in different culture areas. Maslow's hierarchical ordering (self-actualization on top) corresponds to the upper right-hand quadrant of Figure 2. In the lower right-hand quadrant (strong uncertainty avoidance and masculinity), a combination of security and assertiveness needs should be placed on top of a need hierarchy. In the upper left hand quadrant (weak uncertainty avoidance and femininity), social (relationship) needs should be placed on top. In the lower left hand quadrant (strong uncertainty avoidance and femininity), security and relationship needs should be placed on top.

For managers operating internationally it is important for them to realize what countries tend to order human needs differently. Moreover these countries are not necessarily inferior technologically, economically, or in the quality of their management. Some countries may even be superior in some or all of these respects. Japan, a country in which security needs rank very high, has been outperforming the world in recent years. Other East Asian countries follow closely. However, the dominant motivation patterns may affect the type of economic and technological activities at which a country is best. Masculine cultures may have an advantage when it comes to mass production. Feminine cultures may have an advantage when it comes to providing services (such as consulting) and to growing things rather than mass producing them (such as high quality agriculture and biochemistry). For example, the leading companies in the world in the field of penicillin and enzymes are in the Netherlands and Denmark. A truly international management should be able to recognize the strengths and the weaknesses in any country's culture pattern, including the home culture.

Improving the quality of work life often has been interpreted as offering to people satisfactions of needs higher on their need hierarchy. Thus, it should be recognized that different cultures have different need hierarchies. In the lower half of Figure 2, improving the quality of work life probably implies offering more security and possibly more task structure on the job. In the left half of Figure 2, improving the quality of work life implies offering opportunities for creating relationships on the job. In this context a difference is noted between the North American and the North European school of improving the quality of work life (humanization of work, job restructuring). In North America, the dominant objective is to make individual jobs more interesting by providing workers with an increased challenge. This grew out of the earlier "job enlargement" and "job enrichment" movements. In countries such as Sweden and Norway, the dominant objective is to make group work more rewarding by allowing groups to function as self-contained social units (semiautonomous groups) and by fostering cooperation among group members. Humanization of work means "masculinization" in North America, but "femininization" in Sweden (Hofstede, 1980). This shows another aspect of the cultural relativity of the quality of work life.

To the extent the data permitted measurement, the shifts over time on the masculinity-femininity and uncertainty avoidance dimensions were relatively small and inconsistent. There was no sign of convergency among countries, rather there was an indication of increasing divergence (Hofstede, 1980). This means there are not changes premitting one culture's standards for the quality of work life to prevail.

Farewell to Ethnocentrism

Concern for the quality of life is a worthwhile issue in any culture (Alder, 1983). However, researchers approaching the issue in Third World countries have relied too much on definitions of "quality" derived from North American and, to a lesser extent, West European values. Many Third World social scientists have been educated in North America or Western Europe. It is difficult for them to free themselves from the ethnocentricity of the Western approaches. This ethnocentricity is never explicit but is hidden behind "scientific" verbiage. U.S. social scientific theories and instruments, especially have a high status value. It takes considerable personal courage and independence of thought of a Third World researcher —or of an expatriate Western researcher—to suggest these theories and instruments may be wholly or partly inapplicable and irrelevant to another situation. Scientific approaches are never purely "objective." They always have a quasi-religious, symbolic meaning to the initiated. It is highly flattering to the designers of social science theories in the United States and in Western Europe if their ideas become religion to followers in faraway parts of the world. For the longer term this situation serves neither those followers nor their Third World countries. Even social scientists are children of their culture. The patterns of collectivism (loyalty to the scientific reference group at their U.S. or European university) and large power distance (intellectual dependency on the brillant professor) are more likely among Third World social scientists than among those from Western countries.

There are counterforces, however. Western ethnocentrism has become too evidently untenable. Countries trying to transfer Western ideas wholesale have been in trouble—Iran, for example. Countries translating them in a way consistent with their own cultural traditions are now outperforming the West— Japan and Singapore, for example. It is time to bid farewell to ethnocentrism in social science theories in general, and in definitions of the quality of life in particular.

References

Aldler, N. J. Cross-cultural management research: The ostrich and the trend. *Academy of Management Review,* 1983, 8, 226-232.

DeBettignies, L. A., & Hofstede, G. Communauté de travail "Boimondau": A case study on participation. *International Studies of Management and Organization,* 1977, 7, 91-116.

Haire, M., Ghiselli, E. E., & Porter, L. W. *Managerial thinking: An international study.* New York: Wiley, 1966.

Hofstede, G. The colors of collars. *Columbia Journal of World Business,* 1972, 7(5), 72-80.

Hofstede, G. Humanization of work: The role of values in a third industrial revolution. In C. L. Cooper & E. Mumford (Eds.),

The quality of working life in eastern and western Europe. London: Associated Business Press, 1979a, 18-37.

Hofstede, G. Value systems in forty countries: Interpretation, validation, and consequences for theory. In L. H. Eckensberger, W. J. Lonner, & Y. H. Poortinga (Eds.), *Cross-cultural contributions to psychology.* Lisse, Netherlands: Swets & Zeitlinger, 1979b, 398-407.

Hofstede, G. *Culture's consequences: International differences in work-related values.* Beverly Hills, Cal., and London: Sage, 1980.

Hofstede, G. The individual among national, occupational and organizational cultures. Paper presented at the 20th International Congress of Applied Psychology, Edinburgh, Scotland, 1982a.

Hofstede, G. The interaction between national and organizational value systems. Paper presented at the 20th International Congress of Applied Psychology, Edinburgh, Scotland, 1982b.

Hofstede, G. Dimensions of national cultures in fifty countries and three regions. In J. B. Deregowski, S. Dziurawiec, & R. C. Annis (Eds.), *Expiscations in cross-cultural psychology*. Lisse, Netherlands: Swets and Zeitlinger, 1983, 335-355.

Kanungo, R. N. Work alienation and the quality of work life: A cross-cultural perspective. Paper presented at the 20th International Congress of Applied Psychology, Edinburgh, Scotland, 1982.

Kiggundu, M. The quality of working life in developing countries: Beyond the sociotechnical system model. Paper presented at the 20th International Congress of Applied Psychology, Edinburgh, Scotland, 1982.

Maslow, A. H. *Motivation and personality*. New York: Harper & Row, 1954.

McClelland, D. C. *The achieving society*. New York: Van Nostrand Reinhold, 1961.

Morrow, P. C. Concept redundancy in organizational research: The case of work commitment. *Academy of Management Review*, 1983, 8, 486-500.

Singh, J. P. QWL experiences in India: Trials and triumph. Paper presented at the 20th International Congress of Applied Psychology, Edinburgh, Scotland, 1982.

Whyte, W. F. Culture and work. In R. A. Webber (Ed.), *Culture and management*. Homewood, Ill.: Irwin, 1969, 30-39.

Geert Hofstede is Director of the Institute for Research on Intercultural Cooperation, Arnhem, The Netherlands.

[3]

A Buddhist Economic System—in Practice:

The Rules of State Policy Making of the Ideal Kings Sought a 'Middle Way' Between Right and Left

By FREDERIC L. PRYOR*

ABSTRACT. Although there is little discussion of *distributive justice* in the *Theravāda* canon, the *Buddhist State* is advised to provide all people with a minimum income. *Radiation* theory sees the *economy* prospering through the virtuous actions of individuals following the *moral law*. Early Buddhist writings generally accept existing political and economic institutions, even while providing a democratic *social ethos* revolutionary for its time. *King Aśoka,* greatest of all *Indian emperors,* pursued a highly activist *fiscal policy* even though he believed only *meditation* could help people to advance in moral living. But canonical beliefs about economic activity are much more ambiguous than economic literature often indicates. Hence today there are *rightist* and *leftist* Buddhists, differing in interpretation.

ONE CAN INFER economic behavior from the principles of Theravādā Buddhism, as I reported in my previous essay, "A Buddhist Economic System—in Principle" (Pryor, 1990). This leaves the question what influence did they bear on economic behavior as reported in the Theravādā canon. Thus we advance from homilies to annals, and find that this branch of Buddhism was not as "other-worldly" as Max Weber thought.

I

Income Redistribution in the Ideal State

ACCORDING TO LITTLE (1988), Theravādā Buddhism has "nothing comparable" to Western analyses of "distributive justice." Although the Buddhist canon places great stress on gift giving, it is primarily to the monks and the *sangha* (monasteries). "There is, apparently, no . . . Theravādin literature on distributive justice, nor is it the poor as such who are for the Theravādas the primary object of beneficence." Of course, through the laws of *kamma* there is a distributive cycle of cosmic proportions, *i.e.,* one's current social and economic position is

* [Frederic L. Pryor, Ph.D., is professor of economics at Swarthmore College, Swarthmore, PA 19081.]

American Journal of Economics and Sociology, Vol. 50, No. 1 (January, 1991).

due to one's good *kamma* accumulated in a previous existence. This does not mean indifference to the poor, for one's economic status is not only dependent on the laws of *kamma,* but is also complemented by the moral virtues of compassion and generosity.[1] Alms giving to the poor is regarded as increasing one's merit [*viz. Anguttara-Nikāya,* V, iv, 31]. The importance of our active intervention has some important implications for behavior of the "righteous ruler" as well.

It should be added that the revered Buddhist kings are also known for the financial aid which they provided for the poor; indeed, the "Cakkavātti-Sīhanāda Suttanta" advises kings to give their gifts to all who are poor. Moreover, gifts to the monks and to the monasteries do not prevent them from providing a refuge for the destitute or from redistributing such beneficence to the indigent.

Thus although there is little discussion of distributive justice, redistribution of income, either through the public, private, or monastery sectors, is certainly regarded in a favorable light. In order to favor the spiritual improvement of the population, the State is justified in taking steps to provide all people with a minimum income. Whether the motive for redistribution is to spread the *dhamma* (in a Buddhist economy) or to increase distributive justice (in a Western economy) seems a bit irrelevant; in both cases, it should be added, the limits of redistribution are difficult to determine.

II

Radiation: Virtue as a Positive Externality

THE BUDDHIST THEORY of radiation sees the economy prospering through the collective impact of the virtuous actions of individuals following the *dhamma.* In many respects it parallels Leibenstein's conception of X-efficiency as determined by an "atmosphere." This, of course, provides a considerable contrast to the views of Adam Smith who saw an economy prospering through the self-interested, not consciously virtuous, actions of individuals. (Of course, Smith would argue such individual actions would be limited by moral constraints; however, he places less emphasis on the differences between self-interest and greed than do Buddhists who see quite different long-term consequences of the two attitudes).

Buddhists argue that since the economy can ultimately prosper only through virtuous action, ultimately the only hope for prosperity lies in a regeneration of human kind, *e.g.,* through the cultivation of the Four Sublime Abodes (loving kindness, compassion, sympathetic joy, and equanimity). According to Reynolds (1988), Buddhists hold that any appropriate dhammic action inevitably leads to an increase of the material wealth of the community. Further (Reynolds and

Clifford, 1980, p. 62) "As a result of the monk's pure and selfless actions, the laity flourish"; and they stress that it is the interaction between the laity and the monks which brings about such virtue. On the level of the State (p. 66), "the king legitimates his position by displaying his [merit and power] selflessly for the soteriological good of his subjects," especially by supporting the monasteries, and his actions and policies also increase material prosperity. Note that from the standpoint of the king, the primary purpose of the act is to gain individual merit, not further the social good.

A stark contrast to this theory of economic radiation is exemplified by the writings of such Western theologians as Reinhold Niebuhr, who have argued that individual and social progress, in both material and spiritual senses, may be quite different in certain situations; further, personal virtue does not always carry directly over into social virtue.

III

Trade Through the Market

THE MAJOR PARTS of the Buddhist canon does not appear to discuss any alternative means of distributing goods and services beyond the market. Thus their analysis of trade is quite straightforward.

The Buddhist discussion on right livelihood prohibits trade in certain goods and services, which means that all other types of trade are apparently allowed (but not explicitly approved). In an interesting comparison between trading and agriculture as means of livelihood, the Buddha also notes [Discourse 99, *Majjhima-Nikāya*] that both can bring high or low returns, depending on the circumstances; however, trading is an occupation with little to do, few duties, a small administration, and small problems, while agriculture is the reverse. In other parts of the canon (*e.g., Anguttara-Nikāya,* III, ii, 20) the capable merchant is approvingly said to know the value of goods and prices and the profits he obtains; and to buy where the price is low and to sell where the price is high.

One of the most favored of Buddha's disciples was Anāthapiḍika, a merchant who was generous to the cause and who was highly praised for his piety. Some scholars (*e.g.,* Reynolds, 1988) claim that early Buddhism was particularly attractive to merchants, a marginal group adopting a marginal religion which had a strongly democratic nature. In more recent times, anthropologists such as Keyes (1988) have argued that Buddhists in some areas look unfavorably on merchants because they suspect that improper means were used in amassing wealth; however, this has nothing to do with the activity *per se.*

All of this raises a difficult point concerning Buddhist beliefs about the functioning of the market. Certainly Buddhism accepts competition in general in the sense that it is possible to compete without hurting others, *e.g.,* excel in virtue. For instance, King (1964, pp. 241 *ff.*) discusses the work of a Burmese writer on economic issues, U Chan Htoon, who speaks of "prizes in the school of life that each may strive for to obtain. . . . If a man chooses to interpret this as free competition, it is still competition without rivalry, for victory to oneself does not mean the defeat of someone else."

How relevant is this to the economy? If we adopt the reasonable "Austrian" view that the competitive market can not properly function without rivalry, then it can be argued that innovation or "vigorous" market activities can not take place in a Buddhist economy. As Schumpeter pointed out, innovations bring the winds of creative destruction, which can cause economic distress to the non-innovators. Similarly, rivalry in a market where the available demand at an equilibrium price would drive a number of firms out of business would also lead to similar distress. We can lack attachment to our wealth and yet still experience considerable pain in the process of being deprived of our customary livelihood. In both cases, it must be added, the exact incidence and extent of the pain are unanticipated by the participants who are the cause of this distress.

At this point it is important to stress the critical nature of motives in Buddhist ethical thought. Thus, if innovations are made, but not with the intention to ruin a competitor or to amass goods for personal use, but rather to supply goods to the population at a lower cost and to provide gifts to monks and the poor (including, perhaps, former competitors who were not flexible in responding), then innovation can be quite acceptable. Similar arguments can be made in the case of commercial rivalry.

IV

Other Economic Institutions

ACCORDING TO KING (1964, p. 177) the Buddha had little concern for society as such and little conviction of its possible improvability. Certainly society was not to be destroyed and social conditions might help or hinder humans in their search for *nibbāna,* but such conditions could never be *fundamentally* bettered.

One receives the strong impression that early Buddhist writings generally accept existing political and economic institutions, even while providing a democratic social ethos which was revolutionary for its time. For instance, the Buddha did not appear to challenge the general framework of the kingship; and in so far as he did not strongly urge the freeing of slaves (who are mentioned in the canonical sources, even though they did not appear a numerically important group), he appeared to accept the institution of slavery (*e.g.,* the scriptural sources cited by Gard, 1960, p. 225). The Buddha did represent a break from older social traditions in that he did not condemn urban institutions and seemed aligned with such groups as merchants.

It must also be noted, however, that according to the established rules of monastic life, the monks could not have slaves, which suggests that the institution of slavery was uncomfortable to them. In the writings of early Buddhists who are held in particularly high regard, *e.g.,* King Aśoka, there was no call to free slaves, but merely the "proper treatment of slaves and servants" (Nikan and McKeon, 1966, p. 45).

V

Economic Policies

THE "AGGAÑÑA SUTTA" which described the origins of property also discusses the origins of the State. As crime increased after the division of the land, the people elected a king to maintain law and order, paying him for his troubles. This suggests a type of social contract theory, which means that the king has important obligations toward the people.

Some of the discussion about economic policy with such a social contract is too general to be of much help to the policy maker, *e.g.,* Buddhadasa Bhikku's (1986, p. 95) exegesis of the traditional Ten Royal Precepts of Kingship: generosity, morality, liberality, uprightness, gentleness, self-restraint, non-anger, non-hurtfulness, forbearance, and non-opposition.

However, more practical advice can also be found. For instance, one of the canonical sources, the "Kūtadanta Sutta" [Sutta V of *Dīgha-Nikāya*] speaks of the Royal Acts to increase prosperity which include giving of seed corn and food to farmers and of capital to merchants to start or increase their business. The particular source emphasizes that if prosperity increases, economic disorders and crime such as theft decrease.

Additional insight into State economic activities can be gained by examining the records of some of the "righteous rulers" who are revered by the Buddhists. Unfortunately, the economic parts of this literature are not extensive because the monks writing such manuscripts were more concerned with their spiritual lives, rather than their statecraft, an orientation most apparent in the well-known discussion of King Malinda. It should also be noted that because of the participation of the State in the operations of the irrigation systems in many of these countries, the crown had a fairly active role in the economy.

The prototypical important righteous ruler was the revered King Aśoka (Ashoka) (ca. 274–232 B.C.E.), the grandson of the founder of the Mauryan dynasty in India and one of the greatest of the Indian emperors.[2] From Aśoka's edicts it appears that he generally accepted the economic and political institutions of his time. For instance, he did not condemn either torture (although he spoke of the necessity to avoid "unjust torture" or the killing of criminals, Nikam and McKeon, 1966, p. 61), which seems peculiar with regard to his reverence for life, especially of animals.

However, he also took as the goal of statecraft the welfare and happiness of the people (pp. 38, 53) and, although he did not discuss in detail the means, it appears that he adopted a highly activist fiscal policy, both with regard to current and capital expenditures. For instance, he gave gifts to the aged, other needy, and religious orders; he set up public education courses to teach the doctrines of *dhamma;* he cut back on large public festivals; he imported and planted medicinal herbs; and he carried out various public works projects such as digging of wells, planting of trees, construction of rest houses and animal watering stations along main roads in the empire. Some of his edicts appeared to enforce traditional Buddhist beliefs, *e.g.,* bans on slaughtering various animals. The funds spent on the maintenance of the crown and good works were high, *e.g.,* taxes were apparently about one fourth of the revenue of land (p. 69).

However, a curious policy dilemma arises. Aśoka quite specifically noted that "the people can be induced to advance in *dhamma* by only two means: by moral prescriptions and by meditation. Of the two, moral prescriptions are of little consequence, but meditation is of great importance" (p. 40). In short, he saw limits of an activist government in promoting virtue. The definition of such limits has been a source of controversy among Buddhist writers ever since.

Still another righteous ruler was King Ruang (all references refer to Reynolds and Reynolds, 1982), who lived in the 14th century in Thailand, long after the canonical scriptures had been completed. Ruang stated (p. 153) quite clearly that a righteous king brings prosperity to his subjects. He apparently had a much less luxurious court or a less activist governmental expenditure policy than Aśoka, since he advised (p. 151 *ff.*) that taxes should be less than 10 percent of the crop (and less in a drought) and that such taxes should never be higher than those of the preceding king. He also urged (p. 152 *ff.*) that the State provide interest free loans to those wishing to engage in commerce and that no profit taxes should be placed upon such commercial activities.

Of course, the various writings on economic policy are both unsystematic and diffuse; they certainly do not define very exactly what type of economic policies should be followed or, in any very specific sense, the economic principles underlying such action. However, one important assumption behind such policy advice is simple: a king following the *dhamma* and listening to the advice of the monks will know what are the correct policies to follow. These moral policies will bring prosperity according to the doctrine of radiation.

VI

Three Brief Meditations on the Economic Impact of Canonical Buddhism

IT SHOULD BE CLEAR that canonical Buddhist beliefs and attitudes toward economic activity and capital formation are much more ambiguous than often stated in the economic literature (*e.g.*, Ayal, 1963). The purpose of this section is to delve into three economic problems posed within the framework of canonical Buddhism. (The impact of canonical Buddhism on actual economic practices and beliefs in Buddhist countries is a much more complicated subject, especially since these vary considerably from country to country, and they must be left for another occasion.)

The Economic Dialectic Between the Monks and the Laity

As many have suggested, a Buddhist economy comprised only of monks (and nuns) could not last since these people have fully given up occupational and family duties in order to search for *nibbāna,* relying on others to feed them. For a Buddhist economy to survive, there must be both monks and lay people. Simple economic considerations determine the relative numbers of the two groups for a closed Buddhist economy.

If working incentives were not affected by giving away of food to monks, if "radiation" was not important, and if the entire population lived at the subsistence level, then the *maximum* percentage of the population who could live as monks (hereafter "maximum monk-share") would be determined from two factors: the percentage of the economically active lay population (*i.e.*, engaged in production); and the difference between average production and the subsistence level for the family members supported by the person engaged in productive work. To these barebones, other considerations can be taken into account:

Productivity: The higher the level of productivity (due to investment or to a higher level of technology), the greater the maximum monk-share.

Minimum consumption level: It is unlikely that the lay population will be content to maintain just a subsistence level and give their surplus to the monks. The higher the amount of their surplus production they wish to consume before giving any food to the monks, the lower the maximum monk-share.

Disincentives: If the laity must give up a large share of their produce to the monks, they might not work as hard as if all of their food were going to their own consumption. Although diligence is praised in the Buddhist canon, I could find nothing which specified exactly how hard people would work and it is, therefore, likely that less effort would be applied. The greater this disincentive effect, the lower the maximum monk-share.

Radiation: If the laity consume many luxuries, they may become greedy and transgress the laws of *dhamma* so that negative virtue is radiated and the maximum monk-share is lowered. If the monk population follows religious prescriptions in a proper fashion, they and the laity together can radiate virtue, which raises production and increases the maximum monk-share.

Actions of the ruler: The ruler's economic policies affect production and, hence, the maximum monk-share. This raises the problem of what should be policy goals of the ruler. For simplicity of exposition, I assume the policies remain constant and take up the problem of policy goals at the end of the discussion.

An interesting economic problem arises when the number of monks is less than the maximum which can be supported and when the amount of luxury goods consumed by the population corrupts them. Three policy options are open: (a) The luxury foods can be collected and used not for the support of monks (who are not at the maximum number) but for the construction of temples. (Such investment is productive in the sense that it reduces corruption, increases virtue, and raises the production function). (b) The people can be persuaded to work less so that they will have fewer luxury goods, but more time for meditation. This would, of course, lower production. (c) The economic institutions of the society might be rearranged so that productivity would be less, but the possibilities of increasing merit would be greater. For instance, creation of small-scale villages where economies of scale would be lost, but an environment more nurturing of virtuous behavior than that of anonymous city life would be created. The second and third options both entail reduction of consumption, but in quite different ways.

This economic dialectic between the monks and laity has a strong influence on capital formation. More specifically, gifts to the monks would lower the ratio of investment to the GDP if the laity were unwilling to lower their standard of living to an equal amount since the resources would come out of resources previously used in investment, which seems a reasonable assumption. This situation also leads to trade-off between the relative number of current and future monks who can be supported. If a Buddhist government wishes to encourage the achieving of *nibbāna,* it makes good sense to encourage capital formation so that in the long run a higher share of the population can become monks and engage in the necessary contemplation. The exact amount of capital formation depends, of course, on the social discount rate.

What should be the policy goals of a ruler in such Buddhist societies? If achievement of *nibbāna* of as many people as possible were the goal, then policy should be aimed for increasing material prosperity so that more monks could be supported (since they have a higher probability of achieving *nibbāna* and of encouraging as many of the laity as possible (according to the conditions presented in the diagram) to join the monasteries in order to achieve this goal.

This interdependence between laity and monks has some important implications for the nature of Buddhist society. First and foremost, it means that there is a strong complementarity between the nibbanic and the kammic strands of Buddhism. For *nibbāna* to be achieved by some, the others must exist as well; and the two strands of Buddhism are thus inextricably tied.

It also means that many of the interpretations tying Buddhism to lack of economic progress are misguided. As noted in a number of different ways above, Buddhism is not inimical to material prosperity. Further, Buddhism is not just a religion of the monks, but also of the laity; and, therefore, both groups require attention before generalizations can be made about the impact of the religion on the economy.

These rather obvious strictures are not taken into account in many analyses. For instance, in a discussion entitled "The Other-Worldliness of Buddhism and Its Economic Consequences," Max Weber (1968, pp. 627–30) notes that the impact of Buddhism varies from country to country, depending upon the cultural milieu in which it is found. However, in all of them "no motivation toward a rational system for the methodical control of life flowed from Buddhist . . . piety." Although the doctrine does leave "room for the acquisitive drive of the tradesman, the interest of the artisan in sustenance, and the traditionalism of the peasant," it accepts "this world as externally given" and does not provide for a "rationalized ethical transformation" of existing conditions which is necessary either to improve one's own economic condition or that of society in general. Although a type of capitalism has existed in these countries in a modest sense, "there was no development toward 'modern capitalism', nor even any stirrings in that direction. Above all, there evolved no 'capitalist spirit' in the sense that is distinctive of ascetic Protestantism."[3]

Clearly Weber is focusing his attention only on one of the complementary strands of Buddhism. If he had directed his attention to the Buddhist lay people and lay ethic, he might have discovered quite a different economic and social consequence of the religion, *e.g.,* business management and capital accumulation in a "modern fashion," combined with the accumulation of merit by giving away some of the surplus to monks and other poor people. Certainly Zen Buddhism, which has had an extremely strong cultural impact on Japan, has certain important other-worldly aspects, and yet this has not prevented Japan from achieving an impressive degree of economic development. Of course, it is the lay people, not the monks, who are the producers and investors. Nevertheless, the relationships between "other-worldly" Buddhism and economic and political are much more complicated than Weber suggested (a matter explored by a number of writers, *e.g.,* Tambiah [1984], Sarkisyanz [1965]).

Although Weber's exclusive focus on only one of the two complementary social groups in a Buddhist economy appears one-sided, he may well be correct that in certain situations, Buddhism does raise difficulties for economic development, but for quite different reasons than he argued, *e.g.,* where traditional cultural values are antithetical to economic development and where these values and Buddhism are inextricably tied.

The Problem of Needs and Wants

Underlying much of the discussion in the canonical works is a distinction between needs and wants which provides a fulcrum for the doctrinal treatment of consumption. Needs, for instance, are embodied in the Four Requisites (food, clothing, shelter, and medicine). Although asceticism is condemned, the doctrine of non-attachment has been interpreted by many to mean that we should lead a life of simplicity and consume little more than our needs.

How needs are defined is the key question; but I have found little systematic evidence in the canonical scriptures on the matter. An interesting ambivalence appears: *On the one hand,* there appears to be an implicit assumption that our needs are both biological and social, *i.e.,* related to the station of life in which one finds oneself. *On the other hand,* the various stories of generous giving suggest that even those of very high station can live in simplicity consuming only enough to fulfill their basic biological needs after they have disposed of almost all of their wealth to the monastery.

If one's consumption needs are limited, then under normal conditions it may not be necessary to spend much time in work if one is diligent in the few hours when it is necessary to earn one's daily bread. Although Buddhism, in common with the doctrines of other religions, does not appear to treat such incentive problems, this is not worrisome since meditation and other spiritual exercises can be carried out in the greater amount of free time. I have found no evidence of any belief in the Protestant saying that "the devil finds work for idle hands."

Such considerations give rise to a puzzle. What does the Buddhist canon mean by "prosperity" in describing the result of spiritual radiation? Clearly the economic needs of all people are filled and perhaps the quasi-necessities as well. Given the doctrines against attachment and pride, it does not seem likely that luxury consumption should be very high, except in the situation where people are mindful of the impermanence of the situation and would be willing to relinquish all such luxury consumption.

The reduction of consumption to the level of needs—never very clearly defined—has a certain appeal among modern Buddhists and is supported by some interesting arguments. For instance, the Thai monk Buddhadasa Bhikkhu (1986, p. 61) argues that the multiplication of individual wants is always at the expense of society since if people consumed only according to their needs, there would be enough for all and in all times. From the rest of his argument it is clear that he is relying on the story of the creation of property presented above, where the world had sufficient food for all before people started acting with pride and maximizing utility by storing food (and thereby saving daily trips out to the fields).

The Problem of Economic Complexity

In common with all religions which emerged in peasant economies, Buddhism has a number of doctrines which point toward the relationships within a small community as a behavioral ideal. The emphasis on simple living discussed above reinforces this idea. Further, according to Gard (1964, p. 112), Buddhism has a strong personalistic ethic, e.g., a preference for settling questions of equity and justice on a person-to-person basis, rather than by a legalistic technique or stated principles. Their belief that work should enable a person to overcome ego-centredness by joining with others in a common purpose is another sign pointing to the benevolent nature of the small scale community, in contrast to the large, urban community. Modern Buddhists, e.g., Buddhadasa Bhikku (1986, p. 86) or Sivaraksa (1986, pp. 54 ff.) argue that social problems seem to grow as people begin living in larger and larger groups and that such complexity and development leads to an overvaluation of "quantity" and an undervaluation of "quality."

The canonical scriptures appear to provide few direct guideposts for living in highly complicated and impersonal urban complexes. Two approaches are possible to imagine: (a) Traditional doctrines would be extrapolated to meet the new situation, e.g., rightmindedness could be reinterpreted for the needs of such a setting; (b) Attempts would be made to avoid the creation of such conditions. The latter alternate would require the deliberate maintenance of small, face-to-face communities; small factories; considerable self-sufficiency; dampening of the class struggle of workers and property owners by social forces, and maintenance of high direct and indirect barriers to trade with the outside world.

Of course, all of this would be accompanied by a considerable loss of productivity and lower living standards. This, however, would be quite consistent
with the beliefs about production for needs, rather than wants, and for simplicity
of life style. Such self-contained communities would also reduce external trade
and thus reduce the temptation of merchants to deviate from the *dhamma* by
becoming too attached to their profits of trade. In a small community, it may
be easier to enforce social controls to prevent trade profits from being too high.
Finally, the fall in income from the loss of economies of scale which occurs in
small-scale economic communities is, as noted above, one way of reducing the
possible corruption of attachment arising from consumption of luxury goods.

Although I have not seen proposals for such small-scale, autarkic communities
in the Buddhist literature available to me, some—such as Mahatma Gandhi
(who drew upon both Buddhist and Hindu traditions) and E. F. Schumacher
(who drew upon Buddhist ideas)—have viewed this idea with favor. Certain of
Gandhi's disciples (*e.g.,* Das, 1979) have explored at considerable length how
the modern society and economy could be arranged under such a principle
while minimizing the loss of production.

VII

Buddhism as a Guidepost for a Modern Economic System

On a local level the uses of Buddhism are elastic, and doctrinal sources can
be used either to justify the building of yet another temple or to provide religious
support for village development work (*e.g.,* Macy [1983]). On a national level,
a similar doctrinal flexibility is found.

In bygone years some Buddhist social commentators took a very passive view
toward economic policy, arguing that it is even useless to try to correct some
obvious shortcomings of the economy. For instance, in Burma the Buddhist
Shway Yoe, writing at the end of the 19th century (cited by King, 1964, p. 231),
says that the rich and powerful man has a right to govern because in a previous
life he was pious and good; the poor man must be content with his lot because
he must have been bad before he entered this existence.

In more recent times this appears to be changing and a considerable number
of Buddhist intellectuals start their analysis of economic systems with a critique
of the obvious defects of both capitalism and communism, then to argue that
since Buddhism is a doctrine of the Middle Way, it is possible to draw upon the
positive aspects of both types of systems while, at the same time, arranging
matters so as to avoid the general materialism and spiritual sickness which is
found in both systems. The real question, of course, is what must the economy

look like and what must the State do to avoid the various specified evils, while increasing virtue.

The Buddhist canon provides arguments for all sides of the political spectrum for reconstructing the economy. For purposes of illustration it is useful to compare the ideas advanced by the far left (Buddhist socialists or communists) and right (Buddhist traditionalists). Representing the left I draw upon the doctrines of the Buddhist socialists as summarized by Sarkisyanz (1965, 1978); representing the right I draw upon the writings of a Thai monk, Buddhadasa Bhikkhu (1986).[4] I have not been able to locate any intellectual in recent years justifying some type of *laissez faire* capitalism by recourse to the Buddhist canon, although it is not hard to imagine updated versions of the arguments advanced by Shway Yoe (noted above) combined with some notion that it is primarily individual actions, rather than governmental moral prescriptions and policies, which lead to a virtuous society.

Buddhadasa has little discussion of public ownership of the means of production, apparently taking a pragmatic stand in favor of current arrangements based on the necessity of private property arising from human frailities. The Buddhist socialists have favored considerable nationalization of the means of production. For instance, U Nu supported land nationalization by arguing that by eliminating private ownership of land, the class struggle based on the *illusion* about the importance of property could be eliminated as well (Sarkisyanz, 1978). The Burmese government of Ne Win, who overthrew U Nu, carried out considerable nationalization of industry and banks.

Both the right and the left Buddhists favor a certain minimal redistribution of income so that the basic consumption needs of all are covered. However, based on traditional arguments, Bhikkhu can still support the maintenance of class distinctions, albeit based on function and duty rather than inherited wealth. Others on the Buddhist right have argued that redistributing income is "patchwork, like social service" and that true Buddhism takes away the instinct of possessiveness; and that sharing can come only after the overcoming of self. On the left U Nu argued for considerably more redistribution on the grounds that this would increase the number of those economically capable of performing works of piety (Sarkisyanz, 1965, p. 171). Others of the left argued for redistribution, drawing upon arguments about the rough economic equality found in the monastery.

With regard to governmental activism in the economy, the important role of the governments in the irrigation economies of Southeast Asia received mention above. Nevertheless, the dilemma mentioned above concerning King Aśoka— how to define the limits of intervention—is still an unresolved issue.

On the right, Buddhadasa Bhikkhu has drawn those limits rather widely: He called his ideal system "dictatorial dhammic socialism" which, among other things, means that moral governmental policies should be carried out "expeditiously"; this differs from tyranny, he argues, since in the latter the policies carried out do not serve the general interest. In any case he is not shy in urging governmental coercion to force people to contribute their labor to public works construction.

The Buddhists on the left have urged considerable governmental intervention, and both the Burmese governments of U Nu and Ne Win carried out a variety of direct and indirect measures to guide the economy. It also seems possible, however, for a Buddhist to draw upon the canon to urge relatively little intervention, not only on the grounds that "each must find refuge in himself" to achieve virtue but also on the grounds of the effect of such a concentration of political and economic power in the government upon the personnel in the government itself.

In short, the vagueness of the Buddhist canon on economic matters combined with its complexity and length allows room for quite different interpretations of an ideal economic system in modern times, especially since conditions are very much different than they were more than 2000 years ago when the Buddha lived. Of course, this situation is little different from that of Christianity. The really difficult problem is to determine what part of the canon will be taken seriously under what circumstances, but this would require a much different kind of approach than the textual exegesis offered here.

Many of the writings of religious figures applying the ideals of Buddhists to problems of economics are incredibly naive, but this is similar to writings of other religions as well. The Buddhists' moral critiques of modern economies have cogency, as do their investigation of possible alternative economic policies. The increasing interest in Islam has given rise to an exploding literature on Islamic economics; the increasing interest in Buddhism might give rise to a similar development of Buddhist economics as well.

Notes

1. From one perspective, this gives rise to an interesting puzzle: if I give alms to a poor stranger, is such generosity a consequence of his previous behavior and thought, or merely a random event which provides him with pleasure? Is the deed a consequence of my accumulated merit so that our kammic trajectories intersect at this particular point, or is it merely a random event which provides me with unexpected merit?

2. Aśoka's edicts have been collected and systematized by Nikam and McKeon (1966); and my discussion is based on their book. Strong (1988) argues that it is not the historical Aśoka or his writings which are famous and revered, but rather the legendary Aśoka. Although this may well be correct, for purposes of this essay, this is irrelevant.

Buddhism 31

An important righteous ruler before Aśoka was Prince Vessantara, who was Siddhartha Gautama in his immediately previous existence. Of particular note, the Prince gave away all of his wealth to anyone who requested it; this including his children, his wife, his magic white elephant which brought rain, and the kingship itself. He represents the ideal of non-attachment and generosity; it is noteworthy that he did not give funds to monks and their *sangha* since, of course, they did not appear until the Prince in his next life became the Buddha. His other economic policies are not well known.

3. In this passage Weber also makes an argumentative leap from the doctrines of the religion to the actual practices of the society which, as I have indicated above, does not appear warranted. Certainly there is little in the kammic strand of Buddhism which would hinder the development of accounting and other aids to rational business calculation; indeed, the injunctions for good stewardship would encourage such developments. Keyes (1988), for instance, speaks of the "innerworldly asceticism" and "work ethic" of the Buddhists in northeastern Thailand.

4. Although my brief presentation of Bhikkhu's economic ideas make them sound rather similar to doctrines of national socialism in Germany, this connection should not be drawn. Bhikkhu is a strong believer in non-violence and has a profound moral conception of human kind; unfortunately, his economic ideas are naive. Sarkisyanz (1965) presents an interesting summary of active economic policy by Buddhist kings from Aśoka onwards.

References

(For additional references not cited in the text of this article, see the bibliography of my previous article, "A Buddhist Economic System—in Principle," *American Journal of Economics and Sociology,* Vol. 49, No. 3, (July, 1990), pp. 339–49).

Anguttara-Nikāya, Volumes III and IV, trans. by E. M. Hare. *The Book of Gradual Sayings* for Pāli Text Society. London: Luzac, 1961, 1965.

Anguttara-Nikāya, Volumes I and II, trans. by F. L. Woodward, *The Book of Gradual Sayings* for Pāli Text Society. London: Luzac, 1962, 1970.

Ayal, Eliezer, "Value Systems and Economic Development in Japan and Thailand," *Journal of Social Issues,* 19, No. 1 (Jan. 1963), pp. 35–51.

Buddhadasa, Bhikkhu, *Dhammic Socialism,* translated and edited by Donald K. Swearer. Bangkok: Thai Inter-Religious Commission for Development, 1986.

Dīgha-Nikāya, trans. by T. W. Rhys Davids. *Dialogues of the Buddha, Part I,* Pāli Text Society. London: Luzac, 1965.

Dīgha-Nikāya, trans. by T. W. Rhys Davids and C. A. F. Rhys Davids. *Dialogues of the Buddha, Part III,* 5th edition, Pāli Text Society. London: Luzac, 1965.

Das, Amritandanda, *Foundations of Gandhian Economics.* New York: St. Martin's, 1979.

Gard, Richard A., *Buddhism.* New York: George Braziller, 1962.

King, Winston L., *In the Hope of Nibbāna.* LaSalle, Illinois: Open Court, 1964.

Little, David, "Ethical Analysis and Wealth in Theravāa Buddhism: A Response to Frank Reynolds," in Sizemore and Swearer (1988).

Majjhima-Nikāya, Volumes I, II, and III, translated by I. B. Horner for Pāli Text Society. *The Collection of Middle Length Sayings.* London: Luzac, 1957, 1967.

Nikam, N. A. and Richard McKeon, eds. *The Edicts of Aśoka.* Chicago: University of Chicago Press, 1966.

Reynolds, Frank E., "Ethics and Wealth in Theravāda Buddhism: A Study in Comparative Religious Ethics," in Sizemore and Swearer (1988).

————, "Four Modes of Theravāda Action," *Journal of Religious Ethics*, 7, No. 1 (Spring 1979), pp. 12–26.

Reynolds, Frank E. and Regina T. Clifford, "Sangha, Society, and the Struggle for National Identity: Burma and Thailand," in Frank Reynolds and Ludwig, Theodore, eds. *Transition and Transformations in the History of Religions*. Leiden: Brill, 1980, pp. 56–91.

Reynolds, Frank E. and Mani Reynolds, *Three Worlds According to King Ruang: A Thai Buddhist Cosmology*, University of California Research Series 4. Berkeley: Asian Humanities Press, 1982.

Sarkisyanz, E., "Buddhist Backgrounds of the Burmese Socialism," in Bardwell L. Smith, ed. *Religion and the Legitimization of Power in Thailand, Laos, and Burma*. Chambersburg, Pa.: ANIMA Books, 1978.

Sarkisyanz, E., *Buddhist Backgrounds of the Burmese Revolution*. The Hague: Martinus Nijhoff, 1965.

Schumacher, E. F., "Buddhist Economics," in his *Small is Beautiful: Economics as if People Mattered*. New York: Harper and Row, 1973, pp. 53–63.

Sivaraksa, Sulak, *A Buddhist Vision for Renewing Society*. Bangkok: Tienwan Publishing House, 1986.

Tambiah, Stanley Jeyaraja, *The Buddhist Saints of the Forest and the Cult of Amulets: A Study in Charisma, Hagiography, Sectarianism, and Millennial Buddhism*. Cambridge: Cambridge University Press, 1984.

Weber, Max, *Economy and Society,* edited by Guenther Roth and Claus Wittich, Volume II. New York: Bedminster Press, 1968.

Weber, Max, *The Religion of India: The Sociology of Hinduism and Buddhism,* transl. by Hans H. Gerth and Don Martindale. Glencoe: Free Press, 1958.

[4]

Economic Action and Social Structure: The Problem of Embeddedness[1]

Mark Granovetter
State University of New York at Stony Brook

How behavior and institutions are affected by social relations is one of the classic questions of social theory. This paper concerns the extent to which economic action is embedded in structures of social relations, in modern industrial society. Although the usual neoclassical accounts provide an "undersocialized" or atomized-actor explanation of such action, reformist economists who attempt to bring social structure back in do so in the "oversocialized" way criticized by Dennis Wrong. Under- and oversocialized accounts are paradoxically similar in their neglect of ongoing structures of social relations, and a sophisticated account of economic action must consider its embeddedness in such structures. The argument is illustrated by a critique of Oliver Williamson's "markets and hierarchies" research program.

INTRODUCTION: THE PROBLEM OF EMBEDDEDNESS

How behavior and institutions are affected by social relations is one of the classic questions of social theory. Since such relations are always present, the situation that would arise in their absence can be imagined only through a thought experiment like Thomas Hobbes's "state of nature" or John Rawls's "original position." Much of the utilitarian tradition, including classical and neoclassical economics, assumes rational, self-interested behavior affected minimally by social relations, thus invoking an idealized state not far from that of these thought experiments. At the other extreme lies what I call the argument of "embeddedness": the argu-

---

[1] Earlier drafts of this paper were written in sabbatical facilities kindly provided by the Institute for Advanced Study and Harvard University. Financial support was provided in part by the institute, by a John Simon Guggenheim Memorial Foundation fellowship, and by NSF Science Faculty Professional Development grant SPI 81-65055. Among those who have helped clarify the arguments are Wayne Baker, Michael Bernstein, Albert Hirschman, Ron Jepperson, Eric Leifer, Don McCloskey, Charles Perrow, James Rule, Michael Schwartz, Theda Skocpol, and Harrison White. Requests for reprints should be sent to Mark Granovetter, Department of Sociology, State University of New York at Stony Brook, Stony Brook, New York 11794-4356.

American Journal of Sociology

ment that the behavior and institutions to be analyzed are so constrained by ongoing social relations that to construe them as independent is a grievous misunderstanding.

This article concerns the embeddedness of economic behavior. It has long been the majority view among sociologists, anthropologists, political scientists, and historians that such behavior was heavily embedded in social relations in premarket societies but became much more autonomous with modernization. This view sees the economy as an increasingly separate, differentiated sphere in modern society, with economic transactions defined no longer by the social or kinship obligations of those transacting but by rational calculations of individual gain. It is sometimes further argued that the traditional situation is reversed: instead of economic life being submerged in social relations, these relations become an epiphenomenon of the market. The embeddedness position is associated with the "substantivist" school in anthropology, identified especially with Karl Polanyi (1944; Polanyi, Arensberg, and Pearson 1957) and with the idea of "moral economy" in history and political science (Thompson 1971; Scott 1976). It has also some obvious relation to Marxist thought.

Few economists, however, have accepted this conception of a break in embeddedness with modernization; most of them assert instead that embeddedness in earlier societies was not substantially greater than the low level found in modern markets. The tone was set by Adam Smith, who postulated a "certain propensity in human nature . . . to truck, barter and exchange one thing for another" ([1776] 1979, book 1, chap. 2) and assumed that since labor was the only factor of production in primitive society, goods must have exchanged in proportion to their labor costs—as in the general classical theory of exchange ([1776] 1979, book 1, chap. 6). From the 1920s on, certain anthropologists took a similar position, which came to be called the "formalist" one: even in tribal societies, economic behavior was sufficiently independent of social relations for standard neoclassical analysis to be useful (Schneider 1974). This position has recently received a new infusion as economists and fellow travelers in history and political science have developed a new interest in the economic analysis of social institutions—much of which falls into what is called the "new institutional economics"—and have argued that behavior and institutions previously interpreted as embedded in earlier societies, as well as in our own, can be better understood as resulting from the pursuit of self-interest by rational, more or less atomized individuals (e.g., North and Thomas 1973; Williamson 1975; Popkin 1979).

My own view diverges from both schools of thought. I assert that the level of embeddedness of economic behavior is lower in nonmarket societies than is claimed by substantivists and development theorists, and it has changed less with "modernization" than they believe; but I argue

Embeddedness

also that this level has always been and continues to be more substantial than is allowed for by formalists and economists. I do not attempt here to treat the issues posed by nonmarket societies. I proceed instead by a theoretical elaboration of the concept of embeddedness, whose value is then illustrated with a problem from modern society, currently important in the new institutional economics: which transactions in modern capitalist society are carried out in the market, and which subsumed within hierarchically organized firms? This question has been raised to prominence by the "markets and hierarchies" program of research initiated by Oliver Williamson (1975).

OVER- AND UNDERSOCIALIZED CONCEPTIONS OF HUMAN ACTION IN SOCIOLOGY AND ECONOMICS

I begin by recalling Dennis Wrong's 1961 complaint about an "oversocialized conception of man in modern sociology"—a conception of people as overwhelmingly sensitive to the opinions of others and hence obedient to the dictates of consensually developed systems of norms and values, internalized through socialization, so that obedience is not perceived as a burden. To the extent that such a conception was prominent in 1961, it resulted in large part from Talcott Parsons's recognition of the problem of order as posed by Hobbes and his own attempt to resolve it by transcending the atomized, *undersocialized* conception of man in the utilitarian tradition of which Hobbes was part (Parsons 1937, pp. 89–94). Wrong approved the break with atomized utilitarianism and the emphasis on actors' embeddedness in social context—the crucial factor absent from Hobbes's thinking—but warned of exaggerating the degree of this embeddedness and the extent to which it might eliminate conflict:

> It is frequently the task of the sociologist to call attention to the intensity with which men desire and strive for the good opinion of their immediate associates in a variety of situations, particularly those where received theories or ideologies have unduly emphasized other motives. . . . Thus sociologists have shown that factory workers are more sensitive to the attitudes of their fellow workers than to purely economic incentives. . . . It is certainly not my intention to criticize the findings of such studies. My objection is that . . . [a]lthough sociologists have criticized past efforts to single out one fundamental motive in human conduct, the desire to achieve a favorable self-image by winning approval from others frequently occupies such a position in their own thinking. [1961, pp. 188–89]

Classical and neoclassical economics operates, in contrast, with an atomized, *under*socialized conception of human action, continuing in the utilitarian tradition. The theoretical arguments disallow by hypothesis any impact of social structure and social relations on production, distribution, or consumption. In competitive markets, no producer or consumer

American Journal of Sociology

noticeably influences aggregate supply or demand or, therefore, prices or other terms of trade. As Albert Hirschman has noted, such idealized markets, involving as they do "large numbers of price-taking anonymous buyers and sellers supplied with perfect information . . . function without any prolonged human or social contact between the parties. Under perfect competition there is no room for bargaining, negotiation, remonstration or mutual adjustment and the various operators that contract together need not enter into recurrent or continuing relationships as a result of which they would get to know each other well" (1982, p. 1473).

It has long been recognized that the idealized markets of perfect competition have survived intellectual attack in part because self-regulating economic structures are politically attractive to many. Another reason for this survival, less clearly understood, is that the elimination of social relations from economic analysis removes the problem of order from the intellectual agenda, at least in the economic sphere. In Hobbes's argument, disorder arises because conflict-free social and economic transactions depend on trust and the absence of malfeasance. But these are unlikely when individuals are conceived to have neither social relationships nor institutional context—as in the "state of nature." Hobbes contains the difficulty by superimposing a structure of autocratic authority. The solution of classical liberalism, and correspondingly of classical economics, is antithetical: repressive political structures are rendered unnecessary by competitive markets that make force or fraud unavailing. Competition determines the terms of trade in a way that individual traders cannot manipulate. If traders encounter complex or difficult relationships, characterized by mistrust or malfeasance, they can simply move on to the legion of other traders willing to do business on market terms; social relations and their details thus become frictional matters.

In classical and neoclassical economics, therefore, the fact that actors may have social relations with one another has been treated, if at all, as a frictional drag that impedes competitive markets. In a much-quoted line, Adam Smith complained that "people of the same trade seldom meet together, even for merriment and diversion, but the conversation ends in a conspiracy against the public, or in some contrivance to raise prices." His laissez-faire politics allowed few solutions to this problem, but he did suggest repeal of regulations requiring all those in the same trade to sign a public register; the public existence of such information "connects individuals who might never otherwise be known to one another and gives every man of the trade a direction where to find every other man of it." Noteworthy here is not the rather lame policy prescription but the recognition that *social atomization is prerequisite to perfect competition* (Smith [1776] 1979, pp. 232–33).

Embeddedness

More recent comments by economists on "social influences" construe
these as processes in which actors acquire customs, habits, or norms that
are followed mechanically and automatically, irrespective of their bearing
on rational choice. This view, close to Wrong's "oversocialized conception," is reflected in James Duesenberry's quip that "economics is all
about how people make choices; sociology is all about how they don't
have any choices to make" (1960, p. 233) and in E. H. Phelps Brown's
description of the "sociologists' approach to pay determination" as deriving from the assumption that people act in "certain ways because to do so
is customary, or an obligation, or the 'natural thing to do,' or right and
proper, or just and fair" (1977, p. 17).

But despite the apparent contrast between under- and oversocialized
views, we should note an irony of great theoretical importance: both have
in common a conception of action and decision carried out by atomized
actors. In the undersocialized account, atomization results from narrow
utilitarian pursuit of self-interest; in the oversocialized one, from the fact
that behavioral patterns have been internalized and ongoing social relations thus have only peripheral effects on behavior. That the internalized
rules of behavior are social in origin does not differentiate this argument
decisively from a utilitarian one, in which the source of utility functions is
left open, leaving room for behavior guided entirely by consensually determined norms and values—as in the oversocialized view. Under- and
oversocialized resolutions of the problem of order thus merge in their
atomization of actors from immediate social context. This ironic merger is
already visible in Hobbes's *Leviathan,* in which the unfortunate denizens
of the state of nature, overwhelmed by the disorder consequent to their
atomization, cheerfully surrender all their rights to an authoritarian
power and subsequently behave in a docile and honorable manner; by the
artifice of a social contract, they lurch directly from an undersocialized to
an oversocialized state.

When modern economists do attempt to take account of social influences, they typically represent them in the oversocialized manner represented in the quotations above. In so doing, they reverse the judgment
that social influences are frictional but sustain the conception of how such
influences operate. In the theory of segmented labor markets, for example, Michael Piore has argued that members of each labor market
segment are characterized by different styles of decision making and that
the making of decisions by rational choice, custom, or command in upper-primary, lower-primary, and secondary labor markets respectively
corresponds to the origins of workers in middle-, working-, and lower-
class subcultures (Piore 1975). Similarly, Samuel Bowles and Herbert
Gintis, in their account of the consequences of American education, argue
that different social classes display different cognitive processes because

American Journal of Sociology

of differences in the education provided to each. Those destined for lower-level jobs are trained to be dependable followers of rules, while those who will be channeled into elite positions attend "elite four-year colleges" that "emphasize social relationships conformable with the higher levels in the production hierarchy. . . . As they 'master' one type of behavioral regulation they are either allowed to progress to the next or are channeled into the corresponding level in the hierarchy of production" (Bowles and Gintis 1975, p. 132).

But these oversocialized conceptions of how society influences individual behavior are rather mechanical: once we know the individual's social class or labor market sector, everything else in behavior is automatic, since they are so well socialized. Social influence here is an external force that, like the deists' God, sets things in motion and has no further effects—a force that insinuates itself into the minds and bodies of individuals (as in the movie *Invasion of the Body Snatchers*), altering their way of making decisions. Once we know in just what way an individual has been affected, ongoing social relations and structures are irrelevant. Social influences are all contained inside an individual's head, so, in actual decision situations, he or she can be atomized as any *Homo economicus,* though perhaps with different rules for decisions. More sophisticated (and thus less oversocialized) analyses of cultural influences (e.g., Fine and Kleinman 1979; Cole 1979, chap. 1) make it clear that culture is not a once-for-all influence but an ongoing process, continuously constructed and reconstructed during interaction. It not only shapes its members but also is shaped by them, in part for their own strategic reasons.

Even when economists do take social relationships seriously, as do such diverse figures as Harvey Leibenstein (1976) and Gary Becker (1976), they invariably abstract away from the history of relations and their position with respect to other relations—what might be called the historical and structural embeddedness of relations. The interpersonal ties described in their arguments are extremely stylized, average, "typical"— devoid of specific content, history, or structural location. Actors' behavior results from their named role positions and role sets; thus we have arguments on how workers and supervisors, husbands and wives, or criminals and law enforcers will interact with one another, but these relations are not assumed to have individualized content beyond that given by the named roles. This procedure is exactly what structural sociologists have criticized in Parsonian sociology—the relegation of the specifics of individual relations to a minor role in the overall conceptual scheme, epiphenomenal in comparison with enduring structures of normative role prescriptions deriving from ultimate value orientations. In economic models, this treatment of social relations has the paradoxical effect of preserving atomized decision making even when decisions are

Embeddedness

seen to involve more than one individual. Because the analyzed set of individuals—usually dyads, occasionally larger groups—is abstracted out of social context, it is atomized in its behavior from that of other groups and from the history of its own relations. Atomization has not been eliminated, merely transferred to the dyadic or higher level of analysis. Note the use of an oversocialized conception—that of actors behaving exclusively in accord with their prescribed roles—to implement an atomized, undersocialized view.

A fruitful analysis of human action requires us to avoid the atomization implicit in the theoretical extremes of under- and oversocialized conceptions. Actors do not behave or decide as atoms outside a social context, nor do they adhere slavishly to a script written for them by the particular intersection of social categories that they happen to occupy. Their attempts at purposive action are instead embedded in concrete, ongoing systems of social relations. In the remainder of this article I illustrate how this view of embeddedness alters our theoretical and empirical approach to the study of economic behavior. I first narrow the focus to the question of trust and malfeasance in economic life and then use the "markets and hierarchies" problem to illustrate the use of embeddedness ideas in analyzing this question.[2]

EMBEDDEDNESS, TRUST, AND MALFEASANCE IN ECONOMIC LIFE

Since about 1970, there has been a flurry of interest among economists in the previously neglected issues of trust and malfeasance. Oliver Williamson has noted that real economic actors engage not merely in the pursuit of self-interest but also in "opportunism"—"self-interest seeking with guile; agents who are skilled at dissembling realize transactional advantages.[3] Economic man . . . is thus a more subtle and devious creature than the usual self-interest seeking assumption reveals" (1975, p. 255).

[2] There are many parallels between what are referred to here as the "undersocialized" and "oversocialized" views of action and what Burt (1982, chap. 9) calls the "atomistic" and "normative" approaches. Similarly, the embeddedness approach proposed here as a middle ground between under- and oversocialized views has an obvious family resemblance to Burt's "structural" approach to action. My distinctions and approach also differ from Burt's in many ways that cannot be quickly summarized; these can be best appreciated by comparison of this article with his useful summary (1982, chap. 9) and with the formal models that implement his conception (1982, 1983). Another approach that resembles mine in its emphasis on how social connections affect purposive action is Marsden's extension of James Coleman's theories of collective action and decision to situations where such connections modify results that would occur in a purely atomistic situation (Marsden 1981, 1983).

[3] Students of the sociology of sport will note that this proposition had been put forward previously, in slightly different form, by Leo Durocher.

American Journal of Sociology

But this points out a peculiar assumption of modern economic theory, that one's economic interest is pursued only by comparatively gentlemanly means. The Hobbesian question—how it can be that those who pursue their own interest do not do so mainly by force and fraud—is finessed by this conception. Yet, as Hobbes saw so clearly, there is nothing in the intrinsic meaning of "self-interest" that excludes force or fraud.

In part, this assumption persisted because competitive forces, in a self-regulating market, could be imagined to suppress force and fraud. But the idea is also embedded in the intellectual history of the discipline. In *The Passions and the Interests,* Albert Hirschman (1977) shows that an important strand of intellectual history from the time of *Leviathan* to that of *The Wealth of Nations* consisted of the watering down of Hobbes's problem of order by arguing that certain human motivations kept others under control and that, in particular, the pursuit of economic self-interest was typically not an uncontrollable "passion" but a civilized, gentle activity. The wide though implicit acceptance of such an idea is a powerful example of how under- and oversocialized conceptions complement one another: atomized actors in competitive markets so thoroughly internalize these normative standards of behavior as to guarantee orderly transactions.[4]

What has eroded this confidence in recent years has been increased attention to the micro-level details of imperfectly competitive markets, characterized by small numbers of participants with sunk costs and "specific human capital" investments. In such situations, the alleged discipline of competitive markets cannot be called on to mitigate deceit, so the classical problem of how it can be that daily economic life is not riddled with mistrust and malfeasance has resurfaced.

In the economic literature, I see two fundamental answers to this problem and argue that one is linked to an undersocialized, and the other to an oversocialized, conception of human action. The undersocialized account is found mainly in the new institutional economics—a loosely defined confederation of economists with an interest in explaining social institutions from a neoclassical viewpoint. (See, e.g., Furubotn and Pejovich 1972; Alchian and Demsetz 1973; Lazear 1979; Rosen 1982; Williamson 1975, 1979, 1981; Williamson and Ouchi 1981.) The general story told by members of this school is that social institutions and arrangements previously thought to be the adventitious result of legal, historical, social, or political forces are better viewed as the efficient solution to certain economic problems. The tone is similar to that of structural-functional sociology of the 1940s to the 1960s, and much of the argumentation fails the elementary tests of a sound functional explanation laid down by

---

[4] I am indebted to an anonymous referee for pointing this out.

Embeddedness

Robert Merton in 1947. Consider, for example, Schotter's view that to understand any observed economic institution requires only that we "infer the evolutionary problem that must have existed for the institution as we see it to have developed. Every evolutionary economic problem requires a social institution to solve it" (1981, p. 2).

Malfeasance is here seen to be averted because clever institutional arrangements make it too costly to engage in, and these arrangements—many previously interpreted as serving no economic function—are now seen as having evolved to discourage malfeasance. Note, however, that they do not produce trust but instead are a functional substitute for it. The main such arrangements are elaborate explicit and implicit contracts (Okun 1981), including deferred compensation plans and mandatory retirement—seen to reduce the incentives for "shirking" on the job or absconding with proprietary secrets (Lazear 1979; Pakes and Nitzan 1982)—and authority structures that deflect opportunism by making potentially divisive decisions by fiat (Williamson 1975). These conceptions are undersocialized in that they do not allow for the extent to which concrete personal relations and the obligations inherent in them discourage malfeasance, quite apart from institutional arrangements. *Substituting* these arrangements for trust results actually in a Hobbesian situation, in which any rational individual would be motivated to develop clever ways to evade them; it is then hard to imagine that everyday economic life would not be poisoned by ever more ingenious attempts at deceit.

Other economists have recognized that some degree of trust *must* be assumed to operate, since institutional arrangements alone could not entirely stem force or fraud. But it remains to explain the source of this trust, and appeal is sometimes made to the existence of a "generalized morality." Kenneth Arrow, for example, suggests that societies, "in their evolution have developed implicit agreements to certain kinds of regard for others, agreements which are essential to the survival of the society or at least contribute greatly to the efficiency of its working" (1974, p. 26; see also Akerlof [1983] on the origins of "honesty").

Now one can hardly doubt the existence of some such generalized morality; without it, you would be afraid to give the gas station attendant a 20-dollar bill when you had bought only five dollars' worth of gas. But this conception has the oversocialized characteristic of calling on a generalized and automatic response, even though moral action in economic life is hardly automatic or universal (as is well known at gas stations that demand exact change after dark).

Consider a case where generalized morality does indeed seem to be at work: the legendary (I hesitate to say apocryphal) economist who, against all economic rationality, leaves a tip in a roadside restaurant far from home. Note that this transaction has three characteristics that make it

American Journal of Sociology

somewhat unusual: (1) the transactors are previously unacquainted, (2) they are unlikely to transact again, and (3) information about the activities of either is unlikely to reach others with whom they might transact in the future. I argue that it is only in situations of this kind that the absence of force and fraud can mainly be explained by generalized morality. Even there, one might wonder how effective this morality would be if large costs were incurred.

The embeddedness argument stresses instead the role of concrete personal relations and structures (or "networks") of such relations in generating trust and discouraging malfeasance. The widespread preference for transacting with individuals of known reputation implies that few are actually content to rely on either generalized morality *or* institutional arrangements to guard against trouble. Economists *have* pointed out that one incentive not to cheat is the cost of damage to one's reputation; but this is an undersocialized conception of reputation as a generalized commodity, a ratio of cheating to opportunities for doing so. In practice, we settle for such generalized information when nothing better is available, but ordinarily we seek better information. Better than the statement that someone is known to be reliable is information from a trusted informant that he has dealt with that individual and found him so. Even better is information from one's own past dealings with that person. This is better information for four reasons: (1) it is cheap; (2) one trusts one's own information best—it is richer, more detailed, and known to be accurate; (3) individuals with whom one has a continuing relation have an economic motivation to be trustworthy, so as not to discourage future transactions; and (4) departing from pure economic motives, continuing economic relations often become overlaid with social content that carries strong expectations of trust and abstention from opportunism.

It would never occur to us to doubt this last point in more intimate relations, which make behavior more predictable and thus close off some of the fears that create difficulties among strangers. Consider, for example, why individuals in a burning theater panic and stampede to the door, leading to desperate results. Analysts of collective behavior long considered this to be prototypically irrational behavior, but Roger Brown (1965, chap. 14) points out that the situation is essentially an n-person Prisoner's Dilemma: each stampeder is actually being quite rational given the absence of a guarantee that anyone else will walk out calmly, even though all would be better off if everyone did so. Note, however, that in the case of the burning houses featured on the 11:00 P.M. news, we never hear that everyone stampeded out and that family members trampled one another. In the family, there is no Prisoner's Dilemma because each is confident that the others can be counted on.

490

Embeddedness

In business relations the degree of confidence must be more variable, but Prisoner's Dilemmas are nevertheless often obviated by the strength of personal relations, and this strength is a property not of the transactors but of their concrete relations. Standard economic analysis neglects the identity and past relations of individual transactors, but rational individuals know better, relying on their knowledge of these relations. They are less interested in *general* reputations than in whether a particular other may be expected to deal honestly with *them*—mainly a function of whether they or their own contacts have had satisfactory past dealings with the other. One sees this pattern even in situations that appear, at first glance, to approximate the classic higgling of a competitive market, as in the Moroccan bazaar analyzed by Geertz (1979).

Up to this point, I have argued that social relations, rather than institutional arrangements or generalized morality, are mainly responsible for the production of trust in economic life. But I then risk rejecting one kind of optimistic functionalism for another, in which networks of relations, rather than morality or arrangements, are the structure that fulfills the function of sustaining order. There are two ways to reduce this risk. One is to recognize that as a solution to the problem of order, the embeddedness position is less sweeping than either alternative argument, since networks of social relations penetrate irregularly and in differing degrees in different sectors of economic life, thus allowing for what we already know: distrust, opportunism, and disorder are by no means absent.

The second is to insist that while social relations may indeed often be a necessary condition for trust and trustworthy behavior, they are not sufficient to guarantee these and may even provide occasion and means for malfeasance and conflict on a scale larger than in their absence. There are three reasons for this.

1. The trust engendered by personal relations presents, by its very existence, enhanced opportunity for malfeasance. In personal relations it is common knowledge that "you always hurt the one you love"; that person's trust in you results in a position far more vulnerable than that of a stranger. (In the Prisoner's Dilemma, knowledge that one's coconspirator is certain to deny the crime is all the more rational motive to confess, and personal relations that abrogate this dilemma may be less symmetrical than is believed by the party to be deceived.) This elementary fact of social life is the bread and butter of "confidence" rackets that simulate certain relationships, sometimes for long periods, for concealed purposes. In the business world, certain crimes, such as embezzling, are simply impossible for those who have not built up relationships of trust that permit the opportunity to manipulate accounts. The more complete the trust, the greater the potential gain from malfeasance. That such

491

American Journal of Sociology

instances are statistically infrequent is a tribute to the force of personal relations and reputation; that they do occur with regularity, however infrequently, shows the limits of this force.

2. Force and fraud are most efficiently pursued by teams, and the structure of these teams requires a level of internal trust—"honor among thieves"—that usually follows preexisting lines of relationship. Elaborate schemes for kickbacks and bid rigging, for example, can hardly be executed by individuals working alone, and when such activity is exposed it is often remarkable that it could have been kept secret given the large numbers involved. Law-enforcement efforts consist of finding an entry point to the network of malfeasance—an individual whose confession implicates others who will, in snowball-sample fashion, "finger" still others until the entire picture is fitted together.

Both enormous trust and enormous malfeasance, then, may follow from personal relations. Yoram Ben-Porath, in the functionalist style of the new institutional economics, emphasizes the positive side, noting that "continuity of relationships can generate behavior on the part of shrewd, self-seeking, or even unscrupulous individuals that could otherwise be interpreted as foolish or purely altruistic. Valuable diamonds change hands on the diamond exchange, and the deals are sealed by a handshake" (1980, p. 6). I might add, continuing in this positive vein, that this transaction is possible in part because it is not atomized from other transactions but embedded in a close-knit community of diamond merchants who monitor one another's behavior closely. Like other densely knit networks of actors, they generate clearly defined standards of behavior easily policed by the quick spread of information about instances of malfeasance. But the temptations posed by this level of trust are considerable, and the diamond trade has also been the scene of numerous well-publicized "insider job" thefts and of the notorious "CBS murders" of April 1982. In this case, the owner of a diamond company was defrauding a factoring concern by submitting invoices from fictitious sales. The scheme required cooperation from his accounting personnel, one of whom was approached by investigators and turned state's evidence. The owner then contracted for the murder of the disloyal employee and her assistant; three CBS technicians who came to their aid were also gunned down (Shenon 1984).

3. The extent of disorder resulting from force and fraud depends very much on how the network of social relations is structured. Hobbes exaggerated the extent of disorder likely in his atomized state of nature where, in the absence of sustained social relations, one could expect only desultory dyadic conflicts. More extended and large-scale disorder results from coalitions of combatants, impossible without prior relations. We do not generally speak of "war" unless actors have arranged themselves into two

Embeddedness

sides, as the end result of various coalitions. This occurs only if there are insufficient crosscutting ties, held by actors with enough links to both main potential combatants to have a strong interest in forestalling conflict. The same is true in the business world, where conflicts are relatively tame unless each side can escalate by calling on substantial numbers of allies in other firms, as sometimes happens in attempts to implement or forestall takeovers.

Disorder and malfeasance do of course occur also when social relations are absent. This possibility is already entailed in my earlier claim that the presence of such relations inhibits malfeasance. But the *level* of malfeasance available in a truly atomized social situation is fairly low; instances can only be episodic, unconnected, small scale. The Hobbesian problem is truly a problem, but in transcending it by the smoothing effect of social structure, we also introduce the possibility of disruptions on a larger scale than those available in the "state of nature."

The embeddedness approach to the problem of trust and order in economic life, then, threads its way between the oversocialized approach of generalized morality and the undersocialized one of impersonal, institutional arrangements by following and analyzing concrete patterns of social relations. Unlike either alternative, or the Hobbesian position, it makes no sweeping (and thus unlikely) predictions of universal order or disorder but rather assumes that the details of social structure will determine which is found.

THE PROBLEM OF MARKETS AND HIERARCHIES

As a concrete application of the embeddedness approach to economic life, I offer a critique of the influential argument of Oliver Williamson in *Markets and Hierarchies* (1975) and later articles (1979, 1981; Williamson and Ouchi 1981). Williamson asked under what circumstances economic functions are performed within the boundaries of hierarchical firms rather than by market processes that cross these boundaries. His answer, consistent with the general emphasis of the new institutional economics, is that the organizational form observed in any situation is that which deals most efficiently with the cost of economic transactions. Those that are uncertain in outcome, recur frequently, and require substantial "transaction-specific investments"—for example, money, time, or energy that cannot be easily transferred to interaction with others on different matters—are more likely to take place within hierarchically organized firms. Those that are straightforward, nonrepetitive, and require no transaction-specific investment—such as the one-time purchase of standard equipment—will more likely take place between firms, that is, across a market interface.

493

American Journal of Sociology

In this account, the former set of transactions is internalized within hierarchies for two reasons. The first is "bounded rationality," the inability of economic actors to anticipate properly the complex chain of contingencies that might be relevant to long-term contracts. When transactions are internalized, it is unnecessary to anticipate all such contingencies; they can be handled within the firm's "governance structure" instead of leading to complex negotiations. The second reason is "opportunism," the rational pursuit by economic actors of their own advantage, with all means at their command, including guile and deceit. Opportunism is mitigated and constrained by authority relations and by the greater identification with transaction partners that one allegedly has when both are contained within one corporate entity than when they face one another across the chasm of a market boundary.

The appeal to authority relations in order to tame opportunism constitutes a rediscovery of Hobbesian analysis, though confined here to the economic sphere. The Hobbesian flavor of Williamson's argument is suggested by such statements as the following: "Internal organization is not beset with the same kinds of difficulties that autonomous contracting [among independent firms] experiences when disputes arise between the parties. Although interfirm disputes are often settled out of court . . . this resolution is sometimes difficult and interfirm relations are often strained. Costly litigation is sometimes unavoidable. Internal organization, by contrast . . . is able to settle many such disputes by appeal to fiat—an enormously efficient way to settle instrumental differences" (1975, p. 30). He notes that complex, recurring transactions require long-term relations between identified individuals but that opportunism jeopardizes these relations. The adaptations to changing market circumstances required over the course of a relationship are too complex and unpredictable to be encompassed in some initial contact, and promises of good faith are unenforceable in the absence of an overarching authority:

> A general clause . . . that "I will behave responsibly rather than seek individual advantage when an occasion to adapt arises," would, in the absence of opportunism, suffice. Given, however, the unenforceability of general clauses and the proclivity of human agents to make false and misleading (self-disbelieved) statements, . . . both buyer and seller are strategically situated to bargain over the disposition of any incremental gain whenever a proposal to adapt is made by the other party. . . . Efficient adaptations which would otherwise be made thus result in costly haggling or even go unmentioned, lest the gains be dissipated by costly subgoal pursuit. *Governance structures* which attenuate opportunism and otherwise infuse confidence are evidently needed. [1979, pp. 241–42, emphasis mine]

This analysis entails the same mixture of under- and oversocialized assumptions found in *Leviathan*. The efficacy of hierarchical power within the firm is overplayed, as with Hobbes's oversocialized sovereign

Embeddedness

state.[5] The "market" resembles Hobbes's state of nature. It is the atomized and anonymous market of classical political economy, minus the discipline brought by fully competitive conditions—an under-socialized conception that neglects the role of social relations among individuals in different firms in bringing order to economic life. Williamson does acknowledge that this picture of the market is not always appropriate: "Norms of trustworthy behavior sometimes extend to markets and are enforced, in some degree, by group pressures. . . . Repeated personal contacts across organizational boundaries support some minimum level of courtesy and consideration between the parties. . . . In addition, expectations of repeat business discourage efforts to seek a narrow advantage in any particular transaction. . . . Individual aggressiveness is curbed by the prospect of ostracism among peers, in both trade and social circumstances. The reputation of a firm for fairness is also a business asset not to be dissipated" (1975, pp. 106–8).

A wedge is opened here for analysis of social structural influences on market behavior. But Williamson treats these examples as exceptions and also fails to appreciate the extent to which the dyadic relations he describes are themselves embedded in broader systems of social relations. I argue that the anonymous market of neoclassical models is virtually nonexistent in economic life and that transactions of all kinds are rife with the social connections described. This is not necessarily more the case in transactions between firms than within—it seems plausible, on the contrary, that the network of social relations within the firm might be more dense and long-lasting on the average than that existing between—but all I need show here is that there is sufficient social overlay in economic transactions across firms (in the "market," to use the term as in Williamson's dichotomy) to render dubious the assertion that complex market transactions approximate a Hobbesian state of nature that can only be resolved by internalization within a hierarchical structure.

In a general way, there is evidence all around us of the extent to which business relations are mixed up with social ones. The trade associations deplored by Adam Smith remain of great importance. It is well known that many firms, small and large, are linked by interlocking directorates so that relationships among directors of firms are many and densely knit. That business relations spill over into sociability and vice versa, espe-

[5] Williamson's confidence in the efficacy of hierarchy leads him, in discussing Chester Barnard's "zone of indifference"—that realm within which employees obey orders simply because they are indifferent about whether or not they do what is ordered—to speak instead of a "zone of acceptance" (1975, p. 77), thus undercutting Barnard's emphasis on the problematic nature of obedience. This transformation of Barnard's usage appears to have originated with Herbert Simon, who does not justify it, noting only that he "prefer[s] the term 'acceptance' " (Simon 1957, p. 12).

American Journal of Sociology

cially among business elites, is one of the best-documented facts in the sociological study of business (e.g., Domhoff 1971; Useem 1979). In his study of the extent to which litigation was used to settle disputes between firms, Macaulay notes that disputes are "frequently settled without reference to the contract or potential or actual legal sanctions. There is a hesitancy to speak of legal rights or to threaten to sue in these negotiations. . . . Or as one businessman put it, 'You can settle any dispute if you keep the lawyers and accountants out of it. They just do not understand the give-and-take needed in business.' . . . Law suits for breach of contract appear to be rare" (1963, p. 61). He goes on to explain that the

> top executives of the two firms may know each other. They may sit together on government or trade committees. They may know each other socially and even belong to the same country club. . . . Even where agreement can be reached at the negotiation stage, carefully planned arrangements may create undesirable exchange relationships between business units. Some businessmen object that in such a carefully worked out relationship one gets performance only to the letter of the contract. Such planning indicates a lack of trust and blunts the demands of friendship, turning a cooperative venture into an antagonistic horse trade. . . . Threatening to turn matters over to an attorney may cost no more money than postage or a telephone call; yet few are so skilled in making such a threat that it will not cost some deterioration of the relationship between the firms. [Pp. 63–64]

It is not only at top levels that firms are connected by networks of personal relations, but at all levels where transactions must take place. It is, for example, a commonplace in the literature on industrial purchasing that buying and selling relationships rarely approximate the spot-market model of classical theory. One source indicates that the "evidence consistently suggests that it takes some kind of 'shock' to jolt the organizational buying out of a pattern of placing repeat orders with a favored supplier or to extend the constrained set of feasible suppliers. A moment's reflection will suggest several reasons for this behavior, including the costs associated with searching for new suppliers and establishing new relationships, the fact that users are likely to prefer sources, the relatively low risk involved in dealing with known vendors, and the likelihood that the buyer has established personal relationships that he values with representatives of the supplying firm" (Webster and Wind 1972, p. 15).

In a similar vein, Macaulay notes that salesmen "often know purchasing agents well. The same two individuals may have dealt with each other from five to 25 years. Each has something to give the other. Salesmen have gossip about competitors, shortages and price increases to give purchasing agents who treat them well" (1963, p. 63). Sellers who do not satisfy their customers "become the subject of discussion in the gossip exchanged by purchasing agents and salesmen, at meetings of purchasing agents' associations and trade associations or even at country clubs or

496

Embeddedness

social gatherings . . ." (p. 64). Settlement of disputes is eased by this embeddedness of business in social relations: "Even where the parties have a detailed and carefully planned agreement which indicates what is to happen if, say, the seller fails to deliver on time, often they will never refer to the agreement but will negotiate a solution when the problem arises as if there never had been any original contract. One purchasing agent expressed a common business attitude when he said, 'If something comes up, you get the other man on the telephone and deal with the problem. You don't read legalistic contract clauses at each other if you ever want to do business again. One doesn't run to lawyers if he wants to stay in business because one must behave decently'" (Macaulay 1963, p. 61).

Such patterns may be more easily noted in other countries, where they are supposedly explained by "cultural" peculiarities. Thus, one journalist recently asserted,

> Friendships and longstanding personal connections affect business connections everywhere. But that seems to be especially true in Japan. . . . The after-hours sessions in the bars and nightclubs are where the vital personal contacts are established and nurtured slowly. Once these ties are set, they are not easily undone. . . . The resulting tight-knit nature of Japanese business society has long been a source of frustration to foreign companies trying to sell products in Japan. . . . Chalmers Johnson, a professor at . . . Berkeley, believes that . . . the exclusive dealing within the Japanese industrial groups, buying and selling to and from each other based on decades-old relationships rather than economic competitiveness . . . is . . . a real nontariff barrier [to trade between the United States and Japan]. [Lohr 1982]

The extensive use of subcontracting in many industries also presents opportunities for sustained relationships among firms that are not organized hierarchically within one corporate unit. For example, Eccles cites evidence from many countries that in construction, when projects "are not subject to institutional regulations which require competitive bidding . . . relations between the general contractor and his subcontractors are stable and continuous over fairly long periods of time and only infrequently established through competitive bidding. This type of 'quasi-integration' results in what I call the 'quasifirm.' It is a preferred mode to either pure market transactions or formal vertical integration" (1981, pp. 339–40). Eccles describes this "quasifirm" arrangement of extensive and long-term relationships among contractors and subcontractors as an organizational form logically intermediate between the pure market and the vertically integrated firm. I would argue, however, that it is not *empirically* intermediate, since the former situation is so rare. The case of construction is closer to vertical integration than some other situations where firms interact, such as buying and selling relations, since subcon-

American Journal of Sociology

tractors are physically located on the same site as the contractor and are under his general supervision. Furthermore, under the usual fixed-price contracts, there are "obvious incentives for shirking performance requirements" (Eccles 1981, p. 340).

Yet a hierarchical structure associated with the vertically integrated firm does not arise to meet this "problem." I argue this is because the long-term relations of contractors and subcontractors, as well as the embeddedness of those relations in a community of construction personnel, generate standards of expected behavior that not only obviate the need for but are superior to pure authority relations in discouraging malfeasance. Eccles's own empirical study of residential construction in Massachusetts shows not only that subcontracting relationships are long term in nature but also that it is very rare for a general contractor to employ more than two or three subcontractors in a given trade, whatever number of projects is handled in the course of a year (1981, pp. 349–51). This is true despite the availability of large numbers of alternative subcontractors. This phenomenon can be explained in part in investment terms—through a "continuing association both parties can benefit from the somewhat idiosyncratic investment of learning to work together" (Eccles 1981, p. 340)—but also must be related to the desire of individuals to derive pleasure from the social interaction that accompanies their daily work, a pleasure that would be considerably blunted by spot-market procedures requiring entirely new and strange work partners each day. As in other parts of economic life, the overlay of social relations on what may begin in purely economic transactions plays a crucial role.

Some comments on labor markets are also relevant here. One advantage that Williamson asserts for hierarchically structured firms over market transactions is the ability to transmit accurate information about employees. "The principal impediment to effective interfirm experience-rating," he argues, "is one of communication. By comparison with the firm, markets lack a rich and common rating language. The language problem is particularly severe where the judgments to be made are highly subjective. The advantages of hierarchy in these circumstances are especially great if those persons who are most familiar with a worker's characteristics, usually his immediate supervisor, also do the experience-rating" (1975, p. 78). But the notion that good information about the characteristics of an employee can be transmitted only within firms and not between can be sustained only by neglecting the widely variegated social network of interaction that spans firms. Information about employees travels among firms not only because personal relations exist between those in each firm who do business with each other but also, as I have shown in detail (Granovetter 1974), because the relatively high levels of interfirm mobility in the United States guarantee that many workers will be reason-

Embeddedness

ably well known to employees of numerous other firms that might require and solicit their services. Furthermore, the idea that internal information is necessarily accurate and acted on dispassionately by promotion procedures keyed to it seems naive. To say, as Williamson does, that reliance "on internal promotion has affirmative incentive properties because workers can anticipate that differential talent and degrees of cooperativeness will be rewarded" (1975, p. 78) invokes an ideal type of promotion as reward-for-achievement that can readily be shown to have only limited correspondence to existing internal labor markets (see Granovetter 1983, pp. 40–51, for an extended analysis).

The other side of my critique is to argue that Williamson vastly overestimates the efficacy of hierarchical power ("fiat," in his terminology) within organizations. He asserts, for example, that internal organizations have a great auditing advantage: "An external auditor is typically constrained to review written records. . . . An internal auditor, by contrast, has greater freedom of action. . . . Whereas an internal auditor is not a partisan but regards himself and is regarded by others in mainly instrumental terms, the external auditor is associated with the 'other side' and his motives are regarded suspiciously. The degree of cooperation received by the auditor from the audited party varies accordingly. The external auditor can expect to receive only perfunctory cooperation" (1975, pp. 29–30). The literature on intrafirm audits is sparse, but one thorough account is that of Dalton, in *Men Who Manage,* for a large chemical plant. Audits of parts by the central office were supposed to be conducted on a surprise basis, but warning was typically surreptitiously given. The high level of cooperation shown in these internal audits is suggested by the following account: "Notice that a count of parts was to begin provoked a flurry among the executives to hide certain parts and equipment . . . materials *not* to be counted were moved to: 1) little-known and inaccessible spots; 2) basements and pits that were dirty and therefore unlikely to be examined; 3) departments that had already been inspected and that could be approached circuitously while the counters were en route between official storage areas and 4) places where materials and supplies might be used as a camouflage for parts. . . . As the practice developed, cooperation among the [department] chiefs to use each other's storage areas and available pits became well organized and smoothly functioning" (Dalton 1959, pp. 48–49).

Dalton's work shows brilliantly that cost accounting of all kinds is a highly arbitrary and therefore easily politicized process rather than a technical procedure decided on grounds of efficiency. He details this especially for the relationship between the maintenance department and various production departments in the chemical plant; the department to which maintenance work was charged had less to do with any strict time

American Journal of Sociology

accounting than with the relative political and social standing of department executives in their relation to maintenance personnel. Furthermore, the more aggressive department heads expedited their maintenance work "by the use of friendships, by bullying and implied threats. As all the heads had the same formal rank, one could say that an inverse relation existed between a given officer's personal influence and his volume of uncompleted repairs" (1959, p. 34). Questioned about how such practices could escape the attention of auditors, one informant told Dalton, "If Auditing got to snooping around, what the hell could they find out? And if they did find anything, they'd know a damn sight better than to say anything about it. . . . All those guys [department heads] have got lines through Cost Accounting. That's a lot of bunk about Auditing being independent" (p. 32).

Accounts as detailed and perceptive as Dalton's are sadly lacking for a representative sample of firms and so are open to the argument that they are exceptional. But similar points can be made for the problem of transfer pricing—the determination of prices for products traded between divisions of a single firm. Here Williamson argues that though the trading divisions "may have profit-center standing, this is apt to be exercised in a restrained way. . . . Cost-plus pricing rules, and variants thereof, preclude supplier divisions from seeking the monopolistic prices [to] which their sole source supply position might otherwise entitle them. In addition, the managements of the trading divisions are more susceptible to appeals for cooperation" (1975, p. 29). But in an intensive empirical study of transfer-pricing practices, Eccles, having interviewed nearly 150 managers in 13 companies, concluded that no cost-based methods could be carried out in a technically neutral way, since there is "no universal criterion for what is cost. . . . Problems often exist with cost-based methods when the buying division does not have access to the information by which the costs are generated. . . . Market prices are especially difficult to determine when internal purchasing is mandated and no external purchases are made of the intermediate good. . . . There is no obvious answer to what is a markup for profit . . ." (1982, p. 21). The political element in transfer-pricing conflicts strongly affects whose definition of "cost" is accepted: "In general, when transfer pricing practices are seen to enhance one's power and status they will be viewed favorably. When they do not, a countless number of strategic and other sound business reasons will be found to argue for their inadequacy" (1982, p. 21; see also Eccles 1983, esp. pp. 26–32). Eccles notes the "somewhat ironic fact that many managers consider internal transactions to be more difficult than external ones, even though vertical integration is pursued for presumed advantages" (1983, p. 28).

Thus, the oversocialized view that orders within a hierarchy elicit easy

500

Embeddedness

obedience and that employees internalize the interests of the firm, suppressing any conflict with their own, cannot stand scrutiny against these empirical studies (or, for that matter, against the experience of many of us in actual organizations). Note further that, as shown especially well in Dalton's detailed ethnographic study, resistance to the encroachment of organizational interests on personal or divisional ones requires an extensive network of coalitions. From the viewpoint of management, these coalitions represent malfeasance generated by teams; it could not be managed at all by atomized individuals. Indeed, Dalton asserted that the level of cooperation achieved by divisional chiefs in evading central audits involved joint action "of a kind rarely, if ever, shown in carrying on official activities . . ." (1959, p. 49).

In addition, the generally lower turnover of personnel characteristic of large hierarchical firms, with their well-defined internal labor markets and elaborate promotion ladders, may make such cooperative evasion more likely. When many employees have long tenures, the conditions are met for a dense and stable network of relations, shared understandings, and political coalitions to be constructed. (See Homans 1950, 1974, for the relevant social psychological discussions; and Pfeffer 1983, for a treatment of the "demography of organizations.") James Lincoln notes, in this connection, that in the ideal-typical Weberian bureaucracy, organizations are "designed to function independently of the collective actions which can be mobilized through [internal] interpersonal networks. Bureaucracy prescribes fixed relationships among positions through which incumbents flow, without, in theory, affecting organizational operations" (1982, p. 26). He goes on to summarize studies showing, however, that "when turnover is low, relations take on additional contents of an expressive and personal sort which may ultimately transform the network and change the directions of the organization" (p. 26).

To this point I have argued that social relations between firms are more important, and authority within firms less so, in bringing order to economic life than is supposed in the markets and hierarchies line of thought. A balanced and symmetrical argument requires attention to power in "market" relations and social connections within firms. Attention to power relations is needed lest my emphasis on the smoothing role of social relations in the market lead me to neglect the role of these relations in the conduct of conflict. Conflict is an obvious reality, ranging from well-publicized litigation between firms to the occasional cases of "cutthroat competition" gleefully reported by the business press. Since the effective exercise of power between firms will prevent bloody public battles, we can assume that such battles represent only a small proportion of actual conflicts of interest. Conflicts probably become public only when the two sides are fairly equally matched; recall that this rough equality was pre-

American Journal of Sociology

cisely one of Hobbes's arguments for a probable "war of all against all" in the "state of nature." But when the power position of one firm is obviously dominant, the other is apt to capitulate early so as to cut its losses. Such capitulation may require not even explicit confrontation but only a clear understanding of what the other side requires (as in the recent Marxist literature on "hegemony" in business life; see, e.g., Mintz and Schwartz 1985).

Though the exact extent to which firms dominate other firms can be debated, the voluminous literature on interlocking directorates, on the role of financial institutions vis-à-vis industrial corporations, and on dual economy surely provides enough evidence to conclude that power relations cannot be neglected. This provides still another reason to doubt that the complexities that arise when formally equal agents negotiate with one another can be resolved only by the subsumption of all parties under a single hierarchy; in fact, many of these complexities are resolved by implicit or explicit power relations *among* firms.

Finally, a brief comment is in order on the webs of social relations that are well known from industrial and organizational sociology to be important within firms. The distinction between the "formal" and the "informal" organization of the firm is one of the oldest in the literature, and it hardly needs repeating that observers who assume firms to be structured in fact by the official organization chart are sociological babes in the woods. The connection of this to the present discussion is that insofar as internalization within firms does result in a better handling of complex and idiosyncratic transactions, it is by no means apparent that hierarchical organization is the best explanation. It may be, instead, that the effect of internalization is to provide a focus (see Feld 1981) for an even denser web of social relations than had occurred between previously independent market entities. Perhaps this web of interaction is mainly what explains the level of efficiency, be it high or low, of the new organizational form.

It is now useful to summarize the differences in explanation and prediction between Williamson's markets and hierarchies approach and the embeddedness view offered here. Williamson explains the inhibition of "opportunism" or malfeasance in economic life and the general existence of cooperation and order by the subsumption of complex economic activity in hierarchically integrated firms. The empirical evidence that I cite shows, rather, that even with complex transactions, a high level of order can often be found in the "market"—that is, across firm boundaries—and a correspondingly high level of disorder within the firm. Whether these occur, instead of what Williamson expects, depends on the nature of personal relations and networks of relations between and within firms. I claim that both order *and* disorder, honesty *and* malfeasance have more

Embeddedness

to do with structures of such relations than they do with organizational form.

Certain implications follow for the conditions under which one may expect to see vertical integration rather than transactions between firms in a market. Other things being equal, for example, we should expect pressures toward vertical integration in a market where transacting firms lack a network of personal relations that connects them or where such a network eventuates in conflict, disorder, opportunism, or malfeasance. On the other hand, where a stable network of relations mediates complex transactions and generates standards of behavior between firms, such pressures should be absent.

I use the word "pressures" rather than predict that vertical integration will always follow the pattern described in order to avoid the functionalism implicit in Williamson's assumption that whatever organizational form is most efficient will be the one observed. Before we can make this assumption, two further conditions must be satisfied: (i) well-defined and powerful selection pressures toward efficiency must be operating, and (ii) some actors must have the ability and resources to "solve" the efficiency problem by constructing a vertically integrated firm.

The selection pressures that guarantee efficient organization of transactions are nowhere clearly described by Williamson. As in much of the new institutional economics, the need to make such matters explicit is obviated by an implicit Darwinian argument that efficient solutions, however they may originate, have a staying power akin to that enforced by natural selection in the biological world. Thus it is granted that not all business executives "accurately perceive their business opportunities and faultlessly respond. Over time, however, those [vertical] integration moves that have better rationality properties (in transaction cost and scale-economy terms) tend to have better survival properties" (Williamson and Ouchi 1981, p. 389; see also Williamson 1981, pp. 573–74). But Darwinian arguments, invoked in this cavalier fashion, careen toward a Panglossian view of whatever institution is analyzed. The operation of alleged selection pressures is here neither an object of study nor even a falsifiable proposition but rather an article of faith.

Even if one could document selection pressures that made survival of certain organizational forms more likely, it would remain to show how such forms could be implemented. To treat them implicitly as mutations, by analogy to biological evolution, merely evades the issue. As in other functionalist explanations, it cannot be automatically assumed that the solution to some problem is feasible. Among the resources required to implement vertical integration might be some measure of market power, access to capital through retained earnings or capital markets, and appropriate connections to legal or regulatory authorities.

American Journal of Sociology

Where selection pressures are weak (especially likely in the imperfect markets claimed by Williamson to produce vertical integration) and resources problematic, the social-structural configurations that I have outlined are still related to the efficiency of transaction costs, but no guarantee can be given that an efficient solution will occur. Motives for integration unrelated to efficiency, such as personal aggrandizement of CEOs in acquiring firms, may in such settings become important.

What the viewpoint proposed here requires is that future research on the markets-hierarchies question pay careful and systematic attention to the actual patterns of personal relations by which economic transactions are carried out. Such attention will not only better sort out the motives for vertical integration but also make it easier to comprehend the various complex intermediate forms between idealized atomized markets and completely integrated firms, such as the quasi firm discussed above for the construction industry. Intermediate forms of this kind are so intimately bound up with networks of personal relations that any perspective that considers these relations peripheral will fail to see clearly what "organizational form" has been effected. Existing empirical studies of industrial organization pay little attention to patterns of relations, in part because relevant data are harder to find than those on technology and market structure but also because the dominant economic framework remains one of atomized actors, so personal relations are perceived as frictional in effect.

DISCUSSION

In this article, I have argued that most behavior is closely embedded in networks of interpersonal relations and that such an argument avoids the extremes of under- and oversocialized views of human action. Though I believe this to be so for all behavior, I concentrate here on economic behavior for two reasons: (i) it is the type-case of behavior inadequately interpreted because those who study it professionally are so strongly committed to atomized theories of action; and (ii) with few exceptions, sociologists have refrained from serious study of any subject already claimed by neoclassical economics. They have implicitly accepted the presumption of economists that "market processes" are not suitable objects of sociological study because social relations play only a frictional and disruptive role, not a central one, in modern societies. (Recent exceptions are Baker 1983; Burt 1983; and White 1981.) In those instances in which sociologists study processes where markets are central, they usually still manage to avoid their analysis. Until recently, for example, the large sociological literature on wages was cast in terms of "income attainment," obscuring the labor

Embeddedness

market context in which wages are set and focusing instead on the background and attainment of individuals (see Granovetter 1981 for an extended critique). Or, as Stearns has pointed out, the literature on who controls corporations has implicitly assumed that analysis must be at the level of political relations and broad assumptions about the nature of capitalism. Even though it is widely admitted that how corporations acquire capital is a major determinant of control, most relevant research "since the turn of the century has eliminated that [capital] market as an objective of investigation" (1982, pp. 5–6). Even in organization theory, where considerable literature implements the limits placed on economic decisions by social structural complexity, little attempt has been made to demonstrate the implications of this for the neoclassical theory of the firm or for a general understanding of production or such macroeconomic outcomes as growth, inflation, and unemployment.

In trying to demonstrate that all market processes are amenable to sociological analysis and that such analysis reveals central, not peripheral, features of these processes, I have narrowed my focus to problems of trust and malfeasance. I have also used the "market and hierarchies" argument of Oliver Williamson as an illustration of how the embeddedness perspective generates different understandings and predictions from that implemented by economists. Williamson's perspective is itself "revisionist" within economics, diverging from the neglect of institutional and transactional considerations typical of neoclassical work. In this sense, it may appear to have more kinship to a sociological perspective than the usual economic arguments. But the main thrust of the "new institutional economists" is to deflect the analysis of institutions from sociological, historical, and legal argumentation and show instead that they arise as the efficient solution to economic problems. This mission and the pervasive functionalism it implies discourage the detailed analysis of social structure that I argue here is the key to understanding how existing institutions arrived at their present state.

Insofar as rational choice arguments are narrowly construed as referring to atomized individuals and economic goals, they are inconsistent with the embeddedness position presented here. In a broader formulation of rational choice, however, the two views have much in common. Much of the revisionist work by economists that I criticize above in my discussion of over- and undersocialized conceptions of action relies on a strategy that might be called "psychological revisionism"—an attempt to reform economic theory by abandoning an absolute assumption of rational decision making. This strategy has led to Leibenstein's "selective rationality" in his arguments on "X-inefficiency" (1976), for example, and to the claims of segmented labor-market theorists that workers in different mar-

American Journal of Sociology

ket segments have different kinds of decision-making rules, rational choice being only for upper-primary (i.e., professional, managerial, technical) workers (Piore 1979).

I suggest, in contrast, that while the assumption of rational action must always be problematic, it is a good working hypothesis that should not easily be abandoned. What looks to the analyst like nonrational behavior may be quite sensible when situational constraints, especially those of embeddedness, are fully appreciated. When the social situation of those in nonprofessional labor markets is fully analyzed, their behavior looks less like the automatic application of "cultural" rules and more like a reasonable response to their present situation (as, e.g., in the discussion of Liebow 1966). Managers who evade audits and fight over transfer pricing are acting nonrationally in some strict economic sense, in terms of a firm's profit maximization; but when their position and ambitions in intrafirm networks and political coalitions are analyzed, the behavior is easily interpreted.

That such behavior is rational or instrumental is more readily seen, moreover, if we note that it aims not only at economic goals but also at sociability, approval, status, and power. Economists rarely see such goals as rational, in part on account of the arbitrary separation that arose historically, as Albert Hirschman (1977) points out, in the 17th and 18th centuries, between the "passions" and the "interests," the latter connoting economic motives only. This way of putting the matter has led economists to specialize in analysis of behavior motivated only by "interest" and to assume that other motives occur in separate and nonrationally organized spheres; hence Samuelson's much-quoted comment that "many economists would separate economics from sociology upon the basis of rational or irrational behavior" (1947, p. 90). The notion that rational choice is derailed by social influences has long discouraged detailed sociological analysis of economic life and led revisionist economists to reform economic theory by focusing on its naive psychology. My claim here is that however naive that psychology may be, this is not where the main difficulty lies—it is rather in the neglect of social structure.

Finally, I should add that the level of causal analysis adopted in the embeddedness argument is a rather proximate one. I have had little to say about what broad historical or macrostructural circumstances have led systems to display the social-structural characteristics they have, so I make no claims for this analysis to answer large-scale questions about the nature of modern society or the sources of economic and political change. But the focus on proximate causes is intentional, for these broader questions cannot be satisfactorily addressed without more detailed understanding of the mechanisms by which sweeping change has its effects. My claim is that one of the most important and least analyzed of such mecha-

Embeddedness

nisms is the impact of such change on the social relations in which economic life is embedded. If this is so, no adequate link between macro- and micro-level theories can be established without a much fuller understanding of these relations.

The use of embeddedness analysis in explicating proximate causes of patterns of macro-level interest is well illustrated by the markets and hierarchies question. The extent of vertical integration and the reasons for the persistence of small firms operating through the market are not only narrow concerns of industrial organization; they are of interest to all students of the institutions of advanced capitalism. Similar issues arise in the analysis of "dual economy," dependent development, and the nature of modern corporate elites. But whether small firms are indeed eclipsed by giant corporations is usually analyzed in broad and sweeping macropolitical or macroeconomic terms, with little appreciation of proximate social structural causes.

Analysts of dual economy have often suggested, for example, that the persistence of large numbers of small firms in the "periphery" is explained by large corporations' need to shift the risks of cyclical fluctuations in demand or of uncertain R & D activities; failures of these small units will not adversely affect the larger firms' earnings. I suggest here that small firms in a market setting may persist instead because a dense network of social relations is overlaid on the business relations connecting such firms and reduces pressures for integration. This does not rule out risk shifting as an explanation with a certain face validity. But the embeddedness account may be more useful in explaining the large number of small establishments not characterized by satellite or peripheral status. (For a discussion of the surprising extent of employment in small establishments, see Granovetter 1984.) This account is restricted to proximate causes: it logically leads to but does not answer the questions why, when, and in what sectors does the market display various types of social structure. But those questions, which link to a more macro level of analysis, would themselves not arise without a prior appreciation of the importance of social structure in the market.

The markets and hierarchies analysis, important as it may be, is presented here mainly as an illustration. I believe the embeddedness argument to have very general applicability and to demonstrate not only that there is a place for sociologists in the study of economic life but that their perspective is urgently required there. In avoiding the analysis of phenomena at the center of standard economic theory, sociologists have unnecessarily cut themselves off from a large and important aspect of social life and from the European tradition—stemming especially from Max Weber—in which economic action is seen only as a special, if important, category of social action. I hope to have shown here that this Weberian

American Journal of Sociology

program is consistent with and furthered by some of the insights of modern structural sociology.

REFERENCES

Akerlof, George. 1983. "Loyalty Filters." *American Economic Review* 73 (1): 54–63.
Alchian, Armen, and Harold Demsetz. 1973. "The Property Rights Paradigm." *Journal of Economic History* 33 (March): 16–27.
Arrow, Kenneth. 1974. *The Limits of Organization*. New York: Norton.
Baker, Wayne. 1983. "Floor Trading and Crowd Dynamics." In *Social Dynamics of Financial Markets*, edited by Patricia Adler and Peter Adler. Greenwich, Conn.: JAI.
Becker, Gary. 1976. *The Economic Approach to Human Behavior*. Chicago: University of Chicago Press.
Ben-Porath, Yoram. 1980. "The F-Connection: Families, Friends and Firms in the Organization of Exchange." *Population and Development Review* 6 (1): 1–30.
Bowles, Samuel, and Herbert Gintis. 1975. *Schooling in Capitalist America*. New York: Basic.
Brown, Roger. 1965. *Social Psychology*. New York: Free Press.
Burt, Ronald. 1982. *Toward a Structural Theory of Action*. New York: Academic Press.
———. 1983. *Corporate Profits and Cooptation*. New York: Academic Press.
Cole, Robert. 1979. *Work, Mobility and Participation: A Comparative Study of American and Japanese Industry*. Berkeley and Los Angeles: University of California Press.
Dalton, Melville. 1959. *Men Who Manage*. New York: Wiley.
Doeringer, Peter, and Michael Piore. 1971. *Internal Labor Markets and Manpower Analysis*. Lexington, Mass.: Heath.
Domhoff, G. William. 1971. *The Higher Circles*. New York: Random House.
Duesenberry, James. 1960. Comment on "An Economic Analysis of Fertility." In *Demographic and Economic Change in Developed Countries*, edited by the Universities–National Bureau Committee for Economic Research. Princeton, N.J.: Princeton University Press.
Eccles, Robert. 1981. "The Quasifirm in the Construction Industry." *Journal of Economic Behavior and Organization* 2 (December): 335–57.
———. 1982. "A Synopsis of *Transfer Pricing: An Analysis and Action Plan*." Mimeographed. Cambridge, Mass.: Harvard Business School.
———. 1983. "Transfer Pricing, Fairness and Control." Working Paper no. HBS 83-167. Cambridge, Mass.: Harvard Business School. Reprinted in *Harvard Business Review* (in press).
Feld, Scott. 1981. "The Focused Organization of Social Ties." *American Journal of Sociology* 86 (5): 1015–35.
Fine, Gary, and Sherryl Kleinman. 1979. "Rethinking Subculture: An Interactionist Analysis." *American Journal of Sociology* 85 (July): 1–20.
Furubotn, E., and S. Pejovich. 1972. "Property Rights and Economic Theory: A Survey of Recent Literature." *Journal of Economic Literature* 10 (3): 1137–62.
Geertz, Clifford. 1979. "Suq: The Bazaar Economy in Sefrou." Pp. 123–225 in *Meaning and Order in Moroccan Society*, edited by C. Geertz, H. Geertz, and L. Rosen. New York: Cambridge University Press.
Granovetter, Mark. 1974. *Getting a Job: A Study of Contacts and Careers*. Cambridge, Mass.: Harvard University Press.
———. 1981. "Toward a Sociological Theory of Income Differences." Pp. 11–47 in *Sociological Perspectives on Labor Markets*, edited by Ivar Berg. New York: Academic Press.

Embeddedness

————. 1983. "Labor Mobility, Internal Markets and Job-Matching: A Comparison of the Sociological and Economic Approaches." Mimeographed.

————. 1984. "Small Is Bountiful: Labor Markets and Establishment Size." *American Sociological Review* 49 (3): 323–34.

Hirschman, Albert. 1977. *The Passions and the Interests*. Princeton, N.J.: Princeton University Press.

————. 1982. "Rival Interpretations of Market Society: Civilizing, Destructive or Feeble?" *Journal of Economic Literature* 20 (4): 1463–84.

Homans, George. 1950. *The Human Group*. New York: Harcourt Brace & Co.

————. 1974. *Social Behavior*. New York: Harcourt Brace Jovanovich.

Lazear, Edward. 1979. "Why Is There Mandatory Retirement?" *Journal of Political Economy* 87 (6): 1261–84.

Leibenstein, Harvey. 1976. *Beyond Economic Man*. Cambridge, Mass.: Harvard University Press.

Liebow, Elliot. 1966. *Tally's Corner*. Boston: Little, Brown.

Lincoln, James. 1982. "Intra- (and Inter-) Organizational Networks." Pp. 1–38 in *Research in the Sociology of Organizations*, vol. 1. Edited by S. Bacharach. Greenwich, Conn.: JAI.

Lohr, Steve. 1982. "When Money Doesn't Matter in Japan." *New York Times* (December 30).

Macaulay, Stewart. 1963. "Non-Contractual Relations in Business: A Preliminary Study." *American Sociological Review* 28 (1): 55–67.

Marsden, Peter. 1981. "Introducing Influence Processes into a System of Collective Decisions." *American Journal of Sociology* 86 (May): 1203–35.

————. 1983. "Restricted Access in Networks and Models of Power." *American Journal of Sociology* 88 (January): 686–17.

Merton, Robert. 1947. "Manifest and Latent Functions." Pp. 19–84 in *Social Theory and Social Structure*. New York: Free Press.

Mintz, Beth, and Michael Schwartz. 1985. *The Power Structure of American Business*. Chicago: University of Chicago Press.

North, D., and R. Thomas. 1973. *The Rise of the Western World*. Cambridge: Cambridge University Press.

Okun, Arthur. 1981. *Prices and Quantities*. Washington, D.C.: Brookings.

Pakes, Ariel, and S. Nitzan. 1982. "Optimum Contracts for Research Personnel, Research Employment and the Establishment of 'Rival' Enterprises." NBER Working Paper no. 871. Cambridge, Mass.: National Bureau of Economic Research.

Parsons, Talcott. 1937. *The Structure of Social Action*. New York: Macmillan.

Pfeffer, Jeffrey. 1983. "Organizational Demography." In *Research in Organizational Behavior*, vol. 5. Edited by L. L. Cummings and B. Staw. Greenwich, Conn.: JAI.

Phelps Brown, Ernest Henry. 1977. *The Inequality of Pay*. Berkeley: University of California Press.

Piore, Michael. 1975. "Notes for a Theory of Labor Market Stratification." Pp. 125–50 in *Labor Market Segmentation*, edited by R. Edwards, M. Reich, and D. Gordon. Lexington, Mass.: Heath.

————, ed. 1979. *Unemployment and Inflation*. White Plains, N.Y.: Sharpe.

Polanyi, Karl. 1944. *The Great Transformation*. New York: Holt, Rinehart.

Polanyi, Karl, C. Arensberg, and H. Pearson. 1957. *Trade and Market in the Early Empires*. New York: Free Press.

Popkin, Samuel. 1979. *The Rational Peasant*. Berkeley and Los Angeles: University of California Press.

Rosen, Sherwin. 1982. "Authority, Control and the Distribution of Earnings." *Bell Journal of Economics* 13 (2): 311–23.

Samuelson, Paul. 1947. *Foundations of Economic Analysis*. Cambridge, Mass.: Harvard University Press.

American Journal of Sociology

Schneider, Harold. 1974. *Economic Man: The Anthropology of Economics*. New York: Free Press.

Schotter, Andrew. 1981. *The Economic Theory of Social Institutions*. New York: Cambridge University Press.

Scott, James. 1976. *The Moral Economy of the Peasant*. New Haven, Conn.: Yale University Press.

Shenon, Philip. 1984. "Margolies Is Found Guilty of Murdering Two Women." *New York Times* (June 1).

Simon, Herbert. 1957. *Administrative Behavior*. Glencoe, Ill.: Free Press.

Smith, Adam. (1776) 1979. *The Wealth of Nations*. Edited by Andrew Skinner. Baltimore: Penguin.

Stearns, Linda. 1982. "Corporate Dependency and the Structure of the Capital Market: 1880–1980." Ph.D. dissertation, State University of New York at Stony Brook.

Thompson, E. P. 1971. "The Moral Economy of the English Crowd in the Eighteenth Century." *Past and Present* 50 (February): 76–136.

Useem, Michael. 1979. "The Social Organization of the American Business Elite and Participation of Corporation Directors in the Governance of American Institutions." *American Sociological Review* 44:553–72.

Webster, Frederick, and Yoram Wind. 1972. *Organizational Buying Behavior*. Englewood Cliffs, N.J.: Prentice-Hall.

White, Harrison C. 1981. "Where Do Markets Come From?" *American Journal of Sociology* 87 (November): 517–47.

Williamson, Oliver. 1975. *Markets and Hierarchies*. New York: Free Press.

———. 1979. "Transaction-Cost Economics: The Governance of Contractual Relations." *Journal of Law and Economics* 22 (2): 233–61.

———. 1981. "The Economics of Organization: The Transaction Cost Approach." *American Journal of Sociology* 87 (November): 548–77.

Williamson, Oliver, and William Ouchi. 1981. "The Markets and Hierarchies and Visible Hand Perspectives." Pp. 347–70 in *Perspectives on Organizational Design and Behavior*, edited by Andrew Van de Ven and William Joyce. New York: Wiley.

Wrong, Dennis. 1961. "The Oversocialized Conception of Man in Modern Sociology." *American Sociological Review* 26 (2): 183–93.

[5]

The Social Construction of Business Systems in East Asia

Richard D. Whitley

Richard D.
Whitley
Manchester
Business School,
University of
Manchester,
Manchester, U.K.

Abstract

Distinctive forms of business organization have become dominant and successful in Japan, South Korea, Taiwan and Hong Kong over the past 40 years. These different business systems reflect historical patterns of authority, trust and loyalty in Japan, Korea and China. They also vary in their specialization, strategic preferences and patterns of inter-firm co-ordination because of significant differences in their institutional environments, especially the political and financial systems. Similar processes exist in western societies but distinctive business systems are not so sharply bounded between nation states and cultures in Europe and North America.

Introduction: Three Business Systems

The identification of distinctive forms of dominant business organization in Japan, South Korea, Taiwan and Hong Kong over the past few decades (Hamilton et al. 1990; Orru et al. 1988; Whitley 1990) demonstrates the plurality of viable ways of organizing and directing economic activities, as well as the importance of what Maurice (1979) terms the 'societal effect' in generating this pluralism. Dominant economic actors have become established in these societies that are remarkably similar within them yet differ in key respects between them (Hamilton and Biggart 1988). These actors are: the Japanese specialized clan or *kaisha* (Abegglen and Stalk 1985; Clark 1979), the Korean patrimonial bureaucracy or *chaebol* (Amsden 1989; Jones and Sakong 1980; Yoo and Lee 1987) and the Chinese Family Business (Limlingan 1986; Redding 1990). Their major differences were described in an earlier paper in *Organization Studies* (Whitley 1990) and can be explained in terms of the quite different institutional environments in which each business system developed. In this paper, I describe the major social institutions in each economy which together help to account for the distinctive characteristics of these business systems. Essentially, I am arguing that dominant forms of business organization in Japan, South Korea, Taiwan and Hong Kong since the 1950s reflect the nature and interconnections of key social institutions in both pre-industrial Japan, Korea and China and in these contemporary societies.

Organization
Studies
1991, 12/1:
001–028
© 1991 EGOS
0170–8406/91
0012–0001 $1.00

Before continuing to describe these institutions and their connections
with successful business systems, it is worth summarizing the key differences between the three forms of business organization. These can be
subsumed under three broad headings: (a) the system of authoritative
coordination and control, (b) enterprise domain and development, and
(c) the nature of enterprise co-ordination and market organization. They
reflect three key issues which all systems of hierarchy–market relationships have to deal with: how are economic activities coordinated and
controlled through authority hierarchies, what sorts of activities and
resources are authoritatively coordinated in firms, and how are market
connections between firms organized (cf. Imai and Itami 1984)?

These three broad headings can be subdivided into 8 distinct dimensions
which summarize the major differences between East Asian forms of
business organization. Considering first the authority system, there are
major variations in the importance of personal authority and ownership
and, relatedly, the significance of formal co-ordination and control procedures. Managerial styles and authority relations also differ markedly,
as does the nature and extent of employee commitment to the company.
In terms of enterprise domain and development the key variations concern the degree to which businesses specialize in particular economic
activities and capabilities and whether their development is primarily
evolutionary within a given sector or more discontinuous in the activities
and resources controlled. Finally, inter-enterprise co-ordination varies
within and between sectors in its scope and longevity. The extent to which
firms depend on long term and diffuse connections with suppliers and
customers differs considerably, as does their co-ordination of strategies
and new ventures across sectors, either directly or through banks and
state agencies.

These eight dimensions cover important aspects of business organizations
in East Asia which differ markedly between Japan, South Korea, Taiwan
and Hong Kong as summarized in Table 1. Because I am here focusing on
how these differences can be understood in terms of their societal variations and wish to clarify the major ways in which East Asian business
systems vary between themselves, these dimensions differ slightly from
those listed in Table 1 of the earlier *Organization Studies* paper (Whitley
1990). In particular, they highlight the significant variations in preferred
managerial styles and reliance on formal co-ordination procedures as well
as distinguishing more sharply between inter-enterprise connections
within the same sector from those across sectors. These eight do not, of
course, constitute the only ways of contrasting East Asian forms of business organizations, but they do incorporate the major differences which
generate quite distinct business systems. In comparing these with western
hierarchy–market configurations, additional dimensions would become
relevant.

A key feature of any business organization is the basis of managerial
authority. In Korean *chaebol* and the Chinese family business (CFB) this
is much more closely associated with personal ownership than in Japanese

Table 1 East Asian Business Systems	Japanese Kaisha	Korean Chaebol	Chinese Family Business
Authoritative Co-ordination and Control			
Personal authority and owner domination	low	high	high
Significance of formal co-ordination and control procedures	high	medium	low
Managerial style	facilitative	directive	didactic
Employee commitment	emotional	conditional	conditional
Business Domain and Development			
Business specialization	high	low	high within firms medium within families
Evolutionary strategies	high	medium	medium
Inter-Firm Co-ordination			
Relational contracting	high	low	medium
Long-term intersector co-ordination	strong through business groups and state agencies	indirect through state	limited and personal

kaisha where ownership has been separate from managerial control for some time (Abegglen and Stalk 1985: 177; Aoki 1987; Dore 1986: 67–72; Orru et al. 1988; Silin 1976; Yoo and Lee 1987). Linked to this is the formalization of co-ordination and control procedures which tends to be much more significant in Japanese firms — albeit not as great as in large diversified U.S. corporations (Lincoln et al. 1986; Pugh and Redding 1985; Rohlen 1974).

Dominant conceptions of the managerial role and competences also differ in that Japanese managers are not expected to be as remote and aloof from subordinates as are Chinese and Korean ones (Rohlen 1979; Silin 1976; Smith and Misumi 1989). A key part of their role is to maintain high group morale and performance and they are less directive or didactic than managers in Korean and Chinese firms (Liebenberg 1982; Redding and Richardson 1986; Redding and Wong 1986). These differences in managerial authority are echoed by variations in employment policies and practices which together generate conditional loyalties in Chinese and Korean businesses as opposed to what Silin (1976: 127–131) terms 'emotional' loyalties in Japanese *kaisha* (Amsden 1985a; Michell 1988).

In terms of the activities co-ordinated through authority hierarchies, Japanese and Chinese firms tend to restrict them to a relatively narrow range in which their specialized skills and knowledge provide distinctive capabilities. Complementary, but dissimilar activities requiring different skills (Richardson 1972; cf. Mariti and Smiley 1983), are co-ordinated through quasi-market connections (Clark 1979: 62–64; Cusumano 1985: 186–193; Redding and Tam 1985). Korean *chaebol*, in contrast, are much more vertically integrated and control more diverse activities through a common authority hierarchy (Amsden 1989; Orru et al. 1988; Levy 1988; Zeile 1989).

Specialization in Japan is linked to the long-term employment of managers and a preference for evolutionary growth strategies within a particular sector. Diversification thus tends to be limited to related industries (Kagono et al. 1985: 55–87; Kono 1984: 78–80). Korean and Chinese businesses are more susceptible to opportunistic diversification outside their main area of specialization, partly because of the much more personal nature of ownership and control, especially when encouraged to do so by the state as in Korea (Amsden 1989; Kim 1989). Diversified business groups have developed in Taiwan but these are more like family partnerships than authoritatively integrated enterprises (Hamilton et al. 1990; Numazaki 1986).

Business specialization increases the interdependence of enterprises and so the need to co-ordinate activities and strategies to reduce uncertainty. Large Japanese companies are highly dependent on elaborate networks of sub-contractors with whom they have relatively long-term relationships that allow for the extensive sharing of information and technology, together with some commitment to be helpful during crises. Dore (1986: 77–83) describes this as 'relational contracting'. Chinese firms in Taiwan and Hong Kong also depend heavily on sub-contractors but their commitments to them tend to be less extensive and long lasting (Redding and Tam 1985). Because the Korean *chaebol* are more vertically integrated they are less dependent on intra-industry links with other businesses.

In addition to this sort of inter-firm co-ordination there are also considerable variations in the extent to which dominant firms join together in cross-sectoral business groups (Hamilton et al. 1989). Many large Japanese firms are joined together through mutual shareholdings, regular 'presidents' clubs' meetings and the exchange of senior managerial staff across business sectors and with banks, insurance and trust companies to form large, co-operative groups (Futatsugi 1986; Goto 1982; Miyazaki 1980). Similar business groups exist in Taiwan and, to a lesser extent, in Hong Kong but they are much more personal and family based than in Japan (Hamilton and Kao 1987; Numazaki 1986). Korean *chaebol* are more discrete entities which are interconnected through state agencies and political alliances (Kim 1979) rather than by separately institutionalized business networks.

East Asian Business Systems and Pre-industrial China, Korea and Japan

In seeking to explain these differences between business systems in different countries, both current characteristics of dominant social institutions and historical patterns of social development are relevant. Indeed, many of the former cannot be adequately understood without taking account of the latter, as in the case of the relationship between financial institutions and industrial firms in Britain (Ingham 1984). In the analysis of East Asian societies, pre-industrial political and social structures are especially important because of the speed and recentness of their industrialization. In particular, traditional patterns of loyalty, solidarity and trust have substantial consequences for authority patterns within businesses as well as relationships between them and for the organization and policies of state elites. Additionally, because of the weakness of what Pye (1985: 324) terms 'secondary forms of political socialization' after military defeat and occupation in many countries, traditional modes of primary socialization through the family have become more significant in generating and reproducing distinctive attitudes towards authority and power. Thus important aspects of the societal contexts of East Asian business systems include established patterns of obedience, loyalty and trust as well as the structure and legitimacy of the state. Differences in these between Japan, Korea, Taiwan and Hong Kong reflect historical variations in authority relations, political structures and belief systems in addition to patterns of village organization and social co-operation.

The major contrasts between pre-industrial China, Korea and Japan which have affected the contexts in which different business systems developed can be summarized under four headings. First, the historical extent of political pluralism and decentralization of political authority to intermediate levels of organization between the ruler and households. Second, and relatedly, the degree to which privately controlled concentrations of economic power were permitted and became significant loci of political autonomy and influence. Third, the basis on which authority is claimed and obedience justified. Fourth, the degree to which the family was the fundamental unit of social identity, loyalty and production as opposed to broader groupings which crossed kinship boundaries and which were linked to higher levels of authority.

Political Pluralism

One of the most notable differences between Japan, Korea and China is the degree of political pluralism which has developed over the past 1,000 or so years. Both China and Korea were governed by central 'bureaucratic' dynasties which controlled provincial landowners through state officials and made their status dependent on access to state offices (Jacobs 1958, 1985). The Han dynasty in China institutionalized the practice of demoting noble families by one rank each generation and was also able to reduce them to the rank of commoner at any time (Jacobs 1958: 104), a system also practised in Korea to reduce the independence of landowners and make them compete for state appointments (Jacobs 1985: 31). While the effectiveness of these policies has varied, they did prevent the emergence of an independent warrior class which competed for control over the state, as in Japan.

The failure of the Taika reforms (646–858) to replicate the Confucian patrimonial model, and the subsequent separation of the Emperor's personal powers from military control over Japan, led to the distinctive Japanese form of feudalism in which the *de facto* central power was determined by competitive military struggles between clans (Jacobs 1958; Pye 1985). Formal obeisance to the central authority of the Emperor remained important, but effective political and economic power was decentralized to the major clans and, at times, to religious orders such as Buddhist monasteries (Jacobs 1958: 81–83), who controlled land and retainers. The ability of the central political authority to control economic development and capital accumulation was therefore much more restricted in Japan than in China and Korea. Even when the Tokugawa government banned foreign commerce in 1636, feudal lords were able to engage in widespread smuggling and trade, and so increase their wealth substantially (Jacobs 1958: 37–38). In contrast, Chinese rulers could, and did, redistribute land rights to prevent concentrations of landownership and maintained tight control of urban markets and merchant activities (Jacobs 1958: 23–32).

This difference in political pluralism is linked to the existence and significance of a hereditary aristocracy and varied inheritance practices. In Japan and Korea aristocratic status was an important distinction and could not be acquired by passing examinations, whereas in Confucian China elite status was either granted by the ruler as a personal favour or awarded through the education system. Thus a hereditary aristocracy which could develop as an intermediate group between the ruler and his advisors and the mass of the population was prevented from becoming established in China.

Furthermore, whereas inheritance of property in Japan was based on the principle of primogeniture and hence concentrations of resources could be maintained over generations, this was not the case in China and Korea. The general pattern in these countries was to divide an inheritance equally between the sons, or at least equally enough to prevent large amounts of property being conserved and passed on across generations (Jacobs 1958: 149–155). This preference for equal inheritance remains an important feature of Chinese society, which helps to explain the lack of large, stable and successful businesses which have survived over many generations in a comparable manner to Japanese ones.

The combination of equal inheritance, or what Jacobs (1985: 204) terms homoyogeniture, and intergenerational demoting of the nobility in Korea meant that each generation of an aristocratic lineage had to compete for central state offices if they were to restore the family fortunes. Thus, during the Confucian Yi dynasty (1392–1910) local centres of political and economic power based on aristocratic families did not develop to nearly the same extent as in Japan because they depended on the centrally administered examinations and state offices to maintain status and income. As Jacobs (1985: 30) suggests: 'the dominance of the capital over the periphery was assured by preserving the capital as the locus of primary political patrimonial initiative. Hence individuals had to be either physically present or represented at the capital to secure and expand their prestige, power and prebends.' Although, then, the Korean local political elite remained an aristocracy of birth and retained their local power bases, they were too dependent on the centre to mount effective challenges to it and did not mobilize peasants or their retainers to oppose central authority.

Economic Pluralism

The differences in pre-industrial political pluralism between Japan, Korea and China were echoed by variations in economic pluralism. Just as the Confucian elite in China consistently fought any attempt to create local power bases or intermediate political organizations between the central state and the peasantry, so too did they ensure that potential concentrations of private economic power were controlled and limited by strong official control of markets and towns (Jacobs 1958: 30–32). During the Han dynasty, the ruler established his ethical right to prevent the accumulation of monetary power, except under his own control and sponsorship. As a result, any accumulation of property, unless it was for religious purposes or public relief measures, was automatically subject to state confiscation (Jacobs 1958: 57–60). Similar efforts to maintain central state control over mercantile activities and prevent the concentration of private capital occurred in Korea.

In Japan, on the other hand, independent mercantile wealth expanded considerably during the Tokugawa period despite official disdain for merchants and periodic refusals to pay back loans and attacks on merchants' power. By the late 18th century, both the central authority and the feudal lords were so dependent on rich merchants for loans that they could not suppress them and, in some cases, the aristocracy also undertook commercial activities (Hirschmeier and Yui 1981: 14–36). Additionally, many merchants invested their profits in land reclamation, so becoming landowners themselves, and began to blur the formal boundaries between the aristocracy and merchants. By the time of the Meiji restoration (1867–1868) many concentrations of private, family controlled economic power had become established and these dominated the economic system despite their formal subservience to the aristocracy.

The Mitsui family business, for instance, which developed into one of the largest financial holding companies (*zaibatsu*) in pre-war Japan and survives as a giant business group today, was founded in the 17th century and developed into a large chainstore enterprise during the 18th and 19th centuries, which made the family very wealthy (Hirschmeier and Yui 1981: 60–66). While more integrated into, and dependent upon, the prevailing feudal system than their European counterparts, these rich Japanese mercantile families were more powerful, stable and independent than Chinese or Korean ones and were able to establish an effective banking system (Jacobs 1958: 70–74). A further point about the large merchant houses in Tokugawa Japan is that they were organized into powerful guilds that were more stable and autonomous than their Chinese counterparts. These government regulated guilds developed intricate systems of inter-urban, inter-family connections which reinforced their independent economic power, whereas Chinese guilds were primarily local associations of craftsmen with little capital controlled by officials (Jacobs 1958: 38–40; Hirschmeier and Yui 1981: 36–38).

Bases of Claims to Authority and Obedience

In addition to the degree of political and economic pluralism varying considerably between these three pre-industrial societies, there were also major differences in how power was legitimately claimed and obedience justified. Chinese and, later, Korean rulers adopted Confucian ideologies which asserted their superior moral worth and relied on the Confucian elite to legitimate their virtue and hence their right to rule. Japanese leaders, in contrast, acquired central control through military competition between feudal clans and relied on more pragmatic justifications, primarily the ability to sustain political and social order (Jacobs 1958: 77–96). This competitive struggle for power meant that authority was relatively unstable and depended on the effective mobilization of resources and retainers and so on the development and maintenance of loyalty.

Domination in China and Korea was, then, supposed to be derived from the moral virtue of the ruler and his Confucian, virtuous, advisors, so forming a 'virtuocracy' (Pye 1985: 22–24). This meant that the political order was a moral order, so that challenges to it were regarded as attacks on virtue itself. Since state office and authority were reserved for virtuous administrators who had demonstrated their moral worth by mastering the Confucian classics, incumbents had no need to justify their rank and power by being effective administrators or by performing useful services for the uneducated and hence unworthy. By controlling the interpretation of the classics and the examination system, the Confucian 'bureaucratic' elite effectively controlled the definition of virtue, and hence authority, and were able to prevent the emergence of independent power bases by mobilizing resources against evil, unworthy and disruptive accumulations of land or goods.

In contrast, because power in pre-industrial Japan was linked more to military and co-ordinative competence than moral worth, it relied more on actively demonstrating ability and performing some services, rather than a passive exemplification of superior virtue (Pye 1985: 57–58). Feudal lords were able to attract peasants away from Imperial estates during the Taika reform period, for instance, by protecting them against forced labour service for the Imperial authority (Jacobs 1958: 29) and so domination in Japan rested upon some notion of reciprocal service, albeit to a lesser extent than in European feudalism (Moore 1966: 233–234).

A further point about subordination in China is that obedience to the Emperor and his mandarins was more a matter of following norms of filial piety, in an analogous way to fulfilling role obligations to fathers as heads of families, than a personal commitment to an individual superior (Hamilton 1984). Commitment and loyalty to superiors are thus less 'emotional' and more calculating in Chinese society than in Japan, where common identification with collective goals has been facilitated by the institutionalization of feudal loyalties which overrode purely personal and kinship based ones (Moore 1966: 254–266; Silin 1976: 127–138). Because loyalty to collective authority in Chinese society was demanded as a matter of respect for the virtuous as an extension of filial piety in the family, it did not involve active personal commitment. Thus if the leader ceases to manifest his moral superiority by, for example, behaving inappropriately in his private life or failing to be successful in maintaining order, commitment can legitimately be transferred elsewhere (Jacobs 1958: 77).

The plurality of competing clans and alliances in Japan which provided foci of loyalty and identity beyond kinship groups institutionalized collective commitments to relatively large units of social organization in a way that did not happen in Chinese society. The systematic integration of ruling groups with the peasantry, providing military protection in exchange for transferring land tenure rights, ensured that vertical loyalties were less restricted to the household or extended kinship systems than in China where the mandarins rotated and could not claim personal loyalties (Jacobs 1958: 24–27). Because the feudal lords in Japan had to mobilize retainers and peasantry in order to compete effectively, they were more involved with local production systems and social structures than the Korean aristocracy or the Chinese mandarinate who concentrated on the rewards of central favour and preferment. They thus developed integrated hierarchies of control of the peasantry through their retainers and village headmen (Smith 1959: 54–64).

Inter-Family Solidarity and Collaboration

This difference in vertical integration between China and Japan is related to the general significance of the family as the basic unit of social identity and control in East Asian societies and the ease of establishing trust and mutual obligations across family boundaries. As well as vertical loyalties being limited and conditional in Chinese society, so too commitment to horizontal groupings and collective entities which transcend kinship boundaries was restricted by the Confucian concentration on the family as the fundamental unit of harmonious society and model for all authority relations. As Silin suggests (1976: 37): 'Aside from kinship, no coherent model or set of organizing principles exists to govern inter-personal relations within the Confucian conceptual system.' Whereas the Japanese recognized the legitimacy of tensions between family members and allowed ambitious younger sons to leave the family in order to establish a new lineage (Pye 1985: 68–69), thus weakening family boundaries, the Chinese and, to a lesser extent Korean, emphasis on the family as the core institution of society implied strong boundaries between family members and outsiders and the need to maintain solidarity and harmony within families. As Pye (1985: 70) puts it: 'The Chinese were taught to recognise a vivid distinction between family members, who could be relied upon, and non-family people, who are not to be trusted except in qualified ways.'

The pervasiveness of this 'familism' in Chinese culture is demonstrated by the infrequency and limited nature of co-operation across kinship groups in Chinese villages. As Moore (1966: 208) summarizes the situation: 'The Chinese village . . . evidently lacked cohesiveness . . . There were far fewer (than in Japan or Europe) occasions on which numerous members of the village co-operated in a common task in a way that creates the habits and sentiments of solidarity . . . the primary unit of economic production (and consumption as well) was the household.' In contrast, the Japanese village was highly cohesive, with families co-operating in major agricultural tasks, in particular the spring planting of rice (Smith 1959: 50–52). Partly because individual households depended so much on the assistance of others, ostracism and banishment from the village were very powerful sanctions against deviance which, together with the collective responsibility for taxation and criminal law, limited the open expression of conflicts between families and maintained the importance of group solidarity rather than individual wishes (*ibid.*: 60–62).

This contrast between China and Japan is exemplified by the differing results of introducing into the two countries the *pao-chia* system of mutual surveillance, under which ten households were made responsible for each others' conduct. According to Moore (1966: 206, 260), the system was quite ineffective in China, but when the Tokugawa rulers adapted it in 17th century Japan — albeit reduced to five households — it proved highly successful in maintaining order and raising taxes. Such inter-family solidarity and village cohesion was lower in Korea and, in general, the Korean and Chinese families seem to have many features in common. However, although the Korean family is important as the main source of support, the consanguineous lineage is more significant than in China and forms, according to Jacobs (1985: 211), the main intermediary organization between the individual and central, formal authority.

The weakness of inter-family co-operation and solidarity in the traditional Chinese village is echoed by the lack of an effective legal system in China and of institutional processes for regulating exchanges between strangers (Jacobs 1958: 97–99). Together with the Confucian distrust of mercantile wealth which resulted in periodic confiscation and official constraints on economic activities, this meant that personal bonds and familiarity were very important in developing trust and encouraged con-

Table 2
Significant
Differences
Between Pre-
industrial China,
Korea and Japan

	China	Korea	Japan
Political pluralism	low	low	medium
Economic pluralism	low	low	high
Basis of claim to authority	moral worth	moral worth	competitive military success
Inter-family solidarity and integration into larger political units	low	low	high

siderable secrecy and defensiveness. In contrast, pre-industrial Japan began to develop more formal mechanisms for settling disputes as early as the 18th century with the acceptance of the legitimacy of private litigation in 1721.

This growth of impersonality in Japan was assisted by the separation of the warrior class of *samurai* from the land and their employment in towns as the administrative agents of the feudal lords. According to Smith (1988: 136–142), during the Tokugawa period of the 17th, 18th and much of the 19th centuries, traditional feudal ties of personal loyalty between *samurai* and their lords (*daimyo*) became more attenuated, distant and impersonal as the former lost their direct ties to the land and came to depend on the stipends received from the latter for administering their estates. They increasingly saw themselves as loyal administrators of the collective entity, and began to regard merit and competence as the key attributes of superior status and rank rather than inherited positions. While loyalty to superiors remained a necessary attribute of the ideal official, it became less personally focused on the individual leader and had increasingly to be complemented by demonstrated ability (Pye 1985: 161). These differences between pre-industrial China, Korea and Japan are summarized in terms of the four features mentioned earlier in Table 2.

The Institutional Environments of East Asian Business Systems

The differences between China, Korea and Japan described above have had substantial consequences for the institutional environments in which business systems developed. These environments can be summarized in terms of the following interrelated features. First, the system of authority relations, including the degree of vertical integration of loyalties, the importance of personal ties and conceptions of appropriate behaviour. Second, the system for establishing trust and obligation relations between exchange partners and its impact on enterprise loyalties and commitment. Third, the organization and policies of political and bureaucratic state elites, including the extent to which the state dominates the economic system and controls banks as well as co-ordinating firms' strategies. Differences in these features help to explain the development and reproduction of different business systems in East Asia.

The System of Authority Relations

One of the major differences in authority relations between Japanese, Korean and Chinese societies concerns the extent to which loyalties are systematically integrated as a series of mutual commitments between superiors and subordinates in an elaborate vertical hierarchy. Whereas the centralized feudalism of Tokugawa Japan developed a series of intermediate organizations between the state and individual households which integrated vertical loyalties, Confucian China and Korea systematically prevented the establishment of local centres of loyalty and political organization. Thus, obedience and subordination relations in Japan are tied to particular collective entities which, in turn, are subordinate to larger ones. Furthermore, the development of reciprocity norms in Japanese society between superior and subordinate — however asymmetric they may be — has helped to integrate vertical loyalties more than in Chinese or Korean societies, where the rule of collectively self-certified virtuous officials has limited the perceived need to legitimate domination through reciprocal services. While modern Japanese politicians and other leaders are expected to look after their supporters and perform useful services for them in return for deference and support (Eisenstadt and Roniger 1984: 159–162), Chinese and Korean ones restrict their obligation to kinship groupings and do not rely on extensive chains of mutual support. Coupled with the role performance model of filial piety as the exemplar of obedience in Chinese society, this lack of reciprocity and sequential integration of commitments through a succession of superiors and collectivities reduces the intensity of vertical loyalties and their mobilization for collective goals beyond the family unit.

A further difference in the system of authority relations in Japanese, Korean and Chinese societies concerns the relative importance of direct personal subordination to leaders as distinct from obedience to collective and positional authority. This in turn reflects the extent to which authority has become collective and depersonalized in a society. The patrimonial authority system of pre-industrial China and Korea which emphasized the personal moral superiority of the ruler and his advisors inhibited the development of more impersonal forms of authority. As a result, allegiance remains a primarily personal relationship to particular individuals in these societies (Jacobs 1985; Pye 1985).

In contrast, reciprocity and recognition of mutual dependence between superiors and subordinates in modern Japan are combined with strong beliefs in the common commitment to collective goals and the right of superiors to issue commands on the basis of their competence, as assessed by the education system, and subservience to joint interests (Pye 1985: 163–181). Personal commitments to immediate superiors and more senior patrons (Rohlen 1974: 122–134), are greater and more significant than in most western societies, but rest much more on shared loyalties to collective objectives and mutual trust than elsewhere in East Asia.

These variations in loyalty to non-family collectivities are also a result of different conceptions of authority within families which affect expectations about managerial authority and appropriate managerial behaviour (Pye 1985: 73–79). In the Chinese family, the father is supposed to be omnipotent and omniscient so that obedience is owed to him as a superior being who is solely responsible for the family fortunes. The mother is obliged to reinforce his authority and so cannot serve as a focus of different values and modes of conduct (cf. Ho 1986). Authority is thus monolithic and undifferentiated. Similarly, the owner of the CFB is expected to exhibit superior qualities and a didactic leadership style by allowing subordinates to learn the thoughts and beliefs which enable him to be successful (Silin 1976: 127–128). As the head of the family enterprise, he maintains a considerable distance from employees and cannot delegate or share authority because leadership is a moral quality of individuals. Thus managing by consensus in the CFB would be regarded as a sign of incompetence and weakness (Silin 1976: 71). The Korean father is supposed to be similarly omnicompetent and aloof, but authority in the Korean family is more differentiated than in the Chinese one and so children are able to play off paternal and maternal authorities against each other (Pye 1985: 75).

In contrast, the Japanese father can share his responsibilities with others and admit uncertainty. Furthermore, the mother in Japanese families can function as an alternative focus of authority so that children become accustomed to differentiated authority, in particular to what Pye (1985: 74) terms a maternalist image of authority. Together with the need to elicit subordinates' commitment and energies in competitive struggles, this legitimacy of supportive and 'nurturing' forms of authority encourages managerial styles which take account of emotional dependence needs and seek consensus among subordinates and encourage the development of their skills for group goals. Their authority is not threatened by subordinate success in the way that a Chinese or Korean manager's would be. Authority relations in Japanese society then are less focused on direct personal relationships between subordinates and the leader than in Chinese and Korean societies and obedience is owed on the basis of competence and collective loyalties rather than deference to the personal qualities of political leaders.

Trust, Reciprocity and Enterprise Loyalty

The institutionalization of norms of reciprocity and mutual obligation between superiors and subordinates is, of course, a part of the overall development of trust and confidence relationships between increasingly separate individuals and groups in an industrializing society. In considering how such norms and relations differ between Chinese, Korean and Japanese societies it is helpful to use Zucker's (1986) distinction between three major bases for generating trust between exchange partners: reputations for reliability and probity, common ascriptive characteristics such as ethnicity and, third, through some more general social institution such as the professional certification of competences and code of ethics or legal system. The more socially and geographically distant the exchange partners, the more important the formal institutional means of building confidence become, as reputation and ascription cease to be effective where cultural heterogeneity and distances are considerable. Thus the development of large national corporations in the late 19th century U.S.A., after waves of immigration had increased the size and heterogeneity of the population, depended, according to Zucker, on the establishment of formal controls and signalling institutions.

Cultural homogeneity in Japanese, Korean and Chinese societies is greater than in many western countries and so reputational and ascriptive means of developing trust and confidence remain effective over considerable distances through elaborate and extensive reputational networks, as demonstrated by the overseas Chinese (Limlingan 1986; Redding 1990; Yoshihara 1988). However, the growth of more impersonal norms of obligation and objective indicators of performance for officials in the 19th century, together with a strong emphasis among merchants on demonstrating honesty and probity to the public in order to conform with the norms of model citizenship, encouraged more generalized, formal and collective means of establishing trust relations in Japan (Hirschmeier and Yui 1981: 40–48). To be trustworthy across a wide range of transactions became a general and public indication of collective business success and social honour. Confidence in the larger merchant houses grew to the extent that their deposit notes and bills of exchange were often trusted more than cash (Hirschmeier and Yui 1981: 29–30). While not, then, developing the extensive formal mechanisms of trust generation and reproduction found in many western societies, the institutionalization of trust relations between strangers has gone much further in Japan than in Korean or Chinese society.

This more general and collective basis for generating trust in Japan is reflected in the greater ease of establishing mutual obligation relations between members of different groups there (Pye 1985: 71). While Chinese and Korean ties of reciprocal obligations are often based on ascriptive foundations such as common birthplace, school or university class, Japanese ones are more idiosyncratic and situation specific. Thus *guanxi* networks of mutual support in Chinese society are usually tied to common background characteristics (Wong 1988) whereas Japanese obligation networks are formed across such categories as well as within them, and demonstrate an ability to form strong bonds between people with different backgrounds. Reciprocity of favours and obligations is a stronger norm in Japan than in China and Korea and is a more generalized relationship in the sense that it can be developed between Japanese with different ascriptive characteristics. Thus strong loyalties and cohesive bonds can be established between different groups of people to a much greater extent than seems to be feasible in Chinese society where ascriptive ties — especially family — predominate.

These differences are, of course, related to the general pattern of co-operation and solidarity across kinship groups in Japan, Korea and China. As already suggested, the historical nature of the Chinese village and the lack of integration of households in production, consumption or common defence activities have reproduced a sharp distinction between family members and outsiders which makes the development of social cohesion and common identities between families difficult in Chinese societies. Rather, distrust tends to be pervasive, since each person is held to be responsible for his own household and to put its interests ahead of broader objectives.

This primacy of family relationships and identities in Chinese society means that commitment to one's family overrides all other loyalties, and individual prestige is based on family standing rather than being organizational or occupational. Family prestige, in turn, is linked to property ownership as well as to educational and professional success since full membership of the Chinese village was not feasible without owning land and it was also a pre-condition of establishing a family and so gaining respect. In Moore's words (1966: 212): 'no property: no family, no religion'. Especially in societies where political advancement has been inaccessible for many, such as Hong Kong and Taiwan, business success and wealth have become the major sources of family prestige and, for that reason, many managers and technicians leave to start their own businesses when good opportunities arise (Redding and Tam 1985; Tam 1990). Thus, commitment to employers among the expatriate Chinese and Taiwanese is always limited and conditional, unless strong personal obligations exist through family connections.

This limited commitment to employers and companies means that business owners feel unable to trust employees with important decisions unless they are members of the same family or have strong personal obligations and commitments to them. Additionally, since trust is such a personal phenomenon in Chinese society, and people beyond the kinship group are expected to pursue their own family interests even if they fulfil role expectations of obedience to superiors, Chinese entrepreneurs are very concerned to develop personal ties of mutual obligation with key staff and with business partners. Thus personal reputations for honesty and competence and membership of large mutual obligation networks are crucial components of business success in Chinese communities (Limlingan 1986; Ward 1972). The need for strong personal involvement in running the CFB in order to ensure trust and commitment, coupled with the dependence of family prestige on business success and wealth, encourage owner control, highly personal authority relations and centralization of decision-making in the CFB.

In contrast, the greater importance of relatively independent legal procedures for resolving disputes in Japan, and the more widespread and idiosyncratic the processes for establishing mutual obligation ties between

non-family members, have facilitated the development of less personal
forms of control and managerial authority which are not tied to direct
ownership. Additionally, the existence of substantial concentrations of
economic power in feudal Japan and the ability to transform wealth into
political resources meant that owners were not so threatened by political
elites as in China and so did not retain such close personal control over
financial resources and decisions. Loyalty to independent collective entities was institutionalized in Japan well before the Meiji restoration and
the use of unrelated retainers as managers of family businesses was not
uncommon, so that the development of college educated managerial
cadres towards the end of the 19th century did not present a sharp
discontinuity with the Tokugawa period (Hirschmeier and Yui 1981:
165–168).

The weaker sense of family boundaries and historical commitment to
broader collectivities also facilitated the growth of loyalty to firms and a
greater willingness to trust employees (Silin 1976: 131–138). Since family
prestige and worth were derived from the success and prestige of the
collective enterprise, as well as from individual ownership, and personal
identities were as much tied to such enterprises as to specific family
membership, the pressure to establish an independent source of family
status by setting up one's own business is much less than in Chinese
cultures and loyalty to broad, non-family collectives correspondingly
stronger.

State Policies and Financial Systems

Finally, the degree of political and economic pluralism in pre-industrial
China, Korea and Japan has affected the ways in which state agencies and
political elites have dealt with the economic system and promoted
industrialization. In Japan, Korea and Taiwan both bureaucratic and
political elites have been extensively involved in promoting economic
change and growth and have seen the state as a central agent of
modernization and development. In all three countries, the state is
'developmental' and plan rational in Johnson's terms (1982: 17–23)
rather than regulatory and market oriented as in the U.S.A. Thus they
are all concerned with setting substantive social and economic goals
which involve particular industrial policies.

The Hong Kong government, on the other hand, has been overtly distant
from economic affairs and has not sought to manage the process of
economic development. The emergence of a highly efficient and rather
fragmented manufacturing sector since the 1950s has taken place almost
despite the state rather than with its assistance (Haggard and Chen 1987).
However, Deyo (1987) suggests that the leaders of the large banks and
trading companies are strongly integrated into the colonial elite to constitute a British dominated establishment that is supportive of development and fulfils some of the functions of the developmentalist state.
Similarly, Nishida (1990) claims that the British banks and trading houses

provided support for the Shanghaiese cotton spinners in Hong Kong in the 1950s.

Perhaps the major difference in the role of the state between Japan, Korea and Taiwan to be considered here concerns the extent to which it actively intervenes in managing the environment of corporate decision-making and influences individual firms' strategic choices. Whereas the South Korean state since 1961 has pursued a highly interventionist policy aimed at achieving high economic growth and industrial development through state co-ordination of private business, the Japanese bureaucracy has been less inclined to direct corporate decision-making through hierarchical commands and has not been so successful at obtaining compliance since the Second World War. Finally, although the Taiwanese state still controls 18 percent of industrial production and is responsible for half of the gross domestic investment (Amsden 1985), it has not attempted to manage firms' choices in the export sector or allocate resources on a discretionary basis to individual firms (Myers 1986). Thus the extent of state co-ordination of strategies and the direction of economic activities in the export sector over the past 30 years has been highest in South Korea, significant but less directive in Japan, and most indirect — although still important — in Taiwan. Let us first discuss these differences and then consider their consequences for business systems.

The South Korean military regime has assumed direct responsibility for managing economic development, arguably as the means of legitimating its domination (Kim 1988). By controlling access to foreign exchange, bank credit at low interest rates, tax concessions, imposing price controls and threatening tax investigations, the Korean state has manipulated and directed the strategic choices of major firms, especially the *chaebol* (Jones and Sakong 1980: 100–140). Jacobs (1985) has characterized this central direction of the economic system as essentially patrimonial and a continuation of the Confucian system of bureaucratic elitism in which wealth and power depended on the grace of the ruler and his virtuous advisors. However, Kim (1988) suggests that the power of the Korean 'hard state' has declined since the 1960s and the *chaebol* are becoming more autonomous; a view partly borne out by the dispute over the terms for rescuing the Daewoo shipyards (Clifford 1989).

The important role of the state bureaucracy, especially the Ministry of International Trade and Industry (MITI), in guiding Japanese economic development is well known. However, despite the Bank of Japan's strong influence on the credit policies of private banks through the 'overloaning' system (Johnson 1982: 201–204), the ability of the Japanese state to manage economic actors' strategies directly is much more limited than in Korea. This is partly because the bulk of the banking system has been privately owned and controlled, and partly because Japan has had major concentrations of economic power outside the state apparatus for a considerable time. Hence the guidance and co-ordination of private decisions have rarely amounted to direct commands and there have been a number of well publicized rejections of MITI's advice (Abegglen and Stalk 1985; Eads and Yamamura 1987). Generally, the bureaucracy has influenced strategies indirectly through field manipulation of costs and opportunities and has concerned itself more with the collective behaviour of firms and industries, rather than directing the actions of individual firms (Haggard 1988; Johnson 1982, 1987; Wade 1988). It has helped businesses to co-ordinate and plan their strategies but has not, on the whole, intervened in particular decisions of individual firms.

The Taiwanese case is superficially paradoxical because it manifests a high rate of state ownership and control of major banks and industries, with public enterprises contributing 31 percent of gross fixed capital for-mation on average between 1965–1980 compared to 23 percent in Korea and 11 percent in Japan (Wade 1988), at the same time as exercising a much more distant relationship between the state and firms in the export sector. In contrast to South Korea, the Taiwanese state has not sought to co-ordinate firms' strategies, to build up large national champions in particular industries or to direct firms' resources in particular ways, except to encourage investment in plastics and electronics (Myers 1986). Additionally, it has pursued a high interest rate policy in order to control inflation and has not encouraged large-scale lending at privileged interest rates for capital intensive industries (Amsden 1985; Gold 1985; Haggard 1988). Essentially, loss-making state enterprises have subsidized the export sector which has also benefited from general state support for new export such as preferential tariff rates and indicative planning which reduced investment risks (Gold 1985: 87). As Gold (1985: 126) puts it: in Taiwan, planners retained an aloof posture. They met to formulate policy and then relayed their decisions and attendant mechanisms to implement it to the business community, and watched what happened.' Partly as a result, Taiwanese firms have remained relatively small and in industries where flexibility and small size are advantageous (Levy 1988). Lacking strong state support for large, capital-intensive firms, the private sector has been dominated by the CFB and has avoided competing directly with dominant western firms where entry costs are very high (Hamilton and Biggart 1988).

The financial systems in all three countries are based on bank credit for industrial development rather than on capital markets and this has pro-vided the state with substantial leverage over firms' decisions. especially where low real interest rates have stimulated a surplus demand for loans and hence encouraged their administrative rationing (Zysman 1983: 71–72). However, the close association between banks, trust companies and insurance companies with industrial firms in Japanese business groups, seems more equal and interdependent than similar relations in Korea and Taiwan. Furthermore, because the banks are much more state controlled in the latter two countries, many firms have preferred to rely for invest-ment funds on the unofficial 'curb' money markets, even with their attendant exorbitant interest rates, or on personal contacts and family resources (Wade 1988).

In particular, the numerous small and medium sized firms in Taiwan have not developed close links with the state controlled banks and have not formed inter-market business groups through them. Such inter-sector co-ordination as does exist between Taiwanese firms occurs through family connections and strong personal ties between owners (Numazaki 1986). Thus the degree of integration of financial institutions with major firms differs between Japan, Korea and Taiwan although, in all three, it is greater than in capital-market based financial systems such as the U.S.A. While the large Hong Kong banks are not so formally tied to the state or publicly involved in long-term economic development as those elsewhere in East Asia, Haggard and Cheng (1987) suggest that they have played a major role in the long-term funding of manufacturing industries and, more recently, have been critical to the explosion of the financial services industry.

The major significance of state co-ordination and bank involvement in business strategies for the sorts of business recipes that become established concerns risk reduction and sharing, what Pye (1988) terms the 'nationalization of risk'. Particularly with regard to large-scale capital investments in new industries and markets, long-term commitment to enterprise goals by powerful agencies facilitates growth objectives and encourages risky decisions which might not otherwise be taken. Strong state control over labour movements, as in Korea and Taiwan, also encourages major investments because expected profits will be higher than if there is an independent union movement which can challenge owners' rights (Cumings 1987; Haggard 1988).

In the case of Japan, the role of the banks and the General Trading Companies, or *Sogo Shosha*, in business groups facilitated business specialization because many aspects of purchasing, selling and finance functions can be organized on a relational contracting basis with other members of each group (Yoshino and Lifson 1986: 21–53). As a result, firms could concentrate on developing relatively homogenous and specialized skills to achieve high growth rates in particular markets. State support for orderly markets and reducing excessive competition reduced the risks of business specialization and enabled specialized firms to benefit from relatively homogeneous skills and commitments to particular industries, as well as reduced co-ordination costs because of this homogeneity of activities. Thus relatively close and interdependent connection between state agencies, banks, *sogo shosha* and other major actors enabled considerable specialization of capabilities and activities to develop successfully in Japan.

The strong support of the South Korean state for favoured *chaebol*, and the associated preferential allocation of bank loans for politically desired projects (Jones and Sakong 1980: 106–109), clearly encouraged the growth of these large, integrated enterprises and their willingness to move into new, capital-intensive industries in the 1970s (Amsden 1989: 80–85). In effect, the state assumed a substantial proportion of the risks involved and also had the mechanisms for ensuring compliance with its wishes. This close involvement of state agencies also means, though, that *chaebol* are highly dependent on the goodwill of bureaucrats and their masters, which has resulted in their support for government programmes and their strong personal ties to key officials. Shin and Chin (1989) suggest that this need for continued state support and favours helps to explain the high levels of centralized decision-making in the *chaebol* and their reliance on ascriptive criteria for filling senior managerial posts (cf. Yoo and Lee 1987). The paramount need for trust and loyalty in a highly faction ridden society, where personal relationships and connections are critical, encourages the use of kinship and regional criteria for such posts (cf. Jacobs 1985). Centralization within the *chaebol* thus matches the highly centralized nature of authority in Korean society, and the formation of a personally loyal and cohesive group of top managers and advisors facilitates central control of these large enterprises.

The more removed and distant relationships between state agencies and large enterprises in Taiwan, together with a general policy of not directly building up large, integrated businesses to compete with Japanese and western ones in advanced industrial sectors (Myers 1986), have limited the growth of large-scale integrated enterprises in the export sector. Thus, Taiwanese businesses have concentrated on industries and products where economics of scale are less important than flexibility and innovation (Levy 1988). Specialization and extensive sub-contracting are also, of course, a characteristic of the CFB in Hong Kong. The centrifugal tendencies of the CFB appears to have resulted in increasing fragmentation of the industrial structure in the absence of strong central co-ordination of industrial development in Hong Kong (Tam 1990).

To summarize, I am suggesting that the major differences between East Asian business systems, identified in Table 1, result from particular features of their institutional environments. These concern authority relationships, mechanisms for generating and maintaining trust, and obligation relations between non-kin and the structure and policies of state agencies and financial institutions. Variations in these features which help to explain East Asian business systems are listed in Table 3.

Conclusions: Towards the Comparative Analysis of Business Systems

This analysis of the different forms of business organization which have become established and successful in different institutional environments in East Asia highlights both the variability of competitive business systems and their interdependence with their societal contexts. In particular, it emphasizes the continuing influence of pre-industrial political and social structures together with the critical role of state agencies and financial institutions in sharing risks and co-ordinating strategies. Differences between the modern Japanese *kaisha*, Korean *chaebol* and the Chinese family business reflect historical patterns of authority and iden-

Table 3
Major Differences
in the Institutional
Contexts of East
Asian Business
Systems

	Japan	Korea	Taiwan	Hong Kong
Authority Relations				
Vertical integration of loyalties	high	low	low	low
Significance of collective non-personal authority	high	low	low	low
Differentiation of family authority	high	high	low	low
Omnicompetence of father	low	high	high	high
Trust, Reciprocity and Loyalty				
Bases of trust of obligation	institutional	ascriptive	ascriptive and reputational	
Primacy of family commitment	medium	high	high	high
Political and Financial Systems				
Developmental state	high	high	high	low
State coordination of strategies	medium	high	medium	low
Integration of banks with firms	high	high	medium	medium

tity reproduced through current family structures and other institutions as well as variations in state structures and policies during the industrialization process. The extent to which these influences are significant factors in explaining variations between established business systems in other societies differs, however, and it is worthwhile briefly exploring these differences and their implications for a more general comparative analysis of business systems.

The continued importance of pre-industrial political and social structures in East Asian societies, as well as traditional patterns of familial authority, reflects the recentness of their industrialization and the crucial role of the family as the basic social unit. All these 'post Confucian' cultures share the common theme that 'individuals achieved their identity solely through family membership which carried with it not only the obligation of deferring to the collectivity in critical decision-making but of acknowledging that the mortal life of the individual was less important than the immortality of the ancestral family line' (Pye 1985: 62). Despite, then, differences between Japanese, Korean and Chinese family structures and boundaries, consciousness of family identities and of the importance of family relationships is much greater than in most 'western' societies. Furthermore, the relative homogeneity of each culture, which reflects considerable isolation from external influences and migration over several centuries, both encourages and is reproduced by high degrees of similarity of family authority patterns and expectations so that these have a strong influence on attitudes and beliefs within societies.

These points suggest that where industrialization took place over a longer time span and developed before the 20th century, and where the individual has become more detached from the family, pre-industrial structures and attitudes are less directly influential in affecting the sorts of enterprise structure that have developed, and the role of family authority relations is less marked. While the institutional framework in which industrialization took place remains important in understanding present differences between, say, the role of the British and German financial institutions in funding industrial investment, variations in feudal structures do not directly explain differences in the organization of manufacturing firms or in the degree of vertical integration between these countries (cf. Maurice et al. 1980; Sorge and Warner 1986). Similarly, differences in family authority patterns between western countries are less directly significant in explaining variations in co-ordination and control practices than in East Asia because of the greater importance of horizontal groupings and identities based on occupations, as well as the general emphasis on individualism and legal rational modes of authority. Additionally, most western cultures are more heterogeneous than East Asian ones so that family structures are more varied and changeable.

In comparing dominant economic actors in western societies, then, the role of intermediate collective institutions, such as the education and training system (Maurice et al. 1986), and horizontal foci of loyalty and identity are more directly significant. Where skills are formally assessed and certified in a standardized way, and are important bases of identity and labour market boundaries, loyalty to individual employers will be limited and mobility between them correspondingly greater. Because skills are 'owned' by individuals and are separately defined, their integration and co-ordination for particular tasks and problems require more systematic management and organization than if they are derived more directly from particular organizational structures and practices. Thus tasks and responsibilities in 'credential' societies (Collins 1979) tend to be more formally specified, and their performance by individuals more directly monitored and linked to reward systems, than where skills and loyalties are more organization based (Lincoln et al. 1986). Similarly, standardized skills facilitate market determination of wage rates and so the institutionalization of public training and certification of practical skills is associated with market based wage rates rather than with organizationally specific ones (Dore 1973: 71–73, 110–113).

A further feature of the societal context of business systems which becomes highly significant when comparing East Asia with western industrialized countries is the nature of the financial system and the associated extent to which the state performs a market-oriented, regulatory role rather than a plan-oriented developmentalist one. Zysman (1983) has emphasized the differences between capital market and credit-based financial systems for corporate behaviour and for the ability of state agencies to influence firms' policies. Whereas the credit-based system makes firms more directly dependent on the banks and those who can control the availability of loans, capital-market based financial systems inhibit close relations between the state, banks and firms because of, *inter alia*, specialization and competition among financial inter-mediaries. While all East Asian economies have credit-based financial systems and developmentalist states, the U.S.A. and U.K. have strong capital market oriented states which affect the sorts of business systems that have developed.

Firms in these countries are both less constrained by ties to state agencies and banks and less able to claim their support or help in reducing uncertainty than in credit-based systems. Here, the state merely provides the framework for economic activities and does not share risks or co-ordinate plans. Similarly, financial institutions provide funds and own shares on a portfolio basis and so emphasize liquidity and diversification of financial risk rather than interdependence and mutual support. Invest-ment finance is here raised from relatively impersonal and decentralized competitive capital markets, which evaluate the risks and opportunities of a range of investments, rather than from large 'universal' financial institu-tions which are tied to particular businesses and share their particular risks and returns.

These arms' length and impersonal connections between large corpora-tions, state agencies and financial institutions mean that major risks and long-term investments cannot easily be shared with other organizations and market processes are the dominant means by which firms' and banks' activities are co-ordinated. As a result, firms tend to be more risk averse and less likely to undertake major long-term investments than their Japanese or German counterparts. They are also more likely to be con-cerned with increasing their share price and achieving high returns on investment funds supplied by the capital market than with growth and market share objectives because of the much more important market for corporate control in capital market based financial systems (Abegglen and Stalk 1985: 175–178; Lawriwsky 1984: 165–177). Similarly, because they have to manage risk on their own, and are more likely to be taken over and sacked if financial results are regarded by the markets as inferior to others, the dominant coalitions of large U.S. corporations are more positive about diversification into unrelated sectors than are those of large firms in credit-based systems.

The combination of standardized, formally certified skills, legal rational authority principles, a market-oriented state and capital market financial system, then, leads to a quite different form of business organization in Anglo-Saxon societies to those found in East Asia and, in many ways, to those established in some continental European countries. In addition to relying predominantly on formal and impersonal forms of authority and co-ordination, manifesting relatively low levels of employer–employee commitment and loyalty and high levels of task and role differentiation

24   Richard D. Whitley

with performance measures tied to individual efforts, these dominant economic actors incorporate a wide range of skills and activities in diverse markets with few stable, long-term relationships to other firms or banks and tend to make discontinuous, radical changes in growth strategies rather than evolutionary ones (Kagono et al. 1985).

In broadening the comparative analysis of business systems beyond East Asia, this discussion suggests that further important features of institutional environments are: the strength of occupational identities and prevalence of formally assessed and certified skills, the nature of the financial system and the strength and orientation of the state. These help to explain differences in the use of formal co-ordination and control rules and procedures, the extent to which roles and responsibilities are formally specified and allocated to separate individuals as well as the heterogeneity of skills and activities integrated and directed by authority structures, and preferred growth strategies.

As a result of these differences between institutional environments, different kinds of enterprise structures become feasible and successful in particular social contexts, especially where cultures are homogeneous and share strong boundaries with nation states. While not assuming that national contexts determine all aspects of business systems, nor denying the significance of variations between industries in heterogeneous cultures, the comparative analysis of enterprise structures does claim that dominant social institutions generate distinctive business systems which are relatively similar within nation states and strong cultural systems, but vary considerably between them. In this paper, I have suggested how particular features of dominant economic actors in Japan, South Korea, Taiwan and Hong Kong can be understood in terms of their institutional environment as an initial contribution to such a comparative analysis.

References

Abegglen, James C., and George Stalk
1985 *Kaisha, the Japanese corporation.* New York: Basic Books.

Amsden, Alice H.
1985 'The state and Taiwan's economic development' in *Bringing the state back in.* P. B. Evans et al. (eds.), 78–106. Cambridge: Cambridge University Press.

Amsden, Alice H.
1985a 'The division of labour is limited by the rate of growth of the market: the Taiwan machine tool industry in the 1970s'. *Cambridge Journal of Economics* 9: 271–284.

Amsden, Alice H.
1989 *Asia's next giant.* Oxford: Oxford University Press.

Aoki, Masahiko
1987 'The Japanese firm in transition' in *The political economy of Japan, 1: the domestic transformation.* K. Yamamura and Y. Yasuba (eds.), 263–288. Stanford: Stanford University Press.

Berger, Peter, and H.-H. M. Hsiao, *editors*
1988 *In search of an East Asian development model.* New Brunswick, New Jersey: Transaction Books.

Clark, R.
1979 *The Japanese company.* New Haven: Yale University Press.

Clifford, M.
1989 'Shipyard blues'. *Far East Economic Review* (23rd February): 62–64.

Collins, Randall
1979 *The credential society.* New York: Academic Press.

Cumings, Bruce
1987 'The origins and development of the northeast Asian political economy' in *The political economy of the new Asian industrialism.* F. C. Deyo (ed.). Ithaca: Cornell University Press.

Cusumano, Michael A.
1985 *The Japanese automobile industry: technology and management at Nissan and Toyota.* Cambridge, Mass.: Harvard University Press.

Deyo, F. C.
1987 'Coalitions, institutions and linkage sequencing — towards a strategic capacity model of East Asian developments' in *The political economy of the New Asian industrialism.* F. C. Deyo (ed.), 227–247. Ithaca: Cornell University Press.

Dore, Ronald
1973 *British factory — Japanese factory.* London: Allen and Unwin.

Dore, Ronald
1986 *Flexible rigidities.* Stanford: Stanford University Press.

Eads, George C., and Kozo Yamamura
1987 'The future of industrial policy' in *The political economy of Japan, 1: the domestic transformation.* K. Yamamura and Y. Yasuba (eds.), 423–468. Stanford: Stanford University Press.

Eisenstadt, S. N., and L. Roniger
1984 *Patrons, clients and friends.* Cambridge: Cambridge University Press.

Futatsugi, Yusaku
1986 *Japanese enterprise groups.* Kobe University, School of Business Administration.

Gold, T. B.
1985 *State and society in the Taiwan miracle.* Armonk, New York: M. E. Sharpe.

Goto, A.
1982 'Business groups in a market economy'. *European Economic Review* 19: 53–70.

Haggard, Stephen
1988 'The politics of industrialisation in the Republic of Korea and Taiwan' in *Achieving industrialisation in East Asia.* H. Hughes (ed.), 260–282. Cambridge: Cambridge University Press.

Haggard, Stephen, and T.-J. Cheng
1987 'State and foreign capital in the East Asian NICs' in *The political economy of the New Asian industrialism.* F. C. Deyo (ed.), 84–135. Ithaca, New York: Cornell University Press.

Hamilton, Gary
1984 'Patriarchalism in imperial China and western Europe'. *Theory and Society* 13: 393–426.

Hamilton, Gary, and C. S. Kao
1987 'The institutional foundation of Chinese business: the family firm in Taiwan'. Program in East Asian Culture and Development, Working Paper Series, No. 8. Institute of Governmental Affairs, University of California at Davis.

Hamilton, Gary, and N. W. Biggart
1988 'Market, culture and authority: a comparative analysis of management and organisation in the Far East'. *American Journal of Sociology* 94. Supplement: 552–594.

Hamilton, Gary, William Zeile, and W. J. Kim
1990 'The network structures of East Asian economies' in *Capitalism in contrasting cultures.* S. R. Clegg and G. Redding (eds.), 105–130. Berlin: Walter de Gruyter.

Hirschmeier, J., and T. Yui
1981 *The development of Japanese business 1600–1980,* 2nd ed. London: Allen and Unwin.

Ho, David Y. F.
1986 'Chinese patterns of socialisation: a critical review' in *The psychology of the Chinese people.* Michael Bond (ed.), 1–37. Hong Kong: Oxford University Press.

Imai, K., and H. Itami
1984 'Interpretation of organisation and market. Japan's firm and market in comparison with the U.S.'. *International Journal of Industrial Organisation* 2: 285–310.

Ingham, G.
1984   *Capitalism divided? The city and industry in British social development*. London: Macmillan.

Jacobs, Norman
1958   *The origin of modern capitalism and eastern Asia*. Hong Kong: Hong Kong University Press.

Jacobs, Norman
1985   *The Korean road to modernisation and development*. Urbana: University of Illinois Press.

Johnson, Chalmers
1982   *MITI and the Japanese miracle*. Stanford: Stanford University Press.

Johnson, Chalmers
1987   'Political institutions and economic performance: the government–business relationship in Japan, South Korea and Taiwan' in *The political economy of the new Asian industrialism*. F. C. Deyo (ed.), 136–164. Ithaca: Cornell University Press.

Jones, Leroy, and Il Sakong
1980   *Government, business and entrepreneurship in economic development: the Korean case*. Harvard: Harvard University Press.

Kagono, Tadao, Ikujiro Alonaka, Kiyonori Sakakibara, and Akihiro Okumara
1985   *Strategic vs. evolutionary management*. Amsterdam: North Holland.

Kim, Kyong-Dong
1979   *Man and society in Korea's economic growth*. Seoul: Seoul National University Press.

Kim, E. M.
1988   'From dominance to symbiosis: state and *chaebol* in Korea'. *Pacific Focus* 3: 105–121.

Kim, E. M.
1989   'Development, state policy and industrial organisation: the case of Korea's *chaebol*'. Paper presented to the International Conference on Business Groups and Economic Development in East Asia, Hong Kong, June 20–22.

Kono, Toyohiro
1984   *Strategy and structure of Japanese enterprises*. London: Macmillan.

Lawriwsky, Michael L.
1984   *Corporate structure and performance*. London: Croom Helm.

Levy, Brian
1988   'Korean and Taiwanese firms as international competitors: the challenges ahead'. *Columbia Journal of World Business* (Spring): 43–51.

Liebenberg, R. D.
1982   'Japan incorporated' and 'The Korean troops': a comparative analysis of Korean business organisations. Unpublished MA Thesis, Dept. of Asian Studies, University of Hawaii.

Limlingan, Victor S.
1986   *The overseas Chinese in Asean: business strategies and management practices*. Pasig, Metro Manila: Vita Development Corporation.

Lincoln, J. R., M. Hanada, and K. McBride
1986   'Organizational structures in Japanese and U.S. manufacturing'. *Administrative Science Quarterly* 31: 338–364.

Mariti, P., and R. H. Smiley
1983   'Co-operative agreements and the organisation of industry'. *Journal of Industrial Economics* 31: 437–451.

Maurice, Marc
1979   'For a study of "the societal effect": universality and specificity in organisation research' in *Organisations alike and unalike*. C. J. Lammers and D. J. Hickson (eds.), 42–60. London: Routledge and Kegan Paul.

Maurice, Marc, Arndt Sorge, and Malcolm Warner
1980   'Societal differences in organising manufacturing units'. *Organization Studies* 1/1: 59–86.

Maurice, Marc, Francois Sellier, and Jean-Jacques Silvestre
1986   *The social bases of industrial power*. Cambridge, Mass.: MIT Press.

Michell, Tony
1988   *From a developing to a newly industrialised country: the Republic of Korea, 1961–82*. Geneva: ILO.

Miyazaki, Yoshikazu
1980 'Excessive competition and the formation of *keiretsu*' in *Industry and business in Japan*. K. Sato (ed.), 53–73. New York: M. E. Sharpe.

Moore, B.
1966 *The social origins of dictatorship and democracy*. Boston: Beacon Press.

Myers, R. H.
1986 'The economic development of the Republic of China on Taiwan' in *Modes of development*. L. J. Lau (ed.). San Francisco: ICS Press.

Nishida, Judith
1990 *The Japanese influence on the Shanghaiese textile industry and implications for Hong Kong*. M.Phil. Thesis, University of Hong Kong.

Numazaki, I.
1986 'Networks of Taiwanese big business'. *Modern China* 12: 487–534.

Orru, M., Nicole W. Biggart, and Gary Hamilton
1988 'Organisational isomorphism in East Asia: broadening the new institutionalism'. Program in East Asian Culture and Development Research, Working Paper Series, No. 10. Institute of Governmental Affairs, University of California, Davis.

Pugh, Derek S., and Gordon R. Redding
1985 'The formal and the informal: Japanese and Chinese organisation structures' in *The enterprise and management in East Asia*. S. R. Clegg et al. (eds.). University of Hong Kong: Centre for Asian Studies.

Pye, Lucian W.
1985 *Asian power and politics: the cultural dimensions of authority*. Cambridge, Mass.: Harvard University Press.

Pye, Lucian W.
1988 'The new Asian capitalism: a political portrait', in *In search of an East Asian development model*. P. L. Berger and H.-H. M. Hsiao (eds.), 81–98. New Brunswick, N.J.: Transaction Books.

Redding, Gordon
1990 *The spirit of Chinese capitalism*. Berlin: Walter de Gruyter.

Redding, Gordon and S. Richardson
1986 'Participative management and its varying relevance in Hong Kong and Singapore'. *Asia Pacific Journal of Management* 3: 76–98.

Redding, Gordon, and Simon Tam
1985 'Networks and molecular organisations: an exploratory view of Chinese firms in Hong Kong' in *Perspectives in international business*. K. C. Mun and T. S. Chan (eds.). Hong Kong: Chinese University Press.

Redding, Gordon, and Gilbert Y. Y. Wong
1986 'The psychology of Chinese organisational behaviour' in *The psychology of the Chinese people*. M. Bond (ed.), 267–295. Oxford: Oxford University Press.

Richardson, George
1972 'The organisation of industry'. *Economic Journal* 82: 883–896.

Rohlen, Thomas P.
1974 *For harmony and strength: Japanese white-collar organisation in anthropological perspective*. Berkeley: University of California Press.

Rohlen, Thomas P.
1979 'The company work group' in *Modern Japanese organisation and decision-making*. E. F. Vogel (ed.), 185–209. Tokyo: Tuttle.

Shin, E. H., and S. W. Chin
1989 'Social affinity among top managerial executives of large corporation in Korea'. *Sociological Forum* 4: 3–26.

Silin, R. H.
1976 *Leadership and values. The organisation of large scale Taiwanese enterprises*. Cambridge, Mass.: Harvard University Press.

Smith, T. C.
1959 *The agrarian origins of modern Japan*. Stanford: Stanford University Press.

Smith, T. C.
1988 *Native sources of Japanese industri-
      alisation, 1750–1920.* Berkeley:
      University of California Press.

Smith, Peter B., and J. Misumi
1989 'Japanese management. A sun ris-
      ing in the west?' in *International
      review of industrial and organisa-
      tional psychology.* C. L. Cooper and
      I. Robertson (eds.). New York:
      Wiley.

Sorge, A., and Malcolm Warner
1986 *Comparative factory organisation.*
      Aldershot: Gower.

Tam, Simon
1990 'Centrifugal versus Centripetal
      growth processes: contrasting ideal
      types for conceptualising the devel-
      opmental patterns of Chinese and
      Japanese firms' in *Capitalism in con-
      trasting cultures.* S. R. Clegg and G.
      Redding (eds.), 153–183. Berlin:
      Walter de Gruyter.

Wade, Robert
1988 'The role of government in over-
      coming market failure: Taiwan,
      Republic of Korea and Japan' in
      *Achieving industrialisation in East
      Asia.* H. Hughes (ed.), 129–163.
      Cambridge: Cambridge University
      Press.

Ward, Barbara E.
1972 'A small factory in Hong Kong:
      some aspects of its internal
      organisation' in *Economic organisa-
      tion in Chinese society.* W. E.
      Wilmott (ed.), 353–385. Stanford:
      Stanford University Press.

Whitley, Richard
1990 'East Asian enterprise structures
      and the comparative analysis of
      forms of business organisation'.
      Organization Studies 11/1: 47–74.

Williamson, O. E.
1985 *The economic institutions of capital-
      ism.* New York: Free Press.

Wong, Siu-Lun
1988 'The applicability of Asian family
      values to other sociocultural set-
      tings' in *In search of an East Asian
      development model.* P. L. Berger
      and H.-H. M. Hsiao (eds.), 134–
      152. New Brunswick, N.J.: Transac-
      tion Books.

Yoo, S., and S. M. Lee
1987 'Management style and practice in
      Korean *Chaebols*'. *California
      Management Review* 29: 95–110.

Yoshihara, Kunio
1988 *The rise of Ersatz capitalism in
      South East Asia.* Oxford: Oxford
      University Press.

Yoshino, M. Y., and T. B. Lifson
1986 *The invisible link: Japan's Sogo
      Shosha and the organisation of
      trade.* Cambridge, Mass.: MIT
      Press.

Zeile, William
1989 'Industrial policy and organisational
      efficiency: the Korean *chaebol*
      examined'. Program in East Asian
      Culture and Development
      Research, Working Paper Series,
      No. 30. Institute of Governmental
      Affairs, University of California,
      Davis.

Zucker, Lynne G.
1986 'Production of trust: institutional
      sources of economic structure,
      1840–1920'. *Research in Organisa-
      tional Behaviour* 8: 53–111.

Zysman, John
1983 *Governments, markets and growth:
      financial systems and the politics of
      industrial change.* Ithaca: Cornell
      University Press.

Part II
Differences between Countries

[6]

The Cross-Cultural Puzzle of International Human Resource Management

—— André Laurent ——

INTERNATIONAL HUMAN RESOURCE MANAGEMENT: A FIELD IN INFANCY

As noted by Tichy (1983), the human resource field appears to be in a process of gradual and uneven transformation, where different companies may be experiencing different phases of transition: "endings," "in-between," "new beginning." Against this background, what can be said as to the status of the emerging field of International Human Resource Management which is the topic of this Symposium? Is there such a field?

Interestingly, the international dimension of HRM was apparently not retained among the important themes resulting from the previous HRM Symposium held at the University of Michigan two years ago. While the "importance of cultural phenomena" was selected (Tichy, 1983), this theme was framed more in terms of corporate cultures than in terms of national cultures and international implications.

The organizers of this Fontainebleau Symposium must be credited for creative leadership in launching a symbolic event that calls the attention of both executives and researchers on an emerging reality that is neither systematically managed nor extensively researched.

Recent labels like "Human Resource Management" or newer ones like "International Human Resource Management" obviously do not emerge by accident. Even though they often precede our understanding of what they mean, they are social productions that reflect some shared awareness of something important that has not been given enough attention in the past. When the new label is coined, it has the power of inviting people to wonder what it means and to inquire into the underlying reality which the label may be attempting to describe. In the field of organization studies, the concept of organizational culture seems to share a very similar history.

From a more practical point of view, there are some indications sug-

Human Resource Management, Spring 1986, Vol. 25, Number 1, Pp. 91–102
© 1986 by John Wiley & Sons, Inc.   CCC 0090-4848/86/010091-12$04.00

gesting that we are not all caught into some collective illusion. Many organizations are indeed confronted with the issues of managing human resources internationally. "Human Resource Managers" in such organizations are entitled to expect "Professors of HRM" to provide some useful insight on such processes. Yet these new international processes are so complex and so poorly defined and ill-understood at the moment that superficiality remains the mark of most current treatments, including the one attempted during this Symposium. As an illustration of this primitive state of affairs, would it be unfair to suggest that in many cases during this Symposium, participants have made a point of finishing their sentences with the four magic and official words: "within an international context." It remains to be assessed whether the former part of the sentences would have differed in the absence of that ending. If the field of HRM is in a stage of adolescence, International HRM is still at the infancy stage. The intent of this paper is to contribute to the framing of this new domain in building upon the author's inquiry into the cultural diversity of management conceptions across nations.

HRM PRACTICES AS INSTITUTIONALIZED PREFERENCES FOR THE MANAGEMENT OF PEOPLE

Managers in organizations hold particular sets of assumptions, ideas, beliefs, preferences, and values on how to manage people toward the attainment of some organizational goals. Over time these various ideas get translated into particular policies, systems, and practices which in turn may reinforce or alter the original ideas. Furthermore, organizational members have sets of expectations related to those practices which may again reinforce or alter the existing policies. Through this complex process of mutual interaction between various actors' ideas and actions, certain preferred ways of managing people tend to emerge in some organized fashion which we may then call Human Resource Management.

As different organizations have developed different ways of managing their human resources that seem to have been more or less successful, this observation has reinforced the intuition that more strategic thinking was required in this area and that some competitive advantage could be acquired through some form of excellence. Future historians of work organizations may well have a hard time understanding why it took so long to realize the strategic importance of the management of human resources.

If HRM policies and practices reflect managers' assumptions about how to manage people, it becomes very critical to understand such assumptions in order to correctly interpret the meaning of particular policies and practices.

NATIONAL DIFFERENCES IN MANAGEMENT ASSUMPTIONS:
A RESEARCH INQUIRY

In the past few years, we have been interested in systematically exploring management assumptions in an attempt to enrich our understanding of management and organizational processes. The initial research objective was not to explore national differences but to bring into focus some of the implicit management and organizational theories that managers carry in their heads (Laurent, 1981).

As it is very difficult to inquire into beliefs that individuals take for granted, our research strategy has consisted in writing up a large number of possible assumptions about the management of organizations which we inferred from discussing organizational issues with managers. These assumptions were expressed in the form of statements within a standard questionnaire that would seek from respondents their degree of agreement/disagreement with such statements.

Typical survey statements read as follows:

• The main reason for having a hierarchical structure is so that everyone knows who has authority over whom.
• Most managers seem to be more motivated by obtaining power than by achieving objectives.
• It is important for a manager to have at hand precise answers to most of the questions that his subordinates may raise about their work.
• In order to have efficient work relationships, it is often necessary to bypass the hierarchical line.
• Most managers would achieve better results if their roles were less precisely defined.
• An organizational structure in which certain subordinates have two direct bosses should be avoided at all costs.

Successive groups of managers participating in executive development programs at INSEAD (The European Institute of Business Administration) were surveyed. These managers came from many different companies and many different countries.

When their responses were analyzed, it appeared that the most powerful determinant of their assumptions was by far their nationality. Overall and across 56 different items of inquiry, it was found that nationality had three times more influence on the shaping of managerial assumptions than any of the respondents' other characteristics such as age, education, function, type of company . . . etc.

One of the most illustrative examples of national differences in management assumptions was reflected in the respondents' reaction to the following statement:

It is important for a manager to have at hand precise answers to most of the questions that his subordinates may raise about their work.

As indicated in Figure 1, while only a minority of Northern American and Northern European managers agreed with this statement, a majority of Southern Europeans and South-East Asians did. The research results indicated that managers from different national cultures vary widely as to their basic conception of what management is all about (Laurent, 1983).

Conceptions of organizations were shown to vary as widely across national cultures as conceptions of their management did. Across a sample of 10 Western national cultures, managers from Latin cultures (French and Italians) consistently perceived organizations as social systems of relationships monitored by power, authority, and hierarchy to a much greater extent than their Northern counterparts did.

American managers held an "instrumental" view of the organization as a set of tasks to be achieved through a problem-solving hierarchy where positions are defined in terms of tasks and functions and where authority is functionally based. French managers held a "social" view of the organization as a collective of people to be managed through a formal hierarchy, where positions are defined in terms of levels of

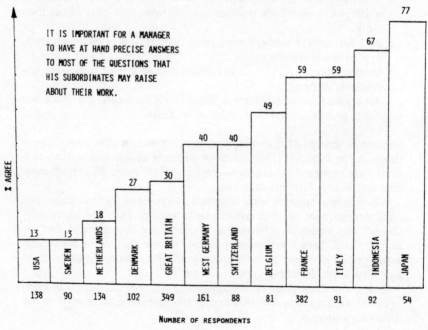

Figure 1.

authority and status and where authority is more attached to individuals than it is to their offices or functions (Inzerilli and Laurent, 1983). Once these results were obtained, the question arose as to whether the corporate culture of multinational organizations would reduce some of the observed national differences and therefore bring some more homogeneity in the picture.

A new research study was designed to test this hypothesis. Carefully matched national groups of managers working in the affiliated companies of a large U.S. multinational firm were surveyed with the same standard questionnaire. The overall results gave no indication of convergence between national groups. Their cultural differences in management assumptions were not reduced as a result of working for the same multinational firm. If anything, there was slightly more divergence between the national groups within this multinational company than originally found in the INSEAD multi-company study. These findings were later replicated with smaller matched national samples of managers in several American and European multinational corporations.

The overall research findings led to the conclusion that deep-seated managerial assumptions are strongly shaped by national cultures and appear quite insensitive to the more transient culture of organizations.

Further exploration was conducted with different methods of inquiry in order to better assess the validity of the findings. In one research study, a large U.S.-based multinational corporation was approached because of its high professional reputation in human resource management. This corporation has implemented for years a standardized worldwide system for the multiple assessment of managerial potential and performance. Open-ended interviews were conducted across a number of affiliated companies in an attempt to identify what managers perceived as being important to be successful in their career. This led to a list of 60 criteria mentioned by managers as being most important for career success. Matched national groups of managers were later asked, in a systematic survey, to select among these 60 criteria those they saw as most important for career success within the firm.

For the American managers, the single most important criterion in order to have a successful career with the company was "Ambition and Drive"—a pragmatic, individualistic, achievement-oriented, and "instrumental" reading of the assessment system. The French managers saw things quite differently. For them the single most important criterion was "Being labelled as having high potential," a more "social" and political reading of the same system. The degree of consensus on what it takes to be successful was significantly higher within the American Affiliate—culturally closer to the designers of the HRM system—than it was in the British, Dutch, German, and French Affiliates.

In spite of the convergence effects that could be expected from a similar and global administrative system of assessment and reward, managed by the U.S. Headquarters on a worldwide basis, a remarkable degree of cultural diversity was observed again across countries in managers' perceptions of the determinants of career success. In a later part of the study, the same national groups of managers were asked to list what they thought were the features of a well-functioning organization, the attributes of effective managers, and the most important things that effective managers should be doing.

The analysis of some of the results can be summarized as follows:

German managers, more than others, believed that creativity is essential for career success. In their mind, the successful manager is the one who has the right individual characteristics. Their outlook is rational: they view the organization as a coordinated network of individuals who make appropriate decisions based on their professional competence and knowledge.

British managers hold a more interpersonal and subjective view of the organizational world. According to them, the ability to create the right image and to get noticed for what they do is essential for career success. They view the organization primarily as a network of relationships between individuals who get things done by influencing each other through communicating and negotiating.

French managers look at the organization as an authority network where the power to organize and control the actors stems from their positioning in the hierarchy. They focus on the organization as a pyramid of differentiated levels of power to be acquired or dealt with. French managers perceive the ability to manage power relationships effectively and to "work the system" as particularly critical to their success.

From the perspective of these various results, international human resource management may only be international in the eyes of the designers.

DISCUSSION

Naive parochialism has plagued the field of Management and Organization Studies for a long time. The societal and cultural context of theories and practices has long been ignored or overlooked by both researchers and practitioners (Hofstede, 1980). Management approaches developed in one particular culture have been deemed valid for any other culture. Models of excellence (Peters and Waterman, 1982) are still being presented with virtues of universality.

A comparative analysis across national cultures brings the startling evidence that there is no such thing as Management with a capital M. The art of managing and organizing has no homeland.

Every culture has developed through its own history some specific and unique insight into the managing of organizations and of their human resources. At the same time, any single cultural model may become pathological when pushed to its extreme, an illustration of the fact that every culture has also developed specific and unique blindspots in the art of managing and organizing. There lie the still largely undiscovered opportunities and threats of international management.

The emerging field of Human Resource Management is not compelled to fall into the trap of universalism. It has the opportunity and the challenge to integrate cultural relativity in its premises. In fact, and given the global context of international business, this field has no choice but to take into full consideration the international dimension of the organizational world.

Comparative research shows that managers from different national cultures hold different assumptions as to the nature of management and organization. These different sets of assumptions shape different value systems and get translated into different management and organizational practices which in turn reinforce the original assumptions. Among such practices, human resource management practices are likely to be most sensitive to cultural diversity as they are designed by culture bearers in order to handle other culture bearers. Thus the assumptions and values of the local designers are likely to be amplified by the expectations of the natives to create a cultural product that may be highly meaningful and potentially effective for the home country but possibly meaningless, confusing, and ineffective for another country.

If we accept the view that HRM approaches are cultural artifacts reflecting the basic assumptions and values of the national culture in which organizations are imbedded, international HRM becomes one of the most challenging corporate tasks in multinational organizations.

With varying degrees of awareness, such organizations are confronted all the time with strategic choices that need to be made in order to optimize the quality and effectiveness of their very diverse human resources around the world. In order to build, maintain, and develop their corporate identity, multinational organizations need to strive for consistency in their ways of managing people on a worldwide basis. Yet, and in order to be effective locally, they also need to adapt those ways to the specific cultural requirements of different societies. While the global nature of the business may call for increased consistency, the variety of cultural environments may be calling for differentiation.

Faced with such a high degree of strategic complexity in managing human resources internationally, corporations have become increasingly seduced by a new and highly attractive dream called corporate culture, that would encapsulate on a worldwide basis their own genuine and unique ways of managing people. What if our corporate culture could act as a "supra-culture" and be expected to supersede some of the annoying specificities of the different national cultures in which we operate?

Indeed different organizations from the same country develop different organizational cultures over time and there is no doubt that the recent recognition of the importance and reality of organizational cultures represents a step forward in our understanding of organizations and of their management. However, and in spite of the interest of the concept, it would probably be illusionary to expect that the recent and short history of modern corporations could shape the basic assumptions of their members to an extent that would even approximate the age-long shaping of civilizations and nations. Indeed the comparative research reported above indicates that the corporate culture of long established large multinationals does not seem to reduce national differences in basic management assumptions across their subsidiaries.

Our tentative interpretation of this finding is that a conceptualization of organizational cultures in terms of basic assumptions (Schein, 1985) may be searching for the reality of organizational culture at a deeper level than it really is. To a certain extent, it may be useful to interpret the current appropriation of the concept of culture in the field of organization studies as a modern attempt at increasing the legitimacy of management in business firms by calling upon a higher order concept of almost indisputable essence. Who can deny the existence of an IBM culture?

Instead of locating the roots of organizational culture at the deepest level of basic assumptions, an alternative and possibly more realistic view would be to restrict the concept of organizational culture to the more superficial layers of implicit and explicit systems of norms, expectations, and historically-based preferences, constantly reinforced by their behavioral manifestations and their assigned meanings. Under this view, organizational members would be seen as adjusting to the behavioral requirements of organizational cultures without necessarily being so deeply immersed into their ideological textures.

Consistent with the previous arguments on the deep impact of national cultures upon organizational theories and practices, our proposed interpretation of the concept of organizational culture probably reflects the Frenchness of the author through his eagerness to differentiate "actors and systems" (Crozier and Friedberg, 1977).

Thus on the international scene, a French manager working in the French subsidiary of an American corporation that insists on an open-door policy may very well leave his office door open—thus adjusting to the behavioral requirements of the corporate culture—without any modification whatsoever of his basic conception of managerial authority. In the French subsidiary of a Swedish firm, whose corporate values include an almost religious reliance upon informality, French shopfloor employees were recently observed as addressing their managers by their first names and using the intimate "tu" form within the boundaries of the firm. The same individuals immediately reverted to "Monsieur le Directeur" and the more formal "vous" form whenever meeting outside the firm.

Similarly the degree of ingeniosity and creativity that can be observed in order to recreate private space and status out of open space offices probably expresses some of the same dynamics whereby organizational members may very well play the expected game without abdicating their own personal values.

Deep-rooted assumptions could then be better understood as the historical result of broader cultural contexts like civilizations and nations. Organizations would only select from the available repertory of their larger cultural context a limited set of ideas that best fit their own history and modes of implementation. This would be called their organizational culture and would strongly reflect national characteristics of the founders and dominant elite of the organization (Hofstede, 1985).

STEPS TOWARD THE INTERNATIONAL MANAGEMENT OF HUMAN RESOURCES

In dealing with other cultures than their home-based culture, international organizations need to recognize more explicitly that they are dealing with different "fabrics of meaning" (Geertz, 1973). Therefore, whatever can be the strength, cohesiveness, or articulated nature of their corporate cultures, the same HRM policy or practice is likely to be attributed quite different meanings by different cultural groups. Behavioral adjustment may occur at a superficial level and provide the designer from Headquarters with an illusory feeling of satisfaction in front of apparent homogeneity across subsidiaries. The dances will appear similar while their actual meaning may be quite different and thus lead to very different outcomes than anticipated. Fortunately, in many other cases, the dances will also be different enough across subsidiaries so as to effectively remind Headquarters that the rest of the world is different from "home."

In the Italian subsidiary, the introduction of a Management-by-Objectives system may be experienced as follows: "We used to be rewarded for our accomplishments and punished for our failures. Why should we now sign our own punishment even before trying?" For the Indonesian affiliate company, the inclusion of negative feedback in performance appraisal interviews may mean "an unhealthy pollution of harmonious hierarchical relationships." The introduction of a matrix-type multiple reporting relationship system may be experienced as a horrible case of divided loyalty in the Mexican subsidiary. Unlike many others, the subsidiaries of Swedish multinational corporations may complain that they do not receive enough "help" from Headquarters. Participative management may mean very different things to Scandinavians and North Americans.

To a large extent, Human Resource Managers who operate internationally know these things and multinational organizations have accumulated wisdom from experience and developed skills to handle cultural diversity. Yet, more often than not, such organizations must have learned by accident or out of necessity how to cope with cultural differences. Only on rare occasions have they explicitly and consciously set out to develop a truly multinational identity by building upon cultural differences in their human resources. How many headquarters genuinely believe that they can learn from their foreign subsidiaries? How many implement such a rare belief by internationalizing headquarters' staff and top management? It may be that recent trends toward multinational cooperative ventures and networks (Lorange, 1985), characterized by a lesser degree of centralized power, will accelerate such development processes.

A truly international conception of human resource management would require a number of critical and painful steps that have not occurred yet in most instances:

- an explicit recognition by the headquarter organization that its own peculiar ways of managing human resources reflect some assumptions and values of its home culture.
- that as such these peculiar ways are neither universally better or worse than others, they are different and they are likely to exhibit strengths and weaknesses particularly when travelling abroad.
- an explicit recognition by the headquarter organization that its foreign subsidiaries may have other preferred ways of managing people that are neither intrinsically better nor worse but that could possibly be more effective locally.
- a willingness from headquarters to not only acknowledge cultural differences but also to take active steps in order to make them discussable and therefore usable.
- the building of a genuine belief by all parties involved that more creative and effective ways of managing people could be developed as a result of cross-cultural learning.

Obviously such steps cannot be dictated or easily engineered. They have more to do with states of mind and mindsets than with behaviors. As such, these processes can only be facilitated and this may represent a primary mission for executives in charge of international human resource management. They may also represent some of the prerequisites and foundations for the development of forward-looking international corporate cultures.

Such cultures could then provide the impetus and the proper framing to address important strategic issues in the area of international HRM such as: how much consistency and which similarity in policies and practices should be developed? How much variety and differentiation and what adaptation should be encouraged? Which policies should be universal and global? Which ones should be local? Which HRM practices should be designed at the center? Locally? By international teams?

Which processes can be invented to reach agreement on objectives and allow variable paths to achieve them? Which passports should key managers have in the headquarter organization and in the main subsidiaries? Home office nationals? Country nationals? Third nationals? How much and which expatriation should occur? How to manage the whole expatriation process? How to properly assess management potential when judgment criteria differ from country to country? How to orchestrate the management of careers internationally? All of these issues require strategic choices that cannot be left to an obscure function as they need to be fully integrated in a global vision of the firm and as they feed and shape that vision.

The challenge faced by the infant field of international human resource management is to solve a multi-dimensional puzzle located at the crossroad of national and organizational cultures. Research is needed on the various strategies that international firms are using as their own attempts at solving the puzzle.

Professor of Organizational Behavior at INSEAD, the European Institute of Business Administration, Fontainebleau, France, André Laurent is a graduate of the Ecole de Psychologues Praticiens de Paris, the University of Paris-Sorbonne (Lisence in Sociology and Doctorate in Psychology) and Harvard University (International Teachers Program). He has been associated for four years with Pechiney as an industrial psychologist in West Africa and for three years with the Institute for Social Research at the University of Michigan as Research Associate and Study Director before joining INSEAD in 1970. Since then he has been a Visiting Scholar at Stanford University, a Visiting Professor at the European Institute for Advanced Studies in Management in Brussels and a consultant to a number of multinational companies.

REFERENCES

Crozier, M., and Friedberg, E. *L'Acteur et le Systeme: Les Contraintes de L'Action Collective*. Paris: Editions du Seuil, 1977.

Geertz, C. *The Interpretation of Cultures: Selected Essays*. New York: Basic Books, 1973.

Hofstede, G. Motivation, Leadership and Organization: Do American Theories Apply Abroad? *Organizational Dynamics*, Summer 1980, 42–63.

Hofstede. G. The Interaction between National and Organizational Value Systems. *Journal of Management Studies*, 1985, 22(4), 347–357.

Inzerilli, G., and Laurent, A. Managerial Views of Organization Structure in France and the USA. *International Studies of Management and Organization*, 1983, XIII(1/2), 97–118.

Laurent, A. Matrix Organizations and Latin Cultures. A Note on the Use of Comparative Research Data in Management Education. *International Studies of Management and Organization*, 1981, X(4), 101–114.

Laurent, A. The Cultural Diversity of Western Conceptions of Management. *International Studies of Management and Organization*, 1983, XIII(1/2), 75–96.

Lorange, P. Human Resource Management in Multinational Cooperative Ventures and Networks. Paper presented at the International Human Resource Management Symposium, Fontainebleau, August 20–23, 1985.

Peters T. J., and Waterman, R. H. *In Search of Excellence*. New York: Harper & Row, 1982.

Schein, E. H. *Organizational Culture and Leadership*. San Francisco: Jossey-Bass Publishers, 1985.

Tichy, N. M. Foreword. *Human Resource Management*, 1983, **22**(1/2), 3–8.

[7]

Discusses the need to understand better cultural diversity in international business.

Culture and Change: Conflict or Consensus?

Bruce Lloyd and Fons Trompenaars

Leadership & Organization Development Journal. Vol. 14 No. 6. 1993. pp. 17-23
© MCB University Press. 0143-7739

In this article, Bruce Lloyd, Head of Strategic and International Management at South Bank University, discusses with Fons Trompenaars, author of Riding the Waves of Culture *(Economist Books, 1993, £20) and Managing Director of the Centre for International Business Studies, the need to better understand cultural diversity in international business.*

BL. Your book is on a vitally important subject. Perhaps we can start with a summary of the key issues in the book.

FT. There are three levels to my answer. First. I hope to make people more aware of differences in culture and their fundamental nature through understanding *themselves*. And you can only understand yourself through others. Extending this first basic point using my own experience. When I went to America for two years. I came back understanding more about the Dutch in me and the French in me than the American culture. It is about basic assumptions that we normally take for granted and suddenly you realize that, in other cultures, your obvious solutions don't work or are not appreciated: that is the first basic point in the book, using anecdotes and humour. The study challenges some of our assumptions that we are taking for granted. Following

from that, there is a second level, which is to generate greater *respect* for other cultures and then different logics: respect tends to increase especially if you can see that most of the cultural variety is in yourself. For example, losing face is not just something for Orientals; it is in all of us and just manifests itself in different ways. Out of the increased awareness I hope to raise respect for differences. The third point I argue is that, from awareness that we are different and that we respect differences, we ask the question, "How can we take better advantage of these differences?" This means the development of processes focusing on the reconciliation of cultural dilemmas. How can we reconcile the dilemma of the rule and the exception, the individual and the group, the future and the past? Such an approach results in a whole area of questioning becoming very different because, if you take the typical traditional Western way of thinking, we seem to choose between extremes such as between centralized and decentralized, between the individual and the group. The key point in my book is that the quality of centralization will determine the quality of decentralization. In a nutshell, awareness, respect and taking advantage of cultural differences are the three basic points I am trying to make in the book.

BL. But what if respect doesn't follow understanding? And how do you ensure that taking advantage doesn't degenerate into exploitation?

FT. Real understanding of cultural differences for me means that you recognize the other's point of view as a part of yourself. Once you see that, respect cannot be avoided; and respect will never lead to exploitation. Obviously, that does not mean that an increased insight cannot lead to exploitation. The advantage, however, of the reconciliation process developed by Charles Hampden-Turner is that it leads to synthesis that includes the thesis of one cultural assumption and the antithesis of another. In other words, while keeping your own cultural preferences, you can enrich them by their opposite. Let me give you an example. An American firm producing microprocessors was continuously looking for the next *universal* chip. Their European subsidiaries were complaining because the particular needs of their clients were seen as a threat to the development of the next universal chip. If we then apply our methodology of reconciling cultural dilemmas, we would approach it as follows: how can we create a situation in which the particular demands of European clients can become an input to the development of a higher quality universal microprocessor that can cope with even more exceptions? American "universalism" is reconciled through European "particularism", while not giving up any of the core cultural values. This is the future challenge of our field . And we need the exceptional creative talents of people. like Charles Hampden-Turner, to lift the field beyond recognition of differences. How we can take advantage of differences is our challenge.

18   **LEADERSHIP & ORGANIZATION DEVELOPMENT JOURNAL 14,6**

BL. Can I start by asking some fundamental questions about the approach you have taken. Is there really a homogeneity of cultural characteristics that can be associated with national or ethnic identities? This is an important issue in its own right but it is also particularly relevant if we are considering the whole area dynamically. Do such characteristics that might exist change over time? And how do they change? Using one illustration: within the US, the UK, France, Nigeria or India there appear to be many regional differences within the national identity that could confuse any study that focuses on using it to define the research boundaries. Of course, national identity is relatively easy to research because there is a well-defined boundary to the definition. But, today, with greater mobility of people (at least some), surely this boundary is getting less and less valid as the vehicle for defining cultural characteristics. Is it really the best definitional vehicle for understanding what is going on and what is changing?

FT. First, let me separate the change issue from the question of national identity. There are two levels. To start with, there is the reality of being Dutch or being British as a level of culture: then there is the way you perceive these differences. The way I explain this is through the use of normal curves, where you see all the variety but it is still a bell shape. If two bell curves overlap there is a tendency to exaggerate the differences. One piece of research I did at Shell, which is not in the book, involved asking questions of the Dutch about what they think the British would do here and, of the British, what do they think the Dutch would do here? The answers tended to double the differences between the two bell distributions and, in that sense, national identity could be focused to say: (1) there is a lot of variety here or (2) there are still significant differences within that bell shape. To take one example: America, where they claim not to really know what I am talking about because there is so much variety: The East Coast is very different from the West and black is different to white. The approach I take identifies both the variety and the common characteristics. The national identity boundary I have drawn is as artificial as any other boundary in terms of culture. In another book, I looked at functional differences, including the famous cultural question: which is closer to each other, the Italian R and D person and the Italian marketing person, or the Italian R and D person and the Dutch R and D person. The issue of change is a subtle one. Once people acknowledge that their survival is at stake, change is very often the result. However, culture is also part of how problems are solved and success, or the lack of crisis, is often the biggest enemy of cultural change. As a result, basic assumptions remain unchallenged. And people who travel more and more often find this leads to a reconfirmation of the superiority of their own value orientations.

BL. This is a very important issue as there is pressure from many directions to break down the whole concept of stereotyping. We are drawn, at one level for example, by equal opportunities legislation and pressure to avoid stereotyping. There is an assumption in your book, and in the approach that you take which could reinforce the whole concept of stereotyping. Is your approach actually in keeping with what many organizations today are actually trying to do?

Stereotyping

FT. Let me reply by making a provocative statement which I very often quote at the beginning of a workshop where we discuss all these issues. For increasing awareness, I have nothing against stereotyping. The problem with stereotyping arises when you don't know you are doing it. On the pedagogical level, I can give an anecdote (and I recognize that anecdotes are stereotypes too) – Italians walk out of the room rather than accept criticism: others laugh and say "Yes, I recognize that." But I know groups of Italians who do not walk out of the room and I know groups of Japanese who also walk out of the room. So I say stereotyping is OK as long as you know you are doing it. The second problem with stereotyping is that we always give it a negative connotation. The French are showing emotions so we say the French are neurotic, and neurotic has negative connotations. The purpose of my book is to use stereotyping to both make a point clear but, more importantly, it will I hope increase understanding and respect so that we can all work together more easily. If we use stereotypes positively no one argues. We must be careful to understand any stereotypes that we use, and then use them positively to further communications: not as an excuse for creating barriers. But, at the same time, I fully accept the risks and criticisms of some of the more traditional approaches to stereotyping. However, my book is not about reinforcing the traditional approach to stereotyping; it is about emphasizing the variety of mankind. All the statistics reflect this variety. There are no cases of 0 per cent or 100 per cent. It is a bit grey – as one would expect. Secondly, I hope people will see that many of the so-called negative stereotypes can flip into something positive if you put another interpretation on them. It is the value judgements that we make about the qualities associated with so-called stereotyping that are the real problem. In workshops, I discuss one of the examples quoted in the book about a car accident and whether you would help a friend in court if you knew he was driving too fast. The figures show that, in general, Venezualians would help their friend while others would call that corrupt because they believe there are rules that ought to be respected and these include not lying, even if it is to protect your friend. But this needs reinterpreting. OK, the Anglo-Saxons and Europeans would say the Venezualians are more corrupt and you cannot trust them because they show a strong tendency to put helping their friends as a high priority. But I then ask the question: What do the Venezualians think about the British? And guess what! They say the British are corrupt and you cannot trust them because they will not even help their friends! What I do is to establish the stereotype then flip it over and challenge the underlying assumptions behind the associations made with the stereotype.

BL. That is a very important example. But what comes out of your comments is that, if there is common understanding and respect over the way that you are using language to communicate, then it is OK to use stereotyped words. But does not part of the cultural issue arise over the use of language and the meaning of words? This is now becoming a particularly sensitive issue in some cultures, which are very concerned with the whole subject under the umbrella of "political correctness" which is an attempt to focus on changing the use of language to change attitudes and behaviours. In some ways this raises even wider cultural issues since, essentially, what is being attempted is to contribute to a change in the culture through changing the use of language. This leads on to one of the particularly fascinating aspects of your book, which is how you come to terms with the dynamic of culture change. For example, if you and I look at our parents' attitudes to many issues when they were our age, and compare them to ours today, we would see many radical changes inside the framework of any particular national culture. How much time-series analysis have you undertaken on the questions you ask, to see how so-called national characteristics are changing over time?

FT. I have done some but it is limited to the past 12 years, which is a relatively short period. On the other hand, if you look at a country like Germany you can see dramatic changes over a very short period. When we did the research initially, just before the Berlin Wall came down, the spread of views was much smaller than when we redid the work after the Wall had come down. At that later stage, they were in turmoil. But before the "revolution" I had the feeling that East Germans were filling in the questionnaires with a much greater emphasis on answers they felt they were suppose to give. From a methodological point of view there are some tricks that can be used to check those uncertainties. The use of little stories and the third person tense rather than the first person. In the turmoil, and immediately afterwards, there were enormous differences in the answers to various questions and I wondered if the cultures would realign again, not out of the "shoulds" versus the "I wants", but they would get closer because they interact so much.

Another interesting phenomenon is that the dynamics within each culture are different. We can see how Americans have changed over the past 12 years, and it is

essentially summed up by the phrase "traumatically unWesternizing". Again, one factor might be that they have become conscious of the way they feel they ought to answer the questions, and they are concerned that they are answering the questions in a too American stereotyped way; they now think more about how they think the Japanese would answer the questions, as opposed to the other possibility that they feel differently about these things without consciously arguing in themselves that they should, and so they really are changing. That is a tricky issue where it would again be necessary to discuss methodology. Other cultures are more stable over time; for example, French views have hardly changed over the past ten years.

BL. Maybe this is a good point to consider methodology because one of the points raised in the data appeared to be that most of your sample are at university graduate level, and it could be that one of the cultural dimensions is the extent to which that group is developing a worldwide homogeneous university graduate "culture" which is being superimposed – if not dominating – national cultures; in a similar way to the functional point you mentioned earlier. This international culture being significantly different to the basic national culture – at least until the widespread advent of the international media which is both developing its own cultural legacy, at the same time as changing traditional cultural patterns.

FT. Methodologically my answer is "yes". If you are considering the workshops I run – more and more of these groups are at university graduate level. But, in the original piece of research, many more levels of society were included. However, if you compare both samples for a particular country, the only thing you see is that the normal curve gets a little narrower for university graduates but the rank order remains the same. In other words, there is some universalization of the culture, but the essential elements still remain identifiable. Then there are gender issues. And my answer to that is that the effect of gender differences on the scores is dependent on the culture you are in. In other words, if we take the US male/female responses, there are much smaller differences than in Holland or the UK. This shows the effect that the more powerful emancipation culture can have on the traditional divisions within male/female subcultures. In some cultures, the men seem to give more general (i.e. broad) responses while, in other cultures, they are more specific (i.e. narrower).

BL. Are you arguing that this has arisen because the American educational system has been more integrated for longer and so it has produced this effect?

FT. In addition to which the pressure for equality is so great in America that both genders should give almost the same answers. In other societies, where they are less integrated throughout the whole educational process,

20   **LEADERSHIP & ORGANIZATION DEVELOPMENT JOURNAL 14,6**

they develop their own subcultures where these differences are accepted, recognized and respected (even if not encouraged) rather than assuming that there is essentially an equality culture and ideology that appears to be the case in the US.

BL. Again, there are not necessarily any problems with differences if these are used positively. However, what you could say is that this kind of analysis is done on subcultures (for instance, gay culture) which could indicate some particular strengths and weaknesses that could require managers to take these differences into consideration when taking particular decisions, such as recruitment. What happens then? How do you deal with this issue?

FT. This is a very important point. I'll give you an example about status – an example which I don't think is in the book. It is about what gives people status. An American company was opening a Turkish marketing office employing only Turks except the person at the top. The US company said that they needed a new infusion of marketing and sales into the Turkish outfit. Their ideal candidate was an American woman with an excellent track record. In theory, ideal. The American company sent her. It is easy to explain why things went wrong – and that could have applied if the person had been gay or black. The issue is the same. What, as a company, do you do with that kind of information? Using this example, there is also the risk now that the woman could have sued you, the company, for discrimination if she had not been sent, if she was the best candidate. That is exactly why my title is *Riding the Waves of Culture*. It is not a matter of just saying the Turks are wrong because they appear to discriminate against women; nor is it an issue about putting the Turks through a crash programme of workshops to explain how we are all equal. The two extremes are, on the one hand, total respect for the local culture, while, at the other extreme, there is the view that we have a corporate culture that must dominate all our thinking and decisions without it becoming a form of cultural colonialism. The question is how can you best reconcile the two viewpoints? It is not easy. Any attempt at reconciliation would show that any cultural dichotomy which does not have the right tension between it will lead to a pathology. So, over-discrimination between males and females leads to a pathology which involves greater differences and less equality between them – you need both. For me the message is reconciling these differences. Charles Hampden-Turner painted it well when he said the issue was how to universalize the particular and, at the same time, how to particularize the universal – to individualize the collective, at the same time as collectivizing the individual. That is the next step. For me, that is a methodology of thinking, a way of thinking, which I think stops all the otherwise unhelpful discussion about the impact and role of so-called minority cultures or even issues about national differences of, say, Nigerians and French.

BL. This is the answer we need to accept in order to work with the material and take the next step. But, to take another dimension. If you are managing a multinational corporation you are looking at it one way – trying to produce homogeneously common criteria – whereas, if you are marketing products you look at it from a different viewpoint. One approach is attempting to integrate the differences, while the other is attempting to exploit them. And many multinationals find it necessary to attempt to do both at the same time. In the end, if you are managing cultural diversity within the same organization, or within organizations that are keen to have relations with each other, there must be some common acceptance of the rules that govern the relationship, like cricket or football. If you don't play by common, accepted rules how can you all play the same game? And even with a general acceptance of rules there is still need for a referee or umpire!

FT. I take the point. But I would argue the higher the quality of the rules, the more variety they can cope with successfully. The metaphor is that of the pendulum. The more you want it to swing at the bottom the higher the quality needed from the nail at the top. The nail is the rule, and I would argue that the quality of the rules established at the top need to be increased so that the pendulum can better swing at the bottom. It is typically Charles Hampden-Turner – the more we expect of decentralization, the more effective has to be the centralization. It is the whole issue of differentiation and integration.

BL. But the paradox that occurs in many organizations is that they don't have the right quality of rules set by the top. What they have is quantity; pretending that makes control more effective.

FT. Exactly. So they have a lot of nails which only end up by limiting the amount of swing in the pendulum.

BL. And this encourages people to play games with the rules, rather than being committed to the core ideas, or spirit, of the process, and relying on trust to implement the ideas. The solution to this dilemma is to get the right people and make sure that the cultural experience of the people is as rich, high quality and integrated with the messages of the corporation and this then enables them to operate effectively, essentially without the rules. Then there is the paradox of trust, which is that you will not be able to trust others if you are not able to be trusted yourself.

FT. I fully agree. What you are doing there is internalizing the rules so that you don't need them anymore. That is what we mean by the corporation's culture.

BL. But this comes back to the theme of your book that we have already touched on. Many people would argue that the IBM corporate culture is more different from the Apple corporate culture, than any differences between national cultures. And that could be generalized as reflecting inherent differences between large mature organizations and small entrepreneurial ones, irrespective of where they operate in the world. This means that much of your methodological approach could equally be applied to examining and integrating different corporate cultures (perhaps after mergers, for example), as well as trying to get national cultures to work better together.

FT. I hope in a synthesizing way. For example, I was working with Shell and I found that wherever I was in the world, it was essentially the same Shell culture; but, at the same time, I felt it was completely different. If you can create a corporate culture like that you can have a real chance of operating successfully in today's multicultural environment.

BL. In many ways, the most challenging corporate issues for the twenty-first century are managing those large corporate culture issues.

Control or Chaos?

FT. And I would add that the quality of the corporate culture is how much cultural variety can it take. Going back to the *law* of Requisite Variety – any system will die if it does not have variety within it to match that of the environment.

BL. So, you come back to the key issue of how you manage cultural diversity.

FT. Essentially as a helix.

BL. Without the centrifugal forces being out of control leading to chaos.

FT. Yes. Managing variety can easily lead to enormous chaos, if you don't get it right.

BL. Absolutely. And that is what the control systems are designed to prevent. The more those at the top understand the patterns they are dealing with, and the more they are able to trust others (and themselves), the easier it will be to have that variety at the same time as retain effective control. Chaos theory almost seems to be part of this new culture. Yet, at the same time, it is part of a new pattern and the difficulty in managing this process comes because those who are responsible for it (i.e. those that control the pins at the top) don't sufficiently understand the fundamental issues they are dealing with.

FT. That's a fair comment. And I make that point in the book.

BL. At the core of the whole subject are issues to do with ethics, values, corruption and integrity. And this can be a (if not *the most*) particularly culturally sensitive subject, as there are a variety of ways different cultures interpret these issues. I wonder how far you can rely on some of the data you obtained because people from certain cultures may feel that they are answering the question on behalf of their cultural identity, rather than a deep-down personal view. For example, one set of questions seems to indicate that the Japanese do not exploit inside information for personal gain. I wonder how far that is actually reflected in their behaviour in their active financial markets, or is it just that they have (like Britain) a sophisticated system of hypocrisy?

FT. First, a mundane answer. Everyone is involved in some hypocrisy. But, as a hypothesis, it could be greater in some societies than others. Who knows? That's why we have more questions, in an attempt to identify where people's loyalties really lie. Is it with their family, their company, society or just with themselves? And how far does the culture within which they live encourage an overlap between these loyalties. Or where are the conflict points? Another much more valid argument is triangulation. This means, please do not rely on all your information coming from a questionnaire; the results are then used only as the basis for further discussion, which is why I make fun of the results sometimes. And, of course, the context and meaning of the questions can be very different.

BL. For example, you had one question on the attitude to the company providing housing that makes this point very well. In some societies there is little movement of workers and, where that happens, it is not surprising that families, rather than companies, look after the housing. The more companies require their employees to move around, the more companies will have to become involved in housing issues. This is more an organizational issue than a cultural one.

FT. Within the questionnaires used, we have been very careful to use multicultural teams to both help draw up the questionnaire and help us with interpretation. Another trick is to double check with other questions and other sources of interviews, such as interviews and independent observations.

BL. Which needs to be done particularly if the answers are to be used to make profound statements, or as the basis of policy decisions. As an aside, I believe there is a fascinating study to be done that shows that all the national characteristics and differences are reflected in their different attitudes to gardens.

22   LEADERSHIP & ORGANIZATION DEVELOPMENT JOURNAL 14,6

FT. That is a very British remark.

BL. Yes and no. I believe it is one reason for Britain's industrial decline. We – particularly the British urban middle classes, following the standards set by the country houses of the establishment – use gardens to reflect our individual identity; while Japanese gardens tend to be more public, where individuals get a feeling of collective identity.

FT. These national attitudes can also be reflected in another apparent correlation, within certain societies, between the number of lawyers and the number of pets. Those who help their friends in a car accident (using one of the questions in the book) tend to be more *particularistic*, and also tend to have fewer lawyers per capita than the *universalists* who use society rules (which have to be enforced by lawyers). One client commented that this was very interesting because there not only appears to be that link, but there is also an apparent link with expenditure on pet food per capita. Of course, there is no relationship with what lawyers eat but, perhaps, there are common roots. Particularist societies have close family links, while universalists are more likely to be living alone; and pets are more likely to be kept by people living alone. Although some people argue we take a lawyer or keep a pet for essentially the same reason – namely that we don't trust other people.

BL. Fascinating. And, while on the subject of pets, there was, I believe, once a piece of research that showed that those at the top of corporations in the US were more likely to have had pets as children than the average of the population. One interpretation was that they learned the concept of responsibility at an early age. Of course, another interpretation is that it is the rich and privileged groups in society who can afford pets.

FT. I have a problem like that with my daughter's pets, which I seem to end up having to look after.

BL. So, at a very early age she has mastered the art of delegation. That should be invaluable later in her life. I believe some of these examples, although they might sound rather flippant and irrelevant, are valuable because, not only is there a lot of change going on in terms of culture within all societies today, but you can often operate in various ways if you want to attempt to manage that cultural change process once you understand what is really going on. Cultural changes sometimes can be generated from very tangential or lateral directions. This is part of both the responsibility of the corporation and society as a whole; and this can then become highly political. Yet, the political dimension of the subject appears to have been almost ignored in your book.

Political Challenge

FT. I agree. It is a whole power issue and this is born out of the fact that the European Community politicians have shown little or no interest in this issue. Yet corporations are taking it all very seriously and that reflects my belief that the EC will be made by business but broken by politicians.

BL. It is almost as if politicians sometimes have a vested interest in ignoring these exercises. They only seem to be interested in how they can use the information to further their individual political ends, rather than use it as a genuine way of improving the way people work together.

FT. One story. A couple of years ago, I could send clients my books across Europe without any invoicing; now, because of the new rules after 1993, I have to send invoices because I need the VAT number of the company ordering it. Since we have lowered the international borders there has been a corresponding, if not greater, increase in the amount of central bureaucracy.

BL. One issue here is that any liberalization process paradoxically needs controls, if chaos is to be avoided and, without a common culture, this has to be some kind of bureaucracy. Then there is another issue as far as rules and regulations are concerned, especially in the public sector, and that is that the people taking the decisions – whether they are politicians or lawyers – are rarely directly involved in any responsibility for the resource implications of their decisions. Such a structure is bound to produce some strange results.

FT. I agree.

BL. How can society best protect itself from these potential excesses? It would be very interesting to take the European Community results of your questionnaires and see how close they really are, because there is unlikely to be effective integration unless there is a coming together over these cultural issues. Or, if there are differences, these need to be either complementary and compatible, or are there specific issues that need to be worked on if we are to further the harmonization process?

FT. This is a tricky issue. If I take it at the corporate level, the Japanese were successful because they produced a corporate culture that was close to, and consistent with, societal culture. The Shell and Unilever examples seem to show that the Dutch and British can work well together, for various reasons. Their differences complement each other, such as the egalitarian, hands on, build it tomorrow Dutch with the more visionary, hierarchical, class-conscious British. In Shell, the British define the refinery of the year 2000, and the Dutch build it tomorrow. I know it is an oversimplification, but what my book attempts to do is provide a language and a vehicle that can be used to increase our understanding of ourselves and others and, through that, it allows us to work more effectively together as a team. Teams can have an enormous amount of variety, but that must be managed on the basis of respect.

BL. But you must be using a basic language that everyone understands and respects.

FT. Which is exactly what is meant by corporate culture.

BL. But, once you get involved in that process, are you not then changing the culture?

FT. Yes. But one of the universal truths in successful corporate cultures is respect for variety. It might sound paradoxical, but those cultures say that "the one thing we have in common is that we respect our differences".

BL. That is easy to say in theory, but difficult to achieve the right balance in practice. It is easy when the differences are not considered to be important to the corporation's short-term success, but it is another thing altogether if they are important, or even perceived to be important.

FT. I agree.

BL. Perhaps we can conclude by summarizing the key issues your book raises for the long term.

FT. First, we need to be thinking more about the longer term. When the Japanese were negotiating to take over the Yosemite National Park, they produced a 250-year business plan and the American reaction was, "Damn it, that's 1,000 quarterly reports". Culture itself needs a long range view and the beauty of this is that this includes the short term, whereas short-termism doesn't necessarily include concern about the long term. So develop these

long-term views, then ensure that these are within an international context which avoids parochialism. International companies must develop their new staff internationally – and, to some extent, that isn't so easy today because of the reduced opportunity for international postings. And, of course, the strategy and implementation of these ideas must be integrated. It is no good having fast decisions that come apart on implementation. Then, finally, we need to change the educational system. These cross-cultural issues need to be addressed very early within an individual's educational and learning experiences. The whole book, and my whole approach, is about how do you live, and manage, with variety without chaos. And that is probably the key challenge facing us all, if we are to survive and be at all successful, in the decades ahead. For many years we have been taught to try to reduce variety. However, the success of Europe will not be dependent on how we get everyone equal, but how we learn to live with and respect the variety. That needs consistency at some levels and leaders who really understand these issues. This is what is needed within leaders today. People who have strong backbones that make them flexible, not rigid. This is the responsibility of both business and political leaders. In business, you will increasingly not survive without these qualities; in politics, I am not so optimistic.

BL. Business appears to be taking these issues and techniques seriously and is working with them, while politicians appear almost to ignore them.

FT. Precisely.

BL. That is a good point on which to end. Riding the waves of culture is certainly going to be an increasingly important part of all our lives in the years ahead and this discussion has only given a flavour of the substance of your book, which I hope will be widely read.

Bruce Lloyd is Head of Strategic and International Management at South Bank University and Fons Trompenaars is the Managing Director of the Centre for International Business, The Netherlands.

[8]

Japanese-Style Management:
Socio-Economic and Cultural Factors

YANG Tien-yi (KAN Toshio)
Faculty of Business Administration, Asia University

Countless treatises on so-called "Japanese-style management," from both Japanese and foreign perspectives, have already appeared in the business administration literature; and when one includes commentaries by observers of current events, the number grows even larger. This paper attempts to bring together this existing research in order to discuss the salient features of Japanese business management from a historical standpoint concentrating on its economic, sociological, and cultural factors.[1] In particular, my intent is to bring into relief special aspects of Japanese management through a comparison of Japanese social characteristics with those of other countries. This approach is only natural, given my belief in the uniqueness of Japanese society.

In contrast to many other countries, which, although comprising a single political entity, consist of a number of parallel, independent cultural systems (including language, religion, and life style) giving rise to a complex social order, Japan displays a degree of linguistic, religious, and racial homogeneity equalled by few other countries. Furthermore, this homogeneous society displays a high degree of integration. Whereas other countries are required by their racial and cultural diversity to spend much of their national energy maintaining their social unity, Japanese society has the inherent advantage of already being socially unified and well organized in every respect. The homogeneous rural (*buraku*) society first created in pre-modern Tokugawa Japan has had its sense of social community further enhanced since the Meiji era by the development of the nationwide administrative system stemming from the centralization of political power and the spread of modern education. When discussing Japanese business management, it is this long experience of social and cultural homogeneity that one should first focus on, for few other countries are endowed with a comparable blessing.

14   EAST ASIAN CULTURAL STUDIES

I. Samurai Influence on Japanese Enterprise

The state-oriented nature of modern industry

According to the Gerschenkron model[2] of the economic process of Western industrialization, the way it proceeds and the way it is managed differ dramatically depending on whether the nation in question is already an advanced nation or still backward, particularly in an international sense, at the time when industrialization begins. When backward nations start industrializing, they can introduce industrial technology, capital, and other institutions from the advanced countries, thus leaping directly into large-scale modern industrial production. On the other hand, it is a historical fact that the more backward a nation, the poorer will be such domestic conditions for industrialization as capital, technology, an educated labour force, and managerial capability, no matter what the international possibilities for cooperation. Industrialization cannot be successful unless this gap between international opportunities and available domestical resources is filled by some kind of "institutional implement." Therefore, the more backward countries will inevitably need to carry out their industrialization policies under the aegis of government guidance. The large-scale and rapid industrialization carried out by the Meiji government fits this model almost perfectly. The guiding principle of this industrialization was also extremely nationalistic, rather than the more individualistic processes seen in more advanced Western countries.

One phenomenon peculiar to industrialization in a non-Western society is exemplified by the enterprises founded rapidly after the Meiji Restoration, which departed radically from the old, indigenous patterns of commerce and industry of traditional Japanese society and adopted an imported, Western format. However, in the case of Meiji Japan, these enterprises did in one sense follow the ideological traditions underlying the projects undertaken by the Tokugawa *bakufu* and the leading feudal clans (*han*)—that is to say, all of the Western-style Meiji era businesses were founded and managed by members of the feudal warrior (*bushi*) class not for their own private gain, but rather in the national interest. In the closed, stratified, agricultural and commercial society of Tokugawa Japan, the samurai played the role of leaders, devoting their life to the common, public good. Money was seen as repugnant; involvement in profit-making activities was to be avoided at all costs. This was expressed in the saying "Merchants may seek profit, samurai seek honour." That the creation and management of the Western-style enterprises in the Meiji era was a "national" undertaking was all the more reason for the samurai to be able to take part in them proudly and unhesitatingly.

To emphasize the difference between these advanced, radical enterprises and the business carried out by the parasitic merchants in Japan's period of isolation, the new leaders guiding the Meiji government invented the term "*jitsugyo*," meaning the industrial activity of production, manufacture, and commerce. Two major contributors praising the progressive image of the new enterprises were Fukuzawa

Yukichi and Shibusawa Eiichi. Shibusawa, in particular, was an advocate of preserving Confucian ethics while encouraging the new enterprises and put forth such ideas as "the Analects and the Abacus" and "Unity of Ethics and Economy." He motivated the samurai to contribute to the state by creating a newly idealized image of the warrior who traded his sword for an abacus.[3] J. Hirschmeier has argued that the motivation of the samurai lay in a nationalism which placed the welfare of the country above all.[4] In summary, the modern Western-style enterprises centred around the samurai between the end of the Tokugawa period and the beginning of Meiji were thought of as organs designed to carry out national tasks; and this view of business management as a national mission, which might be called "managerial nationalism," persists strongly to the current day.

The samurai tradition and ethic in relation to modernization

After the great peace established after the Battle of Sekigahara in 1600, the warrior class was split off from agrarian society and grouped in the castle towns. There they were demilitarized and formed a political and administrative class manning the Tokugawa *bakufu* and leading *han* administrations. In other words, the samurai began to live a simple salaried life, performing certain bureaucratic functions in the feudal administrative organs. This provided an excellent opportunity for them to acquire administrative expertise related to running the bureaucracy.[5] Thus, unlike the landed gentry of Western Europe or the Chinese landowner bureaucrats, they did not need to concern themselves with running an estate, nor were they affected by rulal agrarian village life. This warrior bureaucratization not only greatly facilitated the Meiji Restoration, but also with the dissolution of feudal retainer groups, they were deprived of any possibility of establishing as a Western-style landed aristocracy. The result was that in Japan businessmen could devote themselves exclusively to management, unlike, say, in Britain, where managers were constrained by the aristocratic value system.

The samurai possessed that key managerial ability of "a mature understanding of organization behaviour as administrators and bureaucrats, and a well-developed devotion to their work."[6] Their sense of responsibility towards their defined tasks in the *bakufu* was probably stronger than anywhere else in the world, to the extent that a failure in their work may have led them to take ultimate responsibility by committing suicide. The phenomenon of devoting one's life to society that we come across so frequently in Japanese management has its origin here in samurai society. Japan's rapid industrialization owes much to the existence of this strong sense of devotion and responsibility to the tasks one has been assigned in an organization.

R. P. Dore believes that the reasons for this internalization of a value system based on the responsibility ethic lay in the Confucian education system set up by the Tokugawa administration and has attempted to find therein the roots of Japan's achievement orientation.[7] Based on Dore's work, R. Bendix concluded that the Confucian ideals inculcated in the people by Tokugawa period education and the integral role played by the samurai in the Meiji Restoration are equal in importance to the role played in Western modernization by the Protestant ethic and the ranks of middle-class independent proprietor producers. In other words, the Confucian ethic developed within the feudal education system contained a sort of unique ascetic ethos close to the religious consciousness of M. Weber; that is, for Japan this self-restraint constituted a functional equivalent to Puritanism.[8] But that is not all. It can also be said that this ethos provided a common sounding board between the lower samurai classes and the upper agrarian and town classes, so that by the end of the Tokugawa period the principles and practice of Confucian *bushido* (way of the warrior) had penetrated deeply into the masses. The spread of education was clearly a major factor in furthering this phenomenon. Although the samurai constituted no more than 5% of Japan's population at the beginning of the Meiji era, it is estimated that a full 40% of the male and 10% of the female population were literate.[9] One might say that the samurai ethic was generalized into an ethic for the masses,[10] who, once having internalized this value system, were ready to pour all their energies into the national goal of modernization.

Thus, history's legacy to Japan on the eve of its industrialization included widespread education, the samurai ethic, vocationally-oriented social consciousness, and entrepreneurial talent. The Meiji government used with great effectiveness these qualities and capabilities of a nation sharing the samurai value system.

Entrepreneurs of the Meiji era and social characteristics

Industrialization in non-Western countries has usually commenced with the introduction of modern overseas technology and the transplantation of Western-style industry, rather than through some spontaneous process of automation of traditional craft industries. Japan was no exception, as a great gulf developed between the traditional and modern industrial sectors and between the merchants of the Tokugawa period and the entrepreneurs of Meiji. The ex-samurai were the only group that could gain the understanding of Western industrial culture required for the rapid founding of modern economic sectors such as banking or for the setting up of such foreign trade institutions as trading companies, marine transport and insurance, and warehousing. No one was better endowed to develop into modern entrepreneurs building a new society than these ex-samurai, with their positive outlook vis-à-vis building an advanced economy and their close relationships with the government.

It has been estimated that the ex-samurai, which made up no more than 5% of the population, comprised 48% of Meiji era business founders and entrepreneurs.[11] Of course the origins of the new entrepreneur class were varied. In addition to the ex-samurai, many came from a so-called "boundary class" consisting of the upper strata of the agrarian, merchant, and artisan classes. Due to the reforms at the end of the feudal period, Tokugawa society had become dramatically more fluid, so that people coming from all types of nominal background underwent *bushi*-like education, acquired *bushi*-character, raised their sights and entered that so-called "boundary class," which gave rise to so many leading Meiji entrepreneurs. In addition, the percentage of businessmen who were of ex-samurai extraction gradually increased throughout the Meiji era, due to parents giving their children higher educational opportunities and thus forming a social elite.[12] Higher educational opportunities were all the more important in pursuing international entrepreneurial opportunities, which by any measure were greater than the domestic ones.

One more important aspect of the Gerschenkron model deals with how the "complementary" nature of a backward country's economy strongly influences its process of industrialization. Specifically, when starting industrialization, a country must not only set up leading sectors and adopt import substitution policies, as well as build central trading capabilities to lead the export sector, but in addition, a variety of subsidiary and supplemental functions must be developed, including, for instance, trade finance, insurance, and warehousing. In other words, it is not enough to build a few Western-style industries; a country must also simultaneously set up railroads, banks, foreign trade, and all other infrastructure sectors of a modern economy. But the managerial resources necessary to pursue all these entrepreneurial opportunities are normally lacking in exact proportion to that country's backwardness at the start. One phenomenon that occurs in the case of relative backwardness is that entrepreneurs who succeed in one area will go on to another, with capital, technology, and know-how gradually accumulating and concentrating in their or their families' own hands.[13] This is the family conglomerate seen so frequently in developing countries during their industrialization phase. In Japan, this phenomenon took the form of *zaibatsu* groups, which grew rapidly by diversifying their product lines and businesses during the Meiji era.

In Japan, however, although the overall industrial structure was one of family businesses, management experts without capital and from outside the family quickly came to play an important role in management. This feature distinguishes Japan (1) from some countries of Western Europe where all management power was still concentrated in the hands of owner-managers for up to one full century after the Industrial Revolution, and (2) from the newly industrializing economies, where the family conglomerates dominate. In addition, the managers of Japan's *zaibatsu*, while maintaining their allegiance to the *zaibatsu* families, also in some ways were able to transcend that allegiance. Their loyalty to *zaibatsu* was based on the concept that the maintenance and growth of these organizations would advance the national good, and they did their best to ensure that this would happen.[14] They viewed a *zaibatsu* less as an individual firm, and more as a conceptual part of the state. Even in non-*zaibatsu* industries such as spinning, one sees experts with university degrees entering companies, replacing technically inexperienced stockholders and executives and advancing the state of the art. This is a phenomenon unique to Japan, present in almost all large modern Japanese companies and continuing to the present day. For this reason most Japanese entrepreneurs conform to high standards of spiritual and behavioural ethics; they do not seek mere wealth and are satisfied with a modest life. It is in this sense that Japanese entrepreneurs have been praised for upholding the image of the samurai "men of purpose" who brought about the Meiji Restoration.[15]

Early introduction of joint-stock companies (*kabushiki kaisha*)

By 1880, 153 banks in the form of joint-stock companies had been founded for financing early Meiji industrialization under the National Bank Act (Kokuritsu Ginko Jorei) of 1872 and the revisions of 1876. In addition, during the period from 1878 through 1884, other companies which succeeded in raising public capital were formed as joint-stock companies. They included Tokyo Marine Insurance (Tokyo Kaijo Hoken Kaisha), Japan Railways (Nihon Tetsudo), Osaka Spinning (Osaka Boseki), and Osaka Merchant Marine (Osaka Shosen).[16] In the case of the 153 national banks, the largest contribution to their capitalization was made by the aristocracy and ex-warrior class, amounting to 76% of the total and taking the form of public debentures. Their willingness to invest their own funds boldly in these trust institutions and other sectors was no doubt related to a view of these banks' role as a sort of state institution rather than simple opportunities to earn profits. Here, then, is another distinguishing feature of Japan's industrialization: the creation of enterprises from the start as joint-stock companies.

As business history teaches us, the use of joint-stock companies in England started only after 1880 and was merely limited to cotton spinning and a few other industries. The reason is that there was no need for the joint-stock company's ability to gather external capital, since the resources accumulated during the extended process of industrialization were sufficient enough to allow the firms to continue as family-owned. The length of time in America between the beginning of industrialization and the use of joint-stock companies was somewhat shorter, but even then it was not until the last half of the 1890s that listings of "industrials" began on Wall Street. Therefore, the majority of large American and European companies operated through the greater part of nineteenth century as either individual proprietorships or partnerships.

In Japan, on the other hand, with the exception of *zaibatsu*, almost all Western-style businesses founded during the Meiji era started out as joint-stock companies. The reason is that family-owned companies were ill-adapted to rapid industrialization, and that many of the Western-style businesses were closely related to national goals and received governmental assistance in their growth under such policies as "Shokusan Kogyo" (Domestic Industrial Promotion) plan. In addition, many of their managers came from the ranks of the ex-samurai, and the existence of joint-stock companies made it easier to attract graduates from the imperial universities and top technical colleges. Thus, the tradition of family-owned businesses, deeply rooted in the West, was not a major factor in Japan even from the start of industrialization. In sum, the introduction and spread of the joint-stock company occurred earliest in Japan. In Western Europe, many family-owned businesses still remain, and almost all the large business groups in the newly industrializing countries are in effect family-owned. One might say that in Japan, more than any other country, corporate management could not afford to be hostage to family interests.

The origins of Japanese corporate capital

Not only did Japanese businesses start with social capital raised through the joint-stock corporate form, but many capital needs were also satisfied through bank loans. This tradition of so-called "debt management," another unique feature of Japanese business, goes back to the Meiji era. In the early phases of industrialization, accumulated capital was not sufficient to pursue the great economic opportunities in every sector. In order to meet these urgent needs for capital, the newly formed network of contemporary banks developed new financing techniques. This took the form of long-term loans to growing companies, in addition to the traditional banking services. The banks were forced, contrary to their original plans, to develop into industrial finance institutions, relying on lending with stock as collateral. In those days banks could not hope for large deposits from the poverty-stricken masses, and given the low level of industrial development, commission income from bill discounting was also small, resulting in a weak capital base. As stock-secured lending increased, the banks fell into a position of overlending. Here the large urban-based banks gave to the Bank of Japan their shares of railroad and spinning industry stock as security for funds received in the form of re-discounted bills. This is how the system of close financial co-operation between the banks, industry, and the Bank of Japan emerged within the setting of the national trust. Against the background of this type of indirect financing system, it has been pointed out that stock markets for direct financing remained underdeveloped. The *zaibatsu* firms met their capital requirements indirectly and were not publicly listed. The stock of industrial enterprises was a poor investment, and public savings were invested in time deposits rather than in the stock market.[17] We might add that the tendency for Japanese businesses to depend on bank loans for capital grew even more pronounced after the Second World War. Given the well-known Japanese propensity for saving, this practice of individuals placing their savings in time deposits and the banks relending the money as long-term loans is still with us today.

II. The Corporation as Family and Salient Features of Japanese Society

The economic background for lifetime employment and the seniority system

As discussed above, Japan imported advanced Western technology to build a modern industrial society during the Meiji era. But a noteworthy feature of non-Western modernization is the historical differences between Western industrial technology and the indigenous technologies. This is in contrast to the case in England, for example, where independent artisans served as the first skilled workers in the modern factory system. The Meiji government paid foreign experts high salaries to train the first generation of skilled workers in government-run factories. In time, these government-trained experts fanned out and formed the nuclei of factories in the private sector, but unlike their counterparts in the West, they had no particular view of themselves as craftsmen. Rather than protecting their craft, their interest was in raising their social standing in Japan's rigid, patrimonial (in M. Weber's term) status stratification under the political reality of "government exists above the people." Small in number at that time, these experts became superintendents in the work place or contract work managers in the internal contract work system, and had wide-ranging responsibilities in hiring and supervising general labourers.

Within the favourable economic environment following the Sino-Japanese War, labour shortages emerged and the number of labourers moving from one superintendent to another increased. The number of workers leaving factories reached levels almost intolerable to managers. Growing demand for labour to meet the needs of the more sophisticated industrial structure induced managers to achieve higher levels of discipline and ability and forced them to consider new ways to retain and increase stable work forces. Methods included direct employment of school graduates, internal training, seniority-based promotion and salary systems, a variety of fringe benefit programs, and developing a corporate family spirit. This is the origin of the so-called "corporation as family" approach to labour management.[18] The seniority system and lifetime employment were thus new labour management approaches, developed at the time of the birth of Japan's heavy industries around the First World War and designed to retain scarce skilled labour resources over the long term. The economic reasons that made these approaches inevitably lie in Japan's process of industrialization.

The ideology of corporation as family

Before the Second World War, the traditional family system was an important organizing concept of the state. It is believed that the social value of traditional samurai families and their attendant values were presented by political leaders as the ideal for the nation as a whole.[19] The ultimate expression of this ideal was loyalty expressed in the samurai motto "One's House Above All." The origin of the corporation-as-family idea can be found in this concept and it was generalized and internalized by the merchant classes. As can be seen in the title "The Family-like Nature of Japanese Society," the entire country is viewed as one large family, with the Emperor as its father. Thus, it was natural, or perhaps inevitable, to adopt this view of the corporation as well. The company was one large family, the management its benevolent father, the workers his well-behaved children. When, at the end of the Meiji era, absolute managerial authority was threatened by worker revolts based on emerging socialist ideas, leaders concocted the image of the "respected manager" and borrowed the traditional family system as an ideological framework to reintegrate the new-born industrial labour force and retain its loyalty and dependency over time.[20] In Japan, then, rather than tolerating class confrontation as in the West, an affectionate parent-child–like relationship was raised to the status of social virtue. Workers coming from farm villages were enveloped in this family philosophy, which emphasized how everyone shares the same fate.

On the topic of how managers view labour relations, whereas third or fourth generation managers of family-owned and -operated companies in the West tend to have an extremely strong sense of ownership vis-à-vis the firm, the majority of modern Japanese companies, formed from the start as joint-stock companies and thus making use of society's funds, have almost no such preparation. Even the families owning *zaibatsu*, because they early on entrusted effective management rights to university-trained professional managers, had a low sense of ownership due to the fact that they were not setting the company's directions. The rigid Western sense of management authority, stemming in Europe from a strong sense of ownership and in the United States from a belief in management's high ability, tends to undermine good relations. In Japan, the weak sense of management authority makes it much easier to develop amiable labour relations. The Japanese managers were originally ex-samurai and landowners, who were succeeded by their well-educated children, and thus had an "elite complex" or sense of noblesse oblige, which included a personal responsibility towards the downtrodden working class. What resulted was a corporate environment where the managers treated their workers warmly and responsibly.[21]

In any case, the ideology of corporation as family is a philosophy of managers treating workers in an affectionate, family-like manner, thus increasing the latter's sense of belonging to the corporation. In this view, what is required of the child (worker) is to carry out loyally tasks contributing to the continued existence and prosperity of the family (company) under the direction of the family head (manager).[22] The idea is to transform the corporation as simply a collection of capabilities into a joint familial entity. And the management policies of familism that support this transformation include lifetime employment, salaries based on seniority, and corporate welfare policies for workers.[23] "The trials and tribulations since the Meiji era served to give birth to new management wisdom, and the various approaches were eventually integrated to form a single, unique management philosophy."[24] In that sense these approaches are truly Japanese. This system, deliberately designed to satisfy worker's physical and spiritual needs, including a sense of superiority, has been praised as the jewel of Japan's managerial system.[25] The unparalleled docility of the Japanese people vis-à-vis those in positions of authority probably has its roots in this philosophy and tradition.

In the Japanese sense of the family (*ie*), the home transcends the person; its requirements come before those of the individual. The family business and assets are not meant to satisfy the needs of the individuals making up the family; rather, the head of the household simply manages those assets, ensuring that they can be passed down to succeeding generations. "The concepts of permanency and centrality of the household demand a stringently ascetic attitude on the part of individuals."[26] The overarching importance of preserving the family business and family assets surpasses concerns for the individual happiness of family members. It is an objective institution which transcends the desires of the individual members which compose it. The household also views competence as more important than kinship ties. Performance is the basis of selecting the heir, and the practice of adopting an able son from the outside is well established. It thus promotes goal-orientation. The household, supported by the Japanese ethos of loyalty to organizations, "is a goal-oriented corporation, which values the fruits of one's own labours and its own eternal existence."[27]

This philosophy, which has been extended to view first the corporation and then the entire country as a family, is a social phenomenon peculiar to Japan. The Japanese have developed this tradition of structuring non-family institutions along the lines of the family model with a logical consistency rarely seen elsewhere. The household (*ie*) is the starting point for structuring all secondary institutions, and in that sense represents the core of traditional Japanese social value. This can be expressed of "familial functionalism." Such approaches to thinking and behaviour, surpassing simple blood ties and emphasizing social functions, have flourished on Japanese soil, have proved better adaptable to the tasks of industrializing and modernizing than the traditional (consanguineal) systems seen in other countries, and represent a key resource for managing modern industry. "Corporation as family" can be considered an organizational revolution within Japan's industrialization process.

The concentric nature of Japanese society and the congruence of public and private welfare

In general, Asian religions are distinguished by their emphasis on the unity of god and man and the fusion of nature and self, as opposed to the isolation of man from a transcendent being in Christianity. In other words, Asian people are unconscious of the Weberian *Person*, which is always trying to methodically and systematically idealize the life of an individual standing in a stressful relationship to the outside world. For them, there is no "individual" and thus no conflict between the "individual" and the whole, only a peaceful fusion of the two.

In Japan as well, deeply influenced as it is by the Confucian ethics, the cultural values of religion and economics do not exist for their own sake; and there is no particular conflict between them, nor between them and the area of politics. Particularly in Japan, where political values take precedence,[28] the ideal of loyalty which cut across all social classes is given higher priority than that of filial devotion, as people desire strongly to achieve unity between their individual selves and the body politic. Therefore, in a Japan where the social aggregates of household and state are sanctified and assume a religious flavour, and where the carrying out of one's duties to both one's parents (or ancestors) and political authorities is the ultimate goal, the self has no clear boundaries, and is thus fused into such communal groups as the family and country. These types of communal groups—for example, family, village, prefecture, state, or family, company, nation—form structurally similar sets of concentric rings. Furthermore, the grouping, family–social group–nation, should be arranged on a single plane indicating not a multidimensional loyalty, but rather the fact that the loyalty towards one's family, one's hometown, and one's nation forms an unbroken continuum. This structure of concentric rings means that groupings and institutions in Japanese society are not autonomous, but entirely come under the overall umbrella of the state. Unlike in the West, where the government is simply entrusted with certain limited political and administrative functions and exists parallel to and in competition with other institutions, in Japan the state is the ultimate entity. Under this structure of harmoniously fitting concentric rings, individual needs can only be satisfied through membership in the various aggregates and ultimately through relentless adhesion to the goals of the state. Adhesive structures can exist only due to the special centrally driven nature of Japanese society, by which the part belongs to the whole, the whole cannot function properly but for the sacrifices made by the parts, and the aggregates are frail entities vis-à-vis the central authorities, obeying the latter's dictates almost without hesitation.

It is worth noting that the concentric structure of "leading a moral life, putting one's house in order, governing a state, and reigning over the whole empire" set forth in the Confucian Analects can be found in Japan in a very practical context. The principles set forth by Shibusawa Eiichi in his "Theory of the Unity of Economics and Ethics" establish a connection between this concentric structure and the entrepreneur's pursuit of profit, while placing the quest for business advantage within the framework of improving the position of the aggregate. Group consciousness thus served to blur the distinction between private and public good, and pre-war nationalism thus legitimatized profit making. Post-Meiji business firms were viewed as economic entities whose purpose was to achieve the goal of a "prosperous nation and strong army"; that is, as entities for carrying out the business of the state and as "familial" communities. By emphasizing the public good, the Meiji government attempted to harmonize artificially the pursuit of individual profit with the priority given to the public good. As long as this harmony was maintained, economic activity was aggressively promoted, with many benefits flowing to those industries most closely tied to the public good. At least in this regard, the self-sacrifices required to meet state objectives were in surprising agreement with the pursuit of personal profit and power. Japanese society thus facilitated acquiring private profit through the emphasis and priority placed on the overall welfare of society.

III. THE PRINCIPLE OF GROUPISM AND BUSINESS MANAGEMENT

The post-war principle of groupism

The concept of the family (*ie*) and the village (*mura*), which is thought to form the ideological underpinnings of Japanese-style management, actually began to disappear from Japanese households and farm towns after the Second World War. Nevertheless, the concept of "corporation as family" continued to function effectively in Japanese business management all the same, despite changing its outward appearance to a more "groupistic" orientation. "After the war, familistic management was not destroyed, but rather reformed,"[29] and no major changes were observed at the management policy level.[30] In other words, the concept of social standing remained strong in business organizations, with the seniority system continuing as the basis of management and society. Not only was the lifetime employment system left intact, but employees tended to serve one firm even longer than prior to the war. Salary continued to be based on years of service, and corporate benefit programmes were further expanded.

One thing that did change was management concepts. The pre-war parent-child model gave way to a situation where "at present, labour co-operation at many firms is moving in the direction of being based on a theory of harmonious labour relations for greater corporate prosperity, better living standards for workers, and improved social welfare."[31] This is the shift towards "managerial welfarism," the "groupistic" element in Japanese-style management. Groupism refers to a "way of thinking where the relationship between the individual and the group subordinates the interest of the individual to that of the group,"[32] and the way to reach this goal is to emphasize group members helping each other and depending on one another.[33] "Groupist management" is the term referring to this Japanese behavioural characteristic appearing in the management arena.[34] There is also the view that "support for the organization principle of Japanese-style management can be found in groupism stemming from Japanese psychological characteristics."[35] In other words, "in Japanese society, rather than dividing up responsibilities, individuals form mutual relationships by means of membership in a particular group, thus entering into a specific relationship with society. Individuals in such a society are identified by which group they belong to. Breaking away from the group leaves them powerless and helpless. For this reason, they are loath to confront society directly without the intermediation of their group." This is why they seek a sense of belonging and stability in "a type of group oriented strongly towards stability."[36] It is an article of faith for Japanese that one cannot participate in society without being a member of some organization or other.

The Japanese also strongly believe in the "view that the members of the particular organization to which they belong all share the same fate, and thus it is most important to exploit the capabilities of each member and satisfy his needs, in order for the overall order to continue to thrive, and to achieve overall welfare and happiness for life in the group."[37] The groupist customs in Japanese management are seen as stemming from a "conscious or planned"[38] introduction of traditional groupist consciousness and values found in the family and village into corporate management.

In addition, in most cases of groupism the individual is viewed ideally as one with the organization, rather than as sacrificing his interests to it. The reason is that "if carried out effectively, the organization will be stronger and more flexible than if managed according to an individualist philosophy. That is, the sum of the parts, if actually added up, will turn out to be greater than the whole. It must also be pointed out that this contributes to stable labour relations."[39] All the members of a managed group must co-operate as an organic whole and with a common vision striving to achieve the overall management goals. This explains why in Japanese-style groupism workers co-operate over and above the limits of their assigned jobs in order to meet the organization's goals, since attempting to satisfy their own needs will enhance the welfare of the group. Society was arranged so that individual needs and ambitions could be met more easily through the group than through individualistic effort and responsibility. At least in this respect, post-war groupism, by which mammoth organizations took over the role of the state as an object of loyalty, differs from the pre-war managerial familism. One may compare the "me-society" of the United States, where all actions are triggered by an individual's personal utility function, with the "we-society" of Japan, where the trend is for the activities of all group members to be guided by the organization's utility function. Japanese society does not function at the level of the individual; instead, people act as members of their organizations. "If it's for the company's good, it will end up being for your own good as well."[40]

Characteristics of second-stage groups and group decision making

According to F. L. K. Hsu, who categorized the principles of how secondary groups were organized by the value orientation and cultural style of their members, as well as describing the forms in which they satisfied their social needs, Japanese who left their primary groupings (family and village) and came to the cities formed secondary groupings as a pseudo-familial system based on primary (traditional) principles of amalgamation. These groupings are the *iemoto* system (pseudo-family) in Hsu's prototypical organizations, and the principle on which the organizations were based is called the "kin-tract principle," due to the way it combines the best of both principles of the family and of the contract. When joining a secondary organization after having left a primary (consanguineally based) grouping, the principle of "human relations" (*en* in Japanese) functions strongly, eliminating the possibility of any further transitions.[41] In other words, all Japanese belong completely to one single eternal group. This unilateral belonging includes the elements of what Nakane Chie calls *ba*, or "place," and arises as the human relationship in her "vertical society."[42] Rather than entering into an employment contract, Japanese by nature simply enter a company and create a lifelong relationship with it. They become totally involved in the company, become one with it and depend completely on it.

Given this type of employment relationship, harmony among people in the company will be greatly threatened and the continuing operation of the company hindered if a difference of opinions about management develops into personal confrontations among employees. There is an intimate cause-and-effect relationship between lifetime employment and both the *ringi* (consensus approval) system and *nemawashi* (multilateral internal consultation) prior to formal decision making. Of course the *ringi* system provides a way for lower-ranked staff members to participate in decision making and improves their morale, but there is also the disadvantage that decisions consume large amounts of time, and the distribution of responsibility may degenerate into its abdication. In any case, people in the West talk about "participatory management," but in Japan the traditional value system has always included participation.[43] Including as many people as possible in decision making improves the chances that they will put forth their best efforts in its execution.

Human relations in the company: competition and co-operation

From the perspective of foreign businessman, Japanese companies, while engaging in what could be said to be excess competition both at home and abroad, at the same time undertake co-operative action of the form described by the term "Japan Inc." Competition itself in Japan does not, as in the United States, arise from a direct relationship between the individual and society at large, but rather is exhibited in the battle to expand the capabilities of the entire organization, not the individual, in a never-ending pursuit of greater prestige and prosperity for the organization to which the individuals belong. Japanese management is often described as "tug-of-war competition" or "portable shrine management," but in fact these are competitive principles inherent to Japanese groupism itself. Furthermore, the relationship between individual and company is characterized by the fact that workers are not evaluated on short-term considerations, such as how well they performed some particular job assignment, but rather on their long-term, overall contribution to the company under the lifetime employment system. The result is to strengthen the individual's sense of belonging and loyalty to the company. In the groupist Japanese society, perhaps the only way to extract from people the energy to get some task accomplished is to extract it from the group, focusing on loyalty to the organization in order to better mobilize its resources. And since the measurement of value is made according to the degree of contribution to the group, rather than to internalized individualistic values, people concentrate more and more on attaining the group's goals and engaging in "loyal competition." Thus competition in Japanese society constitutes an intense competition between companies. Just as the people within a company compete over the long term, companies also compete over the long term to survive and grow.

However, viewed from a different angle, the following distinguishing characteristic of the industrialization process in Japan can be observed. There are severe limitations on and tight passages in the route a developing country can take towards industrialization. In order to catch up with the advanced countries, the developing country must navigate this constricted course at high speed. If many companies try to rush down this path at the same time, there is the possibility of mass confusion and mutual destruction. Japan is fortunately better organized than almost any other country in the world, so that this narrow passage to rapid industrialization was traversed in record time by virtue of companies making mutual concessions to each other and in general exhibiting co-operative behaviour.[44] Japan overcame its handicap as a developing nation and achieved its national goal, then, by companies co-operating with affiliated companies and other companies in the same industry, taking advantage of the unique assets of a homogeneous ethnic composition, the samurai tradition, and superb organizational skills.

Organized entrepreneurship and the general trading companies

We have discussed how Japan negotiated the obstacle course of industrialization by each company looking beyond its own interests, taking into consideration the position of other economic entities, and engaging in mutual co-operation. One could not possibly begin to enumerate all the cases in Japan's business history where businessmen acted co-operatively or provided mutual support, but let us give a few representative examples. (1) The way the pressure from foreign traders in raw silk was resisted in the early 1880s at the port of Yokohama through co-operation among local producers and silk traders organized around the Yokohama "Joint Freight Depot." (2) The decisive financial support provided by President Shibusawa Eiichi of the First National Bank to Osaka Spinning Co. to rescue it from difficulties encountered in financing raw cotton purchases. (3) The brilliant co-operation among Japan Mail Steamship Co. (N.Y.K.), Japan Cotton Spinners' Association, and several banks on the occasion of the opening of the sea route to Bombay in 1893. These are all examples of what Nakagawa Keiichiro calls "organized entrepreneurship."[45] In these cases, each economic entity involved kept both the national business horizon and the effects on society in view, resulting in a harmony and identity between social gain and private gain. These entrepreneurs who had a strong sense of the national good have been called "community-centered entrepreneurs," in contrast to the Schumpeterian "auto-centered entrepreneurs" of the West.[46]

As we noted at the beginning, industrialization requires various levels of guidance in the form of institutional implements proportionate to a country's backwardness. In the case of Japan, in addition to the guidance provided by the government, unique overseas trading organizations known as *sogoshosha* (general trading companies) played a central organizing role in industrialization. At the beginning of its industrialization process, Japan needed to import all types of machinery, equipment, and resources, and had to export tea, raw silk, and coal in order to meet foreign exchange requirements. It was for this reason that Mitsui and Co. was formed as a modern trading company. However, Japanese merchants had no experience in or organization for foreign trade and Japan had not yet developed any subsidiary services such as marine transport, marine insurance, foreign exchange, and warehousing required for the import and export business. Therefore, to develop a strong organization competitive enough to deal with the international trading entities of the advanced countries, it was necessary for Mitsui and Co. not only to enter into more diversified commodities transactions but also to provide variety of services associated with foreign trade. This is because if an enterprise could carry out a large amount of diversified transactions, it would become possible to settle a large number of the accompanying bills of exchange internally, thus enabling larger transactions per capital outlay. Handling many commodities also meant that it could keep the company-run ships filled, thus reducing transportation costs. The synergism between engaging in a wide variety of commodities and markets and simultaneously building necessary peripheral businesses enabled the companies to grow to mammoth sizes unheard of elsewhere.[47]

The Japanese *sogoshosha* not only imported and sold technology and equipment but also collected and provided industrial and technical information, thereby playing a major role as organizers in the development of industrialization. This corporate entity has become one of the most unique economic phenomena in the contemporary world.

In Japan, unlike in the advanced countries which accomplished the modernization of all private business sectors through a gradual process of industrialization, certain sectors had to modernize with great haste, while remaining ones continued to operate in their traditional form, giving rise to a pronounced unevenness and a dual structure of economic development. Japan's distribution system is, for example, criticized even now as a type of non-tariff barrier, with its plethora of tiny companies, and complex rules for conducting business, making it impossible for foreign goods to penetrate it. In Japan a complicated and detailed traditional distribution system had grown from the closed-country policy of the Tokugawa *bakufu*, in order to address the unique consumption patterns arising from complex and delicate Japanese sensibilities. These patterns of consumption and the traditional distribution system itself remained impervious to Western cultural and economic influence whether in the areas of clothing, food, or housing. Thus, in sharp contrast to the development of the advanced, efficient *sogoshosha* in the field of foreign trade, the domestic distribution system continued to remain as a "dark continent" within the post-war Japanese economy.[48]

Government-business relationships[49]

Originally Japanese society was less hierarchical than Europe or the United States, since considerations of experience and capability replaced those of fixed social standing and become predominant from the time of Meiji on. Outstanding graduates of the imperial universities entered careers in government and business, guided by a community-centred value system. There they gradually developed a functional set of principles aiming at effective management.

This type of meritocracy contributed greatly to Japan's industrialization and dominated the government administration of industrial activity. Prior to the Second World War, many Diet members were landowners without the capacity to create industrial law, so the tradition emerged where almost all proposed bills relating to industrial issues were drafted by economic bureaucrats in the administrative agencies and presented to the Diet as government proposals of the Cabinet. This is a pattern rarely seen in the West. Moreover, the custom of bureaucrats taking the initiative in policy deliberations remains until the present day. It is also well known that with the post-Meiji emphasis on which university one graduated from, relationships between fellow alumni in government, industry, and academia had important effects on society.

In addition, there were financial circles which played a critical role as intermediaries between government and business by supporting companies in cooperation with national policies. The leading example here is Shibusawa Eiichi, who exercised great influence during the Meiji era as the organizer of the financial world. The co-operation between the public and private spheres in pursuit of national goals became even more pronounced after the war. One of the most interesting parts of the book entitled *Japan as Number One* is its description of the behavioural patterns and policy-making process of Japan's elite groupings, where the system of intimate co-operation among the government, the bureaucracy, and business is graphically portrayed.[50]

IV.   EVALUATION AND APPLICABILITY OF JAPANESE-STYLE MANAGEMENT

Advantages of Japanese-style management

It is well known that interest in Japanese-style management was first raised by J. C. Abegglen in *The Japanese Factory*,[51] where he attempts to find the distinguishing characteristics of Japanese-style management in traditional customs and special cultural character. This book, focusing on lifetime employment practices in large firms of the 1950s, points out that Japan, unlike the West, accomplished its industrialization without major changes occurring in its pre-industrialized social organization and social relationships. It is certainly the case that such practices in Japanese management as lifetime employment, the seniority system, discrimination according to social standing, the individual's feeling of loyalty to his employer, the emphasis on harmony in the work place, the paternalistic concern for the workers' welfare,[52] authoritarian management, consensus decision making, and group responsibility are traditional features which were carried over.[53] However, these traditional practices neither mean that Japan is backward nor did they inhibit its modernization; rather, they constituted an important factor in the development of the Japanese corporation, particularly aiding in industry's post-war rise to prosperity. The reason for the success of Japanese management and part of its uniqueness lie in the way these traditional practices were retained and skillfully used. "The success of Japan's modernization efforts is largely due to the effective use of its traditional value system and a unique social organization. Economically (externally) it has modernized; in human aspects (internally) it is traditional."[54]

Back in 1959 E. F. Vogel surveyed the views about life held by white-collar workers living in the Tokyo suburbs, and concluded that what constituted fundamental value of these Japanese was their group loyalty. Vogel attributed Japanese economic growth to groupism in Japan, which has all members following group goals.[55] It is indeed the case that this feeling of loyalty to the group represents a source of energy to accomplish goals in Japanese society, and Japanese-style management, which values the unity of the group over the capability of the individual, may be considered superior to American management in this regard. Abegglen, trying to locate the source of Japan's economic growth, says that "the Japanese industrial-economic system is the best in the world in terms of achieving high productivity."[56] We can perhaps define Japanese-style management as being the way Japanese firms are predisposed to act, with inborn (traditional) and acquired (modern) aspects forming two sides of the same coin.

P. F. Drucker observes three prominent features of the management style which constituted the main factors for Japan's high economic growth. First, in Japan decision making is done by consensus, so that it takes a great deal of time to make a decision, but once made that decision can be implemented expeditiously. The subject of the decision is as overall direction to be taken, with details left up to the person in charge, thus freeing management from worrying about small problems and permitting it to spend time looking at the big picture. Decision making is of the so-called bottom-up, participative, democratic variety. But although consensus decision making is predominant in Japan, it is not universal. Routinized administrative and supervisory decisions are made by consensus, but even before the war, strategic decisions were made by a small number of members in top management positions.

Secondly, concerning the aligning of corporate and personal objectives, Drucker claims that the American solution of unemployment insurance and seniority rights is superior to the lifetime employment system and seniority system of Japan. But the American system cannot provide the "psychological insurance," or the feeling of trust and peace of mind that Japanese workers possess. Some may say that there is something illogical or unfair about a system like lifetime employment and seniority, where compensation does not necessarily correspond to a worker's duties, but in fact the result is logical and efficient, with the worker's talents, enhanced by in-company training, and the flexibility of the system engendering increased productivity.

Thirdly, fellow alumni cliques exist as informal groups within Japanese companies, and the leaders of the cliques informally look after their younger members. Personnel evaluation depends heavily on information gained through such cliques. This system fosters better mutual understanding and is more effective for management development than systems of education and evaluation within the formal organizational framework.[57] Here Drucker is simply noting with approval one aspect of Japanese management as a guide for American managers in their problem solving.

Abegglen revised his earlier negative position on the lifetime employment and seniority systems after Japan achieved its high economic growth, by praising such institutions for permitting an extremely efficient allocation of labour resources. His reasons were: (1) the seniority-based compensation system encourages growth by reducing labour expenses for companies with relatively more new graduates; (2) young graduates further promote growth through the advanced technical training they bring with them, their youthful vigour, and their management potential; (3) lifetime employment means that graduates make their selection of which company to join with great care—only those companies which can attract the best and brightest will grow.

In other words, the lifetime employment system attracts the most efficient labour resources precisely to those economic sectors which are the most modernized and growing the fastest. The seniority system, meanwhile, facilitates deploying labour resources within the company. Company unions reduce confrontations between management and labour unlike in the West, where workers are forced to choose be-tween the role of company employee and the role of union member. The Japanese form of labour union combines with the lifetime employment system to reduce resistance to the introduction of new technology. This co-operative worker attitude towards cost-cutting and worker readiness to deal with new technology allow the company to accomplish technological innovations with great speed. In contrast to the West, where labour unions impose massive losses on the economy, Japanese-style management is a highly efficient system from which the West could learn in solving its labour problems.[58] In any case, Japan's lifetime employment system is by far more human than that of the West and reduces confrontation. Japanese-style management has been rated highly for the lifetime employment system's economic effectiveness and social value.[59]

The interest of foreign researchers in the subject of Japanese uniqueness grew in the first half of the 1970s. It was at the same time that Abegglen changed his negative view of Japanese employment practices. In its 1973 report on Japanese labour, the OECD (Organization for Economic Co-operation and Development) set forth the three principles of the pure Japanese employment system model to be lifetime employment, the seniority system, and company unions.[60] In the 1977 report it went on to add a fourth element to this list, namely, corporate norms or standards within a firm, distinguished by the three concepts of the firm (or working group) as community, mutually rewarding vertical relationships, and decision mak-ing by consensus.[61]

Confronted with Japan's high labour productivity, foreign researchers were forced starting in the 1970s to broaden their views from the structure and functions of the Japanese labour relations system to encompass the mind-set and behaviour of the workers which supported the system. "The source of Japan's inexpensive, high-quality goods is the worker's loyalty to the firm and his pride in his work." Com-pared with the United States, "Japanese workers almost never take time off from work, almost never go on strikes, . . . work overtime, and do not even use up their paid vacation."[62] This mind-set and concomitant behaviour of the Japanese worker would be noteworthy no matter within what system it had developed. The conclu-sion is that Japan's success depends not on the traditional national characteristics of diligence, persistence, and so on, but rather was accomplished deliberately through the group's ability to accumulate expertise, unique organizational capabilities, policies, and plans.[63] Vogel's emphasis here is on the Japanese-style groupism seen in all sectors, that is, the extent to which Japan can be said to be an intensely managed society.

The American productivity problem cannot be solved through fiscal policies; nor does increasing research and development investment seem to solve the problem. According to W. G. Ouchi the problem will not be solved until the Americans learn how to manage people so that they work effectively together. He looks to Japan for the model that will do this, calling it a new management approach which he dubs the "Z-type" organization.[64] He believes that the following contrasts exist between the prototypical Japanese (J-type) and American (A-type) styles of business

management. Lifetime employment vs. short-term employment; long-term employee evaluation and promotion vs. short-term; promotion as a generalist within
one company vs. promotion as a specialist within an industry; vague management
structure vs. explicit management structure; decision making by groups vs. decision
making by individuals; group responsibility vs. individual responsibility; and full
involvement between people in the company vs. partial involvement. The picture that emerges from this comparison is one of a J-type organization which
emphasizes human relationships and an A-type organization which emphasizes
technology.

In the 1970s the world economy experienced two oil crises, and the Western
economies were bedevilled by inflation and unemployment. Japan, on the other
hand, weathered the crises easily with its flexible response. The greatest contributing factor in this response was Japan's labour relations. Most likely this was
due to the excellent, flexible attitude towards technological progress stemming from
a strong feeling of unity vis-à-vis a crisis in Japan's labour relations.[65] And the high
worker longevity, low absenteeism, voluntary overtime, active participation in
small groups, and co-operative labour relations in the large Japanese firm were supported by the three golden rules of the Japanese labour system (lifetime employment, the seniority system, and company unions). In addition, the Japanese-style
employment system was geared well to economic efficiency. Aspects resembling
Japanese lifetime employment and the seniority system, such as a general tendency
towards greater worker longevity, building up of skills through workers experiencing a variety of tasks in the work place, and internal promotion, were not unheard
of in the West; but in Japanese companies, the Japanese seniority system, or internal promotion system, allowed people to build careers deeper and more broad-
ranging than in the West and encouraged the building up of a variety of skills in the
company's internal labour market, through techniques such as experienced
workers training inexperienced ones on the factory floor. In this sense, it has been
claimed that Japan's labour relations at present are the "most advanced."[66]

Of course, seniority-style labour relations developed through the conjunction
of the seniority-type skills (craftsmen's "sixth sense" and "old tricks"), which
stemmed from the technological backwardness of pre-war and pre–high-growth
Japan, with the company's internal rank system, and as such has its share of
quirks and undemocratic aspects.[67] It goes without saying that Japan's labour relations, unlike those of the United States, are defined on the basis of familism; the seniority system takes the employment relationship itself as its foundation, with an
employee's duties taking on secondary importance, with gaps often existing between one's salary and his responsibilities.[68] These are legitimate problems. They
account for why demands emerged early on for companies to eliminate the all-
encompassing principle of groupism based on the lifetime employment system and
the seniority system, to manage rationally in a performance-based way, to pay fair
salaries for the work performed, to adopt performance-based personnel policies,
and to open up paths for more fluid cross-fertilization in the labour market.[69]

Disadvantages of Japanese-style management

Unlike in the United States, where the work duties required to carry out production activities in factories are determined objectively beforehand and workers with the requisite skills then procured from the marketplace, in Japan new graduates believed to have acquired a certain level of capability are hired en masse, trained and then allowed to develop their skills in various positions within the company. Those believed to have a potential for management, in particular, are given experience from the start in a variety of posts. This approach of not restricting the type of post to which a worker is assigned may be thought of as having its roots in the notion of a warrior in the samurai society. The division of duties in the samurai organizations and on the battlefield was not a formal one; rather, it was designed to maintain mobility at all times. Japan's co-operative working organizations may be said to be the spiritual heirs of the practical approach adopted by these warrior groups. This is why labour management in Japan today deals with workers not labour resource management, and why the labour market is said to have been internalized within the company.

But for exactly that reason, the seniority-based compensation system establishes no direct link between labour performed and compensation; salaries are paid in return for working in general, rather than for some particular type or amount of work provided by the lobourer. This includes a demand for unlimited loyalty on the part of the employee. And this approach is effective to the extent that in a system where the company takes into account concerns about the employee's entire life and compensates him in a way unrelated to his specific duties, the company can legitimately expect unlimited work and loyalty from him. But gaining this effect rests on the condition that compensation be a favour unilaterally bestowed on the employee by the company, rather than an employee's right.[70] This sort of criticism has been directed at the supposedly backward employment system and labour relations in Japan since the beginning of the 1950s.

Among foreign researchers, Abegglen points out that the lifetime employment system attempts to procure people necessary to carry out future tasks rather than current ones, so that a danger of "excess personnel deployment" arises; and getting rid of the deadwood becomes almost impossible. He also presents his doubts that lifetime employment can survive at all if low economic growth continues.[71] It is true that the advantages of Japanese-style management were exploited to the utmost during the period of high economic growth, but come a downturn, Japanese firms cannot lay off workers like American ones can; and since their debt-based management approach dictates that they turn a profit without fail, it is difficult to shut down operations and then start them up again. If this is true, overproduction is likely to aggravate any downturn, more and more exports will have to be pushed overseas, and trade friction with trading partners will worsen, resulting in serious damage done to Japan's world economic position.

In any case, the negative side of Japanese-style management is that it has "many management drawbacks." Perhaps the most fundamental is that "in contrast to individualistic management, the power to motivate workers, especially talented ones, is lacking." "If we pay too much attention to personalities in an attempt to maintain harmony, we just end up hiring faceless zeroes and promoting yes-men . . . and the ones who know they can get the job done get discouraged." A list of the minus factors known all too well to the Japanese themselves would include group irresponsibility, mixing of private and public matters, formation of cliques, creation of yes-men, and feelings of exclusion vis-à-vis the outside. The most serious point is that "group-based management is a major social barrier for Japanese management . . . while both labour and management exist and prosper together within the company, the field of vision of both becomes constricted and they turn selfish."[72] This reminder of the image of the Japanese as only out for themselves is certainly painful for them to hear, but Japanese-style management, depending on how it is implemented, must operate both advantageously and dis-advantageously.

In any case, as is expressed by the contrasting aspects of "belonging vs. contract" or "full participation vs. functional participation," in Japanese management the worker, rather than entering into a contract with the company to receive a fixed salary in return for carrying out some particular assigned task, belongs completely to the company. Unlike in the West, in Japan an employee is first and most a member of the company and only then in charge of some task or other. He is expected to exert every fibre of his being for the company. "Japanese companies are large communal systems belonging to the large family of the state. Employees are public servants in that entity known as the company."[73] The capabilities and characteristics required of these servants in the communal system of shared fate naturally differ substantially from those of the West. The ethics found in the tight feeling of belonging to a particular company, which gives rise to a feeling of "us vs. them," are also different. This collecting of functions within the group, closed to the outside world, may also make it more difficult to rejuvenate the organization.

Since the last half of the 1970s, companies have been forced to explore a variety of ways to address Japan's low economic growth. As one way of promoting the shedding of excess fat, ideas were proposed to introduce performance-based thinking into the lifetime employment system, extending the retirement age, or otherwise overhaul the personnel system in response to population aging. Ways to adjust employment have been adopted such as "while continuing the current managerial organization, personnel systems, and policies, allowing people to choose their own retirement age as a way to eliminate employees in the middle and upper age brackets who have become an obstacle,"[74] or voluntary early retirement plans.

Can Japanese-style management practices be introduced overseas?

How can this style of management so well suited to the Japanese, raised as they were in such an unhierarchical, egalitarian, culturally homogeneous society, be adapted to other societies with their variegated races, religions, and cultures? Japanese-style management know-how is not some universal constant that can be applied as is anywhere, since it is flavoured with aspects limited to one specific culture. There is a one-sided line of thought that Japanese management methods, raised in the soil of Japan's national characteristics, cannot be transplanted intact to a culturally diversified country like the United States, nor is it likely to be easily accepted by peoples, who hold individualism as an article of faith.[75] But is this really the case?

Japanese employees enter a company, not a job, and may take on any post, thus helping or substituting easily for other less talented colleagues. The resulting team-work is thus clearly better than that between American employees, for example, who only think of their particular contractual responsibility. Japanese-style "port-able shrine" has a chance of succeeding in societies where there are many oppor-tunities for human contact and relationships based on familiarity.

There is the case of the overseas joint venture carried out by Matsushita Electric Industries, where the custom of morning greetings and the suggestion system were introduced with resounding success. A unique example is that of YKK (Yoshida In-dustries), where the Japanese employees of its Southeast Asian subsidiary worked and lived alongside the local labour force, thus getting to understand them and con-tributing to the success of the venture. "When a Japanese firm entering the United States introduced Japanese-style management, the feeling of loyalty of the employees towards the company became much stronger than that of workers in other companies, all in the space of a few short years."[76] Other cases have been widely reported, where, for example, American workers entering Japanese firms de-veloped a deeper sense of identity with the firm and greater motivation to do their jobs than when entering American firms. The same holds for the countries of Europe and Southeast Asia. But in large factories where human contact is difficult, one sees more local management practices in use.

The following conclusions have resulted from studies of the effect that the differences in the management and personnel policies of Japanese firms entering the US market and local American firms have had on the attitude and behaviour of American workers. Both managers and labourers employed by the Japanese firms were more productive in their jobs and more satisfied with them than their counterparts hired by American firms. The former also were absent or late less often and resigned of their own accord less frequently.[77] It is hard to deny that these results point to the superiority of group-based management over that based on individualism.

V. THE CORPORATION AS COMMUNITY AND THE RELATIONSHIP BETWEEN THE INDIVIDUAL AND THE FIRM

Groupistic industrialization and the corporation as community

A certain line of research has claimed that the prevailing view of Western-style modernization as being the most representative type should be placed in more relative terms, emphasizing that modernization is a multi-faceted process. For example, Japanese-style modernization should occupy a position distinct from that of the West, in that it is seen as an extension of the "house (*ie*)-type" society. The basis of this multi-faceted process is characterized by the differences in group organization in each society, which is interrelated with differences in the belief systems and religious systems that support and guide each group. According to this opinion, individual-orientation and group-orientation are presented as the two choices for human existence.

This kind of research then goes on to present a view of Japanese history from the group-competition standpoint, depicting it as comprising two cycles, the "clan" (*uji*) society up to the middle ages, followed by the "house-type" groupist society from the inception of samurai society. Four yardsticks for "house-type" society have been presented. (1) The circumstances leading to membership in the group include, in practice, a tendency away from blood relations, but conceptually deepen familiarity with consanguineal logic. In other words, "the principle of group formation rests on the conceptual fiction of blood relations, but in practice transcends blood relations."[78] (2) A "genealogical" nature intended to perpetuate the group's existence. (3) The division of tasks to accomplish group goals forms a "functional hierarchy," which tends to value procedural efficiency. (4) The group is a self-sufficient, autonomous organization, not depending on the outside. These are the fundamental principles of group formation. The picture presented is of Japanese "groupist-style industrialization"[79] as opposed to the "individualistic-style industrialization" in societies of the West. In this line of reasoning, the individualism of the West is far from having been an indispensable element in its industrialization. Groupism, on the other hand, is better suited to industrialization, given the way it can develop sophisticated organizational structures and high degrees of loyalty. This view, still prevalent today, holds that "societies with the central-guidance style of flexible organization and which form consensuses, such as one sees in Japan, are better equipped to deal with the problems of this age"[80] than the social systems of the West, which pursued industrialization based on the individualistic ethic.

According to Hazama,[81] we can call pre-war Japanese-style management "management familism," whereas after the war it developed into "management welfarism" or groupism. In addition, the basis of Japanese-style labour relations, characterized by lifetime employment, the seniority system, and company unions, can be found in the fact that "labour and management co-operate to form a 'community'." Specifically, "in large firms the firm and its management treat employees not as simple labour commodities," but rather the employers watch over the employees, while the employees "give up their lives to the firm," in other words, they satisfy their various desires through recourse to the corporation, so that "in this respect labour and management stand in a relationship of mutual dependence." Both labour and management attempt to make the corporation into a "place where they can lead stable lives," and in this sense the "corporation is a kind of community." It follows that "both lifetime employment and the seniority system are a manifestation of the functions of the corporation as community."

In this way the Japanese corporation becomes an environment in which the employees live their lives. In fact, employees of large firms, no matter where in the country they may be sent, can live in company housing, use the company hospital and credit union, and relax in the company's resort facilities at the ocean or in the mountains. Thus the employees and their families can satisfy all their living needs within the company; there is nothing they require from the outside society. One reason for this is the relative historical poverty of local government in Japan. Since the social infrastructure—roads, water supply, housing, and hospitals—is under-developed, the company takes over creation of these types of welfare facilities for its employees. The result is that the employee's sense of being as a member of the company grows ever larger, while his sense of being as a member of society or as a citizen grows smaller and smaller. In any case, the all-encompassing employment relation between the firm and the employee, and the phenomenon of the employee depending fully upon the organization, can be considered the Japanese version of R. Eells' Metro Corporation (the firm as "womb"),[82] in which the firm's role as community balloons, with regional social functions being subsumed under it.

Tsuda Masumi views Japanese management as a combination of the bureaucratic system, dominated by the logic of impersonality (rationalism and functionalism), and communities, characterized by the logic of individuality (acquiescence and agreement). Unlike in the West, where management is simply a bureaucratic system for the realization of corporate objectives, in Japan the company as community is added to this bureaucratic aspect, and thus forms the outstanding feature of Japanese-style management. Management is a kind of Gesellschaft, fundamentally characterized by the logic of functionalism. In the West, notwithstanding the infiltration of industrialism, the equation where Gemeinschaft equals society at large is of long standing and is the means by which people satisfy their cultural and spiritual needs, relax or find companionship. In Japan, however, the Gemeinschaften of the society at large were dissolved after the war, and no Western-style communities arose; thus the firm, originally a business body functioning as Gesellschaft, was forced to take on the role of Gemeinschaft at the same time. Since in the West a company is nothing more than a place to carry out certain duties in order to earn income, a person finds his reason for living and carries out his social interactions in the context of the society at large. In Japan, however, in addition to its original goal of carrying out production, the corporation has become capable of satisfying social and cultural needs, thus becoming in itself a co-operative system for daily life.

Japanese-style management's spiritual and physical benefits to employees

After the Second World War, the "self-capitalization ratio of the large Japanese firm was under 6%," and "almost 85% of needs for capital are satisfied by borrowing." The fact that "the greatest share of capital needs comes from bank borrowings" is thought to be extremely dangerous in many countries, but "in Japan, it is rather considered to be a source of strength."[83] This was the situation at the end of the 1960s, but it has not changed greatly even now. The situation at the beginning of the 1980s is said to be as follows.

The self-capitalization ratio is still under 20%, with 15% of that coming from funds retained internally and stockholders' equity accounting for a mere 5%, meaning that stockholders have virtually no say in the running of the company. The remaining 80% of total assets comes from outside, the great majority financed by bank loans. This naturally gives banks a major say in how the company is run. Moreover, 97% of the working capital of banks themselves is borrowed, stockholders' equity coming to a minuscule 1% of total assets. In this sense, there are no capitalists in Japan. Even the 5% of the total assets covered by stockholders' equity is so widely dispersed that rarely does any individual stockholder hold more than 1% of the stock. The large stockholders are all institutional investors, such as banks, trust companies, insurance companies, or firms from related industries. This is the phenomenon of cross stockholding among companies. This means that firms are simultaneously each others' owners; there is no clamour for maximizing profits in order to pay high dividends such as one sees in the West with its individual investors. On the other hand, raising dividends to individual investors, resulting in an increase in this type of investor, or an increase in the self-capitalization ratio would deprive the banks of a stable client base for their loan services. This is not a desirable prospect. This accounts for why large Japanese firms are not necessarily interested solely in maximizing profits the way their counterparts in the West are.

We mentioned above how large Japanese enterprises were organized soon after the Meiji Restoration as joint-stock companies, and how specialists took over the reins of management, giving rise to what A. Chandler calls "managerial enterprise."[84] Therefore, from the start there was no room to let the companies be dominated by family concerns. Particularly after the Second World War, the goals of the managers were to have the company grow in sales, market share, and assets, while realizing satisfied employees and gaining authority for themselves, rather than increasing shareholder profit.

In Japan almost all large firms are joint-stock companies; and the separation of ownership and control is more developed than in any other advanced country. The only capitalists that can be said to exist in Japan are the owner-managers of small- and medium-sized firms. Most managers of large Japanese firms are selected from among the university graduates who joined the company thirty to forty years earlier. As a consequence, the manager is, more than anything, a representative of the group of employees. Someone who does not value their welfare could neither reach top management nor stay there. This is a feature found in no other country. In addition, it is common to seek the approval of major stockholders (mainly banks and affiliated companies) before making major strategic decisions, but as long as the company continues to be managed well and make a reasonable profit, the major stockholders will give their approval rather than interfering in the running of the company. If the large financial institutional investors attempt to unduly influence the company, they will grow to be disliked by management and may be displaced in favour of another source of funding. Managers are selected by the stockholders only in a narrow legal sense. In practice, members board choose their own replacements.

In large Japanese firms about 15–20% of net profits are paid to stockholders in the form of dividends. This is a ratio of profits in the narrow sense. Profits in the wider sense include R & D expenditures, employee salaries, and fringe benefits, with only a minuscule portion being distributed to the stockholders. The largest portion of the company's profits is retained internally. Compared to American firms, the propensity to pay dividends in Japan is much lower. The employees overwhelmingly have the upper hand in deciding how to apportion profits. The reasons are that (1) the group made up of the employees headed by a manager in effect controls the company, and the company could not be managed in any other way; (2) as long as an adequate profit is being made, if it is not allocated in ways similar to other companies, recruiting new staff and retaining high-performance workers becomes difficult; (3) internal morale will suffer if profits are not distributed at a commonly accepted level; and (4) the propensity not to pay high dividends is not necessarily detrimental to the stockholders, since greater retained earnings and R & D expenditures will increase the stock price, and contribute to the continuing growth of the firm. Of course, the employee group realizes that taking the lion's share (or all) of the profits will depress the firm's prospects for accelerated growth. In a system of competitive markets, at least part of R & D expenses, market development expenses, and capital investment must come from profits retained inside the company. If the company is growing at a fast pace, the employees will be rewarded in any case with promotions and new posts in addition to their share of the profits.[85]

It is worth noting here that the ratio between the lowest-paid and highest-paid employee in large Japanese firms is a modest 1 to 10, compared with the ratio of 1 to 100 in the United States. Japanese companies with larger ratios are likely to be criticized. The managers of Japan, who operate conspicuously independent from the interests of the owners of capital, seek unending growth for their companies and look for the continuation of the enterprise in the maintenance and development of the communal life system made up of all those participating in it.

The point is that, especially starting from the high-growth era of post-war Japan, company employees have earned ample spiritual and physical benefits and have been rewarded handsomely for their labour. Theoretically speaking, the stockholders are supposed to be the owners of the company, and the profits are supposed to belong to them, but that is not the case in Japan. In Japan the company belongs, rather, to the employees, and they possess a strong sense of identity with it. Under the rallying cry of "our company forever," they lay down their lives on the altar of the company. Foreigners are suspicious of the way the Japanese work so hard for their company, but once the relationship between individual and company discussed so far is understood, there is no longer any reason for amazement. In no other country can one find companies so undominated by the interests of their owners and managed so much with an eye to those of the employees. The process

40   EAST ASIAN CULTURAL STUDIES

is one of communities of interests, communal life organizations, multiplying themselves through "company capitalism." This is perhaps the most important point to recognize when trying to understand Japanese-style management. As long as that flexible machine known as the Japanese economy continues to grow, Japanses-style management will continue to adapt itself to new environments and function successfully.

NOTES

1. I owe much to Prof. Nakagawa Keiichiro, *Hikaku keieishi josetsu* (1981a) and *Nihonteki keiei* (1981b).
2. Gerschenkron 1962.
3. Marshall 1968.
4. Hirschmeier 1964, chap. 5.
5. Dore 1965, p. 305.
6. Nakagawa 1969, pp. 148–49.
7. Dore 1965, pp. 312–13.
8. Bendix 1971, p. 194.
9. Ibid.; and Dore 1965, pp. 317–22.
10. Bellah 1957, chaps. 4 and 5.
11. Ishikawa 1976, p. 142.
12. Hirschmeier and Yui 1977, pp. 129–31.
13. Morikawa 1967.
14. Yasuoka 1975, p. 100.
15. Chosen Nippo 1984.
16. Hirschmeier and Yui 1977, pp. 113–16.
17. Nakagawa 1981b, pp. 62–65; and Imuta 1970, 1969.
18. Hirschmeier and Yui 1977, pp. 167–73, 295–308.
19. Kawashima 1957, chaps. 1 and 2.
20. Bendix 1956, pp. 46–116.
21. Nakagawa 1981a, pp. 175–80.
22. Hazama 1978a, p. 23.
23. Ibid., pp. 81–121.
24. Ibid., p. 41.
25. Yoshino 1975, pp. 91–98.
26. Hazama 1971, p. 93.
27. Hsu 1971, p. 315.
28. Bellah 1957.
29. Hazama 1978a, p. 42.
30. Hazama 1963, pp. 261–62.
31. Ibid., p. 262.
32. Hazama 1971, p. 16.
33. Hazama 1977, p. 44.
34. Hazama 1971, p. 20.
35. Iwata 1977, p. 21.

36. Ibid., pp. 45, 21.
37. Odaka 1981, p. 43.
38. Ibid., p. 59.
39. Hazama 1971, p. 53.
40. Sato 1983.
41. Hsu 1971. See Yang Tien-yi, "Kokusai shakai kara mita Nihon no kigyo to shakai" (Japanese business and society from a foreign perspective), in *Nihon keieishi koza* (Lectures on Japanese business history), vol. 6, *Nihon no kigyo to shakai* (Business and society in Japan) (Tokyo: Nihon Keizai Shinbun-sha, 1977).
42. Nakane 1967.
43. Ballon 1978, chap. 3.
44. Nakagawa 1981b, p. 35.
45. Nakagawa 1967.
46. Ranis 1955.
47. *Taikai tokushu* 1973.
48. Nakagawa 1981b, pp. 49–50.
49. Nakagawa 1981a, chap. 12; and Nakagawa 1980.
50. Vogel 1979.
51. Abegglen 1960.
52. Odaka 1965, p. 9.
53. Odaka 1981, pp. 35–42.
54. Hirschmeier and Yui 1977, pp. 310–14.
55. Vogel 1968.
56. Abegglen 1970, p. 27.
57. Drucker 1971.
58. Abegglen 1974, pp. 20–35.
59. Ibid., p. 46.
60. OECD 1973.
61. OECD 1977.
62. Vogel 1979, p. 160.
63. Ibid., preface, p. 3.
64. Ouchi 1981.
65. Nihon Seisansei Honbu 1981.
66. Koike 1977; and Koike 1981.
67. Tsuda 1967.
68. Sumiya 1976.
69. Takeyama 1965, chap. 3.
70. Ujihara 1966, pp. 118–19.
71. Abegglen 1974, p. 39.
72. Hazama 1971, pp. 53–54.
73. Mito 1981, pp. 18–19; and Mito 1976.
74. Tsuda 1980, p. 270.
75. Taylor 1984.
76. Vogel 1979, pp. 160–61.
77. Pascale 1978.
78. Murakami, Kumon, and Sato 1979, pp. 228–29.
79. Ibid., pp. 53–55, chap. 4.
80. Vogel 1979, p. 293.
81. Hazama 1978b, pp. 7–8.
82. Eells 1974, chap. 3.
83. Abegglen 1970, pp. 7–8.
84. Chandler, Jr. 1977.

85. Nishiyama 1983. See Komiya, R., "Kyoso-teki shijo kiko to kigyo no yakuwari" (Competitively organized markets and the role of the firm) in *Gendai Chugoku no keizai shisutemu* (The economic system of contemporary China), ed. Research and Development Organization (Tokyo: Chikuma Shobo, 1986).

REFERENCES

Abegglen, J. C. 1960. *Nihon no keiei.* Japanese version of *The Japanese factory: Aspects of its social organization* (1958). Tokyo: Daiamondosha.

――. 1970. *Nihon keiei no tankyu: Kabushiki Kaisha Nippon.* Japanese version of *Exploring Japanese management: Japan Inc.* Tokyo: Toyo Keizai Shinposha.

――. 1974. *Nihon no keiei kara nani o manabuka.* Japanese version of *Management of worker* (1973). Tokyo: Daiamondosha.

Ballon, R. J. 1978. *Nihongata bijinesu no kenkyu.* Japanese version of *Studies in Japanese style business.* Tokyo: Purejidentosha.

Bellah, R. N. 1966. *Nihon kindaika to shukyo rinri.* Japanese version of *Tokugawa religion* (1957). Tokyo: Miraisha.

Bendix, R. 1956. *Work and authority: Ideologies of management in the course of industrialization.* New York: Harper & Row.

――. 1971. Japan and the Protestant ethic. In *Scholarship and partisanship: Essays on Max Weber*, ed. R. Bendix and G. Roth. Berkeley: University of California Press.

Chandler, A., Jr. 1977. *The visible hand: The managerial revolution in American business.* Cambridge, Mass.: Harvard University Press.

Chosen Nippo. 1984. *Kankokujin ga mita Nihon* (Japanese from the eyes of the Koreans). Tokyo: Saimaru Shuppankai.

Dore, R. P. 1965. *Education in Tokugawa Japan.* Boston: Routledge & Kegan Paul.

Drucker, P. F. 1971. What we can learn from Japanese management. *Harvard Business Review*, March–April.

Eells, R. 1974. *Bijinesu no miraizo.* Japanese version of *The meaning of modern business* (1960). Tokyo: Yushodo.

Gerschenkron, A. 1962. *Economic backwardness in historical perspective: A book of essays.* Cambridge, Mass.: Harvard University Press.

Hazama, H. 1963. *Nihonteki keiei no keifu* (The roots of Japanese-style management). Tokyo: Nihon Noritsu Kyokai.

――. 1971. *Nihonteki keiei―shudanshugi no kozai* (Japanese-style management: Problems from groupism). Tokyo: Nihon Keizai Shinbunsha.

――. 1977. Nihonjin no kachikan to kigyo katsudo. In *Nihon keieishi koza* (Lectures on Japanese business history), vol. 6, *Nihon no kigyo to shakai* (Business and society in Japan). Tokyo: Nihon Keizai Shinbunsha.

――. 1978a. *Nihon romu kanri-shi kenkyu* (Studies in the history of labour management in Japan). Rev. ed. Tokyo: Ochanomizu Shobo.

――. 1978b. *Nihon ni okeru roshi kyocho no teiryu* (Undercurrents of labour-management harmony in Japan). Tokyo: Waseda Daigaku Shuppankai.

Hirschmeier, J. 1964. *The origins of entrepreneurship in Meiji Japan.* Cambridge, Mass.: Harvard University Press.

Hirschmeier, J., and T. Yui. 1977. *Nihon no keiei hatten: Kindaika to kigyo keiei.* Japanese version of *The development of Japanese business, 1600–1973* (1975). Tokyo: Toyo Keizai Shinposha.

Hsu, F. L. K. 1971. *Hikaku bunmei shakai ron*. Japanese version of *Clan, caste and club* (1963). Tokyo: Baifukan.

Imuta, T. 1969. Meiji-chuki kaisha kigyo no kozo (Structure of mid-Meiji companies). *Shakai keizai shigaku* (Socio-Economic History) 35, no. 2.

———. 1970. Meiji-chuki ni okeru kogyokaisha no shihon kosei (Capital formation in mid-Meiji industrial enterprises). *Osaka Shiritsu Daigaku Keizaigaku Zasshi* (Osaka City University Economic Journal) 62, nos. 4 and 5.

Ishikawa, K. 1976. Kazoku shihon to shizoku keieisha (Aristocratic capital and samurai manager). In *Nihon keieishi koza* (Lectures on Japanese business history), vol. 2, *Kogyoka to kigyosha katsudo* (Industrialization and entrepreneurship). Tokyo: Nihon Keizai Shinbunsha.

Iwata, R. 1977. *Nihonteki keiei no henshu genri* (Organizing principles of Japanese-style management). Tokyo: Bunshindo.

Kawashima, T. 1957. *Ideorogi toshite no kazoku seido* (The family system as ideology). Tokyo: Iwanami Shoten.

Koike, K. 1977. *Shokuba no rodokumiai to sanka* (Labour union and participation in the work place). Tokyo: Toyo Keizai Shinposha.

———. 1981. *Nihon no jukuren* (Skills in Japan). Tokyo: Yuhikaku.

Marshall, B. K. 1968. *Nihon no shihonshugi to nashonarizumu*. Japanese version of *Capitalism and nationalism in Japan*. Tokyo: Daiamondosha.

Mito, T. 1976. *Ko to shi* (Public and private). Tokyo: Miraisha.

———. 1981. *Nihonjin to kaisha* (Japanese and company). Tokyo: Chuo Keizaisha.

Morikawa, H. 1967. Kigyokan taisei to keizai hatten—Tokuni Nihon no baai ni tsuite (Inter-firm relationships and economic development—Looking at the case of Japan). *Keieishigaku* (Japan Business History Review) 2, no. 1.

Murakami, T.; Kumon, S.; and Sato, S. 1979. *Bunmei toshite no ie shakai* (The *ie* society as civilization). Tokyo: Chuo Koronsha.

Nakagawa, K. 1967. Nihon no kogyoka katei ni okeru "soshikika sareta kigyosha katsudo" ("Organized entrepreneurship" in Japan's industrialization process). *Keieishigaku* (Japan Business History Review) 2, no. 3.

———. 1969. *Kigyosha—Kogyoka no ninaite* (Entrepreneurs: The backbone of industrialization). In *Nihon no kogyoka* (The industrialization of Japan), ed. Nakayama I. and Shinohara M. Tokyo: Ushio Shuppan.

———, ed. 1980. Government and business. In *Proceedings of the Fuji Conference*. Tokyo: University of Tokyo Press.

———. 1981a. *Hikaku keieishi josetsu* (Foundations of comparative business history). Tokyo: Tokyo Daigaku Shuppankai.

———. 1981b. *Nihonteki keiei* (Japanese-style management). NHK daigaku koza. Tokyo: Nihon Hoso Shuppan Kyokai.

Nakane, C. 1967. *Tate shakai no ningen kankei* (Human relationships in the vertical society). Tokyo: Kodansha.

Nihon Seisansei Honbu. 1981. *Roshi kankei hakusho—Nihonteki roshi kankei no hyoka to kadai* (White paper on labour-management relations: Evaluation and issues in Japanese-style labour-management relations). Tokyo.

Nishiyama, T. 1983. *Datsu-shihonshugi bunseki* (Analysing post-capitalism). Tokyo: Bunshindo.

Odaka, K. 1965. *Nihon no keiei* (Japanese management). Tokyo: Chuo Koronsha.

———. 1981. *Sangyo shakaigaku kogi: Nihonteki keiei no kakushin* (Lectures on industrial sociology: The revolution of Japanese-style management). Tokyo: Iwanami Shoten.

Organization for Economic Co-Operation and Development. 1973. *OECD report on labour in Japan*. Japanese version. Tokyo: Nihon Rodo Kyokai.

———. 1977. *Development of the labour-management relationship system: What Japan's experience means*. OECD report. Japanese version. Tokyo: Nihon Rodo Kyokai.

Ouchi, W. G. 1981. *Seori Z*. Japanese version of *Theory Z*. Tokyo: CBS Sony Shuppan.

Pascale, R. T. 1978. Personnel practices and employee attitudes. *Human Relations* 31 (July).

Ranis, G. 1955. The Community-centered entrepreneur in Japanese development. In *Explorations in entrepreneurial history*, 1st ser., vol. 8, no. 2.

Sato, R. 1983. *'Me'-shakai to 'we'-shakai: Amerika-shugi Nihon-shugi shihon-shugi* (The Me-society and the We-society: Americanism, Japanism, capitalism). Tokyo: Nihon Keizai Shinbunsha.

Sumiya, M. 1976. *Rodo keizai no riron* (Theory of labour economics). Tokyo: Tokyo Daigaku Shuppankai.

Taikai tokushugo: Sogoshosha ni tsuite. 1973 (Conference on General Trading Companies). *Keieishigaku* (Japan Business History Review) 8, no. 1.

Takeyama, Y. 1965. *Nihon no keiei—Sono fudo to tenbo* (Japanese management—Social climate and prospects). Tokyo: Kajima Shuppankai.

Taylor, J. 1984. *The shadow of Japan*. Japanese version. Tokyo: Kobunsha.

Tsuda, M. 1967. *Nenkoteki roshi kankei ron* (Theory of seniority-style labour-management relations). Tokyo: Mineruva Shobo.

———. 1980. *Nihonteki keiei no daiza* (Japanese-style management on a pedestal). Tokyo: Chuo Keizaisha.

Ujihara, S. 1966. Chingin taikei no ichi kosatsu (Thoughts on the wage system). In *Nihon rodo mondai kenkyu* (Studies in Japanese labour problems). 2d ed. Tokyo: Tokyo Daigaku Shuppankai.

Vogel, E. F. 1968. *Nihon no shin chusankaikyu: Sarariman to sono kazoku*. Japanese version of *Japan's new middle class: Saralied workers and their families* (1963). Tokyo: Seishin Shobo.

———. 1979. *Japan as number one: Lessons for America*. Japanese version. Tokyo: TBS Buritanika.

Yasuoka, S. 1975. *Zaibatsu keisei no bunkateki shakaiteki haikei* (Cultural and social background of formation of the *zaibatsu*). *Keieishigaku* (Japan Business History Review) 10, no. 1.

Yoshino, M. Y. 1975. *Nihon no keiei shisutemu*. Japanese version of *Japan's managerial system* (1968). Tokyo: Daiamondosha.

[9]

CALIFORNIA MANAGEMENT REVIEW
Volume XXIX, Number 4, Summer 1987
© 1987, The Regents of the University of California

Management Style and Practice of Korean Chaebols

Sangjin Yoo   Sang M. Lee

The economic growth of Korea has often been expressed as "The Miracle of the Han River" in comparison to the miracle of the Rhine River (West Germany) and the miracle of the Smida River (Japan).

Over the last two decades, Korea has achieved a truly remarkable economic growth. After World War II, Korea was one of the world's poorest countries, heavily dependent on agriculture and financially dependent upon foreign sources. However, with strong government leadership, sound economic planning, and hard work on the part of her people, Korea has overcome her lack of natural resources and achieved a real annual growth rate of over 9% in GNP. Korea's annual manufacturing output growth rate has been nearly 20% and its export growth rate over 30%. Its per capita income in real terms rose 7.4% annually from only $126 in 1966 to over $2,000 in 1985. [1]

Exports, which reached $100 million for the first time in 1964, amounted to more than $21.6 billion in 1982 and are projected to reach $33 billion in 1986. In 1985, Korean exports ranked 13th in the world and 10 Korean business conglomerates (Chaebols) were ranked in "The Fortune International 500" list. In 1985, Hyundai became the largest exporter of automobiles to Canada in less than 18 months from the introduction of its Ponys.

It is clear that strong leadership and the sound economic planning of the government were important elements of the remarkable economic growth of Korea. However, the efforts of the private business sector, especially those of the Chaebols, have been the real catalysts for Korea's economic development.

According to a report by the Korea Federation of Small Business (KFSB), the number of businesses in Korea totalled 917,321 in 1982, compared to 5,510 in 1947. [2] As of 1981, Korea's 30 largest Chaebols held

96   SANGJIN YOO & SANG M. LEE

289 (0.84%) of the total number of mining and manufacturing operations in Korea and produced 38.7% of the nation's total mining and manufacturing output. The same 289 businesses employed 422,000 workers, 19.8% of the nation's mining and manufacturing employment.[3] Among the 20 largest companies listed in 1983, 15 were owned by the 10 largest Chaebols. In 1984, the five largest Chaebols — Hyundai, Samsung, Lucky-Goldstar, Sunkyung, and Daewoo — had total sales of close to $50 billion, or more than half of the country's GNP. The total exports by eight GTCs (General Trading Companies) owned by the eight largest Chaebols constituted more than 50% of all Korean exports in 1985.[4]

Characteristics of the Korean Chaebols

Evolution of the Korean Chaebols — "Chaebol" stands for a conglomerate or a financial clique in Korea. Korean Chaebols were formed because of the rapid economic growth, although they are different in terms of formation timing and type. Many Chaebols were formed through various support plans initiated by the government. The concept of "Chaebol" originally appeared in Japan, According to Yasuoka, in Japan, the first "Zaibatsu" (Japanese term for Chaebol) — Mitsubishi — was formed in 1893.[5] More Japanese Zaibatsus were established between 1909 and 1920.

Korean Chaebols can be classified in three categories based on the timing of their formation: the late 1950s, the 1960s, and the 1970s.[6] Chaebols of the late 1950s — such as Hyundai, Samsung, and Lucky-Goldstar (formerly Lucky) — were established by self-made founders through governmental support such as preferential allotment of grants, disposal of government-vested properties, and preference in taxation and finance. Chaebols of the 1960s — such as Hanjin, Korea Explosive, Hyosung, Sangyong, and Dong-A — came about because of foreign loans induced for a series of five-year plans. Finally, those of the 1970s — such as Daewoo, Sunkyong, Lotte, Kolon, and Doosan — were formed during the economic boom based on a rapid growth of export and domestic demand.

Even though they produce a larger portion of Korean GDP and consist of many related companies like those in Japan, Korean Chaebols are somewhat different from Japanese Zaibatsus in many aspects, especially in terms of ownership and management.

The Korean "Chaebol" vs. the Japanese "Zaibatsu" — In 1984, the fifty largest Chaebols accounted for about 20% of Korean GDP, with the five largest Chaebols representing about 10% of the total.[7] On the other hand, the total sales percentage of the six largest Zaibatsus in Japan — Mitsui, Mitsubishi, Sumitomo, Huyo, Sangwa, and Daiizikangking — was 16.18% of the total of all 1,791 companies whose stocks were listed in 1983. Their gross capital accounted for 15.30% of the total of all 1,791 listed companies.[8] If we consider only these statistics, it appears that the

MANAGEMENT STYLE & PRACTICE OF KOREAN CHAEBOLS 97

Korean Chaebol and the Japanese Zaibatsu are similar. However, if we take a more analytical look at Chaebols and Zaibatsus, we can find considerable differences between them.

Definition — A Chaebol may be defined as "a business group consisting of large companies which are owned and managed by family members or relatives in many diversified business areas." To be a Chaebol or a Zaibatsu, an organization should satisfy two conditions: it should be owned by family members or relatives; and it should have diversified business operations.[9] Most Korean Chaebols and Japanese Zaibatsus satisfy these two conditions. The owner family of a Chaebol controls 20%-40% of a listed company's total shares.[10] The average market share of each Korean Chaebol in manufacturing, banking, insurance, and construction industries is 3-5%.[11] As indicated, this is also true for the Japanese Zaibatsu.

However, there is one basic difference in the concept of "family members or relatives" between Korea and Japan. In Japan, there are two different types of family concepts.[12] One is a "family" which is formed based upon the blood relationship (consanguinity) concept. The other one is "iae" (household, clan), which does not require the blood relationship. In most cases, family and iae represent the same relationship. Nevertheless, in the case of succession, the gap between these two is clear. In Japan, succession of property is often carried out based on the iae concept. Thus, a successor of the property is not necessarily a blood family member. Under this system, there is no change in the value of the iae's property itself. According to Suzuki, the chief of an iae is a successor of the role or status within the iae rather than the blood.[13]

On the other hand, there is only one family concept in Korea, formed strictly on the blood relationship. Under the Korean concept, the blood relationship is the necessary condition of the family. In the case of succession, the eldest son of the family usually becomes the heir of the business. Of course, the other family members would have their own shares. Thus, the property of the family is divided into several portions. Under the Korean system, unlike that of the Japanese, the chief of a family is a successor of the blood.

Ownership — Japanese Zaibatsus before and after World War II show different characteristics in terms of ownership and management. For comparison purposes, Zaibatsus formed after WW II are probably more suitable than those formed before WW II, since most of these earlier Zaibatsu were broken up and most of the Korean Chaebols were formed after the war.

One of the distinguishing characteristics of Korean management is ownership and management by family. Considering the short history of Korean enterprises, it is understandable that many corporations are still owned by the founder's family members. However, as Table 1 shows, the

Table 1. Korean Chaebols: Distribution of Ownership
(As of 1982)

		Family & Relatives	Affiliated Enterprises	Total	Level of Power†
Chaebol	Top 10*	13.44%	18.99%	32.43%	20.64
	Top 31	19.29%	14.93%	34.22%	29.42
	Top 41	18.65%	10.99%	29.64%	39.16
	Ave.	17.71%	14.96%	32.67%	29.69
Non-Chaebol		20.96%	2.99%	23.95%	— —

*Classified by the amount of paid-in capital. Top 10 means the first 10 Chaebols, Top 31 is the next 21 Chaebols, and Top 41 is the final 10 Chaebols of the study.

†The Unit for the level of power is points and calculated using the following system: Chairman or President = 10; Vice President = 5; representative director = 4; executive director = 3; and director of the affiliated company = 1.

Source: Edited from Tamio Hattori, "Comparison of Large Corporations in Korea and Japan," in Hakjon Lee and Kuhyun Chung, eds., *The Structure and Strategy of Korean Corporations* (Seoul: Bupmunsa, 1986), p. 182.

ratio of family ownership of Chaebols is much higher that those of non-Chaebols. Based on the information provided in Table 1, Chaebols own more than 30% of the listed corporations' stock. Furthermore, larger Chaebols show a relatively higher ratio of family ownership.

Most Korean Chaebols employ one of the following three, somewhat unique structures of ownership:

- sole possession by the owner—the founder or his/her family members and relatives own all affiliated enterprises;
- domination by the core company—the founder or his/her family members or relatives own the core company, which in turn, owns other affiliated enterprises; and
- mutual possession—the founder or his/her family members or relatives own the core company and/or some kind of foundation, which in turn, owns other affiliated enterprises (affiliated enterprises can possess each other's stocks).

Hattori takes Hanjin, Daweoo, and Samsung as respective examples of these three types. [14] Table 2 shows the distribution of ownership within the Samsung Chaebol. As of 1982, the Samsung group had 10 listed companies under its control; 12.73% of the total stocks was possessed by family members; and 20.35% by other affiliated companies in the group. [15]

Japanese Zaibatsus, on the other hand, show different aspects of ownership from those of Korean Chaebols. They have enormous influence on the Japanese economy, just as Korean Chaebols do on the Korean economy. In

Table 2. Stock Distribution of Samsung Group
(As of 1982, in %)

Holder	Company									
	A	B	C	D	E	F	G	H	I	J
Founder	3.40				9.31		2.96		8.17	
2nd Son				2.87				6.20	14.16	
3rd Son	6.02	3.77	5.76				5.30	16.70	1.00	
1st Daughter				2.41		6.99				
2nd Daughter							1.36		0.21	
3rd Daughter		3.46							0.90	
Father-in-law (3rd Son)	0.66	2.18						1.38		
Daughter-in-law										19.28
Company K	1.15			9.47		1.23	9.96	4.60		
Company L	0.50					1.82	2.30			
Company G	3.40		5.75							
Company M	9.66	8.63	9.50	9.47	9.89		8.98	9.60	9.99	
Company J	5.46	4.67		3.86	3.36		1.64			
Company B			22.75	9.54	3.59					
Company H			5.75		9.26		1.00			
Company A					15.24					
Company N							1.39			

Note: Company A through N represent affiliated enterprises of the Samsung Chaebol.

Source: Edited from Tamio Hattori, "Comparison of Large Corporations in Korea and Japan," in Hakjon Lee and Kuhyxn Chung, eds., *The Structure and Strategy of Korean Corporations* (Seoul: Bupmunsa, 1986), p. 189.

1981, the six largest Zaibatsus possessed 25.94% of total Japanese corporations' assets and 15.78% of total Japanese corporations' sales, even though they have only 5.11% of the total number of Japanese corporations' employees. However, unlike Korean Chaebols, the average stock-holding ratio of the six largest Zaibatsus was only 1.78% of 1981.[16] In spite of the relatively low stock-holding ratio, a Zaibatsu can maintain 20–30% of the total stock within a group by mutually possessing each other's stock. For example, in 1983, the ratios of mutual possession were 17.67% for Mitsui, 24.39% for Mitsubishi, and 25.06% for Sumitomo.[17]

Management—To quantify the owners' influence on the Chaebol groups' management, Hattori used a 10-point scale.[18] That is, if the owner or one of the family members is chairman or president that person is given 10 points, the vice president is given 5 points, the representative director 4 points, the executive director 3 points, and the director of the affiliated company 1 point. The far right column of Table 1 shows the point totals.

A study by Lee and Yoo shows that 31% of the executive officers of the top 20 Chaebols in Korea consists of owner's family members.[19] Based upon this information, we may conclude that the owner or his/her family members' influence on management is very strong. However, the power

100   SANGJIN YOO & SANG M. LEE

structure of each Chaebol may be different, based upon the number of
family members and the owner's management philosophy. While the ratio
of family ownership is higher for the larger Chaebols, the owners' influence
on management is stronger in the smaller Chaebols (see Table 1). If the
structure of ownership is sole possession by the owner, the owner or
family members' influence on management is enormous. Even though
some non-family members (such as professional managers) may take
higher management position in Chaebol groups of the other two ownership
types (core company or mutual possession), the most important posts
usually belong to the owner's family members.

According to Okumura, six distinctive characteristics have evolved in
the Japanese Zaibatsu, especially after World War II.[20] They are:

- stock is owned by affiliated companies (members of the council of
  presidents) rather than the owner's family;
- presidents of affiliated companies have become members of the council
  of presidents which makes important decisions in a Zaibatsu;
- an affiliated company owns stock of the other affiliated companies;
- each Zaibatsu owns a bank as its core company to furnish funds;
- each Zaibatsu owns a "Sogoshosha" as its core company (bank and
  "Sogoshosha" are closely related); and
- each Zaibatsu owns affiliated companies in diversified business areas
  rather than in one specific area.

Based upon these characteristics, Japanese Zaibatsus show totally different management structure and style from those of Korean Chaebols.
Almost no owner's family members are involved in management. Rather,
most of the top executives are professional managers who have worked for
a specific company for along time. The ratio of the top executives promoted
from within the company is 78.7% for Mitsui, 69.8% for Mitsubishi, and
73.1% for Sumitomo. On the other hand, the ratio of promotion from other
affiliated companies is 12.2% for Mitsui, 22.6% for Mitsubishi, and 19.4%
for Sumitomo. Outside scouting for the three companies provided 9.1%,
7.6%, and 7.5% of the top executives, respectively.[21]

The Distinctive Management Style of the Korean Chaebol

Founders' Management Philosophy—There are numerous distinctive
management characteristics in Korean Chaebols. Among them, self-made
founders, management by family, and close government relationships are
the most unique features. Before discussing these three in greater detail, an
overview of various top management philosophies helps in understanding
the Chaebols' management style. Following are five founder-owners' philosophies, drawn from among the top 10 Chaebols:

- Choong-Hoon Cho of the Hanjin Group (Korean Airlines, etc.) has
  established enterprises through trust and public credibility. He empha-

MANAGEMENT STYLE & PRACTICE OF KOREAN CHAEBOLS 101

sizes management by family rather than professional management. He also attempts to maintain a lifetime employment system because of his concern for the employees' livelihood. His managerial philosophy is: "Business is an art. To make a good work of art, there should be harmony, just as good as an orchestra's."[22]

- Jong-Hyun Choi of Sunkyong Group is a top manager who has used his academic training in chemistry, economics, and management in establishing and managing his company. He rescued Sunkyong Textile Co., Ltd., which was in a precarious situation, through his knowledge of chemistry. He is one of the top managers who tries to avoid management by family, saying: "A firm should exist through all eternity. Thus, management should leave honorably after serving for a firm."[23]

- Ju-Yung Chung of Hyundai Group is a founder-owner who has expanded his business through his deep commitment to the business and through an aggressive management style for which he is called "the entrepreneur." Based on aggressiveness, he established the Hyundai Group, which consists of construction, automobiles, steel, machinery, shipbuilding, and general trading company (GTC) concerns. He tries to maintain an extremely bureaucratic management system combined with management by family, even though professional managers manage some affiliated companies. He is also very proud of the spirit of the Hyundai Group, as expressed by the slogan: "Be very aggressive and become a strong driving force."[24]

- Woo-Choong Kim of the Daewoo Group established his business through hard work and accurate judgment. His acquisition of failing firms and his use of personal connections (based on graduates from the same high school he attended, instead of using family members), have been the main driving forces for the success of the Daewoo group. He is called "the hardest working man in Korea," and "the best salesman in Korea." As his nickname indicates, his managerial philosophy is based on "hard work." Thus, he always requires subordinates to perform an amount of work commensurate with their pay. To accomplish this, he introduced a quite different management philosophy, "requiring hard work through higher compensation."[25] Kim has said, "We work not because of leisure but because of pride."[26]

- Byung-Chull Lee of Samsung Group is one of the senior businessmen in Korea. He tries to keep his authority through various bureaucratic controls. He is the first top manager in Korea to use a competitive recruiting system. He manages personnel based only on performance and ability. As in the case in almost all Korean Chaebols, family members are the mainstream of management, even though Samsung has the highest ratio of non-family member executives. He attempts to develop elites based on two principles: "the right people to the right position," and "incentive compensation." His managerial philosophy is: "Be the number one."[27]

Self-Made Founders—In Korea, the development of enterprises can be classified in terms of historical periods: [28]

- enterprises formed and continued under Japanese colonial rule (1919–1945);
- enterprises established after WW II even though capital was accumulated during the Japanese colonial rule period;
- enterprises established and modernized during the Korean War (1950–1953); and
- enterprises formed based on either foreign aid in the 1950s or loans in the 1960s.

The inauguration mission of Korean enterprises can be classified into five categories, namely: [29]

- the transfer type—modern entrepreneurs succeeded traditional magnates;
- the imitation type—imitation of the American free enterprise system;
- the endemic type—the traditional Korean businesses;
- the managerial type—organizations based on management theory; and
- the welfare type—intended to improve employees' welfare.

Most Korean enterprises have been founded based on one of these inauguration missions. Almost every early Korean company was established by a self-made founder. These self-made founders inaugurated and managed their enterprises under great difficulties, which stemmed from a lack of capital, technology, experience, and education. There were also political problems, especially during the Japanese colonial rule period. Almost every self-founder has devoted his/her entire life to work. These difficulties and the sweatshop work ethic have led to such common Korean entrepreneurial characteristics as: innate diligence and thrift; creativity; strong impellent force; sincerity and creditability; frontier spirit; preference for harmony among family members and employees; preference for stable and bureaucratic organization; top-down decision making; insensitivity to changes in circumstances; non-scientific management; preference for management by family; and lack of formal education. [30] These common characteristics still have great impact, both positive and negative, on the management style of Korean Chaebols.

Management by Family—Considering the short history of Korean Chaebols, it is understandable that many companies are still managed by the founder-owner. As companies grow and mature, however, many companies face a shift in generation. The "handing over" of an enterprise is not a simple matter, since it is not simply a transfer of wealth but the inheritance of a living project. Thus, the success or failure of the transfer often determines the future of the company. The success or failure of the transfer is often determined by the method of inheritance. Usually, inheritance in Korea has been based on the Confucian tradition of hierarchical order within the family, the highest priority given to the oldest son in the family. In Korea, according to one study,[31] the ratio of inheritance to the first son is 65.9%, to family members other than the first son is 24.4%, and to non-family members is 9.7%.

In addition to the transfer of control, recruiting becomes an important issue for the growth of a company. During the rapid growth of the economy, the company needs to recruit capable managers. Much of the recruiting has been done, not on the basis of ability but on various connections such as family ties, relatives, common hometown/school, or political ties. One study shows that 31% of the executive officers of the top 20 Chaebols in Korea consist of family members, 40% of the executive officers are recruited from outside, while 29% are promoted from within.[32] Another study shows that 25.5% of presidents of Korean companies are founders, 18.5% are the second generation of founders, 21.2% are promoted from within, and 35.1% are recruited from outside.[33] Even though more than 50% of CEOs are not family members, the core positions usually belong to the owner's family.

Table 3 presents the structure and number of executive officers and their influence in the Lucky-Goldstar Chaebol. Points for power have again been calculated using Hattori's 10-point scale. As shown in Table 3, the portion of family members is only 10.8% of the total number of executives. However, they exercise 21.6% of the total influence on management. On the other hand, promoted executives' level of influence is only 1.96 times that of family members' even though the number of promoted executives is 4.88 times the number of family members. This implies management by family, in which the top-down decision-making style of Korean Chaebols originated.

Close Government Relationship—Undeniably, the incredible growth of Korea was initiated and steered by the government. Since many Korean Chaebols owe their success entirely to government support, a close relationship between government and business has been inevitable. For example, a close relationship with the government has been essential for Chaebols to receive the basic benefits that have been critical to their success, such as: preferential disposal of government-vested properties during the period of confusion (1945–Korean War); preferential allotment of foreign aid and grants during the period of reconstruction (after the Korean War–late 1950s); preference for obtaining loans during the period of development (1960s–early 1970s); designation of GTC and export financing during the take-off period (1970s), preference for taxation and financing; and inclusion in the five-year economic development plans of the government.

In addition, the government's control of the banking system since the early 1960s has made it possible to steer big Chaebols into the industries

104   SANGJIN YOO & SANG M. LEE

Table 3. Lucky-Goldstar: Executives and Their Influence
(As of 1982)

Company	Number of Executives			Influence (in Points)		
	Family Member	Promoted Within	Outside Scout	Family Member	Promoted Within	Outside Scout
A	2	15	4	20	29	14
B	4	18	5	26	39	18
C	1	3	4	4	11	17
D	1	6	7	10	13	30
E	2	8	12	5	26	26
F	2	4	4	20	7	13
G		5	1		16	10
H	1	3	2	10	15	4
I	2	13	2	5	41	4
J	1	4	2	10	6	4
K	1	5	4	3	11	13
L	1	3	9	3	12	25
M		1	5		1	16
Total	18	88	61	116	227	194
%	10.8	52.7	36.5	21.6	42.3	36.1

Source: Edited from Tamio Hattori, "Comparison of Large Corporations in Korea and Japan," in Hakjon Lee and Kuhyun Chung, eds., *The Structure and Strategy of Korean Corporations* (Seoul: Bupmunsa, 1986), p. 195.

that the government wanted to develop. Consequently, Chaebols could not help but maintain close relationships with the government if they wanted to be included in the targeted growth areas.

The close government-business relationship in Korea is often referred to as "Korea Inc." However, there are distinct differences between "Korea Inc." and "Japan Inc." For example, "Japan Inc." connoted a government-business partnership in which the policy reflects a consensus between equals. "Korea Inc." means something very different. In Korea, the government sets the policies and businessmen follow, more or less. In this way, Korea is an unusual blend of free enterprise and state direction. The government's strongest weapon is its control of credit. Large Japanese Zaibatsus often have their own banks from which they obtain funds.[34] The Korean government announced banking liberalization plans in 1983, yet the government still does not permit domination of banks by an individual Chaebol.

It is clear that the Korean government's leadership in economic development policy and the close government-business relationship have produced a phenomenal economic growth in Korea. However, government-directed growth policies alone will not achieve *sustained* economic growth, which requires instead a balanced industrial structure, effective competition in the international market, and close cooperation between business and government.

To summarize, the management style of Korean Chaebols consists of:

- clan management
- top-down decision making
- flexible lifetime employment
- a Confucian work ethic
- paternalistic leadership
- loyalty
- compensation based on seniority and merit rating
- bureaucratic conflict resolution
- a very bureaucratic yet low degree of formality and standardized systems
- close government-business relationship
- expansion through conglomeration

Personnel Practice of Korean Chaebols

In general, there are five different concerns in personnel management, which include: security (recruitment), development, compensation, maintenance, and organization. Each area addresses several important issues. For example, recruiting and job assignment are important issues of security, while training, job rotation, performance evaluation, and promotion are important for development policy. Salary, incentives, and welfare are important for compensation, while mobility of workers, retirement policy, and labor relationship are major concerns of maintenance. Finally, task assignment, organization structure, hierarchy, and decision-making style are important issues in the organization area.

According to one study,[35] for security (recruitment), most large Korean corporations classify employees into three categories: core (top management and high-level executives); basic (permanent employees); and temporary. Most Korean companies hire employees through a reference (document) check and a written test for English, knowledge in the major field, and/or common sense. They prefer new college graduates and people with career experience. Once they hire new people, they usually assign the elite group to such core departments as planning, finance, and accounting after a short training period (usually 7–10 days).

For development, Korean corporations adopt uniform training systems for all employees using OJT and experts' lectures. The education and training program is not at all uniform or systematic. It does not closely relate to job assignment, job rotation, and promotion. Thus, employees do not devote themselves to pursuing new knowledge during the education and training period. Naturally, maximum effectiveness of the education and training program is not to be expected. Job rotation in Korean corporations is usually done on an ad hoc basis. Performance evaluation places emphasis on past achievements. Employees in Korean companies are promoted largely

106   SANGJIN YOO & SANG M. LEE

based on seniority, dedication, and relationship with top management rather than on contribution and achievement.

Most Korean companies compensate based on seniority. They determine an employees' base salary considering the level of education and seniority, then add some allowances for gross salary. There is a salary difference between college graduates and high school graduates. In addition to a monthly salary, Korean companies pay seasonal bonuses (such as for New Years, vacations, the Korean Thanksgiving Day, and Christmas). However, most Korean corporations do not yet have complete welfare systems.

In the personnel maintenance area, Korean corporations lay off less important employees (regardless of core, basic, or temporary status) when they face an economic slump. Korean employees retire once they reach a certain age, usually fifty-five. Retiring employees receive a lump sum retirement allowance. They do not usually receive such compensation as a part-time job or consulting position at the company after retirement. In Korea, labor unions have been patterned after the industrial union system. The principle of harmony and paternal authority are emphasized to resolve labor disputes. Labor unions have been kept on a tight leash by law, which forbids outsiders from intervening in a dispute between an employer and his/her workers. These laws make it virtually impossible for a union to help workers bargain with their employers, and regulations on arbitration effectively outlaw strikes.[36]

Finally, in the organization area, most Korean corporations do not have clear job assignment criteria. Usually, middle- or lower-level management do not have much authority to perform their job effectively (more than 80% of the authority resides at the upper management level). Most Korean companies have a people-oriented organization structure. Korean corporations are organized based upon hierarchies with a clear-cut order. Nevertheless, there is no clear description of the relationship between authority and responsibility. Thus, a top-down decision-making style has become typical in Korean corporations. Table 4 shows the distinctive characteristics of the personnel management system in Korea as compared to that of the United States and Japan.

Conclusion

Based on the foregoing discussion, the following conclusions and observations can be made:

- Even though Korean Chaebols are criticized for their "Octopus Arm" style expansion, aggressive infringement in the business areas of small business, lack of business ethics, and the concentration of wealth in a small, select group of people, they have been the backbone of Korean economic growth.

Table 4. Comparison of Personnel Management Systems

Issues	Korea	United States	Japan
Employee Classes	core, basic, temporary	basic, temporary	core, basic, some temporary
Recruitment Criteria	reference check, & written test; prefer both new college	reference check & interview; prefer experienced	interview; prefer new college graduates
Job Assignment	assign elites to important departments	assign based on the job	assign field site or floor first
Training & Education	uniform, OJT, non-systematic	knowledge & technical OJT, university	OJT, job rotation, informal groups
Job Rotation	ad hoc basis	aim at specialists	regular, periodic; aim at generalists
Evaluation	non-systematic, past-oriented	systematic, present-oriented	continuous future-oriented
Promotion	seniority	performance	combination
Salary Criteria	education level & seniority	education level & performance	education level, age, & performance
Incentive System	seasonal bonus (uniform)	performance-based incentive	performance-based incentive
Welfare	no	yes	yes
Employees Lay-Offs	less important people first	temporary people & less important departments first	concentrate on temporary people only
Retirement	age of 55 (inflexible)	age of 65 (flexible)	age of 55-60 (flexible)
Labor Relations	principles of harmony; no strikes	contract-oriented; use strikes as a final method	principles of "wa"; labor disputes start with strike
Job Assignment	no systematic assignment	individual assignment with detailed job descriptions	group assignment job descriptions are not detailed
Structure	people-oriented	work-oriented	combination
Decision Making	top-down	top-down	bottom-up

Source: Edited from Yookeun Shin, *Structures and Problems of Korean Enterprises* (Seoul: Seoul National University Publishing, 1985), pp. 331-359.

108   SANGJIN YOO & SANG M. LEE

- Ownership and management are not separated in most Korean Chaebol groups. This results in management by family even though the proportion of professional managers has increased considerably.
- Many Korean Chaebols adopt certain tactics such as new family ties through marriage to secure their existence and to maintain the family's dominance in management. According to one survey,[37] there are twenty-one marriages between the family members of the top 10 Chaebols.
- Many founders are still in top management position, since Korean Chaebols have had a relatively short history.
- Top-down decision making is common in many Korean Chaebol groups.
- Succession is very important for the success of Korean Chaebols because of their short history and the unique Korean family concept.
- Most Korean Chaebols owe much of their success to government support.
- Most Korean Chaebols' expansion has been largely based upon government policy and with the primary goal of increasing total sales volume rather than profitability.
- Korean Chaebols' management practice reflects many of their unique characteristics.

Korean Chaebols have been able to manage and grow successfully based on their unique characteristics and background. Nevertheless, they may not be able to expect the same favorable situations in the future because: many Korean Chaebols are on the verge of a shift in generation; they are too large to be managed primarily by family members; and the international business environment is becoming increasingly dynamic, with the pressures of protectionism, technological innovation, and stiff international competition.

To manage successfully in this dynamic and difficult environment, Korean Chaebols must devote their efforts to eliminating their weaknesses and making the best use of their strengths. Some of the recommended strategies are:

- continued R&D investment;
- adoption of a continuous training/education concept;
- concentration on high-tech industries;
- improvement of productivity;
- improvement of product quality;
- the fostering of small- and medium-sized firms;
- concentration on technology-intensive industries;
- application of advanced managerial systems;
- positive overseas investment;
- adoption of a permanent employment system;
- the systematization of enterprises;
- positive use of professional management; and
- aggressive international marketing.

MANAGEMENT STYLE & PRACTICE OF KOREAN CHAEBOLS   109

References

1. Dennis Holden, "Bank Liberalization in South Korea," *The Oriental Economist*, Vol. 51, No. 872 (June 1983).
2. Daesuk Hwang and Jungyul Yeon, *History of Korean Management* (Seoul, Korea: Sae Yung Publishing Co., 1978). ,
3. *The Korea Herald*, March 17, 1984.
4. *The Korea Times*, February 18, 1986.
5. Shigeaki Yasuoka, *Zaibatsu of Japan* (Tokyo, Japan: Nikkei Shinbunsha (Nihon Keizai Shinbunsha), 1976), p. 33.
6. Myungsu Hwang, "Study About Korean Business Groups and Entrepreneurs," *The Collection of Papers*, Volume 17 (Seoul, Korea: Dankook University, 1973).
7. Tamio Hattori, "Comparison of Large Corporations in Korea and Japan," in Hakjon Lee and Kuhyun Chung, eds., *The Structure and Strategy of Korean Corporations* (Seoul, Korea: Bupmunsa, 1986), p. 149.
8. Ibid.
9. Ibid., p. 151.
10. Tamio Hattori, "Ownership and Management of Modern Korean Corporations," *Azia Keizai (Asian Economy)* (May/June 1984).
11. Il Sakong, "Economic Growth and Chaebol," *Monthly ChoSun* (Seoul, Korea: Chosun Il Bo Sa, September, 1980).
12. Hattori, "Comparison of Large Corporations in Korea and Japan," in Lee and Chung, eds., op. cit., pp. 152–155.
13. Eitaro Suzuki, "Kacho no Iza (Position of the Head of a Family)," *Nihon Noson Shakai-gaku Genri (The Principle of Japanese Rural Society)* (Tokyo, Japan: Ji-cho sha, 1940 (Showa15)).
14. Hattori, in Lee and Chung, eds., op. cit., p. 183.
15. Ibid., p. 190.
16. Ibid., p. 171.
17. Ibid.
18. Ibid., p. 184.
19. Sang M. Lee and Sangjin Yoo, "The K-type Management: A Driving Force of Korean Prosperity," forthcoming in *International Management Review*, No. 4 (1987).
20. Hiroshi Okumura, *The Largest Six Business Group in Japan* (Tokyo, Japan: Daiyamondo sha (Diamond Publishing Co.), 1976), pp. 20–25.
21. Hattori, in Lee and Chung, eds., op. cit., p. 171.
22. Chosun Il Bo Sa, *The Twenty-Fifth Hour of Korean Chaebols* (Seoul, Korea: Dongkwang Publishing Co. Ltd., 1984), pp. 151–160.
23. Ibid., pp. 113–128.
24. Ibid., pp. 291–324; and Dongsoon Park, *Inauguration Idea of Korean Chaebols* (Seoul, Korea: Sae Kwang Publishing Co. Ltd., 1983), pp. 160–179.
25. Chosun Il Bo Sa, op. cit., pp. 65–92.
26. *The Korea Times*, Chicago Edition, October 22, 1985.
27. Chosun Il Bo Sa, op. cit., pp. 17–50; and Park, op. cit., pp. 85–102.
28. Park, op. cit., pp. 3–6.
29. Ibid.
30. Lee and Yoo, op. cit.
31. Yookeun Shin, *Structure and Problems in Korean Enterprises* (Seoul, Korea: Seoul National University Publishing, 1985), p. 246.
32. Lee and Yoo, op. cit.
33. Shin, op. cit., p. 245.

110   SANGJIN YOO & SANG M. LEE

34. Norman Pearlstine, "How South Korea Surprised The World," *Forbes*, Vol. 123, No. 9, April 30, 1979.

35. Shin, op. cit., pp. 339–359.

36. Hugh Sandeman, "Asia's Most Ambitious Nation," *The Economist*, Vol. 284, No. 7250, August 14, 1982.

37. Kyunghwan Oh, "Marriage Web of Korean Chaebols I, II," *Jeongkyung Yeon Ku (Research in Politics and Economics)* (Seoul, Korea: Kyunghyang Sin Mun Sa, 1986), Vol. 259 (September): 358–377, and Vol. 260 (October): 154–167.

[10]

International Journal of Psychology 25 (1990) 629–641   629
North-Holland

AN EMPIRICAL STUDY OF OVERSEAS CHINESE MANAGERIAL IDEOLOGY *

S.G. REDDING

University of Hong Kong, Hong Kong

Michael HSIAO

National Taiwan University, Taipei, Taiwan

This study of managerial ideology focuses on the question of legitimacy and attempts to reconstruct the way in which the role of the chief executive is perceived in the context of Overseas Chinese economic cultures. The location of the study is Hong Kong, Taiwan and Singapore and those studied were 72 chief executives in Chinese business organizations. Three determinants of present-day beliefs are traced to the socio-historical legacy of China, and these are identified as paternalism, personalism and a defensiveness derived from insecurity. The workings of their influence are traced via perceptions of the self, of relationships, of organization, and of society at large, to explain how executives rationalize their behaviour and their roles.

Studies of management in the case of the Overseas Chinese are now increasing in recognition of their economic significance in East and Southeast Asia, and their potential impact on China itself. The pioneering works of Silin (1976) and Willmott (1960) are now being supplemented by newer full-length studies such as those by Yoshihara (1988), Redding (1989), S.L. Wong (1983) and Limlingan (1986). These rest on a larger base of empirical work of the kind represented in the collection by Lim and Gosling (1983) and Omohundro (1981), and in the current work of scholars such as Hamilton (1989), Tam (1989), and G. Wong (1986).

* The research reported here owes much to the financial and intellectual support of the Institute for the Study of Economic Culture of Boston University, under the directorship of Peter L. Berger. Collaborators in the fieldwork were Theodora Ting Chau of National University of Singapore, and the late Lie Han Hwa in Indonesia. The research assistance of Monica Cartner and the facilities of the Mong Kwok Ping Management Data Bank of the University of Hong Kong are also gratefully acknowledged.

Requests for reprints should be sent to S.G. Redding, Dept. of Management Studies, University of Hong Kong, Pokfulam Road, Hong Kong.

Such literature continues to display the limitations of a still-emerging specialism, and these are (a) a relative paucity of extensive empirical data, and (b) the absence in comparative management generally of an agreed framework to handle the question of culture and causation. Although the contributiion of Hofstede (1980) has served to move enquiry on from the concerns with measuring what culture *is* to an understanding of what it might *do*, there is nevertheless an unnerving variety of models, or of unexplicated causal assumptions, with which to tackle the question of explanation. This is especially problematic when the explanandum is economic growth, as it often is, and the inevitable eventual recourse to multiple and reciprocal determinacy leaves the field full of unresolved challenges.

In that context this paper is an empirical contribution which is located within a framework of reciprocal determinants. It seeks to reconstruct managerial rationalities and investigates how Overseas Chinese chief executives explain their behaviour as chief executives. It takes the notion of managerial ideology as a set of ideas held in common by a group of people who are in positions of power and asks how that power is rationalized (Mannheim 1936). It also seeks to know where their ideas came from, and how they are expressed in behaviour. Above all, it seeks to retain the categories in which they think rather than to impose invented ones.

The underlying point of the enquiry is that the Overseas Chinese have created quite remarkable economic success in Hong Kong, Taiwan,. Singapore, and their sectors of the economies of ASEAN, over the past thirty years. The normal vehicle for their efforts is the Chinese family business and the pattern of its functioning is remarkably consistent across the Asia-Pacific region. The reasons for such distinctively patterned and consistent behaviour are not fully understood. To the extent that these economic institutions are the products of single dominant individuals, the explanation of how and why such structures work should be richly informed by knowledge of what is in the minds of those who own and manage them.

It must of course be acknowledged that individual variation in mind-sets is likely to be very great, and that high levels of consistency would here be suspect. But there is a common heritage, much common experience, and much common environmental background, and it would be reasonable to anticipate some tendencies to see the world in a particular light.

S.G. Redding, M. Hsiao / Overseas Chinese managerial ideology 631

The research process consisted of extensive tape-recorded interviews, with approximately 80 chief executives (for details see Redding 1990), and much attention was paid to creating an atmosphere of cordiality, relaxation, and confidentiality. Most of the interviews were conducted in the private dining room of a hotel, during evenings. A series of probes were used to begin a dialogue between two or three respondents about their 'philosophy' in certain matters, and the conversations taped. The results were frank and open, and inhibitions were rare, although indiscreet questions over matters such as private finance were avoided.

The conversations were then transcribed into 150 pages of extracted dialogue and verbatim statements taken out. These were then placed into the categories of idea which they reflected on, and a picture built up from the raw statements, of what Chinese chief executives think. The themes which emerged are treated according to frequency of occurrence and thus they reflect the mind sets of the respondents in the aggregate. The broad categories of enquiry may be seen as four interacting layers, namely

(1) perceptions of the self,
(2) relationships and kin,
(3) the organization,
(4) society at large.

The ideas which emerged in each of these fields began to take on some coherence as the categories emerged from the statements. It also became possible to see connections between the layers of the model, and also possible to link back into prior determinants in the Chinese cultural heritage. The full model is presented in fig. 1 and acts as the framework for this paper.

It should be noted here that this paper can only be in summary form and is therefore by way of a broad review instead of the detailed exposition which occupies a complete book (Redding 1990).

Influences from traditional Chinese culture

In many ways, the Overseas Chinese preserve traditional Chinese culture. Many of them emigrated to countries where their cohesion as a social group gave them necessary protection, and maintenance of cultural homogeneity has continued to serve a valuable purpose. In the

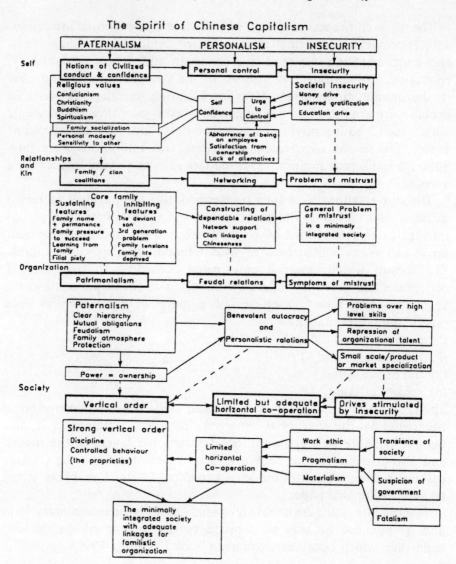

Fig. 1.

case of Taiwan, it has served to symbolise opposition to communism. In all cases the longevity of Chinese civilization has reinforced pride in it for generation after generation and this has served to see its norms perpetuated. Because of this constant carrying forward of tradition, certain cultural baggage is carried along too and with it, three longstanding forces moulding Chinese peoples' thinking and behaviour. These are paternalism, personalism, and insecurity.

Paternalism is a common social force throughout Pacific Asia (Pye 1985) where it serves to maintain sensitivity to hierarchy (Hofstede 1980) and the maintenance of social order via micro units of society such as families, rather than via institutions such as universal law. In the Chinese case, it is the main platform of the Confucian ethic. The power of the paterfamilias, modified and made responsible by the precepts of the doctrine, has served to stabilize society for a remarkably long period, and make it capable of withstandng upheavals of a kind which would have reduced many other societies to anarchy. Because of reliance on this stabilizing force, the vehicle for its expression, i.e. the family, has also remained as the overwhelmingly dominant social unit, and the principle locus of identity for Chinese people.

Personalism refers to the mechanism used by a society to establish reliable connections for the conduct of everyday affairs. The continuum at the end of which it lies has at its opposite end the use of universal, objective, neutral law. Simply put, unless all people are able and willing to abide by universally binding obligations, they must find another way of cementing their connections, reliability of connections being essential in much economic behaviour as well as in other fields. Before the emergence of universally binding institutionalized systems such as law, societies were reliant on personal contact and mutual interpersonal obligation. For the Chinese this traditional form remains normal, and the building and maintenance of such obligation networks a crucial component in social life.

Insecurity comes into play as a determinant of behaviour because the social history of China for some centuries forced people to come to terms with an aloof and exploitative state apparatus, and to develop defence mechanisms now embedded in their world-view. The experience of the Overseas Chinese, many of them in hostile social environments, has, if anything, reinforced this feature. Each family is its own welfare state and the guarantor of its members' long-term security, and there is scant reason to adjust that perception.

These three features of the Chinese heritage do not, of course, provide an exhaustive list of influences, but are simply proposed as being impossible to ignore in understanding present-day thinking, and also being particularly revealing of the mentality of the Chinese businessman, the description of which we now turn to.

634   S.G. Redding, M. Hsiao / Overseas Chinese managerial ideology

Perceptions of the self

The principal theme which emerges in this context is one of a tension played out between, on the one hand, forces which sponsor civilized conduct, and, on the other hand, the pressures deriving from insecurity. The former serve to create an individual with distinctly high levels of self-confidence. The latter create an urge to control events, and the self confidence and the urge to control come together to create a powerful drive towards ownership.

Examining further the inculcation of ideas of civilized conduct, it is possible to discern the deep influences of religious ideals, treating here Confucianism as the functional equivalent of a religion in that it provides a paradigm for the ordering of daily life and relationships. Christianity, Buddhism, and spiritualism were also evident in the cognitive maps of many of these chief executives, but Confucianism more so than any other and commonly in conjunction with another religion.

There are two major themes discernible in the socialization process in question. The first is the hierarchical ordering of relationships, and in particular the learning of roles defined around the key role of paterfamilias. The second is the learning of interpersonal sensitivity and the subsequent capacity to understand 'face' and building of the specific friendship bonds which tie Chinese society together.

It is the absorption of these guides to conduct which is seemingly able to provide the foundation for high levels of self-confidence and also self-discipline so commonly visible in Chinese people. As the rules for how to behave are so clear, and the roles so well specified, much self-doubt can be banished from the scene.

All this takes place, and has for a long time, in a societal context of insecurity. This does not apply in China now, although it did before 1947, but it is endemic for the Overseas Chinese. Only in Singapore can they escape from uncertainty and threat, and there the old values are changing more rapidly than elsewhere much to the consternation of Lee Kuan Yew.

The results of societal insecurity are threefold. Paramount among them is the drive to accumulate wealth, the most obvious security surrogate, and the most direct and obvious determinant of much day to day behaviour, reaching perhaps its most intense levels in Hong Kong where the issue of insecurity is more sharply focused than elsewhere.

The second result is a capacity for deferred gratification, for years of thrifty accumulation of savings in the interests of long-term stability. The third norm stemming from insecurity is the passion for education, seen as the key to upward mobility, and the guarantor of access to the reliable, respectable, stable, and financially rewarding professions.

The urge to control which emerges from the combination of self-confidence and surrounding insecurity is enhanced by a set of reinforcements. There is strong negative feeling, amounting in many to an abhorrence, of being an employee of someone else. The satisfaction of ownership is such that it explains much about the proliferation of small enterprises, and the motivation is at least partly based on an enhanced sensitivity to status and especially the unspoken odium attached to subordination in such a face-conscious, and status-sensitive society.

Relationships and kin

The larger themes visible when analysing perceptions of the self can also be seen at a different level of analysis. Seeing them at work in the social rather than the psychological context reveals other facets of the Overseas Chinese business world and the way it functions. Here the paternalism and Confucianism serve to sponsor strong family and clan coalitions. These are set in an environment of inter-family mistrust, largely stemming from the ambience of insecurity. The tensions which must result are resolved via the mechanism of extensive but very specifically delineated networking.

Relationships for the Chinese have always begun and ended with the core family, the principal, and for many the only locus of security and identity, and the basic building block of society. Despite the forces which support it, however, the Chinese family is not a necessarily stable social system, and it suffers from a number of threats. It exhibits both sustaining and inhibiting features.

Sustaining it are four principal forces: the permanence of the family name is a matter of honour; there is a very strong impetus from within the family to make its members contribute to its long-term security as a sustaining unit; the family remains a main source of social learning and thus of identification; and the power of filial piety as a doctrine remains undiminished, thus perpetuating the responsibility of each succeeding generation for the welfare of its predecessor.

On the other hand, there are forces which conspire to weaken the cohesion of the family: not all children are filially pious, and deviant children can often revolt against the conformity which may be required, especially as security accumulates and freedom can be afforded; the third generation problem is a larger development of this theme and refers to the common break-up of the family as the personal power of the paterfamilias loses its ability to co-ordinate across increasingly distant relationships; family tensions seem inevitable when relationships are forced rather than chosen and when there may be competition for resources or influence; and lastly the discipline required for conformity and the inhibitions which can result from ritualistic deference and conflict avoidance, can result for many individuals in a degree of psychological deprivation which, while seemingly never capable of destroying loyalty, can nevertheless inhibit practical commitment.

Chinese society in Hong Kong has been described by Lau (1982) as 'minimally integrated' and based on 'utilitarianistic familism'. These phrases convey the idea of a mistrusting society constructed of self-serving and thus competing units. In this event it is nevertheless necessary to create enough co-operation for the interactions of economic life to run smoothly. Here personalism comes into play to release the tension by providing for the construction of networks of dependable relationships. Specific trust bonds are developed in which obligations are exchanged and the high salience of trust in this society is a reflection of the critical need for such networks in an otherwise unreliable social environment.

In constructing the networks primary reliance is naturally placed on family and extended family connections, then, as it were, in concentric circles of reliability on clan, then on region of origin. This is not entirely a matter of the natural affiliation of those with an origin in common; it also contains more prosaically the fact that a person who is known as part of a wider social group is more likely to be reliable as he has a reputation to lose if he reneges on a deal. Such reputations are highly significant social and economic currency.

Organization

The beliefs which surround the question of organization continue to reflect the all-pervading nature of paternalism, personalism and insecurity as features of Chinese life. Organizations are familistic in atmosphere and power is exercised in a patrimonial way. At the same time the need to co-opt talent into the organization raises difficulties in the field of co-operation, as it often takes the search for key people outside the boundaries of the family or clan. In this case, special responses come into effect to maintain the co-operation of relative 'outsiders' in key positions as well as the bulk of the workforce whose inclination would normally be towards a utilitarian relationship. The atmosphere created is feudal in nature in that it is based on (a) monopoly ownership of economic resources at the top, (b) high dependence by the majority of subordinates, (c) paternalistic response by the superior, and (d) an exchange of protection downwards and loyalty upwards.

Such a formula does not necessarily guarantee high levels of commitment from non-family members and there are serious practical limitations on how far it can be extended as the obligations which cement it are essentially interpersonal and essentially also centred upon a key chief executive.

In consequence, large-scale co-ordination is the Achilles heel of the Chinese organization and there is a constant battle over trust. The pervading atmosphere of benevolent autocracy is not conducive to the kind of decentralization which sponsors the emergence of talent in lower ranks of organizations, and Chinese family businesses suffer from three constraints directly attributable to problems of trust. The first of these is the problem of senior level talent in generations after the founder. Nepotism serves to keep positions of power in the hands of people whose talents are not always tested in open competition and there is a natural danger of mediocrity. Thus, secondly, talent which would otherwise rise to the top is blocked and its early encouragement stifled by lack of opportunity. The drive to escape into a situation where self-control is possible causes many young executives to start their own companies, and this constant leaching away of talent inevitably weakens what might otherwise be a steadily strengthening organization. The third outcome attributable to mistrust is restriction of organizational complexity. The tendency is to keep activities within the control of the chief executive, at least as far as key decisions are concerned. This leads either to a limited scale of operations or to a narrowing of product or market focus. The former tendency is evident in the typical manufacturing enterprise which has no R&D function, and no marketing function, restricting itself by making to order and concentrating solely on efficient manufacturing. Concentration is evident in the companies which, although they may grow very large, are nevertheless linked to one industry only, examples in shipping or textiles being common.

In making observations about the limitations which flow from mistrust, it must at the same time be acknowledged that efficiencies may also be available at small scale. There are advantages in flexibility when one-man decision-making takes place. There are benefits from the intense managerial dedication which goes with ownership. The endemic nature of mistrust causes high attention to be paid to trust-bonding via personalism, and this can result in a reduction in transaction costs when the alternative apparatus of legal constraint can be dispensed with. The Chinese family business, as an organization, may thus reach high levels of efficiency and this is visibly so when one observes the aggregate results in economic health at the national level.

Society

Overseas Chinese society is visible under a set of different political regimes in Hong Kong, Singapore, Taiwan, and ASEAN, and yet it retains much consistency of character. It perpetuates much Chinese tradition and it continues to display tensions inherited from the pre-modern period.

The respondents in the research offered much evidence illustrating the power of the vertical order. Their discussions of socialization showed how discipline is inculcated, and how behaviour comes to be controlled by notions of propriety. In particular the Confucian doctrines of filial piety continue to work effectively to perpetuate a hierarchy based on paternalism, and the same vertical sense is extended to other fields via a generalized respect for the older person, for those in authority, and for persons who display in their behaviour the almost ritualistic gravitas of the Confucian superior.

This stable vertical structure is set in a context of societal insecurity and serves as an effective coping mechanism, providing core values which serve to maintain both order and co-operation. The insecurity at the societal level is evidenced in a number of ways. Firstly, is the perception of transience. The Overseas Chinese were traditionally sojourners and this heritage is still evident. It reaches its highest point in Hong Kong, but is also visible in other countries. It is exacerbated often by the persistent identification with China as the ultimate spiritual home.

The second indicator of insecurity is the commonly voiced mistrust of government, and the wish to be free, if possible, of dealings with it. In certain circumstances, such as in Indonesia or the Philippines, government protection may be actively sought, as a means of reducing uncertainty, but this is a game only the biggest players can indulge in, and for the average family business owner, officialdom is to be pacified and kept at a distance if possible.

The third indicator of a society not conscious of being in control of its destiny is fatalism, a feature of Chinese thinking which remains important, even in the pragmatic and up-to-the-minute world of business. The residue of superstitions, omens, protective rituals, geomancy, and even astrology, is remarkably common, and although now giving way to increasing rationality, and commonly denied as a belief, is nevertheless practised 'just-in-case'.

In an insecure context, the importance of a guaranteed safe future takes on special significance and the means to its acquisition become core values. The work ethic, pragmatism and materialism are cases in point. They all serve the accumulation of wealth in a competitive context, and they are all clearly espoused by the executives whose views are being considered here.

The final societal issue which emerged, that of restricted but adequate co-operation, finds an echo in a study of peasant societies by Foster (1965), following which he propounded the notion that a society with an 'image of limited good' will not develop extensive systems of co-operation. The argument here is that in a society where the good things in life are perceived as limited and unexpandable, then personal gain must be at the expense of others. In these threatening circumstances there are two routes of escape: maximum co-operation with sanctions against individualism, such as with the communist solution in China, an alternative which requires strong leadership; or extreme individualism with each social unit responsible for its own fate, as in the case of the Overseas Chinese, a solution which may be inevitable in the absence of strong leadership. In this latter case, because of the heightened sense of competitiveness, co-operation between units will be restricted to that which serves the needs of each party's search for security. Thus Overseas Chinese society tends to be, as Lau (1982) has observed, 'minimally integrated'. In the context of business, the notion of 'minimal' has to be qualified by the supplement 'adequate', as the limited bonds of trust are enough to serve the needs for co-operation in the economic sphere.

Conclusions

The purpose of this paper is to outline the reconstructed world view of the Overseas Chinese chief executive. It is based on content analysis of interviews with eighty such executives in Hong Kong, Taiwan, Singapore and Indonesia, and seeks principally to reproduce their perceptions within an analytical framework. It has been possible to reflect on the connections with the Chinese cultural heritage and to speculate on the transfer of old norms and values to the modern context.

In doing so, much is revealed about why Chinese family businesses behave as they do. The principal characteristics of such organizations are as follows (Silin 1976; Tam 1989; Limlingan 1986; Redding 1989):

(1) Small scale, relatively simple organization structure.
(2) Normally focussed on one product or market, with growth by opportunistic diversification.
(3) Centralized decision making with heavy reliance on one dominant executive.
(4) A close overlap of ownership, control, and family.
(5) A paternalistic organizational climate.
(6) Linked to the environment through personalistic networks.
(7) Linked strongly but informally with other organizations.
(8) Cost sensitive, financially efficient.
(9) Relatively weak in large-scale marketing.
(10) High degree of strategic adaptability.

There is no room in the restricted space of this paper to analyse the linkages but in each case it is possible to trace determinacy to the beliefs of the chief executive. In many cases such beliefs will only be contributors to a more complex explanation, as causation is inevitably complex. But organizations which are essentially patrimonial, paternalistic, nepotistic and highly centralized in their decision processes, will be particularly prone to reflect the ideals and ideas of the dominant figure moulding them. It is thus likely that the study of managerial ideology in the case of the Overseas Chinese may be more revealing of organizational characteristics than in many other economic cultures.

References

Foster, G.M., 1965. Peasant society and the image of limited good. American Anthropologist 67, 293–315.

Hamilton, G., 1989. 'The network structures of East Asian economies'. In: S.R. Clegg and S.G. Redding (eds.), Capitalism in contrasting cultures. Berlin: de Gruyter.

Hofstede, G., 1980. Cultures' consequences. London: Sage Publications.

Lau, S.K., 1982. Society and politics in Hong Kong. Hong Kong: Chinese University Press.

Lim, Y.C. and P. Gosling, 1982. The Chinese in Southeast Asia. Singapore: Maruzen Asia.

Limlingan, V.S., 1986. The overseas Chinese in ASEAN. Manila: Vita Development Corporation.

Mannheim, K., 1936. Ideology and utopia. London: Routledge and Kegan Paul.

Omohundro, J.T., 1981. Chinese merchant families in Iloilo. Athens, OH: Ohio University Press.

Pye, L., 1985. Asian power and politics. Cambridge, MA: The Bellknap Press.

Redding, S.G., 1990. The spirit of Chinese capitalism. New York: de Gruyter.

Silin, R.H., 1976. Leadership and values. Cambridge, MA: Harvard University Press.

Tam, S., 1989. 'Centrifugal versus centripetal growth processes: Contrasting ideal types for conceptualizing the developmental patterns of Chinese and Japanese firms'. In: S.R. Clegg and S.G. Redding (eds.), Capitalism in contrasting cultures. Berlin: de Gruyter.

Willmott, D.E., 1960. The Chinese of Semarang. Ithaca, NY: Cornell University Press.

Wong, G., 1986. Interlocking directorates in Hong Kong. Working paper, Department of Management Studies, University of Hong Kong.

Wong, S.L., 1983. Business ideology of Chinese industrialists in Hong Kong. Royal Asiatic Society Journal 23, 137–171.

Yoshihara, K., 1988. The rise of ersatz capitalism in S.E. Asia. Kuala Lumpur: Oxford University Press.

[11]

Int. Studies of Man. & Org., Vol. XVI, No. 2, pp. 37-58
M. E. Sharpe, Inc., 1986

A. I. AHIAUZU (NIGERIA)

The African Thought-System and the Work Behavior of the African Industrial Man

The attention of some researchers in organizational behavior has recently begun to be focused on the work attitudes and general work behavior of the African industrial worker [1-17]. What seems to emerge from most of these studies is that the work attitudes and behavior of the African industrial worker are different in many respects from those of his counterparts in the more industrially advanced parts of the world. In offering an explanation for this phenomenon, I have argued elsewhere [8] that "Any move towards the understanding of the poor attitude to work of the African, which will enable organisational theorists to develop the appropriate administrative and managerial systems for African organisations, should start with the identification of the influences that shape the behaviour of the African at work-places." I further suggested that these influences are very likely "to emanate from historical and cultural origins," which color the perceptual process of the individual.

Kant [9. Pp. 40–42] pointed out that human beings do not perceive the world as it actually is, but rather that our knowledge of reality and reaction to social phenomena are conditioned by certain a priori elements—categories and forms of intuition such as time and space. He argued that these "elements" do not have their source in external reality, but are characteristics of the

---

Dr. Ahiauzu is a Senior Lecturer in Industrial Relations and Organizational Behavior at Rivers State University of Science and Technology, Port Harcourt, Nigeria.

human mind and govern all our perceptions of the world.

Durkheim [10. P. 492], on the other hand, described Kant's "a priori forms" as "collective representations" and argued that their origin was to be found not in the mind per se, as Kant suggested, but in society. In support of this argument, Durkheim pointed out that it is from society that the mind draws "the moulds which are applicable to the totality of things and which make it possible to think of them."

Contributing to this reasoning through exposition of his notion of "cultural relativism," Hanson [11. Pp. 22–23] has argued:

> Thought and behaviour are intelligible only in terms of the *a priori* forms which condition and govern them. Those forms, as collective representations, vary from one society to another. Therefore, ideas, beliefs and actions should be understood from within—in terms of the categories of culture from which they come.

Hanson, in this statement, identifies "thought" and "behavior" as separate elements in human existence that can be meaningful only in the context of the "collective representations" that govern them. He has not given attention to the likely relationship between the two elements. I am inclined to think that in a free society, in which members have a choice between alternative forms of action in their social life, collective representations of the society will govern behavior more effectively only through their conditioning influence on thought. It is therefore possible for a particular type of individual behavior to be traced back to a particular system of thought.

Otite [12. P. 2] has, in fact, pointed out that "The behaviour of a people cannot be fully understood unless one knows their systems of thought." Cole [13. P. vii] also has argued that "The form in which men cast their speculations no less than the ways in which they behave, is the result of the habits of thought and action which they find around them."

On the basis of the foregoing, it is reasonable to argue that the work behavior of the African industrial worker cannot be fully understood unless one considers the African indigenous thought-system.

No social scientist has hitherto addressed his or her attention to examination of the nature of the African thought-system and how this is likely to influence the work behavior of the African industrial worker. I am not assuming here that the reasoning and thinking processes of the African are different from those of other peoples. In fact, I totally reject Lévy-Bruhl's [14. P. 63] claim that primitive mentality, including that of Africans, is "prelogical," by which he meant that "it does not bind itself down . . . to avoiding contradiction." I believe, with Boas [15. P. 135], that the "functions of the human mind are common to the whole of humanity," but agree with Cole and Gay [16. P. 1066] that "The reasoning and thinking processes of different peoples in different cultures do not differ—just their values, beliefs and ways of classifying differ."

Lévi-Strauss, as explained by Cole and Scribner [17. P. 26], put the argument very succinctly by stating that traditional and scientific thought-systems simply represent different "strategies" by which man makes nature accessible to rational inquiry. He pointed out that both "strategies" seek objective knowledge of the universe, and that both "proceed by ordering, classifying and systematizing information; both create coherent systems." Lévi-Strauss claimed that the only difference between the two systems of thought, lay in the "material" used for thought.

My objective here, therefore, is to explore the fundamental source materials and frames of reference the African adopts in ordering, classifying, and systematizing information on social phenomena in his daily life. I shall examine the realms of "common sense" and "theory" in the indigenous African thought-system. My major assumption is that the way people in their "life-world" construct meanings and self-concepts, negotiate their social contexts, and make sense of and order their environment depends largely on their thought-system. Then, having established the important elements that form the bases of the African indigenous thought-system, I shall examine how the thought-

system of the African industrial worker influences his interpretation of organizational and administrative structures and processes
in the modern industrial workplace and results in specific work
attitudes and behavior.

The African thought-system

One question that has attracted the attention of social scientists
interested in African studies is, Does Africa exist? This question
was first posed by Herskovitz[1] in a 1960 symposium at Wellesley
College, Massachusetts. Herskovitz's answer was that Africa
could be "thought of as a separate entity and regarded as a unit
[only] to the degree that the map is invested with an authority
imposed on it by the map makers." He could not consider Africa
as being made up of peoples with any identifiable common racial
and sociocultural characteristics.

Herskovitz was not alone in this line of thinking. N'Daw [18],
reflecting on the African thought-system, observed, "In reality,
the great diversity of our civilisation and the considerable number
of languages spoken would be enough to discourage the most
tenacious analyst who is preoccupied with seizing upon the sin-
gleness of African thought."

Another group of scholars on African studies looked at the
issue differently. Blyden [19] examined the elements that characterize the logic and philosophy that inform the African way of life
and concluded that Africans are very similar in their way of
thinking and general way of life. According to him, the African is
"co-operative, not egotistic or individualistic. We, and not I, is
the law of African life" [19. P. 29].

This view has been extended and presented in detail by Otite
[12. P. 10]:

> The African society is a system of mutually benefitting
> reciprocities. Society to the African exists for the good of all its
> members in a system of role reinforcements. This involves
> myriad reciprocal relationships. . . . The African communa-

listic traditions, like the French Collectivistic traditions and Chinese traditions of Confucian harmonious family-society, provide a peculiar moral context to order their complex systems of reciprocities in contrast to the individual-based principle of the British-American type. The interplay between the moral element and the principle of reciprocal relationships is critical in distinguishing what is African.

It is worth emphasizing that Otite's major argument is that it is the unique moral element in the life of the African and the way he organizes his way of life in a network of reciprocal relationships that clearly identify the African personality.

Sithole [20] has reinforced this argument by emphasizing that the African personality is the sum total of the basic ways the African people feel, think perceive, talk, and behave, which is a result of the specific geographic, historical, cultural, political, and economic setting in Africa; and this is what "distinguishes the African from other human selves," who have different settings in other parts of the world.

From the foregoing it can be concluded that if it is possible to show that the peoples of Africa can be identified by certain common characteristics in their way of life, as suggested by Otite [12], Blyden [19], and a host of other scholars [21–25], then there certainly is an African thought-system.

One of the important attributes of the African thought-system is the high degree of harmony among the elements that underlie the system. For example, John [26] has shown how the word *Ntu* formed the unifying principle of the four elements around which Bantu philosophy and thought revolve; *Muntu* (human being), *Kintu* (thing), *Hantu* (place and time), and *Kuntu* (modality). Adesanya's [27] description of Yoruba thought very well illustrates this attribute of the African thought-system. Commenting on the degree of harmony in the Yoruba thought-system, Adesanya emphasizes that:

. . . this is not simply a coherence of fact and faith, nor of reason and traditional beliefs, nor of reason and contingent facts, but a coherence or compatibility among all the disciplines. A medical theory, for example, which contradicted a theological conclusion, was rejected as absurd and vice-versa. This demand of mutual compatibility among all disciplines considered as a system was the main weapon of Yoruba thinking. . . . Philosophy, theology, politics, social theory, land law, medicine, psychology, birth and burial, all find themselves logically concatenated in a system so tight that to substract one item from the whole is to paralyse the structure of the whole.

To the African, every aspect of life is interrelated, but he distinguishes one aspect from the other by the use of symbols. This brings us to another attribute of the African thought-system: symbolism. Mobana [28] has explained that unlike in other peoples and races of the world, symbolism is the natural expression of the African mind. In his analysis of the African thought-system, Mobana has concluded that the African is:

> . . . symbolistic, universalist or transcendentalist in mentality. His basic tendency or orientation is towards Being as One. We say he is transcendentalist because he does not take the principles of contradiction or identity, with their sequel of almost infinite distinctions, as the starting-point of his thought, but adopts, rather the dialectical and polyvalent principle of the Oneness of Being.

Another aspect of the African thought-system has to do with the way the African organizes his world of common sense. Bullock and Stallybrass [29. P. 115] have defined common sense as "the source or system of those very general beliefs about the world which are universally and unquestioningly taken to be true in everyday life." Every human being makes use of common-sense knowledge while undertaking any articulate act of thinking; and, as argued by Dewey [30], this process has stages. First, the person feels or anticipates a difficulty or problem; he thinks, defines, and locates the problem; he suggests a possible solution;

he then reflects on and tests the validity of possible solutions; and, finally, he arrives at a conclusion by accepting or rejecting the solution he has thought out.

These stages in a normal thinking process apply to every human being in all societies, the only difference being in the nature and sources of the common-sense knowledge that provides the reference material used in the thinking experience. The body of common-sense knowledge in a society forms a major part of the people's social thought.

A major source of the common-sense knowledge in African societies is proverbial social thought. The Pan English Dictionary defines a proverb as "a short saying, usually containing a useful or well-known belief or truth." In all black African societies, proverbs, which express the traditional beliefs and truths about matters, are applied in conversations and in speeches of all kinds. Old people use proverbs more often than the young, and argument that is supported with proverbs is automatically accepted as valid and true, for, as Taiwo [31] explains,

> Proverbs deal with all aspects of life. They are used to emphasize the word of the wise and are the stock-in-trade of old people, who use them to convey precise moral lessons, warnings and advice, since they make a greater impact on the minds than ordinary words. The judicious use of proverbs is often regarded as a sign of wit.

In his study of the nature and role of proverbs in the Fante culture of Southern Ghana, Christensen [32. Pp. 235–38] found examples of how proverbs can be used to support generally accepted norms and values in various areas of social life in a cultural group. Because proverbs are usually handed down from generation to generation, they reflect the sociocultural system of the ancestors of the people. The important place of proverbs in the African thought-system has also been emphasized by Herskovitz [33. P. 453]:

> In African societies it is a mark of elegance to be able to interlard one's speech with . . . aphorisms. Proverbs are cited in the native courts in much the same way as our lawyers cite precedent. . . . The moral they point out gives insight into the basic values of society; they teach us what is held to be right and wrong. They are indeed an index to accepted canons of thought and action.

The proverbs, legends, ballads, and other epitomized experiences that form the social thought of any cultural group in Africa are the product of the interaction among the people, their social heritage (or culture), and their physical environment. Proverbs in African societies are therefore expressions of the traditional values, beliefs, and culturally accepted ways of organizing social life in the respective cultural groups. Because, as pointed out by Otite [12. P. 4], people in preliterate societies, ''live'' their social thought as part of their heritage and preserve their thought through transmissible oral forms as well as through manufactured concrete forms, proverbs constitute an influential source of information and reference materials for the African in his thought-system.

Common-sense information is usually very handy, and thus is an economical tool for coping with a wide range of circumstances in everyday life. But there are certain circumstances in one's thinking process in which common-sense information cannot provide the answers, and the person has no alternative but to jump from common-sense to theoretical thinking. The quest for an explanatory theory in such circumstances is, as Horton [34. P. 51] has put it, ''basically the quest for unity underlying apparent diversity, for simplicity underlying apparent complexity, for order underlying apparent disorder, for regularity underlying apparent anomaly.'' The quest for a theoretical explanation becomes necessary at a certain stage in the thinking process because ''theory,'' as Horton [34. P. 53] goes on to explain, ''places things in a causal context wider than that provided by common-sense.''

The act of seeking a theoretical explanation for a phenomenon in the human environment applies similarly to every human being in all societies of the world. The only difference is in the source usually consulted for the theoretical explanation. Whereas peoples of more scientifically advanced societies consult the results of scientific studies for their required theoretical explanations, those in traditional African societies consult ancestral spirits and gods. Mystical thinking is therefore another aspect of the indigenous African thought-system.

Studies of African cosmologies [22, 35–40] have shown that in every cultural group in Africa, there is a hierarchy of gods and spirits forming a scheme that constitutes a framework within which every aspect of life and the everyday experience of members can be explained. For example, Uchendu [39] has described how different spirits and gods of the Ibo society are responsible for specific aspects of the life of the Ibo. Horton [35] has shown how almost everything that happens to a member of the Kalabari society can be explained in terms of a scheme that postulates three basic kinds of forces—ancestors, heroes, and water-spirits. And Middleton [37] has explained how different forms of opposition and conflict in the daily life of a member of the Lugbara society are interpreted as manifestations of an underlying conflict between ancestors and *adro* spirits.

How the African makes use of common sense and theory in this thought-system can be illustrated by how the African traditionally handles a common occurrence in daily life—sickness or disease. Horton's [34] findings in his field work among the Kalabari of southeast Nigeria offer an interesting example:

> Kalabari recognize many different kinds of diseases, and have an array of herbal specifics with which to treat them. Sometimes a sick person will be treated by ordinary members of his family who recognize the disease and know the specifics. Sometimes the treatment will be carried out on the instructions of a native doctor. When sickness and treatment follow these lines the atmosphere is basically commonsensical. . . . Sometimes, however, the sickness does not respond to treatment, and

it becomes evident that the herbal specific used does not provide the whole answer. The native doctor may rediagnose and
try another specific. But if this produces no result the suspicion
will arise that ''there is something else in this sickness.'' In
other words, the perspective provided by common sense is too
limited. It is at this stage that a diviner is likely to be called in
(it may be the native doctor who started the treatment). Using
ideas about various spiritual agencies, he will relate the sickness to a wider range of circumstances—often to disturbances
in the sick man's general social life. (P. 60)

A noteworthy aspect of the African system of theoretical thinking, which can be deduced from Horton's findings as illustrated
in the above citation, is that the established body of theoretical
tenets the diviner issues as explanations to his clients do not have
alternatives that members of the society are aware of. As soon as
an explanation is offered by a respected diviner, after consulting
the relevant oracles, all inquiries cease, and all effort is directed
toward appeasing angry ancestral spirits and gods through ritualistic activities.

We have indicated above that one of the characteristics that
distinguish the African from other human beings is his unique
thought-system. The important attributes of the African indigenous thought-system have been identified as including symbolism and a high degree of harmony among elements within the
system. It has been shown that African common sense derives
largely from African preliterate social thought, which includes
proverbs, legends, and ballads, and that theoretical thinking in
traditional African society is mystical thinking. Let us now examine the extent to which the African indigenous thought-system is
likely to influence the behavior of the African industrial worker at
the workplace.

The influence of the African
thought-system on work behavior

Viewing man in his ''life-world'' from an existential phenomenological perspective, Haralambos [41] has explained that:

> Unlike matter, man has consciousness—thoughts, feelings, meanings, intentions and an awareness of being. Because of this, his actions are meaningful, he defines situations and gives meaning to his actions and those of others. As a result, he does not merely react to external stimuli, he does not simply behave, he acts. (P. 20)

He illustrates this point as follows:

> Imagine the response of early man to fire caused by volcanoes or spontaneous combustion. He did not simply react in a uniform manner to the experience of heat. He attached a range of meanings to it and these meanings directed his actions. For example, he defined fire as a means of warmth and used it to heat his dwellings; as a means of defense and used it to ward off wild animals; and as a means of transforming substances and employed it for cooking and hardening the points of wooden spears. Man does not just react to fire, he acts upon it in terms of the meanings he gives to it.

The individual constructs and ascribes meanings to aspects of his physical and social environment on the basis of his "assumptive frame of reference" [42]. He then acts upon these aspects of his environment, adopting the meanings he has ascribed to them. It is the individual's mode of "acting" on his environment, which we have shown to be based on the meanings he ascribes to them, that we normally refer to as his "behavior." It is worth pointing out that both the "construction of meaning" and the "acting" take form through the mechanism established by the individual's thought-system.

The African industrial worker has no alternative but to bring his indigenous thought-system to the workplace. He uses this thought-system in interpreting, constructing, and ascribing meanings to things, structures, and processes at the industrial workplace. He acts and reacts to these structures and processes on the basis of the meanings he ascribes to them, and this is what we see as his work behavior.

48   *A. I. AHIAUZU (NIGERIA)*

It is important to mention here that in most black African countries, industrialization is barely twenty years old, or even much less in some countries, the reason being that active industrialization began only following independence. As a result, very few, if any, current industrial workers come from homes in which their parents or other family members previously worked in industry; thus, they have not acquired any sort of industrial culture from them. Most of the industrial workers have left their traditional occupation to enter industry for the first time.

The first thing that probably confronts the African industrial worker is the physical environment of the workplace. The worker sees machines and other complicated equipment arranged in a particular way, totally strange to him. He has to learn to live with the machines; he has to adjust to being part of the strange environment. This process of learning and adjustment involves trying to understand the new environment and reacting to it, which will require adaptation of the worker's thought-system. The problem that faces the African worker is, of course, that, unlike his counterpart in more industrially advanced societies, he has not been used to machines before coming to the industrial workplace and has nothing in his repertoire of ideas or in his experience about complicated machines, such as are usually shown on television, in movies, and in magazines and catalogues. In his adjustment to the strange environment, common-sense knowledge cannot help the African worker; he can only resort to theoretical thinking.

During the field work for our study of workers in a textile factory in the southeastern part of Nigeria, which is reported elsewhere [43], a worker, describing his experience the first day he went to the factory, said, "When I went home at the close of work that day, I told my wife that if she saw the machines in the factory, she would see where the white man's witchcraft did a great work." This was the worker's "theoretical" explanation to this wife, concerning how the complicated machines and equipment at the factory were made. With this type of reasoning, it will certainly take this African textile worker a longer time than it would take his counterpart in a more industrially advanced society to adjust to the physical conditions at the textile factory.

The technology and the industrial mode of work organization create an organizational subculture, with its set of values, norms, and rules at the workplace. Kerr and co-workers [44] have stressed this point by saying that the industrialization phenomenon has its own culture. In the industrial organizational subculture, more emphasis is placed on technical intelligence than on social intelligence, whereas the reverse is the case in African traditional society. Every activity at the industrial workplace is related to time, and the industrial worker has to comply strictly to rules made and enforced by his superiors. An African industrial worker in such a subcultural environment is likely to find it strange and perhaps uncomfortable at first. Blunt [1] reported a Kenyan worker as saying: "At home I am my own boss. Nobody tells me what to do. I have my work, but I can take time off when I like. If it rains I can go indoors. With this type of work, I must stay out in the wet and cold like a goat" (P. 50).

The way the African industrial worker acts or reacts to aspects of this new organizational subculture in which he finds himself, which we see as his work behavior, depends largely on the interpretation and the meanings he ascribes to those aspects; and, as we have explained earlier, this construction of meanings is made through the vehicle of his indigenous thought-system. This does not necessarily mean that the African worker dislikes working in industry, as Blumer [45. P. 10] has suggested. There is, in fact, substantial empirical evidence indicating that most Africans are glad to work in industry [46–48], one of the reasons being that, as Seibel [46] found in her study of 509 industrial workers in the southwestern part of Nigeria, industrial work offers them "the opportunity to learn something new, to gain experience, and to hold a technical job." The African does not, therefore, dislike industrial work. Moreover, his work behavior, from his viewpoint, based on the meanings he ascribes to the circumstances of the industrial workplace, represents quite appropriate actions and reactions.

Another way in which the indigenous thought-system influ-

ences the work behavior of the industrial worker is in the normal
African orientation toward certain concomitants of the mode of
work organization in the modern industrial workplace, such as
work-speed, degree of concentration, complexity of operations,
restrictions in social interaction, and nonrecognition at the workplace of one's social status in the wider society.

The African industrial worker's work-speed seems to underlie
the widely prevalent poor impression critics have of him. The
reason may be that work-speed is normally the first aspect of a
worker's behavior to attract the attention of an observer. The
relatively low work-speed of the average African industrial worker should not be construed as laziness.

Biesheuvel [49] has offered an explanation of this phenomenon. Administering his "General Adaptability Battery" test to a
group of African manual workers and potential supervisors from
among recruits fresh from their country areas, Biesheuvel suggested that one of the factors responsible for the Africans' difficulty in adapting smoothly to industrial life was that they generally had a "preference for slow, modulated action, rather than for
speed." He then argued that as modern industrial production
depends on speed, the African might "be at a disadvantage in
meeting its requirements." This preference for slow, modulated
action by the African is probably, to a large extent, a reflection of
the African thought-system.

The mode of work organization in the industrial workplace
involves complex operations, and performing most of them accurately requires a high level of concentration. To achieve a high
level of concentration in one's thinking process easily, one probably has to develop one's thought-system through a disciplined
and institutionalized form of schooling. The average African
industrial worker is at a disadvantage in this regard because, as
Fortes [50] found in Ghana, and Kibuuka [51] in Uganda, indigenous African systems of education, which takes place mostly in
the homes and in organizations by age-groups in the villages, is
traditionally "informal" and pervades all phases of life at the
same time, instead of being disciplined and institutionalized as
formal schooling.

Viewed through the eyes of the average African, the mode of work organization in the industrial workplace restricts social relations and interractions and does not make any allowance for one's roles and social status in the wider society. The worker has to see his superiors at the workplace merely as supervisors, foremen, and managers and nothing else, and to relate to them in a strictly impersonal manner. Reared in a thought-system developed within the African cultural milieu, in which a person's roles are not normally differentiated [52. P. 8], the African industrial worker, as Banton [53. P. 114] has observed, finds it difficult to adapt readily to the "impersonal relationships of modern industry."

In our study reported elsewhere [8], we narrated an incident in an African industrial workplace in which a supervisor was summoned to appear before the elders of his extended family to answer to a charge proferred against him by a relative of his who was a worker in the same organization. The charge was that the supervisor did not treat him like a "brother" at the workplace. An observer might readily jump to the conclusion that the action of this worker was wrong; but if one considers that it was merely a reflection of the meaning the worker had given to the behavior of the supervisor, on the basis of the worker's thought-system, it is possible to conclude that the worker acted reasonably under the circumstances.

The thought-system of the African industrial worker is also likely to influence his reaction to motivational techniques adopted by management in an African workplace. For example, in his study of 96 Xhosa machine operators, storemen, and book-keepers in South Africa, in which he tested the effects of "Western" versus "tribal" orientations on the relationship between enriched work and job satisfaction and performance, Orpen [54] found that the relationship between enriched work and job satisfaction was higher for Western-oriented workers than it was for tribal-oriented ones. This relationship has been explained in terms of the different norms and values of the two groups. Orpen [54. P. 123], in fact, went on to explain that the Western-oriented worker had acquired "a set of values similar to those of middle-class elites . . . [and as such] these employees tend to develop an orientation to work which stresses the role of work in one's personality and which regards work as a source of gratification of one's most important needs.'' Our explanation of this finding in Orpen's study is that what produced the different results for the two groups of workers was that the ''Western-oriented workers'' had, by association and practice, developed a thought-system similar to that of ''middle-class whites,'' whereas the ''tribal-oriented workers'' still retained their indigenous African thought-system.

In a study reported elsewhere [55], in which we investigated the effectiveness of the motivational techniques adopted by managers in certain workplaces in Port Harcourt (southeastern part of Nigeria), we found that the ''motivational potential'' of an activity in relation to a particular worker depended largely on the circumstances of the worker. By ''motivational potential'' we meant ''the situational capacity of an activity or technique to motivate a particular worker or group of workers.'' The circumstances of a worker found to influence the ''motivational potential'' of a technique included, among others, the ethnic or tribal group of the worker in relation to that of the manager, the educational level of the worker, the duration of the worker's years in wage or industrial employment, the worker's age, and the extent of the worker's fanaticism in his religion. It is pertinent to point out that these circumstances of an African worker do not have a direct influence on his choice of and response to a motivational technique; rather, their influence shapes and conditions his thought-system. It is the meaning the worker ascribes to a motivational technique, on the basis of his thought-system, that determines his response to that technique.

One problem that is likely to result from the nature of the thought-system of the African worker is that, because the meanings (based on his thought-system) he attaches to administrative and managerial processes and other aspects of the industrial workplace determine his actions there, certain aspects of his work behavior may not always meet the expectations of his supervisors. When this happens, the African worker may not find himself advancing in his job as fast as he believes he ought to. His common-sense knowledge may not be able to offer him an acceptable explanation. He immediately resorts to theoretical thinking, which, in the African thought-system, as we have explained, is mystical thinking.

The African worker then consults a diviner for an explanation. Evans-Pritchard [56] has shown, for example, how members of the Luo tribal group of Kenya attribute everything that happens to them to supernatural sources, particularly the spirits of their ancestors and the ghosts of their deceased relations. The diviner consults his supernatural sources and produces an explanation for the worker's failure on the job and a prescription of remedial action to be taken by the worker.

Very often such explanations and prescriptions have little or nothing to do with work behavior or any particular actions the worker performs in his job. Uchendu [39] has described how a member of the Ibo cultural group, in southeastern Nigeria, may endeavor to appease "Mpataku," the spirit of wealth, with ceremonial sacrifices of chickens, locally produced alcoholic drinks, and cola nuts when his business enterprise is not doing well or when he wants to obtain promotion in his employment. But even when all the prescribed sacrifices have been offered, the problem remains, because the required change in work behavior and performance, which is what will actually earn the worker promotion and advancement in his job, may not have occurred, as work behavior and performance in the industrial culture have nothing to do with ancestral spirits or spirits of any kind.

The effectiveness of other administrative and managerial techniques and systems adopted in African industrial workplaces at present are likely to be similarly affected by the nature of the indigenous thought-system of the African worker.

Conclusion and comments

We have examined the nature of the African indigenous thought-system and found tht among the attributes that characterize it are

the use of symbols and the high degree of harmony among elements within the system. We have also found that African common-sense knowledge is based largely on African social thought,
which revolves around proverbs, legends, and ballads, whereas
theoretical thinking in the African thought-system is "mystical
thinking" based on the world of spirits and gods. We have related
this thought-system to the behavior of the African industrial
worker at his workplace and concluded that what we see as his
work behavior is merely a reflection of his thought-system.

This conclusion is based on the argument that the African
industrial worker normally uses his thought-system in interpreting, constructing, and ascribing meanings to things in the physical environment and to managerial and organizational structures
and processes at the industrial workplace. He then acts on and
reacts to these structures and processes on the basis of the meanings he ascribes to them. It is the worker's mode of "acting on"
and "reacting to" these structures and processes at the workplace
that we see as his work behavior.

One major implication of this conclusion is that those who are
involved in the management and supervision of the activities of
the African industrial worker will observe change in his work
behavior only at the rate at which the thought-system of the
African changes. Though he may work in industry, the African
lives in a wider society; and it is from the society outside the
workplace that the elements that constitute the framework within
which the African indigenous thought-system operates derive.

It is therefore reasonable to argue that any conscious effort
aimed at achieving a long-lasting and continuous change in the
work behavior of the African industrial worker has to start with
the wider society. It is worth pointing out that such change cannot
be sudden and traumatic: it has to be gradual, and can result only
from the effects of developmental processes in African societies
on the worker, particularly educational, economic, political, and
sociocultural development.

The situation of the African industrial worker is worsened by
the fact that most, if not all, members of the managerial and
supervisory teams in all industrial workplaces in Africa have, in

one way or another, received managerial and administrative training based on the theories and practices prevalent in the industrially advanced societies of the Eastern and Western worlds and thus are importing foreign managerial theories and practices into the local environment. The manager in the African workplace expects the African industrial worker to respond to these foreign theories and practices in the same way as an American or British worker would. The mistake of the African manager, implied in this study, is that he tends to ignore the fact that, because the African worker and the American worker operate under different thought-systems, they are not likely to respond to the same managerial theories and practices in the same way.

A major solution to this problem is for managers and supervisors in African industrial organizations to be fully and constantly aware of the circumstances of the African worker. Unfortunately, African social scientists have not been of appreciable help to African managers in this regard, because not much empirical investigation has been made of the behavior of Africans at the industrial workplace. It is rather sad to observe that the few research studies of the African industrial worker that have been conducted are mostly by non-African scholars, who are likely to use their own thought-systems and perceptions in interpreting the results of their studies. It is therefore imperative for African social scientists to take up this challenge, and for African governments and large private organizations to provide the required research funds. The more we know about the African worker and his thought-system, the more effective we shall be in managing him.

Note

1. M. J. Herskovitz (1960) "Does 'Africa' Exist?" Presented at a symposium on Africa at Wellesley College, Wellesley, Massachussetts.

References

1. Blunt, P. (1983) *Organisational Theory and Behaviour: An African Perspective*. London: Longman.

56   A. I. AHIAUZU (NIGERIA)

2. Peil, M. (1972) *The Ghanaian Factory Worker: Industrial Man in Africa*. London: Cambridge University Press.

3. Ogionwo, W. (1971) "The Alienated Nigerian Worker: A Test of the 'Generalisation Thesis.'" *The Nigerian Journal of Economic and Social Studies*, *13*(3), 267–84.

4. Oloko, O. (1977) "Incentives and Reward For Effort." *Management in Nigeria*, *15*(5), 62–70.

5. Afonja, S. A. (1979) "Rural-Urban Differences in Work Adaptation: The Case of Some Nigerian Workers." *Rural Sociology*, *44*, 361–69.

6. Ahiauzu, A. I. (1984) "Methods of Job Regulation in Nigerian Workplaces: A Study of Cultural Influences in Industrial Relations." *Genève-Afrique*, *22*(1), 107–122.

7. Ahiauzu, A. I. (1984) "Culture and Workplace Industrial Relations: A Nigerian Study." *Industrial Relations Journal*, *15*(3), 53–63.

8. Ahiauzu, A. I. (1985) "The Influences Shaping Work Behaviour in African Organisations." *Organisation Forum* (University of Lancaster), *1*(2).

9. Kant, I. (1912) In P. Carns (Ed.), *Kant's Prolegomena to any Future Metaphysics*. Chicago: Open Court.

10. Durkheim, E. (1915) *The Elementary Forms of the Religious Life*. London: Allen and Unwin.

11. Hanson, F. A. (1975) *Meaning in Culture*. London: Routledge and Kegan Paul.

12. Otite, O. (1978) "The Study of Social Thought in Africa." In O. Otite (Ed.), *Themes in African Social and Political Thought*. Enugu, Nigeria: Fourth Dimension Publishers.

13. Cole, G. D. H. (1913) In J. J. Rousseau, *The Social Contract and Discourses*. Translated by G. D. H. Cole. London: J. M. Dent and Sons.

14. Lévy-Bruhl, L. (1910) *How Natives Think*. New York: Washington Square Press.

15. Boas, F. (1965) *The Mind of Primitive Man*. New York: The Free Press.

16. Cole, M., and Gay, J. (1972) "Culture and Memory." *American Anthropologist*, *74*, 1066–84.

17. Cole, M., and Scribner, S. (1974) *Culture and Thought: A Psychological Introduction*. New York: Wiley.

18. N'Daw, A. (1966) "Is It Possible to Speak about an 'African Way of Thought?'" *Présence Africaine*, *30*(58).

19. Blyden, E. W. (1908) *African Life and Customs*. London: C. M. Phillips.

20. Sithole, N. (1959) "African Personality." *Voice of Africa*, *1*(8), 18–27.

21. Donohugh, A. C. L. (1935) "Essentials of African Culture." *Africa*, *8*, 329–39.

22. Horton, R. (1964) "Ritual Man in Africa." *Africa*, *34*, 85–104.

23. Busia, K. A. (1967) *Africa in Search of Democracy*. London: Routledge and Kegan Paul.

24. Sithole, N. (1959) *African Nationalism*. Cape Town: Oxford University Press.

25. Wilson, G. (1936) "An African Morality." *Africa*, 9, 75–99.

26. John, J. (1961) *Muntu: The New African Culture*. New York: Grove Press.

27. Adesanya, A. (1958) "Yoruba Metaphysical Thinking." *Journal of West African Studies*, 5, 25–37.

28. Mobana, M. (1960) "Towards an African Philosophy." *Présence Africaine*, 2(30), 73–85.

29. Bullock, A., and Stallybrass. O. (1980) *The Fontana Dictionary of Modern Thought*. London: Fontana Books.

30. Dewey, J. (1910) *How We Think*. Boston: The Free Press.

31. Taiwo, O. (1967) *An Introduction to West African Literature*. London: Thomas Nelson and Sons.

32. Christensen, J. B. (1961) "The Role of Proverbs in Fante Culture." *Africa*, 28.

33. Herskovitz, M. J. (1961) "The Study of African Oral Art." *Journal of American Folklore*, 74.

34. Horton, R. (1967) "African Traditional Thought and Western Science." *Africa*, 37, 50–71.

35. Horton, R. (1962) "The Kalabari World-view: An Outline and Interpretation." *Africa*, 32, 197–220.

36. Lienhardt, G. (1961) *Divinity and Experience: The Religion of the Dinka*. London: Oxford University Press.

37. Middleton, J. (1960) *Lugbara Religion: Ritual and Authority among an East African People*. London: Oxford University Press.

38. Fortes, J. (1959) *Oedipus and Job in West African Religion*. Cambridge: Cambridge University Press.

39. Uchendu, V. C. (1965) *The Igbo of South-East Nigeria*. New York: Holt, Rinehart and Winston.

40. Barber, K. (1981) "How Man Makes God in West Africa: Yoruba Attitudes Towards the Orisa." *Africa*, 51.

41. Haralambos, M. (1980) *Sociology: Themes and Perspectives*. Slough: University Tutorial Press.

42. Tiryakian, E. A. (1973) "Sociological and Existential Phenomenology." In M. Natanson (Ed.), *Phenomenology and the Social Sciences*. Vol. 1. Evanston, IL: Northwestern University Press.

43. Ahiauzu, A. I. (1983) "Cultural Influences on Managerial Industrial Relations Policies: The Case of Hausa and Ibo Workplaces in Nigeria." *Labour and Society*, 8(2), 151–63.

44. Kerr, C., Dunlop, J. T., Harbison, F., and Myers, C. A. (1973) *Industrialism and Industrial Man*. Harmondsworth: Penguin Books.

45. Blumer, H. (1972) "Early Industrialization and the Laboring Class." In J. M. Shepard (Ed.), *Organizational Issues in Industrial Society*. Englewood Cliffs, NJ: Prentice-Hall. Pp. 10–16.

46. Seibel, H. D. (1973) "The Process of Adaptation to Wage Labor." In U. K. Damachi and H. D. Seibel (Eds.), *Social Change and Economic Development in Nigeria*. New York: Praeger.

47. Hutton, C. (1969) "Unemployment in Kampala and Jinja, Uganda." *Canadian Journal of African Studies*, *3*, 431–40.

48. Wober, M. (1967) "Individualism, Home Life and Work Efficiency among a Group of Nigerian Workers." *Occupational Psychology*, *41*, 183–92.

49. Biesheuvel, S. (1952) "The Occupational Abilities of Africans." *Optima*, *2*, 18–22.

50. Fortes, M. (1938) "Social and Psychological Aspects of Education in Taleland." *Africa*, *11*(4).

51. Kibuuka, P. M. T. (1966) Cited by M. Wober (1975) *Psychology in Africa*. London: International African Institute. P. 162.

52. Etukudo, A. (1977) *Waging Industrial Peace in Nigeria*. New York: Exposition Press.

53. Banton, M. (1957) *West African City: A Study of Tribal Life in Freetown*. London: Oxford University Press.

54. Orpen, C. (1979) "The Reactions of Western and Tribal Black Workers to Job Characteristics." *International Review of Applied Psychology*, *28*, 117–25.

55. Ahiauzu, A. I. (1985) "Towards a Diagnostic Approach to Motivating the Nigerian Worker." In E. L. Inanga (Ed.), *Managing Nigeria's Economic System*. Ibadan: Heinemann. Chap. 16.

56. Evans-Pritchard, E. E. (1950) "Ghostly Vengeance among the Luo of Kenya." *Man*, *133*, 86–87.

[12]

Int. Studies of Mgt. & Org., Vol. 21, No. 3, pp. 38–61.
M.E. Sharpe, Inc., 1991

GILLES AMADO AND HAROLDO VINAGRE BRASIL

Organizational Behaviors and Cultural Context: The Brazilian "*Jeitinho*"

1. Introduction

To what extent is it possible to perceive specifically Brazilian organizational behaviors? What are they? Where do they originate?

This paper is within the scope of our previous works, which focused on cultural features, and tries to articulate the human "reality" of organizations which takes root in a sociohistorical analysis that supports the observed and collected data. Concerning the Brazilian case, the data refer to the analysis of both training and development actions in a great number of organizations, as well as to the study of the organizations' images in the minds of managers and the attitudes demonstrated in negotiation processes.

The analysis of such data makes it possible to confirm the "personalist" and "social" dimension of the Latin organizations. Meanwhile, it brings to light typical Brazilian idiosyncracies. Thus, the importance and the original nature of the mediation systems among people are stressed, as well as those between the individual and the organization and between the person and the law.

These specific features are linked to the sociohistorical and anthropological interpretations of Brazil. The "*jeitinho*" category stands out as a hermeneutic key of the Brazilian culture, and is explored in its linkage with the gathered organizational data.

A great Brazilian intellectual, a half-blooded (African-Polish) man, who died recently, Paulo Leminsky, wrote a novel in the Joycean mode of expression, or in the Guimaraes Rosa mode of expression, that is a very significant piece of work on approaching the problems of cultural adaptation. Leminsky (1989) imagines that René Descartes came along on the Maurício de Nassau expedition, at the time of the Dutch occupation in part of the Brazilian Northeastern sites. By metaphorically

Gilles Amado is Professor at HEC Graduate School of Management, Jouy-en-Josas, France. Haroldo Vinagre Brasil is Professor at Fundaçao Dom Cabral, Belo Horizonte, Brazil.

placing Cartesius in the Brazilian tropical environment—a nonrecorded but very plausible fact, for the philosopher wandered, at that time, around the Netherlands—the novelist shows how the "white" European logic collapses under the equatorial latitudes, melting in the heat and before a world that seems hideous and unclassifiable. "How come," asks Leminsky's Descartes, perplexed, "not even nothing is what it seems back there!" "It's a 'pro-return' that goes neither backward nor forward," the philosopher-physicist-mathematician-theologian concludes, in a neologism, a verbal attempt to root itself in reality. In order to live and to survive among so much fauna and flora blending with tropical exuberance, among a procession of Africans and Indians, his rationalism had to be broken up by strokes of nonsense, imagination, fantasy, and surrealism to be able to build up another logic that would be operational down here.

Such allegories are not born by chance. They are symptomatic and paradigmatic, and reflect an underlying reality. The problems of relationships among different cultures are synthesized here. Race, environment, customs, history, and the world viewpoint, in short, determine the personality of the human groups that facilitate or obstruct exchange.

Thus, the Brazilian way of being keeps a close relationship with its history as a colonial dependent and peripheral Third World country with its ethnic formation and geography. So it is a premise that Brazilian development in "adequate" patterns will only happen if Brazilian people are able positively to recognize their "cultural" personality.

One can scarcely find empirical works on the specific matter that might reveal, at the essence of the behaviors, what Celso Furtado calls "the Brazilian cultural being" that has arisen out of the dependent modernization of the country.

Hence, our purpose is to follow a wake that, starting with the analysis of empirical data received from companies—particulary in the negotiation processes, managerial development interventions, and comparative studies with other cultures—should lead to a connection with the historical development and the Brazilians' sociopolitical formation, and help us understand current behaviors in Brazilian organizations better.

2. Organizational behaviors in the Brazilian company

In 1989, A.M. Hostalacio Costa, S.T. Diegues Fonseca, and M.L. Goulart Dourado, members of one of the most important consulting and action-research institutions in Brazil, the Fundaçao Dom Cabral, conceived a report based upon interventions dealing with management and the human relations training of managers in Brazilian companies. The work is based on data gathered from several questionnaires, from observations of role-playing exercises and case discussions in seminars, and also on studies based on interviews with managers from different hierarchical levels. The authors, specialists in the field of organization development, used the North American principles of Hersey and Blanchard, such as

40   AMADO (FRANCE) AND VINAGRE BRASIL (BRAZIL)

"situational leadership," as well as Likert's principle of participative management, Maslow and Herzberg's motivational theories, and Latin and European approaches such as "Institutional Analysis," which was mainly developed in France and Italy, as theoretical and methodological references.

In 1989, in a seminar on leadership, these authors presented their conclusions to a group of thirty executives of several client institutions with which they had worked previously. The conclusions about the way Brazilian organizations are managed were thus articulated as follows:

• Brazilian managerial performance is characterized by an immediatist view, directed toward short-term results with an emphasis on crisis solutions.

• There is a lack of strategic planning and/or a gap in planning between the tactical and the operational management levels.

• Decisions are centralized at superior hierarchical levels, with clear incompatibility between responsibility and authority.

• Organizational structure is excessively hierarchical, and the inner subsystems are excessively segmented, without integration.

• The system of control is partly marked as punitive, composed of follow-up mechanisms that are random and dissociated from a feedback process.

• Negotiations are carried out predominantly in an atmosphere in which winners lose and losers win and the main conflicts are not openly discussed. Attitudes tend to be imposed upon subordinates, and soothing behaviors are employed before superiors.

• Management has trouble occupying its own functional areas, for an inadequate distribution of authority associated with a punitive system of control leads to fear of assuming risks and consequently to a behavior of "pushing the problem upwards"—that is, delegation to a superior.

• The authoritarian-benevolent system within the limits of interaction with the deliberative-consultative one (as in Likert's model) is predominant, even though the organizational discourse tends to be participative. This is when the gap between managerial discourse and practice becomes clearer. "The discourse has to be made a practice"; "Make practical the discourse in which people are the main resources of the company."

Brazilian organizations are predominantly worried about immediate results, achievement, and short-term performance, which are particularly stressed by managers with an engineering background. Results are consequently restricted to a short- and medium-term strategic framework. Such actions impair the purposes and goals of productivity, cost reduction, and quality, as well as organizational efficiency.

When analyzing the organizational, managerial, and individual strengths and weaknesses, the groups have shown a great ease in determining weaknesses and a great difficulty in finding strengths. Primarily, they limit themselves to the professional's personal skill and technical competence, and to each person's commitment to the organization—"we wear the company shirt"—and to one's best intentions of improving and developing.

Within the Brazilian organizational reality, there is a remarkable valorization of managerial positions, to the detriment of technical positions. Salary increases and promotions are closely bound to the executive positions, thus leading to a depreciation of technical duties. There is, however, a paradox in the promotion process, since managers are selected on the basis of their individual technical competence.

One of us, a Frenchman who took part in this seminar, was surprised by two phenomena: first, the findings were rather shocking because of their negative nature; and second, managers received the survey results, which were presented to them in an open and straightforward manner, with a surprising degree of ease. One might rather have expected them to feel crushed by the "verdict."

What to conclude? Was this survey clear and objective and were the Brazilian managers simply not sensitive and not in a defensive position? Or did they tend to submit themselves to the specialists' conclusions in an almost masochistic manner? We shall return to this question.

The above observations are nonetheless very consistent with the results gathered from several surveys conducted by other specialists with company managers. Thus, Cardoso (1964) noted an excessive direct control inside Brazilian organizations, where family control works as a tool to restrain the delegation of authority to subordinates, and to valorize and stress loyalty and trust as desirable characteristics of subordinates.

Prasad (1981), when researching in Brazilian companies and their foreign subsidiaries, concludes with a low opinion of the capacity of subordinates for leadership and initiative, as shown by Brazilian managers. But, surprisingly enough, while he found they were less democratic than the expatriates on leadership issues, they espoused a more democratic belief in internal-control issues.

Amado and Cathelineau (1987–1988) presented a theoretical model and a methodological approach about the meaning of behavior in the context of negotiations. Wey (1987), following this model and methodology, collected data for four years on Brazilian managers (900 from 75 private and state organizations) and different styles of behavior during negotiations. Her findings are summarized in Tables 1 and 2.

These tables show a very clear predominance of the "receptive" style (linking and seducing—63 percent), rather than the so-called active style (persuading and asserting—38 percent), even if such differences are markedly more stressed in state organizations. Everything seems to happen in such a way that Brazilian managers try somehow to fix things up in order to avoid direct confrontation, which is experienced as dangerous (little capacity to withdraw), thus establishing personal relationships and giving signs of an open mind and empathy.

Marcondes et al. confirmed these results in 1989 with the same methodology in a study involving 3, 069 professionals. Their data are summarized in Table 3.

Regarding the submissive and the paternalistic attitudes that are evidently linked to the already mentioned authoritarian and hierarchical features, unpub-

Table 1. Negotiation styles (concepts and behaviors). (From Amado and Cathelineau, 1987–88.)

STYLES	CONCEPTS	TYPICAL BEHAVIORS
	A C T I V E	
PERSUADING	To have others take one's ideas in.	To propose and suggest. To argue, reason and justify.
ASSERTING	To impose and judge others.	To make requirements and rules known. To let one's point of view and wishes be known. To evaluate others and oneself. To punish, reward and yield.
	R E C E P T I V E	
LINKING	To understand the others frame of reference	To encourage participation of others. To search the agreement points. To listen and be empathetic.
SEDUCING	To open one self while trying to involve the others	To influence others through one's own behavior. To seduce, motivate others and raise their spirit. To share information. To admit one's own mistakes.
WITHDRAWAL	To keep a distance from immediate issues	To stay apart, to jump out, to escape difficulties

lished data collected in 1989 by Souza and Wey pointed out that the profile is consistent with the others' findings, with an emphasis on the tendencies listed in Table 4.

In Brazil in 1989, Amado and Cathelineau, in a yet unpublished study, used a case-study methodology based on a negotiation situation between two persons elaborated in France by Cathelineau with French managers in 1989. The 128 Brazilian managers have, overall, shown a very similar profile to that presented by the French investigators. If the latter researchers seem to be a bit more "dialectic" than the Brazilian team (the Cartesian reasoning leads them to be more argumentative), the Brazilians appear more open-minded, more cooperative, more receptive, while their assertiveness and capacity to exert pressure remain weak. (See Figure 1.)

As Graham and Herberger (1983) point out, while the crux of the negotiation process for North American managers is persuasion, in Brazil it is neither information nor persuasion: "Brazilians cannot depend on a legal system to iron out

Table 2.   Most characteristic negotiation styles (from Wey, 1987).

STYLES	THE MOST CHARACTERISTIC STYLES		
	STATE ORGANIZATION	PRIVATE ORGANIZATION	TOTAL
linking	52 %	46 %	(48 %)
persuading	27 %	33 %	(31 %)
seducing	17 %	15 %	(15 %)
asserting	2 %	5 %	(4 %)
withdrawing	2 %	1 %	(1 %)

Table 3.   Negotiation styles (from Marcondes et al., 1989).

Negotiation styles among Brazilian managers - %		Outstanding negotiation styles among Brazilian managers according to their roles - %		
		Director/manager	Superv.	Technicians
Linking	46	49	43	46
Persuading	30	25	35	40
Seducing	18	18	15	10
Asserting	5	6	4	3
Withdrawing	1	2	3	1

Table 4.   Negotiation styles (from Souza and Wey, 1989).

STYLES	STATE ORGANIZATION	PRIVATE ORGANIZATION	TOTAL
linking	59 %	44 %	50,5 %
persuading	18 %	26 %	22,0 %
seducing	16 %	22 %	19,0 %
asserting	6 %	8 %	7,0 %
withdrawing	1 %	--	0,5 %

conflicts, so they depend on personal relationships" (p. 163). That is why they are victims of the "wristwatch syndrome"—the fact that looking at your watch helps get things moving along. Say Graham and Herberger, "impatience causes apprehension, thus necessitating even longer periods of non-task sounding" (p. 163).

Parallel to this study on negotiation, we carried out another study in 1989. Based on the work and methodology developed by Laurent in 1983, this study explored Brazilian managers' conceptions of organizations, compared with those of managers from other countries. Several statements on the management and the structuring of organization were then proposed, and degree of agreement found among managers was recorded, as indicated for each proposal in Figures 2–5.

Many of the results place Brazil in an outstanding position when compared to other nations. The Brazilian representatives seem to dream of eliminating conflicts inside organizations. To the first assertion, that "Most organizations would

44 *AMADO (FRANCE) AND VINAGRE BRASIL (BRAZIL)*

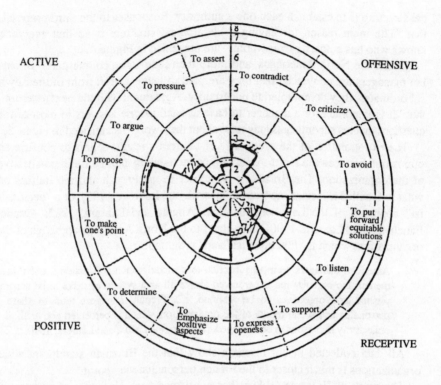

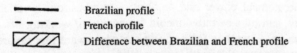

—————— Brazilian profile
- - - - French profile
/////// Difference between Brazilian and French profile

Figure 1. Average profile of Brazilian versus French attitudes in negotiation (from Amado and Cathelineau, 1989). This map is a synthesis of the results of research undertaken with 128 Brazilian managers, and 500 French ones, from a questionnaire presenting 28 situations of interpersonal negotiations with 4 possible solutions each. The results shown here reflect not direct observations but self-reports. When there is only one line on each scale, it means that Brazilian and French managers scored the same.

be better off if conflict could be eliminated forever," managers from various countries tend to answer differently (see Figure 2).

Brazilian managers worry about a precise definition of their roles. Responses to a second assertion, that "Most managers would achieve better results if their roles were less precisely defined," are indicated in Figure 3.

They believe more than the others that the main reason for having a hierarchical structure is to establish each one's authority. Responses to the third proposal, that "The main reason for having a hierarchical structure is so that everyone knows who has authority over whom," are presented in Figure 4.

Unlike the North Americans, and more than their Latin counterparts, Brazilian managers are convinced that they are paid to *know*, and in front of their own subordinates, they do not tolerate uncertainty. Agreement with the next assertion, that "It is important for a manager to have at hand precise answers to most of the questions that his subordinates may raise about their work," is indicated in Figure 5.

The extrapolation of the specificity of Laurent's results seems to confirm an opposition between the North American understanding and the Latin perspective of the organization. The Brazilians are closer to the French and the Italians on what was called a "social" approach (Inzerilli and Laurent, 1983), or a "personalist" approach of the Latin organization (Amado and Laurent, 1982; Amado, Faucheux, and Laurent, 1990), in contrast to the North American approach of the organization, which is "functionalist" and "pragmatic":

> American managers seem to subscribe to a model which is functional and instru-
> mental: the organization is perceived above all as a system of tasks to be accom-
> plished and objectives to be attained. ... French managers tend to share a
> personalist and social model of the organization, which is perceived above all as a
> collectivity of persons to be managed. [Amado, Faucheux, and Laurent, 1990, p. 28]

All data collected in our research show that the Brazilian standpoint about organizations is much closer to the French personalist viewpoint.

The work of Hofstede (1980a) has confirmed such closeness of perspective and suggests the same patterns (see Figures 6 and 7). If the Brazilians are less individualistic than the French and other, richer countries' citizens, they are all marked by the hierarchical power and authority centralization, by attempts to control uncertainty, and by a certain concern for quality of working life and for personal relationships, as well as for a caring attitude toward less favored ones and the working atmosphere (Hofstede calls it "femininity," as opposed to "masculinity," a more "achieving and goal oriented" attitude). Again we find a Latin cluster (the French and the Brazilian outlooks being very close to one another) opposed to an Anglo-Saxon one.

In short, the results of these different research projects are consistent and allow us to define a certain identity of both the Brazilian organization and the behaviors of the employees in it: a Latin pyramid in which a certain dependence (in contrast to France where counterdependence and rebellion prevail) echoes the centralization and control of a hierarchy concerned with asserting itself formally. Brazilian organizations seem to be comprised of members who are faced with the fear of unbearable conflicts, sensitive to the human dimension of work, and who are accustomed to avoiding difficulties thanks to personal interventions, which are the basis of the equilibrium.

This is where the most remarkable difference of the Brazilian man seems to

46 AMADO (FRANCE) AND VINAGRE BRASIL (BRAZIL)

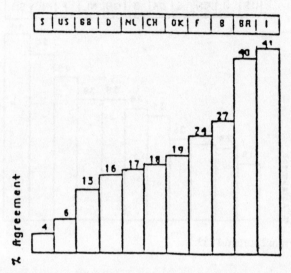

Figure 2. From Laurent, 1983. Abbreviations: US = United States; S = Sweden; GB = Great Britain; NL = The Netherlands; D = Germany; DK = Denmark; CH = Switzerland; B = Belgium; F = France; I = Italy; BR = Brazil.

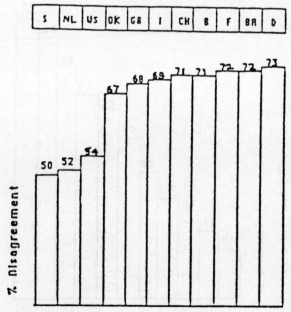

Figure 3. From Laurent, 1983.

ORGANIZATIONAL BEHAVIORS AND CULTURAL CONTEXT   47

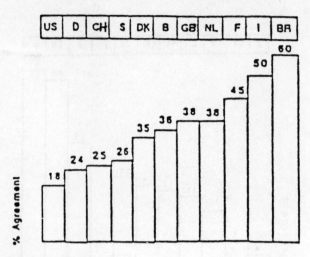

Figure 4.   From Laurent, 1983.

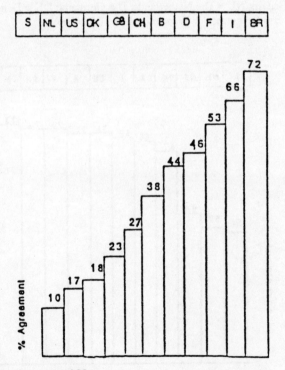

Figure 5.   From Laurent, 1983.

lie. His history and his sociocultural roots are the basis for these intermediations, of which the Brazilian "*jeitinho*"—a special way of managing obstacles in order to find a way out of bureaucracy—makes a paradigmatic synthesis.

3. Sociohistorical roots of the Brazilian culture: an interpretive synthesis

Theoretical background

This study requires as background Max Weber's epistemological principles, in which science does not validate value judgments, but yet it finds its basis in value premises when choosing references and leads to follow. This means that one must be aware that choices and theoretical orientations will be subject, from the beginning, to the researchers' world viewpoint. This fact pervades decisions and reflects cultural values. But this circularity does not invalidate conclusions if it has taken root in reality. Thus, keeping these principles in mind as a reference point makes it possible to reach reliable results, even if they always seem partial and temporary. Nevertheless, it is a mistake to think that these cultural features that are raised will stand together in a harmonic set, or even to think that they form a totally coherent structural model. The Brazilian culture, in particular, is marked by a high level of contradiction because it is young and its components are, just now, in a process of integration. To understand it more adequately, one has to use the similarity and difference methodology of Kant, which entails grasping concepts and categories dialectically in the darkness and lightness of opposition. But, in that process, it is still possible to achieve, at times, several levels of confluence and synthesis that shall come to reveal characteristic totalities.

We therefore see every attempt to search for uniform cultural patterns as stereotyping, and, at times, caricature. A culture itself is a game of transactions through which flow the worldview of people and societies, and even more restrictive groups with unconscious bearings.

When seeking out the origins of the current behavior of the Brazilian—that is, of his culture within this restricted sense—one should study what he says, writes, represents, and does. In this way, Schein (1984) outlines three "windows" through which one may view a culture: the visible signs of its creations, patterns of behavior, and technologies; consciously incorporated values; and unconscious assumptions. The choice of the window (or windows) to which we will turn our eyes is methodologically very important.

It is our intention to find a way, starting with the Brazilian sociopolitical heritage, that will lead to a definition of the influence of the Brazilian culture in the management of organizations founded or based in Brazil. This endeavor will be only a glance through an opening in Schein's window.

In Brazil, the use of the "Best Practices,"[1] which originated in technologically more advanced cultures and in the context of capitalist economies, has proven

ORGANIZATIONAL BEHAVIORS AND CULTURAL CONTEXT   49

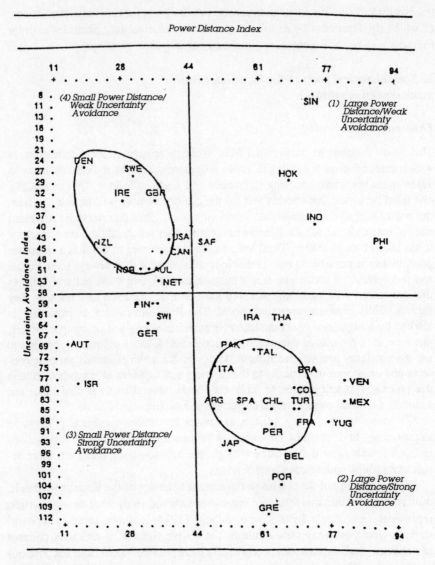

Figure 6.   The position of 40 countries on the power distance and uncertainty scales (from Hofstede, 1980a, p. 51).

that such transpositions are doomed to failure, or take much longer to become functional than is tolerable. And all, it seems, mainly because of cultural diversity. Recent studies carried out by several authors have pointed out that a blind, although well-meaning, use of managerial models might lead to failure and waste of time and money if the local culture is not taken into account. Such

50   AMADO (FRANCE) AND VINAGRE BRASIL (BRAZIL)

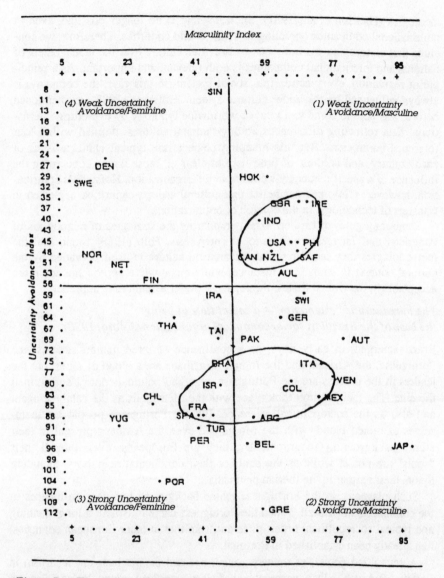

Figure 7.   The position of 40 countries on the uncertainty avoidance and masculinity scales (from Hofstede, 1980a, p. 54).

efforts are frustrating and usually lead to misgivings regarding the companies' modernization actions. Thus, in empirical terms, it is difficult to support the belief expressed by the so-called culture-free line of thought that, in large organizations that are very specialized and formalized, cultural differences are leveled, and this fact brings about a convergence of behaviors thanks to the common ideologies (Hickson et al., 1981). Such leveling is no longer possible, even in multinational companies operating in Third World countries. Therefore, we conclude that research on the influence of Brazilian culture over the management of national and international companies is both relevant and important. As a principle of regulation, every action in a social system (in this case, the company) is always influenced by the wider cultural system. Hofstede (1987), as mentioned before, was able to come to a kind of worldwide typology by exploiting international data reflecting differences among national cultures, defined within four reference parameters. But this mapping neglects the typical characteristics of each country, and is, thus, of little help to clear up those issues concerning the influence of a specific country's culture in the organization. Hofstede's contribution, however, reinforces our belief that cultural aspects cannot be neglected in transfers of technology, in the context of organizations.

Some may go even further. When comparing the strategies of negotiation of American and Japanese multinational enterprises, Hilb (1988) found that the methodologies they use for social research on culture is itself pervaded by the cultural context in study. For instance, while quantitative approaches are more acceptable in the United States, the Japanese prefer a qualitative approach.

The bureaucratic "estamento"—a social state of being:
the base of the Brazilian socioeconomical organization (Faoro, 1958)

Brazil emerged, in early days, as a confluence of three human streams: the Portuguese, the African, and the Indian. Brazilians are a blend of races, but the leaders in the process are the Portuguese, who had political control and formed the elite. The racial fusion took place with the Metropolis as the catalytic agent and also as the sociopolitical reference. But the Portuguese people are themselves of mixed blood, with the Moors and even the Africans present in their ethnic background. Geographically, they are Europeans, even though their "souls" are not as white as the souls of their continental neighbors, including Spain, their partner in the Iberian peninsula.

Such plasticity in the Portuguese ethnic background had deep influences in the colonization of Brazil. When the Portuguese came to Brazil, a long-standing and typical sociopolitical order, different from that in other European countries, had already been established in Portugal.

A centralized power, of military nature, replaced the yet incipient feudalism in Portugal. But such military aggregation had always revolved around the king's power, and the king chose his servants following a mercenary process. He rewarded them with goods and the promise of privileges, appealing simultaneously to the courtiers' greed and adventurous spirit. These servants of wealth did not have to pass through the sieve of the feudal barony which, for that reason, was slowly extinguished.

The state, as a personal enterprise of the prince, had a part in every private business, buying loyalty via the royal treasury, always eager for more contributions. The economy was at that time centralized on the state treasury, which collected revenues and taxes. It was the patriarchal entrepreneur and prince who controlled the kingdom as his own home. Everything was rather different from the rest of Europe, where business was held by private enterprise with a commercial and mercantilist angle.

Nevertheless, it must be stressed that the notion of "state" was fundamental in the *anciens régimes*, and was based upon the old Indo-European distinction between the three states: the church, the army, and the peasants.

Portuguese capitalism flourished like an appendix to the royal house and as a dependent and minor partner. In that structure, traditionalism and centralization predominate and are almost synonymous.

The fundamental element in this machine was the bureaucratic "*estamento*," recruited by the king in order to accomplish his despotic will and goals, in the realm of a patrimonial state.

"*Estamento*," according to Faoro (1958), based on Max Weber, means a group characterized by an aspiration to privileges, which finds its accomplishment in differentiation through honor and the acceptance of individuals. It is different from class, which is the result and product of economic interests tied to the market. It is also different from bureaucracy, which is a simple apparatus of the establishment, its administrative staff performing on the borderlines of rational and professional behaviors. But, even so, *estamento* may sometimes appear as either a class or a bureaucracy, in some ways linked to the state. It cannot be seen as a dysfunction, but better yet as a distortion. It is also different from the political elite, since it is found in all strata.

The *estamento*, on behalf of the prince, is the nation's referee, and also its class's referee. It holds the economy materially as if it were the master of its sovereignty.

Within the limits of every definition, which always tends to be oversimplifying, these considerations describe this social category which the Portuguese transplanted to Brazil.

The country's colonization took place under an "estamental" and patrimonial economic order. Later on, it became a state capitalism, highly supported by the bureaucratic *estamento*.

It was, thus, the country's trademark always to depend on the state, even after the Proclamation of the Republican Regime—theoretically considered as a reaction against monarchy, but which maintained the bureaucratic *estamento* unchanged. But the republic was imposed on the people, who were brought down to the rank of animals, as described by Carvalho (1987). In addition to this, "it boycotted every single opportunity to consolidate citizenship."

This economy, dependent on the state, started with the "*capitanias hereditarias*,"[2] which were a king's donation to his "protégés"; but they were inalienable and indivisible, to such an extent that they would eventually return to the donor's possession. The early explorers in Brazil themselves behaved as contractors and managers of the Power because they were used to being the king's commissioners, despite the fact that they were looking for riches and that they sometimes tried to break their commitments.

Thus, everything in colonial Brazil and in the kingdom of Brazil was delegated. After independence, the empire organized itself as a bureaucratic *estamento* that "nestled into the Executive Power, in the lifelong senate and into the moderating power. This was the first symptom of the mechanism of intermediation and arbitrariness" (Faoro, 1958, p. 204).[3] Lifelong Senates, "bionic senators"[4] are names to label the same reality. The king's "moderating power" or the armed forces are identical categories that bear the purpose of maintaining the "status quo."

Joaquim Nabuco (1915, pp. 280–281) already predicted what is still true today when he wrote: "Since the beginning, the heat, light and life for the larger organizations had come from the Treasury." This fact implicitly includes a high grade of economic and legal regulatory power that the "estamental" state holds, making private enterprise difficult. However, what is even more serious is that organizations found ways to get around such interventionism—that is, they avoided it by associating with the state, standing by its side, and by obtaining subsidies, protectionism, unofficial cartels, and exceptional financing. The government, by subjecting organizations to its will, provided for their needs.

In this way, the *estamento* has embodied the characteristics of a huge *advocacia administrativa*—a way of taking advantage of one's own individual and personal influence before the state in order to get privileges—which has become fundamental to the nation's functioning. Despite the fact that it is necessary to all modern societies, bureaucracy, in Weber's sense, is always conservative. Bureaucracy, in its "estamental" distortion, obstructs the course of change processes because it is an end in itself, a power manipulator, a domination tool. In bureaucracy, formalism predominates in relationships, and it causes the displacement of objectives, a certain accommodation and a disharmony between the written rule and the behavior it induces. Even as a strategy to reduce conflicts, to hide the dualities found in the social structure, and to dissolve downtown-versus-suburb contrasts, such "estamental" bureaucracy is the support of a culture that explains to a great extent the Brazilian people's characteristics and way of life. The popular answer to how to avoid or ignore this spurious usurpation is to create new behavior possibilities (Ramos, 1983) which become, in the course of time, deeply rooted in a culture or in the features of that culture.

The Brazilian "jeitinho" as a hermeneutic key for the Brazilian culture

It is in the conjunction of a society organized in the realm of a conservative, patrimonial, and "estamental" state capitalism of a greatly differentiated ethnic background that the Brazilian man was formed, or is still in the process of being formed. The "*casa grande*" (owner's house on a plantation), in a certain phase of this social and economic evolution, where monoculture (sugar) was prevalent, provided the fusion of these traces to happen, as their components shared the same environment and means of living (Freire, 1954). The *casa grande* complemented by the "*senzala*" (the plantation's slave quarters), represented the whole economic, social, and political system—namely, labor and production, religion and sexual life, which have left

54 AMADO (FRANCE) AND VINAGRE BRASIL (BRAZIL)

marks in the Brazilian people's way of life and behavior. This monocultural system, with supports in slavery and large landed estates—in which the coffee farmer or the *"senhor de engenho"* (the owner and master of large sugarcane fields and sugar mills) was not only the landowner but also the master of men and women—reinforces the ongoing authoritarianism and centralization in the "estamental" government, in colonial, imperial, or even in republican times.

The slavery regime—the base of the entire system—provided the blacks with economic support while they "compounded" with the Portuguese *senhor de engenho*, exchanging culture and blood, and thus incorporating habits, behavior, food, sexuality, and life's rhythm. The *"capoeira"* (a dancelike wrestling practiced by the slaves in Brazil), the merrymaking, the music, most especially the *"samba"* (a popular Brazilian dance of African origin—the center of the yearly *Carnaval*), the *"feijoada"* (a popular Brazilian dish made of black beans boiled with bits of pork and sausage, seasoned with pepper sauce, and served with rice and manioc flour), the *"cocada"* (coconut candy), the seasonings, the *"vatapa"* (a Brazilian dish made of manioc meal, mixed with fish and shrimp), the celebrations, and the religious feasts are clear traces of this racial fusion. Moreover, the cultural syncretism found its way into the official religion of most of the population, Catholicism. The Catholic Church in Brazil has incorporated into its unofficial beliefs the rites and religious practices brought by the blacks from Africa. It is not at all by chance that the patron saint of Brazil, Lady Aparecida, is a black virgin miraculously found in a river (Da Matta, 1986).

All this makes the Brazilian. He is a citizen seeking for his soul in the dialectic profusion of his physical and spiritual components, who has had to develop a flexible, labile, plastic personality in order to survive, live, and build a country. In order to face an oligarchic social system, he developed a *"jogo de cintura"*—a flexibility of body and spirit to deviate from obstacles[5]—an aspect of what can be identified as a key to the Brazilian behavior, the *jeitinho*, a typical cultural feature. We are talking about plasticity and flexibility. The *jeitinho* is the common denominator, the hermeneutic basis from which an interpretation of the Brazilian culture becomes possible. It is not a question of making this one feature absolute, but rather is a matter of using this privileged front door so as to further deepen the exposition. In our analysis, the *jeitinho* provides us with the key for understanding what it means "to be Brazilian," and for deriving some insights into Brazilian management. Of course, the deeper components of *jeitinho* remain to be explored in further research.

Two authors, as far as we know, have elaborated a sociological theory of the *"jeito"*—a way, manner, tact, appearance, adroitness, aptitude, dexterity . . . (*"dar un jeito"*) is a very common expression meaning "to find a way out to")— Guerreiro Ramos (1983) and Roberto Campos (1960).[6] They see *jeito* as the most genuine Brazilian process of problem managing, "despite the contents of the rules, codes and laws," as the latter says, an efficient adaptive process for living in a closed, centralized, "estamental," and formalistic society, with the advantage of avoiding deadlocks, extreme solutions, and paralyzing situations—all outbursts, in short. Because confrontation does not suit the Brazilian social training and way of life, this "cordial"[7] facet of the Brazilian is a consequence of the way he interacts with the sociopolitical environment (Holanda, 1976). Such cordiality—which the European etymology cannot thoroughly translate—is the expression of a rich, overflowing, and sensitive world that rejects ritualism and seeks intimacy, in a different way from the almost religious reverence of the Japanese. Because Brazilians are fond of intimacy, they like to use the diminutive suffix "*inho*"—often used as a term of endearment—beginning with *jeitinho*, which does not mean only and strictly *jeito* (way, manner), but rather, a broadly fresh and intimate game. Thus, Brazilians relate on emotional terms and, even in business, they do not eliminate collective outbursts and nonconformity at the level of the people. Their social rebellions were nearly always cruel, if seen and studied in great depth (Rodrigues, 1982). The cordial man does not necessarily imply kindness, but only the predominance of apparently emotional behaviors; the epitomizing of these behaviors is not reflected on a collective level.

To return to the *jeitinho* as an adaptive answer and as the essence of the behavior the Brazilians have found to deal with this sociopolitical heritage, we notice that it is a highly functional and effective device. It bypasses a legal framework full of "texts out of context—technical elaborations that were not born from customs but from a highly oligarchical power" (Campos, 1960).

This mannerism of the Brazilian personality has brought about typical characters in a society full of mediations: the "*despachante*," a kind of spokesman who represents someone's interests before the bureaucratic establishment (because of the nature of the reigning bureaucracy, Brazilians prefer to hire the services of such an agent, rather than waste their time standing in lines to resolve their issues); the *advocacia administrativa*, the several kinds of brokers and mediators present in business affairs. Each of these mediators takes care of someone else's interests in exchange for pecuniary benefits. As Campos (1960, p. 29) describes them: "They patch up the gap between the law and the fact, making possible the impossible, legal the illegal, and fair the unfair. They grant flexibility to a formal and rigid law with excessive logical strictness."

On the political level, the moderating power, which has acted ever since imperial times, is within this mediating line of behavior, as we have pointed out. At first the emperor strategically ruled conflicts from an upper standpoint, even above the constitution itself. Eventually his rule was assumed by the army. But both always intervened in favor of the oligarchies and of the maintenance of the status quo, as it were.

Setting apart power aspects, these mediators are, in fact, institutionalized *jeitinho*. That is why there are in Brazil some laws that simply do not apply.

The simple fact that *jeitinho* exists allows for discrimination. There are laws for everything, a superabundance of them, in comparison with other countries (especially with Anglo-Saxon ones). Thus, it is easier to choose the one law that protects you or the one that punishes your opponents. "*Aos inimigos a lei, aos amigos as facilidades da lei*" (the law for your enemies, the advantages of the law for your friends), the proverb says.

Conflicts must be avoided at all costs. The Brazilian people appreciate euphemisms

56 AMADO (FRANCE) AND VINAGRE BRASIL (BRAZIL)

(Vinagre Brasil, 1989), which means escaping from the unpleasant, attenuating inconveniences or smoothing over reality. By postponing or watering down conflicts, Brazilians get *around* problems, and that, in a sense, means solving them—in the Brazilian way. Brazilians always escape from the radical standpoints of a confrontation in personal terms. That is why we find such aphorisms as "*deixa estar pra ver como é que fica*" (leave things as they are; wait and see what happens); "*O Brazil é um pais do futuro*" (Brazil is a country that belongs to the future); "*Deus é brasileiro*" (God is Brazilian); "*quem trabalha nao tem tempo de ganhar dinheiro*" (whoever works never finds time to make money); and in a paroxysmal extension, bordering on corruption, these lead to the "*Lei de Gerson*"—Gerson's law—which claims "one must take advantage of every situation,"[8] or that "by giving one receives," which would be a "*lei de Sao Francisco as avessas*,"[9] which was supported by some Brazilian physiologistic politicians (Vinagre Brasil, 1989).

Another very interesting category we may include in Brazil's *jeitinho* culture is that of "*gambiarra*," which is a kind of a nonprofessional, cheap, and quick repair or mending (Paulielo, 1984). *Gambiarra* as a rule "breaks up" in very improper circumstances because the definitive arrangement is always postponed. In this way, a provisory solution becomes a permanent one, despite the risks involved in its adoption.

Brazilians use *gambiarras* to patch up cars, utilities, and even the federal constitution, because it is easier to make a quick repair than it is to give a matter some more thought. In a positive interpretation, *gambiarra* reflects flexibility.

Any analysis of cultural behavior cannot overlook aspects of time and space management. Thus, it is relevant to ask how a Brazilian manages time. We already received some information about this from a North American perspective about the negotiation process. But what do Brazilian anthropologists say? "An hour in Brazil is not enjoyed as it is in the United States regarding rhythm and other living aspects," Ramos (1983) confirms.

According to Da Matta, Brazilian people have differentiated and divergent temporalities: linear time in the outer world, cyclical time at home, and everlasting time in another world. In linear time we are in the realm of organized work, one thing after the other, where routine and repetition predominate; in cyclical time we are at home, all by ourselves, not worried with efficiency or cartesian logic, in a ludic state of mind. These are qualitative dimensions that are inseparable from quantitative ones, and they differentiate and complete each other in the outer world and home spaces. In this way, the Brazilian avoids experiencing a "schizophrenic" time. It is not that other cultures do not incorporate such differences. But here they are much clearer and, paradoxically, more blended because of the importance of the sociopolitical organization, centralized within the state. Following a classification by Ramos (1983), we would say that the utilitarian Taylorian serial time, which makes time a merchandise (time is money), is counterbalanced by the social time one spends at home and during vacations and holidays. The Brazilian escapes from routine and repetition by keeping himself in transit between the two types of time.

Inside organizations, it is during the so-called transitional moments—coffee or conversation breaks—when people arrive or leave work, that one time is inserted into the other. Hence, people mark a wedge in the hierarchichal and anonymous environments of organizations.

This expressive time management reflects how the Brazilian views work and the next day. Because, from the point of view of puritan capitalism transplanted to Brazil in its basic Anglo-Saxon ideology, work does not mean *today* but the *future*, such a viewpoint clashes with the Brazilian reality. The stubborn and oligarchic structure of the "estamental" power makes people live life in a fatalistic manner, as destiny and not as construction. It is a little like the fable of the ant and the grasshopper. Brazilian people are the grasshoppers. That is why neither hurrying nor being punctual is worthwhile. Brazil is more than just a country. It is a continent. Its accomplishment is in the future. Its wealth, to the Brazilian, is inexhaustible and therefore one should not hurry, one should proceed slowly and constantly. Brazilian people believe in charismatic leaders and in magic solutions. It is not by chance that the "*jogo do bicho*," an illegal national lottery,[10] was created—a national institution that, despite its "unofficial" status, is reliable and solidly established. The *estamento*, aware of its existence, creates dozens of lotteries—euphemistic ways of collecting taxes from everyone, including the poor. Then, the future is not history but a game. For the individual, it is not the work that pays off; rather, it is fate that decides if one will be rich or poor. After all, opposites meet . . . but space and time are interdependent. One cannot be managed without the other.

Public time and private time take place in public and in private spaces. Even the "other world's" time is up there and down here in the family memories. In these spaces, intimacy and individuality exist in opposition with depersonalization and anonymity. Behaviors are functions of these spaces and they are inserted inside the logic of these oppositions or of these complementarities.

According to Da Matta (1986), Brazilian society is "relational" because it is integrated through relations between spaces, where it builds transitional bridges. "God is Brazilian," not because with him things will always work out, but, above all, because he is composed—as we are—of three persons or three distinct and absolutely complementary spaces. The father is the outer world, where the state is the relentless universe of impersonal laws, and the son is the home, with his warm relationship, his humanity, and the senses of a person made of flesh and bones. And the holy ghost is the relationship between the two, the other side of the mystery (Da Matta, 1987).

These spaces represented by the home, the outer world, and the other world have activities, specific objects, and time as well-defined and distinct ethics.

Some devices make the transit easier inside these spaces and times, bringing us to the proximity of our daily experiences. They are "breaks" for witticisms and joke telling, to tell about real or imaginary sexual experiences, to have a cup of coffee, to tap someone on the back—in short, to be intimate.

In this three-dimensional world, the *jeitinho* prevails and works as a conflict reducer, smoothing the transit from one environment to another, and thus permitting a conviviality with the dysfunctions of work. The *jeitinho* replaces the law's mediation, which does not work among Brazilians, for the home and the outer world are then self-referential. The "individual" and the "person" at times are one, and at other times are opponents, and only the *jeitinho* can bring harmony to these indefinitions. That is why Brazilian people are obsessed with relationships and with personal bonds, so as always to be able to find the key to their own lives. This distinction between the individual (*o indivíduo*) and the person (*a pessoa*) is another key Da Matta (1987) offers to explain the "Brazilian dilemma." The individual is the impersonal subject of universal laws, while the person is the subject of social relationships, with their emotions and uniqueness. The tendency of Brazilians is therefore to reduce the power of the anonymous individual (or laws) to live and solve processes at a personal level. The outer world, which stands for work, is anonymous, full of surprises, temptations, and insecurity, and is compensated by the home, where Brazilians are personal, have their own bodies, and can keep up the moral dimension of honor, respect, honorability, and shame. This ambiguity is therefore a means of survival. It is also a way of life. "The secret of a correct interpretation of Brazil lies in the possibility of studying what is 'between' things," Da Matta insists (1987, p. 26). The Brazilian *Carnaval* feast is a clear way of linking the home, the outer world, and the other world, or the intimate, the dangerous, and the magical, a typical way of promoting equality by a temporary denial of differences and frontiers.

Even in food, Brazilians care more for pasty dishes. These are "relational" and intermediary, and neither purely solid nor liquid. "*Feijoada*," a stew, "*canjiquinha*," a traditional Brazilian dish of cornmeal and pieces of meat, with pork ribs and cabbage, "*munguza*," a dish of corn with milk, sugar, and cinnamon, with corn and peanuts, "*vatapá*," in which shrimp float on top of the paste, oily with "*dendê*" (an African oilplant grown in Brazil)—these are all almost soups or even solid morsels dipped in something that is almost liquid, in short, pasty.

If the *jeitinho* is taken as a common denominator of oppositions, contrasts, and contradictions, it may not entirely define or explain the behavior of the Brazilians, even if it pictures them realistically. But are we dealing with a matter of definition? The demonstration of Brazilians' sociopolitical and cultural realities by means of the *jeitinho* allows us to find a common root for most of their behavior inside organizations.

These behaviors show a double facet, which makes them contradictory. By being flexible and labile, Brazilians have a chance to face their authoritarian and discriminatory environment, as well as to resist change. This explains why even the negative diagnoses discussed earlier in this paper are accepted, why a certain kind of conflict avoidance is displayed in negotiation, and why the new management technologies (Best Practices) are difficult to implement or do not work out at all.

This double facet of a mediation-type behavior is reflected, in Brazil, through the *jeitinho*. But we cannot ignore the analogies that may come to mind if we turn to other Latin countries. In France and Italy especially, the existence of similar mediation processes is striking. The "system D" in France (where "D" stands for "*débrouillardise*"—resourcefulness) and the "*combinazzione*" in Italy also have this double facet. Both of them are means used by individuals and groups to bypass centralization, an excessive rigidity or amount of laws and regulations, the power of the state, authoritarian modes of leadership. Although the "D" system and the "*combinazzione*" help people to live in a satisfactory way with a real amount of flexibility and creativity, on the other hand they disqualify the power of social rules and lead to anarchy, parallel organizations, or mafias (either terrorist in Italy, or intellectual in France through the elitist castes).

Therefore, beyond its hermeneutic value for the understanding of the cultural Brazilian reality, the *jeitinho* can become the living source of further research on the Latin modes of mediation used by people within organizations and society.

Notes

We would like to express our sincere thanks to the professors of Fundação Dom Cabral: Antônio Mauricio Hostalacio Costa and Sônia Teresa Diegues Fonseca, for having shared with us their vast experience in Brazilian companies gathered during so many years; Professor Roberto Da Matta (Notre Dame University, Kelley Institute), for his precious help in the understanding of the Brazilian culture; Professors Marco Aurélio Spyer Prates and Ulisses Ferreira Diniz e Betânia Tanure de Barros for the "cross-fertilization" of ideas and opinions regarding the research project, "Cultural Reality and Management Systems," being developed at Fundação Dom Cabral; Marc Cathelineau (Thomson and HEC Graduate School of Management) for giving us permission to use his questionnaire about negotiation behaviors and for analyzing the data collected; Professor André Laurent (INSEAD) for permission to use his questionnaire about "organizational mental maps," and for his work, together with Cathy Petts, in the data analysis and editing of this paper; Professor Claude Faucheux (Erasmus University, Rotterdam School of Management, The Netherlands), for his comments and help in the editing of this contribution; HEC Graduate School of Management, its research direction and the "Jouy-Enterprises" Association for their financial and administrative support in the research; Clarissa Rose and Maria Matta Machado for their assistance in the translation of this document; Sylvie Bonneau and Sylvie Metais for their secretarial help; Agnès Melot, director of the HEC library and her colleagues.

  1. Best Practices are linked to administration models—management technologies conceived in developed countries and transferred to the Third World, generally without the necessary adaptation. Examples are: Management by Objectives, Total Quality Control, Just In Time, Zero Defect, among others.

  2. In colonial Brazil, the *capitanias hereditarias* was a jurisdictional division corresponding to a province, allotted to a protégé of the prince.

  3. The moderating power meant that the emperor and, after him, the army, had the role of a referee in the political game, deciding over parties and Congress if the "estamental status quo" was in jeopardy.

  4. The bionic senators were a class of senators nominated by the president during the military government in Brazil. They corresponded to a certain percentage of the Congress that had a greater representation.

  5. This idiomatic expression was originally used to signify the way Brazilians play soccer as if they were dancing the *samba*. They used a swing of their hips to avoid their opponents—to deviate from the opponent's path. In life, it means the Brazilian has to avoid difficult situations.

  6. See also Viera, Da Costa, and Barbosa (1982).

  7. "*O homem cordial*"—the cordial man who reflects the myth of a mixed-blooded society.

60 *AMADO (FRANCE) AND VINAGRE BRASIL (BRAZIL)*

8. Gerson was a world champion Brazilian soccer player who used this expression as a slogan in a cigarette advertisement. The fact that it took on a pejorative connotation at the time upset him.

9. Cardoso Alves, a member of the Brazilian Parlement, first used this expression in an interview in which he supported the *"fisiologismo"* of the politicians—that is, a supportive attitude adopted by some politicians toward the government in exchange for favors. *"As avessas"* means the other way around. San Francis is the author of a well-known prayer that says that by giving, one is already receiving. And Cardoso Alves was giving his support to the government, not taking into consideration the people's interest, but only his own.

10. The *"jogo do bicho"* was created by the Baron of Drummond in Rio de Janeiro to reward the visitors to his zoo. Today it is run by bookmakers. It is a highly reliable lottery network because it never fails to pay the prizes.

References

Amado, G., and Cathelineau, M. (1987–88) "Estudo sobre os comportamentos na negociaçao." *Tendencias do trabalho*, December 1987, pp. 12–16; January 1988, pp. 23–27; February 1988, pp. 15–18.

Amado G.; Faucheux, C.; and Laurent, A. (1990) "Changement organisationnel et réalités culturelles, contrastes franco-américains." In J.F. Chanlat, ed., *L'individu dans l'organisation: les dimensions oubliées*. Québec: Presses de l'Université Laval.

Amado, G., and Laurent, A. (1982) "Organization Development and Change: A Comparison between USA and Latin Countries." IX Annual Conference of SIETAR, San Gimignano, Italy, May.

Blanc, G. (1981) "Culture et management: l'exemple du Brésil." *Cahier de recherche du Centre HEC*, no. 187. Jouy-en-Josas, France: HEC.

Campos, G. (1960) "A Sociologia do 'jeito'." *Revista senhor*, p. 29.

Cardoso, P.H. (1964) *O empresario e o desenvolvimento industrial no Brasil*. São Paulo: Difusao Européia do Livro.

Carvalho, de, J.M. (1987) *Os bestializados*. São Paulo: Companhia das Letras.

Da Matta, R. (1986) *O que faz o Brasil Brasil*. Rio de Janeiro: Rocco.

———. (1987) *A casa e a rua*. Rio de Janeiro: Guanabara.

Faoro, R. (1958) *Os donos do poder*. Porto Alegre: Globo.

Freire, G. (1954) *Casa grande e senzala*, 8th ed. Rio de Janeiro: José Olympio.

Graham, J.L., and Herberger, R., Jr. (1983) "Negotiators Abroad—Don't Shoot from the Hip." *Harvard Business Review*, July–August, pp. 160–168.

Hersey, P., and Blanchard, K. (1969) *Management of Organizational Behavior*. Englewood Cliffs, NJ: Prentice-Hall.

Herzberg, F. (1966) *Work and the Nature of Man*. Cleveland: World.

Hilb, M. (1988) *Japanese and American Multinational Companies: Business Strategies*. Gestion 2000, Université Catholique de Louvain.

Hickson, D.J., et al. (1981) *The Culture Free Context of Organization Structure*. The Aston Programme IV, Guilfort Biddles.

Hofstede, G. (1980a) "Motivation, Leadership and Organisation: Do American Theories Apply Abroad?" *Organisational Dynamics*, Summer, pp. 42–63.

———. (1980b) *Culture's Consequences: International Differences in Work-related Values*. Beverly Hills, CA: Sage Publications.

———. (1987) "Relativité culturelle des pratiques et théories de l'organisation." *Revue Française de gestion*, September–October, pp. 10–21.

Holanda, de, S.B. (1976) *Raizes do Brasil*, 9th ed. Rio de Janeiro: José Olympio.

Hostalacio Costa, A.M., and Diegues Fonseca, S.T. (1989) "Sintese fenomenologica das açoes de desenvolvimento gerencial," Belo Horizonte, Fundaçao Dom Cabral, documento interno.

Inzerilli, G., and Laurent, A. (1983) "Managerial Views of Organizational Structure in France and the USA." *International Studies of Management and Organization*, 8 (1/2), pp. 97–118.

Lapierre, L. (1989) "Imaginario, administraçao e liderança." In *Revista de administraçao de empresas*. São Paulo: Fundaçao Getulio Vargas.

Laurent, A. (1983) "The Cultural Diversity of Western Conceptions of Management." *International Studies of Management and Organization*, 13 (1/2), pp. 75–96.

Leminsky, P. (1989) *Catatau*. Porto Alegre: Sulina.

Likert, R. (1961) *New Patterns of Management*. New York: McGraw-Hill.

Maslow, A.H. (1954) *Motivation and Personality*. New York: Harper and Row.

Nabuco, J. (1915) *Um estadista do império*, vol. 2. Rio de Janeiro: Garnier.

Paulielo, L. (1984) "No pais das gambiarras." *Estado de minas*, Belo Horizonte, June 27.

Prasad, S.B. (1981) "Managers' Attitudes in Brazil: Nationals versus Expatriates." *Management International Review*, 21, pp. 78–85.

Ramos, G. (1983) *Administraçao e contexto Brasileiro*. Rio de Janeiro: Fundaçao Getulio Vargas.

Rodrigues, J.H. (1982) *Conciliaçao e reforma no social*. Rio de Janeiro: Nova Fronteira.

Schein, E.H. (1980) "Coming to a New Awareness of Organizational Culture." *Sloan Management Review*, 25(2), pp. 3–16.

Vieria, C.A.; Da Costa, F.L.; and Barbosa, L.O. (1982) "O 'jeitinho' brasileiro como um recurso de poder." *Revista de administraçao publica* (Rio de Janeiro), 16 (2), pp. 5–31.

Vinagre Brasil, H. (1989) "Patologia da cultura brasileira." *Diario do comércio*, Belo Horizonte, p. 2.

Weber, M. (1965) *Essais sue le théorie de la science*. Paris: Plon.

Wey, V.L. (1987) "Pesquisa revela quem é negociador brasileiro." *Tendências do trabalho*, July, pp. 9–11

[13]

The Iron Law of Fiefs:
Bureaucratic Failure and
the Problem of Govern-
ance in the Chinese
Economic Reforms

Max Boisot
*China-EC Management
Institute, PRC*
John Child
Aston University, England

This paper argues that the current markets and hierarchies framework of transaction-cost economics provides
too limited a set of transactional options to account adequately for many of the organizational problems encountered in developing economies. Focusing on the
codification and diffusion of information, it provides a set
of concepts designed to extend the existing framework.
Applying these concepts to an analysis of the economic
reforms in the People's Republic of China since 1978, the
paper identifies a form of bureaucratic failure that lies
beyond the markets-hierarchies typology and that highlights the important role played by culture and level of
development in shaping transactional preferences.[*]

A key issue for transaction-cost economics concerns the
mode of organization through which transactions are to be
governed. In Williamson's (1975) early analysis, as well as in
that of his predecessors, such as Commons (1934) and Coase
(1937), the choice was seen to fall between governance
through the hierarchical structures of formal bureaucracies or
through the market mechanism. Thus if a bureaucratic governance of transactions failed, the market was presented as
the alternative, and vice versa. While Williamson wrote with
reference to the United States, a developed capitalist
economy, discussions of economic system reform in socialist
countries have also taken as a central theme the postulated
dichotomy between bureaucratic and market transaction-governance structures (e.g., Kornai, 1986).

Recent analyses of the People's Republic of China (PRC),
currently one of the socialist countries in the forefront of economic reform, have accepted this broad parallel (e.g., Tidrick
and Chen, 1987). Indeed, the major official Chinese policy
document on the subject has itself described the reform as
entailing a move from administrative to market coordination
(Communist Party of China, 1984). The examination of the
Chinese case in this article indicates, however, that Williamson's model requires extension to take into account other
transaction-governance possibilities that may be more consistent with the social preferences emanating from a traditional
culture and that are also easier to support with the limited infrastructure of an economically less developed nation. A
focus on the informational aspect of economic transacting
permits this analytical extension to be made.

AN INFORMATIONAL FRAMEWORK FOR ANALYZING
TRANSACTION GOVERNANCE

Information is inherent in transactions for goods and services
because it is a prerequisite for their initiation and completion.
Transactions require the production and exchange of information. The structures through which transactions are governed
differ in the ways they express and distribute information.

Kroeber and Kluckhohn (1952) noted that culture is manifested
in the ways social groups structure and share information
across space and time. This insight leads to a typology based
on the two dimensions of information structuring and sharing
that describes a set of possible combinations within what has
been termed a "culture space" (Boisot, 1986). While this typology is cultural in its inspiration, it also lends itself to a

© 1988 by Cornell University.
0001-8392/88/3304-0507/$1.00.

•

The authors wish to acknowledge the
helpful comments of Professor Tom
Lupton and the *ASQ* editor and anonymous reviewers.

consideration of the possibilities and constraints that derive from economic and technological factors. A particular value of the typology in fact derives from the way that, through a focus on information, it draws attention to the potential interplay of cultural, economic, and technological influences on transaction governance.

The structuring of information is a coding process in which both information compression and loss of information takes place (Bruner, 1974). Uncertainty is reduced and conceptual stability is achieved at the cost of perceptual texture and richness. When the process is a social rather than an individual one, we may refer to it as codification, and since information sharing forms a constituent part of our analysis, we prefer this term to coding. Codification is a matter of degree that reflects the extent to which information is compressed into a specific expression. It is therefore part and parcel of formalization.

The sharing of information can be described by the percentage of a population that possesses it. Since the sharing of information is achieved by a diffusion process, it would be possible to construct a diffusion scale that measures the extent of information sharing within a given population.

The culture space described by the dimensions of codification and diffusion posits distinctive information environments for transactions. It lends itself to the taxonomy of four transaction-governance structures, as shown in Figure 1. Two of these structures correspond to the impersonal order of a (legal-rational) bureaucratic hierarchy and the market. Both rely on a high degree of information codification, but for market transactions the codification has to be widely diffused and understood rather than internal to a particular organization. The other two transaction-governance structures employ relatively noncodified forms of information. One is characterized by transacting with relatively noncodified information that is assymetrically distributed within the relevant population (i.e., has low diffusion). Historically this mode is exemplified by the fief as a social organization, i.e., small numbers, hierarchically structured through face-to-face and personalized power relationships that often have to be charismatically legitimated—by such means as the laying-on of hands, initiation rites, commendation ceremonies, and the like. The fourth category is characterized by transacting with relatively noncodified information that is widely diffused within the relevant population. Examples are "clan" networks and federations. Small close-knit groups whose members transact on an informal basis of shared information, personal trust, and equality also fall within this category; Ouchi (1981) extended the term clan to these. In Williamson's terms these are "small numbers," with information diffusion being high within a small total population.

While this simple fourfold transactional typology has the benefit of symmetry with well-recognized concepts of social organization and exchange, the culture-space framework in fact also allows for the possibility of hybrid forms and of the coincidence of several transactional governance modes that compete or collaborate within one economic entity. It should be borne in mind that codification and diffusion are descriptors

Iron Law of Fiefs

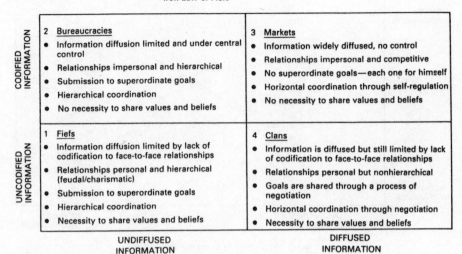

	UNDIFFUSED INFORMATION	DIFFUSED INFORMATION
CODIFIED INFORMATION	**2 Bureaucracies** • Information diffusion limited and under central control • Relationships impersonal and hierarchical • Submission to superordinate goals • Hierarchical coordination • No necessity to share values and beliefs	**3 Markets** • Information widely diffused, no control • Relationships impersonal and competitive • No superordinate goals—each one for himself • Horizontal coordination through self-regulation • No necessity to share values and beliefs
UNCODIFIED INFORMATION	**1 Fiefs** • Information diffusion limited by lack of codification to face-to-face relationships • Relationships personal and hierarchical (feudal/charismatic) • Submission to superordinate goals • Hierarchical coordination • Necessity to share values and beliefs	**4 Clans** • Information is diffused but still limited by lack of codification to face-to-face relationships • Relationships personal but nonhierarchical • Goals are shared through a process of negotiation • Horizontal coordination through negotiation • Necessity to share values and beliefs

Figure 1. Typology of transaction-governance structures.

rather than explanators, albeit that their four main configurations are posited here as necessary conditions for the operation of given transactional modes.

According to this scheme, moreover, the codification and diffusion of information are functionally related. The more information can be compressed into codes, the more quickly and widely it can be transmitted and, hence, diffused. It may take half a lifetime for at most a few acolytes to master the arcane practices of their Zen master, and then only if they live closely together, but it takes only a few seconds for Tokyo to register share-price fluctuations on the Dow Jones. This relationship gives rise to a codification-diffusion curve, as postulated in Figure 2. Its shape is likely to depend in large part on the physical and technological infrastructure available. The functional relation between codification and diffusion implies that to be effective, a high information-diffusion mode of transacting like markets relies on a necessary degree of codification of items such as price, volume, and commodity classifications that enter into transactions, as well as of associated contract law and regulation to prevent abuse. More importantly for our purposes, it also suggests that the alternative to bureaucratic hierarchical governance does not lie exclusively in a shift toward markets and that bureaucratic deficiencies at the system level, such as an inadequate structure of law enforcement and adjudication, might actually inhibit movement in that direction.

Reading Figures 1 and 2 together, then, should make it clear that this taxonomy produces ideal types only and that in the real world intermediate transactional forms are located along both the codification and diffusion dimensions. Moreover, to assign a transaction to a location in the culture space only defines its critical information requirements. In practice, a trans-

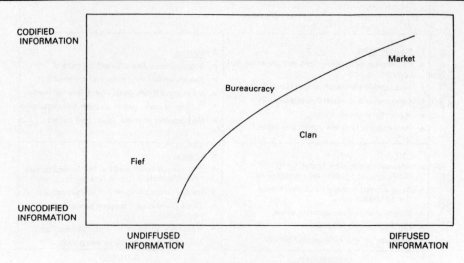

Note: The positioning of the four transaction-
governance structures in this figure is intended
to denote their likely relative levels of
information codification and diffusion.

Figure 2. The codification-diffusion curve of
transaction-governance structures.

action may draw on information scattered throughout the
culture space. Thus, just as the most barren of market data
inevitably harbors a tacit component, so the "eyebrow sema-
phore" that often passes for club rules among established
members may ultimately draw its authority from the existence of some long-forgotten document.

In his more recent work, Williamson (1985, 1987) recognized
a number of transactional governance structures that fall between the extremes of pure hierarchy and pure market.
These can be categorized broadly as forms of either periodic
or continuous contracting. The transactional relationships involved are contractually based but also involve a degree of
particularism, or limited information diffusion, to the set of
partners in question. Other recent analyses have also identified intermediate modes of organizing transactions along the
hierarchy-market continuum, such as federations (Daems,
1983), networks (Thorelli, 1986), and other forms of coordinated contracting (Child, 1987a).

These extensions, however, continue to locate transactions
primarily, if not exclusively, in the codified domain. They focus
on variation along the diffusion dimension of Figure 1 as a
function of the monopolistic possession of information, with
hierarchically governed processes involving restrictions on the
diffusion of information and the classical market relying on
the absence of restrictions on access to relevant information.
Williamson (1985) correctly identified bounded rationality and
opportunism as key transactional variables—"human nature
as we know it"—but he did not relate them to each other in

Iron Law of Fiefs

a rigorous way. To do so would point to the possibility that rationality itself could be bounded by the idiosyncratic and customary nature of particularistic relationships (fiefs), in which impacted, uncodified information can promote noneconomic forms of opportunism, or that economic opportunism may be constrained by clan-like networks such as the Mafia or the Green Gang in Kuomintang China (Seagrave, 1985). Variance along the codification dimension is occasionally hinted at in Williamson's discussions of "atmosphere," and it enters into his joint work with Ouchi (Williamson and Ouchi, 1981), which recognizes the existence of "soft contracting" in which informal noncodified, trust-based relationships provide an additional governance support. It remains, however, to be given as central an analytical place as variance on the information-diffusion dimension.

The unidimensional hierarchy-market continuum underlying Williamson's analysis implies that a response to market failure will lie in the substitution of hierarchical coordination, while a response to bureaucratic failure will lie in greater reliance on the market mechanism. In both capitalist and socialist countries during the past decade there have been strong voices proclaiming bureaucratic failure and the need to give greater play to the market. For example, after 1949 the Chinese leadership expressed an ideological preference for pure hierarchy—the PRC as a single large firm—which has repeatedly come up against existing infrastructural and institutional limitations that undermine the efficiency of hierarchy beyond a certain size (Arrow, 1974). The current economic reforms can be seen in one sense as the leadership's response to bureaucratic failure, and the fact that it is exploring market forms of governance would appear at first sight to speak in favor of Williamson's continuum.

As Williamson (1985: 392) himself noted, however, the study of bureaucratic failure remains very primitive and the associated literature is relatively underdeveloped. One recommendation for dealing with bureaucratic failure that has in recent years gained favor in the West, namely to place greater reliance on organizational "cultures" fostered by top management (Deal and Kennedy, 1982), clearly points to movement toward a fief mode rather than toward the market. Yet, as we shall show, whereas uncodified and more personalized transactions are sought as complements and counterweights to bureaucratic ones that have become inefficiently entrenched and hegemonic in large Western organizations, in the PRC they are re-emerging as opportunistically available traditional alternatives to a bureaucratic order that fails to stabilize for want of formal rationality (Weber, 1968). It is essential therefore to heed Granovetter's (1985) critique of Williamson for failing to take account of the social embeddedness of economic transactions. Williamson's reliance on economic efficiency for explaining the choice of transaction mode not only depends on the assumption of the universal motivational primacy of economic considerations; it also overlooks the extent to which a country's social relations, as the behavioral and structural expressions of its culture and development, support or detract from the efficient operation of different transaction modes.

THE CASE OF CHINA

Before the Reforms

China today inherits a distinct cultural legacy characterized by (1) a respect for hierarchy, (2) a collective orientation, (3) a preference for personal relationships and connections, and (4) a strong sense of national identity (Lockett, 1985; Pye, 1985; Domenach, 1986; Knutsson, 1986; Qian, 1986). Behavior is regulated by appeals to good conduct rather than impersonal recourse to the law, and, consequently, the move from "status" to "contract" that Sir Henry Maine (1986) discerned in Europe at the end of the Middle Ages has yet to occur. Cultural values of this kind imply a preference for face-to-face transactions based on personal trust and mutual obligation.

There is an obvious tension between transactional preferences of this kind, which hail from the uncodified region of the culture space, and those involved in market relations (other than of a purely local kind), which rely substantially on impersonal communications and the force of legal contract, i.e., rules that have been codified and widely diffused. Furthermore, symbolically and administratively China has been a centralized state in which a strong sense of cultural identity compensated for severe limits to the downward extension of state power. "Heaven is high and the Emperor is far away" is an old Chinese saying that helps to explain the state's traditional reluctance to interfere in local affairs except in times of famine. Formal, natural barriers to communication turned the Chinese bureaucracy inward toward the court, leaving the countryside largely free of direct rule and control by superior authority and creating a cellular society of low transactional complexity cemented together by loyalty to the emperor and a simple bureaucracy that was patrimonial rather than rational-legal in character (Weber, 1958). As Reischauer put it, "the government thus was a relatively small, highly centralized body that floated on a sea of isolated peasant communities" (Rodzinski, 1984: 48).

The dominant transaction mode in premodern China was thus arguably fieflike, with problems of bounded rationality and opportunism being kept manageable by a low level of transactional complexity and restrictions to small numbers, both characteristic of an underdeveloped rural economy. If the 1949 revolution sought to break this pattern, it faced the problem that the charismatic leadership style—most effective in the governance of a fief—that Mao had displayed during the "Yenan Period" in the revolutionary base areas could no longer cope on its own with the transactional scale and complexity of national government. The adoption of the well-codified Marxist-Leninist Soviet model signalled an attempted shift from fief to bureaucratic governance.

Fief and bureaucratic governance actively vied with each other as Mao resisted the "routinization" of his charisma. Both the Great Leap Forward of 1958 and the Great Proletarian Cultural Revolution were the outcomes of such transactional competition. In the latter case, Mao lost charismatic control by trying to maintain an uncodified governance structure in spite of large-number conditions. The result, predictably, was clan governance and factionalism.

Iron Law of Fiefs

Our brief examination of the situation up to the 1978 reforms points to a traditional desire by Chinese leaders to maintain their personal authority. To achieve this, they have been prepared, when necessary, to counter moves toward a rational-legal bureacracy that might limit their discretion and to maintain a patrimonial style of governance. This, together with the country's underdeveloped transactional and physical infrastructure—with over twice India's size, the PRC has less than half its road network (World Bank, 1985)—anchors China in the fief quadrant. It was to these recurring "dialectics of leadership" (Schram, 1984) that the economic and enterprise reforms of the last decade were added.

The Economic Reform Program

The reform program initiated in December 1978 by the Third Plenum of the Party Central Committee was an attempt both to rebuild the economy after the depletions of the Cultural Revolution and to transcend the perceived shortcomings of the Soviet economic model developed between 1950 and 1957.

The search began, through a series of experiments that have been detailed by Lee (1987) and Oborne (1986) and that will only be briefly summarized here, for a form of governance that would integrate bureaucratic and market transactions. The search was to be less constrained by socialist ideology, which had tended to channel all transactions, whatever their characteristics, into the bureaucratic mode. Providing that the primacy of bureaucratic transactions, i.e., planning, was not questioned, peaceful co-existence between alternative forms could now be envisaged.

The first experiments in agriculture and industry were instituted in Sichuan Province, where they raised production significantly, and spread to other provinces. By 1980, 6,600 state-owned enterprises in various provinces had assumed new powers over production, marketing, and profit retention. The degree of autonomy for both farmers and firms implied by these measures was extremely modest, however—a move *toward* the market quadrant of the culture space, but not yet an investment *in* it—and even then exceeded the transaction-governance capacity of the system, so that by 1981 some recentralization had occurred.

Nevertheless, the reform momentum was maintained, and in March 1982 selected cities were designated to pioneer urban economic restructuring, particularly to decentralize enterprise management and to create conditions for more effective market transactions. Urban industrial reforms really got into gear after October 1984, when the Central Committee of the Communist Party adopted a major policy document, headed "China's Economic Structure Reform" (Communist Party of China, 1984). The new policy envisaged a further decentralization to industrial enterprises which, within a much reduced state planning framework, were to be fully responsible for profits and losses. The new measures were followed in 1985 by fiscal reforms that replaced profit remissions to the state with tax payments and allowed firms to use retained profits for bonus or worker welfare payments and technical renovation. A bankruptcy law and the sale of shares were both under active discussion by policymakers at this time.

The basic thrust of the reforms described above has been toward a controlled delegation within the state bureaucracy to both provincial and city levels, with priority on the latter, and decentralization to firms, which acquire some freedom to pursue their own economic objectives. In the language of culture space, this implies investing in appropriate transactional infrastructures in the bureaucratic and market regions of the space and either dismantling or neutralizing those institutional practices that lead back into fiefs, in short, lowering the transaction costs, broadly defined, of the former and increasing those of the latter.

In practice, things have not always worked out that way. The central government's inability to set clear operational objectives for subordinate layers of the bureaucracy and to control their implementation testifies to continuing problems of codification and bounded rationality. As predicted by our analytical framework, this failure to handle large-number conditions has increased the level of opportunism in the system and converted what was to be a controlled delegation within a bureaucratic hierarchy into a decentralization in which local goals are substituted for central ones (cf. Krug, 1988). Prefectural and city authorities have been able in many cases to reassert a fieflike dominion over enterprises within their jurisdiction. For example, the absence of a sophisticated administrative mechanism through which the fiscal obligations of industrial enterprises could be computed and revenues collected have pushed the central government to practice a form of tax "farming" in which state revenue requirements are defined and then allocated to provinces, cities, and thence to firms in ways essentially unrelated to their taxable capacity. The resulting fiscal pressure has led a number of city authorities, most notably in Shanghai, to reassert their grip over the state-owned firms under their care and, through a mechanism of "forced allocations," a tight control of enterprise borrowing and of prices, impose on these enterprises noneconomic objectives that often make nonsense of their newly granted freedoms.

The outcome of this dynamic has been the maintenance and, in many cases, the reinforcement of particularism at the enterprise level. The supervising bureaucracy has been able to impose on firms a high level of transaction-specific investment, specific both to sectors and to regions, which keeps exchange idiosyncratic and markets fragmented. Local bureaucracies in many instances have been able to preserve their fiefs through a process of subinfeudation, in which the loyalty of a vassal firm will be secured in exchange for preferential treatment, protection from outside competitors, and negotiable performance goals—what Kornai (1986) in the Hungarian context has labelled the "soft budget constraint" and Boisot (1987) has termed "industrial feudalism."

Thus although the ideological constraint on transactional choices is no longer what it was, the existing institutional structure expressing a cultural inheritance and inadequate infrastructural provision are both working against the emergence of a viable form of governance in the bureaucratic and market regions of the culture space. Delegation and decentralization will only bear fruit if transactions can take root in those regions. Yet, as proved to be the case during the

Iron Law of Fiefs

1950s, the type and extent of codification required to stabilize transactions there appear to go well beyond what is provided for by current policy measures and leadership preferences.

Economic Reforms: The View from the Enterprise

So far we have applied our analytical framework to an examination of the economic reforms at the macro level and concluded that if a more pragmatic approach to ideology has extended China's transactional options beyond a tightly constrained bureaucratic governance, both institutional and infrastructural imperatives appear to channel transactions back into the fief region of the culture space. This is a loosely formulated hypothesis in need of empirical support. Unfortunately, hard evidence of any kind is hard to come by in the PRC, and given the poor reliability of aggregated statistical data, perhaps the best that can be offered is qualitative data at the enterprise level. There is, in any case, a problem in China of defining the boundary between enterprise and macro- or system-level transactions. Chinese enterprises in the state-owned sector were centrally planned and controlled. The reform is attempting to differentiate the two levels more sharply and, through the creation of supporting institutions such as investment banks, to offer enterprises the opportunity to initiate their own external transactions. It is, however, still difficult to obtain hard evidence on the effects of the reform except from case studies of individual enterprises. Since most reform measures are targeted at the state-owned enterprises, which in 1986 accounted for 68.7 percent of industrial output (*Beijing Review,* 5 October 1987: 26), it seems reasonable to assume that many of their effects, even if mediated by the firm's external environment, will be registered there.

The most detailed source of information available to us comes from studies we conducted in the autumn of 1985 with the aid of industrially experienced Chinese MBA students in six industrial state-owned enterprises located in Beijing. Shorter visits were also made in 1986 and 1987 to other enterprises, both in Beijing and in other cities and provinces, and additional interviews were conducted with Chinese managers, researchers, and management-education faculty. Clearly, in discussing enterprise reforms in the PRC today one is aiming at a moving target, so that the information we present may no longer fully describe the current situation. Further information about the Beijing-based enterprises and the method of research is given in Child (1987b). For reasons of confidentiality, enterprises will not be identified by name in what follows.

The Chinese state-owned enterprise, to an even greater extent than the large Japanese enterprise, is something of a total institution to its members, offering housing, health, and schooling services for employees. A key difference between it and the Japanese firm, however, is that whereas the latter offers these services on a voluntary basis in order to secure the loyalty of long-term employees, the Chinese firm has the provision of such services imposed on it by its supervising authority: a city, a provincial, or even the national government. In this way, many services that in Western countries are delivered directly by a municipal authority are in China delivered through enterprises that in a sense are "owned" by their supervising authority. Thus Chinese firms pursue a broader and vaguer, less codified, set of objectives than profit-maximizing Western enterprises.

Obviously, in an environment in which no alternative provision of social services exists and the smaller, more independent collective enterprises operate on the same principle but with a much lower quality of amenity, a worker has everything to gain by being employed in a state-owned firm. Not only the worker but his children and relatives benefit as well, both through welfare provisions and preferential employment opportunities. In an engineering enterprise surveyed by one of the authors, 60 percent of all new recruits were children or relatives of existing employees of the firm.

The key stakeholders in the Chinese state-owned enterprise are the state and the labor force. As has been the case in Hungary and in Yugoslavia (Granick, 1987; Kornai, 1987), the stakeholders compete over the distribution of retained earnings. This competition has intensified since the tax reforms of 1985. Before that time, an enterprise merely handed over its profits to its supervising authority. The introduction of a 55-percent corporation tax (called an "income tax" in the PRC) was designed to inject more clarity and coherence into the relationship between state and enterprise and to create more of an arm's-length, codified relationship between them. The balance of the evidence suggests that this has not yet happened.

The state has a double claim on enterprise profits: as a tax collector and as a shareholder. Some clarity has been established on the tax front, but the state's role as a shareholder remains vague and ambiguous. Officially the state owns the means of production on behalf of "all the people," and in that capacity it is entitled to receive dividends. But enterprise workers have also been repeatedly told that they are "masters of their enterprise" and that they are entitled to the fruits of their efforts. Thus each party feels that legitimacy is on its side, and neither has been willing to subordinate its claim to those of the other.

In practice this has meant that the state has secured its claims primarily through the tax system and has allowed workers to appear as the main beneficiaries of post-tax retained earnings. In the firms that were studied, retained earnings were distributed to bonus payments, welfare expenditures such as housing, schools, and medical facilities, and to an investment fund. These proportions, although in theory fixed, were negotiated on a case-by-case basis with the supervising authority and the local tax and finance bureaus. The enterprise director very much represents the workers' interests in such negotiations. The director's own bonus and that of other senior enterprise managers can only be the average of what is paid to the workforce and the total remuneration of managers as a group cannot exceed 3 percent of the firm's total wage fund. It is usually the supervisory bureau, if it is so minded, that fights to secure funds for reinvestment. It would normally be from such reinvestment funds that the state's dividend claim as a shareholder could be met, but by the time taxes, bonuses, and welfare payments have

Iron Law of Fiefs

been made, the amount left to maintain the firm as a "going concern" is so exiguous that the state has usually preferred to increase its shareholding by ploughing back what it is owed. Since the value of its shares is not calculated in a meaningful way, the state's role as a shareholder is in fact atrophying for lack of clarity. The "main event" is between workers and enterprise managers, on the one hand, and the local authorities, on the other. Each have their own agenda for retained earnings.

Responsibility systems. In the past few years, numerous types of responsibility systems have been introduced to increase enterprise accountability to stakeholders and enhance performance. Usually provincial and city authorities have been left free to choose which variety they wish to promote in the light of local circumstances. They can select from the director-responsibility system, the management-responsibility system, the enterprise-responsibility system, the target-responsibility system, the asset-responsibility system, and so on. Recently they have also been allowed to lease out failing enterprises to new managers who bid for the leases. These various systems can be grouped under two broad headings: (1) those that clarify relationships between the firm and state organs and define their respective obligations: the enterprise will agree to a profit and tax target for the following year, as well as to certain output targets, and the supervising authority will agree to secure for it a certain amount (now diminishing) of scarce raw materials, funds, and so forth; and (2) those that clarify relationships and obligations within the firm itself. Thus, for example, the director-responsibility system has been designed to clarify the relationship between the party secretary and the enterprise director. Such clarifications can be interpreted as an attempt to codify relationships and transactions that have hitherto remained vague and diffuse.

Most of the enterprises surveyed, both in Beijing and in the provinces, were experimenting with one or more of these responsibility systems. In a number of cases the profit target set by the supervising authority for the firm was further broken down and allocated to individual workshops. The reason given for doing this was to create employee involvement. In fact, setting profit targets for individual workshops was often a source of considerable friction, since, in the absence of an external market for their output, no equitable formula for the imputation of profits could be agreed upon. The workshop was a cost center with a profit center responsibility thrust upon it. In many cases, therefore, bonus distribution, which was linked to profits earned, was felt to be arbitrary and often demotivating. One enterprise manager complained that his workshop, with old equipment subject to breakdowns, could only obtain one quarter of the bonuses paid to other, better-equipped workshops in his enterprise.

This inequity was compounded by the fact that profits inside the enterprise were "retained" at the workshop level, so that not only was the distribution of bonuses allocated in an irrational way but so were the welfare payments and the reinvestment fund through which equipment could be modernized. This same manager went on to observe that since pressures for egalitarian distribution were still very strong in his firm, the variation in the distribution of bonuses within each workshop was much lower than that between workshops.

Allocating profit-center responsibilities to workshops is now quite common in Chinese industrial firms and requires comment. First, the practice is consistent with the Marxist tenet that since only labor creates value, workers rather than managers are the source of profit. For this reason, bonus payments to managers are often below what is received by "high-performing" workers, and in general bonus levels are not found to vary according to level of responsibility (Child, 1988). Second, this labor theory of value merges with a concern for industrial democracy that aims to make workers "masters of their enterprise" in a meaningful way.

Managerial role. What then becomes of the managerial role under this scheme? In fact, managers become what they have so often been in the past in the PRC: the fall guys. They are given the responsibility for performance but denied the legitimate authority for achieving it. The increase in managerial rationality and autonomy that could result from reducing the involvement of the supervisory bureaucracy in a firm's operations and clarifying enterprise objectives is immediately drained away by a workforce that has secured for itself large tracts of managerial discretion. Chinese enterprise managers, in effect, are caught today in a pincer movement between the competing claims of a tax-maximizing state and a welfare-maximizing workforce. In these circumstances, and because the state has virtually withdrawn from its shareholding role, long-term profit maximization suffers.

But even when managerial discretion is left intact by the workforce, it remains under more or less permanent threat from the local supervising bureaucracy. "Guidance" planning, for example, was designed to inject some much-needed flexibility into enterprise operations and to reduce the hierarchical weight of the supervising bureau. Yet one bureau interviewed in the city of Guangzhou considered the eight guidance targets that it set for its subordinate firms—output, production, product variety, profits, labor productivity, quality, materials consumption, and safety—as mandatory, to the point that if, say, profit targets were not met, the bureau would secure the required amounts from the firm by reducing either bonus and welfare payments or the investment funds available for equipment renewal. It is not easy for the central government to loosen the grip that bureaus have over their charges.

Some increase in enterprise autonomy seemed implied by the fact that firms were now free to borrow from banks instead of relying as they had done in the past on handouts from the bureaus, and during 1985–1986 much uncontrolled borrowing did in fact take place, stimulated by low interest rates and the tax deductability of principal repayment. Things, however, have now tightened up, and today a bank will not lend to an enterprise without the approval and also quite often the guarantee of its supervising bureau in its pocket. Many bureaus are risk-averse and will only approve those enterprise activities that fall within the plan.

External dependency. Nothing exemplifies the organizational interdependence of supervising bureaucracy and industrial

Iron Law of Fiefs

enterprise as well as the so-called "mother-in-law" problem. Local authorities lack the administrative means to control firms impersonally at a distance. In order to ensure that the various duties they have set their firms are properly carried out, they set up their own offices on the spot. One medium-sized textile firm surveyed in Guangdong Province, for example, is required to provide offices for 22 different municipal agencies and to cover the salary costs of over 400 officials that perform no useful function for the firm itself but work there as representatives of the supervising administration, i.e., the labor bureau, the auditing bureau, the standards and measures bureau, the family planning bureau, and so on. The director of this firm complains that not only do these officials constantly interfere with day-to-day activities and take up a great deal of scarce managerial time in meetings—and sometimes banquets—but their presence prevents him from developing an organizational structure better adapted to operational needs. External dependency has been a common feature of all the enterprises we have studied, with senior organizational members reporting, matrix-fashion, both to the enterprise director and to their external supervisors in the municipal bureaucracy. Indeed, the line that separates a state-owned enterprise from the bureaucracy is perceived to be more hypothetical than real by those required to span it. As one of our interviewees put it, "The manager of a state-owned enterprise is considered to be a government official; the manager of a collective enterprise is not."

The municipal level has its own agenda for its enterprises, and it is not a long-term profit-maximizing one. Chinese cities no less than the central government are dependent on enterprise profits for most of their revenues. The considerable fiscal pressures they are exposed to by the central government—well over 80 percent of the enterprise taxes collected by cities like Shanghai or Wuhan go to the state—and the slenderness of their tax base frequently lead them to impose "forced allocations" on the enterprises within their jurisdiction. Although such allocations have been repeatedly condemned and forbidden by the State Council, the tax bureau of one large municipality estimates that up to 40 percent of a firm's retained earnings can be siphoned off in this way before they are distributed or reinvested. Thus a firm will be asked to pay a "tree planting" fee, a "street cleaning" fee, a "night guard" fee. More covertly, it might be asked to contribute some of its labor force for the carrying out of municipal tasks. The tax bureau has calculated that, on average, 15 percent of a firm's employees might be assigned to such tasks at any one time.

The pattern that emerges thus far is one of the hierarchical exercise of personal power that is characteristic of fiefs. Yet even though vertical interdependency remained strong, all six of the Beijing enterprises studied in the autumn of 1985 reported that there had been some relaxation of control by their higher authorities. In particular, physical output targets were covering a smaller proportion of total output, and the use of profit targets was thought to be helpful. Above-quota production could be priced and marketed with some degree of flexibility, and a detailed analysis of decision-making authority in each enterprise indicated that engagement in market transactions had been facilitated by the decentralization of authority to enterprise managers in certain areas—indeed, subsequent research revealed one large state-owned enterprise in Hubei Province opening up sales offices in New York, Hamburg, and Hong Kong. Four of the six Beijing enterprises were allowed to vary their prices within a 20-percent band of a reference price for all their above-quota production, and a fifth, manufacturing a national-brand electrical product, could freely vary its discounts on nonquota sales. All were free to select their own suppliers for nonstrategic items, and five could now define their own purchasing procedures and contract terms.

None of the firms were as yet free to alter their overall employment establishments or to vary their total wage and salary bill. Recently, however, three-year employment contracts have been introduced for new recruits, and managers have been given more discretion in the setting of worker bonuses. Thus today more freedom has been given to enterprise managers in the selection of new workers, even if the labor and personnel bureaus still define the pool from which the selection is made. In four of the Beijing enterprises, directors were empowered, on paper, to dismiss unsatisfactory workers, although since in a socialist state this remains a delicate matter, they would in practice still secure the prior approval of the enterprise Party Committee as well as a higher authority.

The question is whether this increment of flexibility at the enterprise level points toward the market orientation that the Chinese leadership is seeking to promote. The signals are mixed. For one thing, it is not easy to factor out managerial "passivity" inculcated by years of compliance, a lack of training, and a providential view of the state, from genuine bureaucratic constraints. Some Chinese managers interviewed coped more "entrepreneurially" than others with these constraints: One manager in Guangdong Province, for example, successfully co-opted all the in-house representatives of his "mothers-in-law" and set them to work as employees; another succeeded in by-passing his municipal purchasing organizations by setting up an interprovincial purchasing cooperative. Yet the overall impression gained is that these are the exceptions that prove the rule and that much of the dynamism that underlies the PRC's growth in GNP of 9.8 percent and 9.4 percent in 1986 and 1987, respectively, does not stem from the state-owned sector. Indeed, it could be argued that the greatest stimulus for change in state-owned enterprises today comes only indirectly from the enterprise reforms, in the shape of intensified competition from rural collectives and individual enterprises. These have been growing at more than twice the pace of state-owned enterprises and, being far less controllable by state bureaucracy, have shown a mobility and a vitality that holds promise for the future. If the volume of transactions in the market quadrant of the culture space is on the increase in the PRC today, it may not be because existing state-owned enterprises are changing their transactional style but because small, new, mobile firms are placing their uncommitted transactions there.

Managers of state-owned enterprises, considered by many in the PRC to be the key "field workers" of the reforms, thus face an ambiguous external environment that can be read two

Iron Law of Fiefs

ways. It can be seen as a competitive threat emanating from the market quadrant of the culture space: In many product markets managers face decreasing guaranteed quotas, the need to secure their own inputs, and the need to face up to "interlopers," small undercapitalized new entrants from the rural sector or outlying provinces that are beginning to nibble away at their market share; the closer one gets to consumer goods in the PRC, the more this situation obtains. Alternatively, the environment can be seen as a protective cocoon beckoning from the fief quadrant of the culture space: In spite of the economic reforms, the state-owned enterprise remains a highly privileged player in a protected sector. The preservation of privilege and protection requires that a quasi-feudal relationship with the local bureaucracy be maintained, and the price exacted from the firm for the *guanxi* (privileged relationship) will be compliance and contribution.

Managers and the bureaucracy. Managers of Chinese state-owned enterprises are thus vulnerable. The economic reforms of the past decade have injected some dynamism into almost all sectors of the Chinese economy, but their own has so far been the slowest to respond to the treatment. If they wished to respond to the competitive challenges that threaten their firm, they would need to secure for themselves a greater measure of managerial autonomy than has been vouchsafed them by their supervising bureaucracy. In equipping them for the challenge of market competition, that bureaucracy does not serve them well. First, it possesses precious little information on the firm's external environment outside its own jurisdiction. It is ignorant of market developments, consumer tastes, and market structure. Whatever meager information it does possess, it tends to hoard in order to control enterprise behavior. The continued tendency of the firms studied to rely on their bureaus for the provision of "impacted" and poorly codified information on their external environment was one of the most striking features of their responses to the reforms. Thus the scope for opportunism and the constraints of bounded rationality are both considerable at the bureau level; in fact, operating through the bureau these largely characterize a firm's external environment. Second, by fragmenting the enterprise's objectives and entrusting their implementation in arbitrary fashion to competing groups of workers through the internal contract-responsibility system, the supervising bureaucracy destroys managerial rationality, discretion, and cohesion within the enterprise. The process is rendered complete by the constant interference of municipal "mothers-in-law" in day-to-day operations. Thus the failure to codify a viable and unified set of managerial objectives opens the door to opportunism and bounded rationality inside the firm.

Yet the pursuit of increased autonomy and managerial rationality is only one of the options open to enterprise managers. The other is to "join" the system rather than "beat" it, to accept the protection and security offered by its embrace. The key skills required here are not those of codification but those of negotiation; the name of this game is not to economize on bounded rationality or to exorcise opportunism but to capitalize on them in a linked network of hierarchical face-to-face relationships in which personal power is traded, using loyalty, compliance, and protection as the medium of exchange. Such is the logic of fiefs.

It finds an echo in the "dual dependence" of Hungarian firms as described by Kornai (1987), where the same inability to codify an economically rational and unified set of enterprise objectives in a reform regime opens the door to constant renegotiations and the personalization of power relationships between superior and subordinate organizations. In the Hungarian case, however, the prior existence of a sophisticated administrative infrastructure attenuates the impact of that logic in favor of bureaucracy.

What we see at the enterprise level is a struggle between the two types of rationality identified by Weber (1968, vol. 2: 809ff) as the substantive and the formal. The first is the warm, "involved" rationality of vaguely defined ethical principles applied particularistically. It places a large amount of discretionary power in a few hands and thus opens the door to the twin hazards of bounded rationality and opportunism. The second is the cold, impersonal, and detached rationality of the rule universally applied. Formal rationality, however, only economizes on boundedness by testing itself against the myraid facts of the world; its rules have the character of scientific hypotheses in perpetual need of corroboration. It economizes on opportunism by making transparent the principles on which it operates, through the diffusion of information that follows upon its codification. In the culture space, therefore, formal rationality drives markets and hierarchies, and substantive rationality drives fiefs and clans.

Competing forms of governance are today seeking to secure their dominion over Chinese state-owned enterprises. We have tried to show in this section that although the outcome is by no means settled, fiefs start out having a transactional advantage, with both existing institutional patterns and infrastructure working in their favor. As was argued in the previous section, the economic reforms in the industrial sector, by mishandling delegation and decentralization issues have, if anything, reinforced the transactional bias in favor of fiefs. In short, the recent reform measures are a hypothesis that has so far failed the test for formal rationality and has lowered the marginal cost of transacting in the lower left-hand quadrant of the culture space shown in Figure 1 above.

Since 1949 the pursuit of formal rationality in the PRC was ideologically confined to the bureaucratic region of the culture space where, at best, it managed to create "mock bureaucracies" (Gouldner, 1954) in Marxist-Leninist garb. The limited degree of formal rationality achieved was confined to higher levels. For example, enterprise managers admitted to us that they had formally agreed on an annual plan with their higher authorities and then operated according to their own informal plan.

Formal rationality was not always the goal of the leadership, however, as shown by Mao's encounters with clan governance, which were intentional during the Great Leap Forward when he set up the Communes, but less so during the Cultural Revolution. Only recently has the search broadened to include market forms of governance as well. Yet the policy decision to pursue "socialism with Chinese characteristics"

Iron Law of Fiefs

expresses a strong desire by the leadership to preserve *Gemeinschaft* economic values within a *Gesellschaft* transactional order. Substantive rationality, providing it can be suitably clad, will thus be allowed to keep its seat at the high table. Those who frame the problem of modernization as an exclusive choice of governance structure in the formalized, codified regions of the culture space—bureaucracy for socialists, markets for capitalists—will balk at the search for transactional modes sui generis that is implicit in current Chinese policies. Yet neither the transaction-cost approach in the realm of theory nor the Japanese experience of modernization in the realm of practice suggests that this search is doomed to failure.

CONCLUSION

China today no longer has a planned economy and, indeed, by the more demanding standards of Soviet practice, never really had one. Where Gosplan, the Soviet central planning agency, allocates nearly 20,000 raw materials and attempts to keep track of millions of final goods, the Chinese State Planning Commission now allocates 26 raw materials and tracks 60 final products. Bureaucratic transactions need statistics, large volumes of well-codified information whose diffusion can be carefully controlled by administrative nerve centers, yet China's State Statistical Bureau has never been heavily staffed (*The Economist,* 1987: 15).

Control by central government, historically never very strong, is now weaker than before the reforms. In spite of the fiscal pressures described earlier, central government's share of the taxes paid by state-owned enterprises has fallen from over 60 percent in 1978 to less than 50 percent now, and two provinces (Guandong and Fujien) pay virtually no taxes at all. Its continued inability to push fiscal administration beyond crude methods of tax farming means that at present it has no more than one quarter of all tax revenue under its control. By contrast, the federal share of tax revenues in the United States—no paragon of central planning either—is over 60 percent (*The Economist,* 1987: 16).

A transactional continuum along the lines suggested by Williamson would lead one to predict that such a massive disinvestment in bureaucracy would move the country toward market governance. In both the commercial and the light industrial sector, modest moves toward market governance indeed seem to be taking place. The explanation seems to lie both in the greater remoteness of these sectors from the bureaucracy and in the greater competition from fast-growing rural industries that between 1982 and 1986 have grown by 266 percent and are today almost beyond bureaucratic control.

Yet our own hypothesis is that markets in the PRC at present compete with fiefs for the governance of the uncommitted transaction and that in the urban industrial sector the dynamic of the reforms is pushing toward fiefs as the dominant transactional mode. Patrimonial values have reasserted themselves and are once more imposing a well-tested cellular structure on the Chinese industrial landscape (cf. MacDougall, 1988). Our brief examination of the reform process at work in state-owned enterprises has illustrated this dynamic at the organizational level.

Not only does a deeply rooted cultural preference for personalized hierarchical relations push toward fiefs. The lack of an adequate physical infrastructure that might integrate markets and hence lower transaction costs also favors localism and small-numbers bargaining. At any one time, upward of a million people are travelling across China on trains in search of raw materials or other scarce inputs for their firms. They lack nationally available information on where these might be found, and it can take up to several days to effect telephone calls within the country. Nevertheless, even if information on supplies were available, would-be purchasers could only secure some after a slow process of relationship building. A written order or a telephone call serves little purpose, and suppliers are unwilling to formalize their commitments by setting them down on paper. Only a face-to-face relationship will clinch the deal.

Impersonal contracting is out. When contractual relationships have been made, they are hard to enforce. One enterprise manager recently complained that in spite of a court judgment in his favor following litigation with a supplier, no state agency was willing to enforce the judgment. In the land of fiefs, interpersonal trust is the lubricant that oils exchange relationships, and trust is not built in a day. It is for this reason that many state-owned enterprises are allowed to maintain a "relationship expenses" budget and that those selling scarce consumer goods will allocate up to 10 percent of their total output to those suppliers with whom they need to keep on friendly terms.

Berger (1987) distinguished between governance choices that favor markets or hierarchies and those that simply favor modernization. Our own analysis makes the first type a rich man's choice, only available to countries that have already industrialized and built up stable transactional infrastructures in the upper regions of the culture space where a rational-legal order obtains. Seen in this light, system reform in the Soviet Union genuinely boils down to a choice of the first type and the challenge it faces is to reposition some transactions along Williamson's continuum toward market forms of governance. Even so, the move up the culture space toward greater codification that accompanies modernization may only be a partial one, as the continued presence of bureaucratic fiefdoms in the Soviet Union and the quasi-feudal nature of much Japanese managerial practice (Boisot, 1983) serve to remind us.

The implication we can tease out of Berger's distinction is that China does not yet face a genuine choice of the first type because it has not yet modernized sufficiently. Our own analysis of governance issues at the enterprise level broadly supports this conclusion. Not enough transactions have taken root in the upper, codified regions of the culture space to make Williamson's continuum operational. Chinese bureaucracy, faithful to its traditions, remains patrimonial. It lacks both the codification skills to handle the transactional volumes entailed by bureaucratic and market governance and the legal and information infrastructure that might take it beyond particularistic bargaining. The bounded rationality and information impactedness that result conspire to keep transactional numbers small and relationships personalized and opens the

Iron Law of Fiefs

door to opportunism and "control loss" (Williamson, 1970). China remains a land of fiefs, albeit industrial ones.

Market failure. The extension of transactional analysis represented earlier in Figure 1 points to two ways in which markets can fail. The first occurs when opportunism and information impactedness distribute transactional power differentially to a limited number of players, with no loss of rationality. The result is hierarchical governance either through public or private bureaucracies. The second occurs when bounded rationality itself generates small-numbers bargaining in which opportunism and information impactedness may both be present but are more evenly distributed among those players that have survived the shift away from markets. The outcome is clan governance. Both Robert Michels' (1949) "iron law of oligarchy" and Mancur Olson's (1965) "logic of collective action" are analyses of this move from large- to small-numbers bargaining and its transactional consequences.

Bureaucratic failure. Our analysis of China's economic reforms now allows us to sketch out in propositional form two ways in which a bureaucracy can fail, again employing the framework in Figure 1:

Proposition 1: Bureaucracies give way to market forms of governance when transactionally relevant information loses its impactedness, gains further in codification, and opens the door to large-numbers bargaining. Sooner or later, codified information diffuses.

Proposition 2: Bureaucracies give way to fiefs when bounded rationality is present and the distribution of impacted, uncodified information is skewed in favor of a very few opportunistic players.

If the "iron law of oligarchy" loosely describes one form of market failure (we would prefer the term "oligopoly" but feel that Michels' term adequately covers both market and political processes), then the "iron law of fiefs" covers those bureaucratic failures that can be traced to the same causes, namely, the absence of a transactional infrastructure that can sustain a high degree of codification and hence an adequate level of formal rationality. Both "laws" are illustrated schematically in Figure 3, and clearly neither is derivable from Williamson's continuum.

Bounded rationality and opportunism are responses to an information environment that has been insufficiently specified by Williamson. He has concentrated on information impactedness—degree of nondiffusion in the culture space—and has relegated problems associated with codification under the catch-all term of "atmosphere." What our brief outline of China's experience with its enterprise reforms has tried to show is that the codification variable has an important bearing on the governance options available either at the level of the individual firm or at the broader institutional level.

There are many areas in which this general proposition might be further explored and tested, perhaps through detailed case studies initially and, later, using more formal means. The slow transformation of UNESCO from a professional bureaucracy into an organization in which personal identity and loyalty have come to predominate is a ripe candidate for culture space analysis. Such analysis would also be useful for studying the metamorphosis of financial "clans" in the City of

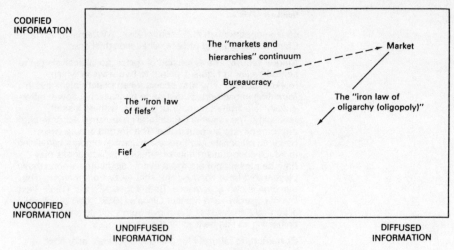

Figure 3. Bureaucratic and market failure in the culture space.

London into an integrated international financial market, which suggests that the "iron law" might work in reverse when a parochial structure is overwhelmed by volumes of well-codified and readily diffusable data. The outcome of such research will help us to assess how far the production and distribution of information impinges on the way that the production and distribution of other goods and services is organized, in short, what case can be made for a political economy of information.

REFERENCES

Arrow, Kenneth
1974 The Limits of Organization. New York: Norton.

Berger, Peter L.
1987 The Capitalist Revolution. Aldershot: Gower.

Boisot, Max H.
1983 "Convergence revisited: The codification and diffusion of knowledge in a British and a Japanese firm." Journal of Management Studies, 20: 159–190.
1986 "Markets and hierarchies in a cultural perspective." Organization Studies, 7: 135–158.
1987 "Industrial feudalism and enterprise reform: Could the Chinese use some more bureaucracy?" In Malcolm Warner (ed.), Management Reforms in China: 217–237. London: Frances Pinter.

Bruner, Jerome S.
1974 Beyond the Information Given. London: Allen and Unwin.

Child, John
1987a "Information technology, organization, and the response to strategic challenges." California Management Review, 30: 33–50.
1987b "Enterprise reform in China: Progress and problems." In Malcolm Warner (ed.), Management Reforms in China: 24–52. London: Frances Pinter.
1988 "The structure of earnings in Chinese enterprises and some correlates of their variation." In John Child and Martin Lockett (eds.), Reform Policy and the Chinese Enterprise. London: JAI Press (forthcoming).

Coase, Ronald H.
1937 "The nature of the firm." Economica, 4: 386–405.

Commons, John R.
1934 Institutional Economics. Madison, WI: University of Wisconsin Press.

Communist Party of China [CPC]
1984 China's Economic Structure Reform—Decision of the CPC Central Committee, October. Beijing: Foreign Languages Press.

Daems, Herman
1983 "The determinants of the hierarchical organisation of industry." In Arthur Francis, Jeremy Turk, and Paul Willmah (eds.), Power, Efficiency and Institutions: 35–53. London: Heinemann.

Deal, Terrence E., and Allen A. Kennedy
1982 Corporate Cultures: The Rites and Rituals of Corporate Life. Reading, MA: Addison-Wesley.

Domenach, Jean-Luc
1986 "Chinese culture: Collective values in the Chinese industrial environment." Paper presented to the Conference on Chinese Culture and Management, organized by The Economist, Paris, January.

Iron Law of Fiefs

The Economist
1987 "A world turned upside down: Survey of China's economy." August 1: 3–22.

Gouldner, Alvin W.
1954 Patterns of Industrial Bureaucracy. Glencoe, IL: Free Press.

Granick, David
1987 "The industrial environment in China and the CMEA countries." In Gene Tidrick and Jiyuan Chen (eds.), China's Industrial Reform: 103–131. New York: Oxford University Press.

Granovetter, Mark
1985 "Economic action and social structure: The problem of embeddedness." American Journal of Sociology, 91: 481–510.

Knutsson, Jan
1986 "Chinese commercial negotiating behaviour and its institutional and cultural determinants." Paper presented to the Conference on Chinese Culture and Management, organized by *The Economist*, Paris, January.

Kornai, Janos
1986 "The Hungarian reform process: Visions, hopes, and reality." Journal of Economic Literature, 24: 1687–1737.
1987 "The dual dependence of the state-owned firm in Hungary." In Gene Tidrick and Jiyuan Chen (eds.), China's Industrial Reform: 317–338. New York: Oxford University Press.

Kroeber, Alfred L., and Clyde Kluckhohn
1952 Culture: A Critical Review of Concepts and Definitions. Cambridge, MA: Peabody Museum of American Archeology and Ethnology, Harvard University.

Krug, Barbara
1988 "Changing economic behaviour under changing constraints: The Chinese manager and economic reforms in the industrial sector." In John Child and Martin Lockett (eds.), Reform Policy and the Chinese Enterprise. London: JAI Press (forthcoming).

Lee, Peter N.S.
1987 Industrial Management and Economic Reform in China 1949–1984. New York: Oxford University Press.

Lockett, Martin
1985 "Culture and the problems of Chinese management." Templeton College Management Research Papers, 85/8, Oxford University.

MacDougall, Colina
1988 "Provinces spurn Peking attempts to rein in economy." *Financial Times*, October 13: 5.

Maine, Sir Henry S.
1986 Ancient Law. Tucson, AZ: University of Arizona Press.

Michels, Robert
1949 Political Parties. Glencoe, IL: Free Press.

Oborne, Michael
1986 "Industrial organisation in China." Paper presented to the Conference on Chinese Culture and Management, organized by *The Economist*, Paris, January.

Olson, Mancur
1965 The Logic of Collective Action. Cambridge, MA: Harvard University Press.

Ouchi, William G.
1981 Theory Z: How American Business Can Meet the Japanese Challenge. Reading, MA: Addison-Wesley.

Pye, Lucian W.
1985 Asian Power and Politics: The Cultural Dimensions of Authority. Cambridge, MA: Harvard University Press.

Qian, Bing Hong
1986 "Social values that influence Chinese organizational behaviour." Unpublished paper, Shanghai Academy of Social Sciences, February.

Rodzinski, Witold
1984 The Walled Kingdom. London: Fontana.

Seagrave, Sterling
1985 The Soong Dynasty. London: Sidgwick and Jackson.

Schram, Stuart R.
1984 Ideology and Policy in China since the Third Plenum 1978–84. London: University of London, School of Oriental and African Studies, Contemporary China Institute.

Thorelli, Hans B.
1986 "Networks: Between markets and hierarchies." Strategic Management Journal, 7: 37–51.

Tidrick, Gene and Jiyuan Chen (eds.)
1987 China's Industrial Reform. New York: Oxford University Press.

Weber, Max
1958 "The Chinese literati." In Hans H. Gerth and C. Wright Mills (eds.), From Max Weber: Essays in Sociology: 416–444. New York: Oxford University Press.
1968 Economy and Society: An Outline of Interpretative Sociology. Guenther Roth and Claus Wittich, trans. New York: Bedminister Press.

Williamson, Oliver E.
1970 Corporate Control and Business Behavior. Englewood Cliffs, NJ: Prentice-Hall.
1975 Markets and Hierarchies. New York: Free Press.
1985 The Economic Institutions of Capitalism. New York: Free Press.
1987 "Economics and sociology: Promoting a dialog." Paper presented to the 8th EGOS Colloquium, Antwerp, July.

Williamson, Oliver E., and William G. Ouchi
1981 "The markets and hierarchies program of research: Origins, implications, prospects." In Andrew H. Van de Ven and William F. Joyce (eds.), Perspectives on Organization Design and Behavior: 347–370. New York: Wiley.

World Bank
1985 China—Long-term issues and options. Report no. 5206-CHA, May. Washington, DC: World Bank.

[14]

Int. Studies of Mgt. & Org., Vol. 20, No. 4, pp. 6–21
M. E. Sharpe, Inc., 1990

GIORGIO INZERILLI

The Italian Alternative:
Flexible Organization and
Social Management

Since the beginning of this century, industrial organization in the Western world has been dominated by ideas, principles, and values developed primarily in the United States. The startling success of mass production techniques, exemplified by the Ford assembly lines of the model T car and used throughout American industry to help the American war effort in the last World War, were compelling reasons for the spread of an American "model" of industrial organization based on large-scale, mass-producing, integrated firms. Speaking of an American model is, of course, an oversimplification. For a long time (and even now), for example, large industrial firms supplying mass markets have coexisted with small firms supplying limited market niches (Granovetter, 1984) in what has been called "economic dualism" (Berger and Piore, 1980). Yet the contribution of small firms to the American economy is quite limited. Only 25.3 percent of its industrial labor force worked in plants with less than one hundred employees in 1977, compared to 58.4 percent in Japan, in 1978 (Granovetter, 1984) and 50.5 percent in Italy, in 1971 (Weiss, 1984). It is also the mass-scale model of production that was (and still is) idealized by many economists as the "modern" sector of the industry as opposed to the "traditional" sector of small firms. And it is the "modern" rather than the "traditional" sector that has typically attracted most of the interest of teachers and researchers of management and organization.

The model is driven by the basic value of rational, economic efficiency achieved by the systematic application of Adam Smith's principles of division of labor, specialization, and standardization, which were refined by Taylor early in this century. The application of these values and principles had several consequences. It led to a search for mass markets, which was helped by the standardization of consumers' tastes (Sabel and Zeitlin, 1982), and the development of railroads (Chandler, 1977). There was a drive toward vertical integration to control supplies and distribution. There was also a drive on the part of management to control more and more a labor force reluctant to accept the de-skilling inherent in Smith and Taylor's principles (Noble, 1986).

The mass production model was also reflected in the contemporary theories of organizations and management. The former were seen as mechanistic systems with different elements and their interrelations rationally designed for the most efficient achievement of organizational objectives. Such a view of organizations tended to give little consideration to the sociocultural characteristics of both their internal and external environment. The dominant management theories, inspired mainly by Taylor, tried to use scientific criteria for the development of work design and for planning, organizing, and controlling work activities. This scientific approach implied that management principles had, ideally, universal validity and could be abstracted, therefore, from the specific context of managerial action.

Hence the dominant theories of both management and organization tended to view work activities as isolated from their social context, in line with the classic economic view that economic activities can be understood in isolation from the social context in which they are embedded (Granovetter, 1985).

Since World War II, economists have started to give substantial consideration to the contextual aspects of economic action (Williamson, 1979). The images or paradigms of organizational analysis have also started to shift from mechanistic models to more behavioral and even phenomenological models (Morgan, 1986). But in the actual practice of management, many aspects of the mass production model still persist in the United States. Taylor's views, for example, are still widespread in American manufacturing, with particular reference to the split between planning and execution (Wheelwright, 1985). The view of management and organization as instrumental to economic, and (in particular) financial performance, is also still quite visible. It can be found, for example, in the use of techniques of bond and stock portfolio management for the management of conglomerates, in the short-term profit orientation for which the Americans are often criticized, and in the growing role of financial experts in the management of American companies (Hayes and Abernathy, 1980). Even more indicative of the vitality of the mass production model is the recent spread of this model to industries, like construction, that by tradition and for technological reasons had been organized along patterns of community and cooperation between labor and management (Piore and Sabel, 1984).

In recent times, there has been a widespread interest for a quite different model of management and organization derived from the study of Japanese firms. This model relies much more on small firms and decentralized production than in the American case, and is based on a conception of organizations as social (rather than instrumental) systems that are integrated with (rather than isolated from) the social context (Dore, 1983). The Japanese model has proved, so far, so successful that efforts have been made to apply some of its elements to Western industries.

Much less attention has been given to another "economic success," that of Italy. Considered not long ago as a developing country, Italy is now the fifth largest economy of the world, after the United States, Japan, Germany, and

8   *GIORGIO INZERILLI (THE NETHERLANDS)*

France. In 1989 its Gross Domestic Product (GDP) was estimated to be 864 billion U.S. dollars, higher than that of England (831 billion U.S. dollars) (OECD, 1989a). In the period 1981–87 the real per capita GDP of Italy grew at an annual (compound) rate of 1.97, higher than that of the United States (1.75), France (1.31), and Germany (1.84) (OECD, 1989b). Italy has historically been burdened by an inefficient government administration, characterized by a high public deficit, and by the relatively undeveloped southern regions (*The Economist*, 1990). Yet the ability of the Italians to improve the efficiency of their economy is shown by the high rate of productivity growth they have achieved in recent years. Between 1979 and 1987, the Italian real GDP per employee has grown by 4 percent, compared to 2.9 for Japan, 2.0 for France, 1.77 for England, 1.49 for Germany, and 0.66 for the United States (OECD, 1989a).

This undeniable success raises the question of which "model" of management and organization has been used by the Italians. Talking of a model is once again an oversimplification. This is particularly true in the case of Italy, which is widely recognized as lacking a homogeneous form of economic organization. The country is, in fact, geographically and economically divided in at least three parts: the south, still relatively undeveloped, the northwest, with high industrialization levels and a concentration of large firms, and the central northeast area, recently industrialized with a proliferation of small firms.

The south is, at this time, economically not relevant enough to search for its own model of management and organization. If there is such model in the industrialized northwest, it probably has substantial elements of the American model. The large size of its industrial firms seems to conform to the American model. It is also in the northwest industrial areas that there has been a history of strong adversarial relationships between labor and management (see Trigilia in the next issue). And it is in these areas that family firms, with few exceptions (e.g., FIAT), have given way to large corporations characterized by the separation of ownership and management that is a prerequisite for rational, efficiency-based management (see Fuá in the next issue). But there is at this time too little research on the managerial culture of the Italian northwest to allow a definition of its specific model of management and organization.

A great deal of research interest has, instead, been attracted recently by the central northeast (CNE) area, for two main reasons. First, the economy of this area has grown more rapidly than that of the more industrialized northwest area. Second, most of this growth is due to small firms, which essentially contradicts the basic tenet of classical economics that industrial growth entails the disappearance of the "traditional" sector in favor of the "modern" sector (Piore and Sabel, 1984).

The economic performance of the central northeast area of Italy

The CNE area comprises seven administrative regions that, taken together, in 1987, were estimated to account for 41.5 percent of the Italian GDP, compared to 34.5 and 23.9 percent, respectively, for the northwest and southern areas (Unioncamere, 1988). The rapid growth of the CNE area in recent years, compared to the highly industrialized northwest and to Italy as a whole, can be seen from three indicators of economic performance: growth of industrial output as measured by manufacturing value added, growth of productivity as measured by value added per employee, and growth of industrial employment. Relevant statistical data for the CNE regions, for the typical, highly industrialized, northwest area of the Piedmont, and for Italy as a whole are available for the periods 1970–76, 1976–80, and 1980–84 and are shown in Tables 1, 2, and 3.

From Tables 1 and 2 it can be seen that in the period 1970–80 industrial output and productivity grew in the CNE regions at a much higher rate than in the Piedmont and at a rate higher than that of Italy as a whole. The number of industrial jobs increased in the CNE regions, while they actually declined in the Piedmont and, in 1976–80, in Italy as a whole.

The period 1980–84 was one of stagnation for Italy as a whole, as indicated by a negative growth rate of value added (Table 1). It was marked, however, by a process of technological innovation (Camagni, 1989), which allowed a continuation of the process of productivity growth (Table 2) that had characterized the Italian industry during the 1970s. Productivity actually grew in the Piedmont more than in the CNE area in the period 1980–84. The Piedmont, however, lost industrial jobs at a rate (–18.7) that was not compensated for by productivity increases (11.4) and was significantly greater than the rate of job losses in the CNE regions (ranging between –15.7 and –9.0). There seems to be convincing evidence, therefore, pointing to the vitality of the economy of the CNE regions compared to a typical highly industrialized region of the Italian northwest.

The size of the industrial firms in the CNE region is quite small. According to the last census (1981), 91 percent of these firms were monoplant with an average of 7.5 employees per plant (Bellandi, 1989). They operate mostly in the traditional industrial sectors. A particular case is that of textile, clothing, footwear, and furnishing sectors. Taken together, they accounted in 1982 for 16.5 percent of Italian exports with a positive export–import balance of 8.7 billion U.S. dollars. By 1988 they accounted for 18.6 percent of Italian exports with a trade balance of 14.5 billion U.S. dollars (Economist Intelligence Unit, 1990). This is all the more remarkable when one considers that wages in the Italian clothing industry are twice those of England, four times those of Hong Kong, and nearly twenty times those of countries such as Sri Lanka (Zeitlin and Totterdill, 1989).

According to many researchers, much of this success is due to a model of industrial organization that is relatively unique to the central northeast area. The model is not typical of all the small firms and industries in the area. But it is typical of some of its successful industries, such as textile, clothing, and leather. It is also not typical only of "traditional" industries, since it can be found in "modern" ones, such as mechanical engineering. And it is not exclusively Italian. It has been found, for example, in the Jutland province of Denmark (textile and

10   *GIORGIO INZERILLI (THE NETHERLANDS)*

Table 1. Real growth rate of manufacturing value added

	1970–76	1976–80	1980–84
Central northeast regions	29.3–48.1[1]	19.7–26.1[1]	–10.4–0.2[1]
Piedmont	18.9	8.2	–9.3
Italy	25.0	17.5	–2.7

[1] Range for all seven central northeast regions.

Source: Camagni (1989).

Table 2. Real growth rate of manufacturing value added per employee

	1970–76	1976–80	1980–84
Central northeast regions	22.8–28.3[1]	21.0–23.8[2]	2.8–10.3[2]
Piedmont	19.8	9.1	11.4
Italy	18.6	17.8	9.1

[1] Range for five regions; rates for remaining two regions are 16.4 and 15.8
[2] Range for all seven central northeast regions.

Source: Camagni (1989).

Table 3. Growth rate of number of industrial employees

	1970–76	1976–80	1980–84
Central northeast regions	3.3–27.8[1]	1.2–3.9[2]	–15.7–9.0[1]
Piedmont	–0.7	–0.8	–18.7
Italy	5.3	–0.2	–10.8

[1] Range for all central northeast regions.
[2] Range for four central northeast regions. Range for remaining three regions is –1.2–0.1.

Source: Camagni (1989).

clothing, machine tools, and ship-building), in the Småland province of Sweden (car components), in Germany's Baden-Würtemberg (textile products and machinery, machine tools, and car components), in France's region of Rhone-Alps (plastic injection, as described by Raveyre and Saglio in this issue), around Madrid (electronic components), and in many regions and industries of Japan (Sabel, 1988). But it is only in Italy that the model can be found in large geographical areas and across a variety of industries that contribute, as we have seen, to such a large proportion of the national economy. It is for this reason that some of the leading students of this phenomenon consider the case of Italy as a prototype of the model (Sabel and Zeitlin, 1982). There is at this time a debate on the specific characteristics of this model (Becattini, in the next issue). There is, however, a general consensus on some of its basic elements, which are outlined in the next sections.

The main characteristics of the model

The essential nature of the model can be understood if one imagines a large-scale corporation where the component elements are made up of independent firms. From the organizational point of view, this means the deverticalization and decentralization of all the major functions of the organization, from purchasing to production and marketing, each of which is assigned to an independent firm. One of these firms usually performs some degree of planning and coordination and, because of this, can be considered as "head firm." It is often the firm that has contact with the market, makes the greater investments, and has the higher risks. Usually, however, the head firm does not have the contractual power to exercise any significant control over the subcontracting firms that make up a "corporation." Furthermore, a firm performing "head" functions at one time may perform, at another time, simple subcontracting functions in another corporation, "headed" by another firm.

More generally, while the functions in the deverticalized process of a "corporation" remain relative stable, the firms performing each function may actually change. Each function can be performed by a variety of firms that replace each other, depending on their production capacity availability, their prices, the technology required by a new product, and so on. Diachronically the firms performing functions for a "corporation" change, even if the functional structure of the "corporation" does not change. At any given time, many "corporations" of this kind operate within a given industry, with all the firms involved usually concentrated in the same geographical area. At any given time, also, each firm works for, and is therefore a member of, different "corporations." Usually, no firm devotes its production capacity to a single "corporation."

What we have, therefore, is an overall system of firms that are *synchronically* members of a set of different "corporations," and that *diachronically* change the set of "corporations" of which they are members. In another sense, each firm is a point of connection between different "corporations" with the connections, however, extending over time to different "corporations."

It should be obvious that, to understand the working of this system, one must not consider the behavior of each individual firm or "corporation," but that of the system as a whole. For example, to assess the economies of scale of a single firm, one cannot consider just its size or that of a single "corporation" for which it is working. Its economies of scale depend, in fact, on the size of all the "corporations" for which it is working at any given time. Hence the whole system determines the economies of scale of an individual firm. Also, the fact that firms are connected to changing sets of "corporations" means that they can

12   GIORGIO INZERILLI (THE NETHERLANDS)

enjoy externalities that are system-specific. Technological innovation and know-how, for example, may spread more easily through these connections than in the case of several large, integrated firms.

It should also be obvious that the regulation and administration of this system cannot be made by administrative, hierarchical authority, not only because each firm is legally independent, but also because the administration of a "corporation" by hierarchical authority would require the stable membership of its constituent firms, which is not the case.

Many researchers see the market as the regulating mechanism, since several firms apparently compete to perform a given function for each "corporation." But a pure market regulation would involve enormous transaction costs. If one considers the variability of the markets in which this system normally operates, the continuously changing web of interdependencies among firms, and the functional specialization of each firm, one should expect very high transaction costs, due, among other things, to uncertainty, specificity of investments, idiosyncratic tasks, and asymmetries of information (Inzerilli, 1989). It may be very difficult to assess these costs (Bellandi, this issue), but their environmental determinants are so strong and pervasive that one could hardly expect that interfirm transactions would be regulated exclusively, or even to a large extent, by the mechanism of the market. Nor can the working of the system be understood in terms of the networks discussed by Thorelli (1986) and Jarillo (1988) because, in this case, networks are essentially characterized by an administrative form of regulation performed by a large firm with strong contractual power vis-à-vis the other firms interacting with it. Networks are, in effect, constellations of weak subcontractors around a strong central firm (Lorenzoni, 1987). Neither the administrative form of regulation nor important differentials of contractual power characterize the Italian model. In this model, there are no strong central firms, for three reasons. First, all the firms in a "corporation" are small. Second, each firm can switch "corporations" relatively easily. And, third, every firm is simultaneously a member of several "corporations," which reduces its dependency on any of them.

It is the internal regulation of the system, therefore, that is most problematic and has attracted most of the interests of researchers in this area. Before discussing this point, it will be useful to consider how the system can be economically viable despite its potentially high transaction costs.

The economic viability of the system

There are a number of contingent factors external to the model just described that have so far supported its economic viability. For example, the Italian small firms enjoy a strong institutional support. Legislation on small firms provides loans and tax incentives. Labor legislation exempts them from union representation. Local governments provide social services, public transportation, industrial land price control, and other forms of assistance. There are also strong industrial associations providing administrative services for small firms at low prices, because of the resulting economies of scale (Inzerilli, 1989).

In the early stages of its development, the system may also have enjoyed externalities such as the government tolerance for tax evasion, pollution, and the unregulated use of homework, as well as the devaluation of the currency that has favored exports. The close proximity of industrial and residential areas may also have facilitated the mobilization of family resources that would not otherwise have entered the economic cycle (see Fuá in the next issue).

But what is most interesting about the Italian model is the economic strength that derives from its internal characteristics. The system is superior to a large, integrated firm in three key respects: economies of scale, flexibility to meet variable market demand, and capacity utilization. In the integrated firm, there are always operations performed at an optimal scale level, while others are not (Becattini, 1979). The recent trend toward externalization of service functions by American companies may be an indication that these services were poorly administered, but also operated below an optimal level by the companies involved (Elfring, 1988).

The Italian model has two advantages in this respect. First, the level at which its firms can reach economies of scale is significantly lower than that of a typical integrated firm. Second, the possibility to increase or decrease the number of "corporations" served by one firm allows it to maintain the utilization of its production capacity close to its optimal level. For its manufacturing operations, the typical large, integrated firm tends to use costly, specialized machines, rigidly linked together in the transfer system and capable of producing only components with fixed specifications. Only mass volumes of production allow them to approach optimal economies of scale, which is why they normally have supplied standardized mass markets. In the Italian model, the typical technology has few indivisibilities, so that the production process can be easily subdivided among different firms. Sabel (1982) has shown that, in this case, economies of scale can be reached even with few machines and relatively low production volumes.

The large, integrated firm is also unable to meet a market demand with variable specifications, because its machines are specialized and because its low-skill labor is incapable of operating different machines and adapting to changing technologies. Instead, the Italians typically use multiple-purpose machines (e.g., numerical control machines) and highly skilled labor, easily adaptable to operating different machines and to mastering new technologies (Lazerson, 1988; Rieser and Franchi, 1986). As a consequence, the Italians have the flexibility to compete successfully in markets with variable-demand styles, such as shoes, leather, and clothing, which are easily prone to fashion.

Low optimal volumes of production still do not shelter the Italian firms from variations of demand volumes and the consequent problems of under- or over-utilization of capacity. But they can cope relatively easily with this problem through the mechanism of shifting "corporation" membership. Thus a firm with excess capacity can always add some "corporations" to the set of those it is already serving. And one with insufficient capacity can always ask a subcontractor to meet its excess production requirements. What is true for a firm, of course, is also true for the parts or all of a "corporation." It is only when the total demand of the system exceeds or is lower than its total capacity that the firm's capacity will be under- or overutilized. We can see, therefore, that the Italian firms enjoy a systemic type of externality that large, integrated firms do not normally have. Unless they are linked to a network of other firms, as in the Italian model, they cannot use other firms as capacity reservoirs to smooth their production requirements. In other words, the Italian system provides a way of managing at the system level the "organizational slack" of individual firms. In this way, the "slack" that would remain unused in the case of an integrated firm is pooled and redistributed among different firms with the likely consequence of a better utilization of the total "slack" of the system. This, of course, may apply not only to production capacity, but also to other resources such as R & D and marketing (Dei Ottati, in the next issue).

How effective the Italian model is for the purpose of optimizing capacity utilization can be seen in the case of the clothing industry, which is prone to variable demand due to fashion. If the styles offered by an integrated firm are rejected by the market, some or (at the limit) all of its production and labor capacity will be made redundant. In the Italian case, instead, there are always many "head" firms specialized in design and marketing of a variety of different styles, and subcontracting most of the production. If the styles offered by one of these firms is rejected by the market, the few machines and workers it employs in packaging and shipping may be made redundant, but the production capacity of the rest of the "corporation" is not. This is because other marketing "head" firms may have been successful in predicting styles and the production capacity of the firms that should have, originally, supplied the first "head" firm will be simply redirected toward the other ones (Brusco, 1982). Production firms will simply shift their "corporation" membership. Furthermore, a large, integrated firm may have to bear most of the labor redundancy costs because of union pressure to avoid layoffs. The small Italian firms, instead, are much less subject to union pressure, thus operating in a freer labor market. In any case, in the Italian system, redundancies of both labor and production capacities will be spread among the several firms involved in the production process of one "corporation" (Brusco, 1982). For all these reasons, it is relatively easy for the overall system to face market demand variations and to absorb potential redundancies.

The regulation of the system

It will be clear from this discussion that the economic viability of this system is partly due to its technology, but also, to a large extent, to the nature of its internal organization. Much of its flexibility and its ability to maintain full capacity utilization at the firm level are due to the peculiar way in which the system is internally organized in terms of the subdivision of the production process among firms and the shifting interconnections among them. It is obvious that a system of this kind presents two basic problems, one of transaction costs and the other of integration and regulation. The higher the number of connections and the more dynamic the shifting pattern of these connections, the higher the transaction costs will be. These could be potentially so high that one could question whether they could be compensated for by the economic advantages described above. Therefore, there must be a form of regulation of the system that can inherently reduce transaction costs. A detailed discussion of these costs in the Italian model can be found in Dei Ottati (in the next issue). How these costs could be reduced by the system's regulation can be understood in terms of Williamson's transaction-cost theory (Williamson, 1979).

It will be recalled that, according to Williamson, one determinant of transaction costs is opportunism, that is, self-interest. A key element of the theory is that all other determinants (such as uncertainty, asymmetries of information, and bounded rationality) produce transaction costs only *in conjunction with* opportunism. "Absent the hazard of opportunism the difficulties would vanish" (Williamson, 1979, p. 241). A basic explanatory hypothesis for the economic viability of the Italian model is, therefore, that in this model opportunism is low. The model would then enjoy all the economic advantages already described, without having to bear the theoretically high transaction costs. The reason for low opportunism, according with this hypothesis, would be that economic relationships, both external and internal to the firm, have more the character of trust-based social exchanges, involving diffuse, informal, and non-contractual obligations typical of familistic associations, than that of opportunistic economic exchanges involving specific and contractual obligations (Blau, 1964). The limited research available provides some indication that this may indeed be the character of economic relationships in the Italian model.

We can see this in relation to both the internal and external relationships of a firm. Let us consider, first, external relationships. As Williamson has suggested, there may be "atmospheric" factors that influence the nature of transactions. Whether there is opportunism or trust in transactions may depend on how they are contextually defined. These definitions are of a cultural nature to the extent that they are collectively shared (Berger and Luckmann, 1967). Bagnasco and Trigilia (in this issue) studied a group of 100 Tuscan firms essentially organized according to the Italian model. When they analyzed subcontracting relationships among these firms, they found that in only 53 cases was there any kind of formal interfirm agreement, and of these only 18 involved legal contracts. When 93 firm owners were asked to describe their relationships with other firms, 56 defined it as one of "trust" or "cooperation," 33 as a "correct market relationship," and 4 as a "hard and sometimes disloyal market relationship." Only a minority, then, saw the relationship as a market transaction and very few described it as characterized by opportunistic behavior.

Bellandi (in this issue) describes interfirm relationships in the leather industry as "nearly always of a personalized and subjective nature, abstracting, therefore, from the logic of pure market relationships."

Similar patterns of cooperation are shown in a survey of 219 mechanical engineering firms (Rieser and Franchi, 1986) and in an in-depth study by Lazerson (1988) of 19 of these firms performing the function of "head firm." In describing the relationship between these firms and their subcontractors Lazerson states:

> The possibility that this increased outsourcing of production might impose higher transaction costs appeared to be a minor consideration unless it compromised the strategic core of the firm's market position, e.g., if outsourcing production risked revealing product and design secrets to competitors with whom a firm might share the same subcontractor. But such sensitive production phases could be kept in-house or entrusted to subcontractors with whom a long relationship of trust had been established. (Lazerson, 1988, p. 339)

The last two studies also provide indications as to the nature of internal relationships between employers and employees. According to Lazerson,

> low trust attitudes on the part of employers toward labor were absent. Only a minority of firms used time clocks, and some that did required everyone, including the partners, to use them. Employees were often permitted some flexibility in working hours. Nor were piece rates or any work-incentive pay systems used, reflecting both the essentially nonrepetitive nature of the work and the employer's preference for self-motivated employees. (Lazerson, 1988, p. 338)

Trust was also a primary factor regulating employees' careers. In the larger study of Rieser and Franchi (1986), it was found that seniority was a primary criterion for promotion, because the employers felt that it reflected the trustworthiness and professionalism of the employees. The same criterion was used for the appointment of partners to help manage the firm. They were usually selected among relatives or senior employees, because their trustworthiness was more important than their potential contributions in terms of capital and skill. Firm owners sometimes even refused to expand if they could not find trustworthy partners (Lazerson, 1988, p. 338).

There also seemed to be a preference for diffuse, informal, and non-contractual relationships, as shown by the fact that the employers who hired mostly people recommended by other firms and friends, "opposed firm-level contracts because of a desire to maintain a direct relationship with their employees and avoid rigid work rules." Finally, employer–employee relationships had a familistic character in that the employers had the widespread view that the relationship should be "permanent," "familial," and "collaborative" (Lazerson, 1988,

p. 337). Most of the employers studied by Rieser and Franchi described the departure of an employee as "trauma."

All this seems to indicate that both internal and external transactions in the Italian model are typified much more by the characteristics of trust-based social exchanges than by those of opportunistic economic exchanges. Hence there is room to believe that the economic viability of the model is strongly supported by lack of significant opportunism and consequently by low transaction costs. It is a social rather than a market form of regulation that allows the system to have an economic viability.

Social forms of regulation of economic transactions have been discussed before by Ouchi (1980). He suggested that types of formal organizations he calls "clans" can generate trust mainly by developing long-term relationships with their members. Transactional disequilibria in favor of one party could then be compensated for over time in favor of the other party. In the case of clans, however, transactions take place *within* a formal organization, where hierarchical authority and the possibility of monitoring behavior have an important role in regulating transactions. Instead, the Italian model refers to transactions *between* organizations, where hierarchical authority is excluded and the possibility of monitoring behavior is vastly reduced.

The trust characterizing economic relationships in the Italian model could be explained by a long-term, opportunistic interest in the stability of these relationships, as suggested by Jarillo (1988) in relation to networks managed by a central firm. But, in this case, interfirm relationships are relatively stable and the number of firms involved is relatively small. Neither of these two conditions is realized, however, in the Italian model, which involves hundreds of firms with shifting (rather than stable) patterns of relationships. Furthermore, the model is found in different geographical areas and across different industries. Trust must, therefore, be a generalized attitude of many individuals that carries over long periods of time across a variety of interactions.

The social bases of economic regulation

A possible explanation for this pervasiveness of trust in the Italian model may be related to the nature of the underlying social organization to which all the actors involved belong. A fundamental mechanism for the development of trust is mutual identification (Erickson, 1959). Among other things, this implies that the individuals involved share a sense of participation in the same community (Tönnies, 1957). Consider again some of Lazerson's descriptions:

> This absence of sharp social conflict between employees and their artisan-employers reflects the social origins of the artisans and the desire of skilled workers to become artisan-employers themselves. The overwhelming majority of artisans surveyed (Rieser and Franchi, 1986, p. 17) had been previously

18 GIORGIO INZERILLI (THE NETHERLANDS)

employed as skilled workers in larger firms, though some had come from artisan enterprises. Indeed, union-shop-stewards surveyed in large firms in the province of Modena defined artisan-owners as members of the working class (Franchi and Rieser, 1983). A similar identity of interests with small-firm owners combined with a hostility toward large industrialists was also expressed in surveys of workers in the neighboring communist region of Tuscany (Bagnasco, 1985, p. 43). (Lazerson, 1988, p. 337)

Consider also the relatively strong political association between employers and employees. On the one hand, a relatively high proportion of the latter belonged to communist-dominated unions (Lazerson, 1988, p. 334). On the other hand, 60 percent of the former were members of the employers' association CNA, which had "close associations with the Communist Party" (Lazerson, 1988, p. 334).

We can see here several mechanisms that can produce mutual identification between employers and employees. First, they come from common social origins, most commonly the working class. Second, this commonality is reinforced through membership in the same political organizations. Finally, the motivational structure provides a basis of identification. A basic aspiration of employees, in fact, is that of becoming themselves entrepreneurs, and hence employers (Lazerson, 1988). Part of their motivation to cooperate with and trust their employers is that they identify with a role they aspire to occupy in the future.

But these identification mechanisms do not help to foster mutual trust only between employers and employees. They also shape interfirm relationships. In fact, the individuals appointed to manage satellite firms were often (as we have seen) relatives or former work colleagues. In a larger study conducted by Rieser and Franchi (1986), 47 percent of business partners were former employees of firm owners.

Thus, trust-generating mechanisms influenced both internal and external relationships so that trust was likely to be a generalized attitude pervading the work relationships of a whole community. This would imply, then, that trust and the underlying basis of mutual identification were not a character of transaction-specific, face-to-face relationships, but represented generalized social attitudes. In this case, behavior would generally manifest itself in forms of collective solidarity, as opposed to individualistic orientations. In fact, "unionization" in these small firms seemed more an affirmation of solidarity with the working class outside the plant rather than a claim to institutionalizing an adverse relationship with the employer inside the plant. Also, "Strikes were usually called to renew regional or national contracts rather than to protest local conditions. . . . . In any case strikes would almost always be followed by employees working overtime to make up lost production" (Lazerson, 1988, p. 337). In other words, strikes were expressions not of social conflict, but of solidarity, horizontally, within one's social class, while the efforts to recover lost production after the strike seem to be an expression of solidarity, vertically, between employers and employees. Collective solidarity, then, as opposed to individualistic opportunism, seems to be a general orientation of the economic actors in the Italian model.

Bagnasco (1985) has outlined several mechanisms that explain this general orientation. In many cases, for example, the development of industrialization in the central northeast of Italy was due to initiatives of families that had prior experience in rural activities such as sharecropping. These families were of an extended type and had developed not only some technical and business skills, but also forms of economic organization that, because of the family ties, were naturally based on mutual trust and cooperation. Since it was often the same family that initially started small industrial firms (many times as a part-time activity), the original model of economic organization was easily transplanted from a rural to an industrial setting (Paci, in the next issue). But the attitudes of collective solidarity tend also to transcend individual firms and families. The social class identity that generates solidarity both vertically (within the firm) and horizontally (across different firms) is reinforced, as we have seen, by political parties that have an interest in maintaining the stability of the local social structure and identity. In the same direction are local public institutions that foster a common cultural identity and mediate potential conflicts internal to the system (Trigilis, in the next issue). The social, cultural, and political contexts, therefore, have a crucial role in maintaining the integration of the system and in fostering a common identity that is the base for trust and cooperation in economic relationships.

Conclusion

There is significant evidence supporting the hypothesis that the Italian model owes much of its economic viability to a form of regulation where economic relationships have the character of trust-based social exchanges and substantially exclude opportunistic behavior and the consequent transaction costs. Trust-based attitudes, however, are not transaction-specific, but are expressions of generalized collective solidarity that is rooted in the social structure and the common cultural background and identification. As we have seen, social, cultural, and political contextual factors perform an important function in the regulation of the system.

But it would be incorrect to say that there is a cause–effect relationship between these contextual factors and the economic effectiveness of the system. As we have seen, in fact, if the context provides a mechanism of integration for the system, the system, in turn, provides the social stability that is instrumental in the maintenance of the integrity of the social context. There is no sharp differentiation, therefore, between the realm of economic activity and its context. It is more appropriate to talk instead of interpenetration of social and economic relations that form an integrated cultural unit.

20 GIORGIO INZERILLI (THE NETHERLANDS)

Beginning with Max Weber, students of economics and sociology have often maintained that the modernization of a society and its economy entails an increasing differentiation between economic and social institutions and structures. The Italian model provides an example of an economic system whose strength derives, to a large extent, not from its differentiation, but from its integration with the social structure. If this is true, then the survival of the system will depend as much on economic factors as on the ability of economic, social, and political actors to maintain a high level of mutual integration.

The Italian model also offers strong support for Granovetter's view that economic systems cannot be adequately understood without reference to the historical and social contexts in which they are embedded (Granovetter, 1985). And it provides a powerful challenge to the classical economic and managerial theories that economic efficiencies and growth can only be achieved with a model of organization based on mass production, standardization, and work specialization.

References

Amin, A. (1989) A Model of the Small Firm in Italy. In E. Goodman and J. Bamford (eds.), Small Firms and Industrial Districts in Italy. London: Routledge.

Bagnasco, Arnaldo (1985) "La costruzione sociale del mercato: strategie di impresa e esperimenti di scala in Italia." Stato e Mercato, 13, pp. 9–45

Becattini, G. (1979) "La cooperazione tra imprese come strumenti di sviluppo economico." Cooperazione di Credito, 68, pp. 130–142.

Bellandi, M. (1989) "The Role of Small Firms in the Development of Italian Manufacturing Industry." In E. Goodman and J. Bamford (eds.), Small Firms and Industrial Districts in Italy. London: Routledge.

Berger, P. L. and Luckmann, Thomas (1967) The Social Construction of Reality. New York: Anchor Books

Berger, Suzanne, and Piore, Michael J. (eds.) (1980) Dualism and Discontinuities in Industrial Societies. Cambridge: Cambridge University Press.

Blau, P. (1964) Exchange and Power in Social Life. New York: John Wiley & Sons.

Brusco, Sebastiano (1982) "The Emilian Model: Productive Decentralisation and Social Integration." Cambridge Journal of Economics, 6, pp. 167–184.

Camagni, R. (1989) "Regional Deindustrialization and Revitalization Processes in Italy." International Conference on Industrial Transformation and Regional Development. Nagoya and Tokyo, Japan.

Chandler, Alfred (1977) The Visible Hand: The Managerial Revolution in American Business. Cambridge: Harvard University Press.

Commission of the European Community, (1989) European Economy (November), p. 42.

Dore, Ronald (1983) "Goodwill and the Spirit of Market Capitalism." British Journal of Sociology, 34, pp. 459–482

Economist Intelligence Unit (1990) Italy–Country Profile, 1989–1990.

Elfring, Tom (1988) "Why Are Business and Professional Services Growing so Rapidly?" Paper presented at the Fifteenth Annual Conference of the European Association for Research in Industrial Economics.

Erikson, Erik (1959) "Identity and the Life Cycle." Psychological Issues, 1 (1).

Franchi, Maura, and Rieser, Vittorio (1983) Esperienza e cultura dei delegati: un indagine nella realta metalmeccanica modenese. Reggio Emilia: Bonhoeffer Edizioni.

Granovetter, Mark (1984) "Small Is Bountiful: Labor Markets and Establishment Size." *American Sociological Review,* 49, pp. 323–334.

———. (1985) "Economic Action and Social Structure: The Problem of Embeddedness." *American Journal of Sociology,* 91, pp. 481–510.

Hayes, R. H., and Abernathy, W. J. (1980) "Managing Our Way to Economic Decline." *Harvard Business Review,* August, pp. 67–77.

Imede–World Economic Forum (1989) *The World Competitiveness Report.*

International Labor Office (1988) *Yearbook of Labor Statistics.*

Inzerilli, G. (1989) Transaction Costs, Opportunism and Social Control. Working paper no. 55. Erasmus University, Rotterdam School of Management.

Jarillo, J. C. (1988) On Strategic Networks. *Strategic Management Journal,* 9, pp. 31–41.

Lazerson, H. Mark (1988) "Organizational Growth of Small Firms: An Outcome of Markets and Hierarchies?" *American Sociological Review,* 53, pp. 330–342.

Lorenzoni, G. 1987. "Costellazione di Imprese e Processi di Sviluppo." *Sviluppo e Organizzazione,* 102, pp. 59–72.

Morgan, G. (1986) *Images of Organizations.* London: Sage.

Noble, D. F. (1986) *Forces of Production.* New York: Oxford University Press.

OECD. (1989a) *Economic Outlook,* 46 (December).

———. (1989b) *National Accounts,* 1, 1960–1988.

Ouchi, W. (1980) "Markets, Bureaucracy and Clans." *Administrative Science Quarterly,* 25, pp. 129–141.

Piore, Michael, and Sabel, Charles (1984) *The Second Industrial Divide: Possibilities for Prosperity.* New York: Basic Books.

Rieser, Vittorio, and Franchi, Maura (1986) Innovazione tecnologica e mutamento organizzativo nell'impresa artigiana: Una ricerca sull'artigianato metalmeccanico di produzione nella provincia di Modena. Unpublished manuscript, along with additional survey results on file with the Confederazione Nazionale dell'Artigianato of Modena.

Sabel, Charles (1982) *Work and Politics. The Division of Labor in Industry.* Cambridge: Cambridge University Press.

———. (1988) "Flexible Specialization and the Re-emergence of Regional Economies." In P. Hirst and J. Zeitlin (eds.), *Reversing Industrial Decline? Industrial Structure and Policy in Britain and Her Competitors.* Oxford: Berg.

Sabel, Charles, and Zeitlin, J. (1982) "Alternative storiche alla produzione di massa." *Stato e Mercato,* 5 (August).

Tönnies, Ferdinand (1957) *Community and Society (Gemeinschaft und Gesellschaft)* (trans. and ed. by Charles P. Loomis). East Lansing: Michigan State University Press.

The Economist (1990) "A Survey of Italy." (May), p. 26.

Thorelli, H. B. (1986) "Networks: Between Markets and Hierarchies." *Strategic Management Journal,* 7, pp. 37–51.

Unioncamere (1988) *Rapporto 1988 sull 'impresa, il sistema pubblico e le economie locali.* Milan: F. Angeli.

Weiss, Linda (1984) "The Italian State and Small Business." *European Journal of Sociology,* 25, pp. 214–241.

Wheelwright, (1985) "Restoring the Competitive Edge in U.S. Manufacturing." *California Management Review,* 27 (3), pp. 57–75.

Williamson, Oliver. 1979. "Transaction Costs Economics: The Governance of Contractual Relations." *Journal of Law and Economics,* 23, pp. 233–261.

Zeitlin, J., and Totterdill, P. (1989) "Markets, Technology and Social Intervention: The Case of Clothing." In P. Hirst and J. Zeitlin (eds.), *Reversing Industrial Decline.* Oxford: Berg.

Part III
Special Aspects of Managing Across Cultures:
Business Environments, Managing Expatriates and Managing Alliances

Competing on the Pacific Rim: High Risks and High Returns

Philippe Lasserre and Jocelyn Probert

When dealing with the Asia Pacific region, Western business executives are often confronted with behaviour of their business partners. customers. suppliers. employees which differs sometimes quite fundamentally from their expectations, their norms, and their way of doing things. Those differences have an important impact on the formulation and implementation of business strategies as well as on the necessary explanations which have to be given to headquarters executives when the time comes for the performance evaluation of Asian operations.

It has been agreed frequently by academic consultants and business managers that 'Asia is different', and should deserve a significant modification in business practices. behaviour. and norms if companies want to build and sustain their competitive advantages in the region. Although it is not unusual in a multinational organization to see each region of the world claiming its differences and requiring 'special treatment', the claim from Asia Pacific appears to be among the most vocal. probably because of the growing strategic importance of this part of the wold in the economic scene.

At the Euro-Asia Centre, we think the assertion of this 'Asia Pacific Difference' needs to be documented. not only by anecdotes but also by an attempt to capture and measure the dimensions of these 'differences' with regard to the elements which constitute the business environment. Already an earlier survey has shown some wide differences in the quality and reliability of business information available for strategic and marketing planning.[1] In the survey published here, our ambitions have been broader. We have tried to measure what constitutes

Western executives must confront attitudes and behaviour among their business partners in the Asia Pacific region that may differ fundamentally from their expectations. This article considers the premises which top management use to formulate strategies to tackle both the competitive context and the political, ethical, and legal dimensions governing the rules of the game in each country. The real challenge for strategic development appears to lie in the adaptation and transformation of corporate organizational behaviour to admit new complexities. Results of a survey conducted among general managers and marketing managers of Western companies operating in the Asia Pacific region are presented.

the 'strategic logic' and 'competitive climate' of the Asia Pacific region.

By 'strategic logic' we mean the premises and models that top management of companies use for the formulation of their strategies. The term includes the definition of purpose (what are the objectives of business). the way one approaches competition. and on what criteria business decisions are made. The 'competitive climate' assessment focuses on the role of governments and on the behaviour of customers and competitors. as well as on the financial environment.

The results presented here are answers given by expatriate managers and in a few instances by local managers of European multinationals operating in the Asia Pacific region. With one possible exception they are not comparative. In other words, we do not know whether the characteristics of the various business environments which emerge from this

Pergamon

0024-6301(93)E0004-A

Long Range Planning Vol. 27. No. 2, pp. 12 to 35. 1994
Copyright © 1994 Elsevier Science Ltd
Printed in Great Britain. All rights reserved
0024-6301/94 $6.00+.00

13

Nothing would be more erroneous than to judge China with our European criteria
Lord Macartney—1793

survey are significantly different from those which would have emerged from a similar survey in Germany, France, Italy, the United Kingdom, or the United States. While this is a serious limitation to the present survey, it seems to us that the results are nevertheless a contribution to the understanding of business conduct in the Asia Pacific region.

The Survey

The survey was mailed to 867 general managers and marketing managers of foreign companies operating in the Asia Pacific region. One hundred and eighty-six valid replies were received by the due date, giving an overall response rate of 21.5 per cent. Among the biggest groups of respondents were from Hong Kong (28) and Singapore (25), reflecting the importance of these locations as bases for foreign business activity.

The distribution of valid responses is shown in Table 1. ('Other' covers 15 additional responses concerning the whole region, or from a variety of countries where unfortunately the response rate was too small to be significant—India, Vietnam, Australia, New Zealand.) The 34 questions can be roughly divided into five topics, with varying degrees of overlap in certain cases between the different themes. These five areas can be categorized as: *government-related issues, blueprints for success, product issues, relationships, and financial issues.*

Government-related Issues

The first question one needs to ask is, 'What is government?' In the Asia Pacific region, the 'government' has many roles. Sometimes the term is used with respect to political involvement; very often it is the bureaucratic function which impinges more on business life. In Japan, for example, the 'government' is far too often blamed for interference in business, when more correctly the ministry bureaucrats are the ones involved (and even then, foreign companies often perceive influences which do not really exist).

Our survey tried to gauge the perceived degree of 'government' involvement in business ('Maintaining smooth and regular contacts with government is an essential part of doing daily business in this country'). The results are shown in Figure 1. Given the *laissez-faire* nature of government in Hong Kong, it comes as no surprise that respondents from the territory disagreed most strongly with this premise. In fact, respondents from all four Asian NIEs* felt that good relationships with the government were not a particularly important factor of doing business, which suggests that business conditions have evolved to the extent that the independence of a foreign firm's activities (within the limits of prevailing regulations) is reasonably well assured.

TABLE 1. Distribution of survey responses.	
Hong Kong	28
Singapore	25
Japan	22
Korea	9
Taiwan	12
China	10
Indonesia	22
Thailand	37
Philippines	6
Malaysia	15
TOTAL	186
Other	15
TOTAL RESPONSES	201

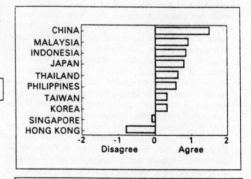

FIGURE 1. Maintaining smooth and regular contacts with government is an essential part of doing business.

*Newly Industrialized Economies.

14

This process has not yet evolved sufficiently among ASEAN nations for businesses to be able to ignore the importance of good government contacts. In China, this is all the more true. Numerous examples exist of foreign firms being unable to develop their business because of faulty contacts with local officials, particularly during times of economic austerity.

Respondents from Japan believed rather firmly that contacts with government needed to be smooth and regular—more so than in Thailand and the Philippines, and only slightly less than in Malaysia and Indonesia. While it may be tempting to deduce that this confirms views of some 'Japan-bashers', for example, that foreign firms are disadvantaged in doing business in Japan because of pervasive government influence over industry, this perception is not strongly borne out by the finding that execcutives demonstrated only slight agreement with the proposition: 'There is a high level of government interference in business' (Figure 2).

A more likely explanation for the need for good government contacts, therefore, is the strength of consensus decision-making as much among Japanese bureaucrats as among Japanese corporate managers. The need for consensus is all the more important if a company (foreign or Japanese) is planning to move into radically new ventures where government officials have relatively little experience. Once accord has been reached, however, the company is unlikely to suffer much interference.

The emphatic disagreement in Hong Kong to the statement that governments exert strong influence over business is completely in line with expectations. The pro-business nature of government in Taiwan appears to leave companies based there relatively free to pursue their own course of action. On the other hand, the weak influence of the Singaporean government over business is surprising in view of the predilection for regulating everything in sight. The government of the remaining NIE, Korea, seems to interfere only slightly less than China in the running of business affairs. The *dirigiste* nature of the Korean government is well documented, for example in the instructions given in 1991 to the *chaebol*† to focus their activities on just three core areas or risk losing preferential interest rate concessions.

The slower move to shed protectionist measures in the governments of the Philippines and of Indonesia provides a plausible explanation for the perception that the authorities are closely involved with business: monopoly privileges remain in some spheres, complicated tariff regimes operate, and foreign firms remain totally barred from some business sectors. Such actions appear to cause less of a problem in Malaysia and Thailand.

The proposal that 'The government here grants preferential advantages to local firms over foreign ones' met with a mixed response (Figure 3). Not

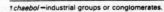

† *chaebol*—industrial groups or conglomerates.

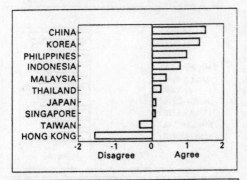

FIGURE 2. There is a high level of government influence in business.

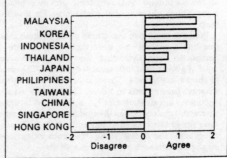

FIGURE 3. The government grants preferential advantages to local firms.

surprisingly, respondents from Hong Kong again disagreed—very few advantages are available to any firm, whether local or foreign. Those from Singapore dissented to some extent, reflecting the positive stance taken by the government ever since the city-state came into being, towards business as a whole and in recognizing the contributions made by foreign influences. It seems unlikely that the government's more recent concern over how to promote Singaporean firms' development abroad will affect its attitude to locally-based business.

The relative lack of integration of the Overseas Chinese community into Malaysian and Indonesian life, and the concern of respective governments to redress perceived imbalances of opportunity for the local population, lie behind the high level of agreement for these countries. In Malaysia particularly, government policy over the last decade has consistently sought to advantage the *bumiputra** businessman—with an indifferent degree of success.

In Korea, foreign firms detect rather a strong discriminatory attitude on the part of government in favour of local firms. Certain industries may be more prone than others: recent events have highlighted particular problems for financial institutions. Surprisingly, given the central planning of the Chinese economy, the government there does not seem to favour state run enterprises over foreign businesses. The case may be different when inputs (raw materials, foreign exchange, financing) are limited. An alternative explanation may be that foreign joint ventures tend to be based in an SEZ† or in the hinterland of Guangdong province behind Hong Kong, where special preferences are given to them.

We have combined the scores given to these three questions relating to government, to create a composite chart indicating the overall perceived level of government influence in business. The result is shown in Figure 4. Three clear tiers of countries emerge: governments in Korea, China, Malaysia and Indonesia are all strategically important to business interests; Japan occupies the middle ground together with the Philippines and Thailand; while in Taiwan, Singapore and Hong Kong the authorities exert negligible influence over business affairs.

*Indigenous.
†SEZ—Special Economic Zone (the Chinese government created five SEZs, which offer preferential treatment to foreign investors, in 1982).

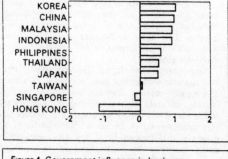

FIGURE 4. Government influence in business.

Blueprints for Success

The proposition that 'In order to be successful here one needs to build up a network of 'contacts'', attracted an uncompromisingly strong degree of acceptance by respondents (Figure 5). Of all responses to questions in the survey, this was the most strongly felt belief among executives replying from Korea, China, the Philippines, Taiwan, and Sinapore. Even in Hong Kong business people believed moderately strongly that an essential factor for success is a good network of connections.

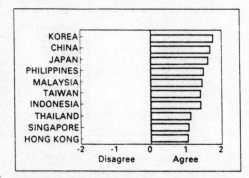

FIGURE 5. In order to be successful one needs to build up a network of 'contacts'.

The importance of a good set of connections has to be recognized at an early stage by a Western company hoping to do business in the region. It is a concept much less well developed in the West and which, at least among countries with a strong Overseas Chinese element, is born of the will to survive against all odds. The implication, of course, is that having connections not only requires time and patience to achieve, but also the ability to convince not just partners but the business community and society as a whole that your company is committed to long term involvement there. This proposal is confirmed by the strong positive response throughout the region to two related questions posed in the survey.

The first, that 'Business relationships based on trust are essential for success but difficult to build', again showed Korea to be the country with the greatest acceptance of the proposition, closely followed by Japan and China (Figure 6). Interestingly, the Philippines ranked just behind these three countries and well ahead of Malaysia, Thailand, and Indonesia. perhaps a reflection of the relative instability of the country in recent years.

Only in Hong Kong and in Singapore, where many foreign multinationals have their regional headquarters, was there a rather lukewarm acceptance of the proposal. While not denying the need for relationships based on trust, it seems that these alliances are easier to forge than elsewhere—perhaps

because of these city-states' long history of foreign involvement and ready acceptance of the presence of foreign influences (passively, in the case of Hong Kong, and actively in Singapore).

The outstanding feature to responses to the second proposal that 'To succeed in this country one has to demonstrate to partners a long term interest in a business venture', was the near 100 per cent strong agreement for Japan. This was the single most strongly held belief in the whole survey, achieving 95 per cent acceptance (Figure 7).

Too many foreign companies in the past have shown a disastrous lack of commitment to Japan—at least in the eyes of the community, if not by head office back home—for example by laying off staff (especially Japanese personnel) during market downturns. A company's commitment to its staff, suppliers, customers is of overriding importance. Any withdrawal, however temporary, suggests that business partners (in the widest sense) run the risk of being let down again in the future. The reputation among Japanese consumers of a foreign product will fall quickly and will prove difficult if not impossible to rebuild if the manufacturer fails to demonstrate his long term commitment.

Outside Japan, the importance of a demonstrable commitment to a business venture appears to be more strongly felt in the Philippines and Korea than in other countries, although all respondents agreed in general on the need for long-termism. The implication of the strong degree of acceptance of the

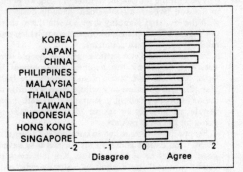

FIGURE 6. Business relationships based on trust are essential for success but difficult and time-consuming to build.

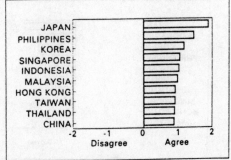

FIGURE 7. One has to demonstrate to partners a long-term interest in a business venture.

17

statement is that the requirement for a truly long term commitment to a market in the Asia Pacific region is not particularly well understood in all corporate headquarters.

Respondents were asked to consider the statement that 'Successful results do not come immediately, but a long time after initial investments have been made'. Managers in Japan agreed, unsurprisingly, rather strongly with this statement. For Indonesia and Korea there was also a fairly strong degree of agreement, perhaps reflecting in Indonesia the relatively bureaucratic business environment where patience is needed to put systems in place. The Korean business environment is commonly regarded by foreign executives as a 'difficult' one for a variety of reasons—regulatory restrictions, labour relations, financing, to name but a few (Figure 8).

Although Taiwanese firms themselves have a reputation for being more entrepreneurial than those in neighbouring countries, answers regarding business results for foreign companies in Taiwan nevertheless indicated that success was a somewhat long term proposition—more so even than in mainland China. While firms in Sinapore and in Hong Kong did not feel particularly strongly that success depended on a long term presence in the market, Malaysia rated this proposition even lower. Agreement was only marginal: the time scale seems not to be as strong a factor here in the attainment of success.

More executives disagreed than agreed with the

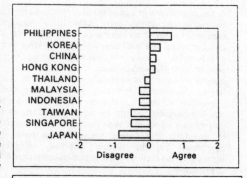

FIGURE 9. Planning does not really work; one needs to be opportunistic.

statement, 'In this country, planning does not really work: one needs to be opportunistic' (Figure 9). Only in four countries—the Philippines, Korea, China and Hong Kong—is the necessity of taking an entrepreneurial attitude to business development thought on balance to be more important than planning. Business executives responsible for the Philippines, who gave the strongest positive response, and those from Korea and China believed in opportunism while at the same time ranking a high level of agreement to the need for an ability to inspire confidence among partners for the long term. Neither in Hong Kong nor in Taiwan (where businessmen actually disagreed with the idea that planning does not work) was there the degree of acceptance of opportunism which one might expect in these countries.

In contrast, and not surprisingly, few people who answered regarding the business environment in Japan felt there was much room for departure from plan. For the question as a whole there was little to divide individual country responses; overall, more people are slightly in favour of planning than of going for the main chance.

Respondents were asked to consider the assertion, 'Here, what counts above all for success is to have a good product or service; factors like low price or good "contacts" are secondary'. Surprisingly, only the Philippines and Hong Kong were slightly in agreement—and neither of these countries would particularly spring to mind as being good illustrations of the statement (Figure 10).

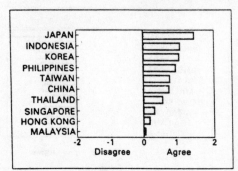

FIGURE 8. Successful results do not come immediately but after a long time.

18

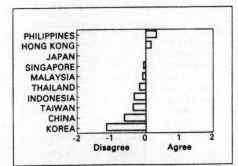

FIGURE 10. What counts above all is to have a product. Price and contacts are secondary.

In Japan, where the quality of a product and/or the service ethic are always cited as important factors for a firm's success, respondents were entirely ambivalent to our premise. Evidently the network of contacts is a balancing factor, although the product is slightly more important than the friend (see Figure 12 below) and the price is certainly not the most important factor (see Figure 11 below).

Singapore, Malaysia, Thailand, Indonesia, and Taiwan all seem to require—in a minor way—advantages of price and/or contacts in order to be successful. In China and Korea, price is clearly more important than product, but friends are just as important as the product. The influence of Japanese investment may perhaps be detected in the appearance of Malaysia in the top right-hand segment of Figure 15, alongside Japan itself, Hong Kong and Singapore; other ASEAN countries have yet to accord the same importance to quality as they do to contacts. Korea gives the most extreme result in favour of contacts and against quality.

Product Issues

Pricing considerations are important product-related issues, and the disparity of attitude between different countries in the Asia Pacific region can have profound implications for a company's pricing strategy. A key question suggested that, 'In this country customers go for the cheapest price with secondary regard for quality'. Emphatic disagreement came from respondents covering Japan, and to a much lesser extent from Singapore, Hong Kong, and even Malaysia (Figure 11). The attitude in Japan comes as absolutely no surprise: sophisticated Japanese consumers have long recognized that there is more to buying a good or service than the simple immediate outlay of money. Western suppliers of luxury goods have traditionally found a ready market there (expensive brands of foreign whisky sell much better than the cheaper varieties, for example), whereas the cheap video recorders and TVs imported from some neighbouring countries failed to find an enduring customer base because of the lack of after sales service. Sophistication levels in Hong Kong and Singapore have risen with the increase in disposable income and status symbols are important in certain sectors of these communities.

Consumers in both the Philippines and Korea tend to be influenced by price rather than quality, even though—in the Philippines at least—they also associate higher prices with higher quality (Figure 13). The Philippines had the highest positive rating to the statement, 'Customers tend to associate higher price with higher quality'. This suggests consumers there are not prepared to pay more, even though they believe they would get a higher quality good by doing so. In Korea the relationship is less clear cut: customers seem more sceptical that paying a higher price will necessarily bring quality advantages—a

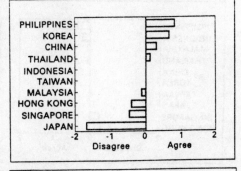

FIGURE 11. In this country customers go for the cheapest price.

19

view which may be influenced by government
campaigns in the past against imported goods
(which can be more expensive than similarly locally-
made products because of customs and excise
duties).

The broad acceptance of the proposal linking
higher prices with higher quality suggests that
people throughout the Asia Pacific region really
believe that 'you get what you pay for'. This belief
seems to be particularly firmly held by the ASEAN
countries (excluding Singapore and Brunei), slightly
more so even than for Japan. Customers in Taiwan,
while not disagreeing with the price/quality link,
nevertheless find it rather weak. Taiwan was also
one of the two countries (with Indonesia) where
customers seem to pay equal attention to price and
quality, to judge from the completely neutral
response in Figure 11 discussed above.

Regarding the relative advantages of a good
product and a good 'friend' ('It is better to have a
good friend in this country than a good product'),
only the Philippines showed a significantly positive
response. In Indonesia the statement was thought to
be true to a small extent, while Hong Kong and
Singapore disagreed somewhat mildly. In these two
countries—and to a lesser extent still, in Japan and
Taiwan—the product is more important than
privileged contacts. Other countries—Malaysia,
Thailand, China, and Korea—were undecided on this
question.

The respondents were presented with the state-

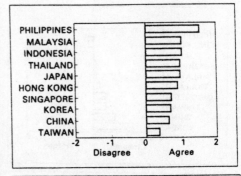

FIGURE 13. Customers tend to associate higher price
with higher quality.

ment, 'Once a customer has developed a good
relationship with a supplier he tends to be loyal
to him, even if his price is higher than others' (Figure
14). Managers replying for Japan demonstrated the
strongest commitment to this principle, based on the
long term business relationships indicated above. In
Korea, where emotional commitment to business
partners may be high, price considerations are even
higher. Hong Kong businessmen demonstrate the
most 'Western' business characteristics in their
readiness to switch loyalties to get a better price.

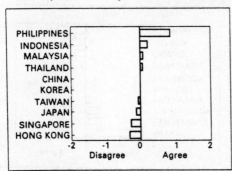

FIGURE 12. It is better to have a good friend than a
good product.

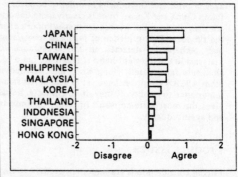

FIGURE 14. Once a customer has developed a good
relationship with a supplier he tends to be loyal
even if prices are higher.

20

Combining the responses to several questions, an overall view of the Quality of Demand in the different countries can be established. We plotted measures of the importance of quality against measures of the importance of contacts, as defined below.

Importance of quality: Scores from Figure 10 ('Here, what counts above all for success is to have a good product or service; factors like low price or good "contacts" are secondary') *Minus* scores from Figure 11 ('In this country customers go for the cheapest price with secondary regard for quality').

Importance of contacts: Scores from Figure 5 ('In order to be successful here one needs to build up a network of "contacts"') *Plus* scores from Figure 14 ('Once a customer has developed a good relationship with a supplier here he tends to be loyal to him, even if his price is higher than others') *Plus* scores from Figure 12 ('It is better to have a good friend in this country than a good product').

Figure 15 shows the result of this composite measure of Quality of Demand.

Sophistication is clearly greatest in Japan. The successful business will require striking an adroit balance between product quality and maintaining a good network of contacts: neither can afford to be sacrificed for the sake of the other. Hong Kong and Singapore again form a small cluster by themselves, according the same importance to a good balance between quality and contacts as found for Japan, but

at a much lower absolute level: the less well developed concept of service compared with Japan and the generally rather unfettered business environment go some way to explain this finding. Malaysia, and with some lag the countries of Indonesia, Taiwan, and Thailand, form the next tier of sophistication. Among these economies, one could speculate on the influence of Japanese investment in Malaysia, Indonesia, and Thailand in raising quality expectations.

The final cluster contains the Philippines, China, and Korea in descending order of refinement of demand. The uncertain times through which the Philippines has passed in the last decade may be a factor here—disrupted business activity over a long period may promote excessive reliance on special relationships. The image received of Korea is not particularly encouraging, and lies at odds with the image local companies are trying to establish for their products overseas. This rating may change over time, but for the present demonstrates an apparent inablity to project a positive image to the outside world.

Marketing

Turning to marketing approaches, there is a widely held belief throughout the region with the exception of China and Singapore that 'Here, if a company successfully launches new products or adopts new marketing approaches it is imitated almost immediately' (Figure 16). This suggests an extremely lively competitive climate—innovative ideas may rapidly become commonplace and the cost of development work apparently wasted in such circumstances, unless the cycle becomes a virtuous cycle of incremental product improvement.

There are numerous examples of products introduced to Japan, particularly, which have been a hit with consumers at first but which have rapidly lost ground to rival products that have used the original idea but have incorporated their own innovations. In Korea, where the problem of imitation is thought (marginally) to be the most severe, locally-based firms will probably undercut the original product on price (and possibly quality as well—although as we have already seen in the responses in Figure 11, the price is the more important factor).

The apparent lack of imitative spirit in Singapore

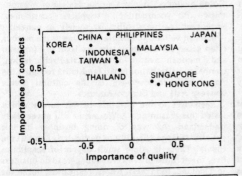

Figure 15. Quality of demand.

21

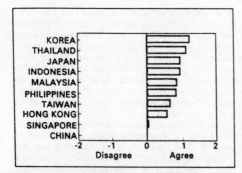

FIGURE 16. Successful products or marketing approaches are imitated almost immediately.

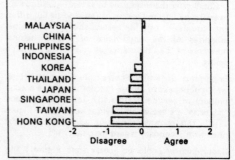

FIGURE 17. Competing is more a matter of playing politics than of marketing mix.

may perhaps be attributed to the lack of 'local' competition, given the dominance of Singaporean industry by multinational corporations; in China, local producers have not had enough time to develop the necessary skills to 'imitate' since the inflow of western products to the country is still relatively recent—although evidence suggests that this situation is changing. In Hong Kong and Taiwan, where the risk of imitation is perceived to be higher than in Singapore or China yet is at the lower end of the scale for the region as a whole, average company size tends to be considerably smaller than the industrial giants of Japan and Korea—which suggests a lack of the capital resources necessary to continually monitor and imitate competitors' moves.

(Another aspect to product imitation, is of course, the question of whether or not it is legitimate: counterfeiting can be a major problem in certain countries where the political will is lacking or general public awareness of intellectual property rights is low.)

Foreign executives are fairly united in their belief that a firm must have a good marketing mix if it is to compete adequately. One question proposed that 'Competing is more a matter of "playing politics" than of "marketing mix"' (Figure 17). While there is a faint echo of 'politicking' in Malaysia (another effect of the *bumiputra* policy, perhaps), even China was very neutral. In the Newly Industrializing Economies of Hong Kong, Taiwan, and Singapore, where gov-

ernments are in one way or another rather benign, there is a clear preference for marketing over politicking: companies are responsible for their own success or failure in the marketplace, through their ability to suit their products and marketing approaches to local needs. Japan might have been expected to show a stronger regard for market forces than the results of our survey suggest.

Relationships

'Doing business' involves a complex set of relationships—with competitors, suppliers, customers, employees, partners, officials, society in general—which can be hard to disentangle. One of the reasons often given for the relatively low level of European and American investment in the Asia Pacific region, compared with that of Japan (and more recently, the Asian NIEs themselves), is the cultural divide between Asia and Europe/America.

Responses to the question in our survey which tested this reasoning, 'A Westerner will never really understand the way of doing business in this country' (Figure 18), did not particularly support the theory. There is some small degree of scepticism over the abilities of Western managers to do business in Thailand, Indonesia, Korea, and China, but in the countries with a history of Western influence—the Philippines (from the US); Singapore, Malaysia, and

22

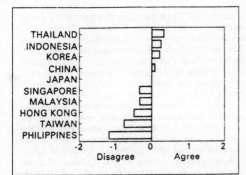

FIGURE 18. Westerners will never really understand the way of doing business here.

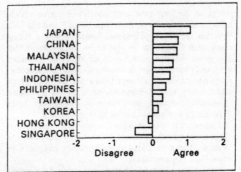

FIGURE 19. Japanese managers are more skilled in dealing with the business environment.

Hong Kong (from the UK)—foreign managers responding to our survey felt at no particular disadvantage. This was particularly the case in the Philippines. Interestingly, Taiwan was not seen to be a particular problem, although managers involved with Japan neither agreed nor disagreed with the statement. Perhaps there are too few well-known examples of foreign businesses racking up successes (compared with failures) for managers to be confident of their abilities.

An alternative reason for the response for Japan may be the relatively high proportion of local (Japanese) managers replying on behalf of their foreign company. This appears to be borne out by the responses to the proposition which questioned Japanese management skills: 'Japanese managers are more skilled than their Western counterparts in understanding and dealing with the business environment in this country'. Inevitably, for Japan itself, there was a reasonably strong 'yes' vote—although not so wholeheartedly as one might have expected (Figure 19).

In Singapore and Hong Kong, Japanese managers are not seen to be more skilful, and in Korea their abilities are seen to be only marginally better than Westerners. On the other hand, in China and in the ASEAN countries which have been major recipients of Japanese foreign investment, Japanese managers are believed to hold some advantage. Even in the Philippines, where relatively little Japanese invest-

ment has been directed and the American position is rather well entrenched, Japanese management is viewed more positively.

We can turn to the statement 'If one applies the business rules of the USA or Europe here, they will not work', to seek some explanation for the higher rating of Japanese managers over Western ones (Figure 20). In every country, Western business methods have to be abandoned or adapted to local business requirements, particularly in China, Japan, and Indonesia. The need for adaptation is least

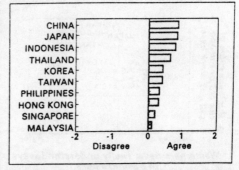

FIGURE 20. Business rules of the USA or Europe will not work in this country.

23

strong in the four countries mentioned above which have historical connections with Europe and the US. Whether the siting of regional headquarters in Hong Kong and Singapore is the cause or effect of the perceived relative acceptance of Western business notions is hard to say. Both are regional communications hubs also. In Singapore one can perhaps point additionally to the preponderance of oil company investments—these tend to have relatively little 'flavour' of any specific style of management.

Figure 21 is another composite graph of responses, which attempts to measure the need for Western firms to adapt their business practices to meet local requirements.

Two clear clusters emerge, separated by a small grouping comprising Taiwan and Korea. The Philippines sits uneasily on the edge, on the one hand ready to agree that Westerners can understand ways of business while on the other agreeing that American or European business methods are not suitable. Japan, China, Indonesia and Thailand are countries where it seems most important to set aside US or European notions if the local business environment is to be penetrated. Hong Kong, Singapore, and Malaysia are economies where Western business assumptions can find greater acceptance.

Ethnic barriers are believed to be a thorny issue for foreign firms in Korea and Japan particularly. The Philippines alone seems not to present this type of problem to foreign business executives. One

question (see Figure 22) suggested that, 'When doing business, it is extremely difficult to "break into" ethnic or classmate informal networks'. In Japan, Old Boy ('OB') connections are tremendously important—by far the most significant being the university classmate system—and represent a thread which runs throughout the fabric of a 'salaryman's' career. In contrast, other countries—which have Overseas Chinese populations that are integrated to a greater or lesser extent into the economy—seem to pose less of a barrier for outsiders. This is perhaps because the network is so loose-knit and informal that outsiders can be absorbed into it eventually; it may also reflect the mercantilist nature of the Chinese who are prepared to do business with anyone (on the right terms); alternatively, it may betray a sense of delusion among foreign managers that they are more readily accepted than in, for example, the much harsher environment of Korea. In explanation of the slightly higher rate of agreement for Indonesia, the ethnic diversity of the country with its many different islands and separate cultures may provide an additional barrier for foreigners to cope with (Figure 22).

China apparently has surprisingly few ethnic barriers to break through; in Hong Kong and Singapore the dependency of the city states on foreign investment to some extent precludes the building of informal barriers. The Philippines, with its generally rather relaxed attitude to business, is the only

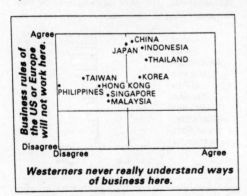

Westerners never really understand ways of business here.

FIGURE 21. Business methods.

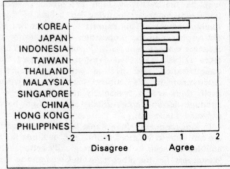

FIGURE 22. It is extremely difficult to 'break into' ethnic or classmate informal networks.

24

country where our respondents disagreed with the statement put forward.

'When dealing with business partners (customers, suppliers, associates ...) there are always some things which are not expressed explicitly, but that one should understand.' Solid agreement across the region was the response to this (Figure 23), emphatic from Korea and China; more mild in the case of Hong Kong and Singapore. The unspoken element is always the hard part for foreigners to grasp: even in the Philippines, which has such a strong American influence, the normal American openness in business (or other) negotiation is not the norm. In the response to this statement we can detect a more unequivocal expression of the response in Figure 20 on US or European business rules, discussed above.

The emotional element in the nature of business in the Asia Pacific region is underlined by the extent of approval with the statement, 'In this country people (employees, suppliers, partners ...) prefer to work on the basis of personal relationships rather than on the basis of rational arguments'. Only in Hong Kong was there marginal disagreement (perhaps as 1997 approaches, heads are ruling more over hearts); for Korea the response was again the strongest. Recognition of this factor does not necessarily mean unfailing comprehension of the message, but it is a step in the right direction. Corporate headquarters, which may be baffled by seemingly in-

congruous decisions made by overseas subsidiaries, need to learn this lesson (Figure 24).

Figure 25 on personal relationships shows an excellent correlation between the answers to the two propositions. Hong Kong and Singapore again emerge as the most friendly environments for 'rational' Westerners: Korea again appears difficult to understand.

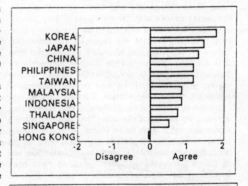

FIGURE 24. People prefer to work on the basis of personal relationships rather than on the basis of rational arguments.

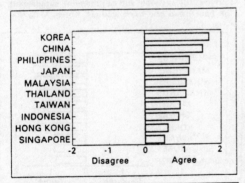

FIGURE 23. When dealing with partners there are always some things not explicitly mentioned but that one should understand.

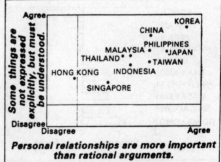

Personal relationships are more important than rational arguments.

FIGURE 25. Personal relationships.

Despite the role of feelings in a business relationship, there remains a role for formal contractual arrangements in some countries. In 6 of the 10 countries covered by the survey respondents disagreed with the statement, 'Legal or contractual agreements are not viewed as definitive and are often interpreted by local business partners as reflecting a lack of trust'. The countries in the region whose legal systems reflect the greatest influence from the UK—Hong Kong, Singapore and Malaysia—showed the strongest variance with the statement (Figure 26).

In contrast, Korea appears to be a country where legal contracts are not well regarded: the emotional links with suppliers and 'contacts' come to the fore. It is also the country where Western influence on business methods is probably the lowest in the region: a reflection of the very strong chauvinistic sentiment to be found there. Taiwan surprisingly came out in agreement with the idea that contractual agreements are not definitive. This may reflect the Confucian ethic also to be found in Japan. Strong tribal influences, especially on Java, will affect attitudes to contractual agreements in Indonesia, but in China Confucian attitudes appear to have been overtaken by socialist principles which demand equality for all.

In Japan, there is room for some agreement with the idea that contracts — distrust, yet as business becomes more international this view is changing. Where foreign firms are involved Japanese firms will now more likely prefer to draw up a formal contract, although there is by no means the same trend towards law suits, as seen in the West. In some industries such as shipping, parties may actually decide tacitly whether a contract is to be 'Japanese-style' (i.e. vaguely worded or even unwritten) or 'Western-style' (i.e. legally watertight).

In contrast to the emotional basis on which some business decisions may be made—the triumph of sentiment over rationality—expressions of anger are clearly not acceptable. The responses to the question which suggested that, 'Overt displays of anger are unacceptable here and can work against companies whose managers express dissatisfaction with anger', reflect the general Western sense of business maturity in Asia Pacific nations—with the possible exception of Taiwan. Hong Kong, and Singapore are the most mature business centres; in Japan, China, and Korea displays of anger may not be welcome, but domestic managers also make then and employees or associates can 'take' it; in the four big ASEAN countries, where the population is 'soft', anger is very badly accepted (Figure 27).

The relative importance of relationships and expert knowledge was investigated through the proposition, 'When doing business, it is often more important to know with "whom" one deals than to have technical expertise' (Figure 28). The overall impression of the region is that technical expertise is fairly readily available and can therefore supplement the benefits of one's connections. Korea, Malaysia,

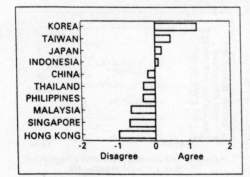

FIGURE 26. Legal or contractual agreements are not viewed as definitive.

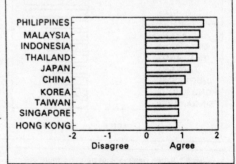

FIGURE 27. Overt displays of anger are unacceptable.

26

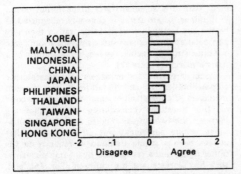

FIGURE 28. It is more important to know with whom one deals than to have technical expertise.

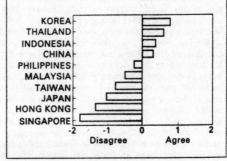

FIGURE 29. Here corruption plays a major role in doing business.

Indonesia, China, and Japan all showed roughly similar levels of agreement with the statement. In these countries, to know people is to have a conduit through which you can provide the technical expertise. In each of the countries also, large government networks and organizations tend to dominate. At the other end of the scale, in Hong Kong, Singapore, and Taiwan, graft is minimal and technical expertise seems to count for more.

These same three countries were among the four most strongly disagreeing with the statement, 'Here corruption plays a major role in doing business' (Figure 29). Disagreement was understandably emphatic in Singapore, where the government has been indubitably successful in rooting out corruption. In Japan, also, corruption is not believed to be an important factor in the normal course of business: recent political scandals show that favour currying does exist, but it has little impact on the average firm—and in public opinion the damage done is at the political level (however briefly it may last). The importance of government backed groups and organizations in Korea, Thailand, Indonesia, and China may explain our respondents' agreement that corruption in these countries is significant.

By combining responses to this question on corruption with the responses charted in Figure 12, concerning the value of a good friend compared with a good product, we can try to establish the relative importance of integrity in business. Figure 30

Good friend better than good product.

FIGURE 30. Integrity in business.

displays the results. In the cluster of countries comprising Korea, Thailand, Indonesia, and China, business principles are clearly different from the more straightforward environment to be found in the cluster formed by Singapore, Hong Kong, Japan, and Taiwan. Malaysia currently falls just outside this group, but might be expected to move to join it over time.

A dispute can be very damaging to the reputation of the foreign firm, which easily risks being cast in a bad light whatever the facts of the matter. The proposition which suggested that 'Indirect communication, sometimes through a third party, is the best way to resolve a dispute or a crisis', found broad agreement except in the more 'Westernized' countries of Hong Kong and Singapore (Figure 31). In China, where third party resolution of conflict was felt to be the most important, political considerations come into play: the régime is extremely sensitive to loss of face, and particularly to any issue which would suggest the country's under-development. Koreans tend also to be extremely vulnerable to any sort of criticism, a result of the historical dependence of the country on either China or Japan. 'Face' is also an important issue in Indonesia (particularly on Java), in Japan, and Thailand.

Three questions in the survey looked at the relationship between employees and the company they work for: two considered the actual relationship between the two groups, while the third reviewed the way in which the connnection is exercised. Confucianism obviously has a role to play in business relationships in the region, though often not to the extent that Western businessmen might believe.

The first of the two questions proposes that, 'In this society a certain social distance should be maintained with employees and business partners, since familiarity makes you vulnerable to loss of authority'. The only country where any real agree-ment with this statement was to be found is the Philippines, where status is generally recognized to be the key factor in a relationship, rather than any particular ability. Perhaps surprisingly, Taiwan came out most strongly against the idea—though only by a narrow margin (Figure 32).

'Local employers and managers have paternalistic responsibilities which are difficult for Western managers to understand or emulate' was the second of the questions considering the relationship between the two groups (Figure 33). In the Philip-pines, where agreement was strongest, there has always been a strong tradition of reliance on the father figure and a recognition by a company owner that his workers are his children. For Thailand, where the degree of agreement was also fairly high, respondents seemed to be reacting to their idea of what local managers do. Responses for China, Japan, Korea, and Indonesia—which were also in agree-ment—appeared to be considering the ability of a Western manager to emulate local managers: he would indeed find it hard to enter into the family life of his employees. In Hong Kong, the attitude is much more one of 'every man for himself', while in Singa-pore the issue is one of government paternalism rather than corporate paternalism.

The third question suggested that, 'Here, it is the duty of a boss to take an active interest in the per-sonal life of his/her employees'. In China, the social responsibilities of the employer are clearly very high;

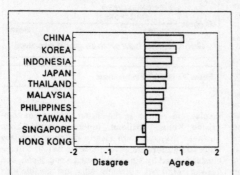

FIGURE 31. Indirect communication is the best way to resolve a dispute or crisis.

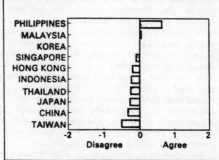

FIGURE 32. In this society a certain social distance should be maintained.

28

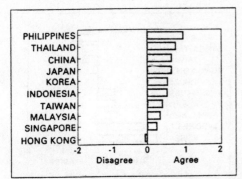

FIGURE 33. Local employers have paternalistic responsibilities which are difficult for Western managers to emulate.

Financial Issues

In some countries where the government and its attendant organizations are very strong, the issue of national development may appear to take priority over shareholders' interests. We tested this idea through the proposition, 'In this country the role of business is more to contribute to national development than to transfer profits to shareholders'.

Only in Korea, China and, to a much smaller extent, Japan did the notion receive any support. The strength of agreement from Korea did not surprise, given that the *chaebol* exist simply for the further-ance of Korea and that nationalist feelings are so strong. In China, where socialism—despite the pace of economic reform—might still have been expected to influence the answers, the concept of the role of business as a contributor to national development received surprisingly low rates of acceptance.

In countries like Malaysia and Indonesia, the government view may well favour the national interest over shareholder interest, but there are sufficient family-owned firms to negate the issue. In Thailand, Taiwan, and (of course) Hong Kong, the government takes a benign attitude to the role of business (Figure 35).

On the question of the motivation of shareholders, we suggested that, 'Shareholders in this country are more interested in long term capital gains than

at the other end of the scale, Hong Kong operates very much on a *laissez-faire* basis. Although some agreement could be found for the proposal in Japan, this probably relates to the obligation on Japanese bosses rather than Western ones: the feeling very much holds true that the Western boss should not become involved. In Korea, where there was only mild support for the proposal, the paternalistic influence is much more tenuous because people tend to change jobs rather frequently (Figure 34).

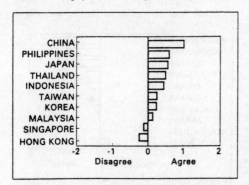

FIGURE 34. It is the duty of a boss to take an active interest in the family life of his/her employees.

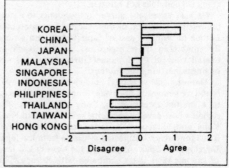

FIGURE 35. The role of business is more to contribute to national development than to transfer profit to shareholders.

29

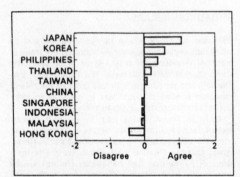

FIGURE 36. Shareholders are more interested in long term capital gains than dividends.

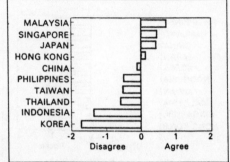

FIGURE 37. The cost of capital is lower than in Europe.

dividends' (Figure 36). The response from Japan, in favour of long term capital gains, can be explained by the overall attitude to business development (which includes reinvestment of profit instead of raising dividends annually), the unwillingness of family businessmen to 'sell the family silver', and the attitude of investors to the stockmarket. Surprisingly, Korean shareholders also appear to be more interested in capital gain than dividends. In Hong Kong, the desire to 'make a fast buck' while the going is good does not surprise.

We also asked our survey respondents to assess the relative attraction of the Asia Pacific region over Europe in terms of cost of capital, risk, and return. By combining these measures, we can reach an overall view of the financial attractiveness of one business location over another.

'Here the cost of capital is lower than in Europe', found agreement in Malaysia, Singapore, Japan and, to a limited extent, Hong Kong (Figure 37). The region's best-developed capital markets are in Hong Kong and Singapore. In Japan, concessionary rate loans for foreign businesses available from the Japan Development Bank supplement the already low level of interest rates there compared with Europe. This alone, however, is not enough to make Japan a low cost business base. Credit squeezes in Korea and, more recently, Indonesia have made these two countries particularly expensive places in which to raise capital. Difficulties for foreign firms in securing

financing locally may be encouraging them to form joint ventures in Korea, in the belief that domestic firms have better access to capital. On the other hand, foreign firms with their own sources of capital are particularly attractive to potential Indonesian partners.

Considering whether 'Financial and business risks are higher than in Europe', political upheavals in the Philippines clearly influence the responses for that country (Figure 38). The high rate of agreement for

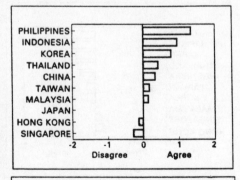

FIGURE 38. Financial and business risks are higher than in Europe.

30

Korea is a measure of the amount of progress the country has yet to make to get itself understood—an acute problem for a country which is so heavily dependent on external trade.

China came out surprisingly favourably in the estimation of our respondents, with risks thought to be only a little higher than in Europe. Business executives are clearly more sanguine about the risk of political reversals than a few years ago, as capitalist business systems become more entrenched. Hong Kong and Singapore again stand out from the rest of the region: risk in these countries is perceived to be lower than in Europe. Confidence in the future role of Hong Kong has clearly been regained.

Figure 39 demonstrates the relative positions of each country when perceptions of the cost of capital are plotted against risk considerations.

Singapore, Hong Kong, Malaysia, and Japan appear in a relatively favourable light, while Korea and Indonesia are seen to be both risky and expensive when compared to Europe. In between these two groups falls another tier, comprising China, Taiwan, and Thailand, where costs and risks are somewhat higher than in Europe.

To the last remaining statement in our survey left to be considered' 'Returns on investments here are higher than in Europe', negative responses were given only for Korea and Japan, with a neutral outcome for the Philippines. Taiwan, Malaysia, and Hong Kong—all of which are generally viewed as

friendly environments for foreign investors—are also thought to give them the best returns (Figure 40).

Figure 41 shows how rates of return and the cost of capital combine to present a slightly different view of a country's attractiveness as an investment location.

Singapore, Hong Kong, and Malaysia appear in a favourable light compared with Japan which offers a rather lower perceived rate of return. Korea again fails to attract, while potential investors in Taiwan, China, and the Philippines may be prepared to

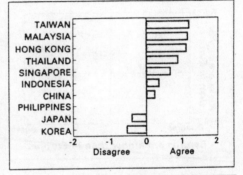

FIGURE 40. Returns on investments are higher than in Europe.

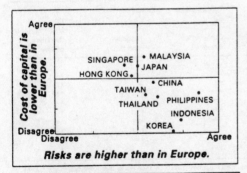

FIGURE 39. Risk and cost of capital.

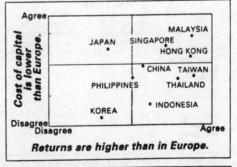

FIGURE 41. Return and cost of capital.

accept slightly higher costs of capital in order to win a higher rate of return.

Our final chart combines measures of risk and return. A group of five countries—Taiwan, Malaysia, Hong Kong, Singapore, and Thailand—seems to offer an attractive balance between the two. Korea again fails to proffer any compelling reason for investment there, while potential investors in Japan may be discouraged by the low rate of return against an average risk consideration (Figure 42).

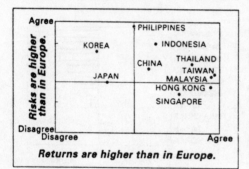

FIGURE 42. Risk/return.

Conclusion

The major features of the business environment in the Asia Pacific region have been summarized in Table 2 according to five main characteristics grouped under two dimensions.

One dimension—referred to as the *Competitive context*—includes characteristics such as the need to enter into a complex network of relationships and the need to decode particular business rules, which make business life more or less familiar to Western participants.

A second dimension, referred to as the *Political, ethical and legal context*, is concerned with the degree of government intervention, the integrity of business practices and the legal framework of business actions, all of which affect the transparency of the rules of the game in different countries.

The mapping of the 10 countries in the region along these two dimensions is represented in Figure 43.

It comes as no surprise that overall, Singapore and Hong Kong are perceived by the respondents of our survey to be the places where the rules of the business game seem the clearest and the most familiar. The position of Korea, which is attributed the worst scores on both dimensions, indicates that Western managers operating in this country experience enormous difficulties in understanding and

TABLE 2. Summary of contextual characteristics in the Asia Pacific region.

| | Competitive context | | Political, legal and ethical context | | |
	(A) Importance of networks and relationships	(B) Ambiguity in understanding business rules	(C) Government influence	(D) Integrity issues	(E) Uncertainty of the rules of law
Hong Kong	•	—	—	—	—
Singapore	•	—	—	—	—
Japan	•••	•••	••	—	••
Korea	•••	•••	•••	••	•••
Taiwan	••	•	•	—	•
China	•••	••	•••	••	•
Indonesia	••	•••	•••	•••	••
Thailand	••	•••	••	•••	•
Philippines	•••	—	••	•••	•
Malaysia	••	•	•••		•

Notes: The stars (*, **, ***) indicate the intensity of the characteristic in each country based on answers to the questions in the survey.
(A) is based on scores to questions in Figures 5, 6, 12, 14, 23, 24, 28.   (D) is based on scores to questions in Figures 12, 29.
(B) is based on scores to questions in Figures 18, 20, 22.   (E) is based on scores to questions in Figures 16, 17, 26, 31.
(C) is based on scores to questions in Figures 1, 2, 3.

32

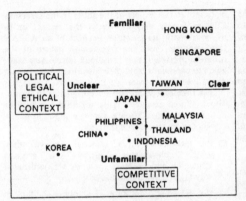

FIGURE 43. The business context in Asia Pacific.

dealing with the business environment. The recent boom in the Southern provinces and their proximity to Hong Kong may explain why China, generally considered to be a difficult country, scores better than Korea and is reasonably close to Indonesia, the Philippines, and Thailand. The position of Japan on this map confirms the disquiet of Western managers in dealing with the complex Japanese industrial environment. In spite of a well developed infrastructure and accessible and reliable sources of data, Japan is still considered to be an unfamiliar country in which to do business. The positive perception of Malaysia with regard to the political, legal, and ethical context is due to the fact that European managers and particularly British ones have a traditional relationship with that country.

Although it may be dangerous to generalize on the basis of a single survey, one can observe that the information extracted from the responses confirms the prevailing idea that, with the exception of Singapore and Hong Kong, Asia Pacific is perceived as complex and unfamiliar to a large proportion of Western managers. This perception may be due to a lack of experience. Since statistics on foreign investments show a weak and only relatively recent flow of European implantations, this explanation of lack of experience seems valid. If this is the case we can expect that with time, education, and experience Asia will lose its mystery for the European executive.

This is what we could call the *adaptation* requirement: in order to understand and deal with the Asian context one needs to learn about it progressively and in consequence adapt one's way of doing things. *One has to do things differently.*

There is an alternative explanation, which posits that the Asian context is so fundamentally foreign to the Western mind—as the quotation of Lord Macartney at the beginning of this article would suggest—that in order to function within it one must change the basic cognitive architecture through which one interprets reality, and accordingly refashion the way one acts. We could call this the *transformation* requirement: in order to cope with Asia one has to transform the way one thinks, the way one judges and evaluates events, and also the way one acts. *One has to do different things.* Rather than being a function of time, a sort of 'cultural revolution' is required.

Probably, as usual, there is a need for both adaptation and transformation, and here lies the real challenge of doing business in Asia Pacific. For companies it implies quite a substantive change in management systems and human resources management practices: domains such as decision-making criteria, strategic planning, evaluation of performances, career management, and training have to take into account this dual need of transformation and adaptation. In our view, the key to future strategic development in the region will belong to those companies which have developed the skill of combining these two requirements in their organizational behaviour.

Implications for Companies and Managers

During the 1980s, many multinational corporations moved to a 'global' approach in managing their operations. This has shifted the power structure from a geographical hierarchy to one which favours the managers in charge of global businesses. However, even for the most 'global-minded' manager it rapidly becomes very obvious, that the sheer variety, strategic distance, and the specific needs of the Asia Pacific competitive climate require a regional perspective to enable companies to gather intelligence, mobilize their forces and focus their energies. The results presented in this survey show that, in this region, 'globalism' reaches its limits. In order to succeed, management needs to develop some sort of 'regional' perspective.

But adapting a regional 'structure' is not enough, because the essence of management problems in Asia Pacific lies in the developing attitudes and 'mind sets' as well as in the enhancing of specific competencies. The building of relationships are not so much the result of organizational structures but rather of internal 'processes'. The experiences of companies like Unilever, Shell, ABB, l'Oréal and Wella which have developed a presence in the region suggest that commitment, attitudes, and information-sharing are important ingredients of success. These are not developed through formal structures or systems but because of the way decisions are made, how priorities are set, how investments are approved and implemented; the mannner in which information is gathered and distributed; how man-power is recruited, trained, and promoted; how control is exercised; and finally, how strategies are debated and formulated.

Four processes require particular attention: strategy formulation, budgeting, evaluation and learning.

or to ignore the impact of the shifts in the Overseas Chinese family network across the region, or to underestimate the potential benefits of an ASEAN joint-venture. Also, the fragmented nature of the different markets makes it difficult for country man-agers to personally 'sell' their ideas to global product executives at the centre.

It is therefore important for companies to formu-late 'regional strategy', tying together the various country strategies. Then a strategic input from the region can be channelled through:

❑ the formulation of a 'regional strategic plan' which consolidates country and product strategies and presents them in a co-ordinated way to corporate headquarters;

❑ the systematic addition of a 'regional plan' to global product plans;

❑ the scheduling of regional strategic meetings where global product managers meet with regional executives and compare their own global plans with the specific local requirements;

❑ the establishment of a review and appeal process by regional managers for global product plans before their sanctioning at the corporate level.

Strategy Formulation
The processes of strategy formulation consist in translating strategic ambition into actions requiring specific allocations of financial and human re-sources. To do this, a variety of tasks must be per-formed. On an analytical level this requires structur-ing and interpreting information, forecasting and calculating possible outcomes, generating alterna-tives, designing sets of choices, and, finally, nego-tiating internally to obtain acceptance and resources. In a multinational corporation, this process takes place at three levels: the business level, the country level, and finally, with endorsement from the corpor-ate level. Three main factors operate in favour of a regional perspective in strategy formulation. First, the region's rapidly changing business climate, and secondly, the 'strategic distance' of the marketing and competitive climates can lead to significant lapses and delays in the time it takes for global managers to grasp the importance of events there. Companies cannot afford to disregard the import-ance of 'grey imports' from one country to another,

Budgeting
Capital and operating budgeting systems are normally well modified in companies. Planning and budgeting procedures define the criteria for capital investments approval and set down the rules for budget preparation. In multinational corporations, rules and procedures tend to be standard and the criteria by which projects and plans are evaluated and approved tend to be the same for every product line and country. If no corrective element is 'brought in' to adjust these budgets for specific regional characteristics, there is a risk of considerable bias in the allocation of resources. In the Asia Pacific region where the business environment is often perceived as more risky than in the US or Europe, with a long term pay-off, and a strong need to spend time and effort to build relationships, etc., a standard approach to budgeting will not provide the resources needed to build a long term presence. Research in several companies in the region has revealed a strong resistance to adapt the rules and procedures, but in practice firms which are successful there

usually have a flexible way of framing budgets.* What counts is the overall Asian ambition of the corporation and also the 'power' of the executives in charge of Asia. However, one can argue that with the multiplicity of opportunities arising from the region, a purely *ad hoc* approach to budgeting is no longer sufficient and that corporations need to acknowledge that a 'different perspective', is needed when it comes to deciding about investments and resource allocation in the region.

Evaluation
The classical criteria for evaluating business performance do not always reflect the peculiarities of Asian environments. For instance, a quick marketing success may be a good yardstick for evaluating a marketing manager in Europe or the United States, but may be totally inappropriate to the Asia Pacific region, where the business cultures often require the gradual building of a network of contacts before a company can expect to see progress reflected in sales. *Political and negotiation skills, the ability to develop team-work, and to recruit and motivate local staff are more relevant criteria than return on business assets.* The argument here is not that managers should neglect return on assets but that if management focus only on immediate profits and if they reward people only on that basis the company is

*In earlier research done at the Euro Asia Centre with three European companies, respondents indicated that they did not modify their budgeting systems for Asia, but it was still possible to make 'strategic investments' there. This is confirmed by many other contacts that the authors have developed in the region over the years. It shows that formal systems are only a minor element of the actual decision-making mechanisms in a corporation, a fact that is well known to organization theorists.

not likely to build a basis for long term success. Just to mention one example: Merlin Gerin, a French producer of electrical equipment, set up a joint venture in Tianjin in 1987. In 1990, the company was doing very poorly and on the basis of profitability should have closed the business. Today it is working very profitably and growing. A similar example is the Xian-Janssen joint venture in the pharmaceutical sector in China or the Bell-Shanghai telecom operation.

Learning
For Western managers, the experience of doing business in Asia and the negative and positive lessons learned are assimilated on an individual level. The problem, for Western firms, is that because these managers are highly mobile, their experiential knowledge of Asia and Asian enterprise cultures is often difficult to institutionalize and retain. One organizational challenge is to find effective mechanisms for translating individual experience and knowledge and incorporating it into an ongoing process of organizational learning and renewal. To cite just a few examples of sucessful methods: certain Western firms have found it useful to do this by preparing *videos* on the Asian corporate culture, or by circulating *case studies* on the firm's experiences in Asia. Another way to conserve organizational learning is to ensure *a better hand-over* between expatriates and their successors, so the expertise of experienced managers is 'recycled' and institutionalized. After expatriate managers are shifted from Asia back to headquarters they should be *debriefed* and asked to share and pass on their Asia Pacific experience in some way.

35

Reference

(1) Philippe Lasserre and Jocelyn Probert, Strategic and Marketing Intelligence in Asia Pacific, Euro-Asia Centre Research Series, No 8, January (1992).

Philippe Lasserre is Professor of Strategy and Management at INSEAD Euro-Asia Centre.

Jocelyn Probert is a Research Analyst at INSEAD Euro-Asia Centre.

[16]

© Academy of Management Review
1991, Vol. 16, No. 2, 291-317.

TOWARD A COMPREHENSIVE MODEL OF INTERNATIONAL ADJUSTMENT: AN INTEGRATION OF MULTIPLE THEORETICAL PERSPECTIVES

J. STEWART BLACK
Dartmouth College
MARK MENDENHALL
University of Tennessee, Chattanooga
GARY ODDOU
San Jose State University

Primarily because of the significant rate and costs of failed international assignments, the attention paid by scholars to the topic of international adjustment has increased recently. Unfortunately, most of the work has been without substantial theoretical grounding. In an effort to move toward a theoretical framework for guiding future research, this article integrates theoretical and empirical work of both the international and the domestic adjustment literatures. This integration provides a more comprehensive framework than might be obtained from either of the literatures alone.

The internationalization of the world's markets has led to a significant increase in the cross-cultural interactions between businesspeople, and in the business world, the use of expatriate managers in this "global village" has led to large numbers of Americans living and working overseas and having to adjust not only to a new work culture, but also to new ways of living. Unfortunately, research shows that many Americans do not succeed in their overseas assignments. Between 16 and 40 percent of all American employees sent overseas return from their assignments early, and each premature return costs a firm roughly $100,000 (Baker & Ivancevich, 1971; Black, 1988; Copeland & Griggs, 1985; Misa & Fabricatore, 1979; Tung, 1982). In addition to these costs, approximately 30 to 50 percent of American expatriates, whose average compensation package is $250,000 per year, stay at their international assignments, but are considered ineffective or marginally effective by their firms (Copeland & Griggs, 1985).

Scholars have only focused their research efforts on the problem of expatriate adjustment and effectiveness since the late 1970s. Previous to that time, some research had been conducted on Peace Corps volunteers and foreign exchange students, but little work was done on expatriate managers (see Church, 1982, for a review). The past decade has seen an increase in research on cross-cultural adjustment; however, to date, little theoretical work has been conducted in the area of international adjustment of expatriates—the existing literature consists mostly of anecdotal or atheoretical empirical efforts to understand the phenomenon (Adler, 1983; Kyi, 1988; Mendenhall & Oddou, 1985; Schollhammer, 1975).

Conversely, the literature in the area of domestic (U.S./Canada) transfers and adjustment is much richer theoretically; researchers in this area have increasingly focused their efforts on understanding how an individual adjusts to a new organizational setting either after a transfer or upon initial entry into the firm (Ashford & Taylor, 1990; Feldman, 1976; Feldman & Brett, 1983; Jones, 1986; Latack, 1984; Louis, 1980a; Nicholson, 1984; Pinder & Schroeder, 1987; Van Maanen & Schein, 1979). To date, scholars in the area of international human resource management have not utilized the domestic adjustment literature in order to formulate theories or models that would assist them in understanding the international adjustment process.

Perhaps this has not occurred because although the theories of adjustment of employees to new organizational settings in the domestic context may have some application to adjustment in the international context, there seem to be substantial differences between domestic and international (or cross-cultural) adjustment. For example, most domestic adjustments do not involve significant changes in the nonwork environment; living in Los Angeles versus New York may be quite different in many ways, but the language, cultural, economic, social, and political contexts are significantly familiar. This is not the norm for international adjustments. Moving from the United States to a foreign country often involves changes in the job the individual performs and the corporate culture in which responsibilities are executed; it can also involve dealing with unfamiliar norms related to the general culture, business practices, living conditions, weather, food, health care, daily customs, and political systems—plus facing a foreign language on a daily basis.

Because the work as well as the nonwork contexts usually change during an international adjustment, not only are unique variables involved, but it also seems possible that different relationships among the variables may also exist. Thus, given (1) the substantial contextual differences between domestic and international adjustment, (2) the relevance of the issue to today's organizations, and (3) the lack of theoretical work in the area of international adjustment, it is appropriate to move toward a theoretical framework and research agenda concerning international adjustment.

This article has three basic objectives. The first is to review the literature on international adjustment, delineating the important variables that scholars have found to influence international adjustment. The second is to review the theoretical literature on domestic adjustment, exploring what it suggests about international adjustment. The third is to integrate what is known and what seems logically compelling from both literatures into a theoretical framework of international adjustment, deriving propositions in an effort to establish a basic research agenda for the future.

REVIEW OF THE INTERNATIONAL ADJUSTMENT LITERATURE

Although international adjustment has received increased scholarly attention, the majority of the writing has been anecdotal in nature, and few scholars have rigorously investigated the phenomenon, empirically or theoretically (Adler, 1983; Black & Mendenhall, 1990; Kyi, 1988; Schollhammer, 1975). Thus, this section summarizes the findings of this empirical research to ascertain if any themes or dimensions exist. Many articles have reviewed parts of the empirical cross-cultural adjustment literature; therefore, we begin by *reviewing the review articles* of the field. Recent empirical articles, which postdated the review articles, are also included.

Five dimensions (or themes) emerged as components of the cross-cultural adjustment process: (1) predeparture training, (2) previous overseas experience, (3) organizational selection mechanisms, (4) individual skills, and (5) nonwork factors. The first three dimensions describe issues that exist before expatriates leave their home countries, and the remaining two deal with issues that become relevant after the expatriates arrive at their foreign assignments.

Predeparture Training

Three review articles have covered the relationship between predeparture training and subsequent cross-cultural adjustment (Black & Mendenhall, 1990; Fiedler, Mitchell, & Triandis, 1971; Mitchell, Dossett, Fiedler, & Triandis, 1972). Black and Mendenhall (1990) subsumed within their review the findings of the previous two, and they also reviewed more comprehensively the entire cross-cultural training effectiveness literature. Additionally, they critiqued the methodology of the studies they reviewed and found that 48 percent included control groups and nearly half of these studies included both the use of control groups and longitudinal designs. These and other studies that had slightly less rigorous designs found support for a positive relationship between cross-cultural training and cross-cultural adjustment, cross-cultural skill development and job performance. They concluded their review of the literature by stating: "Thus, the empirical literature gives guarded support to the proposition that cross-cultural training has a positive impact on cross-cultural effectiveness" (Black & Mendenhall, 1990: 120).

Previous Overseas Experience

It is logical to assume that previous experience living overseas—especially in the same foreign country to which a person is currently assigned—should facilitate adjustment, even though some culture shock will still occur. Church (1982: 549) found in his review of the empirical literature in this area that "empirical findings support the importance of accurate prior cultural experience or prior exposure . . . for sojourner adjustment." Black (1988) discovered that previous overseas work experience was related to work adjustment for expatriates, but not to general adjustment. Torbiorn

(1982) found that specific length of previous overseas experience was not related to higher levels of adjustment; thus, quantity of previous overseas experience does not seem to necessarily relate to current overseas adjustment. Overall, though, previous overseas experience does seem to facilitate the adjustment process. Exactly how that happens or what factors inhibit or magnify the impact of previous experience has yet to be comprehensively determined by scholars in the field.

Organizational Selection Criteria and Mechanisms

In their review of the empirical expatriate selection literature, Mendenhall, Dunbar, and Oddou stated that "MNCs [multinational corporations] consistently overlook key criteria that are predictive of overseas success in their recruiting and screening of potential overseas workers" (1987: 334). Many researchers have noted that American MNCs, despite the evidence that a variety of skills are necessary for success in an overseas assignment, focus only on one selection criterion: technical competence. (For a review, see Mendenhall et al., 1987; also see Hays, 1974; Miller, 1973; Tung, 1981.)

Why firms focus on only one important skill necessary for overseas success is reflected in a statement by a respondent in Baker and Ivancevich's (1971: 40) study: "Managing [a] company is a scientific art. The executive accomplishing the task in New York can surely perform as adequately in Hong Kong." This attitude among managers making selection decisions may reflect why Tung (1981) discovered that only 5 percent of the firms in her sample administered tests to determine the degree to which candidates possessed cross-cultural skills. In a 1987 study, Moran, Stahl, and Boyer, Inc., found that only 35 percent of the American firms in their sample selected expatriates from multiple candidates, and that technical job-related experience and technical job skills were the two most important criteria used in selecting candidates for overseas posts. Thus, the trend of a unidimensional selection practice among American MNCs, first delineated in the early 1970s, has continued throughout the 1980s as well.

Individual Skills

Many researchers have investigated the skills necessary for an executive to be effective in a cross-cultural setting. (For reviews see Brein & David, 1971; Church, 1982; Mendenhall & Oddou, 1985; Stening, 1979.) These skills have been categorized by Mendenhall and Oddou (1985) into three dimensions: (1) the self-dimension, which encompasses skills that enable the expatriate to maintain mental health, psychological well-being, self-efficacy, and effective stress management; (2) the relationship dimension, which constitutes the array of skills necessary for the fostering of relationships with host nationals; and (3) the perception dimension, which entails the cognitive abilities that allow the expatriate to correctly perceive and evaluate the host environment and its actors.

Nonwork Factors

The first nonwork factor that the empirical literature suggests is important to international adjustment is *culture novelty,* or what Mendenhall and Oddou (1985) referred to as *culture toughness.* Some countries' cultures seem to be more difficult to adapt to than others. Church (1982: 547) referred to this phenomenon as *cultural distance* and noted that "empirical studies have generally supported this view" that the more culturally distant or different a host culture is from a person's own, the more difficult it is for him or her to adjust. Mendenhall and Oddou, in their 1985 review, reached the same conclusion. Torbiorn (1982) noted that cultural novelty has its largest impact on expatriates during the first two years of their assignments; after that, the impact of cultural novelty diminishes somewhat.

The second major nonwork factor concerns the adjustment of the spouse and family of the expatriate. Although the expatriate may possess the necessary skills for successful international adjustment, if his or her spouse does not possess these same skills, an aborted assignment may ensue simply because the spouse or family members cannot adjust to the new culture. Past reviews have consistently supported the importance of this nonwork factor (Church, 1982; Mendenhall & Oddou, 1985), and a study by Black and Stephens (1989) provides further support for this conclusion on the basis of a positive and significant relationship between the adjustment of expatriates and spouses for a large sample of American expatriates on assignment in several different countries.

Summary of the International Adjustment Literature

Thus, based on a review of the international adjustment literature three categories of predeparture variables (i.e., previous experience, predeparture training, and candidate selection) and two postarrival variables (i.e., individual skills and nonwork factors) have been identified. It should also be noted that the international adjustment literature has been primarily focused on the degree of overall adjustment to the new culture. Figure 1 provides a rough sketch of how these various categories of variables are conceptually related to international adjustment.

REVIEW OF THE DOMESTIC ADJUSTMENT LITERATURE

Domestic adjustment also involves the basic process of adjusting to a new setting; therefore, this literature may provide important insights for constructing a theoretical framework for international adjustment. Consequently, the following sections briefly review four areas of research that are related to individual adjustment (Ashford & Taylor, 1990): (1) organizational socialization, (2) career transitions and sense making, (3) work role transitions, and (4) relocation/domestic transfers. The relevance of each of these areas of theory and research will be discussed in a later section.

296   *Academy of Management Review*   April

FIGURE 1
Relationships Based on International Adjustment Literature

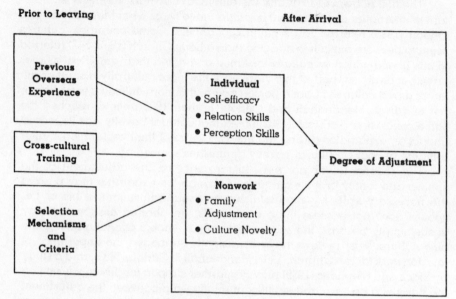

Organizational Socialization Literature

According to Van Maanen and Schein (1979: 211–212), "Organizational socialization refers minimally . . . to the fashion in which an individual is taught and learns what behaviors and perspectives are customary and desirable within the work setting as well as what ones are not." Much of the research on this topic can be divided into two general areas: (1) socialization stages and (2) socialization tactics and individual responses to socialization efforts.

Many scholars have proposed that socialization occurs in stages. Although slight variations exist among the stage models, Fisher's (1986) three-stage model captures most of what has been discussed in this area. The first stage is often referred to as *anticipatory socialization* (Brief, Aldag, Van Sell, & Melone, 1979; Feldman, 1976; Louis, 1980b). In this stage, individuals make anticipatory adjustments to the organization through means such as organizational choice, organizational selection, and expectation formulation. Essentially, the more complete and accurate the anticipatory socialization, the greater the ease and speed of adjustment to the new organization (Fisher, 1986).

The second stage of socialization has been referred to as the *encounter stage* (see Fisher, 1986, for a review). During this phase the individual begins to master the tasks of the job and the relationships with others involved in working in the new organization. At this point, expectations are confirmed or disconfirmed. In general, accurate individual expectations, low role ambiguity, and low role conflict facilitate a person's adjustment to the organization during the encounter stage.

The final stage has been referred to as the *role management* stage by Feldman (1976). During this stage the individual moves toward becoming a fully accepted member of the organization. Adjustments to the organization, such as adopting organizational norms or values, are more incremental in nature at this point.

The second major area of investigation relating to organizational socialization concerns the tactics that organizations use to socialize newcomers and the responses of newcomers to these efforts. Van Maanen and Schein (1979) provided one of the most detailed theoretical discussions of the various tactics organizations use and the expected reactions from newcomers. Though space does not permit a complete review of their theoretical arguments, in general, they suggested that institutional tactics lead to custodial responses by newcomers and that individual tactics lead to innovative responses. With the exception of the relationship between two specific tactics and individual responses, Jones (1986) found general empirical support for Van Maanen and Schein's (1979) arguments. Jones (1986) also found that individuals with high levels of self-efficacy were less influenced by institutional socialization tactics to respond in a custodial manner than individuals with low levels of self-efficacy.

Career Transitions and Sensemaking Literature

This area of study is perhaps best codified in two articles by Louis (1980a, 1980b), who proposed a typology of transitions and a process of how individuals adjust to transitions. Louis's (1980b) typology includes both interrole and intrarole transitions. Louis cited five interrole transitions (i.e., when a new and different role is taken): (1) entry/reentry, (2) intracompany, (3) intercompany, (4) interprofession, and (5) exit. *Entry/reentry* role transitions describe the changes in roles when a person moves from one context to another, such as from school to work or from being single to being married. When a person moves from one division to another within the same company, where co-workers, procedures, and the physical setting are likely to change, this describes an *intracompany* role transition. Similarly, if an individual experiences the same type of changes, but moves from one company to another, this refers to an *intercompany* transition. *Interprofessional* transitions occur when individuals change from one profession to another (e.g., dentist to teacher, attorney to Boy Scouts of America leader). Finally, *exit roles* describe the transitions of individuals who voluntarily or involuntarily leave one organization or context and enter another (e.g., stopping work for parenthood, being fired, joining another organization).

Intrarole transitions, in contrast, describe those situations in which a person takes a new orientation toward an old role. Louis described four intrarole transitions: (1) intrarole adjustment, (2) extrarole adjustment, (3) role/career-stage transition, and (4) life-stage transition. An *intrarole* adjustment represents the changes an individual makes toward his or her role over the duration of time. An *extrarole* adjustment describes the changes a person makes in one role as a result of a new role or changes in an old role. For example, an individual might decide to work fewer hours as a result of getting married due to apparent value changes. Both of the preceding transitions might well be unconscious changes the individual makes. A *role/career-stage* transition represents the changes an individual experiences as a result of progressing through the career life cycle. Finally, when a person experiences the psychological changes of moving from adolescence to adulthood, he or she is going through a *life-stage* transition. In moving through the above roles, then, an individual acts and reacts differently throughout the process. However, there are certain commonalities to the experience and the adjustment process. Louis (1980a) described the adjustment process in terms of three constructs—change, contrast, and surprise—and sensemaking.

Constructs in the adjustment process. *Change* occurs when there is an objective difference in a major feature between the new and old settings. The more such changes occur, the greater the person's unfamiliarity with the new situation, and the greater his or her difficulty in adjusting. These types of changes can be represented by hierarchical or functional differences between the old and new (Schein, 1971) or by status differences. *Contrast*, however, describes changes that are noticed internally and are "perceived products of the individual's experience in the new setting and role (i.e., features identified as figures against the background of a total field)" (Louis, 1980a: 331). The important distinction between change and contrast is that change relates to an external perspective, whereas contrast describes an internal perspective. The third construct, *surprise*, represents the difference between a person's expectations, which might be conscious or unconscious, and what actually occurs.

Sensemaking in the adjustment process. In Louis's model, the pertinent question relates to how an individual makes sense out of his or her new experience. How does the individual cope? To a certain extent, the individual unconsciously acts out of programmed scripts. This is particularly true when the situation confronted is perceived as similar to previous experiences. In other cases, the individual must think and use rational means to understand the situation, and this occurs at a conscious level. Research has indicated that a person uses rational means to sort out confusion when confronted with a novel situation or with a surprise (e.g., unmet expectations) (Abelson, 1976; Langer, 1978). Festinger's (1956) theory of cognitive dissonance explains the action: When what is expected does not happen, individuals must rationalize it through reanalysis, or what Louis referred to as a "need . . . for a return to equilibrium" (1980a: 337).

In summary, when an individual changes roles, certain elements in the total situation bring about confusion. The transition is compounded or simplified by the number and importance of novel or unexpected elements in the situation and by the person's internal reaction to those surprises. Discrepant events require explanations, which are developed, and attributions are made based primarily on an individual's familiarity with past events and his or her expectations about the present situation. Based on this, modifications in the person's expectations are made for future events, and the cycle continues.

The inputs for an individual's attempt to understand the novel or unexpected situation come from several sources: past experiences, a set of cultural assumptions, and input from associates. Unfortunately, these sources are often inadequate because the person does not have enough history in the new context or isn't acquainted with enough or the right people to help interpret the discrepancies or novelties in the novel context.

Work Role Transition Literature

In 1984, Nicholson's article, "A Theory of Work Role Transitions," and Dawis and Lofquist's work, *A Psychological Theory of Work Adjustment*, provided a codification of theoretical ideas on the topic of work role transitions. Although these two works are by no means the only ones on work role transitions, they are key theoretical exemplars and include most of the variables and underlying theoretical arguments of other works in the area. Both works focused on variables that predict how an individual will adjust to the work role change, or *mode of adjustment*, as both Nicholson (1984) and Dawis and Lofquist (1984) called it. Dawis and Lofquist (1984) argued that individuals can adjust by changing the environment in the new situation to more readily correspond to or match their needs and abilities and labeled this mode of adjustment as *active*. They also argued that individuals can adjust to the new situation by changing themselves and labeled this mode of adjustment as *reactive*.

Although Dawis and Lofquist (1984) acknowledged that individuals may not use one or the other of these modes of adjustment exclusively, their theory and research focused primarily on work factors that would predict active or reactive modes of adjustment. In many ways, their notions of active and reactive adjustment are similar to Van Maanen and Schein's (1979) concepts of role innovation and custodial response, respectively. Nicholson (1984) extended these ideas to a two-by-two matrix. Adjustment made by changing neither self nor the situation he termed *replication*. Adjustment made by changing self but not the situation he termed *absorption*. Adjustment made by changing the situation but not self was called *determination*. Finally, adjustment made by changing both self and the situation was termed *exploration*.

According to Dawis and Lofquist (1984), the first set of antecedents of mode of adjustment is the flexibility of the work environment which moderated the mode of adjustment. Nicholson (1984) referred to this notion as *role discretion*, and both sets of scholars argued that greater role discretion leads to modes of adjustment that focus on adjustment through changing the situation rather than changing aspects of the individual. Additionally, Nicholson (1984) concluded that low role novelty leads to modes of adjustment focused on changing the situation and high role novelty leads to modes focused on changing aspects of the individual.

The second set of antecedents of mode of adjustment were addressed by Nicholson (1984), who termed it *induction-socialization processes*. These were essentially the same socialization tactics and predictions made by Van Maanen and Schein (1979), although Nicholson addressed only three of the six sets of tactics. In agreement with Van Maanen and Schein (1979), Nicholson argued that socialization tactics that are sequential and serial and that involve divestiture lead individuals to change aspects of themselves, whereas socialization tactics that are random and disjunctive and that involve divestiture lead individuals to change aspects of their work role.

Nicholson (1984) believed that shifts in role discretion also affect a person's mode of adjustment. Essentially, Nicholson argued that upward shifts in role discretion lead to modes of adjustment focused on individuals making changes in themselves, whereas downward shifts lead to modes focused on individuals changing aspects of the work role. Nicholson also argued that two individual variables also affect mode of adjustment. He asserted that low desire for feedback and low need for control lead to adjustment by changing neither aspects of the work role nor the individual and that high desire for feedback and high need for control lead to adjustment by changes in both aspects of the work role and of the individual.

Although not addressed by Nicholson (1984), Dawis and Lofquist (1984) also defined the degree of adjustment as well as mode of adjustment. They defined degree of adjustment as the gap between the extent to which the work environment meets the needs of the individual (termed *satisfaction*) plus the gap between the extent to which the individual's abilities meet the demands of the work role (termed *satisfactoriness*). The narrower the total gap, the more adjusted the individual was considered to be. Dawis and Lofquist (1984) argued that role ambiguity, role novelty, and role conflict would inhibit the degree of work adjustment because these work variables reduced the ability of the individual and the organization to appropriately match rewards with individual needs and individual abilities with role demands.

Relocation Literature

Many researchers have studied the topic of employee relocation by examining both the effect that relocation has on a number of personal, work, and family outcomes and the factors that affect adjustment after relocation. Studies that have examined the antecedents of adjustment after relocation are the most relevant to the focus of this article. In her review of the literature, Brett stated that "the studies are typically descriptive and atheoretical" (1980: 104). However, Brett (1980) added a theoretical perspective to the topic and asserted that one of the primary processes in relocation adjustment is that of reasserting control through reducing uncertainty. The underlying notion was that the greater the disruption of prior routine caused by the relocation, the greater the resulting uncertainty, and the longer it would take before the uncertainty would be reduced to a comfortable level. Brett (1980) argued that role conflict, role ambiguity, role novelty, and work environment novelty—because these factors tend to increase uncertainty—would be negatively related to adjustment after relocation (i.e., these factors inhibited a smooth and quick adjustment).

On the basis of essentially this theoretical premise (Brett, 1980), Pinder and Schroeder (1987) found that role clarity and social support from supervisor and co-workers facilitated adjustment, and role novelty inhibited adjustment after a relocation transfer. Thus, this area of research suggests that job factors (e.g., role ambiguity, role conflict, role novelty) or organizational factors (e.g., organization culture novelty) that increase uncertainty will inhibit adjustment, whereas job factors (e.g., role clarity) or organization factors (e.g., social support) that reduce uncertainty will facilitate adjustment.

Summary of the Domestic Adjustment Literature

The socialization and work role adjustment literatures, in general, have focused on mode of adjustment as the outcome of interest, whereas the relocation and sensemaking literatures have focused on the degree of adjustment. The research on socialization, relocation, and surprise and sensemaking suggests that individuals make anticipatory adjustments before they actually encounter the new situation; it also suggests the importance of accurate expectations to facilitate adjustment. Further, the socialization literature emphasizes the importance of proper selection criteria and mechanisms relative to effective socialization. Regarding the period after individuals enter the new situation, the work role transition literature and the relocation literature emphasize the importance of job-related variables as antecedents of degree of adjustment. The socialization literature and the work role transition theory, particularly Nicholson (1984), stress the importance of organizational socialization tactics as antecedents to mode of adjustment. The surprise and sensemaking and relocation literatures emphasize the importance of organizational culture or work environment novelty and the social support of co-workers and supervisor as important antecedents of degree of adjustment. Figure 2 provides a rough sketch of how these various factors fit together as antecedents of both mode and degree of adjustment within the domestic context.

THEORETICAL FRAMEWORK AND RESEARCH AGENDA

The domestic and international adjustment literatures have at least one common and underlying thread: In both literatures an individual leaves a familiar setting and enters an unfamiliar one. Because the new setting is unfamiliar, it upsets old routines and creates psychological uncertainty. Scholars from both literatures either argue or imply that individuals generally have a desire to reduce the uncertainty inherent in the new setting, especially concerning new behaviors that might be required or expected

302 *Academy of Management Review* April

FIGURE 2
Relationships Based on Domestic Adjustment Literature

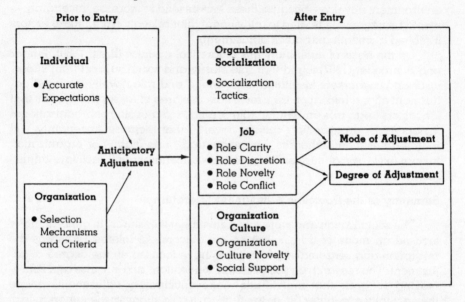

and old behaviors that would be considered unacceptable or inappropriate. Thus, if information concerning these issues is available before people actually enter the new situation, anticipatory adjustments can be made. Once they are actually in the new situation, individuals continue to reduce the uncertainty and discover what behaviors and attitudes are appropriate or inappropriate. Thus, to the extent that various factors either increase or decrease uncertainty, they either inhibit or facilitate adjustment.

However, because international adjustments usually entail greater disruptions of old routines (e.g., work, social, and nonwork routines) than domestic adjustments, the magnitude of uncertainty is usually higher in international versus domestic adjustments. Thus, it should not be surprising that although each literature points to some common important antecedents, each one focuses on unique variables as well. In general, the domestic adjustment literature has focused on pre- and postentry adjustment variables, especially those related to the job and the organization, and mode and degree of adjustment, whereas the international adjustment literature has focused on individual and nonjob variables and on degree of adjustment. We argue that a more comprehensive understanding of international adjustment can be gained by integrating both literatures rather than simply extrapolating from the domestic adjustment literature or from only relying on the extant cross-cultural adjustment literature. Figure 3 represents a schematic integration of both literatures and a more comprehen-

FIGURE 3
Framework of International Adjustment[a]

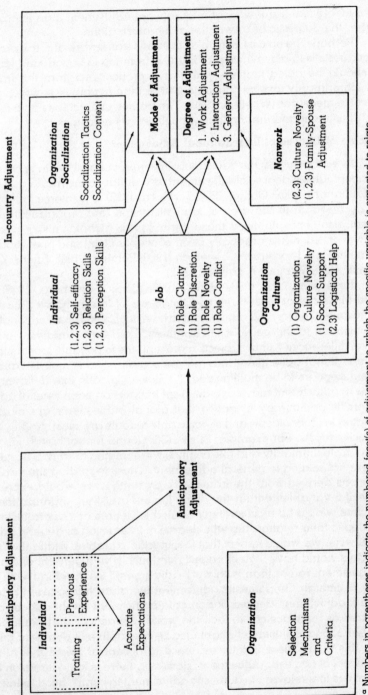

[a] Numbers in parentheses indicate the numbered facet(s) of adjustment to which the specific variable is expected to relate.

sive theoretical framework of international adjustment than is provided by either the domestic or international literature alone.

Perhaps the easiest way to discuss this framework and the propositions it suggests is to move through Figure 3, from top to bottom and left to right. It should be noted that we will derive propositions from the framework, which primarily involve concepts, rather than hypotheses, which primarily involve measures (Whetten, 1989). The framework includes both the degree of adjustment and the mode of adjustment as outcomes.

Facets of Degree of International Adjustment

In early studies on adjustment in cross-cultural settings, researchers conceptualized degree of adjustment as a unitary construct (e.g., Gullahorn & Gullahorn, 1962; Oberg, 1960; Torbiorn, 1982). It is interesting to note that early research in the area of job satisfaction and organizational commitment also conceptualized those variables as global, unitary phenomena; however, each has gradually been conceptualized and operationalized as a multifaceted construct (Gregersen, 1989; Reichers, 1985; Smith, Kendall, & Hulin, 1969; Wanous & Lawler, 1972).

Research in the 1980s (Black, 1988; Black & Stephens, 1989) suggests that there are at least three specific facets of international adjustment: (1) adjustment to work, (2) adjustment to interacting with host nationals, and (3) adjustment to the general environment. Both factor analyses and mean-level differences within subjects regarding these possible facets suggest that international adjustment may not be a unitary construct. Because adjustment appears to be multifaceted, it follows logically that different antecedents to adjustment may have different impacts on each facet of adjustment. There is preliminary evidence that global antecedents are most strongly related to global facets and specific antecedents are most strongly related to specific facets. For example, Black (1988) found that although job variables (e.g., role ambiguity and role conflict) were related to work adjustment, they were not related to general adjustment. Thus, regarding the various propositions derived from the framework presented, we would expect that the specific variables within the "job" factors and the "organization culture" factors, would be most strongly related to degree of work adjustment compared to their relationship with degree of interaction or general adjustment. Likewise, we would expect that the specific variables within the "nonwork" factors would have their strongest relationship with general and interaction adjustment rather than with work adjustment (see [a] in Figure 3).

Although the domestic adjustment literature has focused primarily on work adjustment, degree of domestic adjustment might also be conceptualized as multifaceted. In fact, the work, interaction, and general facets of international adjustment might also be descriptive of domestic adjustment. At this point, there is little evidence to accept or reject this multifaceted concept of domestic adjustment. However, there is logical reason to believe that it is less relevant to domestic adjustment in comparison to international adjustment.

For example, although a person might argue that adjusting to interacting with people from New England is difficult when that individual is from southern California, there is a substantial difference in degree, if not kind, between that interaction and interacting with people from China, whose language, religion, political system, values, daily customs, family structure, economic system, and general world view are significantly different from those in the United States. The same argument could be made regarding general adjustment. To the extent that these facets of adjustment are at least differences in substantial degree between domestic and international adjustment, it raises the probability that the different facets of international adjustment could have greater differential influences on outcome variables relative to domestic adjustment.

For example, general and interaction adjustment might be much stronger predictors of organizational commitment, intent to leave, or turnover in the case of international adjustment versus domestic transitions. Although we have argued that the multifaceted conceptualization of international adjustment is an important change for future research in this area, and perhaps more important than in the domestic adjustment literature, the lack of systematic empirical evidence leaves the question open for future research.

PROPOSITIONS FOR FUTURE RESEARCH

Anticipatory Adjustment

Perhaps one of the greatest contributions gained by examining the domestic adjustment literature for understanding international adjustment concerns the notion of anticipatory adjustment. The basic premise is that if appropriate anticipatory adjustments are made, the actual adjustment in the new international setting will be easier and quicker.

Individual factors. The notion of anticipatory adjustment can be separated into specific factors related to the individual. Work in the socialization, surprise and sensemaking areas suggests that the accuracy of the expectations held by individuals is a key to effective anticipatory adjustment and actual adjustment. The more accurate expectations individuals can form, the more uncertainty they will reduce and the better their anticipatory adjustment will be. The better the anticipatory adjustment, the fewer surprises and negative affective reactions or less culture shock individuals will experience, the more appropriate behaviors and attitudes they will exhibit, and the smoother and quicker their adjustment will be. However, in the case of international adjustments, there are several distinct areas about which individuals might form expectations: (1) the job, (2) the organizational culture, (3) the host-country nationals, (4) the general culture, and (5) daily life in the foreign country (Black, 1988; Bochner, 1982; Brislin, 1981). Based on the previous discussion about facets of adjustment, we would expect, for example, that accurate expectations concerning the job would be most strongly related to the "work" facet of international adjustment.

Proposition 1: Accurate expectations will be positively re-lated to anticipatory adjustment and to degree of international adjustment, and specific types of expectations will have their strongest relationship with conceptually similar facets of degree of international adjustment.

On the basis of the international adjustment literature, it seems reasonable to argue that previous international experience may be an important source of information from which accurate expectations can be formed (Church, 1982). Based on the underlying notion of uncertainty reduction described above, we would expect that several previous international adjustment experiences would provide more information from which uncertainty could be reduced and accurate expectations formed. Additionally, if the previous experiences were in the same (or a similar) culture to the one the individual will enter, they would be a better source from which accurate expectations could be made than previous experiences in a dissimilar culture. Similarly, if the previous experiences were work related, they would facilitate the formation of accurate work expectations, and if the previous experiences were not work related (e.g., study abroad as a student), they would facilitate the formation of nonwork expectations (Church, 1982; Stening, 1979). Although studies of adjustment after a domestic relocation transfer by Pinder and Schroeder (1987) failed to find a significant correlation between the number of previous domestic transfers and adjustment, studies of cross-cultural adjustment by Torbiorn (1982) and Black (1988) provide some support for the following proposition. This difference may stem from the greater number of adjustments that are involved in a cross-cultural adjustment versus a domestic adjustment and, consequently, the number of lessons that may be learned from previous international experiences and applied to the current international transition.

Proposition 2: Previous work-related experiences will facilitate the formation of accurate work expectations, and previous nonwork experiences will facilitate the formation of accurate nonwork expectations.

Just as frequent and relevant previous experiences can facilitate the formation of accurate expectations, so too can predeparture cross-cultural training. Essentially, cross-cultural training provides individuals with useful information for reducing uncertainty associated with the impending international transfer and for forming accurate expectations about living and working in the prospective host country. It is important to note that such training does not necessarily need to be company-sponsored; it could be self-initiated. (This may be important for future empirical research because most U.S. firms do not provide predeparture cross-cultural training.) Additionally, this training need not immediately precede the international transfer, though we would expect more recent training would have the strongest effect (Black & Mendenhall, 1990; Brislin & Pedersen, 1976). (For a more detailed discussion of what types of cross-cultural training would be expected to be more or less effective, see Black & Mendenhall, 1990.)

Proposition 3: Predeparture cross-cultural training will be positively related to accurate expectations.

Organization factors. During the anticipatory phase, perhaps the most important organization factors are the selection criteria and mechanisms. Research in the socialization area suggests that the closer the selected individual matches the needs of the firm, the easier the individual's adjustment after entering the firm. It has already been mentioned that most U.S. MNCs use one dimension (domestic job track record) in selecting individuals for overseas assignments and most do not select the candidate from a pool of competitive or comparable candidates. Thus, we would expect expatriates who have been selected on the basis of a wide array of relevant criteria and from a pool of candidates will experience the easiest and quickest cross-cultural adjustment.

Proposition 4: Individuals who have been selected based on a wide array of relevant criteria will experience easier and quicker cross-cultural adjustment compared to individuals who have been selected on the basis of only job-related criteria.

Proposition 4A: U.S. MNCs that select expatriates based on a wide array of relevant criteria and from a pool of candidates will have lower rates of failed expatriate assignments and lower rates of ineffective expatriates than firms that do not employ these selection criteria or mechanisms.

In-Country Adjustment

Integrating the domestic and international adjustment literatures with the notion of in-country adjustment is somewhat more complicated than was the case for anticipatory adjustment. This is because we must consider both mode of adjustment and degree of adjustment in examining the process of in-country adjustment.

Individual factors. The following three categories of individual factors relating to in-country adjustment were presented in the review article by Mendenhall and Oddou (1985): (1) self-oriented, (2) others-oriented, and (3) perceptual-oriented. One of the underlying issues of the various self-oriented skills discussed by Mendenhall and Oddou (1985) was the ability to believe in oneself and one's ability to deal effectively with the foreign surroundings, even in the face of great uncertainty. This idea is quite similar to what Bandura (1977) and others have consistently referred to as self-efficacy. According to the research on self-efficacy, individuals with higher levels of self-efficacy tend to persist in exhibiting new behaviors that are being learned, even when those efforts are not successful, longer than do individuals with less self-efficacy. The more individuals attempt to exhibit new behaviors in the foreign situation, the more chances they have of receiving feedback, both positive and negative. These individuals can then use this feedback to reduce the uncertainty of what is expected of them and how they are doing, and they can correct their behavior to better correspond to the expectations. This process, in turn, would facilitate degree of adjustment. There may be an interaction effect between self-efficacy and need for feedback (e.g., self-efficacy has the greatest impact on adjustment for individuals with high needs for feedback, Nicholson, 1984), but it would be self-efficacy that would drive the person to persist in exhibiting new behaviors which, in turn, would facilitate degree of adjustment.

> Proposition 5: *Self-efficacy will have a positive relationship with degree of adjustment.*

> Proposition 5A: *Self-efficacy will have its strongest relationship with adjustment for individuals who also have a high need for feedback.*

Relational skills also provide an important means of increasing the cues individuals receive about what is expected and how they are doing regarding those expectations. Consequently, these skills can reduce the uncertainty associated with the foreign environment. The greater individuals' relational skills, the easier it is for them to interact with host nationals (Mendenhall & Oddou, 1985). The more individuals interact with host nationals, the more information they can receive about what is and isn't appropriate in the host culture and how they are doing. Black (1988) found a positive relationship between percentage of time spent with host nationals and general cross-cultural adjustment.

> Proposition 6: *Relational skills will be positively related to degree of in-country adjustment.*

Perceptual skills also provide a significant means of understanding what is appropriate and inappropriate in the host country; these skills, therefore, can reduce the uncertainty associated with the foreign environment. The greater individuals' perceptual skills, the easier it is for them to understand and correctly interpret the host culture (Mendenhall & Oddou, 1985).

> Proposition 7: *Perceptual skills will be positively related to degree of in-country adjustment.*

The integration of the domestic adjustment literature provides a set of propositions regarding the relationship between individual factors and mode of adjustment that are new to the area of international adjustment. For example, Nicholson (1984) suggested that a high desire for control would lead to a mode of adjustment characterized more by adjustment through changing the situation rather than through changing the individual. Nicholson acknowledged that this concept is similar to internal locus of control or high self-efficacy. Thus, we would expect that individuals with high levels of self-efficacy would be more likely to utilize "role innovation" as a means of adjustment than individuals with low levels of self-efficacy.

> Proposition 8: *High levels of self-efficacy will be associated with modes of adjustment that are directed at*

changing the environment (e.g., the work role), whereas
low levels of self-efficacy will be associated with modes
of adjustment characterized by changing the individual.

Job factors. The domestic adjustment literature, in particular, points to the importance of job factors for both degree and mode of adjustment. Regarding job-related variables after arrival in a host culture, theory and past research indicate that role clarity reduces the amount of uncertainty associated with the work situation, which, in turn, would facilitate adjustment at work (Black, 1988; Nicholson, 1984; Pinder & Schroeder, 1987). Theorists of domestic adjustment (Brett, 1980; Dawis & Lofquist, 1984; Nicholson, 1984) also have argued that role discretion allows individuals to adapt their work role and setting to themselves rather than adapting themselves to the situation. Accordingly, greater role discretion makes it easier for individuals to utilize previous behavior patterns, which, in turn, reduces uncertainty in the new situation and facilitates adjustment in the novel setting.

Proposition 9: Role clarity and role discretion will be pos-
itively associated with international adjustment, espe-
cially work adjustment.

In contrast to the positive impact of role clarity and role discretion on work adjustment, conflicting signals about what is expected of individuals in a new work setting (e.g., role conflict) would be expected to increase uncertainty and inhibit adjustment. In a new cultural setting, conflicting signals can generate a high degree of uncertainty because individuals must first understand the messages and then decide which messages to follow or ignore. Once the conflicting messages are sorted out, individuals must then execute appropriate behaviors in the new work role. Additionally, role novelty, which is essentially the degree to which the current role is different from past roles, would increase the uncertainty associated with the job. Consequently, we would expect role novelty to have a negative relationship with adjustment (Black, 1988; Nicholson, 1984; Pinder & Schroeder, 1987). The work by Louis (1980a, 1980b) suggests that one important source of role novelty might be the number of boundaries being traversed in the transfer (e.g., functional, hierarchical, inclusionary).

Proposition 10: Role conflict and role novelty will be neg-
atively associated with international adjustment, espe-
cially work adjustment.

Although little empirical work has been conducted concerning Propositions 9 and 10, there seems to be preliminary evidence to support the facilitating effect of role clarity and role discretion and the inhibiting effect of role conflict and role novelty (Black, 1988; Black & Gregersen, 1989).

On the basis of the theoretical work by Nicholson (1984), we can speculate not only about the relationship between job factors and degree of adjustment but also about the relationship between certain job factors and mode of adjustment. Nicholson (1984: 178) argued that "high discretion roles . . . make it impossible simply to conform to job specifications, role descriptions, or practices of previous incumbents." Therefore, high role discretion would lead to modes of adjustment characterized by efforts to change the situation.

> Proposition 11: International transfers that involve high role discretion will be associated with individuals utilizing modes of adjustment characterized by efforts to change the situation (e.g., the work role), whereas international transfers that involve low role discretion will be associated with individuals utilizing modes of adjustment characterized by efforts to change themselves.

Nicholson (1984: 178) also stated that low novelty in job demands would be associated with modes of adjustment focused on changing the work role because the similarity of the current role compared to the past role would provide "little scope or pressure for change in the person's job-related skills or professional identity."

> Proposition 12: International transfers that involve low role novelty will be associated with individuals utilizing modes of adjustment characterized by efforts to change the situation (e.g., the work role), whereas international transfers that involve high role novelty will be associated with individuals utilizing modes of adjustment characterized by efforts to change themselves.

Organizational culture factors. Based on an integration of both the domestic and international adjustment literatures, three specific organizational culture factors emerge as important in the international adjustment process. First, just as job novelty was expected to increase uncertainty associated with the work role, organizational culture novelty would be expected to increase the uncertainty associated with the work environment in which the work role was carried out (Church, 1982; Mendenhall & Oddou, 1985; Stening, 1979). The greater the difference between the organizational culture of the subsidiary organization in the foreign country compared to the organization in the home country, the more difficult the international adjustment would be.

> Proposition 13: High organizational culture novelty will be negatively associated with degree of international adjustment, especially work adjustment.

An organizational culture that included social support from co-workers and superiors in the subsidiary firm overseas would serve to provide newcomers (transferees) with information about what was acceptable and unacceptable in the new organizational setting. This would reduce uncertainty and thereby facilitate cross-cultural adjustment (Pinder & Schroeder, 1987).

> Proposition 14: Social support from organizational members will be positively associated with degree of international adjustment, especially work adjustment.

Organizations differ in the degree and types of logistical support they provide employees involved in international transfers (Tung, 1984). Logistical support regarding housing, schools, grocery stores, and so on, could potentially reduce uncertainty associated with these significant issues (Baker & Ivancevich, 1971; Copeland & Griggs, 1985; Tung, 1988) and thereby facilitate adjustment (Torbiorn, 1982). Because most logistical support deals with nonwork issues, we would expect logistical support to have a stronger relationship with interaction, and especially general adjustment, rather than with work adjustment.

> *Proposition 15: Logistical support from the organization will be positively associated with degree of international adjustment, especially interaction and general adjustment.*

Organizational socialization factors. The theoretical and empirical literature on organizational socialization has mainly focused on the relationship between organizational socialization tactics and mode of adjustment (Fisher, 1986; Jones, 1986; Van Maanen & Schein, 1979). As mentioned previously, Jones (1986) found support for a significant relationship between institutional socialization tactics and low role innovation as individuals' mode of adjustment and between individual socialization tactics and high role innovation as the mode of adjustment.

> *Proposition 16: Institutional socialization tactics will be associated with low role innovation, and individual socialization tactics will be associated with high role innovation as modes of adjustment during international transfers.*

Although the theoretical arguments regarding socialization tactics presented by Van Maanen and Schein (1979) have influenced both theoretical thinking (e.g., Nicholson, 1984) and empirical work (e.g., Jones, 1986; Zahrly & Tosi, 1989), Fisher (1986), in her review of the literature, argued that in addition to socialization tactics the content of the socialization (or what individuals learn) is important. Thus, in one sense content messages can be communicated both through socialization methods and socialization content. For example, the implicit message of collective socialization tactics (based on Van Maanen and Schein, 1979) is that the roles into which the collective group are about to enter are sufficiently fixed so that it is possible to "process" or socialize the group collectively. This, in turn, influences individuals to respond in a custodial manner (i.e., they do not try to change the definition or content of the role). Theoretically, however, it is possible for the content of the information communicated during the collective socialization process to encourage the group members to innovate and change things. For example, we expect that collective socialization tactics combined with content that encouraged group members to conform would lead to a custodial mode of adjustment, but collective socialization tactics combined with content that encouraged group members to change things would lead to more innovative modes of adjustment.

> *Proposition 17: Institutional socialization tactics and congruent content will be associated with low role innovation, and individual socialization tactics and congruent*

content will be associated with high role innovation as
modes of adjustment during international transfers.

Nonwork factors. Whereas the role of organizational socialization factors stems from the domestic adjustment literature, the role of nonwork factors is derived from the international adjustment literature. In the same way that job novelty and organizational culture novelty were argued to increase uncertainty, so too would the general culture novelty of the host country (Church, 1982; Mendenhall & Oddou, 1985; Stening, 1979). The greater the difference between the culture of the host country compared to the home country, the more difficult would be the international adjustment. Because policies and procedures of the U.S. parent company could dilute the impact of the novelty of the host culture, culture novelty is likely to be most salient in nonwork interactions and activities; therefore, we expect it to have its strongest impact on interaction and general adjustment.

Proposition 18: High culture novelty will be negatively associated with degree of international adjustment, especially interaction and general adjustment.

Bhagat (1983) has argued that nonwork variables can have a spillover effect on employees' adjustment. Perhaps the most important nonwork variable in the international adjustment of U.S. expatriates is the adjustment of family members, especially the spouse, because most U.S. expatriates are married (Black, 1988; Black & Stephens, 1989). We would expect that the uncertainty that could result from poor cross-cultural adjustment of a spouse would inhibit the expatriate's adjustment. In fact, in her survey of U.S. MNC executives, Tung (1981) found that these executives believed that a spouse's inability to adjust to the foreign host culture was the number one reason for expatriate failures. Black (1988) and Black and Stephens (1989), in studies of two separate samples of U.S. managers and spouses, found significant relationships between expatriate and spouse cross-cultural adjustment.

Proposition 19: Family adjustment, especially spouse adjustment, will be positively related to employee international degree of adjustment.

WHAT DID WE LEARN?

In conclusion, it is perhaps helpful to summarize what has been gained by this attempt to provide a theoretical framework of international adjustment. After a careful examination of the last two decades of research on international adjustment, it is clear that most of the work has been anecdotal or atheoretical in nature. Most empirical studies have tried to determine if certain factors were related to international adjustment without a theoretical map of which ones would be expected to be related or why. Given the early stage of development of the international literature in general, and the international adjustment literature in particular, this is perhaps understandable. However, it seems that the lack of an emphasis on theory in the area of international adjustment has perhaps inhibited the field from making as rapid or systematic advances as might otherwise have been possible. Based on the haphazard path of past empirical work over the past two decades, attempts to provide theoretical guidance are important at this stage of the literature's development.

Although the purpose of this paper has been to move toward a more comprehensive theoretical framework of international adjustment and not to provide a framework for both domestic and international adjustment, it is useful to examine some of the differences between the two. Although the fundamental theoretical process is similar between domestic and international adjustment, there are sufficient enough differences that lead to different variables moving from "figure" to "ground" and vice versa for each type of adjustment. For example, because of the generally greater magnitude and breadth of changes involved in international compared to domestic changes, it is expected that predeparture training, especially cross-cultural training (Black & Mendenhall, 1990), would be an important variable (i.e., figure) in international adjustment and much less important (i.e., ground) in domestic adjustment. Likewise, there is preliminary evidence that previous experience is important in international adjustment (Black, 1988) and not in domestic adjustment (Pinder & Schroeder, 1987). Additionally, there is evidence that the adjustment of the spouse is significantly related to the adjustment of the employee during international transfer (Black, 1988; Black & Stephens, 1989); this, in fact, seems to be the primary reason for failed international adjustments (Tung, 1981). In contrast, there is less evidence that the adjustment of the spouse has such a significant impact on the employee during domestic transitions.

We would also expect that culture novelty would be a more important variable during international compared to domestic transitions. Because there is greater variance in culture novelty between, as opposed to within, cultures (Hofstede, 1980), we would expect culture novelty to have a greater impact on adjustment during international transitions. Given the ease of misunderstandings and their serious consequences in a cross-cultural situation (Mendenhall & Oddou, 1985), we might also expect that perceptual skills would be a more important variable during international compared to domestic adjustment transitions. Similar arguments might be made for selection criteria or relational skills; however, the lack of sufficient empirical evidence in the areas of international and domestic adjustment leaves some of these "figure" and "ground" distinctions open to future research.

CONCLUDING COMMENTS

We believe that in addition to pointing out differences and some similarities between international and domestic adjustment that this investigation also provides general guidance for future research in both areas. In the past, scholars in the international adjustment area have relied primarily on the international adjustment literature, neglecting the domestic adjustment literature. We have argued that an integration of the two literatures provides a more comprehensive theoretical framework for understanding international adjustment and for guiding future research. For example, without integrating the domestic.adjustment literature, issues such as anticipatory adjustment, job factors, and organizational factors might continue to be neglected as important predictors of the degree of international adjustment. An important agenda for future international adjustment research would be to attempt more longitudinal studies in order to examine the influence of anticipatory variables relative to in-country variables on in-country adjustment.

Also, few researchers (cf. Black, 1988) have included an examination of job variables; yet, certainly job variables are theoretically critical antecedents of in-country work adjustment. Additionally, without the integration of the domestic literature, researchers in the area of international adjustment might continue to neglect the issue of mode of adjustment and the individual and organizational factors that likely influence mode of adjustment. Little is known about how employees adjust to international transitions in terms of the extent to which they try to change themselves or their environment and the predictors of these different modes of adjustment. This would seem to be an important research agenda for the future.

The integration of the two literatures may also provide direction for future research on domestic adjustment. In the past, the domestic adjustment literature has focused on anticipatory adjustment and work-related issues, and perhaps it has underemphasized nonwork factors. Although nonwork factors may not play as important a role for domestic adjustment compared to international adjustment, they may add significantly to understanding the process. An important addition to the domestic adjustment research agenda may be the investigation of the role of organizational culture novelty. In light of the present importance of strong organizational cultures (i.e., widely shared and firmly held values), one research agenda from a domestic adjustment perspective would be to determine if similar organizational cultures involved in a domestic transfer (which should be related to a strong organizational culture) are positively related to degree of adjustment and if dissimilar organizational cultures are negatively related to degree of domestic adjustment.

Additionally, future empirical work in both areas may benefit from not only examining the methods of socialization but also from examining the content of the messages that are implicitly and explicitly communicated during the socialization process. As was mentioned previously, the international adjustment literature has neglected the issue of mode of adjustment and the role that organizational socialization tactics play. Although this is not true of the domestic adjustment literature, both literatures have neglected the issue of socialization content. Theoretically, socialization content may play as important, or perhaps even more important, a role than socialization tactics. This would seem to be an additional, important research agenda for scholars in both areas.

In conclusion, we believe that although the fundamental process of uncertainty reduction is a common theoretical thread between domestic and international adjustment, there are sufficient contextual differences that some antecedent variables move from figure to ground and vice versa in each type of adjustment. Additionally, the impact of adjustment on other outcome variables such as commitment, intent to leave, or turnover may be different for domestic and international adjustment. This would seem to be a fruitful area for future research. Finally, we believe that a comparison of domestic and international adjustment has contributed to a more comprehensive theoretical framework of international adjustment, but future comparisons and integration are needed to further refine and make more comprehensive theories of international and domestic adjustment.

REFERENCES

Abelson, R. 1976. Script processing in attitude formation and decision making. In J. S. Caroll & J. S. Payne (Eds.), *Cognition and social behavior:* 33–46. Hillsdale, NJ: Erlbaum.

Adler, N. 1983. Cross-cultural management research: The ostrich and the trend. *Academy of Management Review,* 8: 226–232.

Ashford, S. J., & Taylor, M. S. 1990. Understanding individual adaptation: An integrative approach. In K. Rowland & J. Ferris (Eds.), *Research in personnel and human resource management,* vol. 8: 1–41. Greenwich, CT: JAI Press.

Baker, J. C., & Ivancevich, J. M. 1971. The assignment of American executives abroad: Systematic, haphazard, or chaotic? *California Management Review,* 13(3): 39–44.

Bandura, A. 1977. *Social learning theory.* Englewood Cliffs, NJ: Prentice-Hall.

Bhagat, R. S. 1983. Effects of stressful life events on individual performance and work adjustment progress within organizational settings: A research model. *Academy of Management Review,* 8: 660–671.

Black, J. S. 1988. Work role transitions: A study of American expatriate managers in Japan. *Journal of International Business Studies,* 19: 277–294.

Black, J. S., & Gregersen, H. B. 1989. Antecedents of adjustment and turnover in overseas assignments. *Proceedings of the Eastern Academy of Management:* 158–160.

Black, J. S., & Mendenhall, M. 1990. Cross-cultural training effectiveness: A review and theoretical framework for future research. *Academy of Management Review,* 15: 113–136.

Black, J. S., & Stephens, G. K. 1989. The influence of the spouse on American expatriate adjustment in overseas assignments. *Journal of Management,* 15: 529–544.

Bochner, S. 1982. *Cultures in contact: Studies in cross-cultural interaction.* New York: Pergamon Press.

Brein, M., & David, K. H. 1971. Intercultural communication and adjustment of the sojourner. *Psychological Bulletin,* 76: 215–230.

Brett, J. M. 1980. The effect of job transfers on employees and their families. In C. L. Cooper & R. Payne (Eds.), *Current concerns in occupational stress:* 99–136. New York: Wiley.

Brief, A. P., Aldag, R. J., Van Sell, M., & Melone, N. 1979. Anticipatory socialization and role stress among registered nurses. *Journal of Health and Social Behavior,* 20: 161–166.

Brislin, R. W., & Pedersen, P. 1976. *Cross-cultural orientation programs:* New York: Gardner Press.

Brislin, R. W. 1981. *Cross-cultural encounters.* New York: Pergamon Press.

Church, A. T. 1982. Sojourner adjustment. *Psychological Bulletin,* 9: 540–572.

Copeland, L., & Griggs, L. 1985. *Going international.* New York: Random House.

Dawis, R. V., & Lofquist, L. H. 1984. *A psychological theory of work adjustment.* Minneapolis: University of Minnesota Press.

Feldman, D. 1976. A contingency theory of socialization. *Administrative Science Quarterly,* 21: 433–452.

Feldman, D. C., & Brett, J. M. 1983. Coping with new jobs: A comparative study of new hires and job changers. *Academy of Management Journal,* 26: 258–272.

Festinger, 1956. *A theory of cognitive dissonance.* Stanford, CA: Stanford University Press.

Fiedler, F., Mitchell, T., & Triandis, H. 1971. The culture assimilator: An approach to cross-cultural training. *Journal of Applied Psychology,* 55: 95–102.

Fisher, C. 1986. Organizational socialization: An integrative review. *Research in personnel and human resource management,* 4: 101–145. Greenwich, CT: JAI Press.

Gullahorn, J. R., & Gullahorn, J. E. 1962. An extension of the u-curve hypothesis. *Journal of Social Issues,* 3: 33–47.

Hays, R. D. 1974. Expatriate selection: Insuring success and avoiding failure. *Journal of International Business Studies,* 5(1): 25–37.

Hofstede, G. 1980. *Culture's consequences.* Beverly Hills, CA: Sage.

Jones, G. R. 1986. Socialization tactics, self-efficacy, and newcomers' adjustment to the organization. *Academy of Management Journal,* 2: 262–279.

Kyi, K. M. 1988. APJM and comparative management in Asia. *Asia Pacific Journal of Management,* 5: 207–224.

Lagner, E. 1978. Rethinking the role of thought in social interactions. In J. H. Hervey, W. Ickes, & R. F. Kid (Eds.), *New directions in attribution research:* 35–58. Hillsdale, NJ: Erlbaum.

Latack, J. C. 1984. Career transitions within organizations: An exploratory study of work, non-work, and coping. *Organizational Behavior and Human Decision Processes,* 34: 296–322.

Louis, M. R. 1980a. Career transition: Varieties and commonalities. *Academy of Management Review,* 5: 329–340.

Louis, M. R. 1980b. Surprise and sense making: What newcomers experience in entering unfamiliar organizational settings. *Administrative Science Quarterly,* 25: 226–251.

Mendenhall, M., Dunbar, E., & Oddou, G. R. 1987. Expatriate selection, training, and career-pathing: A review and critique. *Human Resource Management,* 26: 331–345.

Mendenhall, M., & Oddou, G. 1985. The dimensions of expatriate acculturation: A review. *Academy of Management Review,* 10: 39–48.

Miller, E. K. 1973. The international selection decision: A study of some dimensions of managerial behavior in the selection decision process. *Academy of Management Journal,* 16: 239–252.

Misa, K. F., & Fabricatore, J. M. 1979. Return on investment of overseas personnel. *Financial Executive,* 47(April): 42–46.

Mitchell, T. R., Dossett, D., Fiedler, F., & Triandis, H. 1972. Cultural training: Validation evidence for the cultural assimilator. *International Journal of Psychology,* 7: 97–104.

Moran, Stahl, & Boyer, Inc. 1987. International human resource management. Boulder, CO: Moran, Stahl, & Boyer, Inc.

Nicholson, N. 1984. A theory of work role transitions. *Administrative Science Quarterly,* 29: 172–191.

O'Brien, G. E., Fiedler, F. E., & Hewett, T. 1970. The effects of programmed culture training upon the performance of volunteer teams. *Human Relations,* 24: 209–231.

Oberg, K. 1960. Culture shock: Adjustment to new cultural environment. *Practical Anthropologist,* 7: 177–182.

Pinder, C. C., & Schroeder, K. G. 1987. Time to proficiency following transfers. *Academy of Management Journal,* 30: 336–353.

Reichers, A. 1985. A review and reconceptualization of organizational commitment. *Academy of Management Review,* 10: 465–476.

Schein, E. H. 1971. The individual, the organization, and the career: A conceptual scheme. *Journal of Applied Behavioral Science,* 7: 401–426.

Schollhammer, H. 1975. Current research in international and comparative management issues. *Management International Review,* 13(1): 17–31.

Smith, P. C., Kendall, L. M., & Hulin, C. L. 1969. *The measurement of satisfaction in work and retirement: A strategy for the study of attitudes.* Chicago: Rand McNally.

Stening, B. W. 1979. Problems of cross-cultural contact: A literature review. *International Journal of Intercultural Relations,* 3: 269–313.

Torbiorn, I. 1982. *Living abroad.* New York: Wiley.

Tung, R. 1981. Selecting and training of personnel for overseas assignments. *Columbia Journal of World Business,* 16(2): 68–78.

Tung, R. 1982. Selecting and training procedures of U.S., European, and Japanese multinational corporations. *California Management Review,* 25(1): 57–71.

Tung, R. 1984. *Key to Japan's economic strength: Human power.* Lexington, MA: Lexington Books.

Tung, R. 1988. *The new expatriates: Managing human resources abroad.* Cambridge, MA: Ballinger.

Van Maanen, J., & Schein, E. 1979. Toward a theory of organizational socialization. In B. M. Staw (Ed.), *Research in organizational behavior,* vol. 1: 209–264. Greenwich, CT: JAI Press.

Wanous, J. P., & Lawler, E. E. 1972. Measurement and meaning of job satisfaction. *Journal of Applied Psychology,* 56: 95–105.

Whetten, D. 1989. What constitutes a theoretical contribution? *Academy of Management Review,* 14: 490–495.

Zahrly, J., & Tosi, H. 1989. The differential effect of organizational induction process on early work role adjustment. *Journal of Organizational Behavior,* 10: 59–74.

J. Stewart Black received his Ph.D. from the University of California, Irvine. He is an assistant professor of business administration at the Amos Tuck School of Business Administration at Dartmouth College. His current research interests include international human resource management.

Mark Mendenhall received his Ph.D. from Brigham Young University. He is the J. Burton Frierson Chair of Excellence in the School of Business at the University of Tennessee, Chattanooga.

Gary Oddou received his Ph.D. from Brigham Young University. He is a professor of management at San Jose University.

[17]

INTERFIRM DIVERSITY, ORGANIZATIONAL LEARNING, AND LONGEVITY IN GLOBAL STRATEGIC ALLIANCES

Arvind Parkhe*
Indiana University

Abstract. Organizational theorists have correctly argued that the emergence and maintenance of robust cooperation between global strategic alliance partners is related to the diversity in the partners' characteristics. Yet previous research has failed to systematically delineate the important dimensions of interfirm diversity and integrate the dimensions into a unified framework of analysis. This paper develops a multilevel typology of interfirm diversity and focuses on organizational learning and adaptation as critical processes that dynamically moderate diversity's impact on alliance longevity and effectiveness.

On March 6, 1990, West Germany's Daimler Benz ($48 billion in sales) and Japan's Mitsubishi Group ($200 billion in sales) revealed that they had held 'a secret meeting in Singapore to work out a plan for intensive cooperation among their auto, aerospace, electronics, and other lines of business. However, combining operations of the two companies seems remote: Daimler's orderly German corporate structure doesn't mesh well with Mitsubishi's leaderless group management approach' [*Business Week* 1990b].

This example illustrates an important paradox in international business today. On one hand, global strategic alliances (GSAs) are being used with increasing frequency in order to, inter alia, keep abreast of rapidly changing technologies, gain access to specific foreign markets and distribution channels, create new products, and ease problems of worldwide excess productive capacity. Indeed, GSAs are becoming an essential feature of companies' overall organizational structure, and competitive advantage increasingly depends not only on a company's internal capabilities, but also on the types of its alliances and

---

*Arvind Parkhe (Ph.D., Temple University) is an Assistant Professor of International Business in the Department of Management, Graduate School of Business, Indiana University (Bloomington). Following an undergraduate degree in chemical engineering, he held corporate management positions with a German company in the United States and Germany. His research focuses on the formation, structuring, and management of interfirm cooperative arrangements, and the impact of national security export control regimes on the global competitiveness of high-technology firms.

This research has been supported by a grant from the School of Business at Indiana University, Bloomington. The author gratefully acknowledges the helpful comments of Charles Schwenk, Janet Near, and the anonymous *JIBS* reviewers.

Received: September 1990; Revised: January & March 1991; Accepted: April 1991.

580   JOURNAL OF INTERNATIONAL BUSINESS STUDIES, FOURTH QUARTER 1991

the scope of its relationships with other companies. On the other hand, GSAs bring together partners from different national origins, with often sharp differences in the collaborating firms' cultural and political bases. As in the above illustration, there may also exist considerable diversity in *firm-specific* characteristics that may be tied to each firm's national heritage.

Interfirm diversity can severely impede the ability of companies to work jointly and effectively [Adler and Graham 1989; Harrigan 1988; Perlmutter and Heenan 1986], since many GSA partners—relative newcomers to voluntary cooperative relationships with foreign firms—have yet to acquire the necessary skills to cope with their differences. Not surprisingly, the rapid growth of GSAs is accompanied by high failure rates [Hergert and Morris 1988; Porter 1986].[1]

Before probing the nexus between diversity and alliance performance, however, it is fruitful to begin with the recognition that (1) in GSAs, significant interfirm diversity is to be expected, and (2) this diversity can be analytically separated into two types. Type I includes the familiar interfirm differences (interdependencies) that GSAs are specifically created to exploit. These differences form the underlying strategic motivations for entering into alliances; an inventory of such motivations is provided, for instance, by Contractor and Lorange [1988: 10]. Thus, Type I diversity deals with the reciprocal strengths and complementary resources furnished by the alliance partners, differences that actually facilitate the formulation, development, and collaborative effectiveness of GSAs.

Type II diversity, the major focus of this paper, refers to the differences in partner characteristics that often negatively affect the longevity and effective functioning of GSAs. Over the life of the partnership, the dynamics of Types I and II are very different, since the two types are differentially impacted by the processes of organizational learning and adaptation. In the case of Type I, learning through the GSA may enable one partner to acquire the skills and technologies it lacked at the time of alliance formation, and eventually rewrite the partnership terms or even discard the other partner. Thus, the GSA becomes a race to learn, with the company that learns fastest dominating the relationship and becoming, through cooperation, a more formidable competitor. Conversely, organizational learning and adaptation can progressively mitigate the impact of Type II differences, thereby promoting longevity and effectiveness. To summarize, a minimum level of Type I differences are essential to the formation and maintenance (raison d'etre) of an alliance, and their erosion destabilizes the partnership. Type II differences, though inevitably present at the initiation of an alliance, may be overcome by iterative cycles of learning that strengthen the partnership.

A large number of previous studies have examined how Type II interfirm differences can play a major role in frustrating the joint efforts of GSA partners. For example, Adler and Graham [1989] found that cross-cultural negotiations are more difficult than intra-cultural negotiations. Several other studies have also established that negotiations between businesspeople of different cultures often fail because of problems related to cross-cultural differences [Adler 1986; Black 1987; Graham 1985; Tung 1984]. Harrigan [1988] studied the influence of sponsoring-firm asymmetries in terms of strategic directions (horizontal, vertical, and relatedness linkages with the venture) on performance. Hall [1984] analyzed the effects of differing management procedures on alliances. Still other researchers have examined the influence of variations in corporate culture [Killing 1982] and national setting [Turner 1987] on successful collaboration. This brief overview, while not exhaustive, conveys the basic directions in which research to date has progressed.

Unfortunately, the usefulness of these important studies in an overall assessment of international interfirm interactions is limited, since they examine the impact of selected aspects of interfirm diversity on cooperative ventures in a piecemeal fashion. The academic literature thus remains fragmented at different levels of analysis, with no overarching theme cohesively pulling together the various dimensions of interfirm diversity in systematic theory-building. Therefore, the main contributions of this paper will be to extend current theory (1) by developing and justifying a typology of the major dimensions of interfirm diversity in the context of GSAs; and, (2) by examining diversity's impact on alliance outcomes through a dynamic model rooted in organizational learning theory. For this purpose, the following questions will be addressed: What are the theoretical dimensions of diversity between GSA partners? In what ways and under what circumstances does each dimension, individually or collectively, translate into reduced collaborative effectiveness? To what extent can deliberate learning/adaptation actions by firms deter expensive alliance failures and promote longevity?

A PREFATORY NOTE ON TERMINOLOGY

It is important at the outset to define terminology. Interfirm cooperative relationships have previously been defined by Borys and Jemison [1989], Schermerhorn [1975], Nielsen [1988], and Oliver [1990]. However, the conceptual domain of GSAs must include the additional properties of being international in scope, mixed-motive (competitive + cooperative) in nature, and of strategic significance to each partner, i.e., tied to the firms' current and anticipated core businesses, markets, and technologies (commonly referred to as the corporate mission). Thus, GSAs are the relatively enduring interfirm cooperative arrangements, involving cross-border flows and linkages that utilize resources and/or governance structures from autonomous organizations headquartered in two or more countries, for the joint accomplishment of individual goals linked to the corporate mission of each sponsoring firm.

This definition delineates GSAs from single-transaction market relationships, as well as from unrelated diversification moves, while accommodating the variety of strategic motives and organizational forms that accompany

582 JOURNAL OF INTERNATIONAL BUSINESS STUDIES, FOURTH QUARTER 1991

global partnerships. For example, GSAs can be used as transitional modes of organizational structure [Gomes-Casseres 1989] in response to current challenges as firms grope to find more permanent structures including, sometimes, whole ownership after the GSA has achieved its purpose. Often, however, longevity is an important yardstick of performance measurement by each parent company [Harrigan 1985; Lewis 1990].

It must be clearly noted that longevity is an imperfect proxy for "alliance success." Longevity can be associated, for instance, with the presence of high exit barriers. And in some alliances, success can also be operationalized in terms of other measures such as profitability, market share, and synergistic contribution toward parent companies' competitiveness (cf. Venkatraman and Ramanujam [1986]). Yet, achievement of these latter objectives can be thwarted by premature, unintended dissolution of the GSA. Furthermore, objective performance measures (e.g., GSA survival and duration) are significantly and positively correlated with parent firms' reported (that is, subjective) satisfaction with GSA performance and with perceptions of the extent to which a GSA performed relative to its initial objectives [Geringer and Hebert 1991], so that for many research purposes the use of longevity as a surrogate for a favorable GSA outcome is probably not too restrictive. With the above limitations acknowledged, we focus mainly on the subset of GSAs where longevity (not planned termination) is sought by each partner, but is threatened by problems stemming from Type II interfirm diversity; however, inasmuch as planned termination represents an important potential alliance outcome involving the deliberate erosion of Type I diversity, it is treated as a special case of a more general diversity/longevity dynamic model later in the paper.

Interfirm diversity refers to the comparative interorganizational differences on certain attributes or dimensions [Molnar and Rogers 1979] that continually shape the pattern of interaction between them [Van de Ven 1976]. In sum, this paper examines the interorganizational interface at which inherent interfirm diversity between GSA partners often makes effective management of pooled resource contributions problematic.

THE PROBLEM OF DIVERSITY

Just as modern business organizations are complex *social* entities (and therefore studied in the ambit of the social sciences), GSAs represent an emerging *social institution*. As researchers in sociology, marketing, and interorganizational relations theory have long noted, dissimilarities between social actors can render effective pairwise interactions difficult, and vice versa.

Evans' [1963] "similarity hypothesis," for example, maintains that "the more similar the parties in a dyad are, the more likely a favorable outcome." The proposed mechanism is: Similarity leads to attraction (sharing of common needs and goals), which causes attitudes to become positive, thus leading to favorable outcomes [McGuire 1968]. Likewise, Lazarsfeld and Merton [1954] identify the tendency for similar values and statuses to serve as bases for social relationships, as a basic mechanism of social interaction. These same principles may explain the characteristics of linkages between organizations [Paulson 1976]. And Whetten [1981:17] argues that ''potential partners are screened to reduce the costs of coordination that increase as a function of differences between the collaborating organizations.''

Although the above literatures primarily focus on problems of surmounting communication difficulties and establishing a common set of working assumptions, a broader set of dimensions is crucial in understanding GSA interactions, given the nature of GSAs as defined above. These dimensions are developed next.

DIMENSIONS OF INTERFIRM DIVERSITY IN GSAs

The major dimensions of Type II interfirm diversity in global strategic alliances are described below; Table 1 summarizes this discussion.[2] In a departure from previous studies that have focused on limited aspects of interfirm diversity, Table 1 spans multiple, critical levels of analysis that are indispensable in providing a fuller understanding of the factors that may lead to friction and eventual collapse of the GSA. In addition, the following discussion also includes an analysis of how each diversity dimension can influence ongoing reciprocal *learning* within the partnership, an important consideration in the study of alliance longevity and effectiveness. Table 1 distinguishes between levels of conceptualization and levels of phenomena. Levels of phenomena refer to dimensions of interfirm diversity that can, with arguable intersubjectivity, be observed and measured. (Hofstede [1983], for example, operationalized culture in four dimensions.) Conceptual levels deal with ideas and theories about phenomena. Thus, the social behavior of interfacing managers from each GSA partner firm is an output of the managers' respective societal (meta), national (macro), corporate-level (meso), and operating-level (micro) influences. While the actual behaviors can be observed, appreciating the often significant differences between them requires an abstraction to the underlying conceptual level of analysis. Finally, it is noted that the dimensions in the typology are often interrelated, and therefore cannot be treated as mutually exclusive.

Societal Culture

The influence of a society's culture permeates all aspects of life within the society, including the norms, values, and behaviors of managers in its national companies. The cross-cultural interactions found in GSAs bring together people who may have different patterns of behaving and believing, and different cognitive blueprints for interpreting the world [Kluckhohn and Kroeberg 1952; Black and Mendenhall 1990]. Indeed, Maruyama [1984]

584   JOURNAL OF INTERNATIONAL BUSINESS STUDIES, FOURTH QUARTER 1991

TABLE 1
Interfirm Diversity in GSAs:
A Summary

Conceptual Level	Phenomenological Level	Dimension of Diversity	Sources of Tension	Coping Mechanisms	Proposition
Meta	Supranational	Societal culture	Differences in perception and interpretation of phenomena, analytical processes	Promote formal training programs, informal contact, behavior transparency	1a, 1b
Macro	National	National context	Differences in home government policies, national industry structure and institutions	Emphasize "rational" (i.e., technological and economic) factors	2
Meso	Top management	Corporate culture	Differences in ideologies and values guiding companies	Encourage organizational learning to facilitate "intermediate" corporate culture	3
Meso	Policy group	Strategic direction	Differences in strategic interests of partners from dynamic external and internal environments	Devise flexible partnership structure	4
Micro	Functional management	Management practices and organization	Differences in management styles, organizational structures of parent firms	Set up unitary management processes and structures	5

argues that cultural differences are at the epistemologic level, that is, in the very structure of perceiving, thinking, and reasoning.

Excellent examples of the deep impact of culture on GSA management can be found in the partners' approaches to problem solving and conflict resolution. In some cultures, problems are to be actively solved; managers must take deliberate actions to influence their environment and affect the course of the future. This is the basis for strategic planning. In contrast, in other cultures, life is seen as a series of preordained situations that are to be fatalistically accepted [Moran and Harris 1982]. Similarly, GSA partners must routinely deal with conflicts in such areas as technology development, production and sourcing, market strategy and implementation, and so on [Lynch 1989]. In some cultures, conflict is viewed as a healthy, natural, and inevitable part of relationships and organizations. In fact, programmed or structured conflict (e.g., the devil's advocate and dialectical inquiry methods) has been suggested as a way to enhance the effectiveness of strategic decision-making (cf. Cosier and Dalton [1990]). But in other cultures, vigorous conflict and open confrontation are deemed distasteful. Embarrassment and loss of face to either party is sought to be avoided at all costs by talking indirectly and ambiguously about areas of difference until common ground can be found, by the use of mediators, and other techniques.

Effective handling of such cultural differences must begin with developing an understanding of the other's modes of thinking and behaving. For example, reflecting on the failed AT&T-Olivetti alliance, AT&T group executive Robert Kavner regretted, ''I don't think that we or Olivetti spent enough time understanding behavior patterns'' [Wysocki 1990]. Avoidance of such preventable mistakes may become increasingly essential, and investments in sophisticated programs to promote intercultural awareness may become increasingly cost-effective, given the accelerating trend of GSA formation and the often enormous losses stemming from failed GSAs.[3] Ethnocentric arrogance (or cultural naivete) and GSAs simply do not mix well.

Nonetheless, Black and Mendenhall [1990] report from their survey of twenty-nine empirical studies that the use of cross-cultural training (CCT) in U.S. multinationals is very limited. Essentially, American top managers believe that a good manager in New York or Los Angeles will be effective in Hong Kong or Tokyo, and that a candidate's domestic track record can serve as the primary criterion for overseas assignment selection. Such a culturally insensitive approach is particularly unfortunate in light of CCT's proven success in terms of enhancing each of its three indicators of effectiveness: cross-cultural skill development, adjustment, and performance [Black and Mendenhall 1990: 115-20]. Clearly, CCT can be a powerful catalyst not only in enhancing intrafirm foreign operations, but also toward overcoming cultural diversity between GSA partners and facilitating ongoing mutual learning that promotes alliance longevity. More formally:

Proposition 1a: Societal culture differences will be negatively related to GSA longevity. However, this relationship will be moderated by formal training programs that enhance intercultural understanding.

Furthermore, bridging the culture gap between GSA partners may be facilitated by effective communication at all interfacing levels. This suggests the need to improve behavior transparency at each level, including effective recognition, verification, and signaling systems between the partners.

Proposition 1b: The relationship between differences in societal culture and longevity of the alliance will be further moderated by structured mechanisms that improve behavior transparency.

National Context

A company's national context primarily includes surrounding industry structure and institutions, and government laws and regulations. The great diversity that exists in the national contexts of global companies can hamper effective collaboration. For instance, disparities in the national context differentially impact global companies' ability to enter and operate GSAs. Of central relevance to this paper are national attitudes about simultaneous competition and cooperation. As noted below, however, national differences notwithstanding, important common patterns may be emerging internationally.

Japanese Context. In Japan, companies have a long history of cooperating in some areas while competing in others, a practice that can be traced primarily to two factors: direction from the Ministry of International Trade and Industry (MITI), and *keiretsu*, or large industrial groups of firms representing diverse industries and skills. However, driven by recent trends in the competitive and political environments, Japanese companies are increasingly entering into GSAs, in the process forsaking their traditionally close *keiretsu* ties. In the context of this paper, the significant implications can be summed up as follows: (1) traditional Japanese industrial associations are in a state of flux; (2) a gradually diminishing role of the *keiretsu* in the future and a greater focus on the individual company; and (3) greater opportunities to enter into GSAs with Japanese firms.[4]

U.S. Context. In the U.S., the federal government has traditionally viewed cooperation between companies with suspicion, particularly if they competed in the same markets. The environment of strict antitrust regulations spawned companies with little experience in successfully managing interfirm cooperation. More recently, however, in an attempt to help correct structural problems in mature industries and to promote international competitiveness in high-tech industries, the U.S. government has adopted more favorable attitudes toward interfirm cooperation, as reflected in its patent, procurement, and antitrust policies. For example, the National Cooperative Research Act of 1984 holds that cooperative ventures between companies are permissible when such arrangements add to the companies' overall efficiency and benefit society at large.

Though intended primarily to benefit U.S. firms, these changes in American national attitudes and policies regarding interfirm cooperation may also have spillover benefits for non-U.S. firms, in that the latter may have greater opportunities to enter into GSAs with U.S. companies.[5] Recent developments in the U.S. may also mean that the ability of U.S. companies to spot, structure, and manage interfirm cooperative relationships will improve over time.

European Context. In Europe, interfirm cooperation historically has been hampered by fragmented European markets, cultural and linguistic differences, diverse equipment standards and business regulations, and nationalist and protectionist government policies. Only in the past several years has the impending threat of a European technology gap against U.S. and Japanese competition compelled European governments to promote the integration of European firms, such as the European Strategic Programme in Information Technologies (ESPRIT). However, such efforts to build a more dynamic, technologically independent Europe do not diminish the fact that Europe is too small to support the risky, multibillion dollar commitments required in many new industries.[6] As Ohmae [1985] argues, companies also need to establish a strong presence in U.S. and Japanese markets to survive.

Three major points emerge from the preceding discussion. First, firms from the Triad regions are heavily influenced by their unique national contexts. Second, cooperating in GSAs may be rendered difficult by the significant differences in national contexts. And third, while these differences are likely to persist, as seen above, they may be progressively overwhelmed by powerful technological and economic factors.

> *Proposition 2*: Differences in partner firms' national contexts and GSA longevity will be negatively related. The effects of these differences on longevity will be moderated by the technological and economic imperatives facing global firms.

Before concluding this discussion of national contexts, it is essential to broach one question that may have a significant bearing on global firms' future partnering abilities and success patterns: Will experience in managing linkages within a firms' home base provide an advantage in building linkages with foreign organizations (cf. Westney [1988])? As just seen, Japanese firms have greater domestic experience in interfirm cooperation than U.S. and European firms, though the latter are also accumulating more local experience. But is this experience transferable to GSAs, where partners typically have more widely varying characteristics? Insufficient evidence currently exists to answer this question; however, systematic research may yield important insights into the differential organizational learning patterns of companies weaned in different domestic contexts.

Corporate Culture

Corporate culture includes those ideologies and values that characterize particular organizations [Beyer 1981; Peters and Waterman 1982]. The notion

588   JOURNAL OF INTERNATIONAL BUSINESS STUDIES, FOURTH QUARTER 1991

that differences in corporate culture matter, familiar to researchers of international mergers and acquisitions [BenDaniel and Rosenbloom 1990], is also crucially important in GSAs. Such firm-specific differences are often interwoven with the fabric of the partners' societal cultures and national contexts, as reflected in the phrases: European family capitalism, American managerial capitalism, and Japanese group capitalism.

Harrigan [1988] argues that corporate culture homogeneity among partners is even more important to GSA success than symmetry in their national origins. (She maintains, for example, that GM's values may be more similar to those of its GSA partner, Toyota, than to those of Ford.) However, studies have shown that a corporation's overall organizational culture is not able fully to homogenize values of employees originating in national cultures [Laurent 1983], indicating the transcending importance of meta- and macro-level variables relative to corporate culture. Although the relative importance of these dimensions must be determined empirically, it is clear that each dimension can be instrumental in erecting significant barriers to effective cooperation.

For example, strikingly different temporal orientations often exist in U.S. versus Japanese corporations. The former, pressed by investors and analysts, may tend to focus on quarterly earnings reports, while the latter focus on establishing their brand names and international marketing channels, a sine qua non of higher order advantage leading to greater world market shares over a period of several years. Thus, Japanese partners may give GSAs more time to take root, whereas their U.S. counterparts may be more impatient.

Significant differences may also exist on the issues of power and control. As Perlmutter and Heenan [1986] assert, Americans have historically harbored the belief that power, not parity, should govern collaborative ventures. In contrast, the Europeans and Japanese often consider partners as equals, subscribe to management by consensus, and rely on lengthy discussion to secure stronger commitment to shared enterprises.

For effective meshing of such diverse corporate cultures, each GSA partner must make the effort to learn the ideologies and values of its counterpart. For managers socialized into their own corporate cultures [Terpstra and David 1990], openness to very different corporate orientations may be difficult. Yet, new forms of business often necessitate the acquisition of new core skills. Among some U.S. firms, for instance, this may mean a reduced emphasis on equity control and an acceptance of slower payback periods on GSA investments in the interest of future benefits over longer time horizons. Among Japanese firms, this may mean a keener recognition of the demands on U.S. managers to show quicker results, with possible modifications in the goals of the GSA and the means used to achieve those goals. Turner [1987] found some support for the emergence of "intermediate" corporate cultures—those characterized by priorities and values between those of the sponsoring firms—as GSA partners made mutual adjustments. However, he did not relate his findings to alliance longevity, and his study was limited to U.K.-Japanese alliances. More empirical work is needed to test the following proposition:

Proposition 3: Corporate culture differences will be negatively related to alliance longevity. This relationship will be moderated by the development of an intermediate corporate culture to guide the GSA.

Finally, corporate culture has a circular relationship with learning in that it creates and reinforces learning and is created by learning; as such, it influences ongoing learning and adaptation within and between GSA partners. Miles and Snow [1978] demonstrate, for example, that a firm's posture (defender, prospector, etc.) is tied closely to its culture, and that shared norms and beliefs help shape strategy and the direction of organizational change. These broad norms and belief systems clearly influence the behavioral and cognitive development that each GSA partner can undergo; in turn, learning and adaptation in organizations often involves a restructuring of these norms and belief systems [Argyris and Schon 1978].

Strategic Directions

As Harrigan [1985] observes, "asymmetries in the speed with which parent firms want to exploit an opportunity, the direction in which they want to move, or in other strategic matters are destabilizing to GSAs" (p.14). Partner screening at the alliance planning stage tests for strategic compatibility by analyzing a potential partner's motivation and ability to live up to its commitments, by assessing whether there may exist probable areas of conflict due to overlapping interests in present markets or future geographic and product market expansion plans. Yet, a revised analysis may become necessary as the partners' evolving internal capabilities, strategic choices, and market developments pull them in separate directions, diminishing the strategic fit of a once-perfect match. Strategic divergence is particularly likely in environments characterized by high volatility, rapid advances in technology, and a blurring and dissolution of traditional boundaries between industries.[7]

One key to managing diverging partner interests may be to build flexibility into the partnership structure, which allows companies to adjust to changes in their internal and external environments. Flexible structures may be attained, for example, by initiating alliances on a small scale with specific, short-term agreements (such as cross-licensing or second sourcing), instead of huge deals that can pose "lock-in" problems with shifting strategic priorities. In a gradually developed relationship, areas of cooperation can be expanded to a broader base to the extent that continuing strategic fit exists. Alternatively, flexibility can be attained by entering into a general (or blanket) cooperative agreement which is activated on an as-needed basis. For example, RCA and Sharp have a long-established cooperative agreement within which they have worked on a series of specific ventures over the years, including a recent $200 million joint venture to manufacture complementary metal oxide semiconductor (CMOS) integrated circuits.

Proposition 4: Divergence in the parents' strategic directions will be negatively related to GSA longevity. The relationship between divergence and longevity will be moderated by structural flexibility that permits adaptation to shifting environments.

Strategy can affect organizational learning, and through learning alliance longevity, in various ways. Since strategy determines the goals and objectives and the breadth of actions available to a firm, it influences learning by providing a boundary to decisionmaking and a context for the perception and interpretation of the environment [Daft and Weick 1984]. In addition, as Miller and Friesen [1980] show, a firm's strategic direction creates a momentum for organizational learning, a momentum that is pervasive and highly resistant to small adjustments.

Management Practices and Organization

The wide interfirm diversity in management styles, organizational structures, and other operational-level variables that exists across firms from different parts of the world can largely be traced to diversity along the first four dimensions discussed above. In turn, these differences, illustrated by the Daimler Benz versus Mitsubishi contrast at the outset of this paper, can heighten operating difficulties and trigger premature dissolution of the GSA. An important issue in this regard is the problem of effectively combining the diverse systems of *autonomous* international firms, each accustomed to operating in a certain manner.

Many researchers in international cooperative strategies have tended, perhaps unwittingly, to focus solely on this final dimension of interfirm diversity (e.g., Dobkin [1988]; Hall [1984]; Pucik [1988]). Among the major differences that have been noted are the style of management (participatory or authoritarian), delegation of responsibility (high or low), decisionmaking (centralized or decentralized), and reliance on formal planning and control systems (high or low). To prevent problems of unclear lines of authority, poor communication, and slow decisionmaking, GSAs may need to set up *unitary* management processes and structures, where one decision point has the authority and independence to commit both partners. Implementation of this recommendation is difficult in cases where both partners are evenly matched in terms of company size and resource contributions to the GSA (cf. Killing [1982]).[8] Yet, agreement on the streamlining of tough operational-level issues must be reached *prior* to commencement of the GSA.

Proposition 5: Diversity in the sponsoring firms' operating characteristics will be negatively related to longevity of the GSA. This relationship will be moderated by the establishment of unitary management processes and structures.

Though structure is often seen as an outcome of organizational learning, it plays a crucial role in determining the learning process itself [Fiol and Lyles 1985]. This observation can be important in the context of GSAs, where one firm's centralized, mechanistic structure that tends to reinforce past behaviors can collide with another firm's organic, decentralized structure that tends to allow shifts of beliefs and actions. More broadly, different management practices and organizational structures can enhance or retard learning, depending upon their degree of formalization, complexity, and diffusion of decision influence.

Theory and practice are linked in Table 2, which illustrates how significant Type II differences between GSA partners can impact the entire spectrum of alliance activities. For the sake of brevity, Table 2 outlines only a select number of characteristics that are derived from the typological dimensions of Table 1. Yet, a review of Table 2 clearly indicates that: (1) the extent of interfirm diversity in global strategic alliances may be high; and (2) as stressed earlier, the various dimensions of diversity are not distinct and unrelated, but rather share a common core that touches GSAs.

Furthermore, Type I and Type II diversity can undergo distinctly different patterns over time, generating different alliance outcomes. The dynamic model of longevity presented in the next section suggests that a pivotal factor in the interfirm diversity/alliance outcome link is organizational learning and adaptation to diversity by the GSA partners.

LONGEVITY IN GSAs: A LEARNING-BASED DYNAMIC MODEL

Organizational theorists [Lyles 1988; Fiol and Lyles 1985] define learning as "the development of insights, knowledge, and associations between past actions, the effectiveness of those actions, and future actions," and adaptation as "the ability to make incremental adjustments." Learning can be minor, moderate, or major. In stimulus-response terms, in minor learning, an organization's worldview (tied to its national and corporate identity) remains the same, and choice of responses occurs from the existing behavioral repertoire. In moderate learning, partial modification of the interpretative system and/or development of new responses is involved. And in major learning, substantial and irreversible restructuring of one or both of the stimulus and response systems takes place [Hedberg 1981]. This conceptualization parallels Argyris and Schon's [1978] single-loop (or low-level) learning that serves merely to adjust the parameters in a fixed structure to varying demands, versus double-loop (or high-level) learning that changes norms, values, and worldviews, and redefines the rules for low-level learning.

Using a contingency theory perspective, we may expect the extent of learning (minor, moderate, or major) necessary for a given level of GSA longevity to be commensurate with the extent of interfirm diversity. Highly similar

592   JOURNAL OF INTERNATIONAL BUSINESS STUDIES, FOURTH QUARTER 1991

TABLE 2

**Selected International Differences
and Impacted Areas of GSA Management**

Characteristic	Value	Country Examples	Description	Impacted Areas of GSA Management
Ownership of Assets	Private	"Free World" Countries	Factors of production predominantly privately owned.	Sourcing strategy, pricing flexibility, quality control, technology transfer, profit repatriation
	Public	East Bloc Countries,[1] Communist China[2]	Factors of production predominantly publicly owned.	
Coordination of National Economic Activity	Market	"Free World" Countries	Consumer sovereignty, freedom of enterprise, equilibration of supply and demand of resources and products by market forces.	Sourcing strategy, pricing flexibility, quality control, technology transfer, profit repatriation
	Command	East Bloc Countries,[1] Communist China[2]	Centralized planning of production quotas, prices, and distribution. Pyramidal hierarchy of control.	
Perceived Ability to Influence Future	Self-determination	USA	Individuals and firms can take actions to influence their environment and improve prospects for the future.	Long-range planning, production scheduling
	Fatalistic	Islamic Countries	People must adjust to their environment. Life follows a preordained course.	
Time Orientation	Abstract, Lineal	USA	The clock serves to harmonize activities of group members. Punctuality is important. Time is money.	Productivity, joint project deadlines
	Concrete, Circular	Argentina, Brazil	Activities are timed by recurring rhythmic natural events such as day and night, seasons of the year.	
Communication	Low Context	USA	Most information is contained in explicit codes, such as spoken or written words. Articulation ("spelling it out") is important.	Initial negotiations, ongoing communications
	High Context	Saudi Arabia	Sending and receiving messages is highly contingent upon the physical context and non-verbal communication.	

TABLE 2
(continued)

Information Evaluation	Pragmatic	U.K.	Emphasis on practical applications of specific details in light of particular goals.	Structure of the GSA management
	Idealistic	Soviet Union	Utilization of abstract frameworks for structuring thinking processes which are molded by a dominant ideology.	
Conflict Management Style	Confrontation	USA	Openness and directness in work relations is promoted. Conflict resolution is preferred over conflict suppression.	Conflict management
	Harmony	Japan	Wa (maintaining harmony in Japanese) is important. Saving face is preferred over direct confrontation and disharmony.	
Decisionmaking[3]	Autocratic	South Korea	Decisions fully formulated before being announced, either individually or with input from experts.	Negotiation and bargaining
	Group	Japan	Information is shared with subordinates, whose input is sought before decisions are made.	
Leadership Style	Task Oriented	West Germany	Enforcement of rules and procedures. Focus on technological aspects.	Decisionmaking, leadership
	People Oriented	Japan	Greater attention to human factors, including morale and motivation. Utilization of group dynamics to reach organizational goals.	
Problem Solving	Scientific	Most Occidental Countries	Logic and scientific method are the means of solving new problems. Accurate data are more important than intuition.	Decisionmaking process
	Traditional	Most Oriental Countries	Solutions to new problems are derived by sifting through past experiences.	

TABLE 2
(continued)

Employment Duration	Variable	Employees can quit to accept better jobs. Employers can terminate low-performing employees.	Human resources management
	Lifetime	Employees are a "family" which cannot be abandoned. Termination causes enormous loss of prestige and must be avoided.	
Power Distance[4]	Low	Relative equality of superiors and subordinates. Greater participation of subordinates in decisionmaking.	GSA structure and communication
	High	Distinct hierarchical layers with formal and restricted interactions. Emphasis on ranks. Top-down communication.	
Uncertainty Avoidance[4]	Low	Uncertainties are a normal part of life. Business risks are judged against potential rewards. Flexibility and innovation are emphasized.	Choice of projects tackled, information and control systems
	High	Business risks lead to high anxiety, leading to mechanisms that offer a hedge against uncertainty: written rules and procedures, plans, complex information systems.	
Individualism[4]	Individualistic	Reliance on individual initiative, self-assertion, and personal achievement and responsibility.	Accountability, performance evaluation systems
	Collectivistic	Emphasis on belonging to groups and organizations, acceptance of collective decisions, values, and duties.	

Country examples: USA, Japan (Employment Duration); Austria, Mexico (Power Distance); Denmark, South Korea (Uncertainty Avoidance); Canada, Singapore (Individualism)

TABLE 2
(continued)

Masculinity[4]	Masculine	Italy	Machismo attitudes. Valued ideals are wealth, power, decisiveness, growth, bigness, and profits. Compensation in monetary rewards, status, recognition, and promotion is expected in proportion to achievement of ideals.	Organizational design, reward systems
	Feminine	Netherlands	Nurturing attitudes. Care of people, interpersonal relations, quality of life, service, and social welfare are valued ideals. Members seek cooperative work climate, security, and overall job satisfaction.	

[1]The situation in the East Bloc countries is in a state of flux, with political reform toward democratization and economic reform embracing free markets and private property. However, Western companies rushing to enter into cooperative ventures with these countries are likely to encounter considerable inertia from past practices (see *Business Week* [1990a]); as such, managers must remain aware of fundamental differences and their implications for alliances.
[2]The international business environment in Communist China has deteriorated considerably following the Tiananmen Square Massacre, forcing corporate strategists to reassess their commitments in the PRC and Hong Kong (see *New York Times* [1990]).
[3]From Kolde [1985].
[4]From Hofstede [1983].

partners would require relatively little mutual adjustment for sustained collaborative effectiveness. Highly dissimilar partners would need to expend greater (double-loop) efforts and resources toward learning, absent which longevity may be expected to suffer.

Moreover, Type I and Type II diversity may shift dynamically along different phases of alliance development. Regarding the former, Porter [1986] observes that:

> Coalitions involving access to knowledge or ability are the most likely to dissolve as the party gaining access acquires its own internal skills through the coalition. Coalitions designed to gain the benefits of scale or learning in performing an activity have a more enduring purpose. If they dissolve, they will tend to dissolve into merger or into an arm's-length transaction. The stability of risk-reducing coalitions depends on the sources of risk they seek to control. Coalitions hedging against the risk of a single exogenous event will tend to dissolve, while coalitions involving an ongoing risk (e.g., exploration risk for oil) will be more durable. [p. 329]

Thus, Type I strategic motivations and organizational learning interact to shape alliance stability and outcome. Similarly, the impact of Type II diversity on alliances can be dynamically altered by organizational learning that itself is an outcome of certain types of deliberate management investments during different phases of alliance development. The pattern of these investments may be a function of the configuration of Type II diversity, i.e., the *degree* and *type* of interfirm differences. If the relatively stable dimensions of societal culture, national context, or corporate culture constitute salient interfirm differences, then organizational learning becomes a threshold condition for alliance success, and management attention must be targeted at the relevant dimensions during the earliest phases of alliance development (such as partner screening and pre-contractual negotiations). In cases where significant diversity arises from the relatively more volatile dimensions of strategic direction and management practices and organization, later adaptive learning under new partner circumstances is a necessary precondition for GSA longevity.

It is evident, then, that the magnitude and timing of Type I and Type II diversity shifts contribute to different alliance outcomes. Specifically, when Type I diversity (mutual interdependency) is larger than Type II diversity, ceteris paribus, longevity will be high. In this situation, additional alliances between the GSA partners become more likely, and ongoing organizational learning in repeated successful collaborative experiences may further reduce Type II diversity, reinforcing the alliancing process.

But when Type II diversity is larger than Type I diversity, ceteris paribus, longevity will be low. This situation can arise in one of two ways: shrinkage of Type I diversity, or escalation of Type II diversity. The first way represents the stepping-stone strategy (planned termination), in which one partner rapidly internalizes the skills and technologies of the other; after the process is completed, that is, when Type I diversity vanishes, little incentive remains for the internalizer firm to remain in the partnership. The second way represents untimely dissolution of the GSA, as a lack of learning and adaptation exacerbates problems of social interaction among managers from the alliance partners. Such unplanned termination is more likely when the partner firms are working together for the first time and have yet to establish a history of prior successful collaborative experiences; differ sharply on one or more of the Type II dimensions; and the efforts and resources committed to learning and adaptation are not commensurate with this diversity.

Thus, the relationship between diversity and longevity is dynamic, and is strongly influenced by the amount of learning and adaptation occurring between the GSA partners. The greater the amount of learning, the greater the negative impact of Type I diversity on longevity, but the smaller the negative impact of Type II diversity on longevity.

IMPLICATIONS AND CONCLUSIONS

The process model of longevity proposed in this paper, drawing upon learning-based management of differences in the properties of the partners, offers rich and exciting opportunities for improved research and practice in GSAs. Only a few of these are touched upon below.

First, there is a need for inductive theory-building (following covariance structure modeling and empirical research) on the relative importance, patterns of interconnectedness, and tension-inducing capacity of the typological dimensions of diversity in a variety of partnering situations, especially in longitudinal studies focusing on the phases of alliance development. Such research will be timely and useful for developing ex post alliance performance generalizations as well as ex ante partner selection criteria. Although preliminary work has been done in both of these areas, as noted above, the research has been fragmented and theory-building in GSAs has been slow, reflecting the lack of systematic conceptualization of a typology of interfirm diversity, much less a dynamic link between diversity and longevity.

The propositions and model developed here draw attention to the crucial aspect of *learning* among interfacing managers of GSA partners; important corollary implications flow from this emphasis. For example, faced with rapid internationalization and even faster growth of interfirm cooperation, how best can global firms quickly enlarge the severely limited cadre of culturally sophisticated, internationally experienced managers (cf. Strom [1990]; Hagerty [1991])? Since coping with interfirm diversity (e.g., formal training programs) is not costless, how are (or methodologically should be) the costs and benefits of such coping efforts assessed by managers or researchers? Fledgling attempts toward institutionalizing learning within the company and enhancing the cumulativeness of cooperative experiences with other companies are already evident, such as General Electric Company's establishment

598   JOURNAL OF INTERNATIONAL BUSINESS STUDIES, FOURTH QUARTER 1991

of GE International in 1988. Created as a special mechanism to efficiently handle the swift growth of GSAs and facilitate organizational learning, GE International's primary roles are to identify and implement GSAs, to promote enhanced international awareness within GE, and to permit the sharing of international partnership expertise throughout the company.

In conclusion, as global firms' technological, financial, and marketing prowess increasingly becomes tied to the excellence of their external organizational relations, "GSA sophistication"—the ability to diagnose important differences between partners and fashion a productive partnership by devising novel solutions to accommodate the differences—is likely to become an imperative. GSAs represent a type of competitive weapon, in that they involve interorganizational *cooperation* in the pursuit of global *competitive* advantage. Sharpening the edge of this competitive weapon may require the adoption of multifirm, multicultural perspectives in joint decisionmaking, a process rendered difficult by the perceptual blinders imposed by culture-bound and corporate-bound thinking (e.g., respectively, the "ugly foreigner" mentality and the NIH, or not invented here, syndrome).[9] Thus, future research on GSA longevity and performance must take into account the partners' cognition of, and adaptation to, the important dimensions of diversity that is an integral, inescapable part of such alliances.

NOTES

1. Although other factors, such as hidden agendas and conceptually flawed logic of the GSA may also account for a portion of these failures, interfirm diversity remains a prime culprit. Moreover, as noted shortly, dissolution of a GSA does not necessarily constitute failure. When GSAs are used as "stepping stones," their termination may be viewed by the parents as a success, not a failure.

2. This typology is suggested as a parsimonious framework to be built upon in future research on GSAs, not as the comprehensive final word. For instance, differences in industry-specific considerations and firm sizes can be significant factors in some cases; these factors are not explicitly considered here.

3. GSAs typically involve commitment of substantial resources on both sides, in cash and/or in kind. Failure can result in a loss of competitive position far beyond merely the opportunity cost of the resources deployed in the GSA itself; synergistic gains and expected positive spillover effects for the parent firm may not be realized.

4. However, the speed with which these changes may occur should not be overestimated, in light of the deeply embedded industry structure and institutions in Japan.

5. One example is the GM-Toyota alliance called New United Motor Manufacturing, Inc. (NUMMI). NUMMI was approved despite strenuous objections from Chrysler and others, whose traditional (antitrust-based) arguments were rejected by the U.S. Department of Justice.

6. This is likely to remain true even after taking into account (a) the move toward a more genuine Common Market in 1992, which creates an integrated economy of 320 million consumers, and (b) the increase in the size of the market arising from East Bloc upheavals.

7. For example, the growing inseparability of data transmission and data processing has created hybrid businesses among companies in computers, telecommunications, office products, modular switchgears, and semiconductors. Similarly, auto firms, driven by cost, quality, and efficiency considerations, increasingly invest in electronics, new materials, aerodynamics, computers, robotics, and artificial intelligence.

8. GSAs must ultimately be guided by careful consideration of the respective management practices and organization of the parents, as well as the operational needs of the venture, such as response time

to market developments and management information systems that accurately reflect the magnitude and scope of the alliance.

9. This problem may be particularly severe for Japanese companies, whose overseas activities until recently strongly emphasized exports and direct investments in wholly owned subsidiaries. The historically closed nature of Japan's society and corporations makes integrating outsiders—even other Japanese—difficult.

REFERENCES

Adler, Nancy, J. 1986. *International dimensions of organizational behavior*. Boston, MA: Kent.

_____ & John L. Graham. 1989. Cross-cultural interaction: The international comparison fallacy? *Journal of International Business Studies*, Fall: 515-37.

Argyris, Chris & Donald A. Schon. 1978. *Organizational learning*. Reading, MA: Addison-Wesley.

BenDaniel, David J. & Arthur H. Rosenbloom. 1990. *The handbook of international mergers and acquisitions*. Englewood Cliffs, NJ: Prentice-Hall.

Beyer, Janice M. 1981. Ideologies, values, and decision making in organizations. In P.C. Nystrom & W.H. Starbuck, editors, *Handbook of organization design*. New York: Oxford University Press.

Black, J. Stewart. 1987. Japanese/American negotiation: The Japanese perspective. *Business and Economic Review*, 6: 27-30.

_____ & Mark Mendenhall. 1990. Cross-cultural training effectiveness: A review and a theoretical framework for future research. *Academy of Management Review*, 15: 113-36.

Borys, Bryan & David B. Jemison. 1989. Hybrid arrangements as strategic alliances: Theoretical issues in organizational combinations. *Academy of Management Review*, 14: 234-49.

Business Week. 1990a. Big deals run into big trouble in the Soviet Union. March 19: 58-59.

_____. 1990b. A waltz of giants sends shock waves worldwide. March 19: 59-60.

Contractor, Farok J. & Peter Lorange (editors). 1988. *Cooperative strategies in international business*. Lexington, MA: Lexington Books.

Cosier, Richard A. & Dan R. Dalton. 1990. Positive effects of conflict: A field assessment. *International Journal of Conflict Management*, January: 81-92.

Daft, Richard L. & Karl E. Weick. 1984. Toward a model of organizations as interpretation systems. *Academy of Management Review*, 9: 284-95.

Dobkin, James A. 1988. *International technology joint ventures*. Stoneham, MA: Butterworth Legal Publishers.

Evans, F.B. 1963. Selling as a dyadic relationship—A new approach. *American Behavioral Scientist*, 6 (May): 76-79.

Fiol, C. Marlene & Marjorie A. Lyles. 1985. Organizational learning. *Academy of Management Review*, 10: 803-13.

Geringer, J. Michael & Louis Hebert. 1991. Measuring performance of international joint ventures. *Journal of International Business Studies*, 22: 249-64.

Gomes-Casseres, Benjamin. 1989. Joint ventures in the face of global competition. *Sloan Management Review*, Spring: 17-26.

Graham, John L. 1985. The influence of culture on the process of business negotiations: An exploratory study. *Journal of International Business Studies*, 16: 81-95.

Hagerty, Bob. 1991. Firms in Europe try to find executives who can cross borders in a single bound. *Wall Street Journal*, January 25: B1, B3.

Hall, R. Duane. 1984. *The international joint venture*. New York: Praeger.

Harrigan, Kathryn R. 1985. *Strategies for joint ventures*. Lexington, MA: Lexington Books.

_____. 1988. Strategic alliances and partner asymmetries. In F.J. Contractor & P. Lorange, editors, *Cooperative strategies in international business*. Lexington, MA: Lexington Books.

Hedberg, Bo. 1981. How organizations learn and unlearn. In P.C. Nystrom & W.H. Starbuck, editors, *Handbook of organizational design*. New York: Oxford University Press.

Hergert, Michael & Deigan Morris. 1988. Trends in international collaborative agreements. In F.J. Contractor & P. Lorange, editors, *Cooperative strategies in international business*. Lexington, MA: Lexington Books.

Hofstede, Geert. 1983. National cultures in four dimensions. *International Studies of Management and Organization*, 13: 46-74.

Killing, J. Peter. 1982. How to make a global joint venture work. *Harvard Business Review*, May-June.

Kluckhohn, C. & A.L. Kroeberg. 1952. *Culture: A critical review of concepts and definitions.* New York: Vintage Books.

Kolde, Endel-Jakob. 1985. *Environment of international business.* Boston: PWS-Kent Publishing Co.

Laurent, Andre. 1983. The cultural diversity of management conceptions. *International Studies of Management and Organization*, Spring.

Lazarsfeld, Paul M. & Robert K. Merton. 1954. Friendship as a social process. In Monroe Berger, Theodore Abel & Charles Page, editors, *Freedom and control in modern society.* New York: Octagon Books.

Lewis, Jordan D. 1990. *Partnerships for profit: Structuring and managing strategic alliances.* New York: Free Press.

Lyles, Marjorie A. 1988. Learning among joint venture-sophisticated firms. In F.J. Contractor & P. Lorange, editors, *Cooperative strategies in international business.* Lexington, MA: Lexington Books.

Lynch, Robert P. 1989. *The practical guide to joint ventures and alliances.* New York: Wiley.

Maruyama, Magoroh. 1984. Alternative concepts of management: Insights from Asia and Africa. *Asia Pacific Journal of Management*, 1(2): 100-11.

McGuire, W.J. 1968. The nature of attitudes and attitude change. In L. Gardner & G. Aronson, editors, *The handbook of social psychology.* Reading, MA: Addison-Wesley.

Miles, Robert E. & Charles C. Snow. 1978. *Organizational strategy, structure and process.* New York: McGraw-Hill,

Miller, D. & P. H. Friesen. 1980. Momentum and revolution in organization adaption. *Academy of Management Journal*, 23: 591-614.

Molnar, Joseph J. & David L. Rogers. 1979. A comparative model of interorganizational conflict. *Administrative Science Quarterly*, 24: 405-24.

Moran, Robert T. & Phillip R. Harris. 1982. *Managing cultural synergy.* Houston: Gulf Publishing Co.

New York Times. 1990. Bush distressed as policy fails to move China. March 11: 1, 11.

Nielsen, Richard P. 1988. Cooperative strategy. *Strategic Management Journal*, 9: 475-92.

Ohmae, Kenichi. 1985. *Triad power.* New York: Free Press.

Oliver, Christine. 1990. Determinants of interorganizational relationships: Integration and future directions. *Academy of Management Review*, 15: 241-65.

Paulson, Steven. 1976. A theory and comparative analysis of interorganizational dyads. *Rural Sociology*, 41: 311-29.

Perlmutter, Howard V. & David A. Heenan. 1986. Cooperate to compete globally. *Harvard Business Review*, March-April: 136-52.

Peters, Thomas J. & Robert H. Waterman. 1982. *In search of excellence.* New York: Warner Books.

Porter, Michael E., editor. 1986. *Competition in global industries.* Boston: Harvard Business School Press.

Pucik, Vladimir. 1988. Strategic alliances with the Japanese: Implications for human resource management. In Farok Contractor & Peter Lorange, editors, *Cooperative strategies in international business.* Lexington, MA: Lexington Books.

Schermerhorn, John R., Jr. 1975. Determinants of interorganizational cooperation. *Academy of Management Journal*, 18: 846-56.

Strom, Stephanie. 1990. The art of luring Japanese executives to American firms. *New York Times*, March 25: F12.

Terpstra, Vern & Kenneth David. 1990. *The cultural environment of international business.* Cincinnati: Southwestern-Publishing Co.

Tung, Rosalie. 1984. *Key to Japan's economic strength: Human power.* Lexington, MA: Lexington Books.

INTERFIRM DIVERSITY IN GLOBAL STRATEGIC ALLIANCES   601

Turner, L. 1987. *Industrial collaboration with Japan*. London: Routledge and Keegan Paul.

Van de Ven, Andrew H. 1976. On the nature, formation, and maintenance of relations among organizations. *Academy of Management Review*, 2: 24-36.

Venkatraman, N. & W. Ramanujam. 1986. Measurement of business performance in strategy research: A comparison of approaches. *Academy of Management Review*, 11: 801-14.

Westney, D. Eleanor. 1988. Domestic and foreign learning curves in managing international cooperative strategies. In F.J. Contractor & P. Lorange, editors, *Cooperative strategies in international business*. Lexington, MA: Lexington Books.

Whetten, David A. 1981. Interorganizational relations: A review of the field. *Journal of Higher Education*, 52: 1-28.

Wysocki, Bernard. 1990. Cross-border alliances become favorite way to crack new markets. *Wall Street Journal*, March 26: A1, A12.

Part IV
Successful Cross-Cultural Management

[18]

The International Journal of Human Resource Management 5:2 May 1994

Expatriate management: lessons from the British in India

Bruce W. Stening

Abstract

In this paper, lessons for the study of expatriate management are drawn from the period of British administration in India. It uses 'the past to study the present' and puts into sharp focus the key issues which confront human resource management researchers and practitioners dealing with expatriate management today. These issues are seen as essentially the same and cover such areas as selection, training, adjustment, appraisal, reward and re-entry.

Introduction

For several hundred years India was ruled by the British and was regarded as the biggest jewel in the English imperial crown. While the structures and procedures for administering this vast, populous country varied somewhat over the period of British rule, for the most part the responsibility for achieving British objectives was in the hands of an élite group whose number never exceeded much more than 1,000, the Indian Civil Service (ICS) (O'Malley, 1965; Woodruff, 1953, 1954).[1] Sent to India in their late teens or early twenties, the men of the ICS (and they were an exclusively male group) typically served for some thirty-odd years in an immensely different, often oppressive and hostile environment. While their titles were different, their functions were first and foremost managerial. Though one might not want to defend the colonialism that underlay all that they did, it must be conceded that the ICS was an impressive outfit: in terms of size and importance it has been compared to the civil services of China under the emperors and of the Ottoman Empire under Suleiman the Magnificent (Woodruff, 1953: 15). As a group and as individuals, they were arguably as influential as the expatriates of any multinational

Bruce W. Stening

corporation. Furthermore, the functions that they undertook and the problems they faced were in many ways analogous to the functions of and problems faced by managers engaged in international business today.

This paper seeks to describe the situation faced by the men of the East India Company and the ICS and then analyse it using contemporary conceptual frameworks, concepts and theories pertaining to expatriate management. Besides providing the basis for an evaluation of expatriate management as practised by the Company and the ICS, the paper is aimed at 'using the past to study the present' (Lawrence, 1984). The supposition underlying this approach, then, is that by reflecting on the management of expatriates in British India it is possible to put into sharper focus the key issues which confront us as human resource management researchers and practitioners dealing with expatriate management today. Those issues are essentially the same for us as they were for the Company and the ICS, namely: Who should be selected for an expatriate assignment and on what basis? How should those selected be trained in order to optimize their effectiveness? Once serving as expatriates, how could they be assisted to adjust to their new environment? On what basis should those expatriates be appraised and rewarded? How might those who had completed their expatriate assignment be assisted to re-enter their home culture?

There is a multitude of contemporary theories and frameworks which can be used in such an historical analysis. Indeed, as various review papers and theory-building books (for example, Black, Gregersen and Mendenhall, 1992a, 1992b; Black and Mendenhall, 1990; Church, 1982; Mendenhall, Dunbar and Oddou, 1987; Mendenhall and Oddou, 1985; Stening, 1979; Torbiorn, 1982) published over the past fifteen or so years have made abundantly clear, the field of expatriate management is one for which there is now a large body of both theory and empirical research. These frameworks will be drawn upon broadly later in the paper to interpret and critique the human resource management practices of the Company and the ICS.

The available material on the British in India, and the ICS in particular, is similarly wide, including: general histories of India and the British in India; histories of the ICS and affiliated institutions such as Haileybury College, the East India Company's expatriate training establishment; official investigations, reports and so forth; handbooks and the like giving advice to those being sent on expatriate assignments to India; official statistics such as those of mental institutions; and biographies, autobiographies, diaries and memoirs of the expatriates themselves and their families. In addition, British colonialism spawned an extensive and rich body of fiction (contributed to by the

Lessons from the British in India

likes of Thackeray, Kipling, Maugham, Orwell and Forster) which can, along the lines suggested by Lewis and Jungman's (1986) anthology dealing with expatriate adjustment, be used to elucidate various matters related to expatriate management. While some of this material (such as more recently published books and journal articles) is available in general libraries, much of it is housed only in the India Office Library in London and was consulted there by this author.[2] While it cannot be claimed that this paper is based on an exhaustive study of the available material (since the amount of information which is available is enormous), it is believed that a sufficiently broad body of material has been surveyed in sufficient depth to provide a rich description and analysis of expatriate management issues in British India.

Setting the scene

Initial British interest in India was solely commercial and was executed through the East India Company from around 1600. These commercial interests eventually required political control and this was gradually assumed by the Company and exercised until 1858 when the Crown assumed direct responsibility for the administration of India.[3] British control over India lasted until independence in 1947. Throughout this long period, British interests were taken care of by various bodies in two broad categories, the army and the public service. As Muttalib (1967: 4) points out, the early titles of the Company's servants indicate that their tasks were clearly mercantile – writers, factors, junior merchants, senior merchants. As their tasks became political as well as commercial, not only did their titles change to reflect this (judges, magistrates, collectors, district officers and many others) but separate services were established (the Indian Civil Service, the Indian Political Service and so on). Of course, besides these various civilian officials there was a large army, and many traders, planters, missionaries and others, all of whom, collectively, constituted 'the British in India'. The overall task of the expatriate civil servants was, as Lord Wellesley pointed out in 1802 in a submission to the Court of Directors of the East India Company (see Ghosal, 1944: 470), immense:

> To dispense justice to millions of people of various languages, manners, usages, and religions; to administer a vast and complicated system of revenue throughout districts equal in extent to some of the most considerable Kingdoms in Europe; to maintain civil order in one of the most populous and litigious regions of the world.

387

Bruce W. Stening

Under the East India Company and then the Crown, there was basically a multidivisional structure based on three presidencies (Bengal, Madras and Bombay) with overall control from London. Below the presidencies there were three levels: provinces, regions and, ultimately, 250 districts, each headed by a district officer. Line control was exercised through this structure by the ICS, assisted by the IPS. Given the enormous difficulties of transport and communication, in the early days of the ICS, in particular, there was a great deal of decentralization, which meant that not only was India fairly autonomous of Britain but that, at the other end of the hierarchy in India, the district officer was often a very powerful individual. Dewey (1973: 267) has commented that 'the Indian civil servant exercised a power for good or evil which no English civil servant – perhaps no functionary in the world – possessed'.

There are numerous accounts of the daily life of a 'typical' ICS official (for example, Campbell, 1893; Keene, 1897; Machonochie, 1926; Trevelyan, 1866). For those who were neither newly arrived and awaiting a field assignment nor permanently assigned to head office in one of the three presidencies, life was mostly likely spent in a relatively remote location, quite possibly without the company of any or many other expatriates. As a district officer or collector, or in another similar role, the expatriate spent much time actually moving around dealing with the Indian population, collecting taxes, dispensing justice or whatever (what was described as 'touring'). Indeed, for such persons, contact with Indians of all levels was both frequent and close. It was essential that the officer speak whatever was the local language, since few if any of the Indians he would come into contact with would speak English. Though Britain's attitude towards India, and the attitudes of expatriates to Indians, altered over time, it was a consistent requirement (if the broad British objectives of commercial gain and political stability were to be achieved) that members of the civil service be both tactful and sympathetic in their relations with the local population; official documents with titles such as 'Memorandum on the subject of social and official intercourse between European officers in the Punjab and Indians' were issued containing such advice (Barrier, 1971). After two or three years in one place, the expatriate would be moved on through promotion to another location (Campbell, 1852), much as an expatriate in a multinational corporation today might move from country to country. This pattern continued until the officer was dismissed (a very rare likelihood), resigned (a fairly uncommon occurrence), died on the job (a more likely possibility) or retired (probably back to Britain, but not necessarily). There could be no mistake, however, that wherever they were, whatever

Lessons from the British in India

their title at that moment and despite occasional internal disputes, the members of the ICS were part of a closely-knit group who saw themselves and were seen by others as the élite corps in India, an attitude intensified by their small number, their intense socialization experiences during training and the fact that there were strong intergenerational family experiences in the service. As Allen (1976: 41–2) has observed, just as Indian society was characterized by a caste system, so too were there castes among the British in India – and the ICS were indisputably the Brahmins.

Besides the isolation which confronted members of the ICS at all levels, there were great hardships and challenges for the expatriates in terms of an oppressive climate, countless untreatable diseases (among them, rabies, cholera, typhoid, dysentery and malaria), separation from families in Britain, foreign languages to be learned and generally harsh living conditions. Over time, with changes brought about by such things as the Suez Canal, telegraph and steam transportation (Spangenberg, 1971: 358), some of these drawbacks were lessened but, until the end, life as an expatriate in India was not an easy one. Indeed, an individual's life expectancy decreased markedly upon assuming their expatriate role; Woodruff (1953: 114) claims that in the 1700s their chances of survival were less than in the trenches in World War I. Certainly one of the most pervasive and touching themes running through the many biographies is the tragedy that befell so many expatriates in India, as, for example, in Keene's (1897: 257) comment that, 'My daughter Emily, a charming girl of seventeen, died in my arms, struck down suddenly by the heat; my wife bore a son who ailed from his cradle to his premature grave; and we all fell into the depths of despair and disease'. Yet, as Woodruff (1954: 203) points out: 'Nor were graves all the cost; much endurance must be counted in as well, much loneliness, hardship, and separation, much toil, much loss of faith, much hardening of the moral arteries'.

Given the practical constraints under which they operated, success in governing India lay in having a very disciplined and efficient civil service. Though there have been criticisms (Ewing, 1984: 33) that by the 1920s 'the complex task of governing India seemed to be beyond the creaking, anachronistic and overworked I.C.S.', it is almost universally credited with having been a remarkably efficient operation. Whatever criticisms might be made of the colonization of India by Britain, it appears that the members of the ICS, and their predecessors, acquitted themselves very well and corruption was rare (Woodruff, 1954: 95).

Bruce W. Stening

Recruitment and selection

As one might expect, the criteria for selection into the ICS varied somewhat over the three centuries that the British were in India. The criteria used were diverse and included: age; personal recommendation; ability to keep accounts and good handwriting; competitive examination scores; morality; health; ability to furnish a security; language competency; 'gentlemanliness'; and ability to ride a horse. In the earliest days of the East India Company, recruitment was by way of straightforward application and, reflecting the commercial nature of the operation, the principal criteria were the ability to keep accounts and good handwriting. By the middle of the eighteenth century there were more applicants than positions available. What developed subsequently was a system of patronage whereby directors of the Company were permitted to recommend individuals personally. This was seen as a means of ensuring that recruits were persons of integrity (Ghosal, 1944: 22). To counter the obvious opportunities for corruption, legislation was passed in 1793 whereby directors had to give reasons for their nomination, state their connections with the nominee and sign a declaration that no payment had been received (Cohn, 1966: 103). From the very earliest days of the Company until the end of British rule in India, members of the civil service had to sign a covenant which set out various matters related to their employment, and had to provide a large financial bond by way of security. Such persons were thus often referred to as covenanted servants, another way in which their status was elevated above that of other expatriate employees.

The system of nomination by directors continued largely without alteration until 1855 when, after considerable debate, the Charter Act of 1853 came into effect requiring selection on the basis of open competition through examination. Clearly, this change created opportunities for a career in the ICS for individuals who had previously stood no chance. While there was widespread support for the change (even more so by the existing civil servants in India than those in London – see Lowell, 1900: 25), there was a widely held fear that the new system would bring in individuals of lower class who would not set the right 'tone', thus not achieve the respect of the Indian population and consequently undermine stability in India. This view is vividly portrayed in the statement (Lowell, 1900: 25) that, 'The Oriental feels and resents at once the rule of a man who has not been surrounded by culture and refinement from his earliest years'. (Perhaps those who held such views might have paused if they could have considered

Lessons from the British in India

Machonochie's later (1926: 256) advice on the dangers of stereotyping: 'And remember Lord Morley's dictum: "The thirst after broad classification works havoc with the truth" . . . Some [Indians] are and some are not, some do and some do not, just as it is with our own people'.)

The basis for the move to a competitive system of selection was the recommendations of a high-powered commission headed by Lord Macaulay which were presented in 1854. The essential recommendations of the commission were, first, that the competitive examination by means of which individuals were selected for the civil service in India should require a high level of general education but no specific knowledge of India; but, second, that, following selection based on the examination of more general matters, there should be a period of not less than one year and not more than two during which those selected would 'give their whole minds to the study in England of their special duties in India' (Lowell, 1900: 19). This specialized training, it was suggested, should include Indian history, languages and law. (These matters will be discussed in more detail in the following section on training.)

Though the details of the competitive examination system were altered from time to time, essentially this remained the basis for the selection of members of the ICS for the next 100 years. It was not a requirement for candidates to prepare for their examinations by attending a university, though almost all did, and of those about three-quarters had studied at either Oxford or Cambridge. It should be noted that, initially at least, those who entered through the new system were often referred to, disparagingly, by officers who had been selected under the old method as competition-wallahs (men), the sentiments about whom are generally reflected in this comment:

> The competition-wallah – the product of cramming – might be more intelligent than his Haileybury predecessors, more prolific and agile with a pen; but was he also a gentleman? Was not his physique so weakened by excessive concentration on the book work needed to succeed in the open examination that his health broke down in India? Of sedentary disposition, could he ride? Could he inspire the same respect in the natives? (Dewey, 1973: 272)

Some time after the introduction of the Charter Act, the Secretary of State for India sought the views of interested parties concerning the appropriate basis for selection for the ICS. Correspondence, notes, memoranda, minutes and the like were published (*Papers relating . . .*, 1876), representing a broad cross-section of views. Beside the question of examination system in principle, one of the matters that most exercised the minds of those who expressed a view was the most appropriate age at which men should take the examination (which obviously

Bruce W. Stening

influenced the age at which they would be sent to India). There was a considerable variation in opinion: of the ninety-six ICS officers who provided their view to the Secretary about this issue, thirty-six wanted to retain the existing limit, twenty-seven wanted to reduce it and thirty-three wanted it increased. Then, as throughout the remaining years of the British in India, there was much debate surrounding the trade-off between youth and education. Blunt (1937: 197) summarized the arguments for higher or lower age limits: the arguments for a lower limit were that younger recruits would be less set in their habits, would be more adaptable to Indian conditions and would be quicker to learn the vernaculars; while the arguments in favour of a higher limit were that men who were somewhat older would have a better education and more developed judgement. As one side of the argument would gain favour over the other, so the requirements for selection would be changed marginally. Fundamentally, however, whatever else they were, the men who constituted the ICS from 1855 were much better educated than their predecessors and had attained their positions through merit rather than connections. It must be said, too, that even before 1855 the process of recruitment and selection was such that overwhelmingly the British civil servants in India were a competent and principled lot, with few 'bad bargains' (Campbell, 1852: 267) among them.

Training

As explained in the previous section, in the period after the introduction of the competitive examination system, those selected then undertook training in Britain for between one and two years in matters that would be of specific relevance to them in carrying out their role in India. However, from the early 1800s formal training had been provided, both in Britain and in India, to the Company's civil servants to prepare them for their expatriate roles. Before that, expatriates were given virtually no other training than some post-arrival instruction in the Indian vernaculars relevant to their posting.

The first formal training requirements were initiated by the then Governor-General of India, Lord Wellesley, who established Fort William College in Calcutta in the early 1800s. He felt that new recruits were inadequately trained, especially since from around this time their functions were administrative rather than commercial. Wellesley wanted a three-year period of training that would be both general and specific to India in nature. As it turned out, for reasons largely resulting from internal politics in the Company (Bowen, 1955:

Lessons from the British in India

109–10), over time the college was scaled back to be principally a language school preparing recruits for the Bengal presidency. Nevertheless, it remained in existence until 1854 and, according to Cohn (1966: 114), added professionalism to the service. Perhaps as much as anything, though, its purpose was in providing a bridge between the home and host country experiences, as reflected in one civilian's comment that the period spent at the college 'made me almost cease to regret the exile from country and family in which I was compelled to pass my days' (Prinsep, quoted in Cohn, 1966: 115). The college also served a real purpose in socializing the new recruits and in forming the basis for a network of relationships which would be important in the performance of each man's job.

In 1804, the Company also established the East India College in Britain (which soon became known as Haileybury, the place where it was located) as a pre-departure training establishment. It trained the recruits in both European and Oriental subjects and was staffed by scholars of very high repute, including Malthus. Monier-Williams was a student there, taught there and ultimately became Professor of Sanskrit at Oxford, but he was just one of the many men who went on to distinguished careers (Danvers, 1894). In fact, over its fifty-two year history it admitted almost 2,000 men, of whom 88 per cent went on to careers as civil servants in India (Stephens, 1900: 304). Those who failed to get through Haileybury were normally put into the Cavalry (O'Malley, 1965: 239). Though it is difficult to assess just how successful it was in transmitting knowledge and skills that were useful to the expatriates in India, like Fort William College it helped to build a strong esprit de corps; as Cohn (1966: 139) points out:

> The students developed peer relations with a group with whom they were to spend their lives working . . . . The British officials in India formed a most unusual kind of society with a fossil culture, cut off from close contact with home . . . . Cut off also from most real contact with Indian society, they had to carry out complex administrative tasks and constantly had to make decisions. It would seem axiomatic that in India they needed an understanding of the values and culture of their peers, superiors and subordinates which the common experience of Haileybury gave them.

While this was largely beneficial, there were some (for example, Trevelyan, 1866: 7) who felt that 'excessive' esprit de corps had the danger of inducing 'a way of thought too exclusively Anglo-Indian'.

As explained in the previous section, after the introduction of the competitive examination system of selection there continued to be training, although it was somewhat more general and less vocational than Haileybury. There were, though, those who doubted 'the universal applicability of occidental methods' and who felt that the

Bruce W. Stening

Macaulay Commission's recommendations had 'insufficient regard for the particulars of the Indian situation' (Dewey, 1973: 267). Of course, the pre-departure training in Britain was only part of what was necessary for the budding ICS expatriate. As Lowell (1900: 46–7) pointed out:

> The young Civilian is not, of course, ready for active duties on his arrival in India. He has still his apprenticeship to serve. He must have some experience of the people and the traditions of administration before he can hold even one of the minor posts, and it is generally assumed that he is merely in training for the first two years after his arrival.

Moreover, throughout British rule in India, much of the training which civil servants received (both work-related and general) was acquired informally through senior colleagues (Woodruff, 1954: 256), through relatives (for the many expatriates who had relatives who had served in India) and from on-the-job experience. Woodruff (1954: 95) quotes G.O. Trevelyan as saying that, 'The real education of a civil servant consists in the responsibility that devolves on him at an early age'.

Adjustment

However careful the selection and intensive the preparatory training, adjustment to life as an expatriate in India was not easy. Compton (1968: 270) claims that, except in broad terms, most expatriates were fairly ignorant about just what India would be like in terms of living conditions and how bad it would be. This was much more so in respect of the general facets of living than in respect of work, though even in relation to the latter there were those (Blunt, 1937) who argued that, after arrival in India, there was not only much for the new expatriate to learn, there were also things to unlearn. As Keene (1897: 328) observed, India is 'a society whose very origin and frame are so different from anything with which we are familiar in Europe'.

To supplement the mainly job-oriented training which the recruits had received, numerous handbooks were published as guides to expatriate life in India (see, for example, Anglo-Indian, 1882; Gilchrist, 1825; Hull and Mair, 1871), providing all manner of practical advice such as how to travel in a palanquin, the best way of expelling weevils, how to handle servants, social customs to be observed, methods of coming to terms with the oppressive climate, rules for the safe consumption of food and beverages, what constituted an appropriate wardrobe and even how to select a mistress. In relation to the matter of what was a suitable 'kit', the list was enormous – included in

394

Lessons from the British in India

Gilchrist's 'necessaries for a lady proceeding to India' were seventy-two chemises, twenty-four pairs of long gloves, twenty-four pairs of short gloves, thirty-six towels and many more items (1825: 527–8).

Much was written both in these guides and in biographies and the like about the difficulties presented by the climate. In line with advice which would typically be given today that intending expatriates should be given a realistic picture of life in the host country, the accounts were stark, to the point where, in the light of such description as that of the 'hot weather' that follows, it is astounding that anyone was attracted:

> Hour after hour, day after day, the heat seems to increase; you get no rest at night, even though you may have had your bed taken out into the compound and a sort of impromptu punkah rigged up over it; you wake with a sense of suffocation; you are irritated beyond measure by trifles; you hate the frogs who croak to each other the lifelong night; the insects of all kinds drive you to distraction, goading you into an almost desperate state. (Anglo-Indian, 1882: 83)

In respect of the climate, as with other difficulties, the expatriates devised various ways of coping. To the extent that was possible (given that work could not stop altogether), expatriates and their families would undertake an annual migration to a hill station to escape the worst of the heat. The best known of these (especially since it attracted the most senior officials) was Simla, but there were many other more localized hill stations throughout India (Allen, 1976: 33). Especially in the days before modern transportation, such a migration, which implied taking not only one's family but also servants and work and so on, was a major undertaking. The men left at their posts not only had to endure the intense heat but extreme isolation, too: 'you might spend months without hearing a lady's voice or speaking your native tongue' (Keene, 1897: 117). Worse still for them, perhaps, was the knowledge that some of the 'grass widows' (women in hill stations without their husbands) had a reputation for having affairs (Allen, 1976: 213).

Besides the climate, the other most significant non-work issue in adjustment to India was family adjustment (an issue which, incidentally, has remained one of the most problematic for sojourners in India – see Useem, 1966). Though there is no evidence to suggest that the divorce rate was very high (or higher than in Britain) or that early return to Britain was common (neither were realistic options during most of the period of the British in India), it is apparent from the many biographies, diaries and histories of women in India that they endured much hardship. While having a large number of servants (forty was not uncommon in the 1800s – a consequence, incidentally,

Bruce W. Stening

not just of the low cost of labour but also of the strict role divisions created by the caste system) had its advantages, it also had its downside insofar as there was often little to do. The children were usually brought up by servants (and, as a result, often learned an Indian language before they learned English – Allen, 1976: 25). Furthermore, once they were old enough they were almost invariably sent back to Britain to be educated. As Diver (1909) wrote sadly:

> One after one the babies grow into companionable children. One after one England claims them, till the mother's heart and house are left unto her desolate.

Since for many women it was feasible to live either in Britain or India, it became a choice of separation from their husband or their children. Those who stayed in India not uncommonly took to horse-riding for recreation and, if they were in a settlement with other Europeans, spent a lot of time engaging in club-based activities.

On the work front, the ICS official faced the dilemma of all expatriates, namely, balancing the need to adjust to the host culture with the need satisfactorily to represent the interests of one's employer (in this case, the British government), what Black, Gregersen and Mendenhall (1992a: Ch. 6) describe as the problem of integrating or balancing dual allegiances. Though, in order to satisfy one's employer's interests, it was necessary to go some way towards localization, it was possible to go too far – and some officials did. In just such a case, a formal regulation was introduced which forbade the wearing of Indian clothes during working hours (Cohn, 1966: 23), said to have been necessary to bring into line a senior person who had 'gone native'.

Largely, however, such behaviour was modified by social control, since the effect of an official deviating too far from English norms was 'to sink him in the estimation of the mass of the community, both Native and European, among whom he resides' (Barrier, 1971: 292). Few people were prepared to endure the isolation which this would imply. There is a view (Braddon, 1872) that a more satisfactory balance (in the direction of fitting in with India) was achieved in the early days of the British in India than was the case by the middle of last century. Braddon attributes this to three factors: the absence of many Englishwomen until around that time (for a long time, most people sent to India were not permitted to take their wives); the isolation by virtue of poor communications and transportation; and the fact that in the early days of the Company the British were essentially traders rather than rulers. Besides Braddon, several writers (Bhatia, 1979; Edwardes, 1967; Keene, 1897; Kincaid, 1938) have commented on the drawbacks to the arrival of large numbers of Englishwomen. Kincaid (1938) went as far as reporting: 'The old-fashioned administrator with his Indian mistress had, it has been argued, a knowledge of the people such as his more virtuous successor could hardly hope to gain'.

Clearly, an ability to get on with Indians at all levels was an essential attribute for the civil servant, a requirement expressed in a variety of ways by the many people who have commented on it, but perhaps captured in this comment of Machonochie (1926: 256):

> The first essential for happiness in India is the ability to get into sympathy with its people. For the man or woman of insular prejudices and antipathies there is no place.

Appraising and rewarding

As with other matters, the basis upon which members of the ICS were appraised and rewarded varied somewhat over the 350-year period. However, although the talents of outstanding individuals were rewarded by rapid advancement, as befitted a civil service (of that period, anyway), promotion was primarily on the basis of seniority rather than merit, even in the earliest days of the Company (Ghosal, 1944: 29). From time to time, the drawbacks associated with such a system were specifically investigated as, for example, in the Lee Commission of 1886 which was set up to enquire into complaints about pay and prospects in the ICS. The complaints were in some instances equity-based, as between ICS officials in the field and those at headquarters, the view being expressed by one in the former group that they 'are generally taken for granted, left in dull places and unwholesome climates, and cheerfully dismissed at the end with no more reward than a pension such as may be earned by the most soulless officer that ever taught a sepoy the goose step' (Keene, 1897: 335). Adjustments were also required occasionally to ensure that comparabilities were maintained between different branches (the executive and the judicial, for instance) of the service (Misra, 1970: 197).

In the 1700s, servants of the company could expect not only a reasonable pension on retirement but to have earned in the order of 30,000 pounds (a small fortune then) through lawful savings (Keene, 1897: ix). Financial moderation came with the establishment of an orthodox civil service in the 1800s. Besides a reasonable initial salary and regular increments based on length of service, members of the ICS were given other allowances as were necessary for the particular host environment in which they were operating. For example, before formal training facilities were established, servants newly arrived in India were given an allowance for employing munshies (Indian

Bruce W. Stening

coaches) to teach them appropriate Indian languages (Ghosal, 1944: 244). Furthermore, there were always allowances for furloughs back in Britain (though these were more generous during some periods than others) and for the education of children there, too. To some extent, the salary an expatriate received was also contingent on being able to demonstrate an ability to cope with local conditions; two examples of this are, first, the necessity of passing language competency tests before being assigned to a position in the field, and, second, the requirement of at least a minimum proficiency in riding before salary could rise above base-level (India List, 1900).

One of the compounding difficulties through the late 1800s into the late 1920s was the falling value of the rupee, the currency in which, by this stage, expatriates received their salary (Ewing, 1984). Indeed, overall, it would seem that the rewards provided were at their relative worst in the 1900s. All of these financial concerns certainly had a negative impact on both morale and recruitment and increased the rate of premature retirement (Spangenberg, 1971), for, while the rewards of service in the ICS might be non-financial (various writers mentioning things such as living in an ancient, exotic and interesting place, the approbation of their country, high levels of responsibility and so on) as well as financial, there were the realities to confront, Machonochie's (1926: 3–4) comments being reflective of many expatriates' feelings:

> While failure to achieve distinction may be accepted with equanimity, penury is another matter. Official worries and personal discomfort are all in the day's work. It is the daily and hourly grinding anxiety as to ways and means that robs a man of his sleep and takes the heart out of his work.

One of the realities that had to be faced increasingly in this century was the pressure for localization. Granted the right to join the ICS in the mid-1800s, by the turn of the twentieth century Indians were gaining more influence and, while it was not that common, it was conceivable that a British member of the service could have an Indian superior, a situation that many expatriates found difficult (Machonochie, 1926: 2).

Repatriating

As explained earlier, a civil servant's life as an expatriate in India was usually a long-term proposition. Permanent re-entry to Britain, then, was likely to occur after a career of some thirty or so years. Of course, furloughs would have been taken several times during the assignment, but this was hardly likely to prepare the returnee for life in a country which had changed enormously. The most obvious differences that had to be confronted were the climate and a life without servants and all the other trappings that went with being 'on top' in India. For some, but it must be said not many, the prospect of returning to Britain was altogether too daunting and they chose to 'stay on' in India. There were some officials who, by virtue of their outstanding performance in India, were repatriated from India at a relatively early age and sent on to undertake even bigger things elsewhere, though they were few in number and less likely to have worked their way up through the ranks than to have come in at an already high level. Unfortunately, less has been written about the repatriation aspects of the ICS officials' expatriate experience than any other.

Of course, ultimate 'repatriation' for the service as a whole came with independence in 1947. Allen (1976: 264), recounts the memories of one expatriate returning to England:

> The final, ritual farewell was made – as always – where the East ended and the West began: 'As we left Port Said and sailed into the open waters everyone was paraded with their topees on deck and at a given signal we all flung our topees into the sea and that was the last of India.'

An overall evaluation: how well did they measure up? what can we learn?

What, then, can a human resource management practitioner or researcher who is concerned with improving the management of an expatriate work-force in the late twentieth century glean from the experience of the British in India? Before endeavouring to answer such a question, it is important to note that the British sent to India were atypical expatriates in certain respects: in particular, their length of service was considerably longer than is usual among modern managerial expatriates, their objectives were broader and their home country held sovereign power in the host country. Nevertheless, in all significant respects, the issues which confronted those who managed the British in India were the same as must be dealt with in, say, multinational corporations today.

In undertaking an evaluation of the British in India, one is faced with the same two fundamental problems as continue to confront us today: the wide variety of criteria by which 'success' can be and is measured (Benson, 1978) and the high reliance on self-reporting of the expatriates themselves as against more objective measures of their per-

Bruce W. Stening

formance. At base, however, then, as now, our evaluation is likely to
be focused on two interrelated but separable matters, the expatriates'
levels of adjustment to and performance in the host culture. In respect
of both aspects, the British in India rate very well.

In relation to overall adjustment, in a comprehensive review of the
empirical literature, Mendenhall and Oddou (1985) stated that there
were four relevant dimensions (which in a subsequent paper
(Mendenhall, Dunbar and Oddou, 1987) they reduced to three) to
expatriate acculturation. The first of these (which they labelled 'self-
orientation') related to 'activities and attributes that serve to
strengthen the expatriate's self-esteem, self-confidence, and mental
hygiene' (Mendenhall and Oddou, 1985: 40) and included stress reduction, reinforcement substitution, physical mobility, technical competence, dealing with alienation, dealing with isolation and realistic
expectations prior to departure. The second (labelled 'others-orienta-
tion') dealt with 'activities that enhance the expatriate's ability to
interact effectively with host nationals' (Mendenhall and Oddou, 1985:
41) and included relationship skills, willingness to communicate, nonverbal communication, respect for others and empathy for others. The
third dimension ('perceptual-orientation') was concerned with understanding why the members of the host culture behave the way they do
and included flexible attributions, broad category width, high tolerance for ambiguity, being non-judgemental, being open-minded and
field-independence. Based on the considerable body of evidence that is
available, it can legitimately be claimed that the British in India
exhibited high levels of achievement on all three dimensions and most
of their constituent elements.

Several factors can be seen to have contributed to the high levels of
adjustment and performance achieved among the members of the
Indian Civil Service (and their predecessors in the East India
Company). Perhaps the most important of these was the tremendously
strong corporate culture which characterized this group throughout its
entire history. This was a group that was (especially measured in relation to their immense tasks) small, difficult to join (even in the days
of patronage), enormously powerful, highly esteemed in all quarters
(even Indian), welded by common adversities, socially quite homogeneous (even after the introduction of a competitive system of entry),
commonly joined by successive generations of the same family, subjected to intensive training and (more broadly) socialization, and governed by an almost Japanese-like system of lifetime employment. All
of these factors contributed to the ICS being a highly cohesive group.
Equally important, the tasks of this group, complex though they were,
were clearly defined, such that it was always possible to re-focus

attention on whether the Service was performing at an optimal level and, if not, to determine what should be done to improve its performance. As we have noted, the means used to achieve the ends changed from time to time. Virtually all such changes were in response to a desire to improve both the general adjustment of the expatriates and their performance in carrying out their tasks. That there was regular debate, both in the Service and outside it, about what were the 'best' methods of selection, training and so forth must be considered a strength and not a weakness. Probably because of the significance of British objectives in India as a whole, enormous resources were invested in ensuring that the Service was well equipped to do its job. This is probably no more evident than in the time and money spent on training the expatriates in the languages, laws, customs and so on of India. Perhaps the only group today that comes close to managing its expatriate work-force as well as the ICS are Japanese multinational corporations; indeed, the strengths ascribed by Tung (1984) to Japanese firms, namely, the importance they assign to human resource management in general, the longer duration of their expatriates' assignments, the broad support system for expatriates in corporate headquarters and the careful attention that they give both to selecting and training their expatriates, were all characteristics of the management of the British officials in India.

In summary, though it had its share of troubles, the ICS stands as an exemplar of expatriate management. Its attention to all aspects of the 'expatriate experience', from beginning to end, provides a multitude of lessons for present-day human resource management practitioners and researchers, particularly, though not exclusively, those concerned with expatriate or remotely located (see Nadkarni and Stening, 1989) work-forces.

Conclusion

Not infrequently, individuals working in any scholarly field are wont to forget not only the work that preceded their era but that new challenges await those who will follow them. Just, then, as the role of, and problems faced by, expatriates in India changed over the period of British rule as a result of various factors, and the issues we confront today are not exactly the same as those which confronted the British in India, the particular problems confronting both expatriates and those who study them will be different in the next century and beyond. However, perhaps those who are concerned with, say, the problems of settling managers on other planets will find some profit in

Bruce W. Stening

examining the issues which exercised our minds and our approaches to handling those issues.

Australian National University
Canberra
Australia

Notes

1   Until 1858, British interests in India were the responsibility of the East India Company, after which they were taken over by the Crown. Those with the responsibility for administering India on behalf of the British were referred to as civil servants (or sometimes just civilians). From 1858 they were, as a body, known as the Indian Civil Service. There were other specialized services including the Indian Forestry Service, the Indian Police Service and the Indian Political Service. However, the ICS was the most important service and, thus, the one for which most data is available. Accordingly, the focus in this paper is the ICS, though expatriates in other services will be referred to as appropriate.
2   Data collection in the India Office Library was undertaken during a period of sabbatical leave. The co-operation of the Library's staff is gratefully acknowledged.
3   By 1856, Britain controlled about two-thirds of the area of pre-partition India (Cohn, 1966: 98), the remaining third being accounted for by the so-called princely states, which maintained a greater degree of autonomy but which were still under the eye of a British Resident or a political agent of the British government.

References

Allen, C. (ed.) (1976) *Plain Tales from the Raj: Images of British India in the Twentieth Century.* London: Futura.
An Anglo-Indian (1882) *Indian Outfits & Establishments: A practical guide for persons about to reside in India, detailing the articles which should be taken out, and the requirements of home life and management there.* London: L. Upcott Gill.
Barrier, N.G. (1971) 'How to Rule India: Two Documents on the I.C.S. and the Politics of Administration', *The Panjab Past and Present*, 5 (2): 276–97.
Benson, P.G. (1978) 'Measuring Cross-Cultural Adjustment: The Problem of Criteria', *International Journal of Intercultural Relations*, 2 (1): 21–37.
Bhatia, H.S. (ed.) (1979) *European Women in India: Their Life and Adventures.* New Delhi: Deep & Deep.
Black, J.S. and Mendenhall, M. (1990) 'Cross-Cultural Training Effectiveness: A Review and a Theoretical Framework for Future Research', *Academy of Management Review*, 15 (1): 113–36.
Black, J.S., Gregersen, H.B. and Mendenhall, M.E. (1992a) *Global Assignments: Successfully Expatriating and Repatriating International Managers.* San Francisco: Jossey-Bass.

Lessons from the British in India

Black, J.S., Gregerson, H.B. and Mendenhall, M.E. (1992b) 'Toward a Theoretical Framework of Repatriation Adjustment', *Journal of International Business Studies*, 23 (4): 737–60.

Blunt, E.A.H. (1937) *The I.C.S.* London: Faber.

Bowen, J. (1955) 'The East India Company's Education of its Own Servants', *Journal of the Royal Asiatic Society*, October: 8–23.

Bradden, E. (1872) *Life in India: A Series of sketches showing something of the Anglo-Indian, the land he lives in, and the people among whom he lives.* London: Longmans, Green & Co.

Brown, H. (ed.) (1948) *The Sahibs: The Life and Ways of the British in India as Recorded by Themselves.* London: William Hodge.

Campbell, G. (1852) *Modern India: A Sketch of the System of Civil Government.* London: John Murray.

Campbell, G. (1893) *Memoirs of my Indian Career*, Vols. I & II. London: Macmillan.

Church, A.T. (1982) 'Sojourner Adjustment', *Psychological Bulletin*, 91 (3): 540–72.

Cohn, B.S. (1966) 'Recruitment and Training of British Civil Servants in India 1600–1860'. In Braibanti, R. (ed.) *Asian Bureaucratic Systems Emergent from the British Imperial Tradition*. Durham, NC: Duke University Press, pp. 87–140.

Compton, J.M. (1968) 'Open Competition and the Indian Civil Service, 1854–1876', *English Historical Review*, 83: 265–84.

Danvers, F.C. *et al.* (1894) *Memorials of Old Haileybury College*. London: Archibald Constable.

Dewey, C.J. (1973) 'The Education of a Ruling Caste: The Indian Civil Service in the Era of Competitive Examination', *English Historical Review*, 88: 262–85.

Diver, M. (1909) *The Englishwoman in India.*

Edwardes, M. (1967) *Raj: The Story of British India.* London: Pan.

Ewing, A. (1984) 'The Indian Civil Service 1919–1924: Service Discontent and the Response in London and Delhi', *Modern Asian Studies*, 18 (1): 33–53.

Ghosal, A.K. (1944) *Civil Service in India under the East India Company: A Study in Administrative Development.* Calcutta: University of Calcutta.

Gilchrist, J.B. (1825) *The General East India Guide and Vade Mecum, for the Public Functionary, Government Officer, Private Agent, Trader or Foreign Sojourner in British India.* London: Kingsbury, Parbury & Allen.

Hull, E.C.P. and Mair, R.S. (1871) *The European in India: A handbook of useful and practical information for those proceeding to or residing in the East Indies, relating to outfits, routes, time for departure, Indian climate and seasons, house-keeping, servants, etc., etc.* London: Henry S. King.

The India List and India Office List for 1900 (1900) [Compiled from official records by direction of the Secretary of State for India in Council] London: Harrison & Sons.

Keene, H.G. (1897) *A Servant of 'John Company': Being the Recollections of an Indian Official.* London: Thacker.

Kincaid, D. (1938) *British Social Life in India, 1608–1937.* London: Routledge & Kegan Paul.

Laurence, B.S. (1984) 'Historical Perspective: Using the Past to Study the Present', *Academy of Management Review*, 9, 2: 307–12.

Lewis, T. and Jungman, R.E. (eds) (1986) *On Being Foreign: Culture Shock in Short Fiction.* Yarmouth, Maine: Intercultural Press.

Lowell, A.L. (1900) *Colonial Civil Service: The Selection and Training of Colonial Officials in England, Holland and France.* New York: Macmillan.

Bruce W. Stening

Machonochie, E. (1926) *Life in the Indian Civil Service*. London: Chapman & Hall.

Mendenhall, M. and Oddou, G. (1985) 'The Dimensions of Expatriate Acculturation: A Review', *Academy of Management Review*, 10 (1): 39–47.

Mendenhall, M.E., Dunbar, E. and Oddou, G.R. (1987) 'Expatriate Selection; Training and Career-Pathing: A Review and Critique', *Human Resource Management*, 26 (3): 331–45.

Misra, B.B. (1970) *The Administrative History of India 1834–1947*. Oxford: Oxford University Press.

Moore, R.J. (1964) 'The Abolition of Patronage in the I.C.S. and the Closure of Haileybury College', *Historical Journal*, 7 (2): 246–57.

Muttalib, M.A. (1967) *The Union Public Service Commission*. New Delhi: Indian Institute of Public Administration.

Nadkarni, S. and Stening, B.W. (1989) 'Human Resource Management in Remote Communities', *Asia Pacific Human Resource Management*, 27 (3): 41–63.

O'Malley, L.S.S. (1965) *The Indian Civil Service 1601–1930*, 2nd edition. London: Frank Cass.

Papers Relating to the Selection and Training of Candidates for the Indian Civil Service (1876) Calcutta: Office of the Superintendent of Government Printing.

Spangenberg, B. (1971) 'The Problem of Recruitment for the I.C.S. during the Late Nineteenth Century', *Journal of Asian Studies*, 30 (2): 341–60.

Stening, B.W. (1979) 'Problems in Cross-Cultural Contact: A Literature Review', *International Journal of Intercultural Relations*, 3 (3): 269–313.

Stephens, H.M. (1900) 'An Account of the East India College at Haileybury (1806–1857)'. In Lowell, A.L. *Colonial Service: The Selection and Training of Colonial Officials in England, Holland and France*. New York: Macmillan, pp. 233–346.

Torbiorn, I. (1982) *Living Abroad*. New York: Wiley.

Trevelyan, G.O. (1866) *The Competition Wallah*, 2nd edition. London: Macmillan.

Tung, R.L. (1984) 'Strategic Management of Human Resources in the Multinational Enterprise', *Human Resource Management*, 23 (2): 129–43.

Useem, R.H. (1966) 'The American Family in India', *Annals of the American Academy*, 368: 132–45.

Woodruff, P. (1953) *The Men who Ruled India: The Founders*. London: Cape.

Woodruff, P. (1954) *The Men who Ruled India: The Guardians*. London: Cape.

[19]

The International Journal of Human Resource Management 5:2 May 1994

Convergence or divergence: human resource practices and policies for competitive advantage worldwide

Paul Sparrow, Randall S. Schuler and Susan E. Jackson

Abstract

The world is becoming far more competitive and volatile than ever before, causing firms to seek to gain competitive advantage whenever and wherever possible. As traditional sources and means such as capital, technology or location become less significant as a basis for competitive advantage, firms are turning to more innovative sources. One of these is the management of human resources. While traditionally regarded as a personnel department function, it is now being widely shared among managers and non-managers, personnel directors and line managers. As the management of human resources is seen increasingly in terms of competitive advantage, the question that arises is: What must we do to gain this advantage? Many of the most successful firms now have to operate globally, and this gives rise to a second question: Do firms in different parts of the globe practice human resource management (HRM) for competitive advantage differently? Because of their importance, these two questions form the primary focus of this investigation. Data from a worldwide respondent survey of chief executive officers and human resource managers from twelve countries are cluster analysed to identify country groupings across a range of human resource policies and practices that could be used for competitive advantage. Differences and similarities on fifteen dimensions of these policies and practices are statistically determined and the results interpreted in the light of relevant literature. This investigation concludes that there is indeed a convergence in the use of HRM for competitive advantage. However, in pursuing this convergence there are some clear divergences, nuances and specific themes in the areas of HRM that will take the fore and in the way in which specific aspects such as culture, work structuring, performance management and resourcing will be utilized. These patterns of HRM bear understanding and consideration in managing human resources in different parts of the world.

Paul Sparrow, Randall S. Schuler and Susan E. Jackson

Introduction

As firms pursue, aggressively, their short-term and long-term goals, they are realizing that their success depends upon a successful global presence (Ghoshal and Bartlett, 1989). In turn, their success as global players is being seen as increasingly dependent upon international human resource management: In a comparative context, human resource management (HRM) is best considered as the range of policies which have strategic significance for the organization (Brewster and Tyson, 1991) and which are typically used to facilitate integration, employee commitment, flexibility and the quality of work life as well as meeting broader business goals such as changing organizational values, structure, productivity and delivery mechanisms. Therefore, in order to explain the various 'brands' of HRM on a worldwide basis in sufficient detail, any analysis must include 'subjects which have traditionally been the concern of personnel management and industrial relations . . . as well as . . . more innovative and strategic approaches to people management' (Brewster and Tyson, 1991: 1). Differences between countries in the historical role and function of the personnel management function make it necessary to take a more strategic perspective of the underlying people issues.

This increasing reliance upon successful HRM as a key to gaining competitive advantage in the global arena is mirroring the same phenomenon that effective firms witnessed during the 1980s on the domestic scene. As technology and capital became commodities in domestic markets, the only thing left really to distinguish firms, and thereby allow them to gain competitive advantage, were skills in managing their human resources (Reich, 1990). While attention has been devoted to international comparisons of production systems and management strategies for many years, the comparison of people management systems has until recently been overlooked (Brewster, Hegewisch and Lockhart, 1991; Pieper, 1990).

Successful global human resource management

If long-run as well as short-run corporate goals are dependent upon successful global HRM, an interesting question is: What is successful global management of human resources? At the risk of oversimplifying, we argue that it is best defined as the possession of the skills and knowledge of formulating and implementing policies and practices that effectively integrate and cohere globally dispersed employees, while at the same time recognizing and appreciating local differences that impact on the effective utilization of human resources.

HRM practices and policies for competitive advantage worldwide

This definition of the successful global management of human resources can be decomposed into two distinct components of international HRM. The first component represents the body of knowledge and action that multinational firms use in allocating, dispersing, developing and motivating their global work-force. The major HRM concerns tend to focus on expatriate assignment, payment schemes and repatriation (Black, Gregersen and Mendenhall, 1992; Dowling and Schuler, 1990). Concerns for third country and local nationals are reflected in issues relating to the management of global operations, such as who is going to run the various geographically dispersed operations. Thus relatively few individuals tend to be encompassed by this component of international HRM.

The second component represents the body of knowledge and action concerned with actually staffing and running the local operations. The topics and issues enacted at this level are essentially focused around an understanding of local differences relevant to attracting, utilizing and motivating individuals (Adler, 1991; Poole, 1986; Punnett and Ricks, 1992).

As Ronen (1986) suggested, for global firms to be successful in managing their worldwide work-forces, they need to have an understanding and sensitivity to several local environments. They must utilize local information and adapt it to a broader set of human resource policies that reflect the firm itself. Of the two components of successful global HRM, this appears to be the lesser developed. Consequently, the focus of this article is on providing a greater understanding of selected aspects of HRM on a worldwide, comparative basis. We should note, however, that many successful organizations have prospered without following a global route.

Human resource practices and concepts for gaining competitive advantage

Porter (1980) suggested the concept of gaining competitive advantage to firms wishing to engage in strategic activities that would be difficult for competitors to copy or imitate quickly. Schuler and MacMillan (1984) applied this concept to HRM. They, and others since (for example, Reich, 1990), have suggested that firms can use HRM to gain competitive advantage because it is difficult for competitors to duplicate. That is, while technology and capital can be acquired by almost anyone at any time, for a price, it is rather difficult to acquire a ready pool of highly qualified and highly motivated employees. It is increasingly difficult to plan strategy in an era of discontinuous change. A number of writers have focused on the importance of underlying competencies –

Paul Sparrow, Randall S. Schuler and Susan E. Jackson

technical, marketing or strategic capabilities – reflected in unique sets of corporate skill and HRM activities (Grant, 1991; Hamel and Prahalad, 1991).

At the global level, firms can seize competitive advantage through the selection and use of human resource policies and practices. The most important questions to ask then are: What human resource policies and practices can firms consider using in their worldwide operations that might assist them in gaining competitive advantage? Are they likely to be the same across countries? Is there some uniformity that firms can pursue in their efforts to manage their worldwide workforces successfully?

Given the analysis by Moss-Kanter (1991) and Porter (1990), it seems reasonable to proceed on the basis that any understanding of comparative HRM would aid firms in seeking to develop and implement human resource policies and practices worldwide to gain competitive advantage.

Key policies and practices in gaining competitive advantage

While there are several specific ways that firms can gain competitive advantage with HRM policies and practices, it is most useful to gather data on generalizable policies and practices that are consistently seen as central to the management of human resources. In order to provide a basis for international comparison, we elected to focus on five major groupings of HRM policies and practices identified in the literature (see Poole, 1990; Schuler, 1992; Walker, 1992). Broadly, these include: culture; organizational structure; performance management; resourcing; and communications and corporate responsibility.

Culture The present study addresses two aspects of culture. The first is the problem of creating a culture of empowerment, of including all employees in the decision making and responsibility of the organization. This aspect of HRM represents a significant trend in a number of US and UK organizations (Lawler, 1991; Wickens, 1987). How important is it worldwide? The second aspect is the promotion of diversity management and the development of a culture of equality. These two practices are tied together by a policy of inclusion, of bringing everyone into the operation and treating them equally with respect. Equality based on diversity covers the recruitment, placement and advancement of all groups (regardless of race, age, sex or religion) in the organization. More specific and detailed concepts of equality are not examined by the research.

270

HRM practices and policies for competitive advantage worldwide

Organization structure Associated with the issue of culture is that of organization structure. Organization structure refers to the relationship among units and individuals in the organization. It can be described as ranging from a hierarchical, mechanistic relationship to a flatter, horizontal and organic relationship (Burns and Stalker, 1961). Obviously, these represent rather contrasting approaches to structuring organizations. Although their impact on individuals has been explored, more investigation specifically related to comparative HRM appears warranted. Are all countries pursuing strategies of reducing the number of vertical layers (delayering) with the same vigour?

Performance management Another important group of HRM policies and practices reflects those associated with performance management. This process links goal setting and rewards, coaching for performance, aspects of career development and performance evaluation and appraisal into an integrated process. As firms seek to 'manage the most out of employees' they are turning their attention to issues associated with employee performance. Because of the nature of international competition, the specific concerns in performance management are with measuring and motivating customer service, quality, innovation and risk-taking behaviour (Peters, 1992).

Resourcing As important as motivating employees once they are employed are issues associated with obtaining the most appropriate individuals (external resourcing); training and developing them with regard to technology and business process change; and managing the size of the work-force through reductions, downsizing and skills reprofiling. Beer *et al.* (1984) describe these issues as part of a human resource flow policy. Seen in aggregate, we also regard them as part of a total resourcing dimension to HRM, as discussed by a number of writers (Boam and Sparrow, 1992; Mitrani, Dalziel and Fitt, 1992; Torrington *et al.*, 1991).

Communication and corporate responsibility The fifth and final group of HRM policies and practices to which we give consideration are those by which firms may seek to describe their philosophy of communication and corporate responsibility. These two aspects of HRM capture the flow and sharing of information, internal and external to the organization (Daft, 1992). Both can be vital as firms seek to empower and include employees in the organization; and as they seek to recognize and incorporate aspects of the external environment such as the general quality of the labour force, legal regulations or concerns about environmental quality and social responsibility.

Paul Sparrow, Randall S. Schuler and Susan E. Jackson

In summary, while these five groupings of HRM policies and practices may not capture all the human resource policies and practices relevant to global firms seeking to gain competitive advantage, they represent some of the major contemporary policies and practices being considered by academics and organizations, and are, therefore, worthy of international comparison.

The current literature suggests that these five aspects of HRM policies and practices may have varying levels of effectiveness throughout the world (Moss-Kanter, 1991; Porter, 1990). Indeed, Whitley (1992a) notes that, as organizations move towards greater integration, there is increasing recognition of national differences in higher level business systems. Despite increasing internationalization within many industries, national institutions remain quite distinct. The role of the state and financial sectors, national systems of education and training, and diverse national cultures, employment expectations and labour relations all create 'national business recipes', each effective in their particular context but not necessarily effective elsewhere. These different national business recipes carry with them a 'dominant logic of action' that guides management practice. This logic of action is reflected in specific management structures, styles and decision-making processes, growth and diversification strategies, inter-company market relationships and market development (Hofstede, 1993). There is also greater recognition of the effects of both sector (Räsäsen and Whipp, 1992) and regional networks (Sabel *et al.*, 1987) in patterning HRM activities.

The institutional argument against unconstrained globalization and business integration runs broadly as follows. There are a number of different and equally successful ways of organizing economic activities (and management) in a market economy (Whitley, 1992a). These different patterns of economic organization tend to be a product of the particular institutional environments within the various nation states. The development and success of specific managerial structures and practices (such as HRM) can be explained only by giving due cognizance to the various institutional contexts worldwide. Not all management methods are transferable. The effectiveness therefore of any worldwide conceptualization of HRM will very likely be constrained by the different institutional contexts for national practice.

Hypotheses and expectations

Based on the world of Moss-Kanter (1991) and Hofstede (1993), two hypotheses are developed in direct relationship to the concept of convergence or divergence of human resource policies and practices. Moss-Kanter (1991) found in her worldwide survey of management

HRM practices and policies for competitive advantage worldwide

practices and expectations that the results could be clustered, not necessarily according to geography but according to culture. Thus she coined the phrase 'cultural allies' to signify results from several countries being identical (e.g. US, UK and Australia) and 'cultural islands' to signify results from individual countries being unique (e.g. Korea; Japan). Using her results and rationale leads to these testable hypotheses:

> *Hypothesis 1:* With regard to using human resource policies and practices for competitive advantage, there will be cultural islands and cultural allies. The cultural islands will be Korea and Japan and the cultural allies will be Europe, North America, UK and Australia; and Latin America.

Our second hypothesis is more tentative, more exploratory than the first. Thus, while we can propose cultural allies and islands to exist, given the existing literature we are unable to make specific predictions about how human resource policies and practices will differ across nations. While it might be argued that they will reflect national cultures (it might also be argued that they will reflect differences in local law, custom and union–management history), we have no guidance suggesting specific relationships between aspects of culture and specific human resource policies and practices. This research is intended to provide such information. Thus, at this time, what we are able to offer is a second and somewhat exploratory hypothesis:

> *Hypothesis 2:* There will be differences in which human resource policies and practices are seen as important for gaining competitive advantage across nations.

Methodology

Questionnaire

To explore these hypotheses, we conducted secondary analyses on data obtained as part of a larger international survey conducted in 1991. This was a worldwide study of human resource policies and practices conducted by IBM and Towers Perrin. The survey data which form the basis of the analysis in this paper have been published elsewhere (Towers Perrin, 1992). In developing the survey questionnaire, some of the authors of this paper were invited to incorporate policies and practices and then write survey items that represented the academic and practitioner research and literature through 1990. These items were reviewed for representation and agreement by a series of other academics and practitioners identified by the IBM Corporation.

Paul Sparrow, Randall S. Schuler and Susan E. Jackson

A major topic addressed in one section of the questionnaire was
'human resource concepts and practices for gaining competitive
advantage'. In this section, respondents were asked to indicate the
degree of importance they attached to each item in their firm's
attempt to gain competitive advantage through human resource policies and practices. They indicated this for the current year (1991) and
for the year of 2000. For the purposes of this study, we have analysed
the data for the year 2000. This allows us to consider the extent to
which future plans and expectations within the firms surveyed are
likely to converge.

The specific firms included were those identified jointly by IBM and
Towers Perrin as being the most effective firms in highly competitive
environments in each of several countries. Details of the sample are
provided by Towers Perrin (1992). In summary, the following information is of relevance in order to draw attention to the nature of the
sample and the limits to which the data may be generalized. Effective
firms in highly competitive environments were identified for each
country surveyed. Given the global nature of firms discussed in the
introduction, major employers in one country were, in some cases,
subsidiaries or divisions of firms headquartered in other countries. In
all cases, Towers Perrin (1992) surveyed two executives from each
firm. Invitation letters and questionnaires were mailed to respondents
in spring 1991. The respondents included the chief operating officers
and the senior human resource officers (2961 respondents or 81 per
cent of the sample). Of these respondents 22 per cent were from firms
that employed over 10,000 employees, 46 per cent were from firms
employing 1,000 to 10,000 employees and 32 per cent were from
firms employing fewer than 1,000 employees. The other 19 per cent of
the sample comprised leading academics, consultants and individuals
from the business media. The total sample of respondents was located
in twelve countries throughout the world (the figures in brackets
denote the sample size for each country): Argentina (42), Brazil (159),
Mexico (67), France (81), Germany (295), Italy (212), the United
Kingdom (261), Canada (120), the United States (1,174), Australia
(94), Japan (387) and Korea (69). The strategy of gathering data from
major employing organizations led to a natural bias in the sample
towards those countries with significant numbers of large organizations (e.g. the United States, Japan, Germany and the United
Kingdom). To overcome the potential bias this might introduce into
the analysis, the statistical tests (as discussed later) used to establish
significant differences between national samples are those that control
for sample size. The analysis that follows then is primarily based upon
responses from respondents in effective firms in highly competitive

274

HRM practices and policies for competitive advantage worldwide

environments in twelve countries worldwide responding to surveys that were translated into the language of the representative country.

When survey responses are used for comparative analysis, there are a number of issues that have to be acknowledged. Different political, economic, social and cultural considerations lead to a reinterpretation of management agendas at a local level. For example, in carrying out the pilot studies for their surveys on European HRM, Brewster, Hegewisch and Lockhart (1991) noted that identical questions about specific HRM tools or issues were interpreted differently by respondents within their national cultural and legal context. For example, the issue of flexible working in Britain and Germany has been linked to demographic change and the need to reintegrate women into the labour market, whereas in France flexible working is seen as a response to general changes in lifestyle and has little to do with female labour force participation. Another problem is that the actual level of rating is difficult to interpret. For example, a low rating to a particular item might reflect the fact that the firm does not think the issue critical because they do not have the competence or desire to pursue the issue, or it might reflect the fact that the firm is very good already in the area under question and so no longer thinks the issue critical (although it will still form part of their activity). Survey findings reflect a pot pourri of past cultural constraints and future expectations based on new practices. Surveys are also cross-sectional and examine perceptions (current or future) at only one point in time. The analysis in this paper is based on expectations and plans for the year 2000, and therefore should not be coloured by short-term factors (such as economic problems) that might influence respondents. This is not to say that short-term factors should be dismissed, but, when considering global patterns of similarity and difference in HRM, the longer-term objectives, directions and pathways provide a more consistent picture. Nevertheless, ratings reflect current mindsets only and these may change over the next ten years as organizations implement the findings of the survey. The data are then not a guarantee of eventual action. Great care is needed in interpreting comparative survey results and where possible we support the survey findings by reference to other published work.

Having noted the methodological constraints of empirical survey work, we would point to the general dearth of large-scale empirical data and the opportunities afforded by an analysis of the Towers Perrin worldwide data. The addition of new empirical data we believe outweighs possible limitations. The statistical analysis in this paper therefore uses the Towers Perrin (1992) survey data to shed light on hypotheses described above:

Paul Sparrow, Randall S. Schuler and Susan E. Jackson

- is there any underlying pattern (i.e. statistical clusters of countries) in the national data on HRM policies and concepts?
- what is the nature of differences between countries or groups of countries across a range of HRM variables?

Statistical analysis

We analysed the responses to thirty-eight questions asked about various HRM practices and concepts. In the first analysis we used the cluster analysis package on S.P.S.S. to ascertain whether there was any pattern in the anticipated HRM policies and concepts across the twelve countries included in the sample. The basic procedure of all agglomerative techniques (such as cluster analysis) is similar. They compute a similarity or distance matrix between a series of variables. Differences between methods arise because of different ways of defining similarity or distance between two groups of dependent variables. The dependent variables for this analysis are the percentage of respondents stating each of the thirty-eight items (human resource concepts or practices) are of critical importance or importance in order to achieve competitive advantage. The successively combined independent variables are the twelve countries. The analysis uses the cosine measure of similarity and fuses countries according to the least 'distance' from their furthest neighbour.

Each fusion decreases by one the number of country groupings or clusters and occurs at a point where increasingly dissimilar countries are being combined (i.e., more and more 'mathematical force' is required to fuse them). Ultimately the data are reduced to a single cluster containing all the original countries. Consequently, great importance is attached to the decision rule that provides the criterion to stop 'forcing' combinations. While such rules are to some extent arbitrary, they are acceptable given that the purpose of cluster analysis is only to classify and interpret differences between countries rather than attributing any further quantitative qualities. The accepted practice is to limit the degree of fusion by calculating coefficients of similarity and stopping the fusion at the point which would require the greatest amount of change (or mathematical force) in this coefficient of similarity once the fusion has begun.

Once the underlying clusters (or grouping of countries) were identified, the differences between the importance these clusters of countries attribute to various HRM policies and practices were analysed. In order to facilitate this analysis of difference, the thirty-eight survey questions were reclassified (on a conceptual basis) into fifteen underlying dimensions. These dimensions identify elements of culture change,

HRM practices and policies for competitive advantage worldwide

structuring the organization, performance management, resourcing, and communication and corporate responsibility. They, therefore, broadly correspond with current conceptualizations of strategic human resource management as discussed in the Introduction (see, for example, Schuler, 1992; Walker, 1992). Questions relating to each of the dimensions examined are listed in Table 1. It is important to note here that we have grouped survey items on a logical basis rather than an empirical basis.

An alternative approach would be to factor analyse the thirty-eight questionnaire items and to create composite scores on the resultant factors. We feel that such an analysis should not be conducted at this stage of investigation, particularly as we do not yet know (but shall test for) significant sub-groupings within the HRM data across countries. The approach we have adopted of creating dimensions based on conceptual similarity, is of more value in linking our comparative analysis back to the academic literature on HRM practices. We shall discuss the possibility of creating categories of HRM practices based on factor analysis later in the paper.

The analyses of statistical differences between the resultant clusters across the fifteen dimensions of HRM were conducted by selecting one (the more representative) country from each cluster. For each of these countries, scores for the fifteen variables were created by averaging the percentage of people who rated the topic as important or very important for achieving competitive advantage across the relevant questions (shown in Table 1). The primary data summary published by Towers Perrin (1992) reported the percentage responses to questions as well as the sample size. A statistical technique had to be chosen that allows for meaningful secondary analysis and comparison. Because country samples have widely varying numbers of respondents it would not be valid to test for simple differences in percentages without controlling for variation in sample size. The most appropriate statistical measure therefore is the Standard Error of Difference between Proportions. This can be used to test whether the percentage difference between any two samples (countries) represents a significant difference or is just due to sampling variation. It is calculated using the formula:

$$\text{Standard error of difference between proportions} = \sqrt{\frac{p_1 q_1}{n_1} + \frac{p_2 q_2}{n_2}}$$

where: p = sample proportion in favour
q = sample proportion against
n = sample size

Paul Sparrow, Randall S. Schuler and Susan E. Jackson

Table 1 *The fifteen HRM dependent variables and the questionnaire items combined to create them*

CULTURE CHANGE VARIABLES:

(1) Promoting an empowerment culture
Facilitate full employee involvement
Require employees to self-monitor and improve
Promote employee empowerment through ownership
(2) Promoting diversity and an equality culture
Promote corporate culture emphasizing equality
Manage diversity through tailored programmes

ORGANIZATION STRUCTURE AND CONTROL VARIABLES:
(1) Emphasis on flexible organization/work practices
Require employee flexibility (i.e. jobs and location)
Flexible cross-functional teams/work groups
Flexible work arrangements
Utilize non-permanent work-force
(2) Emphasis on centralization and vertical hierarchy
Maintain specialized and directed work-force
(3) Emphasis on utilizing IT to structure the organization
Promote advanced technology for communications
Provide more access to information systems
(4) Emphasis on horizontal management
Increase spans of control and eliminate layers
Establish multiple and parallel career paths

PERFORMANCE/PROCESS MANAGEMENT VARIABLES:
(1) Emphasis on measuring and promoting customer service
Reward employees for customer service/quality
Peer subordinate customer ratings
(2) Emphasis on rewarding innovation/creativity
Reward employees for innovation and creativity
Opportunity includes autonomy, creative skills
Reward employees for enhancing skills/knowledge
(3) Link between pay and individual performance
Reward employees for business/productivity gains
Focus on merit philosophy, individual performance
(4) Shared benefits, risks and pay for team performance
Implement pay systems promoting sharing
Flexible benefits
Share benefit risks and costs with employees

HRM practices and policies for competitive advantage worldwide

RESOURCING VARIABLES:
(1) Emphasis on external resourcing
Emphasize quality university hiring programmes
Recruit and hire from non-traditional labour pools
(2) Emphasis on internal resourcing – training & careers
Identify high potential employees early
Emphasize management development/skills training
Require continuous training/retraining
Provide basic education and skills training
(3) Emphasis on internal resourcing – managing outflows
Provide flexible retirement opportunities
Develop innovative and flexible outplacement

COMMUNICATION/CORPORATE RESPONSIBILITY VARIABLES:
(1) Emphasis on communication
Communicate business directions, problems and plans
(2) Emphasis on corporate responsibility
Active corporate involvement in public education
Ensure employees pursue good health aggressively
Offer personal/family assistance
Encourage/reward external volunteer activities
Provide full employment (life-time security)

Given the large number of two-country comparisons that need to be made on any one variable, a more conservative significance level of $p<.01$ is adopted. In order to be significant at the $p<.01$ level, the observed percentage difference has to be 2.58 times greater than the standard error of the difference (3.29 times greater for significance at $p<.001$).

Results

Hypothesis 1

The dendogram in Figure 1 shows the result of the successive fusions of countries, starting from the most similar. There are five resultant clusters of countries. The first cluster initially comprises the Anglo-Saxon business culture countries of the United Kingdom, Australia, Canada and the United States. These countries (the most similar) are subsequently joined by Germany and finally by Italy. The second cluster (a cultural island) consists solely of France. The third cluster is

279

Paul Sparrow, Randall S. Schuler and Susan E. Jackson

another cultural island consisting of Korea. The fourth cluster reveals another set of cultural allies comprising the South American or Latin countries of Brazil, Mexico and Argentina, while the fifth cluster represents another cultural island consisting of Japan alone. These results, which are largely consistent with those we hypothesized, are discussed and interpreted later in this article primarily in relation to two other studies that have considered international patterns in business practice: the work of Hofstede (1980, 1993) on culture and the work of Moss-Kanter (1991) on attitudes towards change.

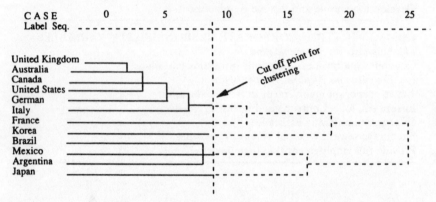

Figure 1 *Rescaled dendogram showing the average for the twelve countries*

Three of the clusters contained only a single country. In order to complete the analysis of HRM differences between the other two clusters, the United States was chosen to represent the Anglo-American cluster (as the largest sample contained within the cluster) and Brazil was chosen to represent the Latin American cluster on the same basis. The results are summarized in Table 2 below. Scores which are significantly 'higher' or 'lower' (using the Standard Error of Difference in Proportions) than those of other countries on each variable are highlighted in the shaded boxes. In some cases, three grades of significant difference existed, i.e. higher, medium and lower.

Exploratory differences on Hypothesis 2

In this section we outline those comparisons that resulted in significant differences regarding HRM practice to be used to gain competitive advantage. Interpretation and discussion of these differences are left until later in the paper. On the *cultural items* Japan scores signifi-

HRM practices and policies for competitive advantage worldwide

cantly lower on 'promoting an empowerment culture' compared to the Anglo-American representative United States (z = −6.40, p<.001) and the Latin American representative Brazil (z = −6.30, p<.001), while the United States scores significantly higher on 'promoting diversity and an equality culture' compared to France (z = 2.98, p<.01) and Japan (z = 3.62, p<.001).

On the *structuring items* the United States scores significantly higher on 'emphasis on flexible work practices' compared to France (z = 3.56, p<.001) and Brazil (z = 2.97, p<.01). Nearly all the comparisons on the 'emphasis on centralization and vertical hierarchy' variable are significant. France and Korea score higher than Japan (z = 3.82, p<.001 and z = 3.25, p<.01), and Japan scores higher than the United States and Brazil (z = 9.87, p < .001 and z = 6.01, p<.001). Variations in the 'emphasis on utilizing IT to structure the organization' are less marked, but Japan scores significantly lower than Korea (z = −2.85, p<.01) and Brazil (z = 3.59, p<.001) and the United States scores lower than Brazil (z = −3.04, p<.01). No significant differences were found between the clusters on the 'emphasis on horizontal management' variable.

Less variation was found between the clusters on the *performance management items*. There were no significant differences on the 'emphasis on rewarding innovation/creativity' and 'link between pay and individual performance' variables. The extent to which emphasis was put on 'customer service' and its measurement varied significantly. France placed significantly higher emphasis on customer service than the United States (z = 3.23, p<.01), while the United States placed more emphasis on customer service than Korea (z = 2.59, p<.01) and Japan (z = 6.06, p<.001). The emphasis placed on 'shared benefits, risks and pay for team performance' also varied significantly. The United States placed greater emphasis on this than Brazil (z = 2.60, p<.01), France (z = 3.79, p<.001), Korea (z = 3.57, p<.001) and Japan (z = 10.84, p<.001). The Japanese score was also significantly lower than that for Brazil (z = −4.34, p<.001).

The *resourcing items* yielded virtually no significant differences. Korea placed a higher 'emphasis on training and career management' than Japan (z = 3.32, p<.001), while Brazil placed greater 'emphasis on managing outflows' of staff than the United States (z = 3.14, p<.01) and Japan (z = 3.54, p.<001).

Finally, there were no significant differences between the cluster country representatives in their emphasis on *communication and corporate responsibility*.

Paul Sparrow, Randall S. Schuler and Susan E. Jackson

Table 2 *Summary of differences in HRM between the five clusters of countries*

Survey items	US Anglo American cluster	France	Japan	Korea	Brazil South American cluster
	Differences between the five clusters of countries on the Culture Change Variables				
Promoting empowerment culture	71.0% HIGHER	64.0%	52.7% LOWER	64.3%	78.7% HIGHER
Promoting diversity and equality culture	53.0% HIGHER	36.5% LOWER	42.5% LOWER	49.5%	47.5%
	Differences between the five clusters of countries on the Structuring Variables				
Emphasis on flexible work practices	59.8% HIGHER	39.8% LOWER	54.5%	53.3%	47.3% LOWER
Emphasis on centralization and vertical hierarchy	6.0% LOWER	53.0% HIGHER	30.0% MEDIUM	51.0% HIGHER	10.0% LOWER
Emphasis on utilizing IT to structure the organization	50.0%	54.5%	46.0% LOWER	64.0% HIGHER	62.5% HIGHER
Emphasis on horizontal management	62.0%	55.5%	61.0%	58.5%	68.5%
	Differences between the five clusters of countries on the Performance Management Variables				
Emphasis on measuring and promoting customer service	67.5% MEDIUM	82.0% HIGHER	50.0% LOWER	51.5% LOWER	66.5%
Emphasis on rewarding innovation/creativity	70.3%	62.7%	66.3%	67.3%	74.0%
Link between pay and individual performance	67.5%	64.5%	72.0%	70.0%	60.5%

HRM practices and policies for competitive advantage worldwide

Survey items	US Anglo American cluster	France	Japan	Korea	Brazil South American cluster
Shared benefits, risks and pay for team performance	71.3% HIGHER	49.7%	40.1% LOWER	49.3%	60.7% MEDIUM
Differences between the five clusters of countries on the Resourcing Variables					
Emphasis on external resourcing	57.5%	50.0%	56.5%	42.0%	52.0%
Emphasis on training and careers	71.0%	60.7%	64.0% LOWER	81.5% HIGHER	73.3%
Emphasis on managing outflows	29.5% LOWER	40.5%	26.5% LOWER	34.0%	42.5% HIGHER
Differences between the five clusters of countries on the Communication and Corporate Responsibility Variables					
Emphasis on communication	85.0%	86.0%	83.0%	72.0%	81.0%
Emphasis on corporate responsibility	39.0%	28.6%	32.4%	37.4%	41.6%

Discussion and summary

There are several ways in which we could discuss the results of this analysis of possible differences among firms from different nations as they seek to gain competitive advantage through their HRM practices. We could look at differences between countries across each of the fifteen dimensions of HRM that have been examined, or focus on overall country strategies (as reflected by the different priorities given to each area of HRM), or consider the relationship between cultural stereotypes of nations and the results obtained in this study. Each of these approaches provides complementary insights, therefore we discuss the findings from all three angles.

Paul Sparrow, Randall S. Schuler and Susan E. Jackson

Relationship to cultural stereotypes

It is useful to compare and contrast the results regarding our hypothesis (particularly the national clusters of countries) with other identified clusters of countries associated with cultural stereotypes (Adler, 1991; Hofstede, 1980, 1993; Phatak, 1992; Johnson and Golembiewski, 1992; and Laurent, 1991) or with studies on the management of change (Moss-Kanter, 1991). The Anglo-American cluster identified in this study contains very similar members to those identified in Moss-Kanter's (1991) study of 12,000 survey respondents worldwide. The United States, Australia, the United Kingdom and Canada were also grouped into a common cluster by Moss-Kanter (1991). There is an Anglo-American or Anglo-Saxon business culture that unites these countries. It is stereotyped in terms of openness and equality. This is reflected in the results on both the culture change items (particularly the 'promoting diversity and equality' variable) on which the Anglo-American cluster scores significantly higher than, for example, France and Japan. Firms in the Anglo-American cluster see this cultural openness as one of their most important ways of gaining competitive advantage, reflecting the academic literature that describes future problems of demography in terms of the need to cope with diversity (Johnston and Packer, 1987). This cultural stereotype of openness and equality is also reflected in the results on the structuring items, where the Anglo-American cluster places a significantly higher emphasis on the criticality of flexible work practices and the lowest emphasis on the need for centralization and vertical hierarchy. It is interesting to note that in Moss-Kanter's (1991) study, Germany formed part of a North European cluster of countries and Italy formed part of a Latin cluster of countries. In contrast, our study suggests that, where people management issues are concerned, the relative emphasis these countries expect to give in the year 2000 to the fifteen dimensions of HRM places them in the Anglo-American camp.

Our study indicated that Japan stands alone with a unique cluster of HRM emphases. This was also the case in Moss-Kanter's (1991) study, which is why she called Japan a cultural island. It is interesting to note that, although Japan faces even more severe demographic problems than the Anglo-American countries, it does not place as high an emphasis on the cultural variables of empowerment, diversity and equality, but places greater emphasis on centralization and vertical hierarchy. Japan gave lowest importance for gaining competitive advantage to promoting empowerment, diversity and equality, reflecting the cultural importance given in Japan to respect for authority and its more homogeneous ethnic culture.

HRM practices and policies for competitive advantage worldwide

In Moss-Kanter's (1991) study France formed part of a North European cluster of countries. The only difference noted in this study is that Germany does not share the same pattern of HRM emphases as France. The results obtained for the French cluster also strongly reflect Hofstede's (1980) findings on culture. In Hofstede's analysis French managers have a higher power distance score (68) in comparison for example with British managers (35). There are greater differences in formal power across management hierarchies in France and managers are more tolerant of such inequalities of power. French managers also have a higher uncertainty avoidance score (86) in comparison to British managers (35) and might be expected to seek to eliminate uncertainty and ambiguity in their tasks. The way in which the manager–subordinate relationship enables them to do this nevertheless remains a delicate point in France (Poirson, 1993). The fear of face to face conflict, the way in which authority is conceived, and the mode of selection of senior managers all act as powerful cultural forces that make it difficult for French organizations readily to adopt Anglo-American management concepts (such as performance management). Rojot (1990) paints French corporate culture as one that creates situations in which subordinate managers seek more responsibility, but in fact remain passive, fear to commit themselves to specific objectives and mostly look for protection from above. Senior managers rule autocratically and see the organization as an élite school in which they are the most intelligent and subordinates therefore cannot conceivably have valid ideas. French managers are therefore more possessive of their individual autonomy. Their reaction is: 'I know my job, if I am controlled, this means they have no confidence in me' (Poirson, 1993). Even where Anglo-American concepts of HRM are adopted, they become 'the stake of a different game' (Rojot, 1990: 98).

Both our study and that of Moss-Kanter (1991) revealed Korea as another cultural island. The Korean results in our study reflect Korea's higher emphasis on protectionism, strong sense of corporate paternalism, preference for centralization and greater optimism for the future, as noted by Moss-Kanter (1991). The utilization of information technology to help do so appears consistent with the image of Korea as a nation that is respectful of authority and very hierarchically organized.

Recently, attention has been directed to the unique features of Latin America in terms of HRM (Baker, Smith and Weiner, 1993; Baker *et al.*, 1992; Nash, 1993). Moss-Kanter (1991) identified a Latin cluster of countries consisting of South American nations, Italy and Spain. Similarly, we found that the South American countries of

Paul Sparrow, Randall S. Schuler and Susan E. Jackson

Mexico, Argentina and Brazil were clustered together. The one difference was that Italy seems to adopt an Anglo-American perspective on
future HRM practices for competitive advantage. Recent analyses of
HRM in Italy and the European Latin countries (Camuffo and Costa,
1992; Filella, 1991) support this finding. The Latin cluster has many
features similar to the Anglo-American cluster, such as promotion of
an empowerment culture, high decentralization, high emphasis on
using IT to support structuring in organizations and a high desire to
seek a sharing of benefits and risks in reward systems which may
reflect the high levels of privatization occurring in those countries.
The Latin cluster differs from the Anglo-American cluster in that it
places more value on the need to manage outflows from organizations
and less emphasis on the need for flexible work practices.

National HRM strategies

In this section we discuss the survey findings in relation to national
patterns of HRM and draw upon other research to provide the necessary context to interpret the survey findings. Naturally, this section
focuses on differences between countries. These differences should not
be overstated, however, for balanced against these are the underlying
convergences that are reducing many of these differences. These convergences will be discussed in the following section.

> European-style class consciousness, a serious socialist movement . . . penetra-
> tion of Marxist ideology in 'old Europe' . . . have variously served to structure
> both the perception and reality of superior–subordinate and management–
> worker relations in industry.
>
> (Lawrence, 1992: 12)

Lawrence (1992) argues that HRM is essentially an Anglo-Saxon construct that has been 'grafted on', but has not 'taken root', in
Continental Europe. Classic HRM functions such as recruitment,
socialization, training and development are determined by different
conceptions of management in Europe, and underpinned by a related
set of values. Historically, HRM has not had the same élan and in
part has been socially and culturally bypassed. When compared with
American (or indeed British) concepts of HRM, a European model
needs to take account of a number of factors. The distinctions drawn
between concepts of HRM prevalent in continental Europe as
opposed to the Anglo-American model (Brewster and Hegewisch,
1993; Pieper, 1990) include more restricted employer autonomy, difficult hiring and firing decisions, lower geographic and professional
employee mobility and a stronger link between type of education and
career progression. There is an increased role of 'social partners' in

HRM practices and policies for competitive advantage worldwide

the employment relationship, a stronger role of trade unions' influence in the setting of HRM policy, collective bargaining at the state and regional level and direct co-determination at the firm level. Finally, there are higher levels of government intervention or support in many areas of HRM, a state role in education through public school and university systems, formal certification systems influencing personnel selection and careers and more comprehensive welfare policies.

It is therefore all the more interesting that Germany and Italy, as two continental European countries, actually fell within the Anglo-American cluster. However, a preliminary analysis of this cluster suggests that, while the constituent members are all more like each other than they are like the other countries (France, Korea, Japan and so forth), there are still likely to be some significant differences in HRM practices within the cluster. Germany and Italy 'joined' the Anglo-American cluster only towards the end of the mathematical forcing process (see Figure 1), and could be considered as worth separate investigation. A useful area for further investigation would be national pathways and statistical differences within the regional clusters.

The characteristics of French HRM (recently discussed by several authors such as Barsoux and Lawrence, 1990; Besse, 1992; Poirson, 1993; Rojot, 1990) as revealed by our analysis support many of the cultural distinctions drawn above. For example, the strong French educational élite, distinct cadres of management and an extremely rigid hierarchical approach to both performance and career management is reflected in the significantly lower rating given to a culture based on diversity and equality as well as a significantly higher emphasis given to centralization and vertical hierarchy. However, the context within which HRM in France is practised has changed considerably over the last ten years (Poirson, 1993; Rojot, 1990). Increased and globalized competition, the growth of multinational organizations, the shortening of product life-cycles and the growing importance of product quality have all provided a new justification of managerial authority in France, and a new language among the employers' associations and bodies has legitimized a number of management and HRM practices, including performance management (Rojot, 1990). A 1987 survey by Hay France of 220 French organizations employing more than 65,000 managers found that 91 per cent had a policy of fixing individual objectives for managers, 81 per cent evaluated performance in relation to these objectives and 87 per cent had an annual performance appraisal review meeting. This renewed fervour for and emphasis on objectives-based performance management is reflected in the French sample high rating for the need to emphasize the promotion and measurement of customer service.

Paul Sparrow, Randall S. Schuler and Susan E. Jackson

Many of our findings reflect the existing competence and perceived priorities in the Japanese HRM system (see Aoki, 1988; Dore, 1986; Koike, 1987) and reveal the unique approach to HRM created by its internal labour market. Japanese HRM has been characterized by hierarchical pyramid-type organizations with bureaucratic control. The Japanese respondents rated an emphasis on centralization and vertical hierarchy as significantly more critical than the Anglo-American cluster (30 per cent compared to 6 per cent). However, the Korean and French samples placed an even greater emphasis on these issues. Performance in Japan is evaluated in the long term and there is a model of life-time employment. Skills are firm-specific and there is a reliance on in-house specific on-the-job training. Not surprisingly, our Japanese sample rated the need to manage outflows from the organization significantly lower than Brazil or France and placed a lower emphasis on training and development (linked to careers as opposed to jobs) given the existing high levels of informal on-the-job training.

Communication in Japan is more informal and relies on managerial networks. Promotion systems (particularly to senior management level) are more geared to an educational élite (Koike, 1987; Whitley, 1992b), female participation rates are low and there is a marked labour market segmentation between core (65 to 90 per cent) employees and lower status, higher mobility, temporary workers. This is reflected in the survey finding that the Japanese sample provided a significantly lower rating to the criticality of promoting a culture that promotes diversity and equality (42 per cent compared to 53 per cent in the Anglo-American cluster).

Japanese wage differentials are based on hierarchy and have remained fairly stable, despite the pressures for change discussed later. Bonuses in Japan are not regarded as a reward or dividend of profit, as in the Anglo-Saxon countries, but are taken more for granted and assumed to be part of regular earnings. Despite the fact they account for around 33 per cent of nominal salaries (Aoki, 1988), they do not decrease even in difficult times (Sano, 1993). Jobs are also highly segmented. The survey data reflected this paradox with the Japanese sample giving a significantly lower rating to pay systems that share risks and benefits or reward team performance (40 per cent compared to 71 per cent in the Anglo-American cluster).

More recently a number of reviews have pointed to growing pressure for change in the Japanese model of HRM (see, for example, Sano, 1993; Sasajima, 1993; Takahaski, 1990). Japanese organizations are facing a crisis and their traditional patterns of HRM are under structural pressure to change. Increasing difficulties are being faced in maintaining employment security and automatic pay increase systems.

HRM practices and policies for competitive advantage worldwide

Demographic pressures have resulted in an ageing work-force with an increasingly long length of service (Sano, 1993), creating fears about skills shortages and upward pressure on labour costs. Education levels have increased markedly, as have female participation and part-time work (these pressures are also apparent in the US and Europe). It is interesting to note that the Japanese sample provided the lowest rating to the importance of promoting an empowerment culture. This could be interpreted in two contrasting ways: a reflection of the fact that the Japanese HRM system already achieves this, and so it is a lower priority for the future, or a recognition by Japanese managers that external pressures may interfere with their ability to maintain this type of culture.

Some authors have argued that in Japan new technology is being used increasingly to deskill jobs and combine business processes because productivity of more senior and skilled employees is falling. However, our survey data do not appear to reflect this concern. The Japanese sample viewed the use of IT to structure the organization as significantly less important compared to, for example, the Korean and Brazilian samples.

Wilkinson (1988) has noted that some features of the Korean labour system resemble those of the Japanese, such as the segmentation of the labour market (our data supported this with both countries rating the need to promote an empowerment culture or culture based on diversity and equality as low) and overall philosophy behind their reward systems (similarly supported by our analysis showing no significant differences between Korean and Japan on any of the four dimensions used to examine performance management). However, a number of writers have noted a number of striking differences between Japanese and Korean labour systems (Biggart, 1989; Chung and Lee, 1988; Deyo, 1989; Michell, 1988; Park, 1992; Sharma, 1991; Shin and Chin, 1989; Whitley, 1992b; Yoo and Lee, 1987). In contrast to Japan, labour turnover in the manufacturing sector in Korea is high (Amsden, 1989) and managerial mobility is high (Biggart, 1989). This is perhaps reflected in our finding that Japan places a low emphasis on the importance of managing outflows from the organization (27 per cent) in comparison to Korea (34 per cent), although the difference is not significant. Similarly, Michell (1988) reported lower employer commitment to employee welfare in Korea than Japan, mainly because its labour-intensive industries (such as textiles) are following cost leadership strategies. Even in capital-intensive industries, lifelong employment is not seen as an ideal. Our analysis revealed that the Korean sample placed a significantly higher emphasis on work structuring through the use of IT and on centralization

289

Paul Sparrow, Randall S. Schuler and Susan E. Jackson

and the vertical hierarchy. These are two dimensions of structure that are often associated with newly industrializing countries and their attempts to drive cost savings and improvements to the business process and productivity.

Attention has also been drawn to the greater scope for manager and owner discretion in Korea, more authoritarian and directive supervisory style focused on task performance as opposed to the facilitation of group performance (Park, 1992; Whitley, 1992b), limited scope for supervisors to organize groups' work and lower levels of autonomy for workers in comparison to Japan (Deyo, 1989). We found only a marginally lower emphasis on the importance of horizontal management in Korea than in Japan and a more marked (but still insignificant) difference in the importance given to communication (72 per cent in Korea, the lowest of all five clusters, compared to 83 per cent in Japan). Perhaps reflecting a national desire to reduce this differential, recent moves towards democratization and the atypical Korean trends towards greater unionization (Park, 1992), the Korean sample placed higher importance on promoting an empowerment culture than did Japan (which, as discussed previously, may feel it has already achieved much in this area).

Recruitment decisions, while based on a university élite as in Japan, also differ in Korea. Shin and Chin (1989) argue that Korean selection and promotion decisions are more influenced by personal and regional networks and relationships than in Japan. Therefore, despite the acute labour shortages experienced in Korea since 1986 (Park, 1992) the lower level of formality in selection is reflected in our results, which show that in Korea only 42 per cent of the sample felt that an emphasis on external resourcing was critical, compared to 57 per cent of the Japanese sample, although again the difference was not significant. Amsden (1989) has also drawn attention to the high wages and fringe benefits (such as company housing, bonus payments and schooling for children) that characterize the Korean reward system. This is essentially a paternalistic system (without the Japanese guarantee of lifelong employment) in which loyalty is less directly incorporated into rewards systems than in Japan. However, as already noted, there were no significant differences between Japan and Korea on the four dimensions of performance management, although the Korean sample placed a lower emphasis on reward systems that share both benefits and risk or pay for team performance, but a higher emphasis on linking pay and individual performance, which seems to reflect the description of reward systems given by Amsden (1989).

HRM practices and policies for competitive advantage worldwide

Predictions about HRM practices for competitive advantage

The comparison of differences thus far have been made using the data for the year 2000. These data were used for two primary reasons. First, using HRM to gain a competitive advantage takes time; thus historical data would not be as much use as data which reflect expectations and plans for the year 2000. Second, data for the year 2000 would enable us to assess the extent to which there is a convergence or divergence occurring worldwide in the practice of HRM.

In making predictions about HRM practices and policies for competitive advantage, it is necessary to establish the baseline from which we started. In this study, the baseline is 1991. If we look at these results in conjunction with the results for the year 2000 we have a better basis not only for prediction but also for comparison across the clusters. Table 3 shows the differences in the importance ratings from respondents for the fifteen dimensions of HRM.

One clear pattern revealed by Table 3 is that the respondents in all the clusters rated all HRM items higher in the year 2000 than they did in the year 1991. This appears to be consistent with the academic and professional literature that suggests that management of people is becoming a more significant force in organizations, particularly now that capital, technology and the like are readily available to everyone. It also reflects the points we made in the section on national strategies which showed that in France and Japan there are increasing pressures to adapt their highly nationalistic models of HRM. Another observation and prediction is that, while people management is becoming important in all the countries surveyed, the countries will continue to exhibit differences, both in degree and in kind. For example, when it comes to promoting an empowerment culture, the Japanese are increasing as are the French, but the Anglo-American cluster is increasing much more (40–71 per cent vs. 40–53 per cent).

When examining Table 3 it is important to keep these percentage differences in mind. They often provide explanatory evidence as to why the differences are indeed different. For the item 'emphasis on communication' both Japan and Korea have small differences compared to the Anglo-American cluster. However, an examination of the original percentage shows that both Japan and Korea had originally rated this item substantially higher than the Anglo-American cluster. Is this suggesting that the Anglo-American cluster is 'playing catch-up'? Are we to assume that an understanding of future events is to be found in the Asian nations? Probably not. These differences more likely still reflect cultural and economic differences. Note that, while Japan and Korea are geographical neighbours to the United States,

Paul Sparrow, Randall S. Schuler and Susan E. Jackson

Table 3 *Differences in HRM between the five clusters: change from 1991–2000*

Survey items	US Anglo American cluster	France	Japan	Korea	Brazil South American cluster
	Differences between the five clusters of countries on the Culture Change Variables				
Promoting empowerment culture	40–71 +31%	38–64 +26%	40–53 +13%	34–64 +30%	41–79 +38%
Promoting diversity and equality culture	31–53 +22%	20–37 +17%	28–43 +15%	18–50 +32%	23–40 +17%
	Differences between the five clusters of countries on the Structuring Variables				
Emphasis on flexible work practices	26–60 +34%	24–40 +16%	32–55 +23%	15–54 +39%	17 47 +30%
Emphasis on centralization and vertical hierarchy	0–6 6%	15–53 +38%	13–30 +17%	25–51 +26%	11–10 –1%
Emphasis on utilizing IT to structure the organization	16–50 +34%	19–55 +36%	21–46 +25%	23–64 +41%	21–63 +42%
Emphasis on horizontal management	36–62 +26%	30–56 +26%	37–61 +24%	30–59 +29%	37–69 +32%
	Differences between the five clusters of countries on the Performance Management Variables				
Emphasis on measuring and promoting customer service	40–68 +28%	47–82 +35%	31–50 +19%	34–52 +18%	36–67 +31%
Emphasis on rewarding innovation/creativity	35–70 +35%	32–63 +31%	41–66 +25%	40–67 +27%	40–74 +34%
Link between pay and individual performance	52–68 +16%	42–65 +23%	44–72 +28%	45–70 +25%	48–61 +13%

HRM practices and policies for competitive advantage worldwide

Survey items	US Anglo American cluster	France	Japan	Korea	Brazil South American cluster
Shared benefits, risks and pay for team performance	40–71 +31%	23–50 +27%	18–40 +22%	23–49 +26%	24–61 +37%
Differences between the five clusters of countries on the Resourcing Variables					
Emphasis on external resourcing	24–58 +34%	37–50 +13%	41–57 +16%	40–42 +2%	23–52 +29%
Emphasis on training and careers	38–71 +33%	43–61 +18%	52–64 +12%	60–82 +22%	59–73 +14%
Emphasis on managing outflows	13–30 +17%	13–41 +28%	7–27 +20%	7–34 +27%	14–43 +29%
Differences between the five clusters of countries on the Communication and Corporate Responsibility Variables					
Emphasis on communication	57–85 +28%	57–86 +29%	74–83 +9%	62–72 +10%	48–81 +33%
Emphasis on corporate responsibility	18–39 +21%	14–29 +15%	16–32 +16%	18–38 +20%	27–42 +15%

overall their results are rather different. In fact, Australia is regarded by some as being in the Asia Pacific region, yet it falls into the Anglo-American cluster in the original analysis.

These observations about Table 3 being so noted, what other predictions about convergence can we offer concerning HRM practices and policies for competitive advantage?

1. The *culture change* dimensions: Firms in all clusters are seeing that it is likely to be useful to empower their employees more than today, and to promote a more diverse and egalitarian culture. As the world's work-force becomes more educated it is demanding more involvement and participation in work-place decisions and events. Tasks and knowledge, as well as employee

Paul Sparrow, Randall S. Schuler and Susan E. Jackson

needs and abilities, appear to be driving this trend in human
resource practices. A related prediction here is that there will be
continued examination of the role of the manager, with continued pressure for change in that role.

2. The *structuring* dimensions: Following from the first prediction is
the second: as the task and knowledge determine the involvement of employees and the role of the manager, they also impact
on the structure of the operation. In particular, they make it necessary for work practices to be more flexible to change as the
skills and abilities needed to do them change. This removes the
sole responsibility for decision making from the hierarchy to
those in the know and those generally nearest the action.

3. The *performance management* dimensions: There is likely to be
enhanced emphasis on obtaining performance and making performance a centre of attention. In particular, performance
related to serving the customer would appear to be of most
importance. This will be closely followed by an emphasis on the
performance related to innovation, new products and services (of
course, designed with the customer in mind). To reinforce these
emphases, remuneration schemes at both the individual and team
level are likely to be implemented in significant numbers during
this decade. There will be a greater sharing of risks and rewards.
With the emphasis on promoting a culture of equality, this might
also mean that greater sharing will occur at all levels of management and non-management employees.

4. The *resourcing* dimensions: Flexibility will be desired and sought
regarding all areas of the business. Just as there is likely to be
more flexibility with regard to job assignments and decisions,
there is likely to be more flexibility regarding staffing decisions,
both at the entry and exit stages. That is, firms might be likely
to seek greater use of part-time or temporary workers to fill
positions, and not bring them into full-time employee status.
Perhaps for the full-time employees, firms will dedicate more
resources to training and retraining. This will make the current
work-force (the one that is more empowered and is making more
decisions) more important to the organization. Nevertheless,
even this work-force may need to be replaced. Knowledge is
doubling every seven years. To capture this, firms may need to
be constantly incorporating new members and new ideas. This
will demand constant change and adaptation by all. For some
this may mean a need to exit from the organization.
Consequently, firms will be equally concerned about managing
the egress of employees. They will want to ensure that this is

HRM practices and policies for competitive advantage worldwide

predictable and that employees with key skills, today and in the future, do not suddenly leave the firm.

5. The *communication and corporate responsibility* dimensions: While organizations are likely to get more involved in community activities, particularly training and education, they are likely still to want employees to focus on the firm. Consequently, they will devote more resources to communicating and sharing the goals and objectives of the organization with all employees. This will facilitate the empowerment of employees and help ensure that the decisions made by employees are as consistent with the needs of the business as those made by top management.

Conclusions

The function of managing people in organizations is perceived as important today for firms to gain competitive advantage. This level of importance, however, pales in comparison to the importance it is expected to have in the year 2000. While this is likely due to greater access organizations have to capital and technology, it is also likely due to a growing recognition that people do make a difference. Thus, this relatively under-utilized resource called 'people' is likely to receive greater attention from organizations throughout this decade, at least for firms seeking to be effective in highly competitive environments.

While 'to receive greater attention' is likely to vary across firms, it is not expected to vary widely concerning several key themes or foci. These include the following: a greater emphasis on empowerment, equality, diversity management, flexibility in job design and assessment, flatter organizational structures, customer-based measures of performance and related remuneration schemes, flexibility in staffing decisions, training decisions and exiting decisions, and greater communication of the objectives and goals of the firm to all employees.

Although the country clusters reported in this study did illustrate differences to these key themes, they also reflected similarity. The differences are probably better described as being more 'in degree' than 'in kind'. Thus, while it might be tempting to conclude that there is clearly a convergence rather than divergence in the practices and policies used by organizations to manage their human resources, this might be overstating the reality (as well as the complexity) of managing human resources effectively. Employees do reflect the larger society and culture from which they come to the organization. From this they bring education and skill, attitude towards work and organization and general expectations about their role and responsibility in the

Paul Sparrow, Randall S. Schuler and Susan E. Jackson

organization. The impact and relevance of these should not be under-stated. Thus, while it may be tempting to conclude by using the term 'convergence', it may be more an attempt to simplify reality prema-turely. Our research findings revealed a number of disjunctures with the academic literature, particularly with regard to the use of new technology in Japan to deskill jobs, differences between Japanese and Korean reward systems, and the level of similarity between German and Italian patterns of HRM and Anglo-American patterns. Such dis-junctures should be noted as areas for further research.

This state of affairs, however, offers opportunity more than it does frustration. It offers competitive advantage to those firms willing to survey systematically their employees and adopt and adapt human resource practices appropriate for the situation. Yet, this situation is likely to reflect the nation in which the operation is located. But, at the end of the day, these reflections may be more at the margin than at the core. Observe the operations of Nissan and Honda in England in comparison to their operations in Japan (Wickens, 1987). Thus organizations seeking to have a truly global operation are likely to pursue the above stated key themes in the work-place with human resource practices that have some cross-cultural variation, but that can all be fitted under a common policy.umbrella.

Paul Sparrow
Manchester Business School
UK
Randall S. Schuler
Susan E. Jackson
New York University
USA

Acknowledgements

The authors wish to thank the IBM Corporation and Towers Perrin for conducting the worldwide study and their report entitled *Priorities for Gaining Competitive Advantage*.

References

Adler, N.J. (1991) *International Dimensions of Organisational Behaviour*. Boston, MA: PWS-Kent.
Amsden, A.H. (1989) *Asia's Next Giant*. Oxford: Oxford University Press.
Aoki, M. (1988) *Information, Incentives and Bargaining in the Japanese Economy*. Cambridge: Cambridge University Press.

HRM practices and policies for competitive advantage worldwide

Baker, S., Smith, G., Weiner, E. and Jacobson, K. (1992) 'Latin America: The Big Move to Free Markets', *Business Week*, 15 June: 50–62.

Baker, S., Smith G. and Weiner, E. (1993) 'The Mexican Worker', *Business Week*, 19 April: 84–92.

Barsoux, J.L. and Lawrence, P. (1990) *Management in France*. London: Cassell Education.

Bartlett, C.A. and Ghoshal, S. (1992) 'What is a Global Manager?', *Harvard Business Review*, 70 (5): 124–32.

Beer, M., Spector, B., Lawrence, P.R., Mills, D.Q. and Walton, R.E. (1984) *Managing Human Assets*. New York: The Free Press.

Besse, D. (1992) 'Finding a New Raison d'Etre: Personnel Management in France', *Personnel Management*, 24 (8): 40–3.

Biggart, N.W. (1989) 'Institutionalised Patrimonialism in Korean Business', Program in East Asian culture and development research, *Working Paper No. 23, Institute of Governmental Affairs*. University of California: Davies.

Black, J.S., Gregersen, H.B. and Mendenhall, P. (1992) *Global Assignments*. San Francisco: Jossey-Bass.

Boam, R. and Sparrow, P.R. (eds) (1992) *Designing and Achieving Competency*. London: McGraw-Hill.

Brewster, C. and Hegewisch, A. (1993) 'Personnel Management in Europe: A Continent of Diversity', *Personnel Management*, 25 (1): 36–40.

Brewster, C. and Tyson, S. (eds) (1991) *International Comparisons in Human Resource Management*. London: Pitman.

Brewster, C., Hegewisch, A. and Lockhart, J.T. (1991) 'Researching Human Resource Management: Methodology of the Price Waterhouse Cranfield Project on European Trends', *Personnel Review*, 20 (6): 36–40.

Burns, T. and Stalker, G.R. (1961) *The Management of Innovation*. London: Tavistock.

Camuffo, A. and Costa, G. (1992) 'Strategic Human Resource Management – Italian Style', *Sloan Management Review*, 34 (2): 59–67.

Chung, K.H. and Lee, H.C. (eds) (1988) *Korean Managerial Dynamics*. London: Praeger.

Daft, R.L. (1992) *Organization Theory and Design*. St Paul, Minneapolis: West Publishing.

Deyo, F.C. (1989) *Beneath the Miracle: Labour Subordination in the New Asian Industrialism*. Berkeley, CA: University of California Press.

Dore, R.P. (1986) *Flexible Rigidities*. Stanford, CA: Stanford University Press.

Dowling, P.J. and Schuler, R.S. (1990) *International Dimensions of Human Resource Management*. Boston: PWS-Kent.

Filella, J. (1991) 'Is There a Latin Model in the Management of Human Resources?', *Personnel Review*, 20 (6): 14–23.

Ghoshal, S. and Bartlett, C.A. (1989) 'The Multinational Corporation as an Interorganisational Network', *Academy of Management Review*, 15 (4): 603–25.

Grant, R.M. (1991) 'The Resource-Based Theory of Competitive Advantage: Implications for Strategy Formulation', *California Management Review*, 33 (3): 114–35.

Hamel, G. and Prahalad, C.K. (1991) 'Corporate Imagination and Expeditionary Marketing', *Harvard Business Review*, 69 (4): 81–92.

Hofstede, G. (1980) *Culture's Consequences: International Differences in Work-Related Values*. London: Sage.

Hofstede, G. (1993) 'Cultural Constraints in Management Theories'. *Academy of Management Executive*, 7 (1): 81–93.

Paul Sparrow, Randall S. Schuler and Susan E. Jackson

Johnson, K.R. and Golembiewski, R.T. (1992) 'National Culture in Organization Development: A Conceptual and Empirical Analysis', *International Journal of Human Resource Management*, 3, 1: 71–84.

Johnston, W.B. and Packer, A.E. (1987) *Workforce 2000: Work and Workers for the 21st Century*. Washington, DC: US Government Printing Office.

Koike, K. (1987) 'Human Resource Development and Labour Management Relations'. In Yamamura, K. and Yashuba, Y. (eds) *The Political Economy of Japan. 2. The Domestic Transformation*. Stanford, CA: Stanford University Press

Laurent, A. (1991) 'Managing Across Cultures and National Borders'. In S.G. Makridakis (ed.) *Single Market Europe: Opportunities and Challenges for Business*. London: Jossey Bass.

Lawler, E.E. (1991) 'The New Plant Approach: A Second Generation Approach', *Organizational Dynamics*, Summer: 5–15.

Lawrence, P. (1992) 'Management Development in Germany'. In Tyson, S., Lawrence, P., Poirson, P., Manzolini, L. and Vincente, C.S. (eds) *Human Resource Management in Europe: Strategic Issues and Cases*. London: Kogan Page.

Michell, T. (1988) *From a Developing to a Newly Industrialised Country: The Republic of Korea, 1961–82*. Geneva: International Labour Organisation.

Mitrani, A., Dalziel, M. and Fitt, D. (eds) (1992) *Competency-Based Human Resource Management*. London: Kogan Page.

Moss-Kanter, R. (1991) 'Transcending Business Boundaries: 12,000 World Managers View Change', *Harvard Business Review*, 69 (3): 151–64.

Nash, N. (1993) 'A New Rush into Latin America', *The New York Times*, 11 April, Sec. 3: 1-6.

Park, D.J. (1992) 'Industrial Relations in Korea', *International Journal of Human Resource Management*, 3 (1): 105–24.

Peters, T. (1992) *Liberation Management: Necessary Disorganisation for the Nanosecond Nineties*. London: Macmillan.

Phatak, A.V. (1992) *International Dimensions of Management.*. Boston, MA: PWS-Kent.

Pieper, R. (ed.) (1990) *Human Resource Management: An International Comparison*. Berlin: de Gruyter.

Poirson, P. (1993) 'The Characteristics and Dynamics of Human Resource Management in France'. In Tyson, S., Lawrence, P., Poirson, P., Manzolini, L. and Vincente, C.S. (eds) *Human Resource Management in Europe: Strategic Issues and Cases*. London: Kogan Page.

Poole, M.J.F. (1986) *Industrial Relations: Origins and Patterns of National Diversity*. London: Routledge.

Poole, M.J.F. (1990) Editorial: 'Human Resource Management in an International Perspective', *International Journal of Human Resource Management*, 1: 1–16.

Porter, M.E. (1980) *Competitive Strategy: Techniques for Analysing Industries and Competitors*. New York: Free Press.

Porter, M.E. (1990) *Competitive Advantage of Nations*. New York: The Free Press.

Punnett, B.J. and Ricks, D.A. (1992) *International Business*. Boston: PSW-Kent.

Räsäsen, K. and Whipp, R. (1992) 'National Business Recipes: A Sector Perspective'. In Whitley, R. (ed.) *European Business Systems: Firms and Markets in National Contexts*. London: Sage.

Reich, R.B. (1990) 'Who is Us?', *Harvard Business Review*, 68 (1): 53–64.

HRM practices and policies for competitive advantage worldwide

Rojot, J. (1990) 'Human Resource Management in France'. In Pieper, R. (ed.) *Human Resource Management: An International Comparison*. Berlin: de Gruyter.

Ronen, S. (1986) *Comparative and Multinational Management*. New York: Wiley.

Sabel, C., Herrigel, G., Deeg, R. and Kazis, R. (1987). 'Regional Prosperities Compared: Massachusetts and Basen-Württemberg in the 1980s', *Discussion Paper of the Research Unit Labour Market and Employment*. Wissenschaftszentrum: Berlin.

Sano, Y. (1993) 'Changes and Continued Stability in Japanese HRM Systems: Choice in the Share Economy', *International Journal of Human Resource Management*, 4 (1): 11–28.

Sasajima, Y. (1993) 'Changes in Labour Supply and their Impacts on Human Resource Management: The Case of Japan', *International Journal of Human Resource Management*, 4 (1): 29–44.

Schuler, R.S. (1992) 'Strategic Human Resource Management: Linking the People with the Strategic Needs of the Business', *Organizational Dynamics*, 21 (1): 18–31.

Schuler, R.S. and MacMillan, I. (1984) 'Creating Competitive Advantage Through Human Resource Management Practices', *Human Resource Management*, 23: 241–55.

Sharma, B. (1991) 'Industrialisation and Strategy Shifts in Industrial Relations: A Comparative Study of South Korea and Singapore'. In Brewster, C. and Tyson, S. (eds) *International Comparisons in Human Resource Management*. London: Pitman.

Shin, E.H. and Chin, S.W. (1989) 'Social Affinity among Top Managerial Executives of Large Corporations in Korea', *Sociological Forum*, 4: 3–26.

Takahashi, Y. (1990) 'Human Resource Management in Japan'. In Pieper, R. (ed.) *Human Resource Management: An International Comparison*. Berlin: de Gruyter.

Torrington, D., Hall, L., Haylor, I. and Myers, J. (1991) *Employee Resourcing*, Wimbledon: Institute of Personnel Management.

Towers Perrin (1992) *Priorities for Gaining Competitive Advantage: A Worldwide Human Resource Study*. London: Towers Perrin.

Walker, J. (1992) *Human Resource Strategy*. New York: McGraw-Hill.

Whitley, R. (ed.) (1992a) *European Business Systems: Firms and Markets in their National Contexts*. London: Sage.

Whitley, R. (ed.) (1992b) *Business Systems in East Asia: Firms, Markets and Societies*. London: Sage.

Wickens, D. (1987) *The Road to Nissan*. London: Macmillan.

Wilkinson, B. (1988) 'A Comparative Analysis'. In *Technological Change, Work Organisation and Pay: Lessons from Asia*. Geneva: International Labour Organization.

Yoo, S. and Lee, S.M. (1987) 'Management Style and Practice of Korean Chaebols', *California Management Review*, 29 (4): 95–110.

[20]

National vs. Corporate Culture: Implications for Human Resource Management

Susan C. Schneider*

Corporate culture has been described as the "glue" that holds organizations together by providing cohesiveness and coherence among the parts. Multinational companies are increasingly interested in promoting corporate culture to improve control, coordination, and integration of their subsidiaries. Yet these subsidiaries are embedded in local national cultures wherein the underlying basic assumptions about people and the world may differ from that of the national and corporate culture of the multinational. These differences may hinder the acceptance and implementation of human resource practices, such as career planning, appraisal and compensation systems, and selection and socialization. This article discusses the assumptions about people and about the world underlying these HRM practices as they may differ from those of the national culture of the subsidiary. Finally, issues concerning the use of corporate culture as a mechanism for globalization will be raised.

Corporate culture has received a great deal of attention in the last five years. Popular books such as *In Search of Excellence* (Peters and Waterman, 1982) and *Corporate Cultures* (Deal and Kennedy, 1982), have sold millions of copies to eager executives in many countries. Although the academic community has taken a more cautious approach, they too are interested (Schein, 1985; Smircich, 1983; see also *ASQ*, September, 1983). While the popular press has implied that excellent companies have strong corporate cultures, the link between strong culture and performance can be challenged. Different environments require different strategies; the corporate culture needs to fit that strategy (Schwartz and Davis, 1981). In the case of the MNC, there is the need to address the fit of corporate culture with the different national cultures of their subsidiaries to assure strategy implementation, particularly HRM strategy.

Corporate culture has been discussed as a means of control for headquarters over their subsidiaries (see special issue of *JIBS*, 1984;

*The author would like to thank Paul Evans, Andre Laurent, Randall Schuler and the anonymous reviewers for their helpful suggestions.

Human Resource Management, Summer 1988, Vol. 27, Number 2, Pp. 231–246
© 1988 by John Wiley & Sons, Inc.   CCC 0090-4848/88/020231-16$04.00

in particular, Baliga and Jaeger; Doz and Prahalad). In this view, corporate culture serves as a behavioral control, instilling norms and values that result in following "the way things are done around here." The methods by which this is accomplished are: recruiting "like-minded" individuals, i.e., those that share the values of the company; socialization through training and personal interaction; and developing strong organizational commitment through various other HR policies such as life time employment, stock option plans, recreational and housing facilities, and expatriate rotation. These methods are frequently used by Japanese firms but also the so-called excellent companies such as IBM, Hewlett-Packard, Digital Equipment known for their strong corporate cultures (Pascale, 1984).

Corporate culture is in part managed through the HRM practices (Evans, 1986). Some of these practices, however, may not be appropriate given the beliefs, values, and norms of the local environment, i.e., the national culture wherein the subsidiary is embedded. Problems arise in transferring corporate culture through these practices in an effort to achieve globalization. More attention needs to be paid to the possible clash of assumptions underlying national and corporate cultures (Laurent, 1986; Adler and Jelinek, 1986).

The purpose of this article is to explore the potential clash of the corporate culture of a multinational organization and the national culture of the local subsidiary, paying particular attention to human resource practices. First, the construct of culture will be reviewed. Then the assumptions underlying human resource management practices will be discussed, questioning their fit within different national cultures. Specific attention will be paid to the implications for human resource management practices such as career planning, performance appraisal and reward systems, selection and socialization, and expatriate assignments. Case examples are used to illustrate the problem. Finally, the article will raise an issue often expressed by multinational companies—what does it mean to be a truly international company? What does "global" really look like? It will also question the use of corporate culture as a homogenizing force and as a mechanism of control.

CULTURE

The construct of culture has caused much confusion. While there are multiple definitions, they tend to be vague and overly general. This confusion is added to by the multiple disciplines interested in this topic, which while increasing richness, does not necessarily increase clarity. Anthropologists, sociologists, psychologists, and others bring with them their specific paradigms and research methodologies. This creates difficulties in reaching consensus on construct definitions as well as their measurement or operationalization.

The model developed by Schein (1985) helps to organize the pieces of the culture puzzle. According to this model, culture is represented at three levels: 1) behaviors and artifacts; 2) beliefs and values; and 3) underlying assumptions. These levels are arranged according to their visibility such that behavior and artifacts are the easiest to observe, while the underlying assumptions need to be inferred. To understand what the behaviors or beliefs actually mean to the participants, the underlying assumptions have to be surfaced. This is most difficult as assumptions are considered to be taken for granted and out of awareness.

This model can be applied to both corporate and national cultures. Laurent (1986) argues, however, that corporate culture may modify the first two levels but will have little impact on the underlying assumptions that are embedded in the national culture. This raises the issue as to whether the behaviors, values, and beliefs prescribed by corporate culture are merely complied with or truly incorporated (Sathe, 1983). This is particularly relevant to concerns regarding motivation, commitment, and the possibility of employees sharing a common "worldview," i.e., the very reasons for promoting a strong corporate culture. Although it can be argued that changes in behavior may result in changes in underlying assumptions over time, the unconscious nature of these assumptions makes this unlikely (Schein, 1985).

The underlying assumptions prescribe ways of perceiving, thinking, and evaluating the world, self, and others. These assumptions include views of the relationship with nature and of human relationships (Schein, 1985; Kluckholn and Strodtbeck, 1961; Wallin, 1972; Hall, 1960; Hofstede, 1980; Laurent, 1983). The relationship with nature reflects several dimensions: 1) control over the environment; 2) activity vs. passivity or doing vs. being; 3) attitudes towards uncertainty; 4) notions of time; 5) attitudes towards change; and 6) what determines "truth." Views about the nature of human relationships include: 1) task vs. social orientation; 2) the importance of hierarchy; 3) the importance of individual vs. group. For example, some cultures, often Western, view man as the master of nature, which can be harnessed and exploited to suit man's needs; time, change, and uncertainty can be actively managed. "Truth" is determined by facts and measurement. Other cultures, often Eastern, view man as subservient to or in harmony with nature. Time, change, and uncertainty are accepted as given. "Truth" is determined by spiritual and philosophical principles. This attitude is often referred to as "fatalistic" or "adaptive."

Assumptions regarding the nature of human relationships are also different. The importance of social concerns over task, of the hierarchy, and of the individual vs. the group are clearly different not only between the East and West, but also within Western cultures. In Eastern cultures, for example, importance is placed on social vs. task concerns, on the hierarchy, and on the group or collective (Hofstede, 1980). By contrast, in Western cultures, the focus is more on task, on the individual and the hierarchy is considered to be of less importance. However, research by Hofstede (1980) and Laurent (1983) demonstrate that along these dimensions there is variance between the U.S. and Europe as well as within Europe.

HUMAN RESOURCE PRACTICES IN MNCs

The differences described above have implications for human resource policies that are developed at headquarters and that reflect not only the corporate culture but the national culture of the MNC. Problems may arise when these policies are to be implemented abroad. According to Schuler (1987), MNCs can choose from a menu of human resource practices that concern: planning and staffing, appraising and compensating, and selection and socialization. Within this menu there are several options which need to be in line with the overall corporate strategy and culture. They also need to take into account the differences in the national cultures of the subsidiaries where they are to be implemented. This section will describe how national culture may affect these choices. In many cases, the description and examples of both corporate and national culture are exaggerated and/or oversimplified. As this is done for purposes of demonstration, it must be remembered that there remains variance within as well as between national and corporate cultures.

Planning and Staffing

Planning can be considered along several dimensions such as formal/informal, and short term/long term. Career management systems represent formal, long term human resource planning. These systems may be inappropriate in cultures where man's control over nature or the future is considered minimal if not sacrilege, e.g., as in the Islamic belief, "Inshallah" (if God wills). Derr (1987) found that national culture was a key determinant of the type of career management systems found within Europe.

Some career management systems assume that people can be evaluated, that their abilities, skills, and traits (i.e., their *net worth* to the company) can be quantified, measured, and fed into a computer. As one British HR manager said, "A lot of that material is highly sensitive; You just don't put it into a computer." On the other hand, Derr (1987) found that the French used highly complex and sophisticated computerized systems. This may reflect a humanistic vs. engineering approach (social vs. task orientation).

Secondly, it may assume that evaluation reflects past performance and predicts future performance, which means that evaluation is based on DOING rather than BEING (active vs. passive). In other words, evaluation is based on *what* you achieve and *what* you know (achievement), and *not* on *who* you are (a person of character and integrity) and *who* you know (ascription). In the U.S., concrete results are the criteria for selection and promotion (Derr, 1987). An American general manager of the U.K. region complained that people around there got promoted because of the schools they went to and their family background, not on what they accomplished. This is also common in France, where ties with the "grandes écoles" and the "grands corps" are important for career advancement.

Third, it may assume that data banks can be created of "skills" that can then be matched to "jobs," that jobs can be clearly defined and that specific skills exist to fit them. One Dutch HR manager said that the major problems of long term planning in high technology industries is that the nature of the job in three to five years is unpredictable. IBM says it hires for careers, not jobs; Olivetti says "potential," not "skills" is most important. These differences may reflect underlying assumptions regarding uncertainty and the relationship between the individual and the group (here, organization), e.g., careers vs. jobs. For example, in Japan job descriptions are left vague and flexible to fit uncertainty and to strengthen the bond between the individual and the company. In the U.S. and France, job descriptions tend to be more specific, which may reduce uncertainty but which permits more job mobility between organizations.

Also, the nature of the skills acquired is a function of the national educational system. In many European countries, particularly France, mathematics and science diplomas have status and engineering is the preferred program of further study. This system encourages highly technical, narrowly focused specialists which may make functional mobility more difficult. In the U.S. and the U.K., psychology and human relations is valued and more generalists are welcomed. Derr (1987) found that in identifying high potentials, the French valued technical and engineering expertise whereas the British preferred "the classical generalist" with a "broad humanistic perspective." Knife and fork tests, assessment of table manners and conversation skills, as well as personal appearance were considered to be important criteria for selection in the U.K.

Many career management systems also assume geographic mobility of the work force. Geographic mobility may reflect assumptions regarding the task vs. social orientation, and the group vs. the individual. Europeans are considered more internationally oriented than

Americans, as they tend to stay longer in each country and move to another country assignment rather than return home (Tung, 1987). Yet, one Belgian general manager stated that the biggest problem in developing leadership was getting people to move; "Belgians would rather commute 2 hours a day to Brussels than to leave their roots. How can you get them to go abroad?" In a survey done in one MNC, the British were most likely to be willing to relocate, while the Spanish were less so, perhaps reflecting economic considerations in Britain and importance of family in Spain. Derr (1987) found 70% of Swedish sample reporting it difficult to relocate geographically due to wives' careers. This is similar to Hofstede's (1980) findings that Sweden has the least differentiation between male and female roles, increasing the likelihood that women would have careers.

Finally, these systems may assume that people want to be promoted. While self-actualization needs are supposedly the same in all countries (Haire et al., 1966), it is not clear that self-actualization means promotion. Nor is it certain that Maslow's hierarchy of needs is universal, as McClelland (1961) found different levels of need for achievement in different societies. In collective societies, wherein the emphasis is on the group over the individual, need for affiliation may be much more important (Hofstede, 1980). In Sweden, egalitarianism as well as the desire to keep a low profile to avoid "royal Swedish envy" (i.e., others covetting your position) may make promotion less desirable. Also, promotion may mean more time must be devoted to work, which means less time for family and leisure, or quality of life. If promotion includes a raise, this may not be desirable due to the Swedish tax structure.

Overall, the notion of career management systems in which people are evaluated in terms of skills, abilities, and traits that will be tested, scored, and computerized may appear impersonal, cold, and objective. These systems may be seen as treating human beings as things, instrumental towards achieving company goals, with no concern for their welfare or for their "soul." Employees should be like family and friends, you don't evaluate them, they are to be unconditionally loved. Even seeing them as "human resources" may be considered questionable.

Appraisal and Compensation

Performance appraisal and compensation systems are also examples of cultural artifacts that are built upon underlying assumptions. As mentioned before, performance appraisal implies that "performance," i.e., what is "done" or "achieved," is important and that it can be "appraised," i.e., measured objectively. What is appraised is thus behavior and not traits. In Japanese firms, however, there is more concern with judging a person's integrity, morality, loyalty, and cooperative spirit than on getting high sales volume. Furthermore, for the Japanese, the notion of "objective" truth is usually neither important nor useful; "objectivity" refers to the foreigners' point of view while "subjectivity" refers to the host's viewpoint (Maruyama, 1984).

Giving direct feedback does not take into account "saving face" so crucial to many Eastern cultures where confronting an employee with "failure" in an open, direct manner would be considered to be "very tactless." The intervention of a third party may be necessary. Appraisal also assumes that the feedback given will be used to correct or improve upon past performance. This requires that individuals receiving the feedback are willing to evaluate themselves instead of blaming others or external conditions for their performance (or lack thereof). This assumes a view of man as having control over the environment and able to change the course of events. It also assumes that what will happen in the future is of importance, that the present provides opportunity, and/or that the past can be used as a guide for future behavior.

Appraisal and compensation systems are often considered to be linked in Western management thinking, as in the case of management by objectives (MBO). Here it is espoused that people should be rewarded based on their performance, what they do or achieve, or for their abilities and skills and not on their traits or personal characteristics. Management by objective (MBO) assumes the following.

1) goals can be set (man has control over the environment);
2) with 3, 6, 12, or 18 month objectives (time can be managed);
3) their attainment can be measured (reality is objective);
4) the boss and the subordinate can engage in a two-way dialogue to agree on what is to be done, when, and how (hierarchy is minimized);
5) the subordinate assumes responsibility to meet the agreed upon goals (control and activity); and
6) the reward is set contingent upon this evaluation (doing vs. being).

Problems with the transfer of MBO to other cultures have been discussed before (Hofstede, 1980; Laurent, 1983; Trepo, 1973). In Germany, MBO was favorably received because of preference for decentralization, less emphasis on the hierarchy (allowing two-way dialogue), and formalization (clear goals, time frames, measurement and contingent rewards). In France, however, this technique was less successfully transferred (Trepo, 1973). Due to the ambivalent views towards authority, MBO was viewed suspiciously as an exercise of arbitrary power and a manipulative ploy of management. Given that power is concentrated in the hands of the boss (importance of hierarchy), subordinates would be held responsible without having the power to accomplish goals. Within this perspective, the notion of the boss and subordinate participating in reaching a decision together is quite foreign. Also, although the French have a preference for formalization, e.g., bureaucreatic systems, things tend to get accomplished outside the system rather than through it—"systeme D" or management by circumvention (Trepo, 1973). Other European managers complain that use of MBO is particularly American as it encourages a short term focus and, as it is tied to rewards, encourages setting lower, more easily attainable goals than necessarily desirable ones.

Tying performance to rewards is also suspect. It would be difficult for most Western managers to consider implementing a system at home whereby the amount that family members are given to eat is related to their contribution to the family income. Yet in the workplace the notion of pay for performance seems quite logical. In African societies, which tend to be more collective, the principles applied to family members apply to employees as well; nepotism is a natural outcome of this logic. One multinational, in an effort to improve the productivity of the work force by providing nutritious lunches, met with resistance and the demand that the cost of the meal be paid directly to the workers so that they could feed their families. The attitude was one of "how can we eat while our families go hungry?"

Preferences for compensation systems and bonuses are clearly linked to cultural attitudes. In one MNC's Danish subsidiary, a proposal for incentives for salespeople was turned down because it favored specific groups, i.e., ran counter to their egalitarian spirit. Furthermore, it was felt that everyone should get the same amount of bonus, not 5% of salary; in fact, there should be no differences in pay. In Africa, savings are managed or bonuses conferred by the group in a "tontine" system wherein everyone gives part of their weekly salary to one group member. Although each member would get the same if they saved themselves, it is preferred that the group perform this function.

The relative importance of status, money, or vacation time varies across countries and affects the motivating potential of these systems. One compensation and benefits manager explained that for the Germans, the big Mercedes wasn't enough; a chauffeur was also needed (status concerns). In Sweden, monetary rewards were less motivating than providing vacation villages (quality of life vs. task orientation). Also, there were different expectations regarding pensions, in part a function of the government and inflation. In Southern European countries the pension expected was 40% of salary, while in the Nordic countries up to 85%, which may reflect different roles of government in society as embedded in the "civic culture" (Almond and Verba, 1963).

Selection and Socialization

One of the major concerns of many multinational companies is the training and development of their human resources. This includes concern for the level of skills at the operating levels, the development of indigenous managerial capability, and the identification and nurturing of "high potentials," i.e., those who will play major future leadership roles. At every level, this requires not only acquiring specific skills, e.g., technical, interpersonal, or conceptual (Katz, 1974), but also acquiring the "way things are done around here"—the behaviors, values, and beliefs and underlying assumptions of that company, i.e., the corporate culture.

Selection is one of the major tools for developing and promoting corporate culture (Schein, 1985). Candidates are carefully screened to "fit in" to the existing corporate culture, assessed for their behavioral styles, beliefs, and values. IBM, for example, may be less concerned with hiring the "typical Italian" than hiring an Italian who fits within the IBM way of doing things. For example, IBM attempts to avoid power accumulation of managers by moving them every two years (it's said that IBM stands for "I've Been Moved"), which may not suit the Italian culture wherein organizations are seen as more "political" than "instrumental" (Laurent, 1983).

One HR manager from Olivetti said that those Italians who want more autonomy go to Olivetti instead of IBM. He described the culture of Olivetti as being informal and non-structured, and as having more freedom, fewer constraints, and low discipline. Recruitment is based on personality and not "too good grades" (taken to reflect not being in touch with the environment). This encouraged hiring of strong personalities, i.e., impatient, more risk-taking and innovative people, making confrontation more likely and managing more difficult.

Socialization is another powerful mechanism of promoting corporate culture. In-house company programs and intense interaction during off-site training can create an "esprit de corps," a shared experience, an interpersonal or informal network, a company language or jargon, as well as develop technical competencies. These training events often include songs, picnics, and sporting events that provide feelings of togetherness. These rites of integration may also be accompanied by initiation rites wherein personal culture is stripped, company uniforms are donned (t-shirts), and humiliation tactics employed, e.g., "pie-in-the-face" and "tie-clipping" (Trice and

Beyer, 1984). This is supposed to strengthen the identification with the company (reinforce the group vs. the individual).

Other examples are to be found in Japanese management development "Hell Camps" wherein "ribbons of shame" must be worn and instruction must be taken from "young females" (*International Management,* January 1985). IBM management training programs often involve demanding, tension-filled, strictly prescribed presentations to "probing" senior managers (Pascale, 1984). These "boot camp" tactics are designed to create professional armies of corporate soldiers. These military metaphors may not be well accepted, particularly in Europe or other politically sensitive regions.

Artifacts of corporate culture campaigns (stickers, posters, cards, and pins) remind members of the visions, values, and corporate goals, e.g., "Smile" campaigns at SAS, Phillips "1 Billion" goal buttons, and G.M. corporate culture cards carried by managers in their breast pockets. Many Europeans view this "hoopla" cynically. It is seen as terribly "American" in its naiveté, enthusiasm, and childishness. It is also seen as controlling and as an intrusion into the private or personal realm of the individual. Statements of company principles on the walls are often referred to sceptically. One HR manager thought that it was "pretty pathetic to have to refer to them." Others feel that it is very American in its exaggeration and lack of subtlety.

Expatriate transfers are also used for socialization and development of an international "cadre" (Edstrom and Galbraith, 1977). The rotation of expatriates from headquarters through subsidiaries and the shipping of local nationals from the subsidiaries to headquarters occur for different reasons, such as staffing, management development, and organization development. These reasons tend to reflect different orientations of headquarters towards their subsidiaries: ethnocentric, polycentric, and geocentric (Ondrack, 1985; Edstrom and Galbraith, 1977; Heenan and Perlmutter, 1979; Evans, 1986).

Differences between American, European, and Japanese firms have been found in the use of transfers for purposes of socialization or as a system of control. U.S. firms rely more on local managers using more formal, impersonal numbers controls, while the European firms rely on the use of the international cadre of managers using more informal, personal control (La Palombara and Blank, 1977; Ondrack, 1985). The Japanese rely heavily on frequent visits of home and host country managers between headquarters and subsidiaries, using both socialization and formalization (Ghoshal and Bartlett, 1987).

Some external conditions affect the use of expatriates, such as local regulations requiring indigenous management and increasingly limited mobility due to the rise of dual career and family constraints. Also, willingness to make work vs. family tradeoffs differ between countries, the Europeans less likely to do so than the Americans (Schmidt and Posner, 1983). It is also reported that the young Japanese managers are less willing to make the same sacrifices to work than their parents were. Therefore, there may be convergence in these trends but for different reasons, e.g., task vs. social orientation or individual vs. group orientation.

This section discussed the assumptions underlying various HRM practices and explored their possible clash with the assumptions of the national cultures of subsidiaries. This clash can cause problems in implementing HRM practices designed at headquarters. The differences in underlying assumptions. however, may provide only the excuse. The extent to which these practices are seen as flowing in one direction, down from headquarters to subsidiaries, may influence the extent to which these practices are adopted and to what extent the behavior, beliefs, and values of the corporate culture are incorporated or even complied with. Ethnocentric vs. geocentric attitudes determine whether there is hope for going global and whether "truly international" is really possible. The next section will discuss some important concerns regarding the use of corporate culture in realizing this global vision.

GOING GLOBAL

Many American multinationals are moving from having international divisions to embracing a "global" or "worldwide" perspective, i.e., stage II to stage III development (Scott, 1973). Even European multinationals having longer histories of international business due to smaller domestic markets, a colonial heritage and greater proximity of "foreign" countries, are asking, "How can we become more international?"

What does international or global really look like? Do they mean the same thing? Some companies point to the reduced number of expatriates in local subsidiaries, the use of third country nationals, and multi-national composition of their top management team as evidence of their "internationalization" (Berenbeim, 1982). Many are clamoring for "corporate culture" to provide the coordination and coherence sought. In one American MNC, the European regional headquarters president saw himself vis-à-vis the national affiliates as "a shepherd that needs to let the flock wander and eat grass but get them all going in one direction—to the barn. You don't want to end up alone in the barn at the end of the day." Is corporate culture necessary for global integration? Will socialization work as a control strategy? Several issues are raised that need careful consideration: need for differentiation vs. integration; autonomy vs. control; and national vs. corporate boundaries.

Differentiation vs. Integration

To what extent can corporate culture override national culture differences to create a global company? Is that desirable or even possible? This raises the issue of the extent to which global vs. local HRM practices are needed to integrate a global company. In the case of global practices, care must be taken so that "geocentric" looks different from "ethnocentric" while remaining sensitive to needs for differentiation. In the case of local, it means determining what needs to be done differently in the context of requirements for integration.

Marketing and HRM have traditionally been functions left decentralized in multinational–subsidiary relationships. Yet, global marketing has been proclaimed the wave of the future (Levitt, 1983) despite obvious local market and customer differences. Global HRM runs along similar logic with similar risks. Is HRM necessarily culture-bound? Does competitive advantage derive from global HRM? Homogenized HRM may weaken competitive advantage by trying to ignore or minimize cultural differences instead of trying to utilize them (Adler, 1986).

Contingency arguments abound. Doz and Prahalad (1984) argue that the simultaneous need for global integration and local responsiveness must be managed. Evans (1986) argues for the product/market logic to determine the socio-cultural strategy for adaptation. Ghoshal and Nohria (1987) argue that the level of environmental complexity and the level of local resources should determine the levels of centralization, formalization, or socialization used for control in headquarters–subsidiary relationships. These prescriptions are all quite rational but may overlook important resistances arising from the following issues regarding autonomy and boundaries.

Control vs. Autonomy

Visions of going global with corporate culture as a strategy for control may have some unforeseen consequences. While Schein (1968) has likened socialization to brainwashing, Pascale (1984) says the maligned "organization man" of the 1960s is now "in." At what point will the push to conform be met with an equal if not stronger push to preserve uniqueness? Dostoyevsky (1960) said that man would even behave self destructively to reaffirm his autonomy. What reactance may be provoked by socialization efforts? Those managers selected out or who "drop out" may be valuable not only by providing their expertise but also by providing an alternative perspective. Certain cultures, both national and corporate, that value conformity over individuality may be better able to use corporate culture as a mechanism for control but may lose the advantage of individual initiative.

Hofstede's (1980) research demonstrates that even within a large multinational, famous for its strong culture and socialization efforts, national culture continues to play a major role in differentiating work values. Laurent (1983) has demonstrated that there is greater evidence for national differences regarding beliefs about organizations in samples of single MNCs than in multicompany samples. These findings may point to a paradox that national culture may play a stronger role in the face of a strong corporate culture. The pressures to conform may create the need to reassert autonomy and identity, creating a cultural mosaic rather than a melting pot.

The convergence/divergence argument (Webber, 1969) states that economic development, technology, and education would make possible globalization whereas differential levels of available resources and national cultures would work against this. A simple comparison of U.S. and Japanese management practices demonstrates that the level of economic development, industrialization, or education is not going to bring about convergence. According to Fujisawa, Founder of Honda, "Japanese and U.S. management is 95% alike and differs in all important aspects."

Equal and opposing forces for unification and fragmentation co-exist (Fayerweather, 1975) as seen within and between countries. The ongoing case of trade policies between Canada and the U.S. (Holsti, 1980) and the hopes for the future of the EEC trade agreements in 1992 rest precariously on this tension. Issues of asymmetry and interdependence between multinationals and host country governments (Gladwin, 1982) and between multinational headquarters and their subsidiaries (Ghoshal and Nohria, 1987) make globalization efforts precarious. Therefore, attempts by headquarters to control subsidiaries through more "subtle" methods, such as corporate culture, should take into account the dependency concerns and autonomy needs of the subsidiary and anticipate their resistance.

For example, efforts to educate Western managers to "understand" Japan met with local resistance (Pucik, personal communication) as ignorance may provide the autonomy zone desired by the local managers. Socialization as a power equalizer as argued by Ghoshal and Nohria (1987) is suspect and will be rejected for precisely this reason. As one general manager of a national subsidiary said regarding the European regional headquarters of a U.S. based MNC, "As long as we give them the numbers they leave us alone." And U.S. headquarters? "They don't have the foggiest idea about what's going on really. They get the numbers. They get 100 million dollars a year in profit and that's probably about as much as they want to know about." Perhaps formal reporting preserves autonomy and will thus be preferred regardless of the logic of globalization.

Boundaries: National vs. Corporate

In the 1960s, multinationals threatened to take over the world; host country governments' sovereignty was at risk (Vernon, 1971; 1977). However, through the transfer of technology and managerial capacity, the power became more symmetrical, even tipping the scale in the other direction as seen at one point in the rash of nationalizations that occurred in the 1970s (Kobrin, 1982). While the balance has subsequently restabilized, larger forces, such as the rise of religious fundamentalism in some areas, threaten this stability.

National boundaries are again threatened. Economic victory in lieu of military victory seems to have created "occupation douce." This is reflected in the anxieties of Americans as they see their country becoming owned by "foreigners" and the Japanese invasion of Wall Street. Mitterand, President of France, said recently that in the future the French might become the museum keepers, relying on tips from Japanese tourists.

The vision of developing an international cadre of executives through frequent and multiple transfers designed to encourage the loss of identification with their country of origin and its transfer to the corporation (Edstrom and Galbraith, 1977) is frightening. In these global "clans," corporate identification may come to override community and even family identification (Ouchi and Jaeger, 1978). These citizens of the world, men and women without countries, only companies, become corporate mercenaries. One story has it that a French IBM executive arriving at JFK airport in New York while searching for his entry visa pulled out his IBM identification card. The customs official, seeing it said, "Oh, it's O.K., you're IBM, you can go ahead." Business schools train these corporate soldiers, dispatching them to multinationals to control the world through finance and management consulting. Perhaps now is the time for academics and practitioners to sit back and reflect about the implications.

Susan C. Schneider is Assistant Professor of Organizational Behavior at INSEAD, The European Institute of Business Administration in Fontainebleau, France.

REFERENCES

Adler, N. J. *International dimensions of organizational behavior.* Belmont, California: Kent Publishing Company, 1986.

Adler, N. J., and Jelinek, M. Is "Organizational Culture" culture bound? *Human Resource Management,* 1986, 25 (1), 73–90.

Administrative Science Quarterly, 1983, 28 (3).

Almond, G. A., and Verba. S. *The civic culture: Political attitudes and democracy in five nations.* Princeton, NJ: Princeton University Press, 1963.

Baliga, B. R., and Jaeger, A. M. Multinational corporations: Control systems and delegation issues. *Journal of International Business Studies,* 1984, 15 (2), 25–40.

Berenbeim, R. *Managing the international company: Building a global perspective.* New York: The Conference Board, Inc., Report no. 814, 1982.

Deal, T., and Kennedy, A. *Corporate cultures: The rites and rituals of corporate life.* Reading, Mass.: Addison-Wesley Publishing Co., Inc., 1982.

Derr, C. Managing high potentials in Europe. *European Management Journal,* 1987, 5 (2), 72–80.

Dostoyevsky. *Notes from the underground.* New York: Dell Publishing Company, Inc., 1960.

Doz, Y., and Prahalad, C. Patterns of strategic control within multinational corporations. *Journal of International Business Studies,* 1984, 15 (2), 55–72.

Edstrom, A., and Galbraith J. Transfer of managers as a coordination and control strategy in multinational organizations. *Administrative Science Quarterly,* 1977, 22, 248–263.

Evans, P. The context of strategic human resource management policy in complex firms. *Management Forum,* 1986, 6, 105–117.

Fayerweather, J. A conceptual scheme of the interaction of the multinational firm and nationalism. *Journal of Business Administration,* 1975, 7, 67–89.

Ghoshal, S., and Bartlett A. Organizing for innovations: Case of the multinational corporation. WP INSEAD No. 87/04, 1987.

Ghoshal, S., and Nohria, N. Multinational corporations as differentiated networks. WP INSEAD No. 87/13, 1987.

Gladwin, T. Environmental interdependence and organizational design: The case of the multinational corporation. WP NYU No. 82-13, 1982.

Haire, M., Ghiselli, E., and Porter, L. *Managerial thinking–An international study.* New York: John Wiley & Sons, Inc., 1966.

Hall, E. T. The silent language of overseas business. *Harvard Business Review,* 1960, 38 (3), 87–95.

Heenan, D. A., and Perlmutter, H. V. *Multinational organization development: A social architectural perspective.* Phillippines: Addison-Wesley Publishing Company, Inc., 1979.

Hofstede, G. *Culture's consequences.* Beverly Hills, CA: Sage Publications, 1980.

Holsti, J. Change in the international system: Integration and fragmentation. In R. Holsti, R. Siverson, and A. George (Eds.), *Change in the International System.* Boulder: Westview Press, 1980, 23–53.

Journal of International Business Studies, Fall 1984.

Katz, R. Skills of an effective administrator. *Harvard Business Review,* 1974, 90–102.

Kluckholn, F., and Strodtbeck, F. *Variations in value orientations.* Evanston, IL: Row, Peterson, 1961.

Kobrin, S. *Managing political risk assessments: Strategic response to environmental change.* Berkeley, CA: University of California Press, 1982.

La Palombara, J., and Blank, S. *Multinational corporations in comparative perspective.* New York: The Conference Board, Report No. 725, 1977.

Laurent, A. The cross-cultural puzzle of international human resource management. *Human Resource Management,* 1986, 25 (1), 91–102.

Laurent, A. The cultural diversity of western conceptions of management. *International Studies of management and Organizations,* 1983, 13 (1–2), 75–96.

Levitt, T. The globalization of markets. *Harvard Business Review,* 1983 (May-June), 92–102.

McClelland, D. *The achieving society.* New York: D. Van Nostrand Company, Inc., 1961.

Maruyama, M. Alternative concepts of management: Insights from Asia and Africa. *Asia Pacific Journal of Management*, 1984, 100–110.

Ondrack, D. International transfers of managers in North American and European MNE's. *Journal of International Business Studies*, 1985, XVI (3), 1–19.

Ouchi, W. G., and Jaeger, A. M. Type Z organization: Stability in the midst of mobility. *Academy of Management Review*, 1978, 3 (2), 305–314.

Pascale, R. The paradox of "Corporate Culture": Reconciling ourselves to socialization. *California Management Review*, 1984, 27 (2), 26–41.

Peters, T., and Waterman, R. *In search of excellence.* New York: Harper & Row, 1982.

Sathe, V. Implications of corporate culture: A manager's guide to action. *Organizational Dynamics*, 1983 (Autumn), 5–23.

Schein, E. H. Organizational socialization and the profession of management. *Industrial Management Review*, 1968, 9, 1–15.

Schein, E. H. *Organizational culture and leadership.* San Francisco: Jossey-Bass Publishers, 1985.

Schmidt, W., and Posner, B. *Management values in perspective.* New York: AMA Publications, 1983.

Scott, B. The industrial state: Old myths and new realities. *Harvard Business Review*, 1973 (Mar.–Apr.), 133–148.

Schuler, R. Human resource management practice choices. In R. Schuler and S. Youngblood (Eds.), *Readings in Personnel and Human Resource Management*, 3rd edition. St. Paul: West Publishing, 1987.

Schwartz, H., and Davis, S. Matching corporate culture and business strategy. *Organizational Dynamics*, 1981 (Summer), 30–48.

Smircich, L. Studying organizations as cultures. In G. Morgan (Ed.), *Beyond Method: Strategies for Social Research.* Beverley Hills, California: Sage Publications, Inc., 1983.

Trepo, G. Management style à la Francaise. *European Business*, 1973 (Autumn), 71–79.

Trice, H. M., and Beyer, J. M. Studying organizational culture through rites and ceremonials. *Academy of Management Review*, 1984, 9 (4), 653–669.

Tung, R. Expatriate assignments: Enhancing success and minimizing failure. *Academy of Management Executive*, 1987, 1 (2), 117–126.

Vernon, R. *Sovereignty at bay.* New York: Basic Books, 1971.

Vernon, R. *Storm over the multinationals.* Cambridge, MA: Harvard University Press, 1977.

Wallin, T. The international executive baggage: Cultural values of the American frontier. *MSU Business Topics*, 1972 (Spring), 49–58.

Webber, R. Convergence or divergence? *Columbia Journal of Business*, 1969, 4 (3).

Part V
The Progress of Understanding

[21]

© Academy of Management Review
1991, Vol. 16, No. 2, 262–290.

THE PAROCHIAL DINOSAUR: ORGANIZATIONAL SCIENCE IN A GLOBAL CONTEXT

NAKIYE AVDAN BOYACIGILLER
San Jose State University
NANCY J. ADLER
McGill University

This article reviews academic management from three global perspectives: contextual, quantitative, and qualitative. Based on multiple methods of assessment, academic management is found to be overly parochial. Cultural values of the United States underlie and have fundamentally framed management research, thus imbuing organizational science with implicit, and yet inappropriate, universalism. Recommendations are made to develop a more globally relevant organizational science in which universal, regiocentric, intercultural, and culture-specific theories and research are clearly demarcated.

Its [culture's] influence for organizational behavior is that it operates at such a deep level that people are not aware of its influences. It results in unexamined patterns of thought that seem so natural that most theorists of social behavior fail to take them into account. As a result, many aspects of organizational theories produced in one culture may be inadequate in other cultures. (Triandis, 1983: 139)

Global business has become a reality. Macro and micro economic statistics daily etch that reality into the decision patterns of political and corporate leaders. Yet the American academic management tradition appears to have fallen behind. Does the creation and dissemination of management knowledge now lag behind economic reality?

Many leaders of the Academy of Management have sounded the international clarion. As president, Richard Steers focused the 1987 National Academy of Management's attention on the international dimensions of management (Steers, 1987, 1989). In 1988, president Don Hellriegel pre-

Earlier versions of this article were presented at the Western Academy of Management meetings in San Francisco and Big Sky, Montana; the Organizational and Strategic Studies Mini-Symposium at the Anderson School of Management at UCLA; the University of California, Berkeley Organizational Behavior Doctoral Seminar; the World Congress of Sociology in Madrid, July 1990; and the Academy of International Business meetings in Toronto, November 1990.

sented internationalization as one of the Academy's four main challenges. Steven Kerr, 1990 president, presided over discussions to join an international federation of academies of management. Similarly, Eastern Academy of Management president Carolyn Dexter moved her region's biannual meetings overseas, arguing that the Academy can no longer remain within the conceptual or geographical borders of the United States. The Western Academy of Management followed suit by convening its unique 1990 meeting in Japan.

This article investigates the global context of management research, education, and theory development in the United States from three perspectives: contextual, quantitative, and qualitative. First, from a contextual perspective, it reviews changes in the external environment that potentially impact academic management, including inherent influences that have resulted from its being a post–World War II, American-based profession. Second, from a quantitative perspective, it reviews the publication of international articles in U.S. management journals, along with American scholars' preparation to conduct such research. Third, and perhaps most important, it reviews a selection of management theories from a qualitative perspective. Although many differences exist between domestic and global management (including myriad issues involving scale, scope, and complexity), given the limits of a single article, we focus on the cultural assumptions that underlie and often frame management research as well as the implicit universalism inherent in much of organizational science.

Parochialism is based on ignorance of others' ways. Ethnocentrism judges foreign ways as inferior to one's own. This article does not criticize American-made organizational science for being ethnocentric. It does not suggest that the main problem is that American theorists view American theories as superior to others' theories. Rather, based on the multiple observations presented, one of our primary conclusions is that of parochialism. Americans have developed theories without being sufficiently aware of non–U.S. contexts, models, research, and values. Our goal, however, is not to extend made-in-America organizational science beyond its current geographical boundaries, but rather to strengthen it by suggesting fundamental changes in how scholars can think about and create theories. The purpose of this article, therefore, is not to castigate the field, its pioneers, or its present leaders; rather, by drawing attention to the forces promulgating parochialism, it reconceptualizes the field's roots and thereby facilitates the creation of a more relevant future. Although the indictments in this article are at times strong, they are attempts to avoid relegating the American academic management tradition to the curiosity of a mid-twentieth-century fossil.

CONTEXTUAL PAROCHIALISM

Industrial Competitiveness: The View Since World War II

In critical reviews of the field, Lawrence (1987) and Pfeffer (1982) underscored the importance of appreciating social context and its influence on theory development. They indicated that the questions organizational theorists have deemed most interesting to study have been a function of managers' concerns and, thus, a *product of the time.* Similarly, such scholars as Kuhn (1962), Merton (1968), and Whitley (1984), among others, suggested that the social system of scientists and the environment of scientific activity constrain knowledge production (Graham & Gronhaug, 1989). According to Merton (1968: 539):

> Social organization of intellectual activity is significantly related to the character of the knowledge which develops under its auspices. . . . Increasingly, it has been assumed that the social structure does not influence science merely by focusing the attention of scientists upon certain problems for research . . . [but also in] the ways in which the cultural and social context enters into the conceptual phrasing of scientific problems.

What is the sociocultural context of academic management? Most management schools and academic management journals are American. They, along with the Academy of Management, grew up as distinctly American institutions in a particular geographical, cultural, and temporal context—that of post–World War II United States. Although the Academy of Management is over 50 years old, two of the most prestigious management journals, *Administrative Science Quarterly* and the *Academy of Management Journal*, were established in 1956 and 1958, respectively, as Whitley (1988: 47) accurately described (based on Gordon & Howell, 1959; Pierson et al., 1959; Smiddy & Naum, 1954; Whitley & England, 1977):

> The encouragement of systematic research into managerial problems and business behavior in the 1950s was based on the widespread belief in the United States at the time that scientific knowledge could provide the foundation for improved managerial decision making and upgrade the quality of business education.

Thus, as William Ouchi presented in his 1990 Western Academy of Management keynote address, management knowledge began to be codified during a particular period of American history. To understand the strengths and limitations of that knowledge base, it is incumbent to understand both its particular historical context as well as the current economic situation.

The United States emerged from World War II as the only major, economically developed nation with its industrial sector unscathed. Immediately following World War II, the United States accounted for 75 percent of the world's GNP (Thurow, 1988). For the next two decades, U.S. multinational corporations dominated world trade. During this period of the United States' postwar economic dominance, American researchers focused on American firms, American perspectives, and those questions most salient to American managers, rather than systematically including either non–U.S. sites or issues. In this context, it was easy for researchers—including non–

U.S. researchers (Servan-Schreiber, 1968)—to assume implicitly that American theories also dominated. We could argue that the field was imprinted with a U.S. orientation (Stinchcombe, 1965). Beechler and Pucik (1989), for example, noted that the Japanese imported American managerial theories primarily during periods of U.S. economic and organizational dominance. Similarly, consulting firms, such as McKinsey and Company, grew rapidly following World War II and actively exported both the structural and process solutions they used for U.S. industry (Blackford, 1988: 124). Today, the United States produces less than one quarter (22%) of the world's GNP. Along with the United States' decline in the global economy, the need to question the previously assumed universality of U.S. theories has become apparent.

Even though some academics and managers believe that American managerial know-how created U.S. economic success—and concomitantly, that Americans must now look to their management systems to regain economic superiority—Thurow (1984, 1988) contends that America was never competitive, but rather, had effortless economic superiority. Ouchi (1984) concurs, describing U.S. corporations during the postwar period as earning monopoly profits and their workers as earning monopoly wages; this was not due to the superiority of American management techniques, but rather it was primarily due to the lack of significant foreign competition. Recognizing the presence today of vigorous foreign competition, Ouchi (1984) predicts that Americans will never again earn the monopoly profits and wages that characterized the decades immediately following World War II. Both Thurow's and Ouchi's arguments suggest an attribution error: The economic success of the United States has been attributed, in part, to Americans' conception of management (a collective internal attribution) rather than to the relative lack of competition (an external attribution).

In the 1990s, American industry faces becoming just another, albeit important, region of the globe. Though corporate and academic performance are certainly not identical, perhaps the time has come for American management professors and faculties to embrace a similar fate. Moreover, perhaps the particular American heritage that facilitated the field's inception and its initial development now hinders its future contributions. To understand better these dynamics, the central institution of American academic management, the Academy of Management, is examined.

The Academy of Management: A Global Perspective

As mentioned, post–World War II economic conditions played a determining role in the way business approached developing, manufacturing, and marketing products and services. In 1966, Vernon proposed a simple, yet widely used, three-phase model for understanding firms' development based on the product life cycle (see also Vernon, 1971). Adding a fourth phase to capture the complexities of today's highly competitive global environment, these phases could be labeled domestic, international, multinational, and global (Adler & Ghadar, 1990). Although the expanded model outlines key aspects of the evolution of multinational enterprises, the four phases also suggest some dimensions for understanding the evolution of American academic management theory, education, and institutions during the same period. Many attributes characterize the four phases, but a few are particularly salient in helping scholars to understand their industry, that is, the creation and dissemination of management knowledge.

The model, in brief, suggests that in the first phase (domestic), firms focus on developing and producing unique new products in and for the domestic market. To a substantial extent, these firms ignore the world outside of their own borders. During the second phase (international), firms focus on marketing. They expand their markets internationally: first by exporting their domestically produced products, next by assembling the products abroad, and finally by producing these products abroad. Using a multidomestic strategy, these firms assess each foreign country separately for its market potential. Because international activities constitute a small and generally less important portion of a firm's overall operations, it commonly relegates the management of such activities to a separate international division. By the third phase (multinational), firms face a much more competitive multinational environment. They therefore emphasize price, that is, developing least-cost production systems by using factor sourcing, production, and distribution that are integrated worldwide. At the third phase, firms frequently organize their substantially larger multinational operations into highly integrated, global lines of business. With the growing importance of economies of scale and scope during this phase, standardization becomes all-important. By the fourth phase (global), firms must operate globally as top-quality, least-cost, state-of-the-art producers and distributors to survive. Strategically and structurally, they must develop flexible systems that are globally coordinated and integrated while remaining highly differentiated and nationally responsive (Bartlett, Doz, & Hedlund, 1990; Bartlett & Ghoshal, 1989; Porter, 1980; Prahalad & Doz, 1987).

Where does the Academy of Management fit when viewed from the evolutionary perspective of this four-phase model? First, scholars produce and disseminate the majority of organizational science research within the United States (Phase 1—domestic). Second, the scope and primary orientation of most theories is American; however, such theories are presented as if they were universally applicable. For example, researchers conduct studies on the job satisfaction of American men and yet use the results to develop and substantiate overall theories on job satisfaction. A few scholars then test these U.S. job satisfaction theories to see if they apply abroad (Slocum & Topichak, 1972). The former is a Phase 1 approach (producing for the home market), while the latter is a Phase 2 approach (i.e., attempting to extend the "market" for U.S. theories abroad). Third, the dominant nationality of the Academy is American. Its leaders, journal editors, and editorial board members are not drawn from scholars worldwide, but rather are predominantly Americans. Fourth, and as most junior scholars at leading U.S. universities know, researchers must publish in top American journals.

Publication in non–U.S. journals (and, to a lesser extent, U.S. journals focusing on international topics) is considered suspect, that is, suspect of being inferior (a Phase 1 assumption). Fifth, international research, rather than being integrated throughout the Academy, constitutes a separate—and in the past, sometimes disparaged—division. The Academy thus echoes the structural dynamics of Phase 2 firms; it too has an international division that is kept organizationally distinct from the mainstream core of the organization. Curiously, because the International Division has been labeled as a separate division, the Academy's Management History, Organization Theory, and Organization Behavior Divisions implicitly become domestic divisions posturing as "universal divisions." Illogical as it seems (except through Phase 2 lenses), at present, international is a subdivision of domestic. Based on these five examples, as well as many similar observations, the Academy currently appears to combine primarily aspects of domestic and international organizations, while exhibiting few multinational or global characteristics.

Given the dramatic shifts in the external economic environment, we recommend that the Academy consider new, more global structures and processes (the final section of this article lists specific recommendations). Although the precise format for "going global" is not important, the result—moving from Phase 1 and 2 structures to those of Phases 3 and 4—is critically important to the future relevance and potential contribution of American academic management.

QUANTITATIVE PAROCHIALISM

Having briefly reviewed the global context, we can now focus directly on the issues addressed and the research produced within that context. Today, between 15 and 30 of the world's 185 countries possess most of its scientific knowledge, while representing less than one third of its population (von Alleman, 1974). If most science is practiced in fewer than 30 countries, all social science is practiced in fewer still, and all organizational science in still fewer (Roberts & Boyacigiller, 1984: 425). The vast majority of management schools are in the United States. The majority of management professors and researchers are American trained. Moreover, as previously mentioned, the vast majority of management research focuses on the United States (see Gergen, 1973, for similar trends in social psychological theory). Lawrence (1987: 2–3) cited 30 key contributions in the development of organizational science, only 5 of which were contributed by non-Americans (6 if Kurt Lewin is included). Additionally, all five of the non–U.S. researchers are European; none are from outside of the occidental tradition (see Adler, Doktor, & Redding, 1986).

Academic institutions (management schools included) produce and disseminate knowledge. The following section reviews the record of American management schools in producing internationally educated managers and professors, as well as the record of those professors in producing internationally focused research.

Management Schools

Several studies have recommended improving the international business education offered to U.S. college graduates in order to improve the performance of American executives working abroad (American Association of School Administrators, 1983; National Advisory Board on Education Programs, 1983; President's Commission on Industrial Competitiveness, 1985; Porter & McKibben, 1988). In 1974, the American Assembly of Collegiate Schools of Business (AACSB) changed its accreditation standards to include a worldwide dimension in the curriculum. By 1979, the AACSB approved an interpretation of that standard, saying, "Every student should be exposed to the international dimension in the curriculum" (Nehrt, 1987). Yet, in 1984, over 20 percent of the AACSB schools' MBA programs had done nothing to internationalize their curricula (Nehrt, 1987). Moreover, at the 1989 global INTERMAN Conference, the only worldwide meeting for management school deans, only 10 deans from the more than 700 American management schools attended, fewer than the number attending from the People's Republic of China. Perhaps even more serious, only 17 percent of the doctoral students had taken an international course; that is, less than one doctoral student in five was prepared in any way to teach the international dimensions of their discipline (Nehrt, 1987).

Similarly, "fewer than half of all colleges and universities now require foreign language study for the bachelor's degree, down from nearly 90% in 1966" (Bowen, 1984: 91), with most doctoral programs counting a computer language as sufficient to meet the foreign language requirement. In the most recent AACSB survey (Thanopoulos, 1986), schools were not even asked if they offered an international organizational behavior course or if they included an international dimension to their regularly required organizational behavior courses (Thanopoulos & Vernon, 1987). Even though the AACSB (1988–1989: 28) now directs business schools to "provide for a broad education preparing the student for imaginative and responsible citizenship and leadership roles in business and society—domestic and worldwide," there is little indication that U.S. business schools are currently able to fulfill the "worldwide" part of their mandate. Given this pattern, it is not surprising that Kobrin (1984) found that most American managers still acquire their international expertise through business experience and not in management seminars and courses.

Management Research

In a survey of 24 journals during the decade 1971 to 1980, Adler (1983) found that less than 5 percent (4.2%) of the organizational behavior articles published in top American management journals focused on cross-cultural or international issues. Of those with a cross-cultural focus, the majority were unicultural, single-country studies (1.9 %). Less than 2 percent (1.4%) compared two or more cultures, and less than 1 percent (.9%) investigated the interaction among people from different cultures, even though interaction is the essence of most international business transactions. Adler (1983) found no increase in the number or proportion of international organizational behavior articles over the decade.

Two studies replicated Adler's results and found no significant increase in the number of cross-cultural organizational behavior articles (Godkin, Braye, & Caunch, 1989a; Peng, Peterson, & Shyi, 1990); this despite the continued commitment of such journals as the *Journal of International Business Studies*, the *Columbia Journal of World Business*, and the newer *Organization Studies*, *Strategic Management Journal*, and *California Management Review* to publish top-quality international management research. This is neither an impressive showing nor a particularly favorable harbinger. Godkin and his colleagues (1989b: 9) concluded that:

> While global economic interdependence has increased and accredited business schools have been required to internationalize their curricula, publication in the field of cross-cultural management seems to lag as in the late 70's. This is a regrettable, but seemingly continuing trend. The dangers inherent in remaining ignorant of our neighbors are disturbing; the ramifications of competing in ignorance more so. The bliss proverbially associated with ignorance and the arrogance accompanying it have a down side.

Why is there such a paucity of international research in organizational science? As described previously, doctoral programs fail in training researchers both to understand international issues and to develop the tools, such as foreign language skills, to conduct such research. Moreover, even if prepared, international research is more difficult to conduct than its domestic counterpart, given the complexity of the multinational environment and the higher monetary and time costs involved in multicountry studies (Adler, 1984; Wind & Perlmutter, 1973: 131). In addition, Graham and Gronhaug (1989) contrasted the lack of fit between the domestic U.S. emphasis on rigorous quantitative methods and internal validity, with the nature of international studies which, by definition, tend to be contextual and therefore demand approaches incorporating high levels of external validity (see Adler, Campbell, & Laurent's [1989] description of the challenges involved in collecting valid survey data in a politically repressive environment). To ignore or to minimize external validity is to assume that theories apply irrespective of context, that is, that they apply under any political, economic, cultural, legal, or historical situation. The general acceptance of laboratory studies in American social science exemplifies this acceptance of context-free methodologies.

Unfortunately, there has been no systematic study of the international aspects of the review process to determine if international research, once produced, gets published. However, as mentioned previously, the preponderance of American journal editors, the paucity of foreign editorial board members, and the lack of recognition of foreign sources is striking. As Whitley (1984: 27–28) recognized:

> A major manifestation of the way reputational control limits the originality of contributions to collective intellectual goals is the necessity of referring to the previous work of colleagues. While this may be necessary to avoid prolix redundancies in the text, it is also a way of exerting social control over novel ideas. . . . In a sense, citations are a way of ritualistically affirming group goals and norms, of demonstrating group membership and identity.

Given that few international articles have been published and that articles published in foreign journals are of suspect quality by many American editorial boards, international researchers are hard pressed to "ritualistically affirm group membership," that is, to cite a sufficient number of relevant articles published in leading American journals to pass the test of "building on prior research" (Graham & Gronhaug, 1989). Arndt (1985: 19) attested to the difficulties of breaking the American-based, logical empiricist mold (in marketing, although the same is certainly true for organizational science): "In our enlightened age, the dissident . . . scientist is not burned at the stake. Instead, he or she is rather likely to suffer the slow burnout of never emerging from the journals' revision purgatories." Graham and Gronhaug's (1989) accurate, and yet discouraging, conclusion is that research methods are driving knowledge production rather than the problems and needs of managers, policy makers, and students.

QUALITATIVE PAROCHIALISM

> The concepts of the field are seldom value-free, and most could be replaced with other concepts carrying far different valuational baggage . . . if our values were otherwise, social conformity could be viewed as pro-solidarity behavior; attitude change as cognitive adaptation; and the risky shift as the courageous conversion. . . . Perhaps our best option is to maintain as much sensitivity as possible to our biases and to communicate them as openly as possible. (Gergen, 1973: 312)

Assumptions about underlying values would be unimportant if either organizational theories were based on universal values or values did not have an impact on organizational behavior (Gonzalez & McMillan, 1961). Neither supposition is tenable given the research substantiating the cultural diversity of values and the impact of such diversity on organizational behavior (e.g., England, 1975; Hofstede, 1980; Kelley & Worthley, 1981; Lane & DiStefano, 1988; Laurent, 1981; Moore, 1974; Oberg, 1963). Child (1981: 347–348) summarized diversity's impact on micro organizational behavior:

> Cultural effects will be most powerful in the process of organizations relating to authority, style, conduct, participation and attitudes, and less powerful in formal structuring and overall strategy. However, we still require a more adequate theory of

organizations which specifies the points at which contingency, culture and the system of economic relationships have their main effects.

Even though values and cultural assumptions profoundly influence micro organizational behavior, they equally clearly influence macro organization theory. For example, Laurent (1983: 75–76) described his difficulty explaining matrix management to French managers:

> The idea of reporting to two bosses was so alien to these managers that mere consideration of such organizing principles was an impossible, useless exercise. What was needed first was a thorough examination and probing of the holy principle of the single chain of command and the managers' recognition that this was a strong element of their own belief system rather than a constant element in nature.

Not surprisingly, Lawrence (1987) credited European researchers (with their more sociological orientation and therefore keen interest in size, technology, structure, and contingency theory) with being the impetus behind the development of the macro side of the field.

Organizational theorists appear to be victims of an attribution error. As described by Jones and Nisbett (1971), the fundamental attribution error posits that individuals are prone to view the behavior of others as determined by their individual characteristics and motivations rather than by characteristics of the environment. Similar to other individuals, organizational theorists seem to have underestimated the extent to which their perceptions and interpretations, and consequently their building of organizational theory, are influenced by the external cultural environment. Cultural biases keep scholars from seeing the full range and diversity of organizational phenomena. For example, in reviewing contributions by leading European scholars, Hofstede (1981: 32) found remarkable differences in focus according to the particular researcher's background: "Authors from Latin Europe, focus on power; from Central Europe, including Germany, on truth; from Eastern Europe, on efficiency; from Northern Europe, on change" (also see Hofstede & Kassem, 1976; Lammers, 1990). Laurent (1983) used British scholars' focus on structure as contrasted with their French counterparts' focus on power to exemplify the same point. Similarly, Roberts and Boyacigiller (1983), in a survey of cross-national researchers, also found national patterns in research emphasis.

Assumed Universality and Organizational Theory

Although important, recognizing culture's profound influence on the development of theories is difficult (Triandis, 1972). If culture is invisible, one's own culture is most invisible (Hall, 1959). As Boulding (1961: 16) eloquently summarized over 25 years ago:

> The development of images is part of the culture or the subculture in which they are developed, and it depends upon all el-

ements of that culture or subculture. Science is a subculture among subcultures. It can claim to be useful. It can claim rather more dubiously to be good. It cannot claim to give validity.

Like all nations, the United States has deeply embedded values that influence the ways in which Americans perceive and think about the world as well as the ways in which they behave within that world. Most American theories, however, have been developed and presented as if they were acultural. Yet, as Berger and Luckman (1966) argued in *The Social Construction of Reality*, acultural perception, observation, interpretation, and theory building have yet to be proven to exist.

As has been noted, most organization theories were "made-in-the-USA" and, therefore, were influenced by the political, economic, and cultural context of the United States. Yet, few researchers have explicitly addressed the influence of American values on U.S.-based organizational science (Adler, 1986; Adler & Jelinek, 1986; Burrell & Morgan, 1979; Hofstede, 1980; Newman, 1972). Rather, most organization theories appear implicitly to assume universality (see Hofstede & Bond, 1988; Lammers & Hickson, 1979, Osigweh, 1989a,b; Smith & Peterson, 1988, for notable exceptions). Even when the applicability of these theories to other cultures is tested, researchers usually select methods that are most acceptable according to American norms, thereby rendering results that are just as culturally conditioned (see Morey & Luthans, 1984; Sekaran, 1983, for exceptions).

Though cultural values potentially have an impact on a range of micro and macro organizational phenomena, the scope of this article limits the number of examples we might cite. The following section offers examples of particularly powerful cultural influences. Because a number of models for examining value orientations are well regarded and increasingly widely used in the field, rather than limiting ourselves to one model, we have chosen examples from three: Kluckhohn and Strodbeck (1961), Hofstede (1980), and Hall (1959). The selected examples demonstrate how U.S. values regarding free will, individualism, and a low-context orientation profoundly affect how the field conceptualizes organizational behavior. The selected examples neither represent all value differences nor the complete range of their impact on organizations and management.

Free Will Versus Determinism: Orientations Toward Power and Efficacy

A prevailing American cultural belief is that individuals can affect their immediate circumstances, are responsible for their actions, and can influence future events (Stewart, 1972). Americans generally see themselves as capable of controlling their own circumstances and, to a substantial degree, their environment:

> While recognizing the influence of both nature and nurture, Americans rarely see themselves as ultimately constrained by their biological or psychological inheritance, their childhood so-

> cialization, or even their prior experience. Instead, they see
> themselves as infinitely capable of self-change, as evident from
> the number of self-help books lining the shelves of popular
> American bookstores. (Adler & Jelinek, 1986: 82)

Similarly, the huge amount ($210 billion) spent annually in the United States on work-related training (American Society for Training and Development, 1989) reflects Americans' confidence in adult learning and, therefore, the possibility of directed change.

By contrast, many other cultures traditionally see causality as determined by factors beyond their control, factors such as God, fate, luck, government, one's social class, or history. Most fundamentalist Moslems, for example, see life as following a path preordained by the will of God (e.g., Harris & Moran, 1979: 46). Similarly, the Chinese invoke "Joss," a combination of luck and fate, to explain events. These more deterministic cultures generally define accountability and responsibility more diffusely than cultures that rely on free will. In deterministic cultures, people cannot assume responsibility for many events because such events are perceived as occurring outside of their control. Perhaps the essentially stable, post–World War II economic, political, social, and legal environment in the United States made it particularly easy for American managers and management theorists to emphasize free will and, thus, personal efficacy and control. For instance, because Americans have not had to contend with major changes or radical breakdown in their legal system, they generally trust the enforceability of contracts. Similarly, because coups, military or otherwise, have not altered the political dynamics of the United States, Americans can reliably predict an environmental stability that is absent in many other parts of the world.

Americans' emphasis on free will and their related belief that people can control and dominate the environment (Kluckhohn & Strodbeck, 1961) profoundly influence their view of organizational design and change (Galbraith, 1973; Miles & Snow, 1978). Most commonly today through organizational culture and leadership models and metaphors, American theorists describe organizations as malleable; that is, given the appropriate intervention, managers can change organizations to create a better alignment with the environment. Similarly, American theorists conceptualize managers as having sufficient power to influence the environment, thus ensuring the continued flow of critical resources (Pfeffer & Salancik, 1978).

By contrast, Kiggundu (1988: 182) notes that in Africa, similar to many other economically developing areas of the world, because of the asymmetrical relationship between the organization and its relevant environment, managing interdependencies with the external environment is much more problematic than it is in the United States. In such cultures, neither the organization as a whole nor the individual manager can strongly influence organizational outcomes.

External environmental determinism is not irrelevant for Americans. It simply fails to have the pronounced, irrefutable relevance that it has for many other cultures. Americans, for instance, used the oil crisis (an external factor perceived to be beyond their control) to explain the U.S. dollar's high value in 1974. Similarly today, in referring to Japanese protectionist legislation, Americans accept a limited determinism in explaining some of their difficulties in resolving the U.S. trade deficit. From the perspective of organizational science, the problem is that most theories fail to sufficiently emphasize external environmental factors in general, or to include such cultural variants as determinism in particular.

Individualism and Collectivism: Orientations Toward Motivation and Commitment

> In what cultural and historical context does the greatest good involve being able to break apart from one's collective base to stand alone, self-sufficient and self-contained? In the context of an individualistic society in which individualism and self-containment is the ideal, the person who most separates self from the group is thereby seen as embodying that ideal most strongly; the person who remains wedded to a group is not our [American] esteemed ideal. (Sampson, 1977: 776)

Hofstede's (1980) research investigating dominant cultural values ranks the United States highest on individualism among his 40-country sample. When this research was extended to over 50 countries, the United States still maintained its first-place position on individualism (Hofstede, 1983). Americans define themselves using personal characteristics and achievements rather than their place within a group or collectivity. Note, for example, the U.S. selection practice of using résumés listing personal achievements rather than hiring relatives, which is pejoratively labeled as nepotism. Sampson (1977: 769) summarized this issue: "Our [American] culture emphasizes individuality, in particular a kind of individual self-sufficiency that describes an extreme of the individualistic dimension."

Many organizational theories reflect this individualist bias. Allen, Miller, and Nath (1988) note that in countries where individualism dominates, individuals view their relationship with the organization from a calculative perspective, whereas in collectivist societies, the ties between the individual and organization have a moral component. Clearly, the concept of organizational commitment (e.g., Staw, 1980) carries very different connotations in collectivist societies than in individualistic societies. Employees who have collectivist values commit to organizations primarily due to their ties with managers, owners, co-workers (collectivism), and much less due to the job itself or the particular compensation scheme (individualistic incentives). Consonant with its individualistic orientation, the United States has the most executive search firms and one of the highest levels of managerial mobility in the world. It is therefore not surprising, and yet highly unfortunate, that American theoretical structures fail to include a full range of explanations for organizational commitment and the lack thereof (see Earley, 1989, for a notable exception).

Similarly, most American theories of motivation reflect a decidedly individualistic perspective. In a review of the motivation literature, Staw (1984: 650–651) states that "whether the driving force is thought to be prior reinforcement, need fulfillment, or expectancies of future gain, the individual is assumed to be a rational maximizer of personal utility." Staw (1984: 651) questions how this individual/calculative view of motivation applies across cultures, suggesting that it "could be a fundamental omission in our motivation theories." Equity theory provides a case in point. According to Sampson (1977: 777), social psychologists continue to search within the psychology of the individual to explain demands for personal equity, rather than within the group or collectivity for less-individualistic explanations. What would our theories of motivation look like if theorists viewed the individual as part of a tightly bound social fabric? What would they look like in a country with more than a quarter of the population unemployed (e.g., in many parts of Africa)? How would our theories explain motivation if scholars viewed jobs as critical not only for the individual's well-being but also for the well-being of the extended family? What would a motivation theory look like in countries where the government assigns people to jobs, rather than allowing individuals to exercise free choice (e.g., for workers in the People's Republic of China)?

Miller and Grush (1988: 119) argued that the popularity of expectancy theory can be explained by "the logical appeal of its underlying assumption that the perceived consequences of actions rationally determine human behavior," and "that conceptual advances can be made in expectancy theory by including additional variables or by identifying the theory's limiting conditions." Cross-culturally based research would facilitate theory development by suggesting additional variables as well as identifying such limiting conditions. The importance of *biaoxian* in evaluating Chinese workers exemplifies this point. *Biaoxian* means

> to manifest something that is an expression of a deeper, hidden quality . . . the term applies to the broad and *vaguely* defined realm of behavior that is subject to leadership evaluation . . . behavior that indicates underlying attitudes and orientations worthy of reward. (Walder, 1983: 60–61, emphasis added)

Incorporating this view and, in particular the vagueness of its measurement, becomes highly problematic for expectancy theory.

The extreme individualism of the U.S. culture also influences leadership theories (see Bass, 1981, for a cross-cultural review). Smith and Peterson (1988: 97) noted that "the particular uniqueness of the USA should alert us to the possibility that the individualistic nature of much American-derived leadership theory is a facet of U.S. culture, rather than a firm base upon which to build leadership theories of universal applicability." For example, although charismatic leadership is valued and studied today by Americans (e.g., Conger, 1989), it is disparaged by Germans.

High- and Low-Context Cultures: Orientations Toward Communication and Understanding

> A high-context communication or message is one in which most of the information is either in the physical context or internalized in the person, while very little is in the coded, explicitly transmitted part of the message. . . . A low-context communication is just the opposite; i.e., the mass of information is vested in the explicit code. . . . Although no culture exists exclusively at one end of the scale, some are high while others are low. (Hall, 1981/1976: 91)

In high-context cultures, the external environment, situation, and nonverbal behavior are crucial for understanding communication. By contrast, in low-context cultures, a much greater portion of the meaning in a given communication comes from the spoken word. In languages spoken in high-context cultures, such as Japanese, Arabic, and Chinese, subtlety is valued. Much of the meaning of messages is derived from the paralanguage, facial expressions, setting, and timing. Alternatively, in low-context cultures, the literal words chosen convey much more of the meaning. The relatively low-context orientation of the United States is evident in Americans' emphasis on written legal documents, whereas many other cultures put more faith in face-to-face personal agreement. In many cultures, the relationship, not the legal document, binds the agreement. Given this orientation, it is not surprising that the United States has the most lawyers per capita in the world: 279 lawyers per 100,000 population, as compared with 114 in the United Kingdom, 77 in West Germany, 29 in France, and 11 in Japan (Council on Competitiveness, 1988: 3). Americans' low-context orientation also underlies their concept of separation, for example, separation of church and state, employees' societal status from their organizational status, and managers' cultural conditioning from their expected behavior at work.

The low-context orientation of the United States (and also England) may explain the minimal emphasis organizational theory historically has placed on such contextual factors as history, social setting, culture, and government. Thus, for the future development of the field, one benefit from scholars' current interest in Japan lies in Japan's high-context culture. Japanese organizational phenomena cannot be understood without using a contextual, institutional framework. Scholars understand Japanese employees only when they understand the organizations and society in which these employees are embedded, including the network of relationships among Japanese government and business organizations (e.g., Gerlach, 1987; Lincoln & McBride, 1987; Ohmae, 1987). The contextual, historical, and institutional approaches necessary to explain Japanese organizational behavior undoubtedly are enriching the study of organizations worldwide.

How would organizational researchers incorporate massive environmental and political change into models of motivation, leadership, and organization structure? Carroll, Delacroix, and Goodstein (1988: 360) note that:

> Although foundations of organizational theory lie within political sociology, current perspectives on organizations show little of this heritage. . . . Curiously, the major intellectual leap from closed to open systems models of organizations has coincided with the de facto dismissal of many of the political issues that concerned many of the early theorists such as Michels (1949), Selznick (1949), and Gouldner (1954).

At the ecological level, Carroll and his colleagues found that political variables had a significant impact, for example, on organizational founding and death rates (Carroll & Delacroix, 1982; Carroll & Huo, 1986; Delacroix & Carroll, 1983). Similarly, at the individual level, ignoring what the 1997 return of Hong Kong to the People's Republic of China means to the Chinese in Hong Kong or what the 1989 violence in Beijing means to the Chinese in the People's Republic of China relative to their work motivation and commitment trivializes any theory's explanatory power.

Together, these three cultural characteristics—free will, individualism, and low-context orientation—also explain much of the emphasis that organizational science places on managers. All three characteristics foster the view that managers have a high degree of discretion and much influence over their organizations. However, surprisingly few empirical studies have tested the actual impact of managerial actions (Lieberson & O'Connor, 1972; Thomas, 1988). Despite the spirited debate in some quarters over the influence of managerial behavior on organizational outcomes (Aldrich, McKelvey, & Ulrich, 1984; Child, 1972), much of organizational science is based on the assumption that managerial behavior makes a difference. The blatancy of this assumption belies the existence of deeply held cultural values.

Important theories exist embodying cultural values other than those discussed above; one example is institutional theory. However, the current interest in institutional theories of organization (DiMaggio & Powell, 1983; Meyer & Rowan, 1977; Meyer & Scott, 1983; Scott, 1987; Zucker, 1988) does not mitigate the fact that since Selznick's classic 1949 work, organizational science has reflected primarily the American cultural values of rationality and free will (see Stinchcombe, 1965, for a notable exception). Some believe that today's emphasis on institutional and ecological perspectives (e.g., Carroll, 1987; Hannan & Freeman, 1989; Zucker, 1988) is, in part, a reaction to Americans' previous overreliance on rational and ahistorical models of organizational behavior. Even though nonrational views of organization have been published, the "rational view steadily gained the upper hand" (Ouchi & Wilkins, 1985: 465). Ouchi and Wilkins (1985), among others, attribute the dominance of rational approaches to the increased emphasis on explicit, quantitative, and computer-aided analysis in the U.S. social sciences. Pfeffer (1982) suggested that forceful cultural values have led us to be more open to certain approaches than others.

RECOMMENDATIONS FOR A MORE INTERNATIONALLY RELEVANT ORGANIZATIONAL SCIENCE

This review focuses on academic management from three perspectives—contextual, quantitative, and qualitative. From all three perspectives, we render the same verdict: inappropriate parochialism. The current body of knowledge and processes for creating that knowledge are bounded and limiting. They lack sufficient breadth and depth to explain the very phenomena that we purport to study. Organizational science has become trapped, that is, trapped within geographical, cultural, temporal, and conceptual parochialism.

Organizational science is in a state of reflection that requires theorists to review the history of the field and critique existing work (e.g., Pinder & Moore, 1979; Van de Ven & Joyce, 1981). Like a weed patch, some theories have been allowed to run rampant due to overgeneralization: They need to be cleared. Overemphasizing particular views of organizational phenomena has caused other perspectives to be underemphasized. As Pfeffer (1982: 1) observed:

> The domain of organization theory is coming to resemble more
> of a weed patch than a well-tended garden. . . . It is often dif-
> ficult to discern in what direction knowledge of organizations is
> progressing—or if, indeed, it is progressing at all.

To date, the development of cross-cultural organizational behavior has helped little to weed the garden because most cross-cultural studies have been unicultural or comparative, designed simply to extend U.S.-developed theories abroad (Adler, 1983; Negandhi, 1975). Rarely has the field focused on the theories themselves.

As described next and summarized in Table 1, we make 13 recommendations for creating a more globally relevant organizational science. Recommendations are made both to individual researchers and to the Academy of Management.

Recommendations: Reflection

For organizational science to continue to develop, we recommend that scholars explicitly address cultural assumptions. Through this reflection, scholars will develop an appreciation of the cultural conditioning of organization theories. Thus, they will become more cognizant of how American values underlie much of organization theory and, consequently, render it constrained. Examining the cultural roots and assumptions is a necessary, but not sufficient, condition for beginning to uncover neglected, overemphasized, and overgeneralized aspects of organizational theory.

TABLE 1
Recommendations for a More Internationally Relevant Organizational Science

Recommendations	Significance
Reflection	
Explicitly address the influence of cultural values on how we conceptualize organization phenomena and construct organization theories.	Helps scholars uncover neglected, overemphasized, and overgeneralized aspects of theories.
Examine the extent to which the organizational sciences reflect U.S. cultural values.	Increases scholars' understanding of American culture and its impact on their perceptions, thoughts and scholarship.
Action Steps for Individual Researchers	
State the cultural and geographical domain of theories and research, as well as indicate other locales in which it applies.	Minimizes implicit universalism.
Indicate the national and cultural characteristics of research samples.	Assists readers of the research to recognize potential limitations.
Research management systems outside of the United States.	Creates new theoretical and methodological approaches not predicated on American assumptions.
Study non–U.S. management systems on their own terms (idiographic research); develop thick descriptions of organizational phenomena and the contexts in which they are embedded.	Increases the organizational forms and contexts with which scholars are familiar, as well as increasing their understanding of the uniqueness of U.S. organizational forms.
Create more multinational and multicultural research teams.	Facilitates recognition of cultural biases in theory development.
Use non–U.S. settings to frame theoretical and methodological approaches.	Expands domain of organizational theories.
Take sabbaticals in foreign countries.	Increases scholars' understanding of foreign cultures and their own cultures, including providing personal thick descriptions of the foreign sabbatical culture.
Organizational Changes	
Journal editors, reviewers, and scholars should question one another regarding their cultural assumptions and research domains.	Rewarding careful exposition of the geographical and cultural domain will check implicit universalism.
Expand editorial boards to include global representation and expertise.	Increases the perspectives represented, both substantively and symbolically.

TABLE 1 (continued)

Recommendations	Significance
Consider forming "global lines of business," strategic alliances, and networks among academic organizations worldwide.	Facilitates internationalization, and, thus, contributes to future relevance.
Select leaders of academic management organizations from multiple nations.	Increases perspectives and knowledge bases represented, thus facilitating frame-breaking change.

Recommendations: Action Steps for Individual Scholars

Miner (1980: 8) identified seven characteristics that a good theory should exhibit. Of the seven, one is particularly relevant:

> There should be a clear delineation of the domain the theory covers. The boundaries of application should be specified so that the theory is not utilized fruitlessly in situations for which it was never intended. This has been an often neglected aspect of theory building in the social sciences generally (Dubin, 1973), including the field of organizational behavior.

To develop a more robust organizational science, we recommend that scholars clearly state the cultural and geographical domain of their theories. By not indicating the domain, scholars inappropriately promulgate a universalistic view of organizational theory.

We support Hofstede's (1980) recommendation that researchers indicate the national and cultural characteristics of their sample so that readers can recognize the potential limitations. For example, Gersick's (1988: 34; 1989) exemplary research shows that "groups use temporal milestones to pace their work and that . . . reaching those milestones pushes groups into transitions." Given the variance in how different cultures view time (Hall, 1959; Kluckholn & Strodbeck, 1961), one must ask to what extent Gersick's findings are a cultural artifact. Clearly Gersick should continue her research. However, replications should be conducted in cultures with very different time orientations. At present, a clarification such as "given the deep-seated differences in how cultures view time, these findings should be viewed with caution outside the United States" would add to her work's contribution to the literature.

We recommend researching cultures and management systems outside of the United States. Especially recommended is research, such as the recent 22-country study (based in the People's Republic of China) of Hofstede and Bond (1988), using non–U.S. settings to frame both the theoretical and methodological approach. Cross-national research forces scholars to question the adequacy of their domestically derived models, thereby encouraging them to create theoretical and methodological approaches not predicated solely on single-culture (especially American) assumptions. Through this process, single-nation researchers can learn much from their cross-national colleagues (e.g., Child & Kieser, 1979; Hamilton & Biggart, 1988; Tannenbaum, Kavcic, Rosner, Vianello, & Wieser, 1974).

In addition, we recommend that scholars study foreign organizations on their own terms (idiographic research). By developing thick descriptions of other cultures (Geertz, 1973) and their management systems, scholars increase the types of organizational forms and environmental contexts with which they are familiar (e.g., Child & Kieser, 1979; Hamilton & Biggart, 1988). Tannenbaum and his colleagues (1974), for example, devoted a full chapter to describing the political, economic, and institutional settings of the countries they studied. Although single-nation studies may not immediately evidence such a need, McKelvey (1982), among others (Roberts, Hulin, & Rosseau, 1978), urged scholars to avoid overgeneralization by describing their research settings in greater detail. This approach increases research-ers' understanding of the uniqueness of U.S. organizational forms (Roberts & Boyacigiller, 1984), thus allowing them to view most previously accepted models as context specific (Clark, Kim, & Freeman, 1989).

We recommend multinational and multicultural research teams to fa-cilitate the recognition of cultural biases in theory development (Evans, 1975). To develop such collaborative relationships, we recommend that scholars take sabbaticals in foreign countries. Spending time abroad not only enhances cross-cultural understanding, but it also deepens cultural self-awareness and, thus, increases recognition of cultural biases in the theories developed. Clark (Clark et al., 1989: 217) provided a provocative example of the value of foreign sabbaticals in describing his initial concern for the relevance of organizational science in Brazil:

> In particular, expectancy theory, equity theory and goal theo-ries appear not to be predictive of successful performance in Brazilian colleges and universities. . . . Similarly, contingency theories of organizational design, including prescriptions for loose/tight coupling, seem to be contradicted by Brazilian insti-tutional practices. . . . Finally, prescriptions resulting from dis-tributive justice theories are also contradicted by the central-ized, yet political and seemingly arbitrary functioning of the governance structure.

Although Clark concluded that basic organizational theories may still ap-ply, given key modifications, it is clear that his Brazilian sabbatical had a great impact on his acceptance of received wisdom.

Recommendations: Organizational Changes

The starting point must be with each individual scholar, but solitary introspection probably is not most effective. Rather, we recommend that scholars, journal editors, and reviewers from a range of countries question one another regarding their cultural assumptions. The following questions should be incorporated into the review process: What is the cultural and geographical domain of this study, and to what extent do the findings apply in other settings? Unless the review process rewards careful exposition of the cultural and geographical domain, implicit universalism will continue.

Given the rate and extent of globalization (Miller, 1988), organizational science appears to be facing a period of frame-breaking change (Tushman, Newman, & Romanelli, 1986). If this is true, incremental efforts at internationalization will be insufficient to meet increasing demands for more relevant organizational research. Rather, more fundamental change is required. Management's elite journals, despite well-intentioned efforts, still do not reflect this globalization. Tushman and his colleagues (1986: 42) found that in only 6 out of 40 cases did current CEOs initiate and implement frame-breaking changes: New leaders were essential to achieve such transformational changes. Thus, we recommend that editorial boards be expanded to include global representation (scholars from a wide range of countries) as well as global process (scholars experienced in researching topics outside of their home countries).

During this period of frame-breaking change (and chaos) the field must accept that leading journals and conferences will refer to many authors, theories, and publications that are as yet unknown and unevaluated by the American research community. At times, mistakes will be made: Quality will be mixed, and scholars will wish that they had not wasted their own or their colleagues' time. However, a more inclusive editorial strategy will infuse the field with new ideas, theories, and authors, thus increasing the chance that frame-breaking advances will be made.

We recommend that academic organizations, such as the Academy of Management, consider forming "global lines of business" (functional divisions with a worldwide orientation), transnational strategic alliances, and networks with professional organizations worldwide (e.g., the German Gesellshaft Fuer Betriebswirtshaft and the Japanese Association of Business Administration). We strongly support the Academy's membership in the newly formed International Federation of Scholarly Associations of Management. In addition, we recommend that academic organizations select their leaders from multiple nations, thus facilitating globalization efforts of a frame-breaking nature and enhancing the field's future relevance and potential contribution. The Academy of Management has made important decisions designed to move it from an excellent domestic organization to an equally excellent global organization. These decisions include creating the International Programs Committee for the entire Academy (rather than limiting it to the International Division); holding regional meetings abroad; discussing the formation of international alliances; supporting workshops on internationalizing the organizational behavior, policy, and strategy curricula; and convening special all-Academy showcase sessions on global issues presented by scholars from several countries.

CONCLUSION

To really understand a culture and to ascertain more completely
the group's values and overt behavior, it is imperative to delve
into the underlying assumptions, which are typically unconscious, but which actually determine how group members perceive, think, and feel. . . . [A]s a value leads to a behavior, and
as that behavior begins to solve the problem which prompted it
in the first place, the value gradually is transformed into an
underlying assumption about how things really are. As the assumption is increasingly taken for granted, *it drops out of
awareness.* (Schein, 1984: 446, emphasis added)

The task before us is a difficult one; for what we are asking of ourselves
and our colleagues is to focus on what has, for most of us, dropped out of
awareness. Yet, the cost of not progressing toward an organizational science that is more internationally relevant is very high. Not only is it unfair
to constituents outside of the United States, but it also falls short of the
mandate to educate and to inform managers inside the United States who
are facing an increasingly multicultural and international workplace.

As the field begins to follow these recommendations, we hope that
major organizational science journals will typically include articles in each
of the following categories and label them as such:

1. *Universally applicable theories:* theories that can apply in widely different cultural
   milieux.

2. *Regiocentric theories:* theories that can apply in a range of cultures sharing certain common characteristics, for example, theories applicable in contiguous geographic areas (e.g., Asia, Latin America, or the Slavic countries) or under similar
   levels of economic development.

3. *Intercultural theories:* theories that explain the interaction among peoples of different cultures.

4. *Intracultural theories:* theories that describe specific cultures (e.g., American, Japanese, Indian).

If these recommendations are followed, theories applicable only to the
United States will be subsidiary to a wider body of universal theories applicable globally. Domestic research will become a subsidiary of more
broadly based research. The era of international research being relegated
to a subsidiary of domestic research will be over.

REFERENCES

Adler, N. J. 1983. Cross-cultural management research: The ostrich and the trend. **Academy of
Management Review,** 8: 226–232.

Adler, N. J. 1984. Understanding the ways of understanding: Cross-cultural management
methodology reviewed. In R. N. Farmer (Ed.), **Advances in international comparative
management,** vol. 1: 31–67. Greenwich, CT: JAI Press.

Adler, N. J. 1986. *International dimensions of organizational behavior.* Boston: Kent Publishing.

Adler, N. J., Campbell, N., & Laurent, A. 1989. In search of appropriate methodology: Outside the People's Republic of China, looking in. *Journal of International Business Studies,* 20(1): 61–74.

Adler, N. J., Doktor, R., & Redding, S. G. 1986. From the Atlantic to the Pacific century: Cross-cultural management reviewed. *Journal of Management,* 12(2): 295–318.

Adler, N. J., & Ghadar, F. 1990. International strategy from the perspective of people and culture: The North American context. In A. Rugman (Ed.), *Research in global strategic management: International business research for the twenty-first century,* vol. 1: 179–205. Greenwich, CT: JAI Press.

Adler, N. J., & Jelinek, M. 1986. Is "organization culture" culture bound? *Human Resource Management,* 25(1): 73–90.

Aldrich, H., McKelvey, B., & Ulrich, D. 1984. Design strategy from the population perspective. *Journal of Management,* 10(1): 67–86.

Allen, D. B., Miller, E. D., & Nath, R. 1988. North America. In R. Nath (Ed.), *Comparative management:* 23–54. Cambridge, MA: Ballinger.

American Assembly of Collegiate Schools of Business. 1988–1989. *Accreditation Council Policies, Procedures & Standards.* St. Louis, MO: American Assembly of Collegiate Schools of Business.

American Association of School Administrators, 3–12. 1983. *The excellence report: Using it to improve your schools.* Arlington, VA: American Association of School Administrators, 3–12. (Contains the report to the President 1982. *A nation at risk: The imperative for educational reform.*)

American Society for Training and Development. 1989. *Training in America: Learning to work for the twenty-first century.* Alexandria, VA: American Society for Training and Development.

Arndt, J. 1985. On making marketing science more scientific: Roles of orientations, paradigms, metaphors, and puzzle solving. *Journal of Marketing,* 49(3): 11–23.

Bartlett, C. A., & Ghoshal, S. 1989. *Managing across borders: The transnational solution.* Boston: Harvard Business School Press.

Bartlett, C. A., Doz, Y., & Hedlund, G. 1990. *Managing the global firm.* London: Routledge & Kegan Paul.

Bass, B. M. 1981. Leadership in different cultures. In B. M. Bass (Ed.), *Stogdill's handbook of leadership:* 552–549. New York: Free Press.

Beechler, S. L., & Pucik, V. 1989. The diffusion of American organizational theory in postwar Japan. In C. A. B. Osigweh (Ed.), *Organizational science abroad: Constraints and perspectives:* 119–134. New York: Plenum Press.

Berger, L., & Luckman, T. 1966. *The social construction of reality.* Garden City, NY: Doubleday.

Blackford, M. G. 1988. *The rise of modern business in Great Britain, the United States and Japan.* Chapel Hill: The University of North Carolina Press.

Boulding, K. E. 1961. *The image.* Ann Arbor: University of Michigan Press/Ann Arbor Paperbacks.

Bowen, E. 1984. Powerful pitch for the humanities. *Time,* December 10: 91.

Burrell, G., & Morgan, G. 1979. *Sociological paradigms and organizational analysis.* London: Heinemann.

Carroll, G. R. 1987. *Ecological models of organizations.* Cambridge, MA: Ballinger.

Carroll, G. R., & Delacroix, J. 1982. Organizational mortality in the newspaper industries of Argentina and Ireland: An ecological approach. **Administrative Science Quarterly,** 27: 169–198.

Carroll, G. R., Delacroix, J., & Goodstein, J. 1988. The political environments of organizations: An ecological view. In B. M. Staw & L. L. Cummings (Eds.), **Research in organization behavior,** vol. 10: 359–392. Greenwich, CT: JAI Press.

Carroll, G. R., & Huo, Y. P. 1986. Organizational task and institutional environments in ecological perspective: Findings from the local newspaper industry. **American Journal of Sociology,** 91: 838–873.

Child, J. 1972. Organization structure, environment and performance: The role of strategic choice. **Sociology,** 6: 2–22.

Child, J. 1981. Culture, contingency and capitalism in the cross-national study of organizations. In B. M. Staw & L. L. Cummings (Eds.), **Research in organizational behavior,** vol. 3: 303–356. Greenwich, CT: JAI Press.

Child, J., & Kieser, A. 1979. Organization and managerial roles in British and West German companies: An examination of the culture-free thesis. In C. J. Lammers & D. J. Hickson (Eds.), **Organizations alike and unlike:** 251–271. London: Routledge & Kegan Paul.

Clark, K. S., Kim, M. V., & Freeman, S. J. 1989. Contradictions between Brazilian and U.S. organizations: Implications for organizational theory. In C. A. B. Osigweh (Ed.), **Organizational science abroad: Constraints and perspectives:** 203–226. New York: Plenum Press.

Conger, J. A. 1989. **The charismatic leader.** San Francisco: Jossey-Bass.

Council on Competitiveness. 1988. Charting competitiveness. **Challenges,** 1(5): 3.

Delacroix, J., & Carroll, G. R. 1983. Organizational foundings: An ecological study of the newspaper industries of Argentina and Ireland. **Administrative Science Quarterly,** 28: 274–291.

DiMaggio, P. J., & Powell, W. W. 1983. The iron cage revisited: Institutional isomorphism and collective rationality in organizational fields. **American Sociological Review,** 48: 147–160.

Dubin, R. 1973. **Theory building.** New York: Free Press.

Earley, P. C. 1989. Social loafing and collectivism: A comparison of the United States and the People's Republic of China. **Administrative Science Quarterly,** 34: 565–581.

England, G. W. 1975. **The manager and his values: An international perspective.** Cambridge, MA: Ballinger.

Evans, W. M. 1975. Measuring the impact of culture on organizations. **International Studies of Management & Organization,** 5(1): 91–113.

Galbraith, J. 1973. **Designing complex organizations.** Reading, MA: Addison-Wesley.

Geertz, C. 1973. **The interpretation of cultures.** New York: Basic Books.

Gergen, K. J. 1973. Social psychology as history. **Journal of Personality and Social Psychology,** 26: 309–320.

Gerlach, M. 1987. Business alliances and the strategy of the Japanese firm. **California Management Review,** 30(1): 126–142.

Gersick, C. J. G. 1988. Time and transition in work teams: Toward a new model of group development. **Academy of Management Journal,** 31: 9–41.

Gersick, C. J. G. 1989. Marking time: Predictable transitions in task groups. **Academy of Management Journal,** 32: 274–309.

Godkin, L., Braye, C. E., & Caunch, C. L. 1989a. U.S. based cross-cultural management research in the eighties. **Journal of Business and Economic Perspectives,** 15(2): 37–45.

Godkin, L., Braye, C. E., & Caunch, C. L. 1989b. *U.S. based cross-cultural management research in the eighties.* Working paper, Lamar University, Beaumont, TX.

Gonzalez, R. F., & McMillan, C., Jr., 1961. The universality of American management philosophy. *Academy of Management Journal,* 41: 33–41.

Graham, J. L., & Gronhaug, K. 1989. Ned Hall didn't get a haircut; or why we haven't learned much about international marketing in the last 25 years. *Journal of Higher Education,* 60(2): 152–157.

Hall, E. T. 1959. *The silent language.* New York: Doubleday.

Hall, E. T. 1981/1976. *Beyond culture.* New York: Doubleday.

Hamilton, G. G., & Biggart, N. W. 1988. Market, culture and authority: A comparative analysis of management organization in the Far East. *American Journal of Sociology,* 94(supplement): 52–94.

Hannan, M. T., & Freeman, J. 1989. *Organizational ecology.* Cambridge, MA: Harvard University Press.

Harris, P., & Moran, R. T. 1979. *Managing cultural differences.* Houston: Gulf.

Hofstede, G. 1980. *Culture's consequences: International differences in work-related values.* Beverly Hills, CA: Sage.

Hofstede, G. 1981. Culture and organizations. *International Studies of Management and Organizations,* 10(4): 15–41.

Hofstede, G. 1983. Dimensions of national cultures in fifty countries and three regions. In J. B. Deregowski, S. Dziurawiec, & R. C. Annis (Eds.), *Explanations in cross-cultural psychology:* 335–355. Lisse, Netherlands: Swets and Zeitlinger.

Hofstede, G., & Bond, M. H. 1988. The Confucius connection: From cultural roots to economic growth. *Organizational Dynamics,* 16(4): 4–21.

Hofstede, G., & Kassem, M. S. 1976. *European contributions to organization theory.* Assen, Netherlands: Von Gorcum.

Inzerilli, G. 1981. Preface: Some conceptual issues in the study of the relationships between organizations and societies. *International Studies of Management and Organization,* 10(4): 3–14.

Jones, E. E., & Nisbett, R. E. 1971. *The actor and the observer: Divergent perceptions of the causes of behavior.* Morristown, NJ: General Learning Press.

Kelley, L., & Worthley, R. 1981. The role of culture in comparative management: A cross-cultural perspective. *Academy of Management Journal,* 25: 164–173.

Kiggundu, M. 1988. Africa. In R. Nath (Ed.), *Comparative management:* 169–244. Cambridge, MA: Ballinger.

Kluckholn, F. R., & Strodbeck, F. L. 1961. *Variations in value orientations.* Evanston, IL: Row, Peterson.

Kobrin, S. J. 1984. *International expertise in American business: How to learn to play with the kids on the street.* New York: Institute of International Education.

Kuhn, T. S. 1962. *The structure of the scientific revolutions.* Chicago: University of Chicago Press.

Lammers, C. J. 1980. Sociology of organizations around the globe: Similarities and differences between American, British, French, German and Dutch brands. *Organization Studies,* 11: 179–205.

Lammers, C. J., & Hickson, D. J. (Eds.). 1979. *Organizations alike and unlike: International studies in the sociology of organization.* London: Routledge & Kegan Paul.

Lane, H., & DiStefano, J. 1988. *International management behavior.* Scarborough, Ontario: Nelson Canada.

Laurent, A. 1981. Matrix organizations and Latin cultures. *International Studies of Management and Organization,* 10(4): 101–114.

Laurent, A. 1983. The cultural diversity of western conceptions of management. *International Studies of Management and Organization,* 13(1–2): 75–96.

Lawrence, P. R. 1987. Historical development of organizational behavior. In J. W. Lorsch (Ed.), *Handbook of organizational behavior:* Englewood Cliffs, NJ: Prentice-Hall.

Lieberson, S., & O'Connor, J. F. 1972. Leadership and organizational performance: A study of large corporations. *American Sociological Review,* 37: 117–130.

Lincoln, J. R., & McBride, K. 1987. Japanese industrial organization in comparative perspective. *Annual Review of Sociology,* 13: 289–335.

McKelvey, W. 1982. *Organizational systematics: Taxonomy, evolution, classification.* Berkeley: University of California Press.

Merton, R. K. 1968. *Social theory and social structure.* New York: Free Press.

Meyer, J. W., & Rowan, B. 1977. Institutionalized organizations: Formal structure as myth and ceremony. *American Journal of Sociology,* 83: 340–363.

Meyer, J. W., & Scott, W. R. 1983. *Organizational environments: Ritual and rationality.* Beverly Hills, CA: Sage.

Miles, R. E., & Snow, C. C. 1978. *Organizational strategy, structure and process.* New York: McGraw-Hill.

Miller, E. L. 1988. *International management: A field in transition, what will it take to reach maturity.* Paper presented at the Research for Relevance in International Management Conference, University of Windsor, Ontario.

Miller, L. E., & Grush, J. E. 1988. Improving predictions in expectancy theory: Effects of personality, expectancies and norms. *Academy of Management Journal,* 31: 107–122.

Miner, J. B. 1980. *Theories of organizational behavior.* Hinsdale, IL: Dryden Press.

Moore, R. 1974. The cross-cultural study of organizational behavior. *Human Organization,* 33: 37–45.

Morey, N., & Luthans, F. 1984. An emic perspective and ethnoscience methods for organizational research. *Academy of Management Review,* 9: 27–36.

National Advisory Board of International Education Programs. 1983. *Critical needs in international education: Recommendations for action.* Washington, DC: National Advisory Board on International Education Programs, December.

Negandhi, A. R. 1975. Comparative management and organization theory: A marriage needed. *Academy of Management Journal,* 18: 334–344.

Nehrt, L. C. 1987. The international studies of the curriculum. *Journal of International Business Studies,* 18(1): 83–90.

Newman, W. H. 1972. Cultural assumptions underlying U.S. management concepts. In J. L. Massie & S. Laytje (Eds.), *Management in an international context:* 327–352. New York: Harper & Row.

Oberg, W. 1963. Cross-cultural perspectives on management principles. *Academy of Management Journal,* 6: 129–143.

Ohmae, K. 1987. *Beyond national borders. Reflections on Japan and the world.* Homewood, IL: Dow Jones-Irwin.

Osigweh, C. A. B. 1989a. *Organizational science abroad: Constraints and perspectives.* New York: Plenum.

Osigweh, C. A. B. 1989b. The myth of universality in transnational organizational science. In

Osigweh, C. A. B. (Ed.), **Organizational science abroad: Constraints and perspectives:** 3–26. New York: Plenum.

Ouchi, W. 1984. **The M-form society.** Reading, MA: Addison-Wesley.

Ouchi, W. G., & Wilkins, A. L. 1985. Organizational culture. **Annual Review of Sociology,** 11: 457–483.

Peng, T. K., Peterson, M. F., & Shyi, Y. P. 1990. Quantitative methods in cross-national management research: Trends and equivalence issues. **Journal of Organizational Behavior:** in press.

Pfeffer, J. 1982. **Organizations and organization theory.** Boston: Pitman.

Pfeffer, J., & Salancik, G. R. 1978. **The external control of organizations.** New York: Harper & Row.

Pinder, C., & Moore, L. F. (Eds.). 1979. **Middle range theory and the study of organizations.** Leiden, Netherlands: Martinus Nijhoff.

Porter, M. E. 1980. **Competitive strategy: Techniques for analyzing industries and competitors.** New York: Free Press.

Porter, L. W., & McKibben, L. E. 1988. **Management education and development: Drift or thrust into the 21st century.** New York: McGraw-Hill.

Prahalad, C. K., & Doz, Y. L. 1987. **The multinational mission.** New York: Free Press.

President's Commission on Industrial Competitiveness. 1985. **Global competition: The new reality** (vol. 1). Washington, DC: U.S. Government Printing Office, January.

Roberts, K. H., & Boyacigiller, N. A. 1983. A survey of cross-national organizational researchers: Their views and opinions. **Organization Studies,** 4: 375–386.

Roberts, K. H., & Boyacigiller, N. A. 1984. Cross-national organizational research: The grasp of the blind men. In B. M. Staw & L. L. Cummings (Eds.), **Research in organizational behavior,** vol. 6: 423–475. Greenwich, CT: JAI Press.

Roberts, K. H., Hulin, C. L., & Rousseau, D. M. 1978. **Developing an interdisciplinary science of organizations.** San Francisco: Jossey-Bass.

Sampson, E. E. 1977. Psychology and the American ideal. **Journal of Personality and Social Psychology,** 35: 767–782.

Schein, E. H. 1984. Coming to a new awareness of organizational culture. **Sloan Management Review,** 25: 3–16.

Scott, W. R. 1987. The adolescence of institutional theory. **Administrative Science Quarterly,** 32: 493–511.

Sekaran, U. 1983. Are U.S. organizational concepts and measures transferable to another culture? An empirical investigation. **Academy of Management Journal,** 2: 409–417.

Selznick, P. 1949. **TVA and the grass roots.** Berkeley, CA: University of California Press.

Servan-Schreiber, J. J. 1968. **The American challenge.** (R. Steel, trans.). New York: Athenum.

Slocum, J. W., & Topichak, P. M. 1972. Do cultural differences affect job satisfaction? **Journal of Applied Psychology,** 56: 177–178.

Smith, P. B., & Peterson, M. F. 1988. **Leadership, organizations and culture.** Beverly Hills, CA: Sage.

Staw, B. M. 1980. Rationality and justification in organizational life. In B. M. Staw & L. L. Cummings (Eds.), **Research in organizational behavior,** vol. 2: 45–80. Greenwich, CT: JAI Press.

Staw, B. M. 1984. Organizational behavior: A review and reformulation of the field's outcome variables. **Annual Review of Psychology,** 35: 627–666.

Steers, R. M. 1987. The international challenge to management education. *Academy of Management Newsletter,* 17(4): 2–4.

Steers, R. M. 1989. Organizational sciences in a global environment: Future directions. In C. A. B. Osigweh (Ed.), *Organizational science abroad: Constraints and perspectives:* 293–304. New York: Plenum Press.

Stewart, E. C. 1972. *American cultural patterns: A cross-cultural perspective.* Chicago: Intercultural Press.

Stinchcombe, A. L. 1965. Social structure and organizations. In J. G. March (Ed.), *Handbook of organizations:* 142–193. Chicago: Rand McNally.

Tannenbaum, A. S., Kavcic, B., Rosner, M., Vianello, M., & Wieser, G. 1974. *Hierarchy in organizations.* San Francisco: Jossey-Bass.

Thanopoulos, J. (with the assistance of J. W. Leonard). 1986. *International business curricula: A global survey.* Cleveland, OH: Academy of International Business.

Thanopoulos, J., & Vernon, I. R. 1987. International business education in the AACSB schools. *Journal of International Business Studies,* 18(1): 91–98.

Thomas, A. B. 1988. Does leadership make a difference to organizations' performance? *Administrative Science Quarterly,* 33: 388–400.

Thurow, L. 1984. Revitalizing American industry: Managing in a competitive world economy. *California Management Review,* 27(1): 9–41.

Thurow, L. 1988. *Keynote address.* Presented at the annual meeting of the Western Academy of Management, Big Sky, MT.

Triandis, H. C. 1972. *The analysis of subjective culture.* New York: Wiley.

Triandis, H. C. 1983. Dimensions of cultural variations as parameters of organizational theories. *International Studies of Management and Organization,* 12(4): 139–169.

Tushman, M. L., Newman, W. H., & Romanelli, E. 1986. Managing the unsteady pace of organizational evolution. *California Management Review,* 29(1): 29–44.

Van de Ven, A. H., & Joyce, W. F. (Eds.). 1981. *Perspectives on organization design and behavior.* New York: John Wiley.

Vernon, R. 1966. International investment and international trade in the product cycle. *Quarterly Journal of Economics,* 80: 190–207.

Vernon, R. 1971. *Sovereignty at bay: The multinational spread of U.S. enterprises.* New York: Basic Books.

von Alleman, H. 1974. International contacts of university staff members: Some problems in the internationality of science. *International Social Science Journal,* 26, 445–457. (Note: von Alleman sites 120 countries but today there are 185 according to *The Statesman's Yearbook* 1989–90 edited by John Paxton. London, England: Macmillan Press, 1989.)

Walder, A. 1983. Organized dependency and cultures of authority in Chinese industry. *Journal of Asian Studies,* 43(1): 51–76.

Whitley, R. 1984. *The intellectual and social organization of the sciences.* Oxford: Clarendon Press.

Whitley, R. 1988. The management sciences and managerial skills. *Organization Studies,* 9: 47–68.

Wind, Y., & Perlmutter, H. V. 1973. On the identification of frontier issues in multinational marketing. *Columbia Journal of World Business,* 12(4): 131–139.

Zucker, L. 1988. *Institutional patterns and organizations: Culture and environment.* Cambridge, MA: Ballinger.

Nakiye Avdan Boyacigiller received her Ph.D. from the University of California, Berkeley. She is an associate professor of international management at San Jose State University. Her current research interests include human resource management issues facing Japanese multinationals in the United States and the influence of national, industry, and organizational factors on the introduction of new products in the Japanese, U.S., and German pharmaceutical industries.

Nancy J. Adler received her Ph.D. in management from the University of California at Los Angeles. She is a professor of organizational behavior and cross-cultural management at the Faculty of Management, McGill University in Montreal, Canada. Her fields of interest include strategic international human resources management, expatriation, women in international management, international negotiating, culturally synergistic approaches to problem solving, and international organization development.

22

RETHINKING ECONOMICS

The gross national product and the gods

The variety of forms that capitalism takes are deeply conditioned by the economic culture of the societies in which it operates

Peter L. Berger

SCHOLARS MAY DISAGREE about why Jesus drove the money-changers from the Temple. But few would question the reality of the tension, implicit in that famous scene, between economics and culture, especially religious culture – the beliefs, values, and orientations toward life through which people organize their existence, search for meaning, and define who they are.

Fewer still would argue that culture actually determines economic behavior in today's industrial societies. (Some anthropologists do, of course, hold such views regarding pre- or non-modern societies, but that is a different matter.) By contrast, numerous economists assert that, since we are "rational actors" in economic affairs, we must be comparably rational in the other areas of our lives. This naturally leads me to wonder why people who have been so remarkably unsuccessful in clarifying, let alone predicting, the workings of the marketplace should be trusted to shape our common interpretations of politics or social life.[1]

Attempts to explain the dynamics of Wall Street in theological terms have been unpersuasive at best; so, too, efforts to provide a strict economic explanation for events like the Iranian revolution. For all practical purposes, therefore, the gulf separating markets from sanctuaries and economic rationality from morals – that is, the gulf between the gross national product and the gods – remains as wide as it was in biblical times.

The idea of economic culture

Must this always be so? Is there no navigable middle course between "culturalism" (where beliefs and values are supposed to explain everything) and "economism" (where politicians, spouses, and Islamic revolutionaries are all assumed to act in accordance with the logic of investment bankers)? Common

---

[1] For a critique of this approach from within the discipline of economics itself, *see* John Nelson, *The Rhetoric of the Human Sciences*, Madison, WI, University of Wisconsin Press, 1987.

THE GROSS NATIONAL PRODUCT AND THE GODS

sense says there is: a perspective focused on what I call "economic culture" – the social and cultural context of economic behavior.[2]

> *Cultural attitudes and habits affect economic behavior and are in turn affected by it in ways that must be studied empirically, case-by-case on the ground*

Such a view of things does not assume that culture determines economics or economics culture. It assumes only that human beings exist in society and that this context, with its baggage of cultural attitudes and habits, affects economic behavior and is in turn affected by it in ways that must be studied empirically, case-by-case on the ground. No matter how much the same capitalist rationality may animate managers from different cultural backgrounds, those differences are not – and cannot be – left conveniently in the cloakroom before discussions or negotiations start. Indeed, they often have as telling an effect on the outcome of such sessions – albeit in a different way – as do cash flow projections or estimates of market size.

A question of advantage

Variations in economic culture matter. In particular settings, they can provide the basis for what my colleagues and I have come to think of as comparative cultural advantage. For historical reasons, to cite one example, modern Japanese capitalism has been more successful than its American counterpart in building large organizations that command intense, sometimes passionate loyalty from their members. Arguably, this has provided Japanese companies a culture-based source of competitive advantage.

> *Variations in economic culture can be a source of comparative advantage*

Now, this does not mean that the Japanese are always successful in this way or that Americans can never be. It means only that, comparatively, the cultural baggage that the Japanese bring with them into the economic arena is differentially helpful in this particular aspect of organization-building. This has, however, a further implication: what may be helpful at one time may be a handicap at another.

The cultural constellation of loyalty and conformism (what the Japanese call "groupism"), which helped create the manufacturing achievements that have

---

[2] The term "economic culture" was coined to delineate the agenda of a research center, the Institute for the Study of Economic Culture at Boston University, of which I have been the director since its founding in 1985. Most of the examples in this paper are from research projects conducted by the Institute. For my own use of the concept within a larger social-scientific interpretation of modern capitalism, *see* Peter Berger, *The Capitalist Revolution*, New York, Basic Books, 1986.

THE GROSS NATIONAL PRODUCT AND THE GODS

been scaring the wits out of Americans and Europeans for so many years, may be much less helpful – may indeed be a source of comparative *dis*advantage – in a "post-industrial" era of high technology and information-driven services.[3] In this new world, Americans may again discover that their economic culture, shaped by individualism and irreverence toward institutions, including the ones that employ them, is a source of cultural advantage.

The Asian riddle

Perhaps the most astounding economic success story of the post-war period has been the development of East Asia, led initially by Japan and now extending in a gigantic crescent of prosperity into the countries of Southeast Asia. Attempts to explain this economic miracle have often stressed the role of East Asian culture – in particular, a presumed Confucian tradition or ethic, which inculcates discipline, hard work, frugality, respect for authority, and a passion for education much as did the so-called "Protestant ethic," that the sociologist Max Weber saw as an important factor in the rise of modern capitalism in the West.[4] But Confucianism is not the only suspect if one seeks cultural explanations of this recent burst of development: Mahayana Buddhism, Shintoism, folk religion, and distinctive features of kinship and household organization are also relevant.

> *Attempts to explain the Asian economic miracle have often stressed the role of East Asian culture – in particular, its presumed Confucian tradition or ethic*

If the economic success of East Asia be explained, even partially, by its culture, the practical implications are immense. It is, for instance, important to know whether the *de facto* model followed by these countries or regions is exportable. If culture is at most a minor factor, then it may make sense for an African country to adopt many of the economic and social policies of, say, Taiwan. But if development success depends largely on cultural traits, then an attempt to transplant them wholesale into a very different cultural milieu is likely to fail. It is one thing for Nigeria to imitate Taiwan in its tax laws; it is quite another to expect Nigerians to adopt the precepts of Confucian morality.

The Overseas Chinese

Clues to solving the riddle of East Asia's economic development are less to be found in ancient texts – few Taiwanese entrepreneurs are steeped in the

---

[3] *See* Kuniko Miyanaga, *The Creative Edge: Emerging Individualism in Japan*, New Brunswick, NJ, Transaction Publishers, 1991.

[4] *See* for example, Roy Hofheinz and Kent Calder, *The Eastasia Edge*, New York, Basic Books, 1982; Michiyo Morishima, *Why has Japan Succeeded?*, Cambridge, Cambridge University Press, 1982; Peter Berger and Hsiu-Huang Hsiao (eds), *In Search of an East Asian Development Model*, New Brunswick, NJ, Transaction Publishers, 1988.

THE GROSS NATIONAL PRODUCT AND THE GODS

Confucian classics – or in time series of data on key economic indicators (which simply reiterate what is already known) than in close, careful, ethnographically-

oriented studies of the sort that anthropologists engage in when they endlessly interview and observe people in a culture they want to understand. This is the kind of study that has been undertaken for several years now by a team of researchers headed by Gordon Redding of the University of Hong Kong.[5] Their research has concentrated on the Overseas Chinese – the approximately fifty million Chinese living outside mainland China who have played a disproportionally large role in driving the capitalist economies of their local societies.

Redding's work has demonstrated in rich detail how distinctive Chinese cultural traits – especially the habits and ethos of the Chinese family – affect the business behavior of Overseas Chinese entrepreneurs-*cum*-managers. Because the great majority of Overseas Chinese firms are family-owned, it is family culture that motivates the dedication, self-denial, sober pragmatism, cohesion, and flexibility of their employees. It also influences their size: most of these firms are small and simply organized.

The explanation lies in the cultural definition of trust. To the question, "Whom can I trust?" the Chinese answer is very clear: close relatives.

This answer is not, however, without its problems: a lack, for instance, of enough talented relatives to fill all the

> *To the question, "Whom can I trust?" the Chinese answer is very clear: close relatives*

required management positions. Even so, the family orientation of these businesses has, to date, been a source mostly of cultural advantage as the Overseas Chinese compete economically with other ethnic groups, such as Malays, in Southeast Asia. But this advantage may not outlive the unique circumstances of this particular moment in the region's economic

---

[5] *See* Gordon Redding, *The Spirit of Chinese Capitalism*, Berlin, Walter de Gruyter, 1990; Stewart Clegg and Gordon Redding (eds), *Capitalism in Contrasting Cultures*, Berlin, Walter de Gruyter, 1990.

THE GROSS NATIONAL PRODUCT AND THE GODS

development. Should it become necessary in the future to create and maintain large, complex organizations, these same Overseas Chinese may find themselves at a considerable *dis*advantage – even as compared to the Malays, who might find sources of broad, trans-familial loyalty and support in a modernized Islamic ethic.

> *The classical Confucian tradition was deeply conservative and disdainful of mercantile values*

Cultural latency

Given this pattern of success, why has the post-Confucian, family orientation of the Overseas Chinese had such massive economic payoffs outside, but not inside, Communist China itself? The answer is simple: even the most dedicated capitalist is going to have a hard time making it in the aboveground portions of a centrally-controlled economy. If the question is posed with regard to pre-Communist China, however, it is not so easy to answer.

Throughout most of its history, China's social and political institutions were intrinsically antagonistic to any form of "modern" economic development. The classical Confucian tradition itself was deeply conservative and disdainful of mercantile values. Moreover, the traditional Chinese family, in its native, pre-emigration form, was embedded in a wide network of kinship obligations that made capital accumulation very difficult. Only by emigrating could the family members escape most of these obstacles to capitalist success.

Once abroad, they did not have to cope with crippling state regulations, disdainful Mandarins, or clamorous relatives eager to stick their noses – and their hands – into the family business.

The key point here is that possessing a given set of cultural traits does not always lead to the same results. In some cases, they may lie dormant or "latent" for long periods of time until the circumstances (economic, political, even ecological) are right for their hidden potential to become manifest. It is not the traits that change, but the external environment. With the Overseas Chinese, a cultural heritage of strong family values may have produced economic stagnation at home but, in the radically altered circumstances of the Chinese Diaspora, has led to very different social and economic outcomes.

The evolution of Iberian Catholicism manifests much the same kind of latency. This religious culture had long been uneasy with modern capitalist development at home as well as in Latin America and the Philippines, the only Catholic society – and the only economic disaster – in capitalist Southeast

THE GROSS NATIONAL PRODUCT AND THE GODS

Asia.[6] In Spain itself, however, the Catholic movement Opus Dei – fiercely conservative in its theology, but very much committed to capitalism – runs two very influential management schools and has played an important role in creating a booming capitalist economy.[7]

> *Japanese and Chinese management styles differ from one another as much as – and possibly more than – either differs from its American counterpart*

"Asian" management

Understanding the futures of different economic cultures is, as these examples suggest, a task for detailed, case-by-case, empirical research. Bold generalizations invite grave misperceptions. Consider the recent talk about the alleged existence of a distinctive "Asian" style of management. In the first place, it is not always clear just what the western boundaries of Asia are supposed to be. The Urals? The Bosphorus?

Even on unambiguous terrain, however, problems exist. Lumping Japanese and Chinese management styles into the same category is a highly questionable act. Both may show influences from the same Confucian moral tradition, and both may be the result of the modernizing of old traditions, (one based on a family-centered ethos, the other on feudal loyalties), but the differences between them are enormous. These styles differ from one another as much as – and possibly more than – either differs from its American counterpart.

And if the idea of Asian management is supposed to include India (let alone the Muslim world), the term quickly loses all meaning. India itself has no simple, overarching economic culture, but rather a great many such cultures, differentiated by region, ethnicity, caste, and religion. Gujerat, for example, is a region that has produced a disproportionate number of successful entrepreneurs among the Marwari caste and the small religious minorities of the Jains and the Parsis. Moreover, as with China, social groups in India that have not evinced much economic dynamism at home have done remarkably well abroad. This is particularly the case in eastern and southern Africa, where Indian businesspeople have played and (where allowed) continue to play a very important role in the economy.

> *Social groups in India that have not evinced much economic dynamism at home have done remarkably well abroad*

---

[6] *See* Lawrence Harrison, *Underdevelopment Is a State of Mind: The Latin American Case,* Lanham, MY, University Press of America, 1985.
[7] A study of Opus Dei by Joan Estruch will be published by Oxford University Press in 1994.

THE GROSS NATIONAL PRODUCT AND THE GODS

Ancient curses

Some observers hold strongly to what might be called the ancient-curse theory of history – the notion that people born into a particular culture are fated to repeat its deep seated patterns over and over again. In this view, whatever the changing context, the Chinese are destined endlessly to re-stage ancient family dramas and the Japanese, dramas of feudal loyalty. Some cultures do, of course, show a remarkable continuity over long stretches of time, a fact best explained by the basic dynamics of socialization through which each new generation absorbs the world of its progenitors. But even in the Chinese and Japanese cases, such a theory grossly oversimplifies.

A multi-million dollar manufacturing company in Taiwan is not simply a peasant clan writ large. Nor is the CEO of a modern Japanese corporation merely a samurai in a three-piece suit. There are cultural echoes, to be sure, but no more than that. More to the point, in some situations people can drastically change their beliefs and their behavior, creating entirely new cultural patterns, often in an amazingly short period of time. When, for example, people are subjected to the intense pressures that arise from the economic and social transformations associated, say, with migration from rural areas into the gigantic pressure-cookers that are the large cities of the Third World, they often create genuinely new cultures with remarkable speed.

> *The pressures of migration often create genuinely new cultures with remarkable speed*

Evangelical Protestantism

One of the most effective agents of such rapid cultural revolution is religious conversion. Contrary to the assumption prevalent in much Western-type higher education, the processes of modernization have not led to a decline of religion in most areas of the world. Just think of the Iranian revolution and its aftermath. With the exception of a few regions (Europe being the most important) and a rather thin cross-national stratum (the graduates of Western universities), the world today is as intensively religious as it ever has been, maybe more so. Passionate religious movements can be found all over the place, some in continuity with the great traditions, others in reaction against them.

> *The world today is as intensively religious as it ever has been, maybe more so*

The Islamic revival (labeled "fundamentalism" by Western observers) is one such movement. Throughout the vast area between the Atlantic Ocean and the China Sea, Islam is visibly inspiring masses of people to change their behavior and, in the process, is shaking up governments and transforming entire societies. Equally important,

THE GROSS NATIONAL PRODUCT AND THE GODS

but perhaps less well recognized, is the gathering power of Evangelical Protestantism (mostly Pentecostal), which is now rapidly spreading over huge areas of Asia, Africa, and Latin America – a geographical scope that is actually wider than that of the Islamic revival.

The origins of this movement are in the United States, where Evangelical Protestantism has for years enjoyed notable growth and, at least since the mid-1970s, active public interest. Current estimates, probably unreliable, put the number of "born-again" Christians in the US at 40 million. Whatever the correct figure, there can be no question that the Evangelical community is already a formidable presence on the American religious scene. Moreover, most of the places outside the US where the Evangelicals' message has taken root (including, significantly, Latin America) now have strong indigenous churches, supporting themselves financially out of their own resources and led by their own indigenous clergy.

> *In Central and South America, the number of Evangelical Protestants rivals that of their co-religionists in the United States*

The movement's scope and dynamism are astounding. It is very strong in Asia, especially in South Korea, but also in Overseas Chinese communities, in the Philippines, and throughout the Pacific archipelagos. It is strong, too, in sub-Saharan Africa, where it has often fused with local, non-Christian, African religions. But its most dramatic and unexpected growth has been in Central and South America, where the number of Evangelical Protestants rivals that of their co-religionists in the United States. Indeed, its greatest success has been in Central America. The best estimates are, for example, that between 25 and 30 percent of the Guatemalan population is now Protestant; but no country in the region has been untouched.

Cultural revolutions

The most careful study of the Evangelical phenomenon is the work by the British sociologist David Martin and his associates, both on the Latin American situation as a whole and on local developments in Brazil and Chile.[8] This work clearly shows that conversion to Protestantism often brings about nothing less than a cultural revolution: the individuals who join these Protestant churches change their behavior abruptly, radically, and – in many cases – permanently. In effect, defying *machismo*-laden stereotypes about Latin American culture, they begin to act like sober, responsible, eighteenth-century English Methodists.

Although most of the pastors in these churches are men, most of the evangelists and organizers are women. As Martin has found, the women influenced by

[8] *See* David Martin, *Tongues of Fire: The Explosion of Protestantism in Latin America*, Oxford, Blackwell Publishers, 1990.

THE GROSS NATIONAL PRODUCT AND THE GODS

this new Protestant ethos insist that their husbands stop drinking, gambling, having women on the side, and spending money on endless celebrations with the godparents of their children. Instead, they must now go to church services (often every night) and contribute a hefty portion of their income to the church, which redistributes it by religious affiliation rather than kinship ties – a very important change. These newly-tightened families also display a strong interest in educating their children – which, as cross-national research clearly shows, is a key factor in upward social mobility.

> *"Max Weber is alive and well and living in Guatemala"*

These social changes are associated with comparable changes in economic behavior. The evidence demonstrates that the people in these churches begin to practice in their lives the same virtues that Weber called the "Protestant ethic." (In fact, one commentator on Martin's work summed up its findings by noting that "Max Weber is alive and well and living in Guatemala.") This is an ethic of discipline and self-denial, hard work, saving rather than consumption, and systematic planning for the future. True, unlike its Anglo-Saxon antecedents, today's Latin American Protestantism is often Pentecostal in character – that is, charged with a highly emotional, even orgiastic style of worship. But this emotionalism does not seem to interfere with – and may even enhance – the new soberness of everyday life.

The long-term economic consequences of this cultural revolution are just beginning to be visible – in places. In countries where the macroeconomic situation does not provide real-world opportunities for improving one's economic situation, it does not much matter *what* one's religious ethic is. Stagnation continues, as in the Northeast of Brazil, for instance, a region of unrelieved economic depression. But where the macroeconomic context *does* provide opportunities, it is clear that these latent Protestant traits are a source of cultural advantage. Chile is a prime case of this. If things go well, an emergent Protestant lower-middle class will evolve into the kind of educated bourgeoisie historically associated in the West with the development of full-blown capitalism.

CARLOS REYES/ANDES PRESSE AGENCY

THE GROSS NATIONAL PRODUCT AND THE GODS

The logic of development

A comparison of the emergent Protestant ethic in Latin America with the post-Confucian ethic of the Overseas Chinese is instructive. Despite the enormous religious and social differences between them, they have important similarities: a self-denying, gratification-delaying, frugal morality that Weber described as "inner-worldly asceticism" (living like a monk, but in the world, not in a monastery); a pragmatic, activist orientation toward life; and a high regard for education. Chinese children may have literacy pounded into them so that they will grow up to be adults who can carry on a wide-ranging business correspondence; Protestant children, so that they can read the Bible. Either way, in economic terms, these children enjoy a cultural advantage over their illiterate, non-Chinese or non-Protestant neighbors.

> *In the early stages of modern economic development, an ethic of self-denial is functionally necessary ...*

This is because, in the early stages of modern economic development, when capital must be accumulated instead of consumed and where much investment must take the form of intense personal effort or "sweat equity," an ethic of self-denial, no matter how legitimated, is functionally necessary. Whether this behavior is motivated by fear of one's mother-in-law or fear of God, *economically speaking*, does not matter.

To some analysts of the contemporary religious scene, the ethics of both the Islamic revival and the new Evangelical Protestantism are roughly comparable. After all, they are both self-denying yet passionate movements. This is not, however, a useful point of similarity: the economic and socio-political consequences of these movements could not differ more.

True, both Islam and Evangelical Protestantism are "reactionary," in that they react against certain aspects of modernity (notably its secularism and alleged immorality) and look back

> *... Whether this behavior is motivated by fear of one's mother-in-law or fear of God, economically speaking, does not matter*

to a supposedly better age in the past. But to *which* age do they look back? For Muslim fundamentalists, it is the golden age of Islam – roughly a thousand years ago. For the Evangelicals, it is the earlier, simpler days of the bourgeois era – only about a century ago. In other words, conservative Islam takes as its ideal an emphatically pre-modern society. By contrast, Evangelical Protestantism extols the virtues of Western culture at precisely the moment when it was in its most dynamic phase of economic modernization. On the

THE GROSS NATIONAL PRODUCT AND THE GODS

evidence to date, Protestant fundamentalism is a modernizing force; Islamic fundamentalism is not.

Counter-culture

Arguably, the most dramatic cultural changes in recent Western history have been those of the late 1960s and early 1970s. During that period, one country after another across the North Atlantic region experienced a series of events that reshaped the established political, social, and cultural scene by exposing it to a constellation of new beliefs, values, and behavior patterns – the so-called counter-culture. But counter to what? Well, counter to the political, social, and cultural *status quo*, certainly, but also to the economic *status quo* – that is, to capitalism.

Broadly speaking, this movement was on the left of the ideological spectrum. Culturally, it opposed the kind of bourgeois society shaped by the Protestant ethic. Instead, it was hedonistic, self-affirming, consumption rather than savings-oriented, averse to systematic discipline or planning, and suspicious of education. As a result, this new cultural ethos looked like bad news for capitalism, indeed for any sort of advanced industrial society. As Marxists used to say, "it was no accident" that these cultural rebels liked to garb themselves in peasant costumes.

> *As Marxists used to say, "it was no accident" that counter-cultural rebels liked to garb themselves in peasant costumes*

This perception of deep hostility to capitalist modernity was shared by the new culture's critics and proponents. In the United States, for example, there was a brief but interesting debate on the question of the so-called "New Class" – supposedly, a new middle class based on the production and distribution of knowledge of a special kind: non-material, symbolic, morally charged. The members of this new knowledge class – educators, therapists, communicators, political activists, bureaucrats, and even some lawyers – were thought to be either the principal agents of the counter-culture or, at least, fellow travellers. They were, after all, mostly to the left – not only of the population in general, but of members of the *old* middle class, which was largely seen to be of a piece with the business community and most of the older professions.

The great question at the time was whether this counter-culture represented the last, best hope for a longed-for revolution, or a decadent force subverting the hard-won economic, political, and moral foundations of society. In retrospect, it is clear that both the hopes and the fears were exaggerated. The basic economic and political structures of "the system," as the cultural revolutionaries called it, certainly survived. What is more, the events that finally culminated

THE GROSS NATIONAL PRODUCT AND THE GODS

in the collapse of the Soviet Union did much to undermine the plausibility of leftism in all its overtly political forms.

Nevertheless, significant cultural shifts *have* occurred in most Western societies, institutionalizing the ethos of the late sixties. Some institutions – notably the universities and some major religious denominations – *have* undergone measurable and apparently permanent change. And so have attitudes about relations between the sexes, interpersonal relations in general, sexuality in all its forms, child-rearing, racial and ethnic differences, health, and the physical environment.

Professional cultures

How have these changes affected the economic culture of the societies in which they took place? A team of social scientists, headed by Hansfried Kellner of the University of Frankfurt, has begun to provide an answer.[9] The team studied various types of "New Class" professionals in the US and Western Europe: consultants in "soft" areas like personnel and corporate public relations, welfare-state bureaucrats, qualitative market researchers, and what the principal American researcher calls "moral entrepreneurs" (for such as anti-smoking and animal rights activists). The values and lifestyles of the counter-culture have heavily influenced these professional cultures, many of whose members had themselves been would-be revolutionaries when younger. What has happened to them since?

> *The values and lifestyles of the counter-culture have heavily influenced "New Class" professional cultures*

For the most part, revolution – in the literal sense of a radical restructuring of economics and politics – is no longer on the agenda. These former rebels have accepted "the system" despite, perhaps, some inner reservations, and they are doing quite well working within it. Still, they have retained many of their earlier beliefs and attitudes about egalitarianism, interpersonal relations, sexuality, and gender, and they are still likely to be on the left of the political spectrum (liberal in the US context, social-democratic in Europe). Twenty years ago, given the ability to peer into the future, they would probably have said of their present selves that they had sold out; their parents, would have said that they had settled down and become more sensible.

To what extent, though, has their personal odyssey meaningfully changed the culture of business? Although the research by Kellner and his team cannot give a quantitative answer, their findings do show, cross-nationally, that certain sectors have been affected to a considerable degree. Indeed, new markets have

[9] *See* Hansfried Kellner and Frank Heuberger (eds), *Hidden Technocrats: The New Class and New Capitalism,* New Brunswick, NJ, Transaction Publishers, 1992.

THE GROSS NATIONAL PRODUCT AND THE GODS

appeared, inspired by counter-cultural values. This is most obviously the case with specific products, such as environment-friendly cosmetics, so-called "natural" foods, equipment for an allegedly healthier lifestyle, and the veritable emporium of utensils (from meditation pillows to folk costumes) serving various "New Age" activities.

Is this kinder, gentler aspect of capitalism likely to add to its international competitiveness?

It has also become possible to make careers and estimable incomes out of helping corporations become more sensitive to various public issues and to the needs of their employees. Setting up affirmative action procedures, running anti-smoking and weight-reduction clinics or day-care facilities for employees' children, and propagating socially responsible corporate images – this is all "New Class" work. But is this kinder, gentler aspect of capitalism likely to add to its international competitiveness?

On the face of it, the answer would seem to be no. East Asian capitalism, to cite one example, is certainly made of harder stuff – and in a contest between hard and soft cultures, it is usually the former that win. Put in more elegant scientific language, hard-nosed SOBs tend to wipe the floor with sensitive types. Nonetheless, as anyone who ever took an introductory sociology course has learned – the famous "Thomas' dictum" – "If people define a situation as real, it *is* real in its consequences." So if people honestly believe that they will produce, say, better telecommunications equipment if they are more appreciative of environmental concerns or of alternative forms of sexual orientation, perhaps they really will – and, along the way, beat out competitors from uptight, insensitive cultures. No one yet knows

"If people define a situation as real, it is real in its consequences"

for sure if the disciplined self-denying ethic that is a source of advantage at earlier stages of modern economic development remains so when the economy moves into a post-industrial or knowledge-driven phase.

*   *   *

Economic culture has endless intellectual fascination; social scientists, in particular, require no motive other than their own curiosity for exploring it. They can paraphrase for their own disciplines the famous toast that used to be offered at the Royal Society of Mathematicians: "To pure mathematics, and may it never be of use to anyone!" But people who must orient their activities by practical results – in business and, increasingly, in government – cannot afford such luxury. They must ask, to what practical application might such insights be put?

THE GROSS NATIONAL PRODUCT AND THE GODS

As I hope this brief sketch of economic culture has made clear, the manifold forms of capitalist activity are intimately connected with the distinctive economic cultures that surround and animate them. In an increasingly borderless world of such varied activity, cultural awareness and understanding rapidly become the most practical of subjects. Q

Professor Peter Berger is Director of the Institute for the Study of Economic Culture at Boston University. Copyright © 1994 McKinsey & Company, Inc. All rights reserved.

23

Comparative Management Theory: Jungle, Zoo or Fossil Bed?*

S. Gordon Redding**

S. Gordon
Redding
University of
Hong Kong
Business School,
Hong Kong

Abstract

Earlier reviews of the state of comparative management theory are considered and summarized and lead to the following conclusions: the literature suffers from an excess of simple empirical reportage; theoretical development is weak in the middle ground and at higher levels; there is a bias away from ethnographic work; perspectives tend to be narrow and partial. Some progress is visible as a result of the unifying work of Hofstede but its contribution also entails new avenues of enquiry about the determinants and consequences of culture. Some middle-range theory building is now occurring in specific fields such as expatriation, leadership, and HRM techniques, but it remains tentative. Dilemmas stemming from alternative frameworks of meaning and complex causation pose severe epistemological challenges and require new approaches to comparison. The economics-based positivist paradigm is seriously inadequate for such challenges, but dangerously imperialist. A new, more theoretically sophisticated, approach is advocated and outlined as a route for progress.

Introduction

The metaphor of the untamed runs through the literature on this subject as a subliminal message expressing exasperation at the subject's refusal to respond to attempts at tidiness and order. The major reviews which have marked its meandering began with Schollhammer's (1969) comparative management theory jungle, then Roberts' (1970) elephant, Adler's (1983) ostrich, and Boyacigiller and Adler's (1991) dinosaur. It seems appropriate now to ask why progress can only be described in terms of movement from a discipline still in the wild to one in danger of being a fossil; or can we at least discern the outline plans of a tidy zoological garden?

The purposes of this paper, then, are (a) to note progress over recent years in clarifying conceptual issues in comparative organizational behaviour theory, (b) to review the quality of such work in terms of relevance, method, and epistemology and (c) to consider its present condition and direction as a discipline. The field itself is that pertaining to individual and group behaviour and interaction within international organizations, and between such organizations and other individuals and groups. The core questions at the normative, practitioner end of the spectrum of enquiry are:

Organization
Studies
1994, 15/3
323–359
© 1994 EGOS
0170–8406/94
0015–0011 $3.00

1. How can multi-cultural organizations be managed?
2. How should the organizations of one culture adapt to the cultural environments and employees of another culture?
3. How can a host culture best accommodate the organizational practices of an outside company?
4. What organizational practices are beneficially transferable from one culture to another?

At the theoretical/epistemological end of the spectrum of enquiry, the key issues are:

1. Ethnocentrism and naive positivism in methods of research.
2. The complexity of multiple and reciprocal determinacy.
3. The highly contingent nature of the core theory of Western organizational behaviour.
4. The lack of nomothetic integration soundly based in empirical support.
5. Inadequate epistemological rigour in defining valid units of analysis for comparative social science.

It will be necessary to conclude that although progress has been made, the discipline has suffered from the excessive repetition of sterile reporting, from theoretical poverty and from a lack of clear direction. The journal literature suggests that, without the unifying and dominant work of Hofstede (1980, 1991) in tackling the core problem of the definition of culture, it would be even more disparate and undisciplined. This theoretical anaemia is seen as an extension of a larger problem in the core discipline of organization theory, viewed by some as directionless and weighed down by useless proliferation (Kochan 1983) and by others (e.g. Sullivan 1992) as polluted by the axiom-based and positivist paradigm espoused by Anglo-Saxon economics in its attempt to cope with its physics-envy. Multi-disciplinary or otherwise innovative solutions to the resolution of such problems are regularly advocated, sporadically organized, but as yet have only rarely contributed to the advance of theory.

The paper will begin with a review of the literature up to 1992 before proceeding to a critique of methods, assumptions, purposes and progress in specific Organizational Behaviour (OB) fields. It will conclude with the outlining of an agenda and a rationale for future work.

Such an analysis is set against a background of proliferating interaction and interdependence between cultures and nations as globalization takes hold. In such a world, the businessman has increasingly urgent needs for assistance from theory. In practice he is forced to run on ahead and let theorizing catch up later if it can. It has been argued that the creation of viable global organizations depends on the redesign of much human-resource management practice. Such redesign is made necessary by two forces: the increasing turbulence and variety of environments is directing new emphasis towards the achievement of controlled diversity and thus new organizational forms; secondly the growth of information technology is affecting the fundamental design of work, making it more conceptual, and causing adjustments in the organizing of tasks, roles, authority relations and sources of power and responsibility (Schein 1986). The field of enquiry and of potential application of new theory is changing rapidly, thus introducing extra complexity to an already complex set of issues. Not surprisingly, it will be complexity which runs as a core through this paper.

The Literature in Comparative Organizational Behaviour

As the purpose of this paper is a critique of the *character* of the literature it is not intended to provide a detailed re-statement of its content. Such detailed reviews are available (e.g. Roberts 1970; Adler 1983, 1984; Barratt and Bass 1976; Bhagat and McQuaid 1982; Drenth 1985; Triandis 1992; Adler, Doktor and Redding 1986; Boyacigiller and Adler 1991; Dunphy and Stening 1984; Beaty and Mendenhall 1990; Child 1981) as are also a number of textbooks which rest upon the incorporation of a wide literature (e.g. Adler 1986; Ronen 1986; Terpstra and David 1985; Dowling and Schuler 1990). In addition, a number of collections of papers in book-form have addressed the issue of comparative management (e.g. Preston 1990; Evans, Doz and Laurent 1989; Clegg and Redding 1990; Joynt and Warner 1985; Jaeger and Kanungo 1990; Lammers and Hickson 1979; Brewster and Tyson 1991; Pieper 1990).

A Review of the Reviews

The early major review by Roberts (1970) was highly critical. Describing the literature as a 'morass', she cited Bass's (1965) comment on U.S. organizational research that there was one group of researchers interested in people without organizations and another group interested in organizations without people. Progress depended on some interaction, but little was evident. She attacked 'mini' theories of culture. She also attacked the 'made in U.S.A.' stamp of much research. More sinister perhaps was her identifying of the scholarly provincialism with which she was 'considerably impressed', and her warning about the limits of a single discipline.

Whitley's (1984) description of management studies as a fragmented adhocracy is relevant here and explains much of the problem of achieving co-ordination in theory building. His taxonomy of scientific fields classifies them by (a) degree of functional dependence, or the need for researchers to use common techniques in order to use each others' work; (b) degree of strategic dependence which is highest when there is monopoly control of a theoretical core and thus of reputation granting; and (c) degree of task uncertainty, or the uncontrollability of work outcomes. The study of management occurs in conditions of low functional dependence, low strategic dependence, and high task uncertainty. Fragmented adhocracy is the organizational response. It leads to a condition where research is personal, idiosyncratic, and only weakly co-ordinated across research sites, and where dependence on reputation cannot justifiably be focused on a dominant core paradigm. Individuals make relatively diffuse contributions to broad, fluid goals because these goals are in turn affected by local and environmental pressures, and by the infiltration of 'lay' ideas, interests, and participants. Paradoxically, however, the case made out in this paper is not so much that the discipline suffers from the looseness implied above, but that the North American practice of it has been colonized by an inappropriate core paradigm which is only pseudo-scientific. The absence of an appropriate core paradigm has caused not so much diffuseness, as distortion.

The review by Barratt and Bass (1976), which focused on individual and group psychology, also saw the literature as fragmented and in need of an integrating framework. They proposed including variables such as: (i) national socialization patterns; (ii) institutions peculiar to the country (e.g. educational structure); (iii) individual traits that are typically formed within a particular nation; (iv) predominant technology; (v) political/socio/economic environment.

They thus advocated a very large contingency model in which specific enquiries could be embedded. For such a model to work, however, progress was needed on operationalizing constructs and standardizing instruments to facilitate comparative study. The literature they reviewed yielded only a small number of studies with a clear theoretical base. The majority of studies simply reported differences or similarities without the ability to illuminate their determinants, and with inadequate attention to reliability.

Child's (1981) review provided a useful parallel to that by Barratt and Bass in that it concentrated more on organizations as units of analysis. Although not central to this paper's concern with organizational behaviour, it is nevertheless worthy of note for its comprehensive attempt to deal with the issue of culture as a determinant of variations in organizational processes and structures. Child began with a review of the problems associated with the use of culture in the cross-national study of organizations and identified five which are commonly found, namely: (a) culture is not clearly defined; (b) cultural boundaries do not necessarily overlap with national boundaries but are usually taken to do so; (c) cultural factors are commonly brought in as explanatory variables without any explanation of their origins in the social history of a society, or of their functioning; (d) not enough has been done to specify which components of which cultures are relevant to organizations, and also which aspects of organizational behaviour are influenced; (e) conceptual and operational problems continue to hinder the measurement of culture. In addition to these handicaps, culture has to compete with two other major sources of explanation: that of the 'culture-free' contingency theorists, and that focusing on modes of production and especially on the capitalism/socialism continuum.

As regards consciously acultural contingency theory, Child concluded that it may well be able to specify boundary constraints on the choice of organization, but these are sufficiently wide to admit various functional equivalents, the evolution of which may be culturally affected. As regards the influence of systems of power relations such as capitalism, it was equally argued that a degree of cultural modification in the operation of economic systems becomes significant at the level of individual organizations. Thus culture remains an essential part of the explanation for international variations in organizing, and the issues return of understanding 'how much' and 'how'.

To this end Child advocated and offered a more sophisticated model than that normally found before then and one which is capable of incorporating the three main fields of determinants (contingency, culture, economic system), seeing them as inevitably interconnected (Figure 1). In re-stating the validity of a culturalist perspective, albeit a necessarily partial contributor to explanation, he then defined the conditions under which research progress might be made. His key points are worthy of note and they are:

1. Culture is best seen as the set of normative and preferential conditions for action, not the action itself. It is the system of meaning within which the conceptually separate social system of organizing human action is

Figure 1
Arguments from Contingency, Culture and Capitalism
(*Source*: Child 1981)

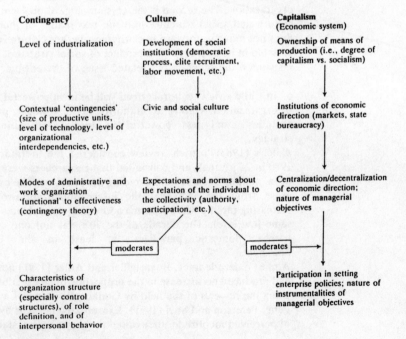

embedded (see also Kessing 1974). The value of such a concept is that it allows for other non-cultural variables to influence action in parallel, as parts of the same explanation.

2. In order to avoid culture being a purely residual black box, it is necessary to identify in advance the cultural characteristics of a country which are considered *a priori* to explain organizational differences, and to demonstrate their concordance with either a national boundary, or an identifiable set of people rather than to infer that culture is visible in the contrasts between sets of research subject responses. These latter may well carry all sorts of non-culture effects and especially the influence of organizational environment.

3. A much richer understanding is needed of the processes of cultural influence in a society and of the stability and persistence of certain cultural transmissions.

4. Industrialization/modernization are arguably expressed with reference to a nation's own tradition and are thus achieved in many different modes. This notion serves to unify the otherwise competing culturalist and 'contingency' schools of thought, and should prove fertile in building necessarily more complete models.

5. Progress in developing the 'organizations within society' approach will need to come to grips with two especially intractable theoretical issues affecting the understanding of comparative organizational behaviour. The first is the variation in the societal understanding of the meanings of authority and of co-operation, each of which has major effects in organization. The second is the epistemological problem that separating culture and social structure into the two realms of thought and action does not move us forward in clarifying whether culture is an explanatory variable in its own right or a product of social structure. This, of course, rests upon the separate but related issue of the adequacy of theories of society.

6. In Child's view, cultural effects will be most powerful in the processes of organization relating to 'authority, style, conduct, participation and attitudes', and less powerful in formal structuring and overall strategy.

Adler's (1983) 'ostrich' review considered the literature from 1971 to 1980 in 24 journals and concluded that researchers were publishing very little, and, in a sense, were avoiding the problem. The ostrich accusation arose from the fact that the internationalization of business was increasing rapidly while research addressing its problems remained at the same low level. The decade of the 70's was not one of progress. The narrow domestic paradigm, at least in the U.S. remained dominant.

Almost a decade later, Boyacigiller and Adler (1991) noted that the 80's had produced no increase in the proportion of cross-cultural OB articles, citing the reviews of the field by Godkin, Braye and Caunch (1989) and Peng, Peterson and Shyi (1991). Exacerbated perhaps by ten more years of perceived ineptitude, they raised the metaphorical stakes from ostrich to 'parochial dinosaur', as the descriptor of American organizational science. Their target, however, was not so much ethnocentrism, in which Americans might view their home-based theory as superior to others, but rather parochialism, or the simple lack of awareness about alternatives. They considered the discipline in danger of becoming a fossil.

Boyacigiller and Adler point to a number of institutional barriers in the discipline which are worthy of recall here because they illuminate the practical dilemmas which stand in the way of dealing with the conceptual challenges.

1. Doctoral programs fail to train scholars for international research.
2. International research is more difficult and more expensive.
3. Domestic research paradigms emphasize quantification and internal validity, whereas international research tends to be contextual, to require external validity, and to be unable to offer laboratory-type, context free methodologies.
4. The review process is parochial.
5. The disdain for foreign journals prevents scholars from engineering a more constructive paradigm shift based on respectable prior research. Thus logical empiricist methodology drives the production of knowledge, and the problems and needs of managers are largely ignored.

These five strictures are made in the North American context and Boyacigiller and Adler raise a significant point in acknowledging the contrasting fertility of European researchers in this field. This is attributed to their generally stronger sociological grounding, and also to the plurality of perspectives that can combine on the basis of common respect (see also Kochan 1983). It is perhaps also inevitable that the cultural variety of European life itself is a pervasive reminder that the issues are real and relevant.

Boyacigiller and Adler's dismal conclusion is that the discipline is trapped within geographical, cultural, temporal and conceptual parochialism. Like organization theory, it resembles a weed patch. To turn it into a well-tended (zoological?) garden requires action. They present thirteen progressive recommendations, reproduced here as Table 1.

Beaty and Mendenhall's (1990) review of what they saw as the 'pre-paradigm' field of international management is also notable for its exposure of the paucity of theory building in the main U.S. journals of the discipline. Qualitative methodologies were clearly disdained and 'empirical opportunism' was rampant.

Triandis (1992) begins his review of 400 studies by acknowledging the parochialism of American organizational psychology and its outcome — an underdeveloped theory of the way culture influences social and organizational behaviour. An indicator of this is the individualist bias in much Western research and the underestimating of the importance of groups, culture and other surrounding features. His analysis of the issues which have to be faced produces the following list of research needs:

1. A rigorous analysis and operationalizing of the concept of culture,

330   S. Gordon Redding

Table 1 Recommendations for a More Internationally Relevant Organizational Science (*Source*: Boyacigiller and Adler 1991)	**Recommendations**	**Significance**
	Reflection	
	Explicitly address the influence of cultural values on how we conceptualize organization phenomena and construct organization theories.	Helps scholars uncover neglected, overemphasized, and overgeneralized aspects of theories.
	Examine the extent to which the organizational sciences reflect U.S. cultural values.	Increases scholars' understanding of American culture and its impact on their perceptions, thoughts and scholarship.
	Action Steps for Individual Researchers	
	State the cultural and geographical domain of theories and research, as well as indicate other locales in which it applies.	Minimizes implicit universalism.
	Indicate the national and cultural characteristics of research samples.	Assists readers of the research to recognize potential limitations.
	Research management systems outside the United States.	Creates new theoretical and methodological approaches not predicated on American assumptions.
	Study non-U.S. management systems on their own terms (idiographic research): develop thick descriptions of organizational phenomena and the contexts in which they are embedded.	Increases the organizational forms and contexts with which scholars are familiar, as well as increasing their understanding of the uniqueness of U.S. organizational forms.
	Create more multinational and multicultural research teams.	Facilitates recognition of cultural biases in theory development.
	Use non-U.S. settings to frame theoretical and methodological approaches.	Expands domain of organizational theories.
	Take sabbaticals in foreign countries.	Increases scholars' understanding of foreign cultures and their own cultures, including providing personal thick descriptions of the foreign sabbatical culture.
	Organizational Changes	
	Journal editors, reviewers, and scholars should question one another regarding their cultural assumptions and research domains.	Rewarding careful exposition of the geographical and cultural domain will check implicit universalism.
	Expand editorial boards to include global representation and expertise.	Increases the perspectives represented, both substantively and symbolically.
	Consider forming 'global lines of business', strategic alliances, and networks among academic organizations worldwide.	Facilitates internationalization, and, thus, contributes to future relevance.
	Select leaders of academic management organizations from multiple nations.	Increases perspectives and knowledge bases represented, thus facilitating frame-breaking change.

including attention to the issue of which dimensions especially influence organizational behaviour.

2. The development of a model able to explain the links between culture and organizational behaviour.

3. Attention to the methodological pitfalls which lie in wait for those doing cross-cultural research, and acknowledgement that it is not so much a choice of which particular method, but of which combination of methods.

4. Acknowledgement of the roles of perception and cognition in the workings of cultural influence, together with the epistemological implications for the definition of the objects of study.

5. The influence of norms in differentiating meanings of apparently common notions.

6. The antecedents and consequences of culturally varied needs, attitudes, motives and values. In this context, Hofstede's (1980, 1991) work remains dominant as a working theory of culture, but Triandis, nevertheless, calls for a deeper understanding of Hofstede's four dimensions, especially 'uncertainty avoidance' and 'masculinity'.

7. Introduction of more dynamic perspectives which illustrate the 'negotiation' processes mediating the interaction of norms, roles, values etc. in each environment.

Triandis concludes that 'our ideas are still quite vague' (p. 54). We are still without a widely accepted definition of culture. We cannot yet clearly separate (a) the psychological from the cultural, (b) the universal from the culture-specific, (c) the single-case specific from the general pattern. Management systems and job designs are known to be culturally influenced but precisely how, and under what conditions, cannot be specified in any comprehensive way.

This review of the major reviews inevitably leads to the conclusion that thirty years' work has made little impression on the immensely complex problem of cultures and organizational behaviour. However, there is strong agreement on the essence of the difficulty, and the nature of the failure, and these may be illustrated in graphic form by relating two of the main dimensions of theory building. Figure 2 proposes that one important dimension is the interpretive–descriptive (or ethnoscience–positivism) dimension. The other is the idiographic–nomothetic dimension, or the theoretical level of analysis from micro analysis to grand theory with middle range theorizing half way.

The main body of work is clustered incompetently, unadventurously, but with comfortable conformity in the positivist micro-mini theory corner. The prototypical work here is the questionnaire survey and report. Outliers exist but in apparently unattractive territory. Understanding lies in moving upwards and outwards, but this requires a more sociological perspective and immediately raises questions about research legitimacy. As Sullivan (1992) has argued, the positivist paradigm of economics has been allowed to define the norms of the science and its reputational criteria. One might extend the argument to say that, in the process, it

Figure 2 Location of the Main Body of Western Comparative Management Research, with Examples of Outliers and a Proposed Re-location

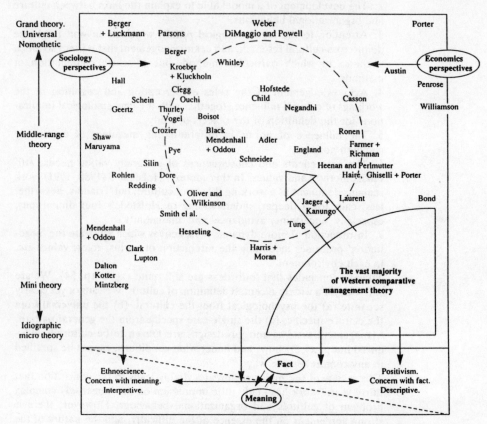

Note: Names cited here do not always refer to specific works but to a general body of work associated with the author(s).

has turned many potentially effective scholars into narrow and unaware conformists, and caused at least thirty years' waste.

In such a context, not much may be expected when we turn to examine more specifically the research on separate aspects of comparative organizational behaviour. It should also be stated that the analyses which follow do not pretend to review comprehensively the literature content. Instead they will concentrate on issues concerned with the process of theory building in order that a more progressive research agenda may be defined. Two general issues will first be addressed, followed by a review of progress in particular OB fields. This paper will then conclude with an examination of epistemological issues and research requirements.

The term 'general issues' refers to those aspects of the study of international OB which are wider in their reach than the traditional subdivisions such as leadership, motivation, etc. The general issues to be considered will be: (a) inter-cultural relations, and (b) human-resource management seen as a whole. More specific aspects will then be addressed, viz: (c) leadership, (d) motivation/needs/attitudes/values, (e) selection/ placement/job design/training, (f) organization development and corporate culture.

These are more focused probes into the literature than the broad review found in the early part of this paper and, by sketching current knowledge boundaries, they will set the stage for the final section which considers how we might proceed with finding out what we currently do not know.

Inter-cultural Relations

Two general prescriptions pervade the field of studies in inter-cultural relations. The first argues by implication that managerial issues are too complex to allow precise advice on anything and the way forward is for each party to understand the other and then take such understanding into account as a contingent factor. It is what one might call a 'recommended empathy' approach, and it is often the only real conclusion emerging from the many studies which describe differences in a theoretical vacuum.

A second, somewhat more constructive, approach is to make the assumption that there is synergy to be sought in cultural variety and that mixtures can result in greater creativity, innovation and responsiveness (Heenan and Perlmutter 1979; Adler 1986; Schein 1986; Cox and Blake 1991). It is possible, using such work, to find out whether and how an organization is culturally heterogeneous, and to work out the procedural steps necessary in the pursuit of synergy. What we do not yet know enough about is how the synergy works and thus how to determine the components of the mixture. As the issue is not one of interpersonal harmony (and may in fact be a matter of using interpersonal tension creatively) it is inevitably very complex. Personality variations also enter the picture to complicate it further.

Looking at the same issue in the context of cross-cultural leader–subordinate relationships, Shaw (1990) has proposed a cognitive categorization model, building on an earlier model by Redding (1980) and the recommendation by Adler, Doktor and Redding (1986) for cognition to be taken seriously in cross-cultural understanding. He presents a case for the cultural creation of prototypes of good/bad role behaviour, and argues that effective relations are achieved when the prototypes can be adjusted to overlap. His contribution is useful middle-range theory building, although it still calls for testing.

The adjustment of managers to foreign assignments is another field which has followed the pattern of being studied extensively but atheoretically, and Black, Mendenhall and Oddou (1991) have usefully proposed new theorizing which makes use of the extensive U.S. domestic literature on transfers and adjustment. They provide a theoretical framework for international managerial adjustment which is capable of sustaining new research effort of an improved kind.

It is of course in the field of joint ventures that inter-cultural relations become especially significant, and here the empirical accounts range from descriptions of problems and failures (e.g. Elashwami 1990; Shenkar and Zeira 1990; Nirenberg 1986; Parnell and Vanderkloot 1989) to claims of successful adaptation (e.g. Rehder, Smith and Burr 1989; Oliver and Wilkinson 1988; Ouchi 1981). Calling for a more rigorous approach to the study of the human-resources issues in international joint ventures, the literature on which they saw as sporadic and limited, Shenkar and Zeira (1987) proposed a preliminary research framework and a set of hypotheses. This uses an open systems approach and concentrates on analyzing personnel problems.

The field of inter-cultural relations, which lies at the core of the most urgent practitioner problems, is beginning to focus now on middle-range model building and hypothesis generation, and progress must be acknowledged.

Human-Resource Management

Laments about the failure to understand theoretically the international dimension of human-resource management are regularly accompanied by claims for its increasing significance. Such claims rest on the fact of globalization and a massive growth of international business (Adler 1986; Ronen 1986) but also more subtly on the increasing strategic significance of human resources as firms enter new modes of competitive behaviour (Tichy 1983; Fombrun et al. 1984; Adler and Ghadar 1990; Evans 1986).

Adler and Ghadar (1988) point to new approaches in managing R & D, production, and marketing and finance, developed in the face of new global realities, but see no equivalent evolution of thought for international human-resources systems. The issues are complex because of the variety of perceptions, value systems and interests (Horwitz 1990), and because of the changes wrought by information technology, organizational destructuring and market turbulence (Schein 1986).

It was noted earlier that practice runs ahead of theory in complex fields and Kidger (1991) provides some useful reflections on this in describing a converging set of HRM practices internationally. He sees increasing standardization in having personnel specialists, policy statements, job evaluation, briefing groups, quality circles, and notes an increase in resources for personnel work. He also argues that there is a closing of the gaps between Japanese, U.S. and European systems, with the Western practices drifting towards an emulation of Japanese lifetime employment ideals, team-working, concern with quality and removal of overt status differences, citing Peters and Waterman (1982), Goldsmith and Clutterbuck (1985), Pang and Oliver (1988) and Purcell (1989). The underlying principles in this process are summarized by Thurley (1990) as those that sponsor (1) dialogue between the social partners in the organization, (2) organizations built on a multicultural basis, (3) opportunities for participation and (4) continuous learning by staff based on objective feedback.

The convergence hypothesis, however, is always controversial and an ample literature exists to indicate that HRM practices do vary substantially in their visible manifestation (e.g. Shackleton and Newell 1991) as well as in the underlying cognitive frameworks which affect them (Al-Faleh 1987; Hayes and Allinson 1988).

Poorly researched issues which are of current concern to practitioners are seen by Kidger (1991) as: (a) the integration of HRM with business strategy; (b) the development of a distinct corporate culture; (c) the creation in different countries of a skilled, flexible, committed workforce, adaptive to change; (d) effects of culture on commitment and on unions.

In endorsing a similar set of research aims, Schein (1986) has pointed out a crucial epistemological stumbling block, well worthy of note before considering the next stages in the development of the discipline. He points out that the meaning of such things as careers and what people get from work varies so substantially across cultures that deeply held concepts about what authority, management, and work are all about in the larger scheme of things, may also vary in critical ways.

A claim can be made that a basic conceptual framework for the HRM field, based on the Harvard model (Beer et al. 1984) is widely accepted by theorists. Concern with the link to strategy has also been analyzed theoretically (e.g. Hendry and Pettigrew 1990; Fombrun, Tichy and Devanna 1984; McKinlay and Starkey 1992). Attention has also been paid to the corporate culture/national culture interaction (e.g. Schneider 1988). A link with organization theory has been proposed as a step towards a general theory of comparative human-resource management (Begin 1992). However, the models offered are somewhat tentative and will require several iterations before their precision approaches the complexity of the explananda. Nor do they fit easily with Schein's concern to include at least some ethnomethodology. Many assumptions still require empirical demonstration and it is perhaps best to conclude this consideration of the general international HRM field with Kidger's (1991) recommendation of research questions, namely: 1. Is there an emerging international body of practices?; 2. Do the practices have the same significance/meaning in different countries?; 3. Do the differences relate to the cultural/educational/political context in such a way that they need to be understood in order to carry out these practices optimally?

Leadership

The massive amount of Western literature on leadership has continued to be enriched with new insights as more ethnographic studies of Western managers (e.g. Mintzberg 1973; Kotter 1982; Bennis and Nanus 1985) supplement the earlier base of largely survey-dependent understanding (e.g. Stogdill 1977). Moving out from this core into the international field has been mainly a matter of extending the survey-type, attitude-oriented methodologies which typify the early descriptive phase of social research and which are well summarized in Ronen (1986). More recent research has now begun to explore the potentially much richer fields of differences in behaviour patterns and in cognitive structures of the kind advocated for study by Adler, Doktor and Redding (1986).

Doktor (1990) has presented data to demonstrate that CEO's use their time differently in Hong Kong, U.S., Japan and Korea, and Stewart (1992) has similarly reported for China. Different ways of using authority have also been reported by Aldemir (1986) as have variations in 'performance management' behaviour between developing countries and Western countries by Mendonca and Kanungo (1990). Sinha (1990) has also developed a normative model for effective leadership behaviour in the Indian context. Japanese structures of leadership behaviour have been extensively studied (for a review see Dunphy 1986) and the occasional ethnographic study (e.g. Rohlen 1974; Clark 1979; Silin 1976) has enriched understanding of the workings of Asian organizational behaviour.

For fuller understanding, more progress will be needed on the question of differences in mental landscapes. Although Hofstede's dimensions provide a useful beginning to an empirical approach to the social construction of reality as classically described by Berger and Luckmann (1966), we are still left with only the broadest hints about the mental frameworks of leaders in various cultures, and there is a clear need for much more indigenous specification of meaning structures of the kind offered by Pye (1985) on authority in Asia. The contribution here of Mendenhall and Oddou (1986) in presenting a guide to the cognitive context of Japanese management is a valuable advance which contains a theory of causation. An empirical extension of such work has been reported by O'Connell, Lord and O'Connell (1990), and an equivalent for the Overseas Chinese is available (Redding 1990).

A significant empirically based investigation of this same issue is now also available (Smith et al. 1989; Smith and Peterson 1988) in which the generalizability of the notion of leadership style across cultures is tested. Using 1177 respondents in Britain, United States, Hong Kong and Japan, and using Misumi's notion of a distinction between a general structure in leadership and variations in its specific expression (Misumi and Peterson 1985), they discovered that, as an example, consideration in an individualist culture might mean respecting subordinate's autonomy, whereas in a collectivist culture it might mean more interaction with them. They also propose that performance and maintenance behaviours are more differentiated from each other in the United States, whereas more overlap may occur elsewhere. The balance of their internal constituents will also vary.

Research of this latter kind is clearly significant in opening up the cognitive dimension. Its potential for enriching theory is also clearly large. However, it is difficult to conduct and, so far, very sparse.

Motivation/Needs/Attitudes/Values

The essential problem in understanding worker motivation cross-culturally is that there are many descriptions of differences, but very little understanding of their local antecedents and causes, or of their implications for appropriate organizational and managerial responses. A comment typifying the outcome is offered by Seddon (1987) who claims: 'It is likely that few appraisal systems are operating effectively in organizations in developing countries'.

The extensive literature on the differences themselves has been well presented by Ronen (1986) and reviewed by Triandis (1992). Beginning with the idea that motives will vary in their dependability and pliability, Triandis opens up the probability that although the structure of motive arousal may be universal to *homo sapiens*, the content of the standards will vary with cultural frames of reference. How this connection works is hardly addressed at all by the extensive literature describing variations. Except, that is, by Hofstede who has written extensively on the antecedents of value systems (Hofstede 1980) and more recently on their organizational and managerial outcomes (Hofstede 1991). A fully worked out theory of culture and its organizational effects is thus available, but as there are inevitable trade-offs between universalism and specificity, it can only offer signposts to the deeper understanding of specific cultures. It must also be acknowledged that variations from Hofstede's set of four values may emerge to make them less universal than they currently appear. An example here is the description of a Chinese values set which suggests a different cognitive structure (Bond and Hofstede 1990; Bond 1988), and this is backed up by other work on Chinese organizational behaviour (Redding and Wong 1986), face (Redding and Ng 1982), trust (Wong 1988) and group dynamics (Tang and Kirkbride 1986).

Hofstede's work has inspired a great improvement in the discipline by specifying a wide-ranging theoretical model which serves to co-ordinate research efforts. Two roads now lead on from it. One is to examine more completely the question of universals and, if necessary, to produce a 'world-map' of value-sets indicating their overlaps and the way they vary in their internal distribution and weighting of factors. The other is to examine more closely the local origins of those value-sets and the mechanics of their influence on behaviour in organizations. One must conclude that such work is in its infancy, although new work by Bond and Schwarz provides hope that breakthroughs may be anticipated (Bond 1991).

Selection/Placement/Training/Job Design

It is inevitable that the paucity of more fundamental understanding of the interaction between culture and organizational behaviour will weaken the precision with which more practical applications are worked out. Thus Bhatt and Miller (1983) found the research field on questions of selection and placement to be 'in disarray'. There is a high failure rate in expatriate assignments (McEnery and Des Harnais 1990) and expatriates either receive no training at all or it is done ineffectively (Derr and Oddou 1991; Adler and Ghadar 1988; Mendenhall and Oddou 1986; Tung 1982; Ronen 1986). Little progress has been made on the issue of which career and personal variables will predict success in foreign assignments (Adler and Graham 1987), although a somewhat disparate literature does exist (reviewed by Brislin 1981; Kealey and Ruben 1983; and Forster 1992).

An attempt to generalize was made by Mendenhall and Oddou (1985) who isolated four variables critical to the processes of selection and training: self-orientation; other orientation; accurate perceptions; and cultural toughness. A much more substantial advance is now available in the comprehensive research model proposed by Black, Mendenhall and Oddou (1991) referred to earlier when discussing inter-cultural relations. Forster's (1992) review of the literature has also led to his proposing a comprehensive model of international job mobility and this is equally likely to assist in focusing future research.

The training of people for work in cross-cultural situations has been reviewed and categorized by Triandis (1992) into four approaches: *self insight* which helps a person to identify his/her own 'cultural baggage'; *attribution training* or learning of the others' frameworks, via culture assimilators; *behavioural training* to re-tune a person's stimuli receptors; *experiential training* or extensive exposure to people from the new host culture. Application of these methods does however appear to need sensitivity to collectivist/individualist differences, and there is also evidence that the sequence in which techniques are used by an individual will influence the effectiveness of a program of sensitization. There appear, however, to be more questions than answers on the issue of cross-cultural training and its effectiveness. Is a general cultural assimilator useful? When should training be given? Who should do it? Should trainers be from the host culture, the home culture, or neutral? How do trainee attributes interact with training? What is the best balance of cognitive versus behavioural training?

The literature on cross-cultural training effectiveness was reviewed by Black and Mendenhall (1990) and their conclusion was that such training was capable of enhancing skill attainment, overall adjustment to a new culture, and job performance, findings which augur well for more attention to this aspect of the field.

The study of job design is a potentially useful field for revealing cross-cultural differences in organizational effectiveness and the determinants thereof. It is here for instance that some of the more dramatic contrasts exist between American and Japanese factories; but understanding remains puny. The Western approach to job design tends to argue that the more variety, task identity and feedback provided by a job, the greater is a worker's satisfaction (Hackman and Oldham 1980). There is however some argument that in collectivist societies, motivation is likely to be influenced by task interdependence and affiliation needs (Morishima and Minami 1983), and that the nature of attachment to the organization and to a job is significantly influenced by culturally deter- mined frameworks of meaning (Redding, Norman and Schlander 1993).

Organization Development and Corporate Culture

There is clear evidence that techniques normally categorized as 'organiza- tion development' need to be consistent with local subjective culture if they are to be effective (Preston 1987; Tainio and Santalainen 1984; Jaeger 1990; Blunt 1988; Feldman 1986; Hayes and Prakasam 1989; Rigby 1987). Their origins as U.S. techniques, although clearly ethnocen- tric, do not necessarily negate their use in other cultures, but do impose a requirement for adaptation (Jaeger 1990). Models for understanding such adaptation are available (e.g. Berry 1980; Harris and Moran 1979; Zeira and Adler 1980) but the empirical testing and refinement of them is still pending.

A similar conclusion applies to the cross-cultural use of the notion of corporate culture. There are well-argued contentions that a corporate culture must be in tune with national culture for an organization to func- tion well (Schneider 1988; Adler and Jelinek 1986; Soeters and Schreuder 1988), and there is some evidence to support the contention empirically (e.g. Lincoln, Hanada and Olsen 1981; Ferris and Wagner 1985; Misumi 1984). There is also valuable work on adaptation of organizational cul- ture, such as that by Ouchi and Jaeger (1978) on the emergence of Type Z as an adaptation from Types A and J.

Further progress in achieving congruence between national and corporate cultures is still dependent, though, on advances in conceptualization of the issues, and in instrumentation to foster fieldwork. Useful contribu- tions to the latter are to be noted from Cooke and Rousseau (1988) and Hofstede et al. (1990).

The various fields within cross-cultural organizational behaviour theory appear then to exhibit different rates of progress towards more fully explicated middle-range theories, and only one universal theory has reached the stage of extensive empirical grounding. The review of theor- etical requirements which now follows must, therefore, take as its agenda (a) the enrichment of the middle range, (b) the sponsorship of alternative grand theory and (c) the refinement of the grand theory whose use is growing.

These theoretical issues will be addressed by examining the debating points which persist in the literature and which remain unresolved. Such debates surround the question of how knowledge should grow and are partly epistemological, partly institutional and partly methodological, usually all at at the same time. As debates they are not always overt, and must be inferred from the behaviour of social scientists across a wide spectrum of disciplines. They may be identified as follows: (1) the specification of the field of enquiry in terms of the key questions being addressed; (2) the specification of the field in terms of the disciplines and schools of thought being brought to bear on it; (3) the issue of alternative frameworks of meaning; (4) questions of epistemology and causation; (5) more progressive research design.

The Field in Terms of Questions Addressed

The more obvious questions of practitioners were identified at the beginning of this paper. Behind them lie the core research questions at the centre of which is the issue of generalizability, of whether there are certain universals in the managing of organizations. A subsidiary issue is that of identifying what varies and what does not. Until we can specify the limits to generalizability, the focusing of research will remain problematic.

It is interesting that the original proponents of the convergence hypothesis (Kerr et al. 1960) have more recently acknowledged that although convergence appears to be occurring in 'the ordinary business of life', i.e. in how a person gets and uses his income, there appears to be little convergence in the realm of the mind; the field of beliefs and values (Kerr 1983).

Those scholars who argue for a single international managerial culture (e.g. Kidger 1991; Everett, Stening and Longton 1982) seem now to be authoritatively outnumbered by those who argue like Laurent (1986) that variety proliferates and that 'the art of managing and organizing has no homeland', but the real questions of what does or does not vary have not been answered. Jorgensen, Hafsi and Kiggundu (1986), Kiggundu (1990) and Jaeger (1990) have produced tentative models of conditions for transferability of organizational systems. Ishida (1986) has treated the transfer of Japanese HRM practices in a similar way. Fairchild (1989) has also perceptively studied the way in which culture causes a re-interpretation of the processes and structures of organizing and the consequent contrasts in the manifestation of bureaucracy. Redding and Whitley's (1990) framework for the analysis of economic systems 'beyond bureaucracy' and Whitley's (1991, 1992) theory of business recipes are beginning to accumulate information from Europe and East Asia which allows for a typology of organizational design clusters, each cluster being understood in terms of a complex of cultural, sociological and institutional determinants. Undoubtedly the new institutionalism in organizational analysis (Powell and DiMaggio 1991) is greatly enhancing understanding.

We observe then an enriching of the field of questions and an ability to specify them with more contingencies and more precision. It is not intended to list them here in detail, but at least those themes that lie at the heart of the field of cross-cultural OB as it now stands and are beginning to claim attention, can be identified, and they are:

1. What are the antecedents and determinants of organizationally relevant values, beliefs, attitudes and motives in specific cultures?
2. Which clusters of values, beliefs, etc. are organizationally relevant in which national contexts?
3. How does culture interact with other factors (e.g. structural contingencies, macro-economic systems, surrounding institutional frameworks) as part of a complex model of multiple and reciprocal determinants of organizational responses?
4. Can organizational responses be clustered to produce a typology? In other words, does a type of organization emerge reciprocally with specific cultural, sociological and institutional conditions.
5. How do the specifics of organizational behaviour reflect the cultural predispositions and meaning systems of members?
6. How may different cultures be blended effectively in the interpersonal, leader–subordinate, organization structural, and operating system frameworks of reference?
7. Which aspects of organizing and managing may be said to be universal and which are most affected by culture (that is, if there is such a construct as managing, which can be disembedded at all).

The Field in Terms of Disciplines and Schools of Thought

The dangers of a field settling prematurely into a normal science straightjacket are manifest in organization theory, as regular warnings indicate (Daft and Lewin 1990; Gioia and Pitre 1990; Sullivan 1992), and the narrowness of focus of many studies in comparative management is a likely outcome of what is taken as normal science, i.e. publishable, in the central disciplines of OT/OB.

The complexity of the domain of study in comparative OB is significantly greater than in the core Western discipline and calls for the incorporation of more explanatory variables, and more diverse models of the management process. The resulting dilemma is that a creative diversity of approaches will hinder even more the achievement of intellectual synthesis and practical research integration; challenges which are already demonstrably problematic.

To examine the nature of this dilemma, it will perhaps be appropriate to consider some maps of how the discipline has so far diffracted, and then some proposals for holding it together with an integrating framework. We shall then be in a position to consider the wider integration initiatives which incorporate other disciplines.

Adler (1984) has usefully identified six alternative ways of doing cross-cultural research: parochial, ethnocentric, polycentric, comparative management, geocentric and synergistic. These vary according to the number of cultures involved, the way similarities and differences are approached, the basic study design and research questions, and the methodology. Synthesis is clearly not fostered in such circumstances.

Another typology by Sechrest (1977) identified three kinds of cross-cultural research: Type I studied the overall impact of culture on organizational behaviour; Type II studied what specific aspects of culture had what effects, using psychological processes as the main object of study; Type III were more anthropological and attempted to study culture itself rather than concentrating on its organizational effects. His observations were that most studies were Type II. Type I studies have to compete with alternative theories claiming different primary determinants. In a comment using this typology, Bhagat and McQuaid (1982) advised beginning with Type I, to achieve some perspective, then proceeding to Type III for greater insight, then Type II for more specific understanding of cause and effect and relative weightings, an iteration between the nomothetic and the idiographic which is also seen by Lammers and Hickson (1979) as the most fruitful means of pursuing understanding in this field.

Assuming that it is possible to accept such advice and dispose oneself as a researcher alternately in ethnographic and hypothesis generating mode, an overarching framework is still required to provide adequate perspective and to suggest perhaps necessary inputs from other disciplines. In a valuable attempt at such integration, Bhatt and Miller (1983) proposed a framework reproduced here as Figure 3. Their Venn diagram identifies three major categories of variables: *enterprise-specific*, a field where organizational and managerial differences can normally be reported, but not explained; *location-specific*, dealing with the institutional and cultural environment and often connecting with descriptions of managerial practices which typify and represent that environment; *international environment-related* which allows the incorporation of cross-national factors affecting organizations such as trade protection, recessions and booms, etc. They also identify fields of overlap or interaction, the most complex being at the centre.

The point of such an exercise in separating fields is that each category has its own accepted research criteria, and is capable of yielding valuable results based on sound existing methodologies and particular disciplinary perspectives. Bhatt and Miller conclude that what is now needed is a moratorium on description and a move towards interdisciplinary theorizing. This plea echoes that of Child (1981) noted earlier, and represented in Figure 1. There is, of course, a long history of such frameworks (c.f. Farmer and Richman 1965; Negandhi and Estafen 1965; Koontz 1969) but it is only recently that researchable specifications of causation have emerged and also that interdisciplinary approaches are beginning to bear fruit. Four examples of this fusion are perhaps worthy of note.

Figure 3
Fields and Types of
Research
(*Source*: Bhatt and
Miller 1983)

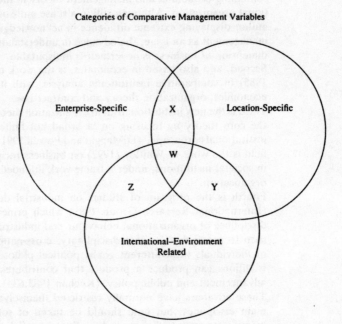

Categories of Comparative Management Variables

Typical Comparative Management Research

Circle or Area	Description
Enterprise-Specific Circle	Variables which describe characteristics, operations, and performance of an enterprise and/or its members
Location-Specific Circle	Variables which describe the nature of institutional and cultural environment in a given location that are relevant to an enterprise and/or its members.
International–Environment-related Circle	Variables which describe the nature of the international environment affecting more than one nation at a given time.
Area X	Studies describing interactions between enterprises and their local institutional/cultural environment
Area Y	Studies describing interactions between local and international environments.
Area Z	Studies describing interactions between enterprise and international environment
Area W	Studies describing interactions among enterprises, their local institutional/cultural environments and the international environment.

At Harvard, Austin (1990) and Porter (1990) are displaying the value of combining economics and management theory in the context of international organization. Although still in a sense anti-sociological, with each author displaying extreme diffidence in acknowledging human-resources management as an issue, the advance in understanding the international dimension of business is nevertheless indisputable.

Second, and also based in economics, is the work of Williamson (1975, 1985) in comparative institutional analysis, with its fusion of work in economics, organization theory and contract law.

Third is the new institutionalism in organization theory which is enriching the core theory by focusing on 'a broad but finite slice of sociology's institutional cornucopia' (DiMaggio and Powell 1991:9). Within this same field is the work of Whitley (1992) on business recipes and their origins in societal institutions, under a framework intended to be a sociology of organization.

Fourth is the program of studies on industrial democracy in Europe (International Research Group 1981) which principally fused the two disciplines of organizational behaviour and industrial relations, and was seen to prove that 'an interdisciplinary, cross-national team composed of individuals with different goals, political philosophies, and research traditions can produce a product that contributes to both theoretical advancement and public policy' (Kochan 1983:634).

These advances have normally restricted themselves to connecting two main disciplines, but note should be taken of some initiatives which incorporate four or five main disciplines in collaboration on a complex question.

Two major projects are now incorporating approaches from history, sociology, economics, organization theory, philosophy and political science, in order to study the success of East Asian economies in recent decades. The underlying assumption is of a link from a society's value systems to its organizations and then to its national performance. They are based respectively at the American Academy of Arts and Science (Tu 1991) and the East-West Center (Dernberger 1989).

Progress may now be identified in matching complex questions with sophisticated frameworks, and the longstanding advocacy of multi-disciplinary approaches is now providing for important advances in understanding. Whether in the longer term they will be seen as major breakthroughs remains uncertain, but they clearly chart a direction worth exploring.

Alternative Frameworks of Meaning

Organizational behaviour theory is a social science and its purpose is the understanding of behaviour. Social science normally achieves its purpose by the study not so much of facts, but of meanings. To understand organizational behaviour comparatively, then, requires access to indigenous frameworks of meaning.

The cross-cultural OB literature offers almost nothing progressive in this regard and to get the issue back onto the research agenda may require a radical ethnographically based challenge, such as those issued by Mintzberg to management theory (1973) and to corporate planning (1990). If leadership 'means' different things in different countries (Smith et al. 1989), if work takes on a variety of 'meanings' by culture (Meaning of Work International Research Team 1987), if organizational behaviour 'means' something different in Japan (Mendenhall and Oddou 1986), if the 'meaning' of organization and how you attach yourself to it is different in Asia from the West (Redding, Norman and Schlander 1993; Yu and Yang in press) then the eventual understanding of organizational behaviour in any 'meaningful' way will have to come to terms with the challenges of ethnoscience.

Nor should it be forgotten in this regard that cognitive frameworks include those that carry the mental processes of understanding and explanation, and that social science itself is a Western cultural artifact, the basic cause-and-effect notion within which is arguably itself ethnocentric (Maruyama 1974).

Epistemology and Causation

There is one central challenge which dominates the field in an epistemological sense and that is the bankruptcy of empirical positivism. More than anything else, it is this which has sent the subject round in circles for thirty years. In considering that issue, it is appropriate to take note of certain questions which surround it, namely (a) the lack of a common observation language and the consequent inevitability of relativism, (b) the imperialism of economics, (c) the weakness of the deterministic mechanical causal model and the false assumptions on which it is based, (d) the implications of causal complexity and reciprocal determinacy and (e) the special nature of the comparative method and the compromises it entails, but finds useful. After considering these issues, a more progressive paradigm shift can be defined.

The main opposition to empiricism comes from the relativist position which holds that a common observation language is impossible in social science. As Geertz (1973:5), arguing from this position, says:

'The concept of culture I espouse . . . is essentially a semiotic one. Believing, with Max Weber, that man is an animal suspended in webs of significance he himself has spun, I take culture to be those webs, and the analysis of it to be therefore not an experimental science in search of law but an interpretive one in search of meaning.'

The dilemma posed by this position is that interpretive approaches resist conceptual articulation and thus systematic modes of assessment. As Geertz (1973:24) points out: 'the tension between . . . the need to grasp and the need to analyze is . . . both necessarily great and essentially irremovable'. Culture theory in this formulation works under three conditions: it must stay close to what it describes and cannot assume a life of its own with freedom to shape its own internal logic; secondly it does not accumulate upon itself, except that an accretion of conceptual tools allows for deeper and more incisive probes into the same things; thirdly it cannot, strictly speaking, be predictive. The role of its theoretical concepts is to provide a vocabulary in which can be expressed what a society's symbolic action has to say about that society. Considering the superficiality of much cross-cultural management understanding, and its manifestation in, for instance, the gulf between the American and Japanese organizational psyche, it is salutary to be reminded of the value of understanding not so much other people, but other people's understanding of themselves.

Geertz's position lies, of course, at one end of the interpretive/descriptive continuum of the discipline, given as the horizontal axis in Figure 2 (for a more elaborate discussion of which see Morgan and Smircich 1980). It is hardly worth dilating on matters at the opposite end, as that is where we have characterized the main part of the discipline as languishing and stranded. It is suffice to say that, as Sullivan (1992) has argued, international business research is dominated by economic theory and what he terms the purposive paradigm. The achievement of this form of intellectual imperialism through the medium of economics can be understood with reference to the sociology of the discipline. Operating as it does to produce novelty under strictly controlled conditions, it uses highly standardized training and certification systems, primarily designed to ensure that future economists will solve artificial puzzles in the approved manner and with formal analytical techniques. Such dogmatic initiation is unchallengeable by neophytes and unchallenged by members, and the end-product is described by Whitley (1986:193) in the following terms:

'As a result, economists share common analytical skills, a standardized symbol system for communicating the results of analytical research, a strong consciousness of the boundaries of economics and of appropriate ways of formulating intellectual problems in the field, and an overwhelming commitment to theoretical goals and priorities since none of the skills they have acquired deal with empirical research or the problems of turning data into information.'

Economics is a 'partitioned bureaucracy' in which the theoretical, analytical work retains its intellectual primacy by marginalizing a number of 'applied' sub-fields which deal with empirical uncertainty. This domination by the high priesthood of neoclassical orthodoxy is maintained via a strict control of significance standards and criteria governing access to key resources (Whitley 1984, 1986). It is thus fortified strongly against both change and reality.

An important concomitant of this, for international business theory, is that progress cannot be achieved by attempting to change Anglo-Saxon economics, or by staying within its paradigm. A fundamentally new discipline is required, with a less self-deceiving and more relevant research agenda. Such a move is advocated, not so much out of pique at having been colonized, but out of a conviction that the deterministic mechanical causal model of the natural sciences is inappropriate for the enterprise of social science, and that economics, in acting as a pseudo-science, has avoided this issue instead of facing it.

There are three substantial objections to the unquestioning transfer of natural science rules to the human sciences: firstly, the purposes of the two forms of science are not identical and different purposes both require and sanction different rules of method; secondly, social science is value-laden and interactive; thirdly, social phenomena vary by their meanings. These points require some elaboration.

Modern Western science follows a dominant ideology in which its core purpose is seen to be understanding which can then lead to the manipulation and control of the natural world. Epistemological validity and progress are seen in terms of prediction and control. Although this same ideology extensively pervades the human sciences, it has no monopoly (Burrell and Morgan 1979), and its legitimacy is weakened by the inadequacy of a mechanical closed system model to account for, and allow control of, social phenomena.

The incursion of values into the processes of social science is manifest in project design, results application, and topic biases. Judgments also enter the descriptions of phenomena, and their critical assessment. A 'managerial' perspective is itself a form of bias, or at least a predisposition to see things from a particular angle, so too would be a Marxist approach. Although conventions exist to foster objectivity in description, they are not designed to transcend the cultural determination of meaning, and there are thus limits to the formulation of universal statements. For instance, to discuss participation, in the context of a society for which it has little meaning, is to impose an inappropriate observation. Thus the search for universal abstract patterns of causation is frustrated both by the observers' interaction with the object of study and by the nature of that object of study. These general social-science problems are exacerbated in cross-cultural work, but are regularly brushed aside in research design.

It was contended earlier that social reality lies in its participants' accounts of it. This requires interaction between the scientist and the object of study in ways which do not apply in the natural sciences. The introduction of participants' conceptions then seriously hinders the construction of a shared observation language for scientists. Also because meanings can change, so therefore do phenomena, and predictive laws cannot remain valid. Changing phenomena will also undermine the stability of criteria set up to control the adequacy of scientific description. Nor will social groups exhibit consensus over meanings, and this makes empirical evidence contestable.

Perhaps the greatest fault, however, in the misapplication of the positivist paradigm — and this leads into our next topic, causation — is the fact that social phenomena are internally related and vary with each other.

To be an employee, for instance, takes meaning from the context of having an employer and colleagues, and a surrounding organization. Change in any one of those components will see an adjustment of meanings and relationships. The nature of the phenomena is contingent on the relationships. Causes and effects cannot thus be ontologically separate, and the most fundamental of positive premises collapses.

An explanation in social science is necessarily a complex of forces, with the following characteristics: (a) multiple; (b) with some more salient than others but not necessarily following precedents in other areas or at other times; (c) interconnected in complex ways; (d) influenced reciprocally by their effects; (e) analyzable via several disciplines; (f) expressed via the meaning structures of actors.

In the face of this, one obvious option is multi-causality, but this can mask evasion. As Kaplan and Manners (1972:160) point out:

'It often happens that multicausalism becomes, in fact, a retreat from explanation, a confession of despair, a final refuge for those who find the birth, life and death of human institutions and the intricacies of human behaviour much too complex to understand.'

Quite simply what is required of the theorist is to stick his neck out, as Weber did, but to do so while respecting the norms of causal explanation in social science. The first of these is to dissociate social science cause from natural science cause, seeing the latter as a particular case of the general principle of determinacy and applying only to the unambiguous influence of external forces (Bunge 1963). The second norm is the acceptance of complexity and non-closure of a system. The third is to study processes as well as objects. The fourth is to use several methods to throw explanatory light from different perspectives on to a common set of phenomena.

The use of the comparative method has, in the vast majority of reported research been simplistic. The standard report says in effect 'Managers in country A believe this; managers in country B believe that. They are different. Isn't that interesting?' A variant is 'We think this is why there are differences but we didn't look at that'. Another is 'We think these are the implications for practice, but more research is needed on that'.

It requires a return to something more radical if comparative organizational behaviour as a social science is to achieve the full potential of the use of comparison which lies at its heart as a discipline. A recent treatment of this issue by Ragin (1987) offers valuable insight, in that he notes the qualitative/quantitative split as being more profound in social science than elsewhere and that it requires some bucking of the trend to attempt a reconciliation. Not to do so means that important research questions will continue to be overlooked or distorted. His solution is the idea of qualitative comparative analysis, in which wholes may be compared as configurations of parts. This integrates the case-oriented and the variable-oriented approaches and allows investigators to retain the complexity of social causation while at the same time acknowledging the variety of social phenomena. The end product is the description of phenomena as clusters of features, or types, within which a rich pattern of interacting determinants can be analyzed. This is clearly a useful starting point for the middle-range theorizing of the kind needed to move the discipline away from its tight little corner.

More Progressive Research Design

The first question to be addressed in considering an improvement to the present condition of international OB is whether to advocate a new paradigm or the amendment of the present one. The encouragement of new initiatives is advocated, for instance by Burrell and Morgan, who identified four major paradigms for the analysis of organizational life (radical humanist, radical structuralist, interpretive, and functionalist — the latter being their term for the one identified here as positivist), and said:

'We firmly believe that each of the paradigms can only establish itself at the level of organizational analysis if it is true to itself. Contrary to the widely held belief that synthesis and mediation between paradigms is what is required, we argue that the real need is for paradigmatic closure. In order to avoid emasculation and incorporation within the functionalist problematic, the paradigms need to provide a basis for their self-preservation by developing on their own account.' (Burrell and Morgan 1979:230)

It is not proposed here that one should be swayed by such an extreme view, but simply that one should note that it is backed up by powerful arguments and that it confronts the problem of intellectual imperialism which runs through this paper. Two factors allow for a less extreme position: firstly the kind of comparative methodology advocated by Ragin would allow for some useful fusion; secondly, a comparative researcher can safely proceed into the middle ground only if he or she is aware of exactly what is going on, and thus chooses consciously to use something better than a single approach. Multiple method research has a major part to play in reinforcing the validity and utility of findings, and in theory development.

It would be inappropriate here to discuss the specifics of research design for middle-range theorizing in this field, and they have been well covered elsewhere (e.g. Ronen 1986; Pasquero 1990). Instead, some pulling together of conclusions will be done with a summary of what it would mean to move, in terms of Figure 2 from the bottom right-hand corner to the centre of the field. These then are the recommendations for progress:
1. Pursue the comparative method via the study of clusters of phenomena or types, the 'interior' of which can be subjected to more idiographic analysis of patterns of determinacy.
2. Search for the kinds of abstract models which can encourage multi-

disciplinary research by rising above the observation languages of the disciplines themselves. For instance, instead of referring to 'lifetime employment' which is anchored in HRM, and also Japan, use the concept 'form of organizational attachment' about which more general theory can be developed.

3. Use the new middle-range theories now emerging in fields such as inter-cultural relations to go into the field ethnographically and refine the models. Find means of encouraging such nomothetic–idiographic iterations.

4. Enrich the current grand theory of Hofstede further by probing into the societal origins of his value clusters, and in terms of outcomes, trace more explicitly the patterns of their organizational consequences.

5. Test further the existence of alternative value clusters, indigenously perceived.

6. Call a halt to closed-system, empirically based positivist reportage.

7. Encourage complex model building of the kind advocated by Child (e.g. analyzing the processes of modernization for their capacity to illuminate the culturalism/contingency debate), but do so without falling into the trap of multi-causalism, i.e. have a leading idea of determinacy.

8. Avoid seeing culture as a single cause of anything and get accustomed to claiming its position as a necessary, but not sufficient, determinant of social outcomes.

9. Do much more ethnographic work on the crucial links between the mental world of culture and the behavioural world of organization, focusing on processes and meanings.

While all this may be going on, the practitioner questions with which we started, remain unanswered. The epistemological questions are also unanswered, but this is not surprising as they can never go away. They are indicators of the need in organizational science for a fusion of approach rather than entrenched specialization, and they also represent the problem of coming to terms with the immense complexity of social life. Movement is now needed if understanding is to increase, and it is at least thirty years overdue. This strangest of animals has been in the wrong cage for too long.

Notes

* An earlier version of the paper was given at the conference, 'Perspectives on International Business: Theory, Research, and Institutional Arrangements', organized by the Centre for International Business Research and Education, University of South Carolina, in May 1992. The paper has benefited greatly in preparation from the support of the Institute for the Study of Economic Culture, Boston University, and its Director, Peter Berger.

** I am most grateful to the following for their helpful comments: Michael Bond, Bob Tricker, Mark Mendenhall, Jeremiah Sullivan, Geert Hofstede, Mark Casson, Nancy Adler, Nakiye Boyacigiller and John Child.

References

Adler, Nancy J.
1980 'Cultural synergy: The management of cross-cultural organizations' in *Trends and issues in OD: current theory and practice*. W. W. Burke and L. D. Goodstein (eds.), 163–184. San Diego: University Associates.

Adler, Nancy J.
1983 'Cross-cultural management research: the ostrich and the trend'. *Academy of Management Review* 8/3: 226–232.

Adler, Nancy J.
1984 'Understanding the ways of understanding: cross-cultural management reviewed' in *Advances in international comparative management*, Vol. 1. R. N. Farmer (ed.), 31–67. Greenwich, CT: JAI Press.

Adler, Nancy J.
1986 *International dimensions of organizational behaviour*. Boston: Kent Publishing.

Adler, Nancy J., R. Doktor and S. G. Redding
1986 'From the Atlantic to the Pacific century: cross-cultural management reviewed'. *Yearly Review of Management of the Journal of Management* 12/2: 295–318.

Adler, Nancy J., and F. Ghadar
1990 'International strategy from the perspective of people and culture: the North American context' in *Research in global strategic management: international business research for the Twenty First Century*. A. M. Rugman (ed.), 179–205. Greenwich, CT: JAI Press.

Adler, Nancy J., and J. L. Graham
1987 'Business negotiations: Canadians are not just like Americans'. *Canadian Journal of Administrative Sciences* 4/3: 211–238.

Adler, Nancy J., and M. Jelinek
1986 'Is "organization culture" culture bound?'. *Human Resource Management* 25/1: 73–90.

Aldemir, M. C.
1986 'The impact of cultural values upon managers' choice of social power base'. *International Journal of Manpower* 7/5: 13–19.

Al-Faleh, Mahmoud
1987 'Cultural influences on Arab management development: a case study of Jordan'. *Journal of Management Development* 6/3: 19–33.

Austin, James E.
1990 *Managing in developing countries*. New York: Free Press.

Barrett, G. V., and B. M. Bass
1976 'Cross-cultural issues in industrial and organizational psychology' in *Handbook of industrial and organizational psychology*. M. D. Dunnette (ed.), 1639–1686. Chicago: Rand McNally.

Bass, Bernard M.
1965 *Organizational psychology*. Boston, MA: Allyn and Bacon.

Beaty, David T., and M. Mendenhall
1990 'Theory building in international management: an archival review and recommendations for future research'. Academy of Management Annual Meeting, San Francisco.

Beer, M., B. Spector, P. R. Lawrence, D. Q. Mills, and R. E. Walton
1984 *Managing human assets*. New York: Free Press.

Begin, J. P.
1992 'Comparative human resource management: a systems perspective'. *International Journal of Human Resource Management* 3/3: 379–408.

Bennis, Warren, and B. Nanus
1985 *Leaders: the strategies for taking charge*. New York: Harper and Row.

Berry, J. W.
1980 'Social and cultural change', in *Handbook of cross-cultural psychology*. H. C. Triandis and R. W. Brislin (eds.), 211–279. Boston, MA: Allyn and Bacon.

Berger, P. L., and T. Luckmann
1966 *The social construction of reality*. London: Pelican.

Bhagat, R. S., and S. J. McQuaid
1982 'The role of subjective culture in organizations: A review and directions for future research'. *Journal of Applied Psychology Monograph* 67: 653–685.

Bhatt, Bhal J., and E. L. Miller
1983 'A framework for upgrading comparative management research'. *Asia Pacific Journal of Management* 1/1: 26–35.

Black, J. Stewart, and M. Mendenhall
1990 'Cross-cultural training effectiveness: a review and a theoretical framework for future research'. *Academy of Management Review* 15/1: 113–136.

Black, J. Stewart, M. Mendenhall, and G. Oddou
1991 'Toward a comprehensive model of international adjustment: an integration of multiple theoretical perspectives'. *Academy of Management Review* 16/2: 291–317.

Blunt, Peter
1988 'Cultural consequences for organization change in a Southeast Asian state: Brunei'. *Academy of Management Executive* 2/3: 235–240.

Bond, M. H.
1988 'Invitation to a wedding: Chinese values and global economic growth' in *Social values and development: Asian perspectives.* D. Sinha and H. S. R. Kao (eds.), 197–209. New Delhi: Sage.

Bond, M. H.
1991 'Cultural influences on modes of impression management: implications for the culturally diverse organization' in *Applied impression management.* R. A. Giacalone and P. Rosenfeld (eds.), 195–215. London: Sage.

Bond, M. H., and G. Hofstede
1990 'The cash value of Confucian values' in *Capitalism in contrasting cultures.* S. R. Clegg and S. G. Redding (eds.), 383–390. New York: de Gruyter.

Boyacigiller, Nakiye, and N. J. Adler
1991 'The parochial dinosaur: organizational science in a global context'. *Academy of Management Review* 16/2: 262–290.

Brewster, C., and S. Tyson, *editors*
1991 *International comparisons in human resource management.* London: Pitman.

Brislin, R. W.
1981 *Cross-cultural encounters.* New York: Pergamon.

Bunge, Mario
1963 *Causality.* Cleveland: Meridien Books.

Burrell, G., and G. Morgan
1979 *Sociological paradigms and organizational analysis.* London: Heinemann.

Child, John
1981 'Culture, contingency and capitalism in the cross-national study of organizations' in *Research in organizational behaviour*, Vol. 3. L. L. Cummings and B. M. Staw (eds.), 303–356. Greenwich, CT: JAI Press.

Clark, Rodney
1979 *The Japanese company.* New Haven: Yale University Press.

Clegg, Stewart R.
1989 *Frameworks of power.* London: Sage.

Clegg, Stewart R., and S. G. Redding
1990 *Capitalism in contrasting cultures.* New York: de Gruyter.

Cooke, R. A., and D. M. Rousseau
1988 'Behavioural norms and expectations: a quantitative approach to the assessment of organizational culture'. *Group and organizational studies* 13: 245–274.

Cox, Taylor, and S. Blake
1991 'Managing cultural diversity: implications for organizational competitiveness'. *The Executive* 5/3: 45–56.

Daft, Richard L., and A. Y. Lewin
1990 'Can organization studies begin to break out of the normal science straightjacket?'. *Organization Science* 1/1: 1–9.

Dernberger, R.
1989 Introduction, Conference on 'Comparative Analyses of the Development Process in East and Southeast Asia: an Integrated Disciplinary Approach'. Honolulu, East-West Center.

Derr, C. B., and G. R. Oddou
1991 'Are US multinationals adequately preparing future American leaders for global competition?'. *International Journal of Human Resources Management* 2/2: 227–244.

DiMaggio, P. J., and W. W. Powell
1991 'Introduction' in *The new institutionalism in organizational analysis*. W. W. Powell and P. J. DiMaggio (eds.), 1–38. Chicago: University of Chicago Press.

Dowling, P. J., and R. S. Schuler
1990 *International dimensions of human resource management*. Boston, MA: PWS-Kent.

Drenth, P. J. D.
1985 'Cross-cultural organizational psychology: challenges and limitations' in *Managing in different cultures*. P. Joynt and M. Warner (eds.), 23–38. Amsterdam: Universitetsforlaget AS.

Dunphy, Dexter C.
1986 'An historical review of the literature on the Japanese enterprise and its management' in *The enterprise and management in East Asia*. S. R. Clegg, D. C. Dunphy and S. G. Redding (eds.), 343–368, 447–479. Hong Kong, Centre of Asian Studies: University of Hong Kong.

Dunphy, Dexter, C., and B. W. Stening
1984 *Japanese organization behaviour and management*. Hong Kong: Asian Research Service.

Elashwami, Farid
1990 'Japanese culture clash in multicultural management'. *Tokyo Business Today* 58/2: 36–39.

Evans, Paul A. L.
1986 'The strategic outcomes of human resource management'. *Human Resource Management* 25/1: 149–167.

Evans, Paul, Y. Doz, and A. Laurent, *editors*
1989 *Human resource management in international firms*. London: Macmillan.

Everett James E., B. W. Stening, and P. A: Longton
1982 'Some evidence for an international managerial culture' *Journal of Management Studies* 19/2: 153–162.

Fairchild, Erika
1989 'National culture and police organization in Germany and the United States'. *Public Administration Review* 49/5: 454–462.

Farmer, Richard N., and B. M. Richman
1965 *Comparative management and economic progress*. Homewood, Ill.: Irwin.

Feldman, Steven P.
1986 'Management in context: an essay on the relevance of culture to the understanding of organizational change'. *Journal of Management Studies* 23/6: 587–607.

Ferris, G. R., and J. A. Wagner
1985 'Quality circles in the United States: a conceptual re-evaluation'. *Journal of Applied Behavioural Science* 21: 155–167.

Fombrun, C. J., N. M. Tichy, and M. A. Devanna, *editors*
1984 *Strategic human resources management*. New York: Wiley.

Forster, N.
1992 'International managers and mobile families: the professional and personal dynamics of transnational career pathing and job mobility in the 1990s'. *International Journal of Human Resource Management* 3/3: 605–623.

Geertz, Clifford
1973 *The interpretation of cultures*. New York: Basic Books.

Gioia, D. A., and E. Pitre
1990 'Multiparadigm perspectives on theory building'. *Academy of Management Review*. 15/4: 584–602.

Godkin, L., C. E. Braye, and C. L. Caunch
1989 'US based cross-cultural management research in the eighties'. *Journal of Business and Economic Perspectives* 15/2: 37–45.

Goldsmith, W., and D. Clutterbuck
1985 *The winning streak*. Harmonds-
      worth: Penguin.

Hackman, J. R., and G. R. Oldham
1980 *Work redesign*. Reading, MA:
      Addison-Wesley.

Harris, Philip R., and R. T. Moran
1979 *Managing cultural differences*. Hou-
      ston: Gulf Publishing.

Hayes, John, and C. W. Allinson
1988 'Cultural differences in the learning
      styles of managers'. *Management
      International Review* 28/3: 75–80.

Hayes, J., and R. Prakasam
1989 'Culture: the efficiency of different
      modes of consultation'. *Leadership
      and Organization Development
      Journal* 10/1: 24–32.

Heenan, David A., and H. Perlmutter
1979 *Multinational organization develop-
      ment*. Reading, MA: Addison-
      Wesley.

Hendry, Chris, and A. Pettigrew
1990 'Human resource management: an
      agenda for the 1990's'. *International
      Journal of Human Resource Man-
      agement* 1/1: 17–44.

Hofstede, G.
1980 *Culture's consequences*. London:
      Sage.

Hofstede, Geert, B. Neuijen, D. D.
Ohayv, and G. Sanders
1990 'Measuring organizational cultures'.
      Administrative Science Quarterly 35:
      286–316.

Hofstede, G.
1991 *Cultures and organizations: software
      of the mind*. London: McGraw-Hill.

Horwitz, F.
1990 'HRM: an ideological perspective'.
      Personnel Review 19/2: 10–15.

International Research Group
1981 *Industrial democracy in Europe*.
      Oxford: Clarendon Press.

Ishida, Hideo
1986 'Transferability of Japanese human
      resource management abroad'.
      Human Resource Management 25/1:
      103–120.

Jaeger, Alfred M.
1990 'The applicability of Western man-
      agement techniques in developing
      countries: a cultural perspective' in
      *Management in developing coun-
      tries*. A. M. Jaeger and R. N.
      Kanungo (eds.), 131–145. London:
      Routledge.

Jaeger, Alfred M., and R. N. Kanungo,
editors
1990 *Management in developing coun-
      tries*. London: Routledge.

Jorgensen, Jan J., T. Hafsi, and M. N.
Kiggundu
1986 'Towards a market imperfections
      theory of organizational structure in
      developing countries'. *Journal of
      Management Studies* 23/4: 417–442.

Joynt, Pat, and M. Warner, *editors*
1985 *Managing in different cultures*.
      Amsterdam: Universitetsforlaget
      AS.

Kaplan, D., and R. A. Manners
1972 *Culture theory*. Englewood Cliffs,
      NJ: Prentice-Hall.

Kealey, D. J., and B. D. Ruben
1983 'Cross-cultural personnel selection:
      criteria, issues and methods' in
      Handbook of intercultural training,
      Vol. 1, 155–175. New York:
      Pergamon.

Kerr, C.
1983 *The future of industrial societies*.
      Cambridge, MA: Harvard Univer-
      sity Press.

Kerr, Clark, J. T. Dunlop, F. H. Harbison,
and C. A. Myers
1960 *Industrialism and industrial man*.
      Cambridge, MA: Harvard Univer-
      sity Press.

Kidger, Peter J.
1991 'The emergence of international
      human   resource   management'.
      *International Journal of Human
      Resource Management* 2/2: 149–163.

Kiggundu, Moses
1990 'Managing structural adjustment in
      developing countries: an organiza-
      tional perspective' in *Management
      in developing countries*. A. M.
      Jaeger and R. N. Kanungo (eds.),
      46–61. London: Routledge.

Kochan, Thomas A.
1983 Review of *Industrial democracy in Europe* (International Research Group, Oxford, Clarendon Press 1981). *Administrative Science Quarterly* 28/4: 629–634.

Koontz, H.
1969 'A model for analysing the universality and transferability of management'. *Academy of Management Journal* 12/4: 415–429.

Kotter, John P.
1982 *The general managers*. New York: Free Press.

Lammers, Cornelis J., and D. J. Hickson
1979 *Organizations alike and unlike*. London: Routledge and Kegan Paul.

Laurent André
1986 'The cross-cultural puzzle of international human resource management'. *Human Resource Management* 25/1: 91–102.

Lincoln, J. R., M. Hanada, and J. Olsen
1981 'Cultural orientations and individual reactions to organizations: a study of employees of Japanese-owned firms'. *Administrative Science Quarterly* 26: 93–115.

Maruyama, M.
1974 'Paradigmatology and its application to cross-disciplinary, cross-professional, and cross-cultural communication'. *Dialectica* 28/3–4: 135–196.

Meaning of Work International Research Team
1987 *The meaning of work*. London: Academic Press.

Mendenhall, M., and G. Oddou
1985 'The dimensions of expatriate acculturation: a review'. *Academy of Management Review* 10: 39–48.

Mendenhall, M., and G. Oddou
1986 'The cognitive, psychological and social contexts of Japanese management'. *Asia Pacific Journal of Management* 4/1: 24–37.

Mendonca, Manuel, and R. N. Kanungo
1990 'Performance management in developing countries' in *Management in developing countries*. A. M. Jaeger and R. N. Kanungo (eds.), 223–251. London: Routledge.

Mintzberg, Henry
1973 *The nature of managerial work*. New York: Harper and Row.

Mintzberg, Henry
1990 'The design school: reconsidering the basic premises of strategic management'. *Strategic Management Journal* 11/3: 171–195.

Misumi, J.
1984 'Decision making in Japanese groups and organizations' in *International perspectives on organizational democracy*. B. Wilpert and A. Sorge (eds.). New York: Wiley.

Misumi, J., and M. F. Peterson
1985 'The Performance-Maintenance (PM) theory of leadership: review of a Japanese research program'. *Administrative Science Quarterly* 30: 198–223.

Morgan, Gareth, and L. Smircich
1980 'The case for quantitative research'. *Academy of Management Review* 5/4: 491–500.

Morishima, M., and T. Minami
1983 'Task interdependence and internal motivation: application of job characteristics model to collectivist cultures'. *Tetsugaku* 77: 133–147.

McEnery, Jean, and G. Des Harnais
1990 'Culture shock'. *Training and Development Journal* 44/4: 43–47.

McKinlay, A., and K. Starkey
1992 'Strategy and human resource management'. *International Journal of Human Resource Management* 3/3: 435–450.

Negandhi, Anant R., and B. D. Estafen
1965 'A research model to determine the applicability of American management know-how in differing cultures and/or environments'. *Academy of Management Journal* 8/4: 309–318.

Nirenberg, John
1986 'Understanding the failure of Japanese management abroad'. *Journal of Managerial Psychology* 1/1: 19–24.

O'Connell, M. S., R. G. Lord, and M. K. O'Connell
1990 'Differences in Japanese and American leadership prototypes: implications for cross-cultural training'. Working Paper, Dept. of Psychology, University of Akron.

Oliver, Nick, and B. Wilkinson
1988 *The Japanization of British industry*. Oxford: Blackwell.

Ouchi, W. G.
1981 *Theory Z: how American business can meet the Japanese challenge*. Reading, MA: Addison-Wesley.

Ouchi, W. G., and A. M. Jaeger
1978 'Type Z organization: stability in the midst of mobility'. *Academy of Management Review* 5: 305–314.

Pang, K., and N. Oliver
1988 'Personnel strategy in eleven Japanese manufacturing companies in the UK'. *Personnel Review* 17/3: 16–21.

Parnell, Myrtle, and J. Vanderkloot
1989 'How to build cross-cultural bridges'. *Communications World* 6/8: 4–42.

Pasquero, Jean
1990 'Comparative research: the case for middle range methodologies' in *International and comparative corporation and society research*. L. E. Preston (ed.), 93–121. Greenwich, CN: JAI Press.

Peng, T. K., M. F. Peterson, and Y. P. Shyi
1991 Quantitative methods in cross-national management research: trends and equivalence issues'. *Journal of Organizational Behaviour* 2: 87–107.

Peters, Thomas J., and R. H. Waterman
1982 *In search of excellence*. New York: Harper and Row.

Pieper, R., editor
1990 *Human resource management: an international comparison*. Berlin: de Gruyter.

Porter, Michael E.
1990 *The competitive advantage of nations*. London: Macmillan.

Powell, Walter W., and P. J. DiMaggio
1991 *The new institutionalism in organizational analysis*. Chicago: University of Chicago Press.

Preston, J. C.
1987 'Cultural blinders: take off before attempting international organizational development'. *Organizational Development Journal* 5: 50–56.

Preston, Lee L., editor
1990 *International and comparative corporation and society research*. Greenwich, CN: JAI Press.

Purcell, John
1989 'The impact of corporate strategy on human resource management' in *New perspectives on human resource management*. J. Storey (ed.), 67–91. London: Routledge.

Pye, L.
1985 *Asian power and politics*. Cambridge, MA: Harvard University Press.

Ragin, C. C.
1987 *The comparative method*. Berkeley: University of California Press.

Redding, S. G.
1980 'Cognition as an aspect of culture and its relation to management processes: an exploratory view of the Chinese case'. *Journal of Management Studies* 17/2: 127–148.

Redding, S. G.
1990 *The spirit of Chinese capitalism*. New York: de Gruyter.

Redding, S. G., and M. Ng
1982 'The role of "face" in the organizational perceptions of Chinese managers'. *Organization Studies* 3/3: 201–219.

Redding, S. G., A. Norman, and A. Schlander
1993 'The nature of individual attachment to the organization: a review of East Asian variations' in *Handbook of industrial and organizational psychology*, Vol. 4. M. D. Dunnette (ed.), 647–688. Palo Alto: Consulting Psychologists Press.

Redding, S. G., and R. D. Whitley
1990 'Beyond bureaucracy: towards a comparative analysis of forms of economic resource co-ordination and control' in *Capitalism in contrasting cultures*. S. R. Clegg and S. G. Redding (eds.), 79–104. New York: de Gruyter.

Redding, S. G., and G. Y. Y. Wong
1986 'The psychology of Chinese organizational behaviour' in *The psychology of the Chinese people*. M. H. Bond (ed.), 267–295. Hong Kong: Oxford University Press.

Rehder, Robert, M. Smith, and K. Burr
1989 'A salute to the sun: cross-cultural organizational adaptation and change'. *Leadership and Organization Development Journal* 10/4: 17–27.

Rigby, J. Malcolm
1987 'The challenge of multinational team development'. *Journal of Management Development* 6/3: 65–72.

Roberts, Karlene H.
1970 'On looking at an elephant: an evaluation of cross-cultural research related to organizations'. *Psychological Bulletin* 74/5: 327–350.

Rohlen, Thomas P.
1974 *For harmony and strength: Japanese white-collar organization in anthropological perspective*. Berkeley: University of California Press.

Ronen, Simcha
1986 *Comparative and multinational management*. New York: Wiley.

Schein, Edgar
1986 'International human resource management: new directions, perpetual issues, and missing themes'. *Human Resource Management* 25/1: 169–176.

Schneider, Susan
1988 'National vs corporate culture: implications for human resource management'. *Human Resource Management* 27/2: 231–246.

Schollhammer, Hans
1969 'The comparative management theory jungle'. *Academy of Management Journal* 12: 81–97.

Sechrest, L.
1977 'On the dearth of theory in cross-cultural psychology: there is madness in our method' in *Basic problems in cross-cultural psychology*. Y. H. Poortinga (ed.), 73–82. Amsterdam: Swets and Zeitlinger.

Seddon, John
1987 'Assumptions, culture and performance appraisal'. *Journal of Management Development* 6/3: 47–54.

Shackleton, V. V., and S. Newell
1991 'Management selection: a comparative survey of methods used in top British and French companies'. *Journal of Occupational Psychology* 64/1: 23–36.

Shaw, James B.
1990 'A cognitive categorization model for the study of intercultural management'. *Academy of Management Review* 15/4: 626–645.

Shenkar, Oded, and Y. Zeira
1987 'Human resources management in international joint ventures: directions for research'. *Academy of Management Review* 12/3: 546–557.

Shenkar, Oded, and Y. Zeira
1990 'International joint ventures: a tough test for HR'. *Personnel* 67/1: 26–31.

Silin, Robert H.
1976 *Leadership and values: the organization of large-scale Taiwanese enterprises*. Cambridge, MA: Harvard University Press.

Sinha, Jai B. P.
1990 'A model of effective leadership styles in India' in *Management in developing countries*. A. M. Jaeger and R. N. Kanungo (eds.), 252–263. London: Routledge.

Smith, Peter B., and M. Peterson
1988 *Leadership in context.* London: Sage.

Smith, Peter B. et al.
1989 'On the generality of leadership style measures across cultures'. *Journal of Occupational Psychology* 62: 97–109.

Soeters, Joseph, and H. Schreuder
1988 'The interaction between national and organizational cultures in accounting firms'. *Accounting, Organizations and Society* 13/1: 75–85.

Stewart, Sally
1992 'China's managers'. *The International Executive* 34: 2.

Stogdill, R. M.
1977 *Leadership abstracts and bibliography 1904 to 1974.* Columbus, Ohio: Ohio State University.

Sullivan, Jeremiah
1992 'Theory development in international business research; the decline of culture'. Conference, Perspectives on International Business, University of South Carolina, 1992.

Tainio, R., and T. Santalainen
1984 'Some evidence for the cultural relativity of organizational development programs'. *Journal of Applied Behavioural Sciences* 20: 95–111.

Tang, Sara F. Y., and P. S. Kirkbride
1986 'The development of conflict-handling skills in Hong Kong: some cross-cultural issues'. Working paper, City Polytechnic of Hong Kong.

Terpstra, Vern, and K. David
1985 *The cultural environment of international business.* Dallas: Southwestern.

Thurley, Keith
1990 'Towards a European approach to personnel management'. *Personnel Management* 22/9: 54–57.

Tichy, Noel M.
1983 *Managing strategic change.* New York: Wiley.

Triandis, Harry C.
1992 'Cross-cultural industrial and organizational psychology' in *Handbook of industrial and organizational psychology,* Vol. 4. M. D. Dunnette (ed.), 103–172. Palo Alto, CA: Consulting Psychologists Press.

Tu, Wei-ming
1991 'The rise of East Asia: the challenge of the post-Confucian states'. Working Paper, American Academy of Arts and Sciences.

Tung, Rosalie L.
1982 'Selection and training procedures of U.S., European, and Japanese multinationals'. *California Management Review* 25/1: 57–71.

Vogel, Ezra F.
1979 *Japan as number one: lessons for America.* New York: Harper and Row.

Weber, Max
1958 *The protestant ethic and the spirit of capitalism.* New York: Scribners.

Whitley, R. D.
1984 *The intellectual and social organization of the sciences.* Oxford: Clarendon Press.

Whitley, R. D.
1986 'The structure and context of economics as a scientific field'. *Research in the History of Economic Thought and Methodology* 4: 179–209.

Whitley, R. D.
1991 'The social construction of business systems in East Asia'. *Organization Studies* 12/1: 1–28.

Whitley, R. D.
1992 *Business systems in East Asia: firms, market and societies.* London: Sage.

Williamson, Oliver E.
1975 *Markets and hierarchies.* New York: Free Press.

Williamson, Oliver E.
1985 *The economic institutions of capitalism.* New York: Free Press.

Wong, Siu-lun
1988 *Emigrant entrepreneurs: Shanghai industrialists in Hong Kong.* Hong Kong: Oxford University Press.

Yu, An-Bang, and K. S. Yang
1992 'The nature of achievement motivation in collectivistic societies' in *Individualism and collectivism: social and applied issues*. S. C. Choi, C. Kagitcibasi and U. Kim (eds.), (in press). London: Sage.

Zeira, Y., and N. J. Adler
1980 'International organizational development: goals, problems and challenges'. *Group and Organizational Studies* 5: 295–309.

Name Index